NCERT
SOLUTIONS
Mathematics

CLASS
VI

by
RK Behl
Nitika Singh Bisla

✳arihant
Arihant Prakashan (School Division Series)

✳arihant

Arihant Prakashan (School Division Series)

All Rights Reserved

ꭍ Administrative & Production Offices

Regd. Office

'Ramchhaya' 4577/15, Agarwal Road, Darya Ganj, New Delhi -110002
Tele: 011- 47630600, 43518550

ꭍ   Head Office

Kalindi, TP Nagar, Meerut (UP) - 250002
Tel: 0121-7156203, 7156204

ꭍ Sales & Support Offices

Agra, Ahmedabad, Bengaluru, Bareilly, Chennai, Delhi, Guwahati, Hyderabad, Jaipur, Jhansi, Kolkata, Lucknow, Nagpur & Pune.

ꭍ ISBN   978-93-27197-08-2

PO No : TXT-XX-XXXXXXX-X-XX

Published by Arihant Publications (India) Ltd.

For further information about the books published by Arihant, log on to www.arihantbooks.com or e-mail at info@arihantbooks.com

Follow us on

Preface

Feeling the immense importance and value of NCERT books, we are presenting this book, having the **NCERT Exercises' Solutions.** This book presents not only solutions but also detailed explanations. Through these detailed explanations, students can learn the concepts which will enhance their thinking and learning abilities. Along with the solutions, we have covered the text material of NCERT books in Notes form covering all Definitions, Formulae, Important Points, etc.

We have introduced some Additional Features with the solutions which are given below:

- All questions covered including questions given in-between the chapter; **Try These and all the Chapter Exercises.**

- This book also covers solutions to selected problems of **NCERT Exemplar Problems.**

- **Explanatory Solutions** Along with the solutions to questions we have given all the points that tell how to approach to solve a problem. All formulae and hints are discussed in full detail.

- **Tips** have been added with questions to cover all those loopholes which may lead to confusion.

For such a wonderful work, a special note of thanks goes to our Authors (RK Behl & Nitika Singh Bisla) and our production team.

We are confident that this book will be highly useful for the students. Suggestions for the improvement of the book shall be received with great appreciation and gratitude.

Publisher

Contents

Chapter 1

Knowing Our Numbers

Important Points

- The numbers which are written in figures are called numerals.
- **Comparing numbers** Let two or more numbers be given, then a number having greater number of digits will be greatest and a number having smaller number of digits will be smallest.

  If the number of digits in two or more numbers is same, then that number will be larger, which has a greater leftmost digit. If this digit also happens to be the same, we look at the next digit and so on.

  e.g.

  (i) Let 92 and 395 be given numbers. It is clear that number 395 has greater number of digits. Hence, 395 is greatest number.

  (ii) Let 395 and 424 be given numbers. Here, both given numbers have same number of digits. But 424 has a greater leftmost digit. Hence, 424 is greatest number.

- **Arrangement of numbers** Suppose some digits say n are given to form greatest number and smallest number, then for greatest number, we arrange the given digits in descending order of their values and for smallest number. We arrange the given digits in ascending order of their values.

  Note In forming numbers, we should be careful to see that the conditions, under which the numbers are formed, are satisfied.

  (i) **Ascending order** It means, arrangement from the smallest to the greatest number.

(ii) **Descending order** It means, arrangement from the greatest to the smallest number.

▪ On adding 1 to the greatest n-digit number, we would get the smallest $(n+1)$-digit number.

e.g. Greatest 2-digit number $+ 1 =$ Smallest 3-digit number

i.e. $\qquad\qquad\qquad\qquad 99 + 1 = 100$

   (i) Greatest 3-digit number $= 999$

      ∴ Smallest 3-digit number $= 100$

  (ii) Greatest 4-digit number $= 9999$

      ∴ Smallest 4-digit number $= 1000$

 (iii) Greatest 5-digit number $= 99999$

      ∴ Smallest 5-digit number $= 10000$

 (iv) Greatest 6-digit number $= 999999$

      ∴ Smallest 6-digit number $= 100000$

  (v) Greatest 7-digit number $= 9999999$

      ∴ Smallest 7-digit number $= 1000000$

 (vi) Greatest 8-digit number $= 99999999$

      ∴ Smallest 8-digit number $= 10000000$

▪   (i) One hundred $= 10$ tens

  (ii) One thousand $= 10$ hundreds $= 100$ tens

 (iii) One lakh $= 100$ thousands $= 1000$ hundreds

 (iv) One crore $= 100$ lakhs $= 10000$ thousands

  (v) One million $= 1000$ thousands $= 10$ lakhs

 (vi) One billion $= 1000$ millions

▪ **Indian System of Numeration** In this system, we use ones, tens, hundreds, thousands, lakhs and crores. Here, commas are used to mark thousands, lakhs and crores.

The first comma comes after three digits from the right (i.e. after hundreds place), the second comma comes two digits later (i.e. after ten thousands place) and third comma comes after another two digits (i.e. after ten lakh place).

e.g. We have, 50801592

Thus, Indian system of numeration $= 5, 08, 01, 592$

- **International System of Numeration** In this system, we use ones, tens, hundreds, thousands and then millions. Here, commas are used to mark thousands and millions. It comes after every three digits from the right. The first comma marks thousands and the next comma marks millions.

  e.g. We have, 60801892

  Thus, International system of numeration = 60, 801, 892

- The units **kilo** is the greatest and **milli** is the smallest. Also, kilo shows 1000 times greater, milli shows 1000 times smaller and centi shows 100 times smaller.

  (i) 1 kilometre = 1000 metre

  (ii) 1 kilogram = 1000 grams

  (iii) 1 metre = 10 decimetre = 100 centimetres = 1000 millimetres

  (iv) 1 gram = 10 decigrams = 100 centigrams = 1000 milligrams

  (v) 1 litre = 10 decilitres = 100 centilitres = 1000 millilitres

  Note

  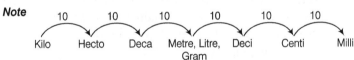

  In the above figure, each unit has the difference of 10.

  i.e. 1 kilometre (km) = 10 hectometres

  and 1 kilometre (km) = 10 × 10 = 100 decametres

- **Estimation** Estimation involves approximating a quantity to an accuracy required e.g. 4117 may be approximated to 4100 a to 4000. i.e. to the nearest hundred on to the nearest thousand depending on your need.

- **Rounding off Numbers**

  (i) For rounding off a number to the **nearest tens**, we examine the digit at ones place.

  If the digit at ones place is less than 5, then replace the ones digit by 0 and keep the other digits as they are.

  e.g. We rounding off 12 to 10.

  If the digit at ones place is 5 or more than 5, then replace the ones digit by 0 and increase tens digit by 1.

  e.g. We rounding off 78 to 80.

(ii) For rounding off a number to the **nearest hundreds,** we examine the digit at tens place.

If the digit at tens place is less than 5, then replace the digits at tens and ones place by 0 and keep all other digits as they are.

e.g. We rounding off 2546 to 2500.

If the digit at tens place is 5 or more than 5, then replace the digits at tens and ones place by 0 and increase the digit at hundreds place by 1.

e.g. We rounding off 5750 to 5800.

(iii) For rounding off a number to the **nearest thousands,** we examine the digit at hundreds place.

If the digit at hundreds place is less than 5, replace each one of the digits at hundreds, tens and ones by 0 and keep all other digits as they are.

e.g. We rounding off 65437 to 65000.

If the digit at hundreds place is 5 or more than 5, then replace each one of the digits at hundreds, tens and ones by 0 and increase the digit at thousands place by 1.

e.g. we rounding off 2573 to 3000.

- **Some Facts**

    (i) There are no rigid rules to estimate the outcomes of numbers. The procedure depends on the degree of accuracy required and how quickly the estimate is needed. The most important thing is, how sensible the guessed answer would be.

    (ii) To estimate sum or difference, the general rule is round off each factor to its greatest place, then sum or difference the rounded off factors. e.g.

    (a) As for 5,290 + 17,986

         5,290 is round off to 5,000

         17,986 is rounded off to 18,000

         ∴   Estimated sum = 18,000 + 5,000 = 23,000

    (b) As for 5,673 − 436

         5,290 is rounded off to 6,000

         436 is rounded off to 0

         ∴ Estimated sum = 6,000 − 0 = 6,000

(iii) To estimate products, the general rule is round off each factor to its greatest place, then multiply the rounded off factors. e.g. As for 63×182, we rounded off 63 to tens and 182 to hundreds. i.e. 63 is rounded off to 60 and 182 to the nearest hundred, i.e. 200, we get

Estimated product $= 60 \times 200 = 1,200$

(iv) Brackets are symbols used in pairs of groups things together. Various types of groups are

(a) Parenthesis or round brackets '()'

(b) Curly brackets or set brackets '{}'

(c) Square brackets or box brackets '[]'

We use the brackets to avoid the confusion and first, turn everything inside the brackets into a single number and then do the operation outside the brackets.

■ **Roman Numerals** One of the early systems of writing numerals is the system of Roman numerals. This system is still used in many places as in clocks, in the school time table, etc.

Some main roman numerals are as follows:

I	V	X	L	C	D	M
1	5	10	50	100	500	1000

The first ten roman numerals are

1	2	3	4	5	6	7	8	8	10
I	II	III	IV	V	VI	VII	VIII	IX	X

Other roman numerals can be made with the help of these numerals.

The rules for the system are as follows :

(i) If a symbol is repeated, its value is added as many times as it occurs, as III is equal to 3 and XXX is equal to 30.

(ii) A symbol is not repeated more than three times. Also, the symbols V, L and D are never repeated.

(iii) If a symbol of smaller value is written to the right of a symbol of greater value, its value gets added to the value of greater symbol.

e.g. $XIII = 10 + 3 = 13$ and $LXV = 50 + 10 + 5 = 65$.

(iv) If a symbol of smaller value is written to the left of a symbol of greater value, its value is subtracted from the value of the greater symbol.

e.g. $IX = 10 - 1 = 9$ and $XC = 100 - 10 = 90.$

(v) The symbols V, L and D are never written to the left of a symbol of greater value i.e. V, L and D are never subtracted.

Note The symbol I can be subtracted from V and X only. The symbol X can be subtracted from L, M and C only. There is no symbol for 'Zero'. 4 and 9 has been written by subtraction. 2, 3, 6, 7 and 8 has been written by addition and repetition of symbol.

Try These (Page 2)

Que 1. Can you instantly find the greatest and the smallest numbers in each row?

     (a) 382, 4972, 18, 59785, 750
     (b) 1473, 89423, 100, 5000, 310
     (c) 1834, 75284, 111, 2333, 450
     (d) 2853, 7691, 9999, 12002, 124

Was that easy? Why was it easy?

TIPS A number having greater number of digits will be greatest and a number having smaller number of digits will be smallest.

Sol. (a) 59785 is the greatest number because it has highest number of digits i.e. 5 and 18 is the smallest number because it has least number of digits i.e. 2.

    (b) 89423 is the greatest number because it has highest number of digits i.e. 5 and 100 is the smallest number because it has least number of digits i.e. 3.

    (c) 75284 is the greatest number because it has highest number of digits i.e. 5 and 111 is the smallest number because it has least number of digits i.e. 3.

    (d) 12002 is the greatest number because it has highest number of digits i.e. 5 and 124 is the smallest number because it has least number of digits i.e. 3.

        Yes, it was easy. We just identify the number of digits and locate the greatest and smallest numbers because greatest number has more digits.

Que 2. Find the greatest and the smallest numbers.
     (a) 4536, 4892, 4370, 4452
     (b) 15623, 15073, 15189, 15800
     (c) 25286, 25245, 25270, 25210
     (d) 6895, 23787, 24569, 24659

> **TIPS**
> If two numbers contain the same number of digits, the number having smaller number of digits will be smaller and the number having greater digit at the leftmost place will be greater. If the leftmost digits are also same, we compare the next digit from left and so on.

Sol. (a) We have, 4536, 4892, 4370, 4452.

Here, each of the given numbers is containing 4-digits and their digits at thousand places are also same.

So, we compare the hundreds place digit.

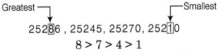

Greatest ——┐   ┌—Smallest

4536, 4⌷8⌷92, 4⌷3⌷70, 4452

∵   8 > 5 > 4 > 3

∴ The greatest number is 4892 and the smallest number is 4370.

(b) We have, 15623, 15073, 15189, 15800

Here, the two leftmost digits 15 i.e. digits at thousand and ten thousands place are same in each numbers.

So, we compare the hundreds place digit.

Greatest ——┐   ┌— Smallest

15189, 15⌷8⌷00, 15623, 15⌷0⌷73

∵   8 > 6 > 1 > 0

∴ The greatest number is 15800 and the smallest number is 15073.

(c) We have, 25286, 25245, 25270, 25210

Here, the three leftmost digits 252 are same in each number.

So, we compare the tens place digit.

Greatest ——┐   ┌—Smallest

252⌷8⌷6 , 25245, 25270, 252⌷1⌷0

8 > 7 > 4 > 1

∴The greatest number is 25286 and the smallest number is 25210.

(d) We have, 6895, 23787, 24569, 24659

Here, 6895 is a 4-digits number and other numbers are 5 digits, so it is clear that 6895 is the smallest number.

Now, in remaining three numbers, the digit at ten thousands place is same in each number.

So, we compare the thousands place digit.

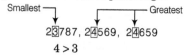

Smallest ──┐   ┌── Greatest

2③787, 2④569, 2④659

∵   4 > 3

Again, in two numbers, digit at thousands place is same.

So, we compare the hundreds place digit.

Smallest ──┐   ┌── Greatest

24⑤69, 24⑥59

∵   6 > 5

∴ The greatest number is 24659 and smallest number is 6895.

Try These (Page 3)

Que 3. Use the given digits without repetition and make the greatest and smallest 4-digit numbers.

    (a) 2, 8, 7, 4   (b) 9, 7, 4, 1   (c) 4, 7, 5, 0   (d) 1, 7, 6, 2

    (e) 5, 4, 0, 3

TIPS

For greatest number, we arrange the given digits in descending order of their values and for smallest number, we arrange the given digits in ascending order of their values.

Sol. (a) Here, descending order of the given digits is 8, 7, 4, 2

    ∴   Greatest number = 8742

    and ascending order of the given digits is 2, 4, 7, 8

    ∴   Smallest number = 2478

    (b) Here, descending order of the given digits is 9, 7, 4, 1.

    ∴   Greatest number = 9741

    and ascending order of the given digits is 1, 4, 7, 9.

    ∴   Smallest number = 1479

    (c) Here, descending order of the given digits is 7, 5, 4, 0

    ∴   Greatest number = 7540

    and ascending order of the given digits is 0, 4, 5, 7

    But, 0457 is a three-digit number, so we have to interchange the place of 4 and 0. i.e. 4057

    ∴   Smallest number = 4057

    (d) Here, descending order of the given digits is 7, 6, 2, 1.

    ∴   Greatest number = 7621

    and ascending order of the given digits is 1, 2, 6, 7.

    ∴   Smallest number = 1267

(e) Here, descending order of the given digits is 5, 4, 3, 0.

∴ Greatest number = 5430

and ascending order of the given digits is 0, 3, 4, 5.

But 0345 is a three-digit number. So, we have to interchange the place of 3 and 0. i.e 3045.

∴ Smallest number = 3045

Que 4. Make the greatest and the smallest 4-digit numbers by using any one digit twice.

(a) 3, 8, 7   (b) 9, 0, 5   (c) 0, 4, 9   (d) 8, 5, 1

> We will use the greatest digit twice and then arrange in descending order to get the greatest 4-digit number. Similarly, we will use the smallest digit twice and then arrange in ascending order to get the smallest 4-digit number.

Sol. (a) Given digits are 3, 8 and 7.

Here, descending order of the given digits is 8, 8, 7, 3.

[∵ greatest digit 8 is taken twice]

∴Greatest 4-digit number = 8873

and ascending order of the given digits is 3, 3, 7, 8.

[∵ smallest digit 3 is taken twice]

∴Smallest 4-digit number = 3378

(b) Given digits are 9, 0 and 5.

Here, descending order of the given digits is 9, 9, 5, 0.

[∵ greatest digit 9 is taken twice]

∴Greatest 4-digit number = 9950

and ascending order of the given digits is 0, 0, 5, 9

[∵ smallest digit 0 is taken twice]

Then 4-digit number = 0059

But 0059 is a 2-digit number because '0' at first two leftmost places is meaningless. So, keeping 5 (instead of 0) at the leftmost place and taking the smallest digit 0 twice i.e. 5009.

∴Smallest 4–digit number = 5009

(c) Given digits are 0, 4 and 9.

Here, descending order of the given digits is 9, 9, 4, 0.

[∵ greatest digit 9 is taken twice]

∴Greatest 4-digit number = 9940

and ascending order of the given digit is 0,0,4,9.

[∵ smallest digit 0 is taken twice]

Then, 4-digit number = 0049

But 0049 is a 2-digit number because '0' at first two leftmost places is meaningless. So, keeping 4 (instead of 0) at the leftmost place and taking the smallest digit 0 twice, we get 4009.

∴Smallest 4-digit number = 4009

(d) Given digits are 8, 5 and 1.

Here, descending order of the given digits is 8, 8, 5, 1.

[∵ greatest digit 8 is taken twice]

∴Greatest 4-digit number = 8851

and ascending order of the given digits is 1, 1, 5, 8,

[∵ smallest digit 1 is taken twice]

∴Smallest 4-digit number = 1158

Que 5. Make the greatest and the smallest 4-digit numbers using any four different digits with conditions given below

   (a) Digit 7 is always at ones place
   (b) Digit 4 is always at tens place
   (c) Digit 9 is always at hundreds place
   (d) Digit 1 is always at thousands place

Sol. Digits in ascending order are 0, 1, 2, 3, 4, 5, 6, 7, 8 and 9. And digits in descending order are 9, 8, 7, 6, 5, 4, 3, 2, 1 and 0. Also, we know that 0 can never be taken at the left most place.

   (a) Keeping the digit 7 at ones place, we can fill other places tens, hundreds and thousands by remaining numbers.

   Greatest number | 9 | 8 | 6 | 7 | [Keeping the greatest digits i.e. 9 , 8 and 6 at thousands, hundreds and tens place]

   Smallest number | 1 | 0 | 2 | 7 | [Keeping the smallest digits i.e. 0 , 1 , 2 at hundreds, thousands and tens place. If keep 0 at thousands place, then number will be equal to 3-digits number]

   (b) Keeping the digit 4 at tens place, we can fill other places thousands, hundreds and ones place by remaining number.

   Greatest number | 9 | 8 | 4 | 7 | [Keeping the greatest digits i.e. 9 , 8 and 7 at thousands, hundreds and tens place]

   Smallest number | 1 | 0 | 4 | 2 | [Keeping the smallest digits i.e. 9 , 8 and 7 at thousands, hundreds and tens place]

   (c) Keeping the digit 9 at hundreds place, we can fill thousands, tens and ones place by remaining digits.

   Greatest number | 8 | 9 | 7 | 6 | [Keeping the greatest digit i.e. 8 , 7 and 6 at thousands tens and ones place]

   Smallest number | 1 | 9 | 0 | 2 | [Keeping the smallest digit i.e. 1 , 0 and 2 at thousands, tens and ones place]

(d) Keeping the digit 1 at thousands place, we can fill hundreds, tens and ones place digit by remaining digits.

Greatest number | 1 | 9 | 8 | 7 | — [Keeping the greatest digit i.e. 9 , 8 and 7 at hundreds, tens and ones place]

Smallest number | 1 | 0 | 2 | 3 | — [Keeping the smallest digit i.e. 0 , 2 and 3 at hundreds tens and ones place]

Que 6. Take two digits, say 2 and 3. Make 4-digit number using both the digits equal number of times.

(i) Which is the greatest number?

(ii) Which is the smallest number?

(iii) How many different numbers can you make in all?

Sol. Two given digits are 2 and 3. We want to make 4-digit numbers using both the digits equal number of times.

The possible 4-digit numbers are 2233, 3322, 2332, 3223, 2323 and 3232.

(i) The greatest number is 3322.

(ii) The smallest number is 2233.

(iii) We can make 6 different numbers in all.

In Text (Page 4)

Que 7. Who is the tallest? Who is the shortest?

(a) Can you arrange them in the increasing order of their heights?

(b) Can you arrange them in the decreasing order of their heights?

Ramhari (160 cm) Dolly (154 cm) Mohan (158 cm) Shashi (159 cm)

Sol. (i) From the given figure, it is clear that 160 > 159 > 158 > 154
∴ Ramhari is the tallest because he has the height of 160 cm.

(ii) From the given figure, it is clear that 154 < 158 < 159 < 160
∴ Dolly is the shortest because she has the height of 154 cm.

We can arrange height from two types.

(a) Yes, we can arrange their heights in increasing order as follows: Dolly (154 cm) < Mohan (158 cm) < Shashi (159 cm) < Ramhari (160 cm)

(b) Yes, we can arrange their heights in decreasing order as follows: Ramhari (160 cm) > Shashi (159 cm) > Mohan (158 cm) > Dolly (154 cm)

Note Here, we have used two symbols i.e. < and >. '<' is used to represent less than value and '>' is used to represent greater than value.

Que 8. Sohan and Rita went to buy an almirah. There were many almirahs available with their price tags.
    (a) Can you arrange their prices in increasing order?
    (b) Can you arrange their prices in decreasing order?

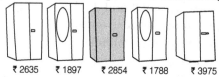

    ₹ 2635   ₹ 1897   ₹ 2854   ₹ 1788   ₹ 3975

Sol. (a) Yes, prices can be arranged in increasing order as follows:
    ₹ 1788 < ₹ 1897 < ₹ 2635 < ₹ 2854 < ₹ 3975
    (b) Yes, prices can be arranged in decreasing order as follows:
    ₹ 3975 > ₹ 2854 > ₹ 2635 > ₹ 1897 > ₹ 1788

Try These (Page 4)

Que 9. Think of five situations, where compare three or more quantities.

Sol. Five more situations may be
    (i) Prices of 4 different kinds of branded shoes are ₹ 4225, ₹ 3835, ₹ 2620 and ₹ 2230 respectively.
    (ii) The weight of 4 students of class VI are 33 kg, 38 kg, 35 kg and 37 kg respectively.
    (iii) Marks obtained by 4 students in Mathematics out of 100 are 87, 88, 90 and 78 respectively.
    (iv) The tution fee paid by 4 students of different classes are ₹ 170, ₹ 190, ₹ 150 and ₹ 200 respectively.
    (v) The runs scored by 4 players A, B, C and D in an innings are 75, 60, 25 and 82 respectively.

Try These (Page 5)

Que 10. (i) Arrange the following numbers in ascending order.
    (a) 847, 9754, 8320, 571   (b) 9801, 25751, 36501, 38802
    (ii) Arrange the following numbers in descending order.
    (a) 5000, 7500, 85400, 7861
    (b) 1971, 45321, 88715, 92547

Sol (i) (a) We have, 847, 9754, 8320, 571
    Ascending order of given numbers is as follows:
    571 < 847 < 8320 < 9754

(b) We have, 9801, 25751, 36501, 38802

Ascending order of given numbers is as follows:

9801 < 25751 < 36501 < 38802

(ii) (a) We have, 5000, 7500, 85400, 7861

Descending order of given numbers is as follows:

85400 > 7861 > 7500 > 5000

(b) We have, 1971, 45321, 88715, 92547

Descending order of given numbers is as follows:

92547 > 88715 > 45321 > 1971

Try These (Page 6-7)

Que 11. Read and expand the numbers wherever there are blanks.

Number	Number name	Expansion
20000	Twenty thousand	2 × 10,000
26000	Twenty six thousand	2 × 10,000 + 6 × 1,000
38400	Thirty eight thousand four hundred	3 × 10,000 + 8 × 1,000 + 4 × 100
65740	Sixty five thousand seven hundred forty	6 × 10,000 + 5 × 1,000 + 7 × 100 + 4 × 10
89324	Eighty nine thousand three hundred twenty four	8 × 10,000 + 9 × 1,000 + 3 × 100 + 2 × 10 + 4 × 1
50000		
41000		
47300		
57630		
29485		
29085		
20085		
20005		

Sol. The remaining blanks are shown as below with appropriate number, name and expansion.

Number	Number name	Expansion
50000	Fifty thousand	5 × 10000
41000	Forty one thousand	4 × 10000 + 1 × 1000
47300	Forty seven thousand three hundred	4 × 10000 + 7 × 1000 + 3 × 100

Number	Number name	Expansion
57630	Fifty seven thousand six hundred thirty	$5 \times 10,000 + 7 \times 1000 + 6 \times 100 + 3 \times 10$
29485	Twenty nine thousand four hundred eighty five	$2 \times 10,000 + 9 \times 1000 + 4 \times 100 + 8 \times 10 + 5 \times 1$
29085	Twenty nine thousand eighty five	$2 \times 10,000 + 9 \times 1000 + 8 \times 10 + 5 \times 1$
20085	Twenty thousand eighty five	$2 \times 10,000 + 8 \times 10 + 5 \times 1$
20005	Twenty thousand five	$2 \times 10,000 + 5 \times 1$

Que 12. Read and expand the numbers wherever there are blanks.

Number	Number name	Expansion
3,00,000	Three lakh	$3 \times 1,00,000$
3,50,000	Three lakh fifty thousand	$3 \times 1,00,000 + 5 \times 10,000$
3,53,500	Three lakh fifty three thousand five hundred	$3 \times 1,00,000 + 5 \times 10,000 + 3 \times 1,000 + 5 \times 100$
4,57,928		
4,07,928		
4,00,829		
4,00,029		

Sol. The remaining blanks are shown as below with appropriate number, name and expansion.

Number	Number name	Expansion
(i) 4,57,928	Four lakh fifty seven thousand nine hundred twenty eight	$4 \times 10,00,00 + 5 \times 10,000 + 7 \times 1000 + 9 \times 100 + 2 \times 10 + 8 \times 1$
(ii) 4,07,928	Four lakh seven thousand nine hundred twenty eight	$4 \times 1,00,000 + 7 \times 1000 + 9 \times 100 + 2 \times 10 + 8 \times 1$
(iii) 4,00,829	Four lakh eight hundred twenty nine	$4 \times 1,00,000 + 8 \times 100 + 2 \times 10 + 9 \times 1$
(iv) 4,00,029	Four lakh twenty nine	$4 \times 1,00,000 + 2 \times 10 + 9 \times 1$

Try These (Page 8)

Que 13. (a) What is $10 - 1 = ?$ (b) What is $100 - 1 = ?$

(c) What is $10000 - 1 = ?$ (d) What is $100000 - 1 = ?$

(e) What is $10000000 - 1 = ?$

Sol. (a) $10 - 1 = 9$ (b) $100 - 1 = 99$
   (c) $10000 - 1 = 9999$ (d) $100000 - 1 = 99999$
   (e) $10000000 - 1 = 9999999$

Que 14. Give five examples, where the number of things counted would be more than 6-digit number.

Sol. The least 6-digit number is 100000 (one lakh).
Now, five examples, where the number of things counted would be more than 6-digit number are as follows:
  (i) The number of people in a big city.
 (ii) The number of stars in a clear dark night.
(iii) The number of motor cycles in a big town.
(iv) The number of grains in a sack full of wheat.
 (v) The number of pages of notebooks of all students in a big town.

Que 15. Starting from the greatest 6-digit number, write the previous five numbers in descending order.

Sol. The greatest 6-digit number $= 999999$
   1st previous number $= 999999 - 1 = 999998$
   2nd previous number $= 999999 - 2 = 999997$
   3rd previous number $= 999999 - 3 = 999996$
   4th previous number $= 999999 - 4 = 999995$
   5th previous number $= 999999 - 5 = 999994$
   Now, descending order of these numbers is as follows
       $999998 > 999997 > 999996 > 999995 > 999994$

Que 16. Starting from the smallest 8-digit number, write the next five numbers in ascending order and read them.

Firstly, write the smallest 8-digit number i.e. 10000000 and then add 1, 2, 3, 4, 5 to get required next five numbers.

Sol. The smallest 8-digit number $= 10000000$
  ∴ 1st next number $= 10000000 + 1 = 10000001$
     2nd next number $= 10000000 + 2 = 10000002$
     3rd next number $= 10000000 + 3 = 10000003$
     4th next number $= 10000000 + 4 = 10000004$
     5th next number $= 10000000 + 5 = 10000005$
     Now, ascending order of these numbers is as follows
       $10000001 < 10000002 < 10000003 < 10000004 < 10000005$

Try These (Page 11)

Que 17. Read these numbers. Write them using placement boxes and then write their expanded forms.

    (i) 475320   (ii) 9847215   (iii) 97645310   (iv) 30458094

    (a) Which is the smallest number?

    (b) Which is the greatest number?

    (c) Arrange these numbers in ascending and descending orders.

Sol. After reading these numbers, we have

    (i) **475320** Four lakh seventy five thousand three hundred twenty.

    (ii) **9847215** Ninety eight lakh forty seven thousand two hundred fifteen.

    (iii) **97645310** Nine crore seventy six lakh forty five thousand three hundred ten.

    (iv) **30458094** Three crore four lakh fifty eight thousand ninety four.

The placement boxes is shown as below :

Number	Crore	Ten lakh	Lakh	Ten thousand	Thousand	Hundred	Tens	Ones
475320	—	—	4	7	5	3	2	0
9847215	—	9	8	4	7	2	1	5
97645310	9	7	6	4	5	3	1	0
30458094	3	0	4	5	8	0	9	4

Expanded forms of given numbers are as follows :

    (i) **475320** $= 4 \times 100000 + 7 \times 10000 + 5 \times 1000 + 3 \times 100 + 2 \times 10 + 0 \times 1$

    (ii) **9847215** $= 9 \times 1000000 + 8 \times 100000 + 4 \times 10000 + 7 \times 1000$
$$+ 2 \times 100 + 1 \times 10 + 5 \times 1$$

    (iii) **97645310** $= 9 \times 10000000 + 7 \times 1000000 + 6 \times 100000 + 4 \times 10000$
$$+ 5 \times 1000 + 3 \times 100 + 1 \times 10 + 0 \times 1$$

    (iv) **30458094** $= 3 \times 10000000 + 4 \times 100000 + 5 \times 10000 + 8 \times 1000$
$$+ 0 \times 100 + 9 \times 10 + 4 \times 1$$

    (a) The smallest number = 475320

    (b) The greatest number = 97645310

    (c) Ascending order of given numbers is as follows :
$$475320 < 9847215 < 30458094 < 97645310$$
Descending order of given numbers is as follows :
$$97645310 > 30458094 > 9847215 > 475320$$

Que 18. Read these numbers
  (i) 527864 (ii) 95432   (iii) 18950049 (iv) 70002509
  (a) Write these numbers using placement boxes and then using commas in Indian system of numeration as well as International system of numeration.
  (b) Arrange these in ascending and descending orders.

Sol. After reading these number, we have
  (i) **527864** Five lakh twenty seven thousand eight hundred sixty four.
  (ii) **95432** Ninety five thousand four hundred thirty two.
  (iii) **18950049** One crore eighty nine lakh fifty thousand forty nine.
  (iv) **70002509** Seven crore two thousand five hundred nine.
  (a) By using placement boxes, given number can be written as

Number	Crore	Ten lakh	Lakh	Ten thousand	Thousand	Hundred	Tens	Ones
527864	—	—	5	2	7	8	6	4
95432	—	—	—	9	5	4	3	2
18950049	1	8	9	5	0	0	4	9
70002509	7	0	0	0	2	5	0	9

By using commas, given numbers can be written as

Number	Number using commas in Indian system of numeration	Number using commas in International system of numeration
527864	5,27,864	527,864
95432	95,432	95,432
18950049	1,89,50,049	18,950,049
70002509	7,00,02,509	70,002,509

  (b) Ascending order of these numbers are as follows:
      95432 < 527864 < 18950049 < 70002509
  Descending order of these numbers are as follows:
      70002509 > 18950049 > 527864 > 95432

Que 19. You have the following digits 4, 5, 6, 0, 7 and 8. Using them, make five numbers each with 6-digits.
  (a) Put commas for easy reading.
  (b) Arrange them in ascending and descending orders.

Sol. Given digits are 4, 5, 6, 0, 7 and 8.
We can make many numbers by using these digits, five of them are as follows :
    876540, 867540, 876450, 876045 and 867405

(a) After putting commas, numbers are as follows :
   (i) 8,76,540   (ii) 8,67,540   (iii) 8,76,450
   (iv) 8,76,045   (v) 8,67,405
(b) Ascending order of numbers is as follows :
      867405 < 867540 < 876045 < 876450 < 876540
   Descending order of numbers is as follows :
      876540 > 876450 > 876045 > 867540 > 867405

Que 20. Take the digits 4, 5, 6, 7, 8 and 9. Make any 3 numbers each with 8-digits. Put commas for easy reading.

Sol. Given digits are 4, 5, 6, 7, 8 and 9.
We can make many numbers by using these digits, three of them are as follows :
      98877456, 98877465 and 98877654
Using commas, numbers can be rewritten as
(i) 9,88,77,456   (ii) 9,88,77,465   (iii) 9,88,77,654

Que 21. From the digits 3, 0 and 4, make five numbers each with 6-digits. Use commas.

Sol. Given digits are 3, 0 and 4.
We can make many numbers by using these digits, five of them are as follows :
(i) 330443   (ii) 343404   (iii) 344430
(iv) 434043   (v) 344034
Using commas, these numbers can be rewritten as
(i) 3,30,443   (ii) 3,43,404   (iii) 3,44,430
(iv) 4,34,043   (v) 3,44,034

Exercise 1.1

Que 1. Fill in the blanks.
   (a) 1 lakh = ___ ten thousand
   (b) 1 million = ___ hundred thousand
   (c) 1 crore = ___ ten lakh
   (d) 1 crore = ___ million.
   (e) 1 million = ___ lakh.

Sol. (a) We know that,
      1 lakh = 100000 (in digits) = 10 × 10000
            = ten × ten thousand   (in number name)
      1 lakh = **ten** ten thousand

(b) We know that, 1 million = 1000000 (in digits) = 10×100000
  = ten × hundred thousand (in number name)
  ∴ 1 million = **ten** hundred thousand

(c) We know that,
  1 crore = 10000000 (in digits) = 10×1000000 = ten × ten lakh
  (in number name)
  ∴ 1 crore = **ten** ten lakh

(d) We know that, 1 crore = 10000000 (in digits) = 10×1000000
  = ten × one million (in number name)
  ∴ 1 crore = **ten** million

(e) We know that.
  1 million = 1000000 (in digits) = 10×100000 = ten × one lakh
  (in number name)
  ∴ 1 million = **ten** lakh

Que 2. Place commas correctly and write the numerals :

(a) Seventy three lakh seventy five thousand three hundred seven

(b) Nine crore five lakh forty one

(c) Seven crore fifty two lakh twenty one thousand three hundred two

(d) Fifty eight million four hundred twenty three thousand two hundred two

(e) Twenty three lakh thirty thousand ten.

Sol. Numbers after commas are as follows:

(a) 73, 75, 307   (b) 9, 05, 00, 041   (c) 7, 52, 21, 302
(d) 58, 423, 202   (e) 23, 30, 010

Que 3. Insert commas suitably and write the names according to Indian System Numeration.

(a) 87595762 (b) 8546283   (c) 99900046   (d) 98432701

Sol. We can draw a table to show these operations

	Number	Number, using commas in Indian system numeration	Number name
(a)	87595762	8,75,95,762	Eight crore seventy five lakh ninety five thousand seven hundred sixty two
(b)	8546283	85,46,283	Eighty five lakh forty six thousand two hundred eighty three
(c)	99900046	9,99,00,046	Nine crore ninety nine lakh forty six
(d)	98432701	9,84,32,701	Nine crore eighty four lakh thirty two thousand seven hundred one

Que 4. Insert commas suitably and write the name according to International System of Numeration.

(a) 78921092   (b) 7452283   (c) 99985102   (d) 48049831

Sol. We can draw a table to show these operations

	Number	Number, using commas in International system of numeration	Number name
(a)	78921092	78,921,092	Seventy eight million nine hundred twenty one thousand ninety two
(b)	7452283	7,452,283	Seven million four hundred fifty two thousand two hundred eighty three
(c)	99985102	99,985,102	Ninety nine million nine hundred eighty five thousand one hundred two
(d)	48049831	48,049,831	Forty eight million forty nine thousand eight hundred thirty one

Try These (Page 12)

Que 1. How many centimetres make a kilometre?

Sol. We know that,   1 km = 1000 m = 1000 × 100 cm   [∵ 1 m = 100 cm]

= 100000 cm

Que 2. Name five large cities in India. Find their population. Also, find the distance (in kilometres) between each pair of these cities.

Sol. The names of five large cities in India are Delhi, Bangalore, Kolkata, Hyderabad and Chennai.

Process of making the pair of cities are given below :

We have, Delhi, Bangalore, Kolkata, Hyderabad and Chennai

First, we take Delhi as base city.

So,   Delhi   Bangalore   Kolkata   Hyderabad   Chennai

Now, we take Bangalore as base city.

So,   Delhi   Bangalore   Kolkata   Hyderabad   Chennai

Now, we take Kolkata as base city.

So,

| Delhi | Bangalore | Kolkata | Hyderabad | Chennai |

Now, we take Hyderabad as base city.

So,

| Delhi | Bangalore | Kolkata | Hyderabad | Chennai |

Their respective population can be taken from a book of general awareness. However, the distance (in kilometres) between each pair of these cities is given below.

Cities in pair	Distance between two cities (in km)
Delhi - Bangalore	2019
Delhi - Kolkata	1442
Delhi - Hyderabad	1453
Delhi - Chennai	2157
Bangalore - Kolkata	1883
Bangalore - Hyderabad	566
Bangalore - Chennai	334
Kolkata - Hyderabad	1516
Kolkata - Chennai	1678
Hyderabad - Chennai	704

These are the national distances between the cities.

Try These (Page 13)

Que 3. How many milligrams make one kilogram?

Sol. We know that, $1 \text{ kg} = 1000 \text{ g} = (1000 \times 1000) \text{ mg}$ [$\because 1 \text{ g} = 1000 \text{ mg}$]
$$= 1000000 \text{ mg}$$
∴ 1000000 milligrams make one kilogram.

Que 4. A box contains 2,00,000 medicine tablets each weighting 20 mg. What is the total weight of all the tablets in the box in grams and in kilograms?

Sol. Given, weight of one tablet $= 20 \text{ mg}$
Total weight of 200000 tablets in the box $= 200000 \times 20 \text{ mg}$
$$= 4000000 \text{ mg}$$
Now,   weight in gram $= \dfrac{4000000}{1000} \text{ g} = 4000 \text{ g}$ $\left[\because 1 \text{mg} = \dfrac{1}{1000} \text{ g}\right]$

Now, weight in kilograms $= \dfrac{4000}{1000} \text{ kg} = 4 \text{ kg}$ $\left[\because 1 \text{g} = \dfrac{1}{1000} \text{ kg}\right]$

Try These (Page 13-14)

Que 5. A bus started its journey and reached different places with a speed of 60 km/h. The journey is shown below.

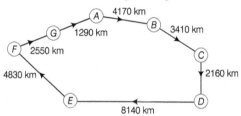

(i) Find the total distance covered by the bus from A to D.

(ii) Find the total distance covered by the bus from D to G.

(iii) Find the total distance covered by the bus, if it starts from A and returns back to A.

(iv) Can you find the difference of distances from C to D and D to E?

(v) Find out the time taken by the bus to reach

    (a) *A* to *B*   (b) *C* to *D* (c) *E* to *G*   (d) Total journey

Sol. From the given figure,

(i) Total distance covered by bus from *A* to *D*

= $AB + BC + CD$ = 4170 + 3410 + 2160 = 9740 km

(ii) Total distance covered by bus from *D* to *G*

= $DE + EF + FG$ = 8140 + 4830 + 2550 = 15520 km

(iii) Total distance covered by bus = Distance from *A* to *D*

+ Distance from D to *G* + Distance from *G* to *A*

= 9740 + 15520 + 1290   [from (i) and (ii) parts]

= 26550 km

(iv) Distance from *C* to *D* = 2160 km

Distance from *D* to *E* = 8140 km

∴ Difference of distances from *C* to *D* and *D* to *E*

= 8140 – 2160 = 5980 km

(v) To find out the time for individual places, we will use the formula of time

i.e. $\text{Time} = \dfrac{\text{Distance}}{\text{Speed}}$

(a) Time taken by bus to reach from *A* to *B*

$= \dfrac{\text{Distance from } A \text{ to } B}{\text{Speed}} = \dfrac{4170}{60} = \dfrac{139}{2} = 69\dfrac{1}{2}$ h

(b) Time taken by bus to reach from C to D
$$= \frac{\text{Distance from } C \text{ to } D}{\text{Speed}} = \frac{2160}{60} = 36 \text{ h}$$

(c) Time taken by bus to reach from E to G
$$= \frac{\text{Distance from } E \text{ to } G}{\text{Speed}} = \frac{4830 + 2550}{60} = \frac{7380}{60} = 123 \text{ h}$$

(d) Time taken by bus for total journey $= \dfrac{\text{Total distance covered}}{\text{Speed}}$

$$= \frac{26550}{60} \text{ h} = \frac{885}{2} = 442\frac{1}{2} \text{ h}$$

Que 6.

Raman's shop	
Things	**Price**
Apples	₹ 40 per kg
Oranges	₹ 30 per kg
Combs	₹ 3 for one
Tooth brushes	₹ 10 for one
Pencils	₹ 1 for one
Note books	₹ 6 for one
Soap cakes	₹ 8 for one

The sales during the last year	
Apples	2457 kg
Oranges	3004 kg
Combs	22760
Tooth brushes	25367
Pencils	38530
Note books	40002
Soap cakes	20005

(a) Can you find the total weight of apples and oranges Raman sold last year?

Weight of apples = _____kg

Weight of oranges = _____kg

Therefore, total weight = ____kg +____kg = ____ kg

(b) Can you find the total money Raman got by selling apples?

(c) Can you find the total money Raman got by selling apples and oranges together?

(d) Make a table showing how much money Raman received from selling each item? Arrange the entries of amount of money received in descending order. Find the item which brought him the highest amount. How much is this amount?

Sol. (a) Weight of apples sold during the last year = 2457 kg

Weight of oranges sold during the last year = 3004 kg

∴ Total weight of apples and oranges Raman sold, during the last year = 2457 + 3004 = 5461 kg

(b) Total money Raman got by selling apples
$$= \text{Total number of apples} \times \text{Cost per kg}$$
$$= 2457 \times 40 = ₹\,98280$$

(c) Total money Raman got by selling oranges
$$= \text{Total number of oranges} \times \text{Cost per kg}$$
$$= 3004 \times 30 = ₹\,90120$$

∴ Total money Raman got by selling apples and oranges together $= 98280 + 90120 = ₹\,188400$

(d) Following table shows the money received from selling items

Items	Sales	Rate	Money Received
Apples	2457	₹ 40 per kg	$2457 \times 40 = ₹\,98280$
Oranges	3004	₹ 30 per kg	$3004 \times 30 = ₹\,90120$
Combs	22760	₹ 3 for one	$22760 \times 3 = ₹\,68280$
Tooth brushes	25367	₹ 10 for one	$25367 \times 10 = ₹\,253670$
Pencils	38350	₹ 1 for one	$38350 \times 1 = ₹\,38350$
Note books	40002	₹ 6 for one	$40002 \times 6 = ₹\,240012$
Soap cakes	20005	₹ 8 for one	$20005 \times 8 = ₹\,160040$

The entries of amount of money received in descending order are as follows :

₹ 253670 > ₹ 240012 > ₹ 160040 > ₹ 98280 > ₹ 90120 > ₹ 68280 > ₹ 38350

The item which brought him the highest amount is tooth brushes. This amounts ₹ 253670.

Exercise 1.2

Que 1. A book exhibition was held for four days in a school. The number of tickets sold at the counter on the first, second, third and final days was respectively 1094, 1812, 2050 and 2751. Find the total number of tickets sold on all the four days.

Sol. Given, number of tickets sold on the first day = 1094

Number of tickets sold on the second day = 1812

Number of tickets sold on the third day = 2050

Number of tickets sold on the fourth day = 2751

∴ Total number of tickets sold on all the four days
$$= 1094 + 1812 + 2050 + 2751 = 7707$$

Hence, there are 7707 tickets sold on all the four days.

Que 2. Shekhar is a famous cricket player. He has so far scored 6,980 runs in test matches. He wishes to complete 10,000 runs. How many more runs does he need?

Sol. Given, number of runs scored by Shekhar = 6,980

Target of runs to be scored = 10,000

∴ Number of runs needed more = Target of runs – Run scored yet

= 10,000 – 6,980 = 3,020

Que 3. In an election, the successful candidate registered 5,77,500 votes and his nearest rival secured 3,48,700 votes. By what margin did the successful candidate win the election?

Sol. Given, votes registered by the successful candidate = 5,77,500

Votes registered by the nearest rival = 3,48,700

∴ Margin, by which the successful candidate won

= Votes of successful candidate – Votes of nearest rival

= 5,77,500 – 3,48,700 = 2,28,800

Que 4. Kirti bookstore sold books worth ₹ 2,85,891 in the first week of June and book worth ₹ 4,00,768 in the second week of the month. How much was the sale for the two weeks together? In which week was the sale greater and by how much?

Sol. Given, sale of books in Ist week = ₹ 2,85,891

Sale of books in IInd week = ₹ 4,00,768

Total sales of two weeks = Sale of Ist week + Sale of IInd week

= 2,85,891 + 4,00,768 = ₹ 6,86,659

Since, 4,00,768 > 2,85,891

Thus sale in the second week is greater.

∴ Difference in the sales amount = 4,00,768 – 2,85,891 = ₹ 1,14,877

Hence, sale in the second week was greater by ₹ 1,14,877.

Que 5. Find the difference between the greatest and the least numbers that can be written using the digits 6, 2, 7, 4, 3 each only once.

Sol. Using the digits 6, 2, 7, 4 and 3, we get

Greatest number = 76,432 and least number = 23,467

∴ Difference = Greatest number – Least number

= 76,432 – 23,467 = 52,965

> **Note** We can form a greatest number with individual digits by arranging them in descending order from right and similarly, we can form a least number by arranging them in ascending order from right.

Que 6. A machine, on an average, manufactures 2,825 screws a day. How many screws did it produce in the month of January 2006?

Sol.   Number of screws manufactured by the machine in one day = 2825

We know that, Number of days in the month of January = 31

∴ Number of screws produced by the machine in the month of January, 2006 = 2,825 × 31 = 8,7575

Hence, number of screws produced by the machine in the month of january, 2006 are 87,575.

Que 7. A merchant had ₹ 78,592 with her. She placed an order for purchasing 40 radio sets at ₹ 1,200 each. How much money will remain with her after the purchase?

Sol.   Given, cost of one radio set = ₹ 1200

Number of radio sets to be purchased = 40

∴ Cost of 40 radio sets = Cost of one radio set × Number of radio sets
$$= 40 \times 1200 = ₹\,48{,}000$$

∵ Total money with the merchant = ₹ 78,592

∴ Money left with the merchant after purchase of 40 radio sets
$$= \text{Total money} - \text{Cost of 40 radio sets}$$
$$= 78{,}592 - 48{,}000 = ₹\,30{,}592$$

Hence, ₹ 30592 will remain with her after the purchase.

Que 8. A student multiplied 7,236 by 65 instead of multiplying by 56. By how much was his answer greater than the correct answer?

Sol.   If a student multiplies 7,236 by 65, he will get = 7,236 × 65
$$= 4{,}70{,}340$$

According to the question,

Student multiplies 7236 by 56 and he will get = 7,236 × 56 = 4,05,216

Now, required difference = Actual answer − Wrong answer
$$= 4{,}70{,}340 - 4{,}05{,}216 = 65{,}124$$

Que 9. To stitch a shirt 2 m 15 cm cloth is needed. Out of 40 m cloth, how many shirts can be stitched and how much cloth will remain?

Sol. Total length of cloth = 40 m = 40 × 100 cm   [∵ 1 m = 100 cm]
$$= 4000 \text{ cm}$$

Cloth needed for one shirt = 2 m 15 cm = (2 × 100) cm + 15 cm
$$= (200 + 15) \text{ cm} = 215 \text{ cm}$$

∴ Number of shirts stitched out of total cloth

$$= \frac{\text{Total length of cloth}}{\text{Cloth needed for stitched shirt}}$$

$$= \frac{4000}{215} = 18\frac{130}{215}$$

```
215) 4000 (18
     215
     1850
     1720
      130
```

Hence, 18 shirts can be stitched and cloth left over is 130 cm i.e. 1 m 30 cm.

Que 10. Medicine is packed in boxes, each weighing 4 kg 500g. How many such boxes can be loaded in a van which cannot carry beyond 800 kg?

Sol. Given, van can carry a weight of 800 kg

i.e. 800×1000 g $= 800000$ g   [∵ 1 kg = 1000 g]

According to the question,

Weight of one packet $= 4$ kg 500 g $= 4 \times 1000 + 500$

$$= 4000 + 500 = 4500 \text{ g}$$

```
45) 8000 (177
    45
    350
    315
    350
    315
     35
```

∴ Number of packets that can be loaded in the van

$$= \frac{\text{Total weight strength of the van}}{\text{Weight of one packet}} = \frac{800000}{4500} = \frac{8000}{45}$$

Hence, only 177 boxes can be loaded in the van.

Que 11. The distance between the school and the house of a student's house is 1 km 875 m. Everyday she walks both ways. Find the total distance covered by her in six days.

Sol. Given, distance between the school and the house

$= 1$ km 875 m $= 1 \times 1000 + 875 = 1000 + 875 = 1875$ m [∵ 1 km = 1000 m]

∴ Distance covered by the student in one day

$= 2 \times 1875 = 3750$ m [∵ She walks both ways in one day]

∴   Distance covered in 6 days $= 6 \times 3750 = 22500$ m

$= (22 \times 1000 + 500)$ m $= 22$ km 500 m [∵ 1 km = 1000 m]

Que 12. A vessel has 4 L and 500 mL of curd. In how many glasses, each of 25 mL capacity, can it be filled?

Sol. Given, capacity of vessel $= 4$ L 500 mL

$= 4 \times 1000 + 500 = 4000 + 500 = 4500$ mL [∵ 1 L = 1000 ml]

and capacity of one glass $= 25$ mL

∴ Number of glasses of curd filled out of vessel

$$= \frac{\text{Capacity of a vessel}}{\text{Capacity of a glass}} = \frac{4500}{25} = 180$$

Hence, curd can be filled in 180 glasses.

Try These (Page 19)

Que 1. Round off these numbers to the nearest tens.

28 32 52 41 39 48
64 59 99 215 1453 2936

TIPS

The numbers 1, 2, 3 and 4 are nearer to 0 than 10. So, we round off 1, 2, 3 and 4 as 0. Numbers 6, 7, 8 and 9 are nearer to 10, so we round off them as 10. Number 5 is equidistant from both 0 and 10. It is a common practice to round off it as 10. Hence, we will follow this method and get required answer.

Sol. We can arrange it as a table

Number	Rounding off	Number	Rounding off
28	30	64	60
32	30	59	60
52	50	99	100
41	40	215	220
39	40	1453	1450
48	50	2936	2940

Que 2. Check, if the following rounding off is correct or not.

(i) 841 → 800   (ii) 9537 → 9500
(iii) 49730 → 49700   (iv) 2546 → 2500
(v) 286 → 200   (vi) 5750 → 5800
(vii) 168 → 200   (viii) 149 → 100
(ix) 9870 → 9800

Correct those which are wrong.

TIPS

Numbers 1 to 49 are closer to 0 than 100, so they are rounded off to 0. Numbers 50 to 99 are closer to 100 than 0, so they are rounded off to 100.

Sol. On checking the rounding off in respect of given numbers, we find that, the rounding off of 286 and 9870 are incorrect. Their correct result should be 300 and 9900, respectively.

Que 3. Check if the following rounding off is correct or not.

(i) 2573 → 3000   (ii) 53,552 → 53,000
(iii) 6404 → 6000   (iv) 65,437 → 65,000
(v) 7805 → 7000   (vi) 3499 → 4000

Correct those, which are wrong.

Numbers 1 to 499 are nearer to 0 than 1000. So, they are rounded off to 0. Numbers 500 to 999 are nearer to 1000 than 0. So, they are rounded off to 1000.

Sol. On checking the rounding off in respect of given numbers, we find that the rounding off of 7805, 53552 and 3499 are incorrect. Their correct results should be 7800, 54000 and 3000, respectively.

Try These (Page 20)

Que 4. Round off the given numbers to the nearest tens, hundreds and thousands.

Given number	Approximate to nearest	Rounded form
75847	Tens	
75847	Hundreds	
75847	Thousands	
75847	Ten thousands	

Sol. The complete table is shown as below

Given number	Approximate to nearest	Rounded form
75847	Tens	75850
75847	Hundreds	75800
75847	Thousands	76000
75847	Ten thousands	80000

Try These (Page 22)

Que 5. Estimate the following products.

(a) 87×313 (b) 9×795 (c) 898×785 (d) 958×387

Sol. (a) 87×313

∵ $\qquad 87 \to 90 \qquad$ [rounding off to nearest tens]
$\qquad 313 \to 300 \qquad$ [rounding off to nearest hundreds]
∴ Estimated product $= 90 \times 300 = 27{,}000$

(b) 9×795

∵ $\qquad 9 \to 10 \qquad$ [rounding off to nearest tens]
$\qquad 795 \to 800 \qquad$ [rounding off to nearest hundreds]
∴ Estimated product $= 10 \times 800 = 8{,}000$

(c) 898×785

∵ $898 \to 900$ [rounding off to nearest hundreds]
                  $785 \to 800$ [rounding off to nearest hundreds]
∴   Estimated product $= 900 \times 800 = 7,20,000$

(d) 958×387

∵ $958 \to 1000$ [rounding off to nearest hundreds]
                  $387 \to 400$ [rounding off to nearest hundreds]
∴   Estimated product $= 1000 \times 400 = 4,00,000$

Exercise 1.3

Que 1. Estimate each of the following using general rule.

   (a) $730 + 998$ (b) $796 - 314$
   (c) $12,904 + 2888$ (d) $28,292 - 21,496$

Sol. (a) $730 + 998$

∵ $730 \to 700$ [rounding off to nearest hundreds]
                  $998 \to 1000$ [rounding off to nearest hundreds]
∴   Estimated sum $= 700 + 1000 = 1700$

(b) $796 - 314$

∵ $796 \to 800$ [rounding off to nearest hundreds]
                  $314 \to 300$ [rounding off to nearest hundreds]
∴   Estimated difference $= 800 - 300 = 500$

(c) $12,904 + 2888$

∵ $12904 \to 13000$ [rounding off to nearest thousands]
              $2888 \to 3000$ [rounding off to nearest thousands]
∴   Estimated sum $= 13000 + 3000 = 16000$

(d) $28,292 - 21,496$

∵ $28,292 \to 28,000$ [rounding off to nearest thousands]
              $21,496 \to 21,000$ [rounding off to nearest thousands]
∴   Estimated difference $= 28000 - 21000 = 7000$

Que 2. Give a rough estimate (by rounding off to nearest hundreds) and also a closer estimate (by rounding off to nearest tens).

   (a) $439 + 334 + 4317$ (b) $1,08,734 - 47,599$
   (c) $8325 - 491$ (d) $4,89,348 - 48,365$

Sol. (a) We have, $439 + 334 + 4317$

$$\left.\begin{array}{l} 439 \to 400 \\ 334 \to 300 \\ 4317 \to 4300 \end{array}\right\}$$ [rounding off to nearest hundreds]

∴Rough estimate = 439 + 334 + 4317 = 400 + 300 + 4300 = 5000

$$439 \rightarrow 440$$

Again, $334 \rightarrow 330$ [rounding off to nearest tens]

$$4317 \rightarrow 4320$$

and closer estimate = 439 + 334 + 4317 = 440 + 330 + 4320 = 5090

(b) We have, 1,08,734 – 47599

∵ $1,08,734 \rightarrow 1,08,700$

$47,599 \rightarrow 47,600$ [rounding off to nearest hundreds]

∴ Rough estimate = 1,08,734 – 47,599 = 1,08,700 – 47,600 = 61,100

Again, $1,08,734 \rightarrow 1,08,730$

$47,599 \rightarrow 47,600$ [rounding off to nearest tens]

and closer estimate = 1,08,734 – 47,599 = 1,08,730 – 47,600 = 61,130

(c) We have, 8325 – 491

∵ $8325 \rightarrow 8300$

$491 \rightarrow 500$ [rounding off to nearest hundreds]

∴ Rough estimate = 8325 – 491 = 8300 – 500 = 7800

Again, $8325 \rightarrow 8330$

$491 \rightarrow 490$ [rounding off to nearest tens]

and closer estimate = 8325 – 491 = 8330 – 490 = 7840

(d) We have, 4,89,348 – 48,365

∵ $489348 \rightarrow 4,89,300$

$48,365 \rightarrow 48,400$ [rounding off to nearest hundreds]

∴Rough estimate = 4,89,348 – 48,365 = 4,89,300 – 48,400 = 4,40,900

Again, $4,89,348 \rightarrow 4,89,350$

$48,365 \rightarrow 48,370$ [rounding off to nearest tens]

and closer estimate = 4,89,348 – 48,365 = 4,89,350 – 48,370 = 4,40,980

Que 3. Estimate the following products using general rule.

(a) 578×161 (b) 5281×3491

(c) 1291×592 (d) 9250×29

Sol. (a) We have, 578×161

$578 \rightarrow 600$ [rounding off to nearest hundreds]

$161 \rightarrow 200$ [rounding off to nearest hundreds]

∴ Estimated product = $600 \times 200 = 1,20,000$

(b) We have, 5281×3491

$5281 \rightarrow 5000$ [rounding off to nearest thousands]

$3491 \rightarrow 3500$ [rounding off to nearest hundreds]

∴ Estimated product = $5000 \times 3500 = 1,75,00,000$

(c) We have, 1291×592

$$1291 \rightarrow 1300 \qquad \text{[rounding off to nearest hundreds]}$$
$$592 \rightarrow 600 \qquad \text{[rounding off to nearest hundreds]}$$

∴ Estimated product $= 1300 \times 600 = 7,80,000$

(d) We have, 9250×29

$$9250 \rightarrow 9000 \qquad \text{[rounding off to nearest thousands]}$$
$$29 \rightarrow 30 \qquad \text{[rounding off to nearest tens]}$$

∴ Estimated product $= 9000 \times 30 = 2,70,000$

Try These (Page 23)

Que 1. Write the expressions for each of the following using brackets.

    (a) Four multiplied by the sum of nine and two.

    (b) Divide the difference of eighteen and six by four.

    (c) Forty five divided by three times the sum of three and two.

Sol. (a) According to the question, Sum of 9 and $2 = 9 + 2$

Now, mutiplying it by 4, we have $4 \times (9 + 2)$

This is the required expression.

    (b) According to the question, Difference of 18 and $6 = (18 - 6)$

Now, dividing this difference by 4, we have $(18 - 6) \div 4$

This is the required expression.

    (c) According to the question, Sum of 3 and $2 = (3 + 2)$

Now, multiplying it by 3, we get $3 \times (3 + 2)$

Again, divide 45 by this result, we have $45 \div 3 \times (3 + 2)$

This is the required expression.

Que 2. Write three different situations for $(5 + 8) \times 6$. (One such situation is Sohani and Reeta work for 6 days; Sohani works 5 hours a day and Reeta 8 hours a day. How many hours do both of them work in a week?)

Sol. We can make many situations of this kind, three situations of them are as follows :

Situation 1. Prabha read 5 pages of a novel in the evening and 8 pages in the morning. How many pages did Prabha read in 6 days?

Situation 2. Meena and Reena work for 6 days. Meena earns ₹ 5 per day and Reena earns ₹ 8 per day. What do they earn together in 6 days?

Situation 3. Ram and Shyam walk for 6 days. Ram walks 5 km in a day and Shyam walks 8 km in a day. How many kilometres do both of them walk in 6 days?

Que 3. Write five situations for the following, where brackets would be necessary.

    (a) 7 (8 − 3)   (b) (7 + 2) (10 − 3)

Sol. We can make many situations of this kind, five situations of them are as follows :

  (a) **Situation 1.** Marry is a maid (servant). She charges ₹ 8 per day to clean a house but gives back ₹ 3 to the house owner for saving. What amount does she carry in her hand from 7 houses?

      Situation 2. Ankit's pocket money is ₹ 8 per day. He spents ₹ 3 daily. Find his total saving in 7 days.

      Situation 3. What will be the seven times the difference of eight and three?

      Situation 4. A clerk works 8 h daily in an office but he remains absent for 3 h daily. In a week, for how many hours did he work?

      Situation 5. Seven children with ₹ 8 each went to market. Each of them bought pencils costing ₹ 3. What is total money left with them?

  (b) **Situation 1.** There are 7 adults and 2 children in each of 10 houses in a street. On Sunday, 3 houses were locked. How many persons were present on Sunday?

      Situation 2. A team of 7 sales girls and 2 managers work 10 h daily in a mobile shop. On Saturday, the shop was closed 3 h early. How many total number of hours the team worked in the shop?

      Situation 3. Rahul gets ₹ 10 per day as pocket money. He spends ₹ 3 per day. In December, he got a bonus pocket money for 2 days. What is his saving for the month of December?

      Situation 4. Sohan and Mohan are two brothers. Both takes ₹ 10 each from their father and make an expenditure of ₹ 3 each. Find the total savings of Sohan of 7 days and Mohan of 2 days.

      Situation 5. 7 persons hired a van upto a metro station for ₹ 10 per head. The van driver added 2 more passengers and reduced the fare by ₹ 3 per head. What was the driver's total collection as fare?

Try These (Page 25)

Que 4. Write in Roman numerals.

    (i) 73   (ii) 92

Sol. In Roman numerals, there are seven basic symbols to write any numeral. These symbols are given as below :

Roman numeral	I	V	X	L	C	D	M
General numeral	1	5	10	50	100	500	1000

Now, we will break the given numbers into small numbers in such a way, that these numbers can be written in place of those numbers.

(i) Here, 73 can be written as sum of 50, 10, 10, 1, 1 and 1. Also, we can replace these numbers by Roman numerals easily.

∴ $73 = 70 + 3 = 50 + 10 + 10 + 1 + 1 + 1$

Hence, Roman numerals = LXXIII

(ii) Similarly, $92 = 90 + 2 = 90 + 1 + 1 = (100 - 10) + 1 + 1$

Hence, Roman numerals = XCII

(If we subtract the smaller value from greater value then, we write symbol for smaller value to the left of symbol of greater value)

Selected **NCERT Exemplar Problems**

Directions *In questions 1 and 3 out of the four options, only one is correct. Write the correct answer.*

Que 1. The product of the place values of two 2's in 428721 is

(a) 4   (b) 40000   (c) 400000   (d) 40000000

Sol. We know that, the place value of a digit changes according to the change of its place.

Here, digit 2 is at two places i.e. tens and ten thousands.

Thus, the place values of 2's in 428721 are 20 and 20000.

∴ The product of 20 and 20000 $= 20 \times 20000 = 400000$

Hence, option (c) is correct.

Que 2. Keeping the place of 6 in the number 6350947 same, the smallest number obtained by rearranging other digits is

(a) 6975430   (b) 6043579   (c) 6034579   (d) 6034759

Sol. The digits in the given number 6350947 are (6, 3, 5, 0, 9, 4, 7) keeping the digit 6 at ten lakh place, the rest of the digits fill other places lakh, ten thousands thousand, hundreds and ones place. To get a smallest number, we write rest of the digits in decreasing order (i.e. 0, 3, 4, 5, 7, 9) Hence, the required smallest number is 6034579.

Que 3. Which of the following numbers in Roman numerals is incorrect?

(a) LXXX   (b) LXX   (c) LX   (d) LLX

Sol. We know that, the symbols V, L and D are never repeated.

So, option (d) is incorrect.

Directions *In questions 4 to 6, state true and false. If the given statement is false, then give the correct statement.*

Que 4. In Roman numeration, if a symbol is repeated, its value is multiplied as many times as it occurs.

Sol. False because if a symbol is repeated, its value is added as many times at it occurs.

Que 5. $82546 = 8 \times 1000 + 2 \times 1000 + 5 \times 100 + 4 \times 10 + 6$.

Sol. False because in the given number, 8 is at ten thousands place. The true statement is as follows:

$82546 = 8 \times 10000 + 2 \times 1000 + 5 \times 100 + 4 \times 10 + 6 \times 1$

$82546 = 8 \times 10000 + 2 \times 1000 + 5 \times 100 + 4 \times 10 + 6$

Que 6. The largest six digit telephone number that can be formed by using digits 5, 3, 4, 7, 0, 8 only once is 875403.

Sol. False because the largest six-digit telephone numbers that can be formed by using digits 5, 4, 4, 7, 0 and 8 only once is 875430.

Directions *In questions 7 to 9 fill in the blanks to make the statement true.*

Que 7. By reversing the order of digits of the greatest number made by five different non-zero digits, the new number is the .... number of five digits.

Sol. By reversing the order of digits of the greatest number made by five different non-zero digits, the new number is the smallest number of five digits.

Que 8. In Roman numeration, the symbol X can be subtracted from ...... M and C only.

Sol. We know that, In Roman numeration, the symbol X can be subtracted from L, M and C only.

Que 9. India's population has been steadily increasing from 439 millions in 1961 to 1028 millions in 2001. Find the total increase in population from 1961 to 2001. Write the increase in population in Indian System of Numeration, using commas suitably.

Sol. Given, population of India in 1961 = 439 millions

$$= 439 \times 1000000 = 439000000 \qquad [\because 1 \text{ million} = 1000000]$$

and population of India in 2001 = 1028 millions

$$= 1028 \times 1000000 = 1028000000 \qquad [\because 1 \text{ million} = 1000000]$$

∴ Total increase in population from 1961 to 2001

$$= \text{Population in 2001} - \text{Population in 1961}$$
$$= 1028000000 - 439000000 = 589000000$$
$$= 589 \times 1000000 = 589 \text{ millions}$$

And the increase in population in Indian system of numeration
$$= 58,90,00,000$$

Que 10. Radius of the Earth is 6400 km and that of Mars is 43,00,000 m. Whose radius is bigger and by how much?

Sol. Given, radius of the Earth = 6400 km = 6400 × 1000 m = 64,00,000 m

$$[\because 1 \text{ km} = 1000 \text{ m}]$$

and radius of Mars = 43,00,000 m

It is clear that radius of the Earth is bigger than the radius of Mars.

∴ Difference = 64,00,000 − 43,00,000 = 21,00,000 m

Que 11. A person had ₹ 10,00,000 with him. He purchased a colour TV for ₹ 16580, a motor cycle for ₹ 45,890 and a flat for ₹ 8,70,000. How much money was left with him?

Sol. Given, total money = ₹ 10,00,000

Money spent on a colour TV = ₹ 16,580

Money spent on a motor cycle = ₹ 45,890

and money spent on a flat = ₹ 8,70,000

Total amount spent = 16,580 + 45,890 + 8,70,000 = ₹ 9,32,470

∴ Money left with him = 10,00,000 − 9,32,470 = ₹ 67,530

Hence, ₹ 67,530 was left with him.

Que 12. Chinmay had ₹ 6,10,000. He gave ₹ 87,500 to Jyoti, ₹ 1,26,380 to Javed and ₹ 3,50,000 to John. How much money was left with him?

Sol. Given, Chinmay's total money = ₹ 6,10,000

Money given to Jyoti by Chinmay = ₹ 87,500

Money given to Javed by Chinmay = ₹ 1,26,380

Money given to John by Chinmay = ₹ 3,50,000

∴ Money left with Chinmay = Total money − Distributed money

$$= 6,10,000 - (87,500 + 1,26,380 + 3,50,000) = 6,10,000 - 5,63,880 = 46,120$$

Hence, ₹ 46,120 was left with him.

Que 13. Find the difference between the largest number of seven digits and the smallest number of eight digits.

Sol. We know that,

Largest 7-digit number = 9999999

and smallest 8-digit number = 10000000

∴ Difference = 10000000 − 9999999 = 1

Que 14. A mobile number consists of ten digits. The first four digits of the number are 9, 9, 8 and 7. The last three digits are 3, 5 and 5. The remaining digits are distinct and make the mobile number, the greatest possible number. What are these digits?

Sol. Given, first four numbers = 9, 9, 8 and 7

and last three numbers = 3, 5 and 5

∴ Greatest possible mobile number = 9987642355

[∵ a mobile number consists of 10-digits]

Hence, the remaining digits are 6, 4 and 2.

Que 15. In a five digit number, digit at ten's place is 4, digit at unit's place is one fourth of ten's place digit, digit at hundred's place is 0, digit at thousand's place is 5 times of the digit at unit's place and ten thousand's place digit is double the digit at ten's place. Write the number.

Sol. According to the question,

Digit at ten's place = 4

Digit at unit's place = $\frac{1}{4}$ of ten's place digit = $\frac{1}{4} \times 4 = 1$

Digit at hundred's place = 0

Digit at thousand's place = 5 × Digit of unit's place = 5 × 1 = 5

Digit at ten thousand's place = 2 × Digit of ten's place = 2 × 4 = 8

∴ Required number = 85041.

Que 16. Find the sum of the greatest and the least six digit numbers formed by the digits 2, 0, 4, 7, 6, 5 using each digit only once.

Sol. Given digits are 2, 0, 4, 7, 6 and 5.

Descending order of the given digits is 7, 6, 5, 4, 2, 0

∴ Greatest six digits number = 765420

and ascending order of the given digits is 0, 2, 4, 5, 6, 7

But 024567 is a 5-digit number because 0 at first left most place is meaningless. So, keeping 2 (instead of 0) at the left most place and then taking the smallest digit 0 i.e. 204567.

∴ Smallest 6-digit number = 204567

Now,   Sum = 765420 + 204567 = 969987

Que 17. A factory has a container filled with 35,874 L of cold drink. In how many bottles of 200 mL capacity each, can it be filled?

Sol. Given, capacity of container = 35,874 L

$$= 35,874 \times 100 \times 10 = 3,58,74,000 \text{ mL} \quad \begin{bmatrix} \because 1 \text{ litre} = 100 \text{ centilitres} \\ 1 \text{ centilitre} = 10 \text{ millilitres} \end{bmatrix}$$

Capacity of a bottle = 200 mL

∴ Number of bottles $= \dfrac{\text{Capacity of a container}}{\text{Capacity of a bottle}} = \dfrac{3,58,74,000}{200} = 1,79,370$

Que 18. The population of a town is 4,50,772. In a survey, it was reported that one out of every 14 persons is illiterate. In all, how many illiterate persons are there in the town?

Sol. Given, total population of a town = 450772

According to the survey, one person is illiterate out of every 14 persons.

∴ Number of illiterate persons $= \dfrac{\text{Total Population}}{\text{Ratio of illiterate persons}}$

$$= \dfrac{4,50,772}{14} = 32,198$$

Hence, there are 32198 illiterate persons in the town.

Que 19. How many grams should be added to 2 kg 300 g to make it 5 kg 68 g?

Sol. We will get the required weight by subtracting 2 kg 300 g from 5 kg 68 g.

Hence, 2768 g or 2 kg 768 g should be added to 2 kg 300 g to make it 5 kg 68 g.

	kg	g
	5	068
−	2	300
	2	768

Que 20. A box contains 50 packets of biscuits each weighing 120 g. How many such boxes can be loaded in a van, which cannot carry beyond 900 kg?

Sol. Given, weight of one packet of biscuit = 120 g

∴ Total weight of 50 packets of biscuits = 120 × 50 = 6000 g

$$= \dfrac{6000}{1000} \text{ kg} = 6 \text{ kg} \qquad \left[\because 1 \text{ g} = \dfrac{1}{1000} \text{ kg} \right]$$

Van can carry a weight of 900 kg.

∴ Number of packets that can be loaded in the van

$$= \frac{\text{Total weight strength of van}}{\text{Weight of one packet}} = \frac{900}{6} = 150$$

Hence, 150 boxes can be loaded in the van.

Que 21. How many lakhs make five billions?

Sol. We know that, 1 billion = 1000 millions

$$1 \text{ million} = 1000 \text{ thousands}$$
$$\therefore \quad 1 \text{ billion} = 1000 \times 1000 \text{ thousands}$$
$$= 1000000 \text{ thousands}$$
$$= 1000000 \times 1000$$
$$= 10000 \text{ lakh}$$

Now, 5 billions $= 5 \times 10000$ lakh
$$= 50000 \text{ lakh}$$

Que 22. How many millions make 3 crores?

Sol. We know that, 1 crore $= 10000000 = 10 \times 1000000$ [in digits]
$$= 10 \text{ million} \quad [\because 1 \text{ million} = 1000000]$$
$$\therefore \quad 3 \text{ crore} = 3 \times 10 \text{ millions} = 30 \text{ millions}$$

Que 23. The population of a town was 78,787 in the year 1991 and 95,833 in the year 2001. Estimate the increase in population by rounding off each population to nearest hundreds.

Sol. Given, population of town in 1991 = 78,787

and population of town in 2001 = 95833

$$\because \quad 78787 \rightarrow 78800 \quad [\text{rounding off to nearest hundreds}]$$
$$95833 \rightarrow 95800 \quad [\text{rounding off to nearest hundreds}]$$
$$\therefore \quad \text{Estimated increase} = 95,800 - 78,800 = 17,000$$

Que 24. A garment factory produced 2,16,315 shirts, 1,82,736 trousers and 58,704 jackets in a year. What is the total production of all the three items in that year?

Sol. According to the question,

A garment factory produced shirts = 2,16,315

Produced trousers = 1,82,736, Produced jackets = 58,704

∴ Total production of all the three items in that year

$$= \text{Sum of all items} = 2,16,315 + 1,82,736 + 58,704$$
$$= 4,57,755$$

Hence, the total production of all the three items in that year is 4,57,755.

Chapter **2**

Whole Numbers

Important Points

■ **Natural numbers** The counting numbers 1, 2, 3, 4, ... are known as natural numbers. The collection of natural numbers is denoted by N.

$$N = \{1, 2, 3, 4...\}$$

If we add 1 to any natural number, then we get the next number, which is called its **successor.**

If we subtract 1 from any natural number, then we get the previous number, which is called its **predecessor.**

> **Note** Every natural number has a successor and every natural number except 1 has a predecessor. (1 has no predecessor) 1 is the smallest natural number. There is no last and greatest number i.e. we have, infinite natural numbers.

■ **Whole numbers** The natural numbers along with zero form the collection of whole numbers. i.e. numbers 0, 1, 2, 3, 4, ... are called whole numbers. The collection of whole numbers is denoted by W.

$$W = \{0, 1, 2, 3, 4, ...\}$$

All natural numbers are whole numbers but all whole numbers are not natural numbers.

(∵ zero is a whole number but not a natural number)

> **Note** Every whole number has a successor and every whole number except 0 has a predecessor. There is no last and greatest whole number i.e. we have, infinite whole numbers.

- **The number line** We can represent whole numbers on a line called number line. To represent whole numbers on a number line, draw a straight line and mark a point on it and label it 0. Starting from 0 on the line mark equal intervals (of unit length) to the right of 0 and label them as 1, 2, 3, ... The distance between these points labelled as 0, 1 is called as unit distance.

  Thus, we represent whole number on the number line as shown below

  On the number line, the number on the right of the other number is the greater number and the number on the left of the other number is the smaller number.

- **Addition on number line** When we add any number to a given number, we move towards right on the number line.

- **Subtraction on number line** When we subtract any number from a given number, we move towards left on the number line.

- **Multiplication on number line** For multiplication, we make jumps of equal distance starting from origin.

Properties of Whole Numbers

    (i) **Closure property** The sum of any two whole numbers is a whole number and multiplication of two whole numbers is also a whole number. Thus, we can say that, whole numbers are closed under addition and under multiplication. This property is known as **closure property**.

    e.g. Let 8 and 5 are two whole numbers.

    Then, sum $= 8 + 5 = 13$, which is a whole number.

    Similarly, multiplication $= 8 \times 5 = 40$, which is a whole number.

> **Note** Whole numbers are not closed under subtraction and division, and division of a whole number by 0 is not defined.

    (ii) **Commutative property** Addition and multiplication are commutative for whole numbers. i.e. we can add or multiply two whole numbers in any order. This property is known as **commutative property**.

    For any two whole numbers a and b.

    $a + b = b + a$ and $a \times b = b \times a$

    e.g. As 3 and 4 are two whole numbers.

    Then, sum $3 + 4 = 4 + 3$ and multiply $3 \times 4 = 4 \times 3$

Note Subtraction and division are not commutative for whole numbers.

i.e. $\qquad a - b \neq b - a$ and $\dfrac{a}{b} \neq \dfrac{b}{a}$

(iii) **Associative property** Addition and multiplication are associative for whole numbers i.e. sum or multiplication of three or more than three whole numbers remains same on changing the grouping of the numbers and we group the numbers for convenience of adding or multiplication. This property is known as **associativity under addition** or **multiplication** for whole numbers.

For three whole numbers a, b and c.

$$a + (b + c) = (a + b) + c$$
$$a \times (b \times c) = (a \times b) \times c$$

e.g $\qquad 2 + (3 + 4) = (2 + 3) + 4$, both are equal to 9.

$\qquad 2 \times (3 \times 4) = (2 \times 3) \times 4$, both are equal to 24.

(iv) **Distributive property** Let a, b and c are three whole numbers.

Then $\quad a \times (b + c) = (a \times b) + (a \times c)$

e.g. $\qquad 2 \times (3 + 4) = (2 \times 3) + (2 \times 4)$, both are equal to 14.

This is known as **distributivity of multiplication over addition.**

(v) **Identity** Zero is the identity for addition of whole numbers and 1 is the identity for multiplication of whole numbers.

In other words, zero is the **additive identity** become on adding zero to a whole number it does not change i.e. its identity remain same and 1 is the **multiplicative identity** for whole numbers become on multipling one to whole number, it does not change i.e. its identity remain same.

Note Zero has a special role in multiplication, if any whole number is multiplied by zero, the product is always be zero.

These properties of whole numbers are useful (or helpful) in simplifying calculations.

- **Patterns in whole numbers** Every number can be arranged in one of these elementary shapes (i) a line, (ii) a rectangle, (iii) a square and (iv) a triangle.

  (i) Every number can be arranged as a line. • • •

  (ii) Some numbers like 6, 8, 12, ... can be shown as rectangle.

  • • •

  • • •

(iii) Some numbers like 4, 9, 16, ... can be shown as square.

• •

• •

(iv) Some numbers like 3, 6, 10, ... can be shown as triangle.

•

• •

The patterns of numbers are useful for verbal calculations and help us to understand properties of numbers better.

Try These (Page 28)

Que 1. Write the predecessor and successor of 19, 1997, 12000, 49 and 100000.

TIPS
To get predecessor of a number, we subtract 1 from that number and for successor, we add 1 to that number.

Sol.

	Given number	Predecessor	Successor
(a)	19	19 – 1 = 18	19 + 1 = 20
(b)	1997	1997 – 1 = 1996	1997 + 1 = 1998
(c)	12000	12000 – 1 = 11999	12000 + 1 = 12001
(d)	49	49 – 1 = 48	49 + 1 = 50
(e)	100000	100000 – 1 = 99999	100000 + 1 = 100001

Que 2. Is, there any natural number that has no predecessor?

Sol. Yes, the smallest natural number 1 has no predecessor, because predecessor of 1 is (1 – 1 = 0) zero and zero is not a natural number.

Que 3. Is, there any natural number, which has no successor? Is there a last natural number?

Sol. (i) No, there is no natural number which has no successor. Because each natural number has a successor.
e.g. Successor of 4 = 4 + 1 = 5
Successor of 5 = 5 + 1 = 6 and so on.

(ii) There is no last natural number, because natural number starts from 1 and goes upto infinite.

Try These (Page 29)

Que 4. Are all natural numbers also whole numbers?

Sol. Yes, all the natural numbers are also whole numbers.

Que 5. Are all whole numbers also natural numbers?

Sol. No, all whole numbers are not natural numbers. Because 0 is a whole number but it is not a natural number.

Que 6. Which is the greatest whole number?

Sol. Since, every whole number has a successor. So, there is no greatest whole number.

Try These (Page 30)

Que 7. Find using the number line.

    (i) 4 + 5   (ii) 2 + 6

    (iii) 3 + 5   (iv) 1 + 6

TIPS

When we add positive integer to a given number, we move towards right on the number line.

Sol.   (i) **To find 4 + 5**

Let us start from 4. Since, we have to add 5 to this number, we make 5 jumps to the right of 4. Each jump being equal to 1 unit. After five jumps, we reach at 9.

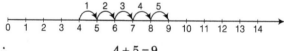

∴   4 + 5 = 9

(ii) **To find 2 + 6**

Let us start from 2. Since, we have to add 6 to this number, we make 6 jumps to the right of 2. Each jump being equal to 1 unit. After six jumps, we reach at 8.

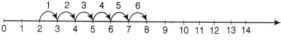

∴   2 + 6 = 8

(iii) **To find 3 + 5**

Let us start from 3. Since, we have to add 5 to this number, we make 5 jumps to the right of 3. Each jump being equal to 1 unit. After five jumps, we reach at 8.

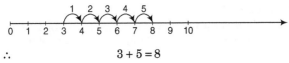

$\therefore$ $\qquad\qquad\qquad 3 + 5 = 8$

(iv) **To find 1 + 6**

Let us start from 1. Since, we have to add 6 to this number, we make 6 jumps to the right of 1. Each jump being equal to 1 unit. After six jumps, we reach at 7.

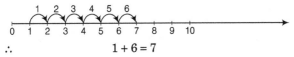

$\therefore$ $\qquad\qquad\qquad 1 + 6 = 7$

Que 8. Find using the number line.

(i) $8 - 3$ (ii) $6 - 2$ (iii) $9 - 6$

TIPS

When we subtract a negative integer from a given number, we moves towards left on the number line.

Sol. (i) **To find 8 – 3**

Let us start from 8 and make 3 equal jumps to the left of 8. Each jump is equal to 1 unit. Now, we reach at 5.

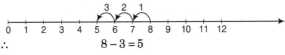

$\therefore$ $\qquad\qquad\qquad 8 - 3 = 5$

(ii) **To find 6 – 2**

Let us start from 6 and make 2 equal jumps to the left of 6. Each jump is equal to 1 unit. Now, we reach at 4.

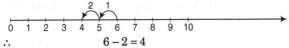

$\therefore$ $\qquad\qquad 6 - 2 = 4$

(iii) **To find 9 – 6**

Let us start from 9 and make 6 equal jumps to the left of 9. Each jump is equal to 1 unit. Now, we reach at 3.

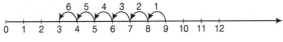

$\therefore$ $\qquad\qquad 9 - 6 = 3$

Try These (Page 31)

Que 9. Find using the number line.

    (i) 2×6 (ii) 3×3 (iii) 4×2

Sol.   (i) **To find 2×6**

We have to multiply 2 by 6 i.e. 2 units $\times 6$ (or 2 units 6 times).
Let us start from 0, move 2 units to the right of 0.

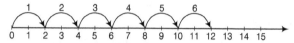

After making such 6 moves, we reach at 12.

∴ $2 \times 6 = 12$

  (ii) **To find 3×3**

We have to multiply 3 by 3 i.e. 3 units $\times 3$ (or 3 units 3 times).
Let us start from 0, move 3 units to the right of 0.

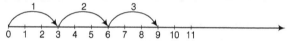

After making such 3 moves, we reach at 9.

∴ $3 \times 3 = 9$

  (iii) **To find 4×2**

We have to multiply 4 by 2 i.e. 4 units $\times 2$ (or 4 units 2 times).
Let us start from 0, move 4 units to the right of 0.

After making such 2 moves, we reach at 8.

∴ $4 \times 2 = 8$

Exercise 2.1

Que 1. Write the next three natural numbers after 10999.

Sol. The next three natural numbers, after 10999 are as follows:
   $10999 + 1 = 11000;\ 11000 + 1 = 11001;\ 11001 + 1 = 11002$
   i.e. 11000, 11001 and 11002.

Que 2. Write the three whole numbers occurring just before 10001.

Sol. The three whole numbers occurring just before 10001 are as follows :
   $10001 - 1 = 10000;\ 10000 - 1 = 9999;\ 9999 - 1 = 9998$
   i.e. 10000, 9999 and 9998.

Que 3. Which is the smallest whole number?

Sol. The smallest whole number is zero (0).

Que 4. How many whole numbers are there between 32 and 53?

Sol. Whole numbers between 32 and 53 are as follows:

33, 34, 35, 36, 37, 38, 39, 40, 41, 42, 43, 44, 45, 46, 47, 48, 49, 50, 51 and 52.

Hence, total number of whole numbers between 32 and 53 is 20.

Alternate Method

We can find the total number by using $(b - a) - 1$.

Where, a = First number and b = Last number

Here, $a = 32$, $b = 53$

Whole numbers between 32 and 53 = $(b - a) - 1$
$$= (53 - 32) - 1 \qquad \text{[putting the values of } a \text{ and } b]$$
$$= 21 - 1 = 20$$

Que 5. Write the successor of

    (a) 2440701   (b) 100199   (c) 1099999   (d) 2345670

Sol. We know that, successor is the next value of any number which is obtained by adding 1 on that number.

Hence, the successor of given number is as follows:

Given number	Successor
(a) 2440701	2440701 + 1 = 2440702
(b) 100199	100199 + 1 = 100200
(c) 1099999	1099999 + 1 = 1100000
(d) 2345670	2345670 + 1 = 2345671

Que 6. Write the predecessor of

    (a) 94   (b) 10000   (c) 208090   (d) 7654321

Sol. We know that, predecessor is the previous value of any number which is obtained by subtracting 1 from that number.

Hence, the predecessor of given number is as follows:

Given number	Predecessor
(a) 94	94 − 1 = 93
(b) 10000	10000 − 1 = 9999
(c) 208090	208090 − 1 = 208089
(d) 7654321	7654321 − 1 = 7654320

Que 7. In each of the following pairs of numbers, state which whole number is on the left on the other number on the number line. Also, write them with the appropriate sign (>, <) between them.

    (a) 530, 503   (b) 370, 307

    (c) 98765, 56789   (d) 9830415, 10023001

TIPS

The smaller number is to the left of bigger number on the number line and the bigger number is to the right of smaller number on the number line.

Sol. (a) On the number line, whole number 503 is on the left of 530.
Because 530 is greater than 503 i.e. 530 > 503.

  (b) On the number line, whole number 307 is on the left of 370.
Because 370 is greater than 307 i.e. 370 > 307.

  (c) On the number line, whole number 56789 is on the left of 98765.
Because 98765 is greater than 56789 i.e. 98765 > 56789.

  (d) On the number line, whole number 9830415 is on the left of 10023001.
Because 9830415 is less than 10023001 i.e. 9830415 < 10023001.

Que 8. Which of the following statements are true (T) and which are false (F)?

    (a) Zero is the smallest natural number.

    (b) 400 is the predecessor of 399.

    (c) Zero is the smallest whole number.

    (d) 600 is the successor of 599.

    (e) All natural numbers are whole numbers.

    (f) All whole numbers are natural numbers.

    (g) The predecessor of a two digit number is never a single digit number.

    (h) 1 is the smallest whole number.

    (i) The natural number 1 has no predecessor.

    (j) The whole number 1 has no predecessor.

    (k) The whole number 13 lies between 11 and 12.

    (l) The whole number 0 has no predecessor.

    (m) The successor of a two digit number is always a two digit number.

Sol. (a) False, because zero is not a natural number. It is a whole number.
(b) False, because predecessor of 399 is $399 - 1 = 398$.
(c) True, because whole numbers start with zero (0).
(d) True, because successor of 599 is $599 + 1 = 600$.
(e) True.
(f) False, because 0 is not a natural number.
(g) False, because predecessor of 10 is $10 - 1 = 9$, which is a single digit number.
(h) False, because 0 is the smallest whole number.
(i) True, because if we subtract 1 from 1, then we get 0 $(1 - 1 = 0)$, which is not a natural number.
(j) False, because predecessor of 1 is $1 - 1 = 0$ and 0 is a whole number.
(k) False, because 13 is greater than 12.
(l) True.
(m) False, because successor of two digit number 99 is $99 + 1 = 100$, which is a three digit number.

Try These (Page 37)

Que 1. Find   (i) $7 + 18 + 13$ (ii) $16 + 12 + 4$

Sol. (i) We have, $7 + 18 + 13 = (7 + 13) + 18$ [by associative property]
$$= 20 + 18 = 38$$
(ii) We have, $16 + 12 + 4 = (16 + 4) + 12$ [by associative property]
$$= 20 + 12 = 32$$

Que 2. Find   (i) $25 \times 8358 \times 4$ (ii) $625 \times 3759 \times 8$

Sol. (i) We have, $25 \times 8358 \times 4 = (25 \times 4) \times 8358$ [by associative property]
$$= 100 \times 8358 = 835800$$
(ii) We have, $625 \times 3759 \times 8 = (625 \times 8) \times 3759$
[by associative property]
$$= 5000 \times 3759 = 18795000$$

Try These (Page 39)

Que 3. Find using distributive property.
(i) 15×68 (ii) 17×23 (iii) $69 \times 78 + 22 \times 69$

Sol. (i) We have, $15 \times 68 = 15 \times (60 + 8) = 15 \times 60 + 15 \times 8$
[by distributive property of multiplication over addition]
$$= 900 + 120 = 1020$$

(ii) We have, $17 \times 23 = 17 \times (20 + 3) = 17 \times 20 + 17 \times 3$
                    [by distributive property of multiplication over addition]
                    $= 340 + 51 = 391$

(iii) We have, $69 \times 78 + 22 \times 69 = 69 \times (78 + 22)$

                    [taking 69 as a common term]
                    $= 69 \times 100 = 6900$

Exercise 2.2

Que 1. Find the sum by suitable rearrangement.

    (a) $837 + 208 + 363$ (b) $1962 + 453 + 1538 + 647$

> **TIPS**
> Sum of three or more than three whole numbers remains same on changing the grouping of the numbers and we group the numbers for convenience of adding. This property is known as associativity of addition for whole numbers.

Sol. (a) We have, $837 + 208 + 363 = (837 + 363) + 208$

                    [by associative property]

                    $= 1200 + 208 = 1408$

    (b) We have, $1962 + 453 + 1538 + 647 = (1962 + 1538) + (453 + 647)$
                    $= 3500 + 1100 = 4600$

Note We rearrange the number in such a way that new number obtained after rearrangement has zero.

Que 2. Find the product by suitable rearrangement.

    (a) $2 \times 1768 \times 50$ (b) $4 \times 166 \times 25$

    (c) $8 \times 291 \times 125$ (d) $625 \times 279 \times 16$

    (e) $285 \times 5 \times 60$ (f) $125 \times 40 \times 8 \times 25$

> **TIPS**
> First, we multiply those two numbers, which can give us zero (0) like 100, 1000 etc. Because, to multiply any number with these numbers is simple.

Sol. (a) We have, $2 \times 1768 \times 50 = (2 \times 50) \times 1768$
                    $= 100 \times 1768 = 176800$

    (b) We have, $4 \times 166 \times 25 = (4 \times 25) \times 166 = 100 \times 166 = 16600$

    (c) We have, $8 \times 291 \times 125 = (8 \times 125) \times 291$
                    $= 1000 \times 291 = 291000$

(d) We have, $625 \times 279 \times 16 = (625 \times 16) \times 279$
$$= 10000 \times 279 = 2790000$$

(e) We have, $285 \times 5 \times 60 = (5 \times 60) \times 285 = 300 \times 285 = 85500$

(f) We have, $125 \times 40 \times 8 \times 25 = (125 \times 40) \times (8 \times 25)$
$$= 5000 \times 200 = 1000000$$

Que 3. Find the value of the following.

(a) $297 \times 17 + 297 \times 3$

(b) $54279 \times 92 + 8 \times 54279$

(c) $81265 \times 169 - 81265 \times 69$

(d) $3845 \times 5 \times 782 + 769 \times 25 \times 218$

Sol. (a) We have, $297 \times 17 + 297 \times 3 = 297 \times (17 + 3) = 297 \times 20 = 5940$
[taking 297 as a common term]

(b) We have, $54279 \times 92 + 8 \times 54279 = 54279 \times (92 + 8)$
[taking 54279 as a common term]
$$= 54279 \times 100 = 5427900$$

(c) We have, $81265 \times 169 - 81265 \times 69 = 81265 \times (169 - 69)$
[Taking 81265 as a common term]
$$= 81265 \times 100 = 8126500$$

(d) We have, $3845 \times 5 \times 782 + 769 \times 25 \times 218$
$= 3845 \times 5 \times 782 + (769 \times 5) \times 5 \times 218$ $[\because 25 = 5 \times 5]$
$= 3845 \times 5 \times 782 + 3845 \times 5 \times 218 = 3845 \times 5 \times (782 + 218)$
$= 3845 \times 5 \times 1000 = 19225 \times 1000 = 19225000$

Que 4. Find the product using suitable properties.

(a) 738×103 (b) 854×102

(c) 258×1008 (d) 1005×168

Sol. (a) We have, $738 \times 103 = 738 \times (100 + 3) = 738 \times 100 + 738 \times 3$
[by distributive property of multiplication over addition]
$$= 73800 + 2214 = 76014$$

(b) We have, $854 \times 102 = 854 \times (100 + 2) = 854 \times 100 + 854 \times 2$
[by distributive property of multiplication over addition]
$$= 85400 + 1708 = 87108$$

(c) We have, $258 \times 1008 = 258 \times (1000 + 8) = 258 \times 1000 + 258 \times 8$
[by distributive property of multiplication over addition]
$$= 258000 + 2064 = 260064$$

(d) We have, $1005 \times 168 = (1000 + 5) \times 168 = 168 \times (1000 + 5)$
$$= 168 \times 1000 + 168 \times 5$$
[by distributive property of multiplication over addition]
$$= 168000 + 840 = 168840$$

Que 5. A taxidriver filled his car petrol tank with 40 litres of petrol on Monday. The next day, he filled the tank with 50 litres of petrol. If the petrol costs.₹ 44 per litre, how much did he spend in all on petrol?

Sol. Given, quantity of petrol filled on Monday = 40 L
Quantity of petrol filled on the next day i.e. Tuesday = 50 L
Total quantity of petrol = 40 + 50 = 90 L
Cost of petrol = ₹ 44 per litre
Total cost of petrol = Cost per litre × Total quantity of petrol
$$= 44 \times 90 = ₹ 3960$$
Hence, total cost of petrol is ₹. 3960.

Que 6. A vendor supplies 32 litres of milk to a hotel in the morning and 68 litres of milk in the evening. If the milk costs. ₹15 per litre, how much money is due to the vendor per day?

Sol. Given, milk supplied in the morning = 32 L
Milk supplied in the evening = 68 L
Total milk supplied to a hotel in the morning and evening
$$= 32 + 68 = 100 \text{ L}$$
Money due to vendor per day = Total quantity of milk × Cost per litre
$$= 100 \times 15 = ₹ 1500$$

Que 7. Match the following.

(i) 425 × 136 = 425 × (6 + 30 + 100)	(a) Commutativity under multiplication
(ii) 2 × 49 × 50 = 2 × 50 × 49	(b) Commutativity under addition
(iii) 80 + 2005 + 20 = 80 + 20 + 2005	(c) Distributivity of multiplication over addition

Sol. (i) We have, $425 \times 136 = 425 \times (6 + 30 + 100)$
$$= 425 \times 6 + 425 \times 30 + 425 \times 100$$
It is distributivity of multiplication over addition.
Hence, (i) belongs to (c).

(ii) We have, $2 \times 49 \times 50 = 2 \times 50 \times 49$
Here, we have changed the place of 49 and 50.
So, it comes under commutativity under multiplication.
Hence, (ii) belongs to (a).

(iii) We have, $80 + 2005 + 20 = 80 + 20 + 2005$
Here, we have changed the place of 20 and 2005.
So, it comes under commutativity under addition.
Hence, (iii) belongs to (b).

Try These (Page 42)

Que 1. Which numbers can be shown only as a line?

Sol. Every numnber can be shown as a line. Some of them are 2, 5, 7, 11, 13, ... e.g. 5 can be shown as • • • • •

Que 2. Which number can be shown as square?

Sol. A number which is square of a number can be shown as square. So, numbers that can be shown as squares are 4, 9, 16, 25,... e.g. 9 can be shown as

Que 3. Which numbers can be shown as rectangle?

Sol. Numbers that can be shown as rectangle are 6, 8, 10, 12,.... e.g. 8 can be shown as

Que 4. Write down the first seven numbers that can be arranged as triangle e.g. 3,6, ...

Sol. First seven numbers that can be arranged as triangle are 3, 6, 10, 15, 21, 28 and 36. e.g. 3 and 6 can be shown as

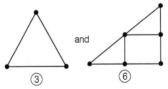

Que 5. Some numbers can be shown by two rectangles, e.g.

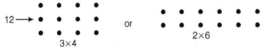

Give at least five other such examples.

Sol. There are many examples of such type. Five of them are as follows:

(i)

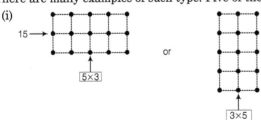

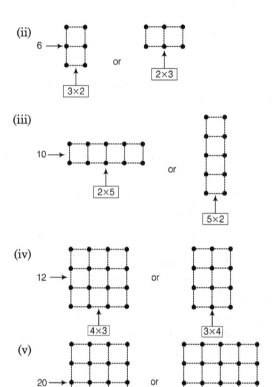

Exercise 2.3

Que 1. Which of the following will not represent zero?

(a) $1 + 0$ (b) 0×0 (c) $\dfrac{0}{2}$ (d) $\dfrac{10 - 10}{2}$

Sol. (a) $1 + 0 = 1 \neq 0$ (b) $0 \times 0 = 0$

(c) $\dfrac{0}{2} = 0 \times \dfrac{1}{2} = 0$ (d) $\dfrac{10 - 10}{2} = \dfrac{0}{2} = 0$

Thus, only option (a) does not represent zero.

Que 2. If the product of two whole numbers is zero, can we say that one or both of them will be zero? Justify through examples.

Sol. Yes, if the product of two whole numbers is zero, then one or both of them will be zero. Since, we know that the product of any whole number with zero is always zero i.e. $a \times 0 = 0$, where a is any whole number and $0 \times 0 = 0$. Some examples are as follows:

Whole number	Product (a × 0)	Product (0 × a)	Is the product zero?
5	5 × 0 = 0	0 × 5 = 0	Yes
3	3 × 0 = 0	0 × 3 = 0	Yes
0	0 × 0 = 0	0 × 0 = 0	Yes
4	4 × 0 = 0	0 × 4 = 0	Yes
25	25 × 0 = 0	0 × 25 = 0	Yes

Que 3. If the product of two whole numbers is 1, can we say that one or both of them will be 1? Justify through examples.

Sol. We know that, on multiplying any whole number by 1, we get the same whole number.

i.e. $5 \times 1 = 5; 20 \times 1 = 20; 1 \times 0 = 0; 1 \times 1 = 1$

Hence, the product of two whole numbers will be equal to 1, if and only if both whole numbers are 1.

Que 4. Find using distributive property.

 (a) 728×101 (b) 5437×1001 (c) 824×25

 (d) 4275×125 (e) 504×35

Sol. (a) We have, $728 \times 101 = 728 \times (100 + 1) = 728 \times 100 + 728 \times 1$

      [by distributive property of multiplication over addition]
        $= 72800 + 728 = 73528$

 (b) We have, $5437 \times 1001 = 5437 \times (1000 + 1)$

          $= 5437 \times 1000 + 5437 \times 1$

      [by distributive property of multiplication over addition]
        $= 5437000 + 5437 = 5442437$

 (c) We have, $824 \times 25 = 824 \times (20 + 5) = 824 \times 20 + 824 \times 5$

      [by distributive property of multiplication over addition]
        $= 16480 + 4120 = 20600$

(d) We have, $4275 \times 125 = 4275 \times (100 + 20 + 5)$
$$= 4275 \times 100 + 4275 \times 20 + 4275 \times 5$$
[by distributive property of multiplication over addition]
$$= 427500 + 85500 + 21375 = 513000 + 21375 = 534375$$

(e) We have, $504 \times 35 = 35 \times 504$ [by commutative property]
$$= 35 \times (500 + 4) = 35 \times 500 + 35 \times 4$$
[By distributive property of multiplication over addition]
$$= 17500 + 140 = 17640$$

Que 5. Study the pattern.

$$1 \times 8 + 1 = 9$$
$$1234 \times 8 + 4 = 9876$$
$$12 \times 8 + 2 = 98$$
$$12345 \times 8 + 5 = 98765$$
$$123 \times 8 + 3 = 987$$

Write the next two steps. Can you say how the pattern works?

(**Hint** $12345 = 11111 + 1111 + 111 + 11 + 1$)

Sol. It is clear that the next two steps will be

$123456 \times 8 + 6 = 987654$ and $1234567 \times 8 + 7 = 9876543$

Pattern of the working is given below

$$11 + 1 = 12$$
$$111 + 11 + 1 = 123$$
$$1111 + 111 + 11 + 1 = 1234$$
$$11111 + 1111 + 111 + 11 + 1 = 12345$$

$\therefore$
$$1 \times 8 + 1 = 9 = 1 \times 8 + 1$$
$$12 \times 8 + 2 = 98 = (11 + 1) \times 8 + 2$$
$$123 \times 8 + 3 = 987 = (111 + 11 + 1) \times 8 + 3$$
$$1234 \times 8 + 4 = 9876 = (1111 + 111 + 11 + 1) \times 8 + 4$$
$$12345 \times 8 + 5 = 98765 = (11111 + 1111 + 111 + 11 + 1) \times 8 + 5$$

and the next two steps will be work as $123456 \times 8 + 6 = 987654$
$$= (111111 + 11111 + 1111 + 111 + 11 + 1) \times 8 + 6$$

$$1234567 \times 8 + 7 = 9876543$$
$$= (1111111 + 111111 + 11111 + 1111 + 111 + 11 + 1) \times 8 + 7$$

Selected **NCERT Exemplar Problems**

Directions *In questions 1 to 5 out of the four options, only one is correct. Write the correct answer.*

Que 1. The product of successor and predecessor of 999 is

    (a) 999000 (b) 998000   (c) 989000   (d) 1998

Sol. Successor of 999 = 999 + 1 = 1000

    Predecessor of 999 = 999 − 1 = 998

∴ Product = 1000 × 998 = 998000

    Hence, option (b) is correct.

Que 2. The product of a non-zero whole number and its successor is always

    (a) an even number   (b) an odd number

    (c) a prime number   (d) divisible by 3

Sol. The product of a non-zero whole number and its successor is always an even number.

    e.g.   A non-zero whole number   = 1

                    Successor of 1   = 1 + 1 = 2

    ∴   Product   = 1 × 2 = 2 (even)

    Hence, option (a) is correct.

Que 3. A whole number is added to 25 and the same number is subtracted from 25. The sum of the resulting numbers is

    (a) 0   (b) 25   (c) 50   (d) 75

Sol. Let, a whole number = 2

    According to the question,

    A whole number is added to 25 = 25 + 2 = 27

    and a whole number is subtracted from 25 = 25 − 2 = 23

    ∴ The sum of resulting numbers = 27 + 23 = 50

    Hence, option (c) is correct.

Que 4. Which of the following statements is not true?

    (a) $0 + 0 = 0$ (b) $0 - 0 = 0$

    (c) $0 \times 0 = 0$ (d) $0 \div 0 = 0$

Sol. We know that, if a is a whole number then $a \div 0$ is not defined.

    So, option (d) is not true.

Que 5. The greatest number, which always divides the product of the predecessor and successor of an odd natural number other than 1, is

    (a) 6   (b) 4   (c) 16   (d) 8

Sol. Let, an odd natural number other than 1 be 3.

2	2, 4
2	1, 2
	1, 1

        Predecessor of 3 $= 3 - 1 = 2$
        Successor of 3 $= 3 + 1 = 4$
∴   Product $= 2 \times 4 = 8$
Now, LCM of predecessor and successor $= 2 \times 2 = 4$

∴ The greatest number which always divides the product of predecessor and successor of an odd natural number other than 1 is 4. Hence, option (b) is correct.

Directions *In questions 6 to 14, state whether the given statement is true (T) or false (F).*

Que 6. Successor of a one digit number is always a one digit number.

Sol. False, because successor of a one-digit number is not always a one digit number.

e.g. Let one digit number be 9.

∴ Successor of $9 = 9 + 1 = 10$, which is a two digit number.

Que 7. Predecessor of a two digit number is always a two digit number.

Sol. False, because predecessor of a two digit number is not always a two digit number.

e.g.   Let a two digit number be 10.

∴   Predecessor of $10 = 10 - 1 = 9$, which is a one digit number.

Que 8. Between any two natural numbers, there is one natural numbers.

Sol. False, because between any two natural numbers, there are many (one or more than one) natural numbers.

Que 9. The smallest 4-digit number is the successor of the largest 3-digit number.

Sol. True, the smallest 4-digit number is the successor of the largest 3-digit number. e.g. Largest 3-digit number = 999

∴   successor of $999 = 999 + 1$

                            $= 1000$ (smallest four digit number)

Que 10. There is a whole number which when added to a whole number, gives the number itself.

Sol. True, because there is a whole number which when added to a whole number, gives the number itself.
e.g. Let a whole number be 0.
Other whole number be 1.
∴ $0 + 1 = 1 + 0 = 1$

Que 11. If a whole number is divided by another whole number, which is greater than the first one, the quotient is not equal to zero.

Sol. True, if a whole number is divided by another whole number which is greater than the first one, the quotient is not equal to zero.

Que 12. A whole number divided by another whole number greater than 1 never gives the quotient equal to the former.

Sol. True, a whole number divided by another whole number greater than 1 never gives the quotient equal to the former.

Que 13. Sum of two whole numbers is always less than their product.

Sol. False, because sum of two whole numbers is not always less than their product.
e.g. (i) Let two whole numbers be 2 and 3.
Sum $= 2 + 3 = 5$ Product $= 2 \times 3 = 6$
∴ Sum of two whole numbers < Product of two whole numbers
Again, let two whole numbers be 1 and 2.
∴ Sum $= 1 + 2 = 3$ Product $= 1 \times 2 = 2$
∴ Sum of two whole numbers > Product of two whole numbers

It is clear that the sum of two whole numbers is not always less than their product.

Que 14. If the sum of two distinct whole numbers is odd, then their difference also must be odd.

Sol. True, if the sum of two distinct whole numbers is odd then their difference also must be odd.
e.g.   Let two distinct whole numbers be 5 and 8
∴   Sum $= 5 + 8 = 13$ Difference $= 8 - 5 = 3$

Directions *In questions 15 to 19, fill in the blanks to make the statements true.*

Que 15. .... is the successor of the largest 3-digit number.

Sol. Largest 3-digit number $= 999$

∴ Successor of $999 = 999 + 1 = 1000$

Hence, **1000** is the successor of the largest 3-digit number.

It is clear that, if 0 is subtracted from a whole number, then the result is the number itself.

Que 16. The smallest 6-digit natural number ending in 5 is ....

Sol. Smallest 6-digit number $= 100000$

∴ Smallest 6-digit number ending in $5 = 100000 + 5 = 100005$

It is clear that the smallest 6-digit numb

Que 17. $1001 \times 2002 = 1001 \times (1001 + ...)$.

Sol. $1001 \times 2002 = 1001 \times (1001 + \underline{1001})$.

Que 18. $786 \times 3 + 786 \times 7 = ...$.

Sol. $786 \times 3 + 786 \times 7 = 786 \times (3 + 7) = 786 \times 10 = \underline{7860}$.

Que 19. $24 \times \underline{25} = 24 \times \overline{4} = 600$

Sol. $24 \times 25 = 24 \times \dfrac{100}{4} = 600$

Que 20. Determine the sum of the four numbers as given below:

    (a) successor of 32

    (b) predecessor of 49

    (c) predecessor of the predecessor of 56

    (d) successor of the successor of 67

Sol. (a) Successor of $32 = 32 + 1 = 33$

    (b) Predecessor of $49 = 49 - 1 = 48$

    (c) Predecessor of $56 = 56 - 1 = 55$

        Again, predecessor of $55 = 55 - 1 = 54$

    (d) Successor of $67 = 67 + 1 = 68$

        Again, successor of $68 = 68 + 1 = 69$

    ∴ Sum $= 33 + 48 + 54 + 69 = 204$

Chapter **3**

Playing with Numbers

Important Points

- **Factors and multiples** A factor of a number is an exact divisor of that number. e.g. 1, 2, 3 and 6 are exact divisors of 6. So, 1, 2, 3 and 6 are factors of 6.

  A number is a multiple of each of its factors.

  e.g. 6 is a multiple of 2 and 3.

  (i) 1 is a factor of every number.

  (ii) Every number is a factor of itself.

  (iii) Every factor is less than or equal to the given number.

  (iv) Number of factors of a given number are finite.

  (v) Every multiple of a number is greater than or equal to that number.

  (vi) The number of multiples of a given number is infinite.

  (vii) Every number is a multiple of itself.

- **Perfect number** If sum of all factors of a number is equal to twice the number, then the number is called a perfect number.

  e.g. All factors of 28 are 1, 2, 4, 7, 14 and 28.

  Their sum $= 1 + 2 + 4 + 7 + 14 + 28 = 56 = 2 \times 28$.

  So, 28 is a perfect number.

- **Prime numbers** The numbers other than 1, whose only factors are 1 and the number itself are called prime numbers. Some prime numbers are 2, 3, 5, 7 and 11, etc.

- **Composite numbers** The numbers having more than two factors are called composite numbers. Some composite numbers are 4, 6, 8, 9 and 10, etc.

  Note 1 is neither a prime number nor a composite number, because it has one factor.

- **Even numbers** The numbers which are multiple of 2 are called even numbers. e.g. 0, 2, 4, 6, ..., etc., are even numbers.

  Or

  The numbers which are completely divided by 2 are known as even numbers.

- **Odd numbers** The numbers which are not completely divided by 2 are known as odd numbers. e.g. 1, 3, 5, 7, ..., etc., are odd numbers because, these numbers are not completely divided by 2. In the words, a number with 1, 3, 5, 9 at the one's place is an odd number

  Note 2 is the smallest prime number which is even and every prime number except 2 is odd.

- **Tests for divisibility of numbers**
    - (i) A number is **divisible by 2**, if it has any of the digits 0, 2, 4, 6 or 8 in its ones place.
    - (ii) A number is **divisible by 3**, if the sum of its digits is divisible by 3.
    - (iii) A number with 3 or more digits is **divisible by 4**, if the number formed by its last two digits (i.e. ones and tens) is divisible by 4.
    - (iv) A number is **divisible by 6**, if the number is divisible by 2 and 3 both.
    - (v) A number is **divisible by 5**, if it has either 0 or 5 in its ones place.
    - (vi) A number with 4 or more digits is **divisible by 8**, if the number formed by the last three digits is divisible by 8.
    - (vii) A number is **divisible by 9**, if the sum of its digits is divisible by 9.
    - (viii) A number is **divisible by 10**, if it has 0 in its ones place.
    - (ix) A number is **divisible by 11**, if the difference between the sum of the digits at odd places (from the right) and the sum of the digits at even places (from the right) of the number is either 0 or divisible by 11.

- **Co-prime numbers** Two numbers, which have only 1 as a common factor are called co-prime numbers.

Note Any two prime numbers are always co-primes, but two co-primes need not be be both prime numbers.

- **Some more divisibility rule**
  (i) If a number is divisible by another number, then it is divisible by each of the factors of that number. e.g. 18 is divisible by 9 and the factors of 9 i.e. 1, 3 also divide 18.
  (ii) If a number is divisible by two co-prime numbers, then it is divisible by their product also. e.g. 80 is divisible by 4 and 5. It is also divisible by $4 \times 5 = 20$ and 4, 5 are co-primes numbers.
  (iii) If two given numbers are divisible by a number, then their sum is also divisible by that number.
  e.g. 24 and 30 are both divisible by 6 and the sum of these number 24+30=54 is also divisible by 6.
  (iv) If two given numbers are divisible by a number, then their difference is also divisible by that number.
  e.g. The numbers 16 and 36 are both divisible by 4. The difference 36 −16 = 20 is also divisible by 4.

- **Prime factorisation** The process in which a number is expressed as product of prime factors is called a prime factorisation.
  e.g. Prime factorisation of $24 = 2 \times 2 \times 2 \times 3$

  Here, 2 and 3 both are prime numbers.

  Note Prime factorisation of a number is always unique, i.e. it can be factorised into prime in only one way.

- **Highest Common Factor** (HCF) The highest common factor of two or more given numbers is the highest (or greatest) factor out of their common factors. It is also known as **Greatest Common Divisor** (GCD).

- **Lowest Common Multiple** (LCM) The lowest common multiple of two or more given numbers is the lowest (or smallest or least) multiple out of their common multiples.

Try These (Page 48)

Que 1. Find the possible factors of 45, 30 and 36.

We know that, a factor of a number is an exact divisor of that number. So, for finding factors of given number, we divide it by 1, 2, 3, ... one by one and note the quotient (If remainder = 0). The number, which divides given number and corresponding quotient, both will be the factors of that number.

Sol. (i) We have, 45

On dividing 45 by 1,

We get, divisor $= 1$ and quotient $= 45$

i.e. $1 \times 45 = 45$

So, **1 and 45 are factors of 45.**

Now, on dividing 45 by 3,

We get, divisor $= 3$ and quotient $= 15$

i.e. $3 \times 15 = 45$

So, **3 and 15 are factors of 45.**

Again, on dividing 45 by 5,

We get, divisor $= 5$ and quotient $= 9$

i.e. $5 \times 9 = 45$

So, **5 and 9 are factors of 45.**

Again, on dividing 45 by 9, we get quotient 5

i.e. $9 \times 5 = 45$

But it is repetition of above step, so we will stop this process here.

Hence, factors of 45 are 1, 3, 5, 9, 15 and 45.

$$\begin{array}{r} 1\overline{)45}(18 \\ \underline{4} \\ 5 \\ \underline{5} \\ 0 \end{array}$$

$$\begin{array}{r} 3\overline{)45}(15 \\ \underline{3} \\ 15 \\ \underline{15} \\ 0 \end{array}$$

$$\begin{array}{r} 5\overline{)45}(9 \\ \underline{45} \\ 0 \end{array}$$

Note Here, on dividing 45 by 2, 4, 6, 7, ..., we get remainder. So, we will not consider these cases.

(ii) We have, 30

On dividing 30 by 1,

We get, divisor $= 1$ and quotient $= 30$

i.e. $1 \times 30 = 30$

So, **1 and 30 are factors of 30.**

Now, on dividing 30 by 2,

We get, divisor $= 2$ and quotient $= 15$

i.e. $2 \times 15 = 30$

So, **2 and 15 are factors of 30.**

Again, on dividing 30 by 3,

We get, divisor $= 3$ and quotient $= 10$

i.e. $3 \times 10 = 30$

So, **3 and 10 are factors of 30.**

Again on dividing 30 by 5,

We get, divisor $= 5$ and quotient $= 6$

i.e. $5 \times 6 = 30$

So, **5 and 6 are factors of 30.**

$$\begin{array}{r} 1\overline{)30}(30 \\ \underline{30} \\ 0 \\ 0 \\ \overline{0} \end{array}$$

$$\begin{array}{r} 2\overline{)30}(15 \\ \underline{2} \\ 10 \\ \underline{10} \\ 0 \end{array}$$

$$\begin{array}{r} 3\overline{)30}(10 \\ \underline{3} \\ 0 \\ \underline{0} \\ 0 \end{array}$$

$$\begin{array}{r} 5\overline{)30}(6 \\ \underline{30} \\ 0 \end{array}$$

Again, on dividing 30 by 6, we get quotient 5.

But it is the repetition of above step, so we will stop this process here.

Hence, factors of 30 are 1, 2, 3, 5, 6, 10, 15 and 30.

(iii) We have, 36

On dividing 36 by 1,

We get, divisor = 1 and quotient = 36

i.e. $1 \times 36 = 36$

So, **1 and 36 are factors of 36.**

Now, on dividing 36 by 2,

We get, divisor = 2 and quotient = 18

i.e. $2 \times 18 = 36$

So, **2 and 18 are factors of 36.**

Again, on dividing 36 by 3,

We get, divisor = 3 and quotient = 12

i.e. $3 \times 12 = 36$

So, **3 and 12 are factors of 36.**

Again, on dividing 36 by 4,

$$\begin{array}{r} 4\overline{)36}(9 \\ \underline{36} \\ 0 \end{array}$$

We get, divisor = 4 and quotient = 9 i.e. $4 \times 9 = 36$

So, **4 and 9 are factors of 36.**

Again, on dividing 36 by 6,

We get, divisor = 6 and quotient = 6

i.e. $6 \times 6 = 36$

So, **6 and 6 are factors of 36.**

Again, on dividing 36 by 9, we get quotient 4.

But it is the repetition of above second last step, so we will stop this process here.

Hence, factors of 36 are 1, 2, 3, 4, 6, 9, 12, 18 and 36.

$$\begin{array}{r} 1\overline{)36}(36 \\ \underline{3} \\ 6 \\ \underline{6} \\ 0 \end{array}$$

$$\begin{array}{r} 2\overline{)36}(18 \\ \underline{2} \\ 16 \\ \underline{16} \\ 0 \end{array}$$

$$\begin{array}{r} 3\overline{)36}(12 \\ \underline{3} \\ 6 \\ \underline{6} \\ 0 \end{array}$$

$$\begin{array}{r} 6\overline{)36}(6 \\ \underline{36} \\ 0 \end{array}$$

Exercise 3.1

Que 1. Write all the factors of the following numbers

(a) 24   (b) 15   (c) 21

(d) 27   (e) 12   (f) 20

(g) 18   (h) 23   (i) 36

Sol. (a) We have, 24

$$24 = 1 \times 24; 24 = 2 \times 12; 24 = 3 \times 8; = 4 \times 6$$

∴ Factors of 24 are 1, 2, 3, 4, 6, 8, 12 and 24.

(b) We have, 15

$$15 = 1 \times 15; 15 = 3 \times 5$$

∴ Factors of 15 are 1, 3, 5 and 15.

(c) We have, 21

$$21 = 1 \times 21; 21 = 3 \times 7$$

∴ Factors of 21 are 1, 3, 7 and 21.

(d) We have, 27

$$27 = 1 \times 27; 27 = 3 \times 9$$

∴ Factors of 27 are 1, 3, 9 and 27.

(e) We have, 12

$$12 = 1 \times 12; 12 = 2 \times 6; 12 = 3 \times 4$$

∴ Factors of 12 are 1, 2, 3, 4, 6 and 12.

(f) We have, 20

$$20 = 1 \times 20; 20 = 2 \times 10; 20 = 4 \times 5$$

∴ Factors of 20 are 1, 2, 4, 5, 10 and 20.

(g) We have, 18

$$18 = 1 \times 18; 18 = 2 \times 9; 18 = 3 \times 6$$

∴ Factors of 18 are 1, 2, 3, 6, 9 and 18.

(h) We have, 23

$$23 = 1 \times 23$$

∴ Factors of 23 are 1 and 23.

(i) We have, 36

$$36 = 1 \times 36; 36 = 2 \times 18; 36 = 3 \times 12; \ 36 = 4 \times 9; 36 = 6 \times 6$$

∴ Factors of 36 are 1, 2, 3, 4, 6, 9, 12, 18 and 36.

Que 2. Write first five multiples of

   (a) 5   (b) 8   (c) 9

Sol. (a) Multiples of 5,

$$5 \times 1 = 5; 5 \times 2 = 10; 5 \times 3 = 15; 5 \times 4 = 20; 5 \times 5 = 25$$

∴ First five multiples of 5 are 5, 10, 15, 20 and 25.

(b) Multiples of 8,

$$8 \times 1 = 8; 8 \times 2 = 16; 8 \times 3 = 24; 8 \times 4 = 32; 8 \times 5 = 40$$

∴ First five multiples of 8 are 8, 16, 24, 32 and 40.

(c) Multiples of 9, $9 \times 1 = 9; 9 \times 2 = 18; 9 \times 3 = 27; 9 \times 4 = 36 ; 9 \times 5 = 45$

∴ First five multiples of 9 are 9, 18, 27, 36 and 45.

Note We can also write the 'Table' of required number to get the multiples of that number.

Que 3. Match the items in column 1 with the items in column 2.

	Column 1		Column 2
(i)	35	(a)	Multiple of 8
(ii)	15	(b)	Multiple of 7
(iii)	16	(c)	Multiple of 70
(iv)	20	(d)	Factor of 30
(v)	25	(e)	Factor of 50
		(f)	Factor of 20

Sol. (i) Factors of 35 are 5 and 7 and we know that, a number is a multiple of each of its factor. Hence, 35 is a multiple of 7.

(ii) We know that, a factor of a number is an exact divisor of that number.

Here, 30 is divided by 15. So, 15 is a factor of 30.

(iii) Factors of 16 are 2 and 8 and we know that, a number is a multiple of each of its factor. Hence, 16 is a multiple of 8.

(iv) We know that, every number is a factor of itself. So, 20 is a factor of itself i.e. 20.

(v) We know that, a factor of a number is an exact divisor of that number. Here, 50 is divided by 25. So, 25 is a factor of 50.

Now, matching of these items is as follows:

(i) $\rightarrow$ (b)   (ii) $\rightarrow$ (d)   (iii) $\rightarrow$ (a)
(iv) $\rightarrow$ (f)   (v) $\rightarrow$ (e)

Que 4. Find all the multiples of 9 upto 100.

Sol. Multiples of 9 upto 100 are as follows:

$9 \times 1 = 9;$ $9 \times 4 = 36;$ $9 \times 7 = 63;$ $9 \times 10 = 90$
$9 \times 2 = 18;$ $9 \times 5 = 45;$ $9 \times 8 = 72;$ $9 \times 11 = 99$
$9 \times 3 = 27;$ $9 \times 6 = 54;$ $9 \times 9 = 81$

Hence, all the multiples of 9 upto 100 are 9, 18, 27, 36, 45, 54, 63, 72, 81, 90 and 99.

Try These (Page 52)

Que 1. Observe that $2 \times 3 + 1 = 7$ is a prime number. Here, 1 has been added to a multiple of 2 to get a prime number. Can you find some more numbers of this type?

Sol. Some more numbers of this type are as follows :

$2 \times 2 + 1 = 5; 2 \times 5 + 1 = 11; 2 \times 6 + 1 = 13$
$2 \times 8 + 1 = 17; 2 \times 9 + 1 = 19; 2 \times 11 + 1 = 23$

Here, all numbers 5, 11, 13, 17, 19 and 23 are prime numbers and 1 has been added to a multiple of 2 to get these prime numbers.

Exercise 3.2

Que 1. What is the sum of any two (a) odd numbers?
(b) even numbers?

 TIPS We know that a number is called an even number, if it is completely divided by 2 (i.e. remainder = 0). Otherwise, it is an odd number.

Sol. (a) Let the two odd numbers be 5 and 7.

$$\text{Sum} = 5 + 7 = 12 \qquad \text{(even number)}$$

Taking one more example,

Let the two odd numbers be 3 and 7.

$$\text{Sum} = 3 + 7 = 10 \qquad \text{(even number)}$$

Hence, we can say, sum of any two odd numbers is an even number.

(b) Let the two even numbers be 4 and 8.

$$\text{Sum} = 4 + 8 = 12 \qquad \text{(even number)}$$

Taking one more example,

Let the two even numbers be 6 and 20.

$$\text{Sum} = 6 + 20 = 26 \qquad \text{(even number)}$$

Hence, we can say, sum of any two even numbers is an even number.

Que 2. State whether the following statements are true or false.

(a) The sum of three odd numbers is even.

(b) The sum of two odd numbers and one even number is even.

(c) The product of three odd numbers is odd.

(d) If an even number is divided by 2, the quotient is always odd.

(e) All prime numbers are odd.

(f) Prime numbers do not have any factor.

(g) Sum of two prime numbers is always even.

(h) 2 is the only even prime number.

(i) All even numbers are composite numbers.

(j) The product of two even numbers is always even.

Sol. (a) False, because the sum of three odd numbers is always odd.

e.g. $3 + 5 + 7 = 15$ and $9 + 11 + 13 = 33$ (odd)

(b) True, because the sum of two odd numbers and one even number is always an even number.

e.g. $\underset{\underset{\text{Odd}}{\downarrow}}{3} + \underset{\underset{\text{Odd}}{\downarrow}}{7} + \underset{\underset{\text{Even}}{\downarrow}}{6} = 16$ (even)

(c) True, because product of three odd numbers is always odd.

e.g. $3 \times 5 \times 7 = 105$ (odd)

(d) False, because if an even number is divided by 2, the quotient is always an even number.

e.g. $$\frac{24}{2} = 12$$ (even)

(e) False, because 2 is only even prime number. So, all prime numbers are not odd.

(f) False, because prime numbers have two factors, which are 1 and number itself.

e.g. 5 is a prime number and has two factors 1 and 5.

(g) False, because sum of two prime numbers is either odd or even.

e.g. $2 + 3 = 5$ (odd) and $3 + 7 = 10$ (even)

(h) True,

(i) False, because all even numbers are not composite numbers.

e.g. 2 has the factors 1 and 2 only, so it is a prime number but not a composite number.

(j) True, the product of two even numbers is always even.

e.g. $2 \times 4 = 8$ (even)

Que 3. The numbers 13 and 31 are prime numbers. Both these numbers have same digits 1 and 3. Find such pairs of prime numbers upto 100.

Sol. All prime numbers upto 100 are 2, 3, 5, 7, 11, 13, 17, 19, 23, 29, 31, 37, 41, 43, 47, 53, 59, 61, 67, 71, 73, 79, 83, 89 and 97. Out of these prime numbers, a pair of prime numbers having same digits are

(i) 13, 31   (ii) 17, 71   (iii) 37, 73   (iv) 79, 97

Hence, there are 4 pairs of such types.

Que 4. Write down separately the prime and composite numbers less than 20.

Sol. Prime numbers are those numbers whose only factors are 1 and the number itself.

So, prime numbers less than 20 are 2, 3, 5, 7, 11, 13, 17 and 19.

Composite numbers are those numbers which have more than two factors.

So, composite numbers less than 20 are 4, 6, 8, 9, 10, 12, 14, 15, 16 and 18.

Que 5. What is the greatest prime number between 1 and 10?

Sol. Prime numbers between 1 and 10 are 2, 3, 5 and 7. Therefore, the greatest prime number between 1 and 10 is 7.

Que 6. Express the following as the sum of two odd primes.

    (a) 44   (b) 36   (c) 24   (d) 18

Sol. We know that, every prime number except 2 are odd numbers.

    (a) We have, 44

$$44 = 13 + 31 \text{ or } 44 = 3 + 41$$

    (b) We have, 36

$$36 = 5 + 31 \text{ or } 36 = 13 + 23$$

    (c) We have, 24

$$24 = 5 + 19 \text{ or } 24 = 11 + 13$$

    (d) We have, 18

$$18 = 7 + 11 \text{ or } 18 = 5 + 13$$

Que 7. Give three pairs of prime numbers whose difference is 2. [**Remark** Two prime numbers whose difference is 2 are called twin primes].

Sol. Three pairs of prime numbers whose difference is 2 are as follows:

    (i) 5, 7   i.e. $7 - 5 = 2$

    (ii) 11, 13   i.e. $13 - 11 = 2$

    (iii) 17, 19   i.e. $19 - 17 = 2$

Que 8. Which of the following numbers are prime?

    (a) 23   (b) 51   (c) 37   (d) 26

 TIPS To check these given numbers, firstly we divide each number individually by the prime numbers, less than each.
If any number is not completely divided by prime numbers, it would be a prime number.

Sol. (a) We find that 23 is not exactly divisible by any of the prime numbers 2, 3, 5, 7, 11, 17 and 19. So, it is a prime number.

    (b) We find that 51 is divisible by 3. So, it is not a prime number.

    (c) We find that 37 is not exactly divisible by any of the prime numbers 2, 3, 5, 7, 11, 13, 17, 19, 23, 29 and 31. So, it is a prime number.

    (d) We find that 26 is exactly divisible by 2 and 13. So, it is not a prime number.

Que 9. Write seven consecutive composite numbers less than 100 so that there is no prime number between them.

Sol. Seven composite numbers of such type are as follows:

$$90, 91, 92, 93, 94, 95 \text{ and } 96$$

Que 10. Express each of the following numbers as the sum of three odd primes.

    (a) 21   (b) 31   (c) 53   (d) 61

Sol. (a) We have, 21 $\Rightarrow$ $21 = 3 + 5 + 13$

        where 3, 5 and 13 are odd prime numbers.

  (b) We have, 31 $\Rightarrow$ $31 = 3 + 5 + 23$

      where 3, 5 and 23 are odd prime numbers.

  (c) We have, 53 $\Rightarrow$ $53 = 13 + 17 + 23$

      where 13, 17 and 23 are odd prime numbers.

  (d) We have, 61 $\Rightarrow$ $61 = 7 + 13 + 41$

      where 7, 13 and 41 are odd prime numbers.

Que 11. Write five pairs of prime numbers less than 20, whose sum is divisible by 5. (**Hint** $3 + 7 = 10$)

Sol. Prime numbers less than 20 are 2, 3, 5, 7, 11, 13, 17 and 19.

    Here, $2 + 3 = 5$ (divisible by 5); $2 + 13 = 15$ (divisible by 5)

              $3 + 7 = 10$ (divisible by 5); $3 + 17 = 20$ (divisible by 5)

              $7 + 13 = 20$ (divisible by 5)

Hence, five pairs of prime numbers whose sum is divisible by 5 are

    (i) 2, 3   (ii) 2, 13   (iii) 3, 7 (iv) 3, 17   (v) 7, 13

Que 12. Fill in the blanks.

    (a) A number which has only two factors is called a__.

    (b) A number which has more than two factors is called a __.

    (c) 1 is neither__ nor__.

    (d) The smallest prime number is ___.

    (e) The smallest composite number is ___.

    (f) The smallest even number is ____.

Sol. (a) A number which has only two factors is called a **prime number**.

  (b) A number which has more than two factors is called a **composite number**.

  (c) 1 is neither **prime** nor **composite number**.

  (d) The smallest prime number is **2**.

  (e) The smallest composite number is **4**.

  (f) The smallest even number is **2**.

Exercise 3.3

Que 1. Using divisibility tests, determine which of the following numbers are divisible by 2 ; by 3 ; by 4 ; by 5 ; by 6; by 8 ; by 9 ; by 10 ; by 11 (say, yes or no)?

Number		Divisible by								
		2	3	4	5	6	8	9	10	11
(i)	128	Yes	No	Yes	No	No	Yes	No	No	No
(ii)	990									
(iii)	1586									
(iv)	275									
(v)	6686									
(vi)	639210									
(vii)	429714									
(viii)	2856									
(ix)	3060									
(x)	406839									

Sol. We know that, a number is divisible by
2, if it has digits 0, 2, 4, 6 or 8 in ones place.
3, if the sum of the digits is a multiple of 3 or it is divisible by 3.
4, if last two digits of the number is completely divisible by 4.
5, if a number has 0 or 5 in its ones place.
6, if it is divisible by 2 and 3 both.
8, if last three digits of the number is completely divisible by 8.
9, if the sum of the digits of the number is divisible by 9.
10, if a number has 0 in its ones place.
11, if the difference of sum of the digits of even place and sum of the digits at odd place is either 0 or multiple of 11.
Now, complete table is shown as below

Number		Divisible by								
		2	3	4	5	6	8	9	10	11
(i)	128	Yes	No	Yes	No	No	Yes	No	No	No
(ii)	990	Yes	Yes	No	Yes	Yes	No	Yes	Yes	Yes
(iii)	1586	Yes	No	No	No	No	No	No	No	No
(iv)	275	No	No	No	Yes	No	No	No	No	Yes
(v)	6686	Yes	No	No	No	No	No	No	No	No
(vi)	639210	Yes	Yes	No	Yes	Yes	No	No	Yes	Yes
(vii)	429714	Yes	Yes	No	No	Yes	No	Yes	No	No
(viii)	2856	Yes	Yes	Yes	No	Yes	Yes	No	No	No
(ix)	3060	Yes	Yes	Yes	Yes	Yes	No	Yes	Yes	No
(x)	406839	No	Yes	No	No	No	No	No	No	No

Que 2. Using divisiblity tests, determine which of the following numbers are divisible by 4 and 8?

(a) 572   (b) 726352   (c) 5500   (d) 6000
(e) 12159   (f) 14560   (g)21084   (h) 31795072
(i) 1700   (j) 2150

Sol. We know that, a number is divisible by 4, if the number formed by last two digits i.e. tens and ones place digits are divisible by 4.

Number is divisible by 8, if the number formed by last three digits i.e. its hundreds, tens and ones place digits are divisible by 8.

(a) We have, 572

$$4\overline{)72}(18$$

   (i) Divisibility by 4

      Number formed by last two digits = 72

      On dividing 72 by 4, we get

      Remainder = 0

      ∵ 72 is divisible by 4, so 572 is also divisible by 4.

$$\begin{array}{r} 4 \\ \hline 32 \\ 32 \\ \hline \times \end{array}$$

   (ii) Divisibility by 8

      Number formed by last three digits = 572

      On dividing 572 by 8, we get

      Remainder ≠ 0

      ∴ 572 is not divisible by 8.

$$8\overline{)572}(71$$
$$\begin{array}{r} 56 \\ \hline 12 \\ 8 \\ \hline 4 \end{array}$$

(b) We have, 726352

   (i) Divisibility by 4

      Number formed by last two digits = 52

      On dividing 52 by 4, we get

      Remainder = 0

$$4\overline{)52}(13$$
$$\begin{array}{r} 4 \\ \hline 12 \\ 12 \\ \hline \times \end{array}$$

      ∵ 52 is divisible by 4, so 726352 is also divisible by 4.

   (ii) Divisibility by 8

      Number formed by last three digits = 352

      On dividing 352 by 8, we get

      Remainder = 0

      ∵ 352 is divisible by 8

      ∴ 726352 is also divisible by 8.

$$8\overline{)352}(44$$
$$\begin{array}{r} 32 \\ \hline 32 \\ 32 \\ \hline \times \end{array}$$

(c) We have, 5500

   (i) Divisibility by 4

      Number formed by last two digits = 00 which is divisible by 4.

      ∴ 5500 is divisible by 4.

(ii) Divisibility by 8

Number formed by last three digits = 500

On dividing 500 by 8, we get

Remainder ≠ 0

∵ 500 is not divisible by 8

∴ 5500 is not divisible by 8.

$$8\overline{)500}(62$$
$$\underline{48}$$
$$20$$
$$\underline{16}$$
$$4$$

(d) We have, 6000

(i) Divisibility by 4

Number formed by last two digits = 00 which is divisible by 4.

∴   6000 is divisible by 4.

(ii) Divisibility by 8

Number formed by last three digits = 000 which is divisible by 8.

∴ 6000 is divisible by 8.

(e) We have, 12159

(i) Divisibility by 4

Number formed by last two digits = 59

On dividing 59 by 4, we get

Remainder ≠ 0

∵ 59 is not divisible by 4, so 12159 is not divisible by 4.

$$4\overline{)59}(14$$
$$\underline{4}$$
$$19$$
$$\underline{16}$$
$$3$$

(ii) Divisibility by 8

Number formed by last three digits = 159

On dividing 159 by 8, we get

Remainder ≠ 0

∵ 159 is not divisible by 8,

∴ 12159 is not divisible by 8.

$$8\overline{)159}(19$$
$$\underline{8}$$
$$79$$
$$\underline{72}$$
$$7$$

(f) We have, 14560

(i) Divisibility by 4

Number formed by last two digits = 60

On dividing 60 by 4, we get

Remainder = 0

∵   60 is divisible by 4, so 14560 is also divisible by 4.

$$4\overline{)60}(15$$
$$\underline{4}$$
$$20$$
$$\underline{20}$$
$$\times$$

(ii) Divisibility by 8

Number formed by last three digits = 560

On dividing 560 by 8, we get

Remainder = 0

∵ 560 is divisible by 8.

∴ 14560 is also divisible by 8.

$$8\overline{)560}(70$$
$$\underline{56}$$
$$0$$
$$\underline{0}$$
$$\times$$

(g) We have, 21084

$\quad$(i) Divisibility by 4

$\qquad$Number formed by last two digits = 84

$\qquad$On dividing 84 by 4, we get

$\qquad$Remainder = 0

$\qquad$∵ 84 is divisible by 4, so 21084 is divisible by 4.

$$4\overline{)84}(21$$
$$\underline{8}$$
$$4$$
$$\underline{4}$$
$$×$$

$\quad$(ii) Divisibility by 8

$\qquad$Number formed by last three digits = 084 = 84

$\qquad$On dividing 084 by 8, we get

$\qquad$Remainder ≠ 0

$\qquad$∵ 084 is not divisible by 8.

$\qquad$∴21084 also not divisible by 8.

$$8\overline{)84}(10$$
$$\underline{8}$$
$$4$$
$$\underline{0}$$
$$4$$

(h) We have, 31795072

$\quad$(i) Divisibility by 4

$\qquad$Number formed by last two digits = 72

$\qquad$On dividing 72 by 4, we get

$\qquad$Remainder = 0

$\qquad$∵ 72 is divisible by 4.

$\qquad$∴31795072 is also divisible by 4.

$$4\overline{)72}(18$$
$$\underline{4}$$
$$32$$
$$\underline{32}$$
$$×$$

$\quad$(ii) Divisibility by 8

$\qquad$Number formed by last three digits = 072 = 72

$\qquad$On dividing 072 by 8, we get

$\qquad$Remainder = 0

$\qquad$∵ 072 is divisible by 8, so 31795072 is also divisible by 8.

$$8\overline{)72}(9$$
$$\underline{72}$$
$$×$$

(i) We have, 1700

$\quad$(i) Divisibility by 4

$\qquad$Number formed by last two digits = 00, which is divisible by 4.

$\qquad$∴ 1700 is also divisible by 4.

$\quad$(ii) Divisibility by 8

$\qquad$Number formed by last three digits = 700

$\qquad$On dividing 700 by 8, we get

$\qquad$Remainder ≠ 0

$\qquad$∵ 700 is not divisible by 8.

$\qquad$∴ 1700 is also not divisible by 8.

$$8\overline{)700}(87$$
$$\underline{64}$$
$$60$$
$$\underline{56}$$
$$4$$

(j) We have, 2150

$\quad$(i) Divisibility by 4

$\qquad$Number formed by last two digits = 50

$\qquad$On dividing 50 by 4, we get

$\qquad$Remainder ≠ 0

$\qquad$∵ 50 is not divisible by 4, so 2150 is also not divisible by 4.

$$4\overline{)50}(12$$
$$\underline{4}$$
$$10$$
$$\underline{8}$$
$$2$$

(ii) Divisibility by 8

Number formed by last three digits = 150

On dividing 150 by 8, we get

Remainder $\neq 0$

$\because$ 150 is not divisible by 8

$\therefore$ 2150 is also divisible by 8.

$$8\overline{)\,150\,}(18$$
$$\underline{8}$$
$$70$$
$$\underline{64}$$
$$6$$

Que 3. Using divisibility tests, determine which of the following numbers are divisible by 6?

(a) 297144   (b) 1258   (c) 4335   (d) 61233

(e) 901352   (f) 438750   (g) 1790184   (h) 12583

(i) 639210   (j) 17852

Sol. We know that, a number is divisible by 6, if it is divisible by 2 and 3 both. Also, a number is divisible by 2 if it has any of the digits 0, 2, 4, 6 or 8 in its ones place and number is divisible by 3, if the sum of the digits is a multiple of 3.

(a) We have, 297144

   (i) Divisibility by 2

      $\because$ Units digit of number = 4, so 297144 is divisible by 2.

  (ii) Divisibility by 3

      Sum of digits of given number = 2 + 9 + 7 + 1 + 4 + 4 = 27

      $\because$ 27 is divisible by 3, so 297144 is also divisible by 3.

      Now, we see that 297144 is divisible by 2 and 3 both.

      Hence, it is divisible by 6.

(b) We have, 1258

   (i) Divisibility by 2

      $\because$ Units digit of number = 8, so 1258 is divisible by 2.

  (ii) Divisibility by 3

      Sum of digits of given number = 1 + 2 + 5 + 8 = 16

      16 is not divisible by 3, so 1258 is not divisible by 3.

      Now, we see that 1258 is divisible by 2 but not divisible by 3.

      Hence, it is not divisible by 6.

(c) We have, 4335

   (i) Divisibility by 2 $\because$ Units digit of number = 5

      which is not any of the digits 0, 2, 4, 6 or 8.

      $\therefore$ 4335 is not divisible by 2.

  (ii) Divisibility by 3

      Sum of digits of given number = 4 + 3 + 3 + 5 = 15

      $\because$ 15 is divisible by 3, so 4335 is divisible by 3.

      Now, we see that 4335 is divisible by 3 but not divisible by 2.

      Hence, it is not divisible by 6.

(d) We have, 61233

   (i) Divisibility by 2

      $\because$ Units digit of number = 3

      which is not any of the digits 0, 2, 4, 6 or 8.

      $\therefore$ 61233 is not divisible by 2.

      Now, we have no need to check the given number is divisible by 3 or not because it is not divisible by one of the factors of 6. Hence, the given number 61233 is not divisible by 6.

(e) We have, 901352

   (i) Divisibility by 2

      $\because$ Units digit of number = 2, so 901352 is divisible by 2.

   (ii) Divisibility by 3

      Sum of digits of given number $= 9 + 0 + 1 + 3 + 5 + 2 = 20$

      $\because$ 20 is not divisible by 3, so 901352 is not divisible by 3.

      Now, we see that 901352 is divisible by 2 but not divisible by 3.

      Hence, it is not divisible by 6.

(f) We have, 438750

   (i) Divisibility by 2

      $\because$ Units digit of number = 0, so 438750 is divisible by 2.

   (ii) Divisibility by 3

      Sum of digits of given number $= 4 + 3 + 8 + 7 + 5 + 0 = 27$

      $\because$ 27 is divisible by 3, so 438750 is divisible by 3.

      Now, we see that 438750 is divisible by 2 and 3 both.

      Hence, it is divisible by 6.

(g) We have, 1790184

   (i) Divisibility by 2

      $\because$ Units digit of number = 4, so 1790184 is divisible by 2.

   (ii) Divisibility by 3

      Sum of digits of given number $= 1 + 7 + 9 + 0 + 1 + 8 + 4 = 30$

      $\because$ 30 is divisible by 3, so 1790184 is divisible by 3.

      Now, we see that 1790184 is divisible by 2 and 3 both.

      Hence, it is divisible by 6.

(h) We have, 12583

   (i) Divisibility by 2

      $\because$ Units digit of number = 3

      which is not any of the digits 0, 2, 4, 6 or 8.

      $\therefore$ 12583 is not divisible by 2.

Now, we **have no need to check** the given number is divisible by 3 or not because it is not divisible by one of the factors of 6. Hence, the given number 12583 is not divisible by 6.

(i) We have, 639210
    (i) Divisibility by 2
        ∵ Units digit number = 0, so 639210 is divisible by 2.
    (ii) Divisibility by 3
        Sum of digits of given number = 6 + 3 + 9 + 2 + 1 + 0 = 21
        ∵ 21 is divisible by 3, so 639210 is divisible by 3.
        Now, we see that 639210 is divisible by 2 and 3 both.
        Hence, it is divisible by 6.
(j) We have, 17852
    (i) Divisibility by 2
        Units digit of number = 2, so 17852 is divisible by 2.
    (ii) Divisibility by 3
        Sum of digits of given number = 1 + 7 + 8 + 5 + 2 = 23
        ∵ 23 is not divisible by 3, so 17852 is not divisible by 3.
        Now, we see that 17852 is divisible by 2 but not divisible by 3.
        Hence, it is not divisible by 6.

Que 4. Using divisibility tests, determine which of the following numbers are divisible by 11?

    (a) 5445   (b) 10824   (c) 7138965
    (d) 70169308   (e) 10000001   (f) 901153

> **TIPS**
> Firstly, find the difference between the sum of the digits at odd places (from the right) and the sum of the digits at even places (from the right) of the number. If the difference is either 0 or divisible by 11, then the number is divisible by 11, otherwise not.

Sol. (a) We have, 5445

$$5 \quad 4 \quad 4 \quad 5$$
$$\downarrow \downarrow \downarrow \downarrow$$
$$E \quad O \quad E \quad O$$

where, O = Odd and E = Even
Sum of digits at odd places from right = 5 + 4 = 9
Sum of digits at even places from right = 4 + 5 = 9
Now, difference = 9 − 9 = 0, so 5445 is divisible by 11.

(b) We have, 10824

$$1 \quad 0 \quad 8 \quad 2 \quad 4$$
$$| \quad | \quad | \quad | \quad |$$
$$O \quad E \quad O \quad E \quad O$$

Sum of digits at odd places from right = 4 + 8 + 1 = 13

Sum of digits at even places from right = 2 + 0 = 2
Now, difference = 13 – 2 = 11, so 10824 is divisible by 11.

(c) We have, 7138965

$$7 \quad 1 \quad 3 \quad 8 \quad 9 \quad 6 \quad 5$$
$$| \quad | \quad | \quad | \quad | \quad | \quad |$$
$$O \quad E \quad O \quad E \quad O \quad E \quad O$$

Sum of digits at odd places from right = 5 + 9 + 3 + 7 = 24
Sum of digits at even places from right = 6 + 8 + 1 = 15
Now, difference = 24 – 15 = 9
∵ 9 is not a multiple of 11, so 7138965 is not divisible by 11.

(d) We have, 70169308

$$7 \quad 0 \quad 1 \quad 6 \quad 9 \quad 3 \quad 0 \quad 8$$
$$| \quad | \quad | \quad | \quad | \quad | \quad | \quad |$$
$$E \quad O \quad E \quad O \quad E \quad O \quad E \quad O$$

Sum of digits at odd places from right = 8 + 3 + 6 + 0 = 17
Sum of digits at even places from right = 0 + 9 + 1 + 7 = 17
Now, difference = 17 – 17 = 0
∴ 70169308 is divisible by 11.

(e) We have, 10000001

$$1 \quad 0 \quad 0 \quad 0 \quad 0 \quad 0 \quad 0 \quad 1$$
$$| \quad | \quad | \quad | \quad | \quad | \quad | \quad |$$
$$E \quad O \quad E \quad O \quad E \quad O \quad E \quad O$$

Sum of digits at odd places from right = 1 + 0 + 0 + 0 = 1
Sum of digits at even places from right = 0 + 0 + 0 + 1 = 1
Now, difference = 1 – 1 = 0, so 10000001 is divisible by 11.

(f) We have, 901153

$$9 \quad 0 \quad 1 \quad 1 \quad 5 \quad 3$$
$$| \quad | \quad | \quad | \quad | \quad |$$
$$E \quad O \quad E \quad O \quad E \quad O$$

Sum of digits at odd places from right = 3 + 1 + 0 = 4
Sum of digits at even places from right = 5 + 1 + 9 = 15
Now, difference = 15 – 4 = 11, so 901153 is divisible by 11.

Que 5. Write the smallest digit and the greatest digit in the blank space of each of the following numbers, so that the number formed is divisible by 3:

(a) __6724   (b) 4765__2

TIPS Firstly, find the sum of digits of given number, then subtract it from those multiples of 3, which are greater than this sum to get smallest and greatest digit.

Sol. (a) We have, __6274

Sum of the given digits $= 6 + 7 + 2 + 4 = 19$

∵ Multiples of 3 greater than 19 are 21, 24, 27, 30,...

∴ $21 - 19 = 2; 24 - 19 = 5; 27 - 19 = 8; 30 - 19 = 11$

But 11 is not a single digit.

∴ Smallest digit $= 2$ and greatest digit $= 8$

(b) We have, 4765 __ 2

Sum of the given digits $= 4 + 7 + 6 + 5 + 2 = 24$

∵ 24 is a multiple of 3, so smallest digit $= 0$

Now, multiples of 3 greater than 24 are 27, 30, 33, 36, ...

∴ $27 - 24 = 3; \ 30 - 24 = 6; \ 33 - 24 = 9; \ 36 - 24 = 12$

But 12 is not a single digit.

∴ Smallest digit $= 0$ and greatest digit $= 9$

Que 6. Write a digit in the blank space of each of the following numbers, so that the number formed is divisible by 11.

  (a) 92__389   (b) 8__9484

TIPS
Firstly, assume the blank space digit as x, then find the sum of odd places and even places digits (from the right) separately. Now, take difference of sum of odd places digits and sum of even places digits equal to 0 or 11 and simplify to get the value of x.

Sol. (a) Let the required unknown digit be x.

Then, number be

$$9 \quad 2 \quad x \quad 3 \quad 8 \quad 9$$
$$\downarrow \ \downarrow \ \downarrow \ \downarrow \ \downarrow \ \downarrow$$
$$E \quad O \quad E \quad O \quad E \quad O$$

where, O = odd and E = even

Sum of digits at odd places from right $= 9 + 3 + 2 = 14$

Sum of digits at even places from right $= 8 + x + 9 = 17 + x$

∵ Number is divisible by 11.

∴ Difference of digits will be 0 or 11.

⇒ $(17 + x) - 14 = 0$ or 11

⇒ $17 + x - 14 = 0$ or $11 \Rightarrow x + 3 = 0$ or 11

Taking difference 0, $x + 3 = 0$

⇒ $x = 0 - 3 = -3$ (not possible)

Taking difference 11, $x + 3 = 11$

⇒ $x = 11 - 3 = 8$

So, required digit to write in the blank space is 8.

(b) Let the required unknown digit be x.

	8	x	9	4	8	4
Then, number be	↓	↓	↓	↓	↓	↓
	E	O	E	O	E	O

Sum of digits at odd places from right $= 4 + 4 + x = 8 + x$

Sum of digits at even places from right $= 8 + 9 + 8 = 25$

∵ Number is divisible by 11.

∴ Difference of digits will be 0 or 11.

⇒ $\qquad\qquad 25 - (8 + x) = 0$ or 11

⇒ $\qquad\qquad 25 - 8 - x = 0$ or $11 \Rightarrow 17 - x = 0$ or 11

Taking difference 0, $\quad 17 - x = 0 \Rightarrow x = 17 + 0 \Rightarrow x = 17$

$\qquad\qquad$ [but 17 is not a single digit number, so it is not possible]

Taking difference 11, $\quad 17 - x = 11$

⇒ $\qquad\qquad\qquad x = 17 - 11 = 6$

So, required digit to write in the blank space is 6.

Try These (Page 58)

Que 1. Find the common factors of

(a) 8, 20 $\qquad\qquad\qquad$ (b) 9, 15

TIPS $\quad$ Firstly, write all the factors of given numbers separately, then take common numbers out of them as common factors.

Sol. (a) Factors of 8 and 20 are as follows :

$\qquad 8 = 1 \times 8; 8 = 2 \times 4$

$\qquad$ and $\ 20 = 1 \times 20; 20 = 2 \times 10; 20 = 4 \times 5$

Now, all factors of $8 = \boxed{1}, \boxed{2}, \boxed{4}, 8$

and all factors of $20 = \boxed{1}, \boxed{2}, \boxed{4}, 5, 10, 20$

∴ Common factors $= 1, 2, 4$

Hence, common factors of 8 and 20 are 1, 2 and 4.

(b) Factors of 9 and 15 are as follows :

$\qquad\qquad\qquad 9 = 1 \times 9; \ 9 = 3 \times 3$

and $\qquad\qquad\qquad 15 = 1 \times 15; 15 = 3 \times 5$

Now, all factors of $9 = \boxed{1}, \boxed{3}, 9$

and all factors of $15 = \boxed{1}, \boxed{3}, 5, 15$

∴ Common factors $= 1, 3$

Hence, common factors of 9 and 15 are 1 and 3.

Exercise 3.4

Que 1. Find the common factors of

    (a) 20 and 28   (b) 15 and 25

    (c) 35 and 50   (d) 56 and 120

Sol. (a) Factors of 20 and 28 are as follows :

$$20 = 1 \times 20; 20 = 2 \times 10; 20 = 4 \times 5$$

and $\qquad 28 = 1 \times 28; 28 = 2 \times 14; 28 = 4 \times 7$

Now, all factors of 20 = $\boxed{1}$, 2, $\boxed{4}$, 5, 10, 20

and all factors of 28 = $\boxed{1}$, 2, $\boxed{4}$, 7, 14, 28

∴ Common factors = 1, 2, 4

Hence, common factors of 20 and 28 are 1, 2 and 4.

(b) Factors of 15 and 25 are as follows :

$$15 = 1 \times 15; 15 = 3 \times 5$$

and $\qquad 25 = 1 \times 25; 25 = 5 \times 5$

Now, all factors of 15 = $\boxed{1}$, 3, $\boxed{5}$, 15

and all factors of 25 = $\boxed{1}$, $\boxed{5}$, 25

∴ Common factors = 1, 5

Hence, common factors of 15 and 25 are 1 and 5.

(c) Factors of 35 and 50 are as follows :

$\qquad 35 = 1 \times 35; 35 = 5 \times 7$

and $\quad 50 = 1 \times 50; 50 = 2 \times 25; 50 = 5 \times 10$

Now, all factors of 35 = $\boxed{1}$, $\boxed{5}$, 7

and all factors of 50 = $\boxed{1}$, 2, $\boxed{5}$, 10, 25, 50

∴ Common factors = 1, 5

Hence, common factors of 35 and 50 are 1 and 5.

(d) Factors of 56 and 120 are as follows:

$$56 = 1 \times 56; 56 = 2 \times 28; 56 = 4 \times 14; 56 = 7 \times 8$$

and $\qquad 120 = 1 \times 120; 120 = 2 \times 60; 120 = 3 \times 40; 120 = 4 \times 30$

$$120 = 5 \times 24; 120 = 6 \times 20; 120 = 8 \times 15; 120 = 10 \times 12$$

Now, all factors of 56 = $\boxed{1}$, $\boxed{2}$, $\boxed{4}$, 7, $\boxed{8}$, 14, 28, 56

and all factors of 120 = $\boxed{1}$, $\boxed{2}$, 3, $\boxed{4}$, 5, 6, $\boxed{8}$, 10, 12, 15, 20

$$24, 30, 40, 60, 120$$

∴ Common factors = 1, 2, 4, 8

Hence, common factors of 56 and 120 are 1, 2, 4 and 8.

Que 2. Find the common factors of

    (a) 4, 8 and 12   (b) 5, 15 and 25

Sol. (a) We have 4, 8 and 12

$$4 = 1 \times 4; 4 = 2 \times 2$$

∴Factors of 4 are 1, 2 and 4.

Now, $\qquad 8 = 1 \times 8; 8 = 2 \times 4$

∴Factors of 8 are 1, 2, 4 and 8.

and $\qquad 12 = 1 \times 12; 12 = 2 \times 6; 12 = 3 \times 4$

∴Factors of 12 are 1, 2, 3, 4, 6 and 12.

Now, all factors of 4 = $\boxed{1}$, $\boxed{2}$, $\boxed{4}$

all factors of 8 = $\boxed{1}$, $\boxed{2}$, $\boxed{4}$, 8

and all factors of 12 = $\boxed{1}$, $\boxed{2}$, 3, $\boxed{4}$, 6, 12

Hence, common factors of 4, 8 and 12 are 1, 2 and 4.

(b) We have 5, 15 and 25

$$5 = 1 \times 5$$

∴ Factors of 5 are 1 and 5.

Now, $\qquad 15 = 1 \times 15; 15 = 3 \times 5$

∴ Factors of 15 are 1, 3, 5 and 15.

and $\qquad 25 = 1 \times 25; 25 = 5 \times 5$

∴ Factors of 25 are 1, 5 and 25.

Now, all factors of 5 = $\boxed{1}$, $\boxed{5}$

all factors of 15 = $\boxed{1}$, 3, $\boxed{5}$, 15

and all factors of 25 = $\boxed{1}$, $\boxed{5}$, 25

Hence, common factors of 5, 15 and 25 are 1 and 5.

Que 3. Find first three common multiples of

    (a) 6 and 8   (b) 12 and 18

Sol. (a) Some multiples of 6 = 6, 12,18, $\boxed{24}$, 30, 36, 42, $\boxed{48}$ 54, 60, 66, $\boxed{72}$, ...

Some multiples of 8 = 8, 16, $\boxed{24}$, 32, 40, $\boxed{48}$, 56, 64, $\boxed{72}$, 80, 88, 96, ...

Hence, first three common multiples are 24, 48 and 72.

(b) Some multiples of 12 = 12, 24, $\boxed{36}$, 48, 60, $\boxed{72}$ 84, 96, $\boxed{108}$, 120, 132, ...

Some multiples of 18 = 18, $\boxed{36}$, 54, $\boxed{72}$, 90, $\boxed{108}$, 126, 144, ...

Hence, first three common multiples are 36, 72 and 108.

Que 4. Write all the numbers less than 100 which are common multiples of 3 and 4.

Sol. Multiples of 3 which are less than 100 are as follows :

    3, 6, 9, $\boxed{12}$, 15, 18, 21, $\boxed{24}$, 27, 30, 33, $\boxed{36}$, 39, 42, 45, $\boxed{48}$, 51, 54, 57, $\boxed{60}$, 63, 66, 69, $\boxed{72}$, 75, 78, 81, $\boxed{84}$, 87, 90, 93, 96 , 99

Multiples of 4 which are less than 100 are as follows :

4, 8, $\boxed{12}$, 16, 20, $\boxed{24}$, 28, 32, $\boxed{36}$, 40, 44, $\boxed{48}$, 52, 56, $\boxed{60}$, 64, 68, $\boxed{72}$, 76, 80, $\boxed{84}$, 88, 92, 96

Hence, common multiples of 3 and 4 are 12, 24, 36, 48, 60, 72, 84 and 96.

Que 5. Which of the following numbers are co-prime?

    (a) 18 and 35   (b) 15 and 37   (c) 30 and 415

    (d) 17 and 68   (e) 216 and 215   (f) 81 and 16

> **TIPS**
> Firstly, write the factors of given numbers. If two numbers have only 1 as common factor, then they are called co-prime numbers otherwise not.

Sol. (a) We have, 18 and 35

$$18 = 1 \times 18; 18 = 2 \times 9; 18 = 3 \times 6$$

Factors of 18 are 1, 2, 3, 6, 9 and 18.

and $35 = 1 \times 35; 35 = 5 \times 7$

Factors of 35 are 1, 5, 7 and 35.

∵ Common factor of 18 and 35 is only 1.

So, 18 and 35 are co-prime numbers.

    (b) We have, 15 and 37

$$15 = 1 \times 15; 15 = 3 \times 5$$

Factors of 15 are 1, 3, 5 and 15.

and $37 = 1 \times 37$

Factors of 37 are 1 and 37.

∵ Common factor of 15 and 37 is only 1.

So, 15 and 37 are co-prime numbers.

    (c) We have, 30 and 415

$$30 = 1 \times 30; 30 = 2 \times 15; 30 = 3 \times 10; 30 = 5 \times 6$$

Factors of 30 are 1, 2, 3, 5, 6, 10, 15 and 30.

and $415 = 1 \times 415; 415 = 5 \times 83$

Factors of 415 are 1, 5, 83 and 415.

∵ Common factors of 30 and 415 are 1 and 5.

So, 30 and 415 are not co-prime numbers.

    (d) We have, 17 and 68

$$17 = 1 \times 17$$

Factors of 17 are 1 and 17.

and $68 = 1 \times 68; 68 = 2 \times 34; 68 = 4 \times 17$

∴ Factors of 68 are 1, 2, 4, 17, 34 and 68.

∵ Common factors of 17 and 68 are 1 and 17.

So, 17 and 68 are not co-prime numbers.

(e) We have, 216 and 215

$216 = 1 \times 216; 216 = 2 \times 108; 216 = 3 \times 72; 216 = 4 \times 54$

$216 = 6 \times 36; 216 = 8 \times 27; 216 = 9 \times 24; 216 = 12 \times 18$

Factors of 216 are 1, 2, 3, 4, 6, 8, 9, 12, 18, 24, 27, 36, 54, 72, 108 and 216.

and $215 = 1 \times 215; 215 = 5 \times 43$

Factors of 215 are 1, 5, 43 and 215

∵ Common factor of 216 and 215 is only 1.

So, 216 and 215 are co-prime numbers.

(f) We have, 81 and 16

$$81 = 1 \times 81; 81 = 3 \times 27; 81 = 9 \times 9$$

Factors of 81 are 1, 3, 9, 27 and 81.

and $16 = 1 \times 16; 16 = 2 \times 8; 16 = 4 \times 4$

Factors of 16 are 1, 2, 4, 8 and 16.

∵ Common factor of 81 and 16 is only 1.

So, 81 and 16 are co-prime numbers.

Que 6. A number is divisible by both 5 and 12. By which other number will that number be always divisible?

Sol. The given number will be divisible by the product of 5 and 12.

i.e. it is always divisible by $5 \times 12 = 60$.

Note If a number is divisible by two co-prime numbers, then it is divisible by their product also.

Que 7. A number is divisible by 12. By what other numbers will that number be divisible?

Sol. If any number is divisible by 12, then this number will also be divisible by the factors of 12. i.e. $12 = 1 \times 12; 12 = 2 \times 6; 12 = 3 \times 4$

Factors of 12 are 1, 2, 3, 4, 6 and 12.

∴Number will be divisible by 1, 2, 3, 4, 6 and 12.

Try These (Page 61)

Que 1. Write the prime factorisations of 16, 28, 38.

Sol. When a number is expressed as a product of its factors, in which all numbers are prime, is called prime factorisation.

(i) We have, 16

∴ Prime factorisation of 16

$= 2 \times 2 \times 2 \times 2$

2	16
2	8
2	4
2	2

(ii) We have, 28

$$
\begin{array}{r|r}
2 & 28 \\
\hline
2 & 14 \\
\hline
7 & 7 \\
\hline
 & 1
\end{array}
$$

∴   Prime factorisation of $28 = 2 \times 2 \times 7$

(iii) We have, 38

∴   Prime factorisation of $38 = 2 \times 19$

$$
\begin{array}{r|r}
2 & 38 \\
\hline
19 & 19 \\
\hline
 & 1
\end{array}
$$

Exercise 3.5

Que 1. Which of the following statements are true?

(a) If a number is divisible by 3, it must be divisible by 9.

(b) If a number is divisible by 9, it must be divisible by 3.

(c) A number is divisible by 18, if it is divisible by both 3 and 6.

(d) If a number is divisible by 9 and 10 both, then it must be divisible by 90.

(e) If two numbers are co-prime, atleast one of them must be prime.

(f) All numbers which are divisible by 4 must also be divisible by 8.

(g) All numbers which are divisible by 8 must also be divisible by 4.

(h) If a number exactly divides two numbers separately, it must exactly divide their sum.

(i) If a number exactly divides the sum of two numbers, it must exactly divide the two numbers separately.

Sol. (a) False, because there are plenty of numbers, which are divisible by 3 but not divisible by 9. e.g. 30 is divisible by 3, but not divisible by 9.

(b) True, because if a number is divisible by any number, then it is divisible by each factor of that number. Here, 3 is a factor of 9.

e.g. $\dfrac{27}{9} = 3$ and $\dfrac{27}{3} = 9$

(c) False, e.g. Number 30 is divisible by 3 and 6 both but not divisible by 18.

(d) True, because if a number is divisible by two co-prime numbers, then it is divisible by their product also.

(e) False, we know that, two numbers having only 1 as a common factor are called co-prime numbers. So, it is not necessary that one of them must be prime.

e.g. numbers 8 and 15 are co-prime numbers, since both have only 1 as a common factor, but no one is a prime number.

(f) False, e.g. number 36 is divisible by 4 but not divisible by 8.

(g) True because if a number is divisible by any number, then it is divisible by each factor of that number. Here, 4 is a factor of 8.

So, all numbers divisible by 8 must also be divisible by 4.
e.g. Number 56 is divisble by 8 as well as divisible by 4.

(h) True, if two given numbers are divisible by a number, then their sum is also dividible by that number. e.g. number 13 is exactly divides number 52 and 65 also divide their sum 117.

(i) False, e.g. Number 5 is exactly divides the sum of number 2 and 3 but not exactly divides these two numbers.

Que 2. Here are two different factor trees for 60. Write the missing numbers.

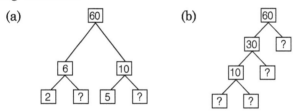

Sol. (a) ∵ $6 = 2 \times 3$ and $10 = 5 \times 2$

Hence, missing numbers are 3 and 2.

(b) ∵ $60 = 30 \times 2$

$30 = 10 \times 3$

and $10 = 5 \times 2$

∴ Hence, missing numbers are 5, 2, 3 and 2.

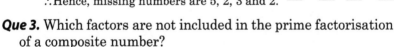

Que 3. Which factors are not included in the prime factorisation of a composite number?

Sol. Factor 1 and that number itself are not included in the prime factorisation of a composite number.

Que 4. Write the greatest 4-digit number and express it in terms of its prime factors.

Sol. The greatest 4-digit number = 9999

　Now,

3	9999
3	3333
11	1111
101	101
	1

∴ Prime factors of 9999 $= 3 \times 3 \times 11 \times 101$

Que 5. Write the smallest 5-digit number and express it in the form of its prime factors.

Sol. The smallest 5-digit number = 10000

　Now,

2	10000
2	5000
2	2500
2	1250
5	625
5	125
5	25
5	5
	1

∴ Prime factors of 10000 $= 2 \times 2 \times 2 \times 2 \times 5 \times 5 \times 5 \times 5$

Que 6. Find all the prime factors of 1729 and arrange them in ascending order. Now, state the relation, if any, between two consecutive prime factors.

Sol. Prime factors of 1729 $= 7 \times 13 \times 19$

Ascending order of prime factors of 1729 are 7, 13 and 19. Here, $19 - 13 = 6$ and $13 - 7 = 6$
So, it is clear that difference of two consecutive prime factors is 6.

7	1729
13	247
19	19
	1

Que 7. The product of three consecutive numbers is always divisible by 6. Verify this statement with the help of some examples.

Sol. We know that, a number is divisible by 6, if the number is divisible by 2 and 3 both.

Example 1 Let the three consecutive numbers be 7, 8 and 9.

Product of numbers = $7 \times 8 \times 9 = 504$

Units digit of number = 4, so it is divisible by 2.

Now, sum of the digit = $5 + 0 + 4 = 9$, which is a multiple of 3.

So, 504 is divisible by 3.

∵ 504 is divisible by both 2 and 3, so 504 is divisible by 6.

Example 2 Let the three consecutive numbers be 11, 12 and 13.

Product of numbers = $11 \times 12 \times 13 = 1716$

Units digit of number = 6, so it is divisible by 2.

Now, sum of the digit = $1 + 7 + 1 + 6 = 15$, which is a multiple of 3.

So, 1716 is divisible by 3.

∵   1716 is divisible by both 2 and 3.

∴   1716 is divisible by 6.   **Hence, verified.**

Que 8. The sum of two consecutive odd numbers is divisible by 4. Verify this statements with the help of some examples.

Sol. Let us consider the following examples

Consecutive odd numbers	9 and 11	103 and 105
Sum	9 + 11 = 20	103 + 105 = 208
Number formed from the last two digits of the sum	20, which is divisible by 4	08, which is divisible by 4

We observed that, the numbers formed from the last two digits is divisible by 4. Hence, the sum of two consecutive odd numbers are also divisible by 4.   **Hence, verified.**

Que 9. In which of the following expressions, prime factorisation has been done?

    (a) $24 = 2 \times 3 \times 4$ (b) $56 = 7 \times 2 \times 2 \times 2$

    (c) $70 = 2 \times 5 \times 7$ (d) $54 = 2 \times 3 \times 9$

Sol. (a) We have, $24 = 2 \times 3 \times 4$

    Here, 4 is not a prime number.

    So, number 24 does not have prime factorisation.

  (b) We have, $56 = 7 \times 2 \times 2 \times 2$

    Here, 2 and 7 are prime numbers.

    So, number 56 have prime factorisation.

  (c) We have, $70 = 2 \times 5 \times 7$, Here, 2, 5 and 7 all are prime numbers.

    So, number 70 have prime factorisation.

  (d) We have, $54 = 2 \times 3 \times 9$, Here, 9 is not a prime number.

    So, number 54 does not have prime factorisation.

Que 10. Determine, if 25110 is divisible by 45.

[**Hint** 5 and 9 are co-prime numbers. Test the divisibility of the number by 5 and 9].

 TIPS If a number is divisible by two co-prime numbers, then it is divisible by their product also.

Sol. We have, $45 = 5 \times 9$, also 5 and 9 are co-prime.

Now, 25110 is divisible by 5 because its units digit is 0.

Again, sum of the digits $= 2 + 5 + 1 + 1 + 0 = 9$

∵ Sum of the digits is divisible by 9, so 25110 is also divisible by 9.

Since, 25110 is divisible by both 5 and 9, where 5 and 9 are co-primes.

∴ 25110 is divisible by 5×9 i.e. by 45.

Que 11. 18 is divisible by both 2 and 3. It is also divisible by $2 \times 3 = 6$. Similarly, a number is divisible by both 4 and 6. Can we say that the number must also be divisible by $4 \times 6 = 24$? If not, give an example to justify your answer.

Sol. We know that, if a number is divisible by two co-prime numbers, then it is divisible by their product also.

Here, 2 and 3 are co-prime numbers. So, 18 is divisible by their product i.e. 6 but 4 and 6 are not co-prime numbers, so the number divisible by 4 and 6 will not be divisible by $4 \times 6 = 24$.

e.g. Take the number 60.

It is divisible by both 4 and 6, but it is not divisible by its product.

i.e. $6 \times 4 = 24$

Que 12. I am the smallest number, having four different prime factors. Can you find me?

Sol. Since the number is smallest, so different four smallest prime factors are 2, 3, 5 and 7

∴ Smallest number having four different prime factors
$$= 2 \times 3 \times 5 \times 7 = 210$$

Try These (Page 63)

Que1. Find the HCF of the following

    (i) 24 and 36   (ii) 15, 25 and 30

    (iii) 8 and 12   (iv) 12, 16 and 28

 TIPS To find the HCF of given numbers. First we find their common factors by prime factorisation. Thus, the multiplication of these common factors would be the HCF of those numbers.

Sol. (i) We have, 24 and 36

2	24
2	12
2	6
3	3
	1

2	36
2	18
3	9
3	3
	1

Prime factorisation of $24 = \boxed{2} \times \boxed{2} \times 2 \times \boxed{3}$
Prime factorisation of $36 = \boxed{2} \times \boxed{2} \times 3 \times \boxed{3}$
Common factors of 24 and 36 are 2 (occurring twice) and 3.
Thus, HCF of 24 and 36 $= 2 \times 2 \times 3 = 12$

(ii) We have, 15, 25 and 30

3	15
5	5
	1

5	25
5	5
	1

2	30
3	15
5	5
	1

Prime factorisation of $15 = 3 \times \boxed{5}$
Prime factorisation of $25 = 5 \times \boxed{5}$
Prime factorisation of $30 = 2 \times 3 \times \boxed{5}$
Common factor of 15, 25 and 30 is 5.
Thus, HCF of 15, 25 and 30 $= 5$

(iii) We have, 8 and 12

2	8
2	4
2	2
	1

2	12
2	6
3	3
	1

Prime factorisation of $8 = \boxed{2} \times \boxed{2} \times 2$
Prime factorisation of $12 = \boxed{2} \times \boxed{2} \times 3$
Common factor of 8 and 12 is 2 (occurring twice).
Thus, HCF of 8 and 12 $= 2 \times 2 = 4$

(iv) We have, 12, 16 and 28

2	12
2	6
3	3
	1

2	16
2	8
2	4
2	2
	1

2	28
2	14
7	7
	1

Prime factorisation of $12 = \boxed{2} \times \boxed{2} \times 3$
Prime factorisation of $16 = \boxed{2} \times \boxed{2} \times 2 \times 2$
Prime factorisation of $28 = \boxed{2} \times \boxed{2} \times 7$
Common factor of 12, 16 and 28 is 2 (occurring twice).
Thus, HCF of 12, 16 and 28 $= 2 \times 2 = 4$

Exercise 3.6

Que 1. Find the HCF of the following numbers.

    (a) 18, 48   (b) 30, 42   (c) 18, 60   (d) 27, 63

    (e) 36, 84   (f) 34, 102   (g) 70, 105,175 (h) 91, 112,49

    (i) 18, 54, 81 (j) 12, 45, 75

Sol. (a) Prime factorisation of $18 = \boxed{2} \times 3 \times \boxed{3}$

    Prime factorisation of $48 = \boxed{2} \times 2 \times \boxed{3} \times 2 \times 2$

    Common factors of 18 and 48 are 2 and 3.

    Thus, HCF of 18 and 48 $= 2 \times 3 = 6$

  (b) Prime factorisation of $30 = \boxed{2} \times \boxed{3} \times 5$

    Prime factorisation of $42 = \boxed{2} \times \boxed{3} \times 7$

    Common factors of 30 and 42 are 2 and 3.

    Thus, HCF of 30 and 42 $= 2 \times 3 = 6$

  (c) Prime factorisation of $18 = 2 \times \boxed{3} \times \boxed{3}$

    Prime factorisation of $60 = 2 \times \boxed{2} \times \boxed{3} \times 5$

    Common factors of 18 and 60 are 2 and 3.

    Thus, HCF of 18 and 60 $= 2 \times 3 = 6$

  (d) Prime factorisation of $27 = \boxed{3} \times \boxed{3} \times 3$

    Prime factorisation of $63 = \boxed{3} \times \boxed{3} \times 7$

    Common factor of 27 and 63 is 3 (occurring twice)

    Thus, HCF of 27 and 63 $= 3 \times 3 = 9$

  (e) Prime factorisation of $36 = \boxed{2} \times \boxed{2} \times \boxed{3} \times 3$

    Prime factorisation of $84 = \boxed{2} \times \boxed{2} \times \boxed{3} \times 7$

    Common factors of 36 and 84 are 2 (occurring twice) and 3.

    Thus, HCF of 36 and 84 $= 2 \times 2 \times 3 = 12$

  (f) Prime factorisation of $34 = \boxed{2} \times \boxed{17}$

    Prime factorisation of $102 = \boxed{2} \times \boxed{17} \times 3$

    Common factors of 34 and 102 are 2 and 17.

    Thus, HCF of 34 and 102 $= 2 \times 17 = 34$

  (g) Prime factorisation of $70 = 2 \times \boxed{5} \times \boxed{7}$

    Prime factorisation of $105 = 3 \times \boxed{5} \times \boxed{7}$

    Prime factorisation of $175 = 5 \times \boxed{5} \times \boxed{7}$

    Common factors of 70, 105 and 175 are 5 and 7.

    Thus, HCF of 70, 105 and 175 $= 5 \times 7 = 35$

  (h) Prime factorisation of $91 = \boxed{7} \times 13$

    Prime factorisation of $112 = \boxed{7} \times 2 \times 2 \times 2 \times 2$

    Prime factorisation of $49 = \boxed{7} \times 7$

    Common factor of 91, 112 and 49 is 7

    Thus, HCF of 91, 112 and 49 = 7.

(i) Prime factorisation of $18 = 2 \times \boxed{3} \times \boxed{3}$
Prime factorisation of $54 = 2 \times \boxed{3} \times \boxed{3} \times 3$
Prime factorisation of $81 = 3 \times \boxed{3} \times \boxed{3} \times 3$
Common factor of 18, 54 and 81 is 3 (occurring twice).
Thus, HCF of 18, 54 and $81 = 3 \times 3 = 9$

(j) Prime factorisation of $12 = 2 \times 2 \times \boxed{3}$
Prime factorisation of $45 = 5 \times 3 \times \boxed{3}$
Prime factorisation of $75 = 5 \times 5 \times \boxed{3}$
Common factor of 12, 45 and 75 is 3.
Thus, HCF of 12, 45 and $75 = 3$

Que 2. What is the HCF of two consecutive

  (a) numbers?   (b) even numbers?
  (c) odd numbers?

Sol. (a) Let the two consecutive numbers be 8 and 9.
Now, prime factorisation of $8 = 2 \times 2 \times 2$
Prime factorisation of $9 = 3 \times 3$
Common factor of 8 and $9 = 1$
Thus, HCF of 8 and 9 is 1.

Note The HCF of two consecutive numbers is 1.

(b) Let the two consecutive even numbers be 10 and 12.
Now, prime factorisation of $10 = \boxed{2} \times 5$
Prime factorisation of $12 = \boxed{2} \times 2 \times 3$
Common factor of 10 and $12 = 2$
Thus, HCF of 10 and 12 is 2.

Note The HCF of two consecutive even numbers is 2.

(c) Let two consecutive odd numbers be 3 and 5.
Prime factorisation of $3 = \boxed{1} \times 3$
Prime factorisation of $5 = \boxed{1} \times 5$
Common factor of 3 and $5 = 1$
Thus, HCF of 3 and 5 is 1.

Note The HCF of two consecutive odd numbers is 1.

Que 3. HCF of co-prime numbers 4 and 15 was found as follows by factorisation. $4 = 2 \times 2$ and $15 = 3 \times 5$, since there is no common prime factor, so HCF of 4 and 15 is 0. Is the answer correct? If not, what is the correct HCF?

Sol. No, the answer is not correct. Because 0 (zero) cannot be factor of any number. If there is no common factor means 1 is the common factor.
∴ HCF of 4 and $15 = 1$

Exercise 3.7

Que 1. Renu purchases two bags of fertiliser of weights 75 kg and 69 kg. Find the maximum value of weight, which can measure the weight of the fertiliser exact number of times.

Sol. For getting the maximum value of weight, we have to find out the HCF of 75 kg and 69 kg.

i.e.

3	75
5	25
5	5
	1

3	69
23	23
	1

∴ Prime factorisation of $75 = \boxed{3} \times 5 \times 5$
   Prime factorisation of $69 = \boxed{3} \times 23$
   Common factor of 75 and 69 is 3.
   Thus, HCF of 75 kg and 69 kg = 3 kg
   Hence, required maximum value of weight is 3 kg.

Que 2. Three boys step off together from the same spot. Their steps measure 63 cm, 70 cm and 77 cm, respectively. What is the minimum distance each should cover, so that all can cover the distance in complete steps?

Sol. Here, the required minimum distance will be equal to LCM of measures of their steps. because, the minimum distance each boy should walk must be the least common multiple of the measure of their steps.

So, we have to find out the LCM of 63, 70 and 77 cm.

i.e.

2	63, 70, 77
3	63, 35, 77
3	21, 35, 77
5	7, 35, 77
7	7, 7, 77
11	1, 1, 11
	1, 1, 1

∴ LCM of 63, 70 and $77 = 2 \times 3 \times 3 \times 5 \times 7 \times 11 = 6930$
   Hence, required minimum distance = 6930 cm

Que 3. The length, breadth and height of a room are 825 cm, 675 cm and 450 cm, respectively. Find the longest tape, which can measure the three dimensions of the room exactly.

Sol. For the longest tape, which can measure dimensions of room exactly, we have to find out the HCF of dimensions. i.e.

3	825		3	675		2	450
5	275		3	225		3	225
5	55		3	75		3	75
11	11		5	25		5	25
	1		5	5		5	5
				1			1

∴ Prime factorisation of $825 = \boxed{3} \times \boxed{5} \times \boxed{5} \times 11$
Prime factorisation of $675 = \boxed{3} \times \boxed{5} \times \boxed{5} \times 3 \times 3$
Prime factorisation of $450 = \boxed{3} \times \boxed{5} \times \boxed{5} \times 3 \times 2$

∴ Common factors of 825, 675 and 450 are 3 and 5 (occurring twice).

Thus, HCF of 825, 675 and $450 = 3 \times 5 \times 5 = 75$

Hence, required measure of longest tape = 75 cm

Que 4. Determine the smallest 3-digit number which is exactly divisible by 6, 8 and 12.

Sol. Firstly, we have to find out the LCM of 6, 8 and 12.

2	6, 8, 12
2	3, 4, 6
2	3, 2, 3
3	3, 1, 3
	1, 1, 1

∴ $LCM = 2 \times 2 \times 2 \times 3 = 24$

We know that, smallest three digit number is 100.

On dividing 100 by 24,

$$24) \overline{100} (4$$
$$\underline{96}$$
$$4$$

We find that, when 100 is divided by 24, we get remainder 4.

Now, required three digit number which is exactly divisible by 24 = (Smallest 3-digit numbers + Divisor – Remainder)

$= 100 + 24 - 4 = 120$

Que 5. Determine the greatest 3-digit number exactly divisible by 8, 10 and 12.

Sol. Firstly, we have to find out the LCM of 8, 10 and 12.

2	8, 10, 12
2	4, 5, 6
2	2, 5, 3
3	1, 5, 3
5	1, 5, 1
	1, 1, 1

$$120 \overline{)999} (8$$
$$\underline{960}$$
$$39$$

∴ LCM $= 2 \times 2 \times 2 \times 3 \times 5 = 120$

We know that, largest 3-digit number = 999

On dividing 999 by 120,

We find that, when 999 is divided by 120, we get remainder 39. Now, required three digit number which is exactly divisible by 120 = (Greatest 3-digit number – Remainder) = 999 – 39 = 960

Que 6. The traffic lights at three different road crossings change after every 48 seconds 72 seconds and 108 seconds respectively. If they change simultaneously at 7 a.m., at what time will they change simultaneously again?

Sol. The time period after which the traffic lights at three different road crossing changes simultaneously again will be the LCM of 48, 72 and 108.

2	48, 72, 108
2	24, 36, 54
2	12, 18, 27
2	6, 9, 27
3	3, 9, 27
3	1, 3, 9
3	1, 1, 3
	1, 1, 1

∴ LCM $= 2 \times 2 \times 2 \times 2 \times 3 \times 3 \times 3 = 432$

$$= \frac{432}{60} \text{ min} = 7 \text{ minute 12 second}$$

$$\left[\begin{array}{l} \because \quad 1 \text{ min} = 60 \\ \text{and} \quad 1 \text{ s} = \frac{1}{60} \text{ min} \end{array} \right]$$

So, time when they will change again = 07 : 00 : 00

$$\underline{+ \quad 07 : 12}$$
$$07 : 07 : 12$$

i.e. 7 min 12 s past 7 a.m.

Que 7. Three tankers contain 403 Litres 434 Litres and 465 Litres of diesel, respectively. Find the maximum capacity of a container, that can measure the diesel of the three containers exact number of times.

Sol. Here, maximum quantity of container will be equal to the HCF of 403, 434 and 465.

13	403		2	434		3	465
31	31		7	217		5	155
	1		31	31		31	31
				1			1

Prime factorisation of $403 = 13 \times \boxed{31}$
Prime factorisation of $434 = 2 \times 7 \times \boxed{31}$
Prime factorisation of $465 = 3 \times 5 \times \boxed{31}$
Common factor of 403, 434 and 465 is 31.
∴ Maximum capacity of container = HCF of 403, 434, and 465
$$= 31 \text{ Litres}$$

Que 8. Find the least number which when divided by 6, 15 and 18 leave remainder 5 in each case.

Sol. First, we have to find out the LCM of 6, 15, 18.

2	6, 15, 18
3	3, 15, 9
3	1, 5, 3
5	1, 5, 1
	1, 1, 1

∴ LCM $= 2 \times 3 \times 3 \times 5 = 90$
Now, required number = LCM + Remainder $= 90 + 5 = 95$
Hence, the required number is 95.

Que 9. Find the smallest 4-digit number which is divisible by 18, 24 and 32.

Sol. First, we have to find out the LCM of 18, 24, and 32.
∴ LCM $= 2 \times 2 \times 2 \times 2 \times 2 \times 3 \times 3 = 288$
We know that, smallest 4-digit number is 1000.
On dividing 1000 by 288,

$$288)\overline{1000}(3$$
$$\underline{864}$$
$$136$$

2	18, 24, 32
2	9, 12, 16
2	9, 6, 8
2	9, 3, 4
2	9, 3, 2
3	9, 3, 1
3	3, 1, 1
	1, 1, 1

When we divide 1000 by 288, we get 136 as remainder.

∴ Required smallest 4-digit number which is exactly divisible by 18, 24 and 32 = (Smallest 4-digit number + Divisor – Remainder)
= 1000 + 288 – 136 = 1152

Que 10. Find the LCM of the following numbers

(a) 9 and 4   (b) 12 and 5   (c) 6 and 5   (d) 15 and 4

Observe a common property in the obtained LCM. Is LCM the product of two numbers in each case?

Sol.   (a) LCM of 9 and 4

2	9, 4
2	9, 2
3	9, 1
3	3, 1
	1, 1

∴   LCM = $2 \times 2 \times 3 \times 3 = 36$

(b) LCM of 12 and 5

2	12, 5
2	6, 5
3	3, 5
5	1, 5
	1, 1

∴   LCM = $2 \times 2 \times 3 \times 5 = 60$

(c) LCM of 6 and 5

2	6, 5
3	3, 5
5	1, 5
	1, 1

∴   LCM = $2 \times 3 \times 5 = 30$

(d) LCM of 15 and 4

2	15, 4
2	15, 2
3	15, 1
5	5, 1
	1, 1

∴   LCM = $2 \times 2 \times 3 \times 5 = 60$

Here, we see that in each case LCM of given numbers is a multiple of 3 and 2.

Yes, in each case LCM = Product of two given numbers.

Que 11. Find the LCM of the following numbers in which one number is the factor of the other.

    (a) 5, 20   (b) 6, 18   (c) 12, 48   (d) 9, 45

What do you observe in the results obtained?

Sol. (a) LCM of 5 and 20

$$
\begin{array}{r|l}
2 & 5, 20 \\
\hline
2 & 5, 10 \\
\hline
5 & 5, 5 \\
\hline
& 1, 1
\end{array}
$$

    $\therefore$ LCM $= 2 \times 2 \times 5 = 20$

(b) LCM of 6 and 18

$$
\begin{array}{r|l}
2 & 6, 18 \\
\hline
3 & 3, 9 \\
\hline
3 & 1, 3 \\
\hline
& 1, 1
\end{array}
$$

    $\therefore$ LCM $= 2 \times 3 \times 3 = 18$

(c) LCM of 12 and 48

$$
\begin{array}{r|l}
2 & 12, 48 \\
\hline
2 & 6, 24 \\
\hline
2 & 3, 12 \\
\hline
2 & 3, 6 \\
\hline
3 & 3, 3 \\
\hline
& 1, 1
\end{array}
$$

    $\therefore$ LCM $= 2 \times 2 \times 2 \times 2 \times 3 = 48$

(d) LCM of 9 and 45

$$
\begin{array}{r|l}
3 & 9, 45 \\
\hline
3 & 3, 15 \\
\hline
5 & 1, 5 \\
\hline
& 1, 1
\end{array}
$$

    $\therefore$ LCM $= 3 \times 3 \times 5 = 45$

Here, we observe that in all parts, LCM of the given numbers is the larger of two numbers because one number is the factor of the other number.

Selected **NCERT Exemplar Problems**

Directions *In questions 1 to 9, out of the four options, only one is correct. Write the correct answer.*

Que 1. Number of even numbers between 58 and 80 is
    (a) 10   (b) 11   (c) 12   (d) 13

Sol. We know that, all the multiples of 2 are called even numbers.
So, even numbers between 58 and 80 are 60, 62, 64, 66, 68, 70, 72, 74, 76, 78.
∴ Number of even numbers between 58 and 80 is 10.
Hence, option (a) is correct.

Que 2. Sum of the number of primes between 16 to 80 and 90 to 100 is
    (a) 20   (b) 18   (c) 17   (d) 16

Sol. We know that, the numbers other than 1 whose any factors are 1 and the number itself are called prime numbers.
So, prime numbers between 16 to 80 are 17, 19, 23, 29, 31, 37, 41, 43, 47, 53, 59, 61, 67, 71, 73, 79.
∴ Number of prime numbers between 16 to 80 = 16
And prime numbers between 90 to 100 is 1. i.e. 97
∴ Now, the sum of the number of primes between 16 to 80 and 90 to 100 = 16 + 1 = 17. Hence, option (c) is correct.

Que 3. Which of the following statement is not true?
    (a) The HCF of two distinct prime numbers is 1.
    (b) The HCF of two co-prime numbers is 1.
    (c) The HCF of two consecutive even numbers is 2.
    (d) The HCF of an even and an odd number is even.

Sol. The HCF of an even and an odd number is an odd number.
e.g. Let an even number be 2 and an odd number be 3.
Now, HCF of 2 and 3 = 1 (which is odd). Hence, option (d) is not true.

Que 4. The number of distinct prime factors of the largest 4-digit number is
    (a) 2   (b) 3   (c) 5   (d) 11

Sol. We know that, largest 4-digit number $= 9999$
Prime factors of 9999

3	9999
3	3333
11	1111
101	101
	1

i.e. $\qquad 9999 = 3 \times 3 \times 11 \times 101$

∴ The number of distinct prime factors of the largest 4-digit number is 3. Hence, option (b) is correct.

Que 5. The number of distinct prime factors of the smallest 5-digit number is

(a) 2   (b) 4   (c) 6   (d) 8

Sol. We know that, smallest 5-digit number $= 10000$
Prime factors of 10000

2	10000
2	5000
2	2500
2	1250
5	625
5	125
5	25
5	5
	1

i.e. $10000 = 2 \times 2 \times 2 \times 2 \times 5 \times 5 \times 5 \times 5$

∴ The number of distinct prime factors of the smallest 5-digit number is 2. Hence, option (a) is correct.

Que 6. If the number 7254*98 is divisible by 22, the digit at * is

(a) 1   (b) 2   (c) 6   (d) 0

Sol. We know that, if a number is divisible by two co-prime numbers, then it is divisible by their product also.

Here, the number 7254 *98 is divisible by 22. It means the given number is divisible by 2 and 11 also.

The units place of given number is 8. Hence, it is divisible by 2.

Now, we check this number for 11.

$$7 \quad 2 \quad 5 \quad 4 \quad * \quad 9 \quad 8$$
$$\downarrow \quad \downarrow \quad \downarrow \quad \downarrow \quad \downarrow \quad \downarrow \quad \downarrow$$
$$O \quad E \quad O \quad E \quad O \quad E \quad O$$

Sum of the digits at odd places from right $= 8 + * + 5 + 7 = 20 + *$

Sum of the digits at even places from right $= 9 + 4 + 2 = 15$

According to the test of divisibility by 11,

$$20 + * - 15 = 11 \quad \Rightarrow \quad 5 + * = 11$$
$$* = 11 - 5 \Rightarrow \quad * = 6$$

Hence, the value of $* = 6$

Hence, option (c) is correct.

> **Note** A number is divisible by 11, if the difference of the sum of its digits in odd places (from the right) and the sum of its digits in even places (from the right) is either 0 or a multiple of 11.

Que 7. The largest number which always divides the sum of any pair of consecutive odd numbers is

    (a) 2   (b) 4   (c) 6   (d) 8

Sol. The largest number which always divides the sum of any pair of consecutive odd numbers is 4.

e.g. Let any pair of consecutive odd number is 3 and 5.

Sum of 3 and 5 $= 3 + 5 = 8$ which is divisible by 4.

So, 4 is the largest number, which always divides the sum of any pair of consecutive odd number. Hence, option (b) is correct.

Que 8. A number is divisible by 5 and 6. It may not be divisible by

    (a) 10   (b) 15   (c) 30   (d) 60

Sol. The given number will be divisible by the product of 5 and 6.

i.e. it is always divisible by $5 \times 6 = 30$

But $30 \div 60$ (not possible). Hence, option (d) is correct.

Que 9. The sum of the prime factors of 1729 is

    (a) 13   (b) 19   (c) 32   (d) 39

Sol. We have, 1729

Thus, the prime factors of $1729 = 7 \times 13 \times 19$

∴ The sum of the prime factors of 1729

$$= 7 + 13 + 19 = 39$$

Hence, option (d) is correct.

7	1729
13	247
19	19
	1

Directions *In questions 10 to 21, state whether the given statements are true (T) or false (F).*

Que 10. Sum of two consecutive odd numbers is always divisible by 4.

Sol. True, e.g. Let two consecutive odd numbers be 3 and 5.

$\therefore$ $\qquad\qquad$ Sum $= 3 + 5 = 8; 8 \div 4 = 2$

Que 11. If a number is divisible both by 2 and 3, then it is divisible by 12.

Sol. False, e.g. Let a number be 48.

Here, units digit $= 8$, which is divisible by 2.

So, 48 is divisible by 2.

Now, sum of the digits of $48 = 4 + 8 = 12$ which is divisible by 3.

Now again, check it for 12.

Here, tens digit $= 4$ and units digit $= 8$.

So, 48 is divisible by 12.

Now, take another example.

Let a number be 210.

Here, units digit $= 0$.

So, 210 is divisible by 2.

Now, sum of the digit of $210 = 2 + 1 + 0 = 3$ which is divisible by 3

Here, tens digit $= 1$ and units digit $= 0$.

So, 10 is not divisible by 4.

Thus, 210 is not divisible by 12.

Hence, we can say that it is an exceptional case.

Que 12. A number with three or more digits is divisible by 6, if the number formed by its last two digits (i.e. ones and tens) is divisible by 6.

Sol. False, e.g. Let two numbers be 1284 and 1384. Its last two digits (ones and tens digit) are divisible by 6. But 1284 is divisible by 6 and 1384 is not divisible by 6.

Que 13. All numbers which are divisible by 4 may not be divisible by 8.

Sol. True, e.g. 16, 20 and 24 are divisible by 4 but 20 is not divisible by 8.

Que 14. The highest common factor of two or more numbers is greater than their lowest common multiple.

Sol. False, the highest common factor of two or more numbers is not greater than their lowest common multiple.

e.g. Let two numbers be 24 and 30.

2	24
2	12
2	6
3	3
	1

2	30
3	15
5	5
	1

$\therefore$

$$24 = \boxed{2} \times 2 \times 2 \times 3$$
$$30 = \boxed{2} \times 3 \times 5$$

$\because$ Common factors = 2, 3

HCF $= 2 \times 3 = 6$ and LCM $= 2 \times 2 \times 2 \times 3 \times 5 = 120$

i.e. HCF is not greater than LCM.

Que 15. LCM of two numbers is 28 and their HCF is 8.

Sol. False, as we know that, LCM of two or more numbers is always divisible by the HCF of those number.

Here, LCM of two numbers (28) is not divisible by HCF (8).

Que 16. LCM of two or more numbers may be one of the numbers.

Sol. True, LCM of two or more numbers may be one of the numbers.

e.g. Let two numbers be 24 and 120. LCM of 24 and 120

2	24, 120
2	12, 60
2	6, 30
3	3, 15
5	1, 5
	1, 1

$\therefore$ LCM of 24 and 120 $= 2 \times 2 \times 2 \times 3 \times 5 = 120$

Que 17. HCF of two or more numbers may be one of the numbers.

Sol. True, HCF of two or more numbers may be one of the numbers.

e.g. Let two numbers be 12 and 24.

Prime factorisation of 12 and 24

2	12
2	6
3	3
	1

2	24
2	12
2	6
3	3
	1

$$12 = \boxed{2} \times \boxed{2} \times \boxed{3}$$
$$24 = \boxed{2} \times \boxed{2} \times 2 \times \boxed{3}$$

Common factors = 2, 2 and 3 ∴ HCF = $2 \times 2 \times 3 = 12$

Que 18. If the HCF of two numbers is one of the numbers, then their LCM is the other number.

Sol. True, let two numbers be 18 and 36.

2	18
3	9
3	3
	1

2	36
2	18
3	9
3	3
	1

$$18 = \boxed{2} \times \boxed{3} \times \boxed{3}$$
$$36 = \boxed{2} \times \boxed{3} \times \boxed{3} \times 2$$

Common factors are 2, 3 and 3.

∴ HCF = $2 \times 3 \times 3 = 18$ and LCM = $2 \times 3 \times 3 \times 2 = 36$

It is clear that, if the HCF of two numbers is one of the numbers, then their LCM is the other number.

Que 19. The HCF of two numbers is smaller than the smaller of the numbers.

Sol. True, the HCF of two numbers is smaller than the smaller of the numbers. e.g. Let two numbers be 14 and 30.

Prime factorisation of 14 and 30

2	14
7	7
	1

2	30
3	15
5	5
	1

$$14 = \boxed{2} \times 7$$
$$30 = \boxed{2} \times 3 \times 5$$

Here, common factor is 2.

∴ HCF = 2

It is clear that, the HCF of two numbers is smaller than the smaller of the numbers.

Que 20. The LCM of two numbers is greater than the larger of the numbers.

Sol. False, the LCM of two numbers is not always greater than the larger of the numbers. e.g. Let two numbers be 14 and 28.
LCM of 14 and 28

$$
\begin{array}{c|c}
2 & 14, 28 \\
\hline
2 & 7, 14 \\
\hline
7 & 7, 7 \\
\hline
& 1, 1
\end{array}
$$

$$\text{LCM} = 2 \times 2 \times 7 = 28$$

Que 21. The LCM of two co-prime numbers is equal to the product of the numbers.

Sol. True, e.g. Let two co-prime numbers be 2 and 3.
∴ Their product $= 2 \times 3 = 6$ and LCM of 2 and $3 = 6$
It is clear that, the LCM of two co-prime numbers is equal to the product of the numbers.

Directions *In questions 22 to 24, fill in the blanks to make the statements true.*

Que 22. Two numbers having only 1 as a common factor are called ...... number.

Sol. co-prime

Que 23. The LCM of two or more given numbers is the lowest of their common ..... .

Sol. multiple

Que 24. The HCF of two or more given numbers is the highest of their common ..... .

Sol. factors

Que 25. Determine the least number which when divided any 3, 4 and 5 leaves remainder 2 in each case.

Sol. We have,

∴ LCM of 3, 4 and $5 = 2 \times 2 \times 3 \times 5 = 60$

Since, 60 is the least number exactly divisible by 3, 4 and 5.

To get the remainder 2,

The least number $= 60 + 2 = 62$

$$
\begin{array}{c|c}
2 & 3, 4, 5 \\
\hline
2 & 3, 2, 5 \\
\hline
3 & 3, 1, 5 \\
\hline
5 & 1, 1, 5 \\
\hline
& 1, 1, 1
\end{array}
$$

Que 26. A merchant has 120 L of oil of one kind, 180 L of another kind and 240 L of a third kind. He wants to sell the oil by filling the three kinds of oil in tins of equal capacity. What should be the greatest capacity of such a tin?

Sol. The greatest capacity of the required measure will be equal to the HCF of 120, 180 and 240 L.

Prime factorisation of 120, 180 and 240.

2	120
2	60
2	30
3	15
5	5
	1

2	180
2	90
3	45
3	15
5	5
	1

2	240
2	120
2	60
2	30
3	15
5	5
	1

$$120 = \boxed{2} \times \boxed{2} \times 2 \times \boxed{3} \times \boxed{5}$$
$$180 = \boxed{2} \times \boxed{2} \times 3 \times \boxed{3} \times \boxed{5}$$
$$240 = \boxed{2} \times \boxed{2} \times 2 \times 2 \times \boxed{3} \times \boxed{5}$$

Common factors of 120, 180 and 240 $= 2 \times 2 \times 3 \times 5 = 60$

Hence, greatest capacity of tin $= 60$ L

Que 27. A box contains 5 strips having 12 capsules of 500 mg medicine in each capsule. Find the total weight in grams of medicine in 32 such boxes.

Sol. Given, in each strip their are 12 capsule

Also, given weight of one capsule is 500 mg

Weight of 12 capsule $= 12 \times 500 = 6000$ mg

∴ Weight of 1 strip = weight of 12 capsule $= 6000$ mg

∴ weight of 5 strips $= 5 \times$ weight of 1 strip $= 5 \times 6000 = 30000$ mg

∴ weight of 1 box = weight of 5 strips $= 30000$ mg

∴ weight of 32 box $= 32 \times$ weight of 1 box $= 32 \times 300000$ mg

$$= 960000 \text{ mg}$$

$$= \frac{960000}{1000} \text{ grams} \quad \begin{bmatrix} \because 1 \text{ gram} = 1000 \text{ mg} \\ \therefore 1 \text{ mg} = \dfrac{1}{1000} \text{ gram} \end{bmatrix}$$

$$= 960 \text{ grams}$$

Hence, the total weight of 32 medicine box is 960 grams.

Que 28. Find a 4-digit odd number using each of digits 1, 2, 4 and 5 only once such that when the first and last digits are interchanged, it is divisible by 4.

Sol. We know that 4-dight number is said to be an add number, if the place digit is an odd number (i.e. 1 or 5)

Total such add numbers are,

4125, 4215, 1245, 1425, 2145, 2415, 4251, 4521, 5241, 5421, 2451, 2541

Also we know that any four digits number be divisible by 4, if the last two digits number is divisible by 4.

Consider a number 4521, if we interchage the first and the last digit, the new number will be 1524. Here we see that the last two dights (i.e. 24) which is divisibley 4. Hence the number 1524 is divisible by 4.

Hence, the required four digits number is 4521.

Que 29. The floor of a room is 8m 96cm long and 6m 72cm broad. Find the minimum number of square tiles of the same size needed to cover the entire floor.

Sol. Given,   length of the floor = 8 m 96 cm

$$= 8 \times 100 \text{ cm} + 96 \text{ cm} \qquad [\because 1 \text{ m} = 100 \text{ cm}]$$

$$= (800 + 96) \text{ cm} = 896 \text{ cm}$$

and breadth of the floor = 6 m 72 cm

$$= 6 \times 100 \text{ cm} + 72 \text{ cm} \qquad [\because 1 \text{ m} = 100 \text{ cm}]$$

$$= (600 + 72) \text{ cm} = 672 \text{ cm}$$

Now, size of the square tile = HCF of 896 and 672

Prime factorisation of 896 and 672

2	896
2	448
2	224
2	112
2	56
2	28
2	14
7	7
	1

2	672
2	336
2	168
2	84
2	42
3	21
7	7
	1

$$896 = \boxed{2} \times \boxed{2} \times \boxed{2} \times \boxed{2} \times \boxed{2} \times 2 \times 2 \times \boxed{7}$$
$$672 = \boxed{2} \times \boxed{2} \times \boxed{2} \times \boxed{2} \times \boxed{2} \times 3 \qquad \times \boxed{7}$$

Common factors of 896 and 672 = $2 \times 2 \times 2 \times 2 \times 2 \times 7 = 224$

$\therefore$ Minimum number of square tiles $= \dfrac{\text{Area of floor}}{\text{Area of square tile}}$

$= \dfrac{896 \times 672}{224 \times 224}$ [$\because$ area of square $= (\text{side})^2$]

$= \dfrac{896 \times 3}{224} = 4 \times 3 = 12$

Que 30. In a school library, there are 780 books of English and 364 books of Science. Ms Yakang, the librarian of the school wants to store these books in shelves such that each shelf should have the same number of books of each subject. What should be the minimum number of books in each shelf?

Sol. Given, number of English books = 780

Number of Science books = 364

For getting the minimum number of books in each shelf, we have to find the HCF of 780 and 364.

$\Rightarrow$ Prime factorisation of 780 and 364

2	780
2	390
3	195
5	65
13	13
	1

2	364
2	182
7	91
13	13
	1

$780 = \boxed{2} \times \boxed{2} \times 3 \times \boxed{13} \times 5$
$364 = \boxed{2} \times \boxed{2} \times 7 \times \boxed{13}$

Common factors of 780 and 364 $= 2 \times 2 \times 13 = 52$

Que 31. In a colony of 100 blocks of flats numbering 1 to 100, a school van stops at every sixth block while a school bus stops at every tenth block. On which stops will both of them stop if they start from the entrance of the colony?

Sol. Given, in a colony block numbering 1 to 100. Here school van and bus stop at the same stopage means it is the LCM of both stopage
$\therefore$ LCM of 6 and 10 $= 2 \times 3 \times 5 = 30$

It shows that first time they both meets at 30 th stopage and the next time they again meet at a multiples of 30.

Hence, the both of them meet the stopage on 30, 60 and 90.

Chapter 4

Basic Geometrical Ideas

Important Points

- The term 'Geometry' is the English equivalent of the Greek word 'Geometron'. 'Geo' means earth and 'metron' means measurement.
- **Point** A point determines a location. It is denoted by a single capital letter like A, B, C etc. A point has no length, breadth or height.
- **Line segment** A line segment corresponds to the shortest distance between two points.

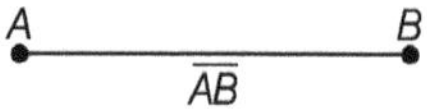

  The line segment joining points A and B (ray) is denoted by $\overline{AB}$ or $\overline{BA}$. The point A and B are called the end points of the line segment.
- **Line** A line is obtained, when a line segment say $\overline{AB}$ is extended on both

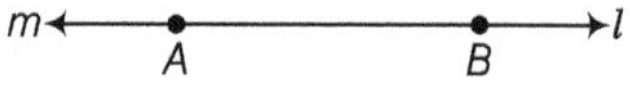

  sides indefinitely. A line is denoted by $\overleftrightarrow{AB}$ and sometimes it is denoted by single letter as l, m.

  Two points are enough to fix a line.
- **Intersecting lines** If two lines have one common point, then they are called intersecting lines.

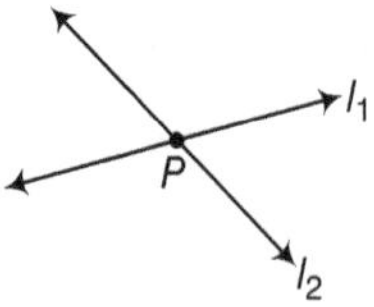

  In the figure, lines l_1 and l_2 are intersecting lines, which intersect at point P.
- **Parallel lines** Two lines in a plane, which do not meet, even when produced (extended) indefinitely in either direction, are called parallel lines.

▪ e.g. The opposite edges of ruler (or scale) are parallel.

▪ **Ray** A ray is a portion of a line, which starts at one point (known as starting point) and goes endlessly in a particular direction.

In the figure, $\overrightarrow{AP}$ is a ray, whose starting point is A and P is a point on the path of the ray. Here, the arrow indicates that the ray $\overrightarrow{AP}$ is endless in the direction from A to P.

▪ **Curve** Any drawing (straight or non-straight) done without lifting the pencil may be called a curve. If we take a piece of paper and it is just doodled. Then, the pictures obtained as a result of doodling are curves. A line is also a curve.

▪ **Types of Curve**
   (i) If a curve does not cross itself, then it is called a **simple curve**.
   (ii) A curve, which does not cut itself, is called an **open curve**.
        In other words, when the ends of a curve are not joined, then it is called an open curve.
   (iii) A curve, which cuts itself, is called a **closed curve**.
        In other words, when the ends of a curve are joined, then it is called closed curve.
        In a closed curve, there are three parts, which are as follows:
        (a) Interior (inside) of the curve
        (b) Boundary (on) of the curve
        (c) Exterior (outside) of the curve

▪ **Polygon** A simple closed figure made up entirely of line segments is called a polygon. In the given figure, $ABCDE$ is a polygon.
   (i) The end points of the same side of a polygon are called the **adjacent vertices**.
        In polygon $ABCDE$, A and B, B and C, C and D, D and E, E and A are adjacent vertices.
   (ii) The meeting point of a pair of sides is called its **vertex**. In polygon $ABCDE$, A, B, C, D and E are vertices.

(iii) Any two sides with a common end point (vertex) are called the **adjacent sides** of the polygon.

In polygon *ABCDE*, one pair of adjacent sides is *AB* and *BC* (where, *B* is a common vertex).

(iv) The line segments, forming a polygon are called its **sides**. In polygon *ABCDE*, *AB*, *BC*, *CD*, *DE* and *EA* are its sides.

(v) The line segments are obtained by joining vertices, which are not adjacent, are called the **diagonals** of the polygon.

In polygon *ABCDE*, *AC*, *AD*, *BD*, *BE* and *CE* are diagonals.

■ **Angle** Two rays together are said to form an angle, if they have a common end point. Two rays forming the angle are called the **arms** or **sides** of the angle and common end point is the **vertex** of the angle.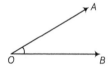

In the figure, *AOB* is an angle and it is denoted by ∠*AOB* or ∠*BOA* or ∠*O*. *OA* and *OB* are arms or sides of angle and *O* is the vertex of the angle.

(i) In specifying the angle, the vertex is always written as the middle letter.

(ii) An angle leads to three divisions of a region. i.e. on the angle, the interior of the angle and the exterior of the angle. In this diagram, *X* is in the interior the angle. Point *P*, *S*, *R* are on an the angle and point y is in exterior of the angle

■ **Triangle** A triangle is a three sided polygon.
In Δ*ABC*, three sides are $\overline{AB}$, $\overline{BC}$ and $\overline{CA}$. Three angles are ∠*BAC*, ∠*ABC* and ∠*BCA*. Three vertices are *A*, *B* and *C*. It can also be written Δ*CBA* or Δ*BCA* or Δ*BAC*.

Note Triangle is a polygon with the least number of sides.

■ **Quadrilateral** A polygon having four sides is called a quadrilateral.
In quadrilateral *ABCD*, four sides are $\overline{AB}$, $\overline{BC}$, $\overline{CD}$ and $\overline{DA}$. Four angles are ∠*A*, ∠*B*, ∠*C* and ∠*D* or ∠*ABC*, ∠*BCD*, ∠*CDA* and ∠*DAB*. Four vertices are *A*, *B*, *C* and *D*.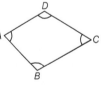

Also, $\overline{AB}$ and $\overline{CD}$, $\overline{BC}$ and $\overline{AD}$ are opposite sides. $\angle A$ and $\angle C$, $\angle B$ and $\angle D$ are opposite angles. $\angle A$ and $\angle B$, $\angle B$ and $\angle C$, $\angle C$ and $\angle D$, $\angle D$ and $\angle A$ are adjacent angles.

▪ **Circle** A circle is the path of a point, moving at the same distance from a fixed point. This fixed point is called **centre,** the fixed distance is called **radius** and the distance around the circle is called **circumference** of the circle.

In the figure, O is the centre and

$\overline{OP} = \overline{OC} = \overline{OD}$, each are the radius of a circle.

(i) A **chord** of a circle is a line segment joining any two points on the circle. In figure, AB is a chord of the circle.

(ii) A chord of a circle, which passes through the centre of the circle, is called **diameter** of the circle. In figure, CD is the diameter of circle.

(iii) An **arc** is a portion of a circle. In figure, AB is an arc of the circle.

(iv) A region in the interior of a circle enclosed by an arc on one side and a pair of radii on the other two sides is called a **sector** of circle.

In the figure, MON is a sector of the circle.

(v) A region in the interior of a circle enclosed by a chord and an arc is called a **segment** of the circle.

In the figure, RQS is a segment of the circle.

Note Diameter of a circle is double the radius of the circle. The diameter of a circle divides it into two parts, each part is called **semi-circle.** Diameter is the longest chord of the circle and equal to each other so the diameter of a circle are congruent because the centre is a common point. The plural of radius is radii.

Try These (Page 70)

Que 1. With a sharp tip of the pencil, mark four points on a paper and name them by the letters A, C, P, H. Try to name these points in different ways. One such way could be this

A•   •C

P•   •H

Sol. We can give the name to these given points in different ways as follows :

(i) • • • •
    M N P R

(ii) R•   •S

    P•   •T

(iii) P•   •Q

     R•   •S

(iv) T• •P

     Q•   •R

(v) S•   •M

    T•   •R

Que 2. A star in the sky also gives us an idea of a point. Identify atleast five such situations in your daily life.

Sol. Five situations of a point in our daily life are as follows :

   (i) Tip of an ice cone.   (ii) An edge of a table.

  (iii) Corner of a room.   (iv) Corner of a desk.

   (v) Corner of a paper.

Try These (Page 71)

Que 3. Name the line segments in the figure. Is *A*, the end point of each line segment?

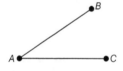

Sol. We know that, the shortest distance between two points is called a line segment. The line segment joining two points *A* and *B* is denoted by $\overline{AB}$ or $\overline{BA}$. The line segment in the given figure are as follows :

   (i) $\overline{AB}$ (or $\overline{BA}$)   (ii) $\overline{AC}$ (or $\overline{CA}$)

Yes, from the figure, it is clear that point *A* is the end point of each line segment.

Do This (Page 72)

Que 4. Take a sheet of paper. Make two folds (and crease them) to represent a pair of intersecting lines and discuss.

   (a) Can two lines intersect in more than one point?

   (b) Can more than two lines intersect in one point?

Sol. We know that, if two lines have one common point, then they are called intersecting lines. By making two folds of a sheet of paper and crease them, we get the following figure.

   (a) From figure, it is clear that line *l* and *m* intersect at one point *O* (say) only. So, two lines cannot intersect in more than one point.

(b) Now, we again fold the paper diagonally (i.e. fold the paper three times) and crease them. We get the following figure.

In the figure, four lines *l*, *m*, *n* and *o* are intersecting at one point *O* (say) only. So, it is clear from the above figure, that more than two lines intersect in one point.

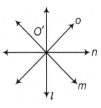

Try These (Page 74)

Que 5. (a) Name the rays given in this picture.

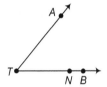

(b) Is *T* a starting point of each of these rays?

Sol. We know that, a ray is a part of a line which starts at one point and goes endlessly in a direction.

(a) In the given figure, there are four rays namely $\overrightarrow{TA}$, $\overrightarrow{TN}$, $\overrightarrow{NB}$ and $\overrightarrow{TB}$.

(b) No, *T* is not a starting point of each of these rays. *T* is a starting point of $\overrightarrow{TA}$, $\overrightarrow{TB}$ and $\overrightarrow{TN}$ only but not of $\overrightarrow{NB}$.

Exercise 4.1

Que 1. Use the figure to name
  (a) five points.   (b) a line.
  (c) four rays.   (d) five line segments.

Sol. From the given figure,

(a) Five points are *B*, *C*, *D*, *E* and *O*.

(b) A line is $\overleftrightarrow{BD}$ (or $\overleftrightarrow{OB}$).

(c) Four rays are $\overrightarrow{OB}$, $\overrightarrow{OC}$, $\overrightarrow{OE}$ and $\overrightarrow{OD}$.

(d) Five line segments in the given figure are $\overline{OB}$, $\overline{OC}$, $\overline{OE}$, $\overline{OD}$ and $\overline{DE}$.

Note Two points are enough to fix a line. Hence, we can say that two points determine a line.

Que 2. Name the line given in all possible (twelve) ways, choosing only two letters at a time from the four given letters.

Sol. We know that, a line is a line segment which can extend indefinitely in both directions. Name of lines in all possible ways are as follows :

(i) By taking A, all possible ways are $\overleftrightarrow{AB}$, $\overleftrightarrow{AC}$ and $\overleftrightarrow{AD}$

(ii) By taking B, all possible ways are $\overleftrightarrow{BC}$, $\overleftrightarrow{BD}$ and $\overleftrightarrow{BA}$

(iii) By taking C, all possible ways are $\overleftrightarrow{CD}$, $\overleftrightarrow{CA}$ and $\overleftrightarrow{CB}$

(iv) By taking D, all possible ways are $\overleftrightarrow{DA}$, $\overleftrightarrow{DB}$ and $\overleftrightarrow{DC}$

Que 3. Use the figure to name

(a) line containing point E.

(b) line passing through A.

(c) line on which O lies.

(d) two pairs of intersecting lines.

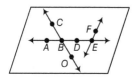

Sol. (a) Here, two lines contain point E, one of them is $\overleftrightarrow{AE}$.

(b) Here, one line is passing through A, i.e. $\overleftrightarrow{AE}$.

(c) Line on which O lies, is $\overleftrightarrow{CO}$ or $\overleftrightarrow{OC}$.

(d) There are two pairs of intersecting lines. i.e. are $\overleftrightarrow{CO}$, $\overleftrightarrow{AE}$ and $\overleftrightarrow{AE}$, $\overleftrightarrow{EF}$.

Que 4. How many lines can pass through

(a) one given point?   (b) two given points?

Sol. (a) Infinite number of lines can pass through one given point.

Let there be a point O on a surface. Now, we can draw infinite lines through it,

(b) Exactly one and only one line can pass through two given points (say A and B) i.e.

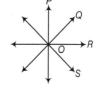

Que 5. Draw a rough figure and label suitably in each of the following cases.

(a) Point P lies on $\overline{AB}$.

(b) $\overleftrightarrow{XY}$ and $\overleftrightarrow{PQ}$ intersect at M.

(c) Line l contains E and F but not D.

(d) $\overleftrightarrow{OP}$ and $\overleftrightarrow{OQ}$ meet at O.

Sol. A rough figure in each of the cases is given below

(a) Point P lies on $\overline{AB}$.

(b) $\overleftrightarrow{XY}$ and $\overleftrightarrow{PQ}$ intersect at M.

(c) Line l contains E and F but not D.

(d) $\overleftrightarrow{OP}$ and $\overleftrightarrow{OQ}$ meet at O.

Que 6. Consider the following figure of line $\overleftrightarrow{MN}$. Say whether following statements are true or false in context of the given figure.

(a) Q, M, O, N, P are points on the line $\overleftrightarrow{MN}$.

(b) M, O, N are points on a line segment $\overline{MN}$.

(c) M and N are end points of line segment $\overline{MN}$.

(d) O and N are end points of line segment $\overline{OP}$.

(e) M is one of the end points of line segment $\overline{QO}$.

(f) M is point on ray $\overrightarrow{OP}$.

(g) Ray $\overrightarrow{OP}$ is different from ray $\overrightarrow{QP}$.

(h) Ray $\overrightarrow{OP}$ is same as ray $\overrightarrow{OM}$.

(i) Ray $\overrightarrow{OM}$ is not opposite to ray $\overrightarrow{OP}$.

(j) O is not an initial point of $\overrightarrow{OP}$.

(k) N is the initial point of $\overrightarrow{NP}$ and $\overrightarrow{NM}$.

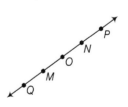

Sol. (a) True, because points M, O and N lie on the line $\overleftrightarrow{MN}$ and points Q and P lie on the extended portion of $\overleftrightarrow{MN}$ on both sides.

    (b) True, because points M, O, N lie on the line segment $\overline{MN}$.

    (c) True, because M to N is the shortest route of line segment $\overline{MN}$.

    (d) False, because it is clear from figure that point N is between O and P.

    (e) False, because it is clear from figure that point M is between Q and O.

    (f) False, because M is outside from ray $\overrightarrow{OP}$.

    (g) True, because all the rays have their own existence.

    (h) False, because rays $\overrightarrow{OP}$ and $\overrightarrow{OM}$ are in opposite directions.

    (i) True, because it is clear from figure that rays $\overrightarrow{OM}$ and $\overrightarrow{OP}$ are opposite.

    (j) False, because it is clear from figure that point O is the initial point of $\overleftrightarrow{OP}$.

    (k) True, because it is clear from figure that line segment $\overline{NP}$ and $\overline{NM}$ start from point N.

Do This (Page 77)

Que 1. Try to form a polygon with

    (i) five matchsticks.   (ii) four matchsticks.

    (iii) three matchsticks.   (iv) two matchsticks.

Sol. We know that, if a closed simple figure is made up entirely of line segments, then it is called a polygon.

    (i) Polygon with five matchsticks

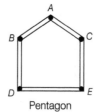

Pentagon

    (ii) Polygon with four matchsticks

Quardrilateral

(iii) Polygon with three matchsticks

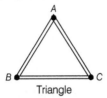

Triangle

(iv) We know that, a polygon is a closed plane figure, bounded by line segments. So, with the help of two matchsticks, it is not possible to make a close plane figure. Hence, no polygon is formed by two matchsticks.

Exercise 4.2

Que 1. Classify the following curves as (i) open or (ii) closed.

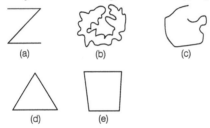

(a)   (b)   (c)

(d)   (e)

 TIPS A simple curve is one, that does not cross itself. Besides, when the ends of a curve are joined, it is called a **closed curve**. If its ends are not joined, it is called an **open curve**.

Sol. Now, from the figure, (a) and (c) are open curves and (b), (d) and (e) are closed curves.

Que 2. Draw rough diagram to illustrate the following
   (a) open curve.   (b) closed curve.
Sol. (a) The curve given below is an open curve, since its ends are not joined.

(b) The curve given below is a closed curve, since its ends are joined.

Que 3. Draw any polygon and shade its interior.

 We know that a simple closed figure made up entirely of line segments is called a polygon and in a closed curve, the interior is inside of the curve.

Sol. Thus, *ABCD* is a polygon, where interior is shaded as given below

Que 4. Consider the given figure and answer the questions.

    (a) Is it a curve?

    (b) Is it closed?

 Any drawing drawn without lifting the pencil from the paper is called a curve. A curve is said to be a closed curve, if its ends are joined.

Sol. (a) Yes, it is a curve.   (b) Yes, it is closed.

Que 5. Illustrate, if possible, each one of the following with a rough diagram.

    (a) A closed curve that is not a polygon.

    (b) An open curve made up entirely of line segments.

    (c) A polygon with two sides.

Sol. (a) This figure shows a closed curve but not a polygon because a polygon is made by line segments only.

(b) This figure shows an open curve made up entirely of line segments.

(c) It is not possible because a polygon of two sides cannot be drawn.

Exercise 4.3

Que 1. Name the angles in the given figure.

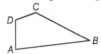

Sol. We know that, an angle is made up of two rays starting from a common end point. So, the angles in given figure are as follows :

   (i) $\angle A$ or $\angle DAB$ (ii) $\angle B$ or $\angle ABC$

  (iii) $\angle C$ or $\angle DCB$ (iv) $\angle D$ or $\angle ADC$

Que 2. In the given diagram, name the point(s).

   (a) In the interior of $\angle DOE$.

   (b) In the exterior of $\angle EOF$.

   (c) On $\angle EOF$.

Sol. (a) In given figure, point A lies between the sides OD and OE. So it is in the interior of $\angle DOE$.

  (b) In given figure, point C, A and D are in the exterior of $\angle EOF$.

  (c) In given figure, point E, B, O and F lie on the sides OE and OF of $\angle EOF$, so these points are on $\angle EOF$.

Que 3. Draw rough diagrams of two angles such that they have

   (a) one point in common.   (b) two points in common.

   (c) three points in common.   (d) four points in common.

   (e) one ray in common.

Sol. (a) The diagram is shown as below
     Here, $\angle ROQ$ and $\angle QOP$ have one point O in common.

  (b) The diagram is shown as below
     Here, $\angle MON$ and $\angle ONR$ have two ponts O and N in common.

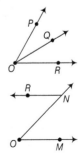

(c) Drawing a diagram of two angles, such that they have three points in common, is not possible.

(d) Drawing a diagram of two angles, such that they have four points in common, is not possible.

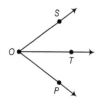

(e) In the figure given below, ∠SOT and ∠POT have one ray $\overrightarrow{OT}$ in common.

Exercise 4.4

Que 1. Draw a rough sketch of a ΔABC. Mark a point P in its interior and a point Q in its exterior. Is the point A in its exterior or in its interior?

Sol. (i) A triangle is a three sided polygon. A rough sketch of a ΔABC is given.

(ii) Now, from the figure

Point P is inside the ΔABC and point Q is outside the ΔABC. The point A is neither in the exterior nor in the interior of ΔABC because point A is the vertex of ΔABC, so it lies on the ΔABC.

Que 2. (a) Identify three triangles in the figure.
(b) Write the names of seven angles.
(c) Write the names of six line segments.
(d) Which two triangles have ∠B as common?

Sol. (a) We know that, a triangle is a three sided polygon. So, three triangles in the given figure are as follows :
    (i) ΔABD   (ii) ΔADC   (iii) ΔABC

(b) An angle is made up of two rays starting from a common end point here the names of seven angles are as follows :
    (i) ∠BAD   (ii) ∠BAC   (iii) ∠CAD   (iv) ∠ABD
    (v) ∠ACD   (vi) ∠ADC   (vii) ∠ADB.

(c) The names of six line segments are as follows :
    (i) AB   (ii) BD   (iii) DC   (iv) CA   (v) AD   (vi) BC

(d) From the given figure, it is clear that ∠B is common of ΔABD and ΔABC.

Exercise 4.5

Que 1. Draw a rough sketch of a quadrilateral *PQRS*. Draw its diagonals, name them. Is the meeting point of the diagonals in the interior or exterior of the quadrilateral?

Sol. The joins of the vertices, which are not adjacent i.e. opposite to each other, are called diagonals of quadrilateral.

A rough sketch of a quadrilateral *PQRS* with its diagonals and their name is given.

Here, *PR* and *QS* are its diagonals. They intersect each other at point *O*. So, point *O* is in the interior of the quadrilateral *PQRS*.

Que 2. Draw a rough sketch of a quadrilateral *KLMN*. State,

     (a) two pairs of opposite sides.

     (b) two pairs of opposite angles.

     (c) two pairs of adjacent sides.

     (d) two pairs of adjacent angles.

Sol. A rough sketch of a quadrilateral *KLMN* is given here

   Now, from the figure

   (a) *KL, MN* and *LM, NK* are two pairs of opposite sides.

   (b) $\angle K$, $\angle M$ and $\angle L$, $\angle N$ are two pairs of opposite angles.

   (c) *KL, LM* and *LM, MN* are two pairs of adjacent sides because end point of one line is starting point of another line.

   (d) Two angles are called adjacent angles, if they have common vertex. Hence, $\angle K$, $\angle L$ and $\angle L$, $\angle M$ are two pairs of adjacent angles because they have the common vertex *L*.

Que 3. Investigate Use strips and fasteners to make a triangle and a quadrilateral. Try to push inward at any one vertex of the triangle. Do the same to the quadrilateral? Is the triangle distorted? Is the quadrilateral distorted? Is the triangle rigid? Why is it that structures like electric towers make use of triangular shapes and not quadrilaterals?

Sol. On pushing inward at any one vertex of the triangle, we find that the triangle is not distorted. Whereas doing so with the quadrilateral, we find that it is distorted. Triangle is rigid. Thus, we use triangular shapes in making structures like electric towers as triangular shapes.

Exercise 4.6

Que 1. From the figure, identify
    (a) the centre of circle   (b) three radii
    (c) a diameter   (d) a chord
    (e) two points in the interior (f) point in the exterior
    (g) a sector   (h) a segment

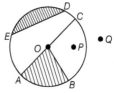

Sol. (a) In the given figure, point O is the centre of the circle.

  (b) Three radii of circle in the given figure are OA, OB and OC.

  (c) Here, OA and OC are radii such that OA and OC are in a line.
     So, AC is the diameter i.e. diameter $= 2 \times$ radius.

  (d) In the given figure, ED is a chord of circle.

  (e) Points P and O are in the interior of circle.

  (f) Point Q is in the exterior of circle.

  (g) A region in the interior of a circle enclosed by an arc on one side
     and a pair of radii on the other two sides is called a sector. In
     given figure, OAB is a sector.

  (h) A region in the interior of a circle enclosed by a chord and an arc
     is called a segment of the circle. In given figure, region enclosed
     by ED is a segment.

Que 2. (a) Is every diameter of a circle also a chord?
      (b) Is every chord of a circle also a diameter?

Sol. (a) Yes, every diameter of a circle is also a chord because a chord is a
     line segment connecting two points on a circle.
     Also, diameter is the longest chord.

  (b) No, every chord of a circle is not also a diameter because
     diameter of a circle is double of the radius i.e. passes through the
     centre.

Que 3. Draw any circle and mark
    (a) its centre   (b) a radius
    (c) a diameter   (d) a sector
    (e) a segment   (f) a point in its interior
    (g) a point in its exterior   (h) an arc

Sol. In the adjoining figure,

(a) *O* is the centre of the circle.

(b) *ON*, *OA* and *OM* are the radii of the circle.

(c) *MN* is the diameter of the circle.

(d) *AON* is a sector of the circle.

(e) *ST* is a segment of the circle.

(f) *R* is a point which is in its interior.

(g) *Q* is a point which is in its exterior.

(h) *EF* is an arc of the circle.

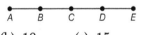

Que 4. Say true or false.

(a) Two diameters of a circle will necessarily intersect.

(b) The centre of a circle is always in its interior.

Sol. (a) True, because each diameter passes through the centre of a circle.

(b) True, as the centre of a circle is always in its interior.

Selected **NCERT Exemplar Problems**

Directions *In questions 1 to 6 out of the four options only one is correct. Write the correct answer.*

Que 1. Number of line segments in figure are

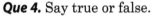

(a) 5   (b) 10   (c) 15   (d) 20

Sol. (b) We know that, a line segment corresponds to the shortest distance between two points.

Here, the number of line segment are 10 in the given figure.

Hence, option (b) is correct.

Que 2. In the given figure, point *A* is shifted to point *B* along the ray *PX* such that *PB* = 2*PA*, then the measure of ∠*BPY* is

(a) greater than 45°   (b) 45°

(c) less than 45°   (d) 90°

Sol. (b) If point *A* is shifted to point *B* along the ray *PX*, such that *PB* = 2*PA*, then the measure of ∠*BPY* = 45°.

[∵ points, *P*, *A*, *B*, and *X* are collinear].

Hence, option (b) is correct.

Que 3. The number of angles in the given figure are

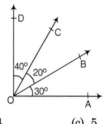

(a) 3   (b) 4   (c) 5   (d) 6

Sol. From the given figure,

$$\angle AOB = 30° ; \angle AOC = 30° + 20° = 50°$$
$$\angle AOD = 30° + 20° + 40° = 90°$$
$$\angle BOC = 20° ; \angle BOD = 20° + 40° = 60°$$

and $\angle COD = 40°$

Thus, the number of angles is 6. Hence, option (d) is correct.

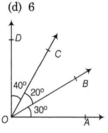

Que 4. If the sum of two angles is greater than 180°, then which of the following is not possible for the two angles?

    (a) One obtuse angle and one acute angle
    (b) One reflex angle and one acute angle
    (c) Two obtuse angles
    (d) Two right angles

Sol. (d) We know that, the sum of three angles of a triangle is 180°.

    If the sum of two angles is greater than 180°, then two right angles is not possible for the two angles.

    Hence, option (d) is correct.

Que 5. A polygon has prime number of sides. Its number of sides is equal to the sum of the two least consecutive primes. The number of diagonals of the polygon is

    (a) 4   (b) 5   (c) 7   (d) 10

Sol. (b) We know that, two least consecutive prime numbers are 2 and 3.

    ∴ Sum $= 2 + 3 = 5$

    Hence, option (b) is correct.

Direction *In questions 6 to 10, fill in the blanks to make the statement true.*

Que 6. In figure, points lying in the interior of the triangle *PQR* are ___, that in the exterior are___ and that on the triangle itself are ___.

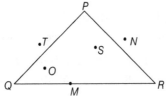

Sol. Points lying in the interior of the triangle *PQR* are *O* and *S* i.e. The exterior are *T* and *N* and that on the triangle itself are *P, Q, M* and *R*.

Que 7. A polygon of six sides is called a ....

Sol. A polygon of six sides is called a **hexagon**.

Que 8. A triangle with all its sides of unequal lengths is called a .... triangle.

Sol. A triangle with all its sides of unequal lengths is called a **scalene** triangle.

Que 9. The number of common points in the two angles marked in figure is ___.

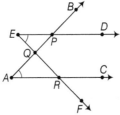

Sol. The number of common points in the two angles marked in figure is three (i.e. *P, Q, R*).

Que 10. The number of common points in the two angles marked in figure is___.

Sol. The number of common points in the two angler marked in figure is four (i.e. *E, E, G* and *F*).

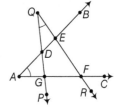

Directions *In questions 11 to 12 state whether the given statement is true (T) or false (F).*

Que 11. Two non-parallel line segments will always intersect.

Sol. False, because two non-parallel line segments will intersect, when they are produced (extended).

Que 12. Angle of 0° is an acute angle.

Sol.   False, because measure of acute angle is between 0° and 90°.

Que 13. In the given figure, $PO \perp AB$ and $PO = OQ$. Is PQ the perpendicular bisector of line segment AB ? Why or why not?

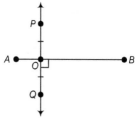

Sol. PQ is not the perpendicular bisector of line segment AB because $AO \neq BO$.

Que 14. In the given figure, if $AC \perp BD$, then name all the right angles.

Sol. There are four right angles in the given figure. They are $\angle APD$, $\angle APB$, $\angle BPC$ and $\angle CPD$.

Que 15. The number of common points in the two angles marked in figure is _____.

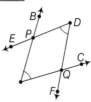

Sol. We know that, the intersection of two lines meets at a common point. The number of common point in two angles marked in figure is two i.e. P and Q.

Que 16. The number of common points in the two angles marked in figure is ____.

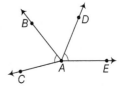

Sol. The number of common points in the two angles marked is figure is one (i.e. A).

Que 17. State the mid points of all the sides of figure.

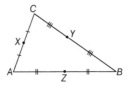

Sol. It is clear form the figure that mid points of all the sides of a triangle are X, Y and Z.

Que 18. Look at figure and mark a point

(a) A, which is in the interior of both $\angle 1$ and $\angle 2$.

(b) B, which is in the interior of only $\angle 1$.

(c) C in the interior of $\angle 1$.

Now, state whether points B and C lie in the interior of $\angle 2$ also.

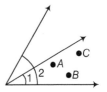

Sol. Yes, it is clear from given figure, that the points B and C lie in the interior of $\angle 2$ also.

Que 19. What is common in the following figures (i) and (ii)?

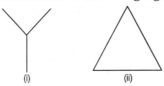

Is figure (i) that of a triangle? if not, why?

Sol. Both figures have 3 line segments.

No, figure (i) is not a triangle because it is not a closed figure.

Que 20. In figure, O is the centre of the circle.

    (a) Name all chords of the circle.

    (b) Name all radii of the circle.

    (c) Name all chords, which is not the diameter of the circle.

    (d) Shade the sectors OAC and OPB.

    (e) Shade the smaller segment of the circle formed by CP.

Sol. (a) All the chords of the circle are PC and AB, because it is joining any two points on a circle.

    (b) All radii of the circle are OP, OC, OA and OB.

    (c) Only PC is the chord, which is not the diameter of the circle.

    (d) shading sectors of OAC and OPB is shown in the figure.

    (e) The shade part of the smallest segment of the circle formed by CP is shown in the figure.

Que 21. Write the name of

    (a) vertices   (b) edges, and

    (c) faces of the prism shown in figure.

Sol. (a) The vertices in a figure are A, B, C, D, E and F.

    (b) The edges in a figure are $AB, AC, BC, BD, CF, DF, DE, EF$ and AE.

    (c) The faces of the prism shown in figure are $ABC, DEF, AEFC, ABDE$ and $BDFC$.

Understanding Elementary Shapes

Important Points

- **Line segment** A line segment is a fixed portion of a line. The measure of each line segment is a unique number called its length.

- **Ruler and divider** A graduated ruler and the divider are useful to compare lengths of line segments. One side of a ruler is divided into 15 parts. Each of these 15 parts is of length 1 cm. Each centimetre is divided into 10 subparts. Each subpart of the division of a cm is 1 mm.

  Note If A, B and C are any three points on a line such that $AC + CB = AB$, then point C will lie between point A and B. Its converse is also true.

- **Angle** An angle is a figure formed by two rays with the same initial point, it is increased in degrees the common initial point is also known as vertex of angle.

  Right angle An angle which is equal to $90°$ is called right angle.

  Straight angle An angle which is equal to $180°$ is called straight angle.

  Note There are four main directions **North** (N), **South** (S), **East** (E) and **West** (W). South is opposite to North and West is opposite to East. The turn from North to East or East to South or South to West or West to North is a **right angle** (i.e. 90°).

  Angle between two adjacent directions is one right angle. Also, the turn from North to South or East to West are two right angles or a **straight angle** (i.e. 180°).

Complete angle Turning by two straight angles (or four right angles) in the same direction makes a full turn. This one complete turn is called **one revolution** and the angle for one revolution is a complete angle (i.e. 360°).

Acute angle An angle is smaller than a right angle is called an acute angle.

Obtuse angle An angle is larger than a right angle, but less than a straight angle is called an obtuse angle.

Reflex angle An angle is larger than a straight angle is called a reflex angle.

▪ **Degree** One complete revolution is divided into 360 equal parts. Each part is a degree and we write 360° to say 'three hundred sixty degrees.

Thus, in a clock, 12 divisions = 360°.

To find the measure of an angle, we use protractor. The curved edge of protractor is divided into 180 equal parts. Each parts is equal to a degree. The markings start from 0° on the right side and ends with 180° on the left side and *vice-versa*.

▪ **Perpendicular** If two lines intersect each other and the angle between them is a right angle, then these lines are said to be perpendicular.

▪ **Perpendicular bisector** The perpendicular bisector of a line segment is a perpendicular to the line segment, that divides it into two equal parts.

▪ **Triangle** Least side polygon is called triangle.

Classification of Triangles

　(i) **On the basis of sides**

　　　• A triangle having all three sides unequal is called a **scalene triangle**.

　　　• A triangle having two sides equal is called an **isosceles triangle**.

　　　• A triangle having all three sides equal is called an **equilateral triangle**.

(ii) **On the basis of angles**
  - If each angle of a triangle is less than 90°, then the triangle is called anx **acute angled triangle.**
  - If any one angle of a triangle is a right angle, then the triangle is called a **right angled triangle.**
  - If any one angle of a triangle is greater than 90° but less than 180°, then the triangle is called an **obtuse angled triangle.**

- **Quadrilaterals** A quadrilateral is a polygon which has four sides.
  (i) A quadrilateral in which two sides (or one pair of sides) are parallel is called a **trapezium.**
  (ii) A quadrilateral in which opposite sides (or two pair of sides) are parallel and equal is called a **parallelogram.**
  (iii) A parallelogram in which all four angles are right angle is called a **rectangle.**
  (iv) A parallelogram in which all four sides are of equal length is called a **rhombus.**
  (v) A rhombus in which all four angles are right angles is called a **square.**

Properties	Name of Quadrilateral
One pair of parallel sides	Trapezium
Two pairs of parallel sides	Parallelogram
Parallelogram with 4 right angles	Rectangle
Parallelogram with 4 sides of equal length	Rhombus
A rhombus with 4 right angles	Square

- **Polygons** Polygons are classified according to the number of their sides as follows :

Number of sides	Name of polygons
3	Triangle
4	Quadrilateral
5	Pentagon
6	Hexagon
7	Heptagon
8	Octagon
9	Nonagon
10	Decagon

- **Face, edge and vertex** Each side of the cube is a flat surface called a flat face (or simply a face). Two faces meet at a line segment, which is called an edge and three edges meet at a point which is called a vertex.
- **Triangular prism** A triangular prism has two identical bases (triangle in shape) and its other faces are rectangles.
- **Rectangular prism** If the prism has a rectangular base, then it is a rectangular prism.

Exercise 5.1

Que 1. What is the disadvantage in comparing line segments by mere observation?

Sol. The disadvantage in comparing line segments by mere observation is that, sometimes the difference in lengths between two line segments may not accurate. So, we cannot always be sure about our usual judgment.

In the figure, the line segments $\overline{PQ}$ and $\overline{RS}$ seems to be equal but actually they are not equal.

Que 2. Why is it better to use a divider than a ruler, while measuring the length of a line segment?

Sol. When we measure the length of a line segment by ruler, there may be some errors due to its thickness and angular viewing. These errors can be removed by measuring a line segment with the help of a divider. Hence, the use of a divider is better than a ruler.

Que 3. Draw any line segment, say $\overline{AB}$. Take any point C lying in between A and B. Measure the lengths of AB, BC and AC. Is $AB = AC + CB$?

Sol. Let AB be the line segment of length 6 cm and point C lying between A and B.

On measuring the lengths of line segments AB, AC and CB using ruler, we find that $AB = 6$ cm, $AC = 4$ cm and $CB = 2$ cm

Now, $AC + CB = 4 + 2 = 6$ cm $= AB$

i.e. $AC + CB = AB$

So, we can say that C lies between A and B.

Que 4. If A, B and C are three points on a line such that $AB = 5$ cm, $BC = 3$ cm and $AC = 8$ cm, which one of them lies between the other two?

Sol. Firstly, draw a line AC of 8 cm. Take a point B on AC such that $AB = 5$ cm.

$$\underset{A \qquad\qquad\quad B \qquad C}{\overset{\overset{\text{5 cm} \qquad\qquad \text{3 cm}}{\rule{4cm}{0.4pt}}}{\underset{\text{8 cm}}{\xleftrightarrow{\hspace{4cm}}}}}$$

Now, distance of $BC = AC - AB = 8 - 5 = 3$ cm

Thus, $AB + BC = AC$

So, the point B lies between points A and C.

Que 5. Verify, whether D is the mid-point of $\overline{AG}$.

$$\underset{0 \ \ 1 \ \ 2 \ \ 3 \ \ 4 \ \ 5 \ \ 6 \ \ 7}{\overset{A \ B \ C \ D \ E \ F \ G}{\longleftrightarrow}}$$

 TIPS Firstly, find the distance of D from A and G i.e. AD and DG. If $AD = DG$, then D is the mid-point of AG otherwise not.

Sol. From the given figure, it is clear that

$$AD = AB + BC + CD = 1 + 1 + 1 = 3 \text{ units}$$

and $DG = DE + EF + FG = 1 + 1 + 1 = 3$ units

Now, $AG = AD + DG = 3 + 3 = 6$ units

and $AD = DG = 3$ units

$\because$ D lies between A and G. Thus, D is the mid-point of $\overline{AG}$.

Que 6. If B is the mid-point of $\overline{AC}$ and C is the mid-point of $\overline{BD}$, where A, B, C and D lie on a straight line, say why $AB = CD$?

Sol. Given, B is the mid-point of $\overline{AC}$.

$\therefore$ $AB = BC$ ...(i)

and C is the mid-point of $\overline{BD}$.

$\therefore$ $BC = CD$ ...(ii)

i.e. $\underset{A \quad B \quad C \quad D}{\longleftrightarrow}$

Now, on adding Eqs. (i) and (ii), we get

$$AB + BC = BC + CD$$

$\therefore$ $AB = CD$ **Hence proved.**

Que 7. Draw five triangles and measure their sides. Check in each case, if the sum of the lengths of any two sides is always less than the third side.

Sol. (i) Here, we draw a $\triangle ABC$.

In which, $AB = 3$ cm, $BC = 3.5$ cm and

$\qquad AC = 3.9$ cm

Now, by adding two sides of $\triangle ABC$

i.e. $\qquad AB + BC = 3 + 3.5 = 6.5$ cm

Clearly, $AB + BC > AC$

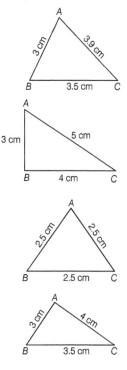

(ii) Here, we draw a $\triangle ABC$ in which

$AB = 3$ cm, $BC = 4$ cm and $AC = 5$ cm

Now, by adding two sides of $\triangle ABC$

i.e. $\qquad AB + BC = 3 + 4 = 7$ cm

Clearly, $AB + BC > AC$

(iii) Here, we draw a $\triangle ABC$ in which

$AB = BC = AC = 2.5$ cm

Now, by adding two sides of $\triangle ABC$

i.e. $\qquad AB + BC = 2.5 + 2.5 = 5$ cm

Clearly, $AB + BC > AC$

(iv) Here, we draw a $\triangle ABC$ in which

$AB = 3$ cm, $BC = 3.5$ cm and $AC = 4$ cm

Now, by adding two sides of $\triangle ABC$

i.e. $\qquad AB + BC = 3 + 3.5 = 6.5$ cm

Clearly, $AB + BC > AC$

(v) Here, we draw a $\triangle ABC$ in which

$\qquad\qquad AB = 2$ cm,

$\qquad\qquad BC = 4$ cm

and $\qquad\qquad AC = 4.5$ cm

Now, by adding two sides of $\triangle ABC$

i.e. $\qquad AB + BC = 2 + 4 = 6$ cm

Clearly, $AB + BC > AC$

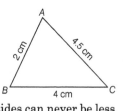

From all these conclusions, we observe that in each case, the sum of the lengths of any two sides is greater than the third side. So, the sum of the lengths of any two sides can never be less than the third side.

Try These (Page 91)

Que 1. What is the angle name for half a revolution?

Sol. We know that, 1 revolution = 2 straight angles

Now, dividing by 2 on both sides, we get
$$\frac{1}{2} \text{ revolution} = \frac{2}{2} \text{ straight angle} = 1 \text{ straight angle}$$

Hence, the angle name for half a revolution is straight angle or two right angles.

Que 2. What is the angle name for one-fourth revolution?

Sol. We know that, 1 revolution = 4 right angles

Now, dividing by 4 on both sides, we get
$$\frac{1}{4} \text{ revolution} = \frac{4}{4} \text{ right angles}$$

$$\frac{1}{4} \text{ revolution} = 1 \text{ right angle}$$

Hence, the angle name for one-fourth revolution is one right angle.

Que 3. Draw five other situations of one-fourth, half and three-fourth revolution on a clock.

Sol. (i) **One-fourth revolution** For one-fourth revolution, the clock hand moves in many individual routes. Some of these situations on a clock are as follows :

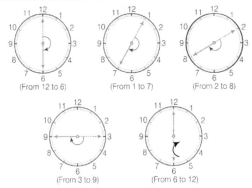

(From 12 to 6)　　(From 1 to 7)　　(From 2 to 8)

(From 3 to 9)　　(From 6 to 12)

(ii) **Half revolution** For a half revolution, the clock hand moves in many individual routes. Some of these situations on a clock are as follows :

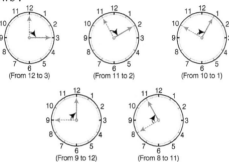

(iii) **Three-fourth revolution** For three-fourth revolution, the clock hand moves in many individual routes. Some of these situations on a clock are as follows :

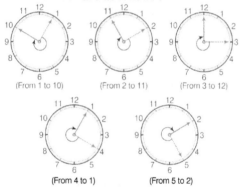

Exercise 5.2

Que 1. What fraction of a clockwise revolution does the hours hand of a clock turn through, when it goes from

    (a) 3 to 9   (b) 4 to 7   (c) 7 to 10

    (d) 12 to 9   (e) 1 to 10   (f) 6 to 3

Sol. (a) The situation from 3 to 9 on clock is given in the figure.

Hence, from 3 to 9, hour hand turns through 1/2 of a revolution, clockwise.

(b) The situation from 4 to 7 on clock is given in the figure.

Hence, from 4 to 7, hour hand turns through 1/4 of a revolution, clockwise.

(c) The situation from 7 to 10 on clock is given in the figure.

Hence, from 7 to 10, hour hand turns through $\frac{1}{4}$ of a revolution, clockwise.

(d) The situation from 12 to 9 on clock is given in the figure.

Hence, from 2 to 9, hour hand turns through $\frac{3}{4}$ of a revolution, clockwise.

(e) The situation from 1 to 10 on clock is given in the figure.

Hence, from 1 to 10, hour hand turns through $\frac{3}{4}$ of a revolution, clockwise.

(f) The situation from 6 to 3 on clock is given in the figure.

Hence, from 6 to 3, hour hand turns through $\frac{1}{4}$ of a revolution, clockwise.

Que 2. Where will the hand of a clock stop if it
   (a) starts at 12 and makes 1/2 of a revolution, clockwise?
   (b) starts at 2 and makes 1/2 of a revolution, clockwise?
   (c) starts at 5 and makes 1/4 of a revolution, clockwise?
   (d) starts at 5 and makes 3/4 of a revolution, clockwise?

TIPS The hand of a clock makes two right angles in 1/2 of a revolution, one right angle in 1/4 of a revolution and three right angles in 3/4 of a revolution.

Sol. (a) If the hand of a clock starts at 12 and makes 1/2 of a revolution, clockwise, i.e. two right angles, it reaches at 6.

(b) If the hand of a clock starts at 2 and makes $\frac{1}{2}$ of a revolution, clockwise, i.e. two right angles, it reaches at 8.

(c) If the hand of a clock starts at 5 and makes $\frac{1}{4}$ of a revolution, clockwise, i.e. one right angles, it reaches at 8.

(d) If the hand of a clock starts at 5 and makes $\frac{3}{4}$ of a revolution, clockwise, i.e. three right angles, it reaches at 2.

Que 3. Which direction will you face, if you start facing

(a) East and makes $\frac{1}{2}$ of a revolution, clockwise?

(b) East and makes $1\frac{1}{2}$ of a revolution, clockwise?

(c) West and makes $\frac{3}{4}$ of a revolution, anti-clockwise?

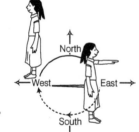

(d) South and makes one full revolution?
(Should we specify clockwise or anti-clockwise for this last question? Why not?)

TIPS   We know that, the angle between two adjacent directions is one right angle. Use this result to find required position.

Sol. (a) We have,
If we starts facing East and makes 1/2 of a revolution clockwise i.e. Two right angles, we will face West.

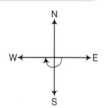

(b) We have,

If we starts facing East and makes $1\frac{1}{2}$ of a revolution clockwise i.e. One complete revolution and two right angles, we will face West.

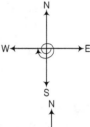

(c) We have,

If we starts facing West and makes 3/4 of a revolution anti-clockwise.

i.e. Three right angles, we will face North.

(d) We have,

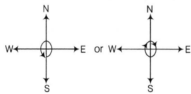

If we starts facing South and makes one full revolution either clockwise or anti-clockwise, we will face South again.

There is no need to specify clockwise or anti-clockwise for the last question because one full revolution will bring us back to the original position.

Que 4. What part of a revolution have you turned through if you stand facing

(a) East and turn clockwise to face North?

(b) South and turn clockwise to face East?

(c) West and turn clockwise to face East?

Sol. (a) Here, the turn from East to South is one right angle from South to West is one right angle and from West to North is one right angle. So, the turn from East to North is three right angles.

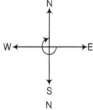

Hence, 3/4 of a revolution is required to turn from East to North.

(b) Here, the turn from South to West is one right angle, from West to North is one right angle and from North to East is one right angle. So, the turn from South to East is three right angles.

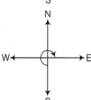

Hence, 3/4 of a revolution is required to turn from South to East.

(c) Here, the turn from West to North is one right angle, from North to East is one right angle. So, the turn from West to East is two right angles.

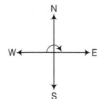

Hence, 1/2 of a revolution is required to turn from West to East.

Que 5. Find the number of right angles turned through by the hour hand of a clock, when it goes from

    (a) 3 to 6   (b) 2 to 8   (c) 5 to 11

    (d) 10 to 1   (e) 12 to 9   (f) 12 to 6

Sol. We know that, in a clock, the hour hand moves from first digit to next three digits by making a right angle.

    (a) Here, the hour hand moves from 3 to 6. It starts from 3 and covers digits 4, 5 and 6. So, hour hand turned by one right angle.

    (b) Here, the hour hand moves from 2 to 8. It starts from 2 and covers digits 3, 4, 5, 6, 7 and 8. So, hour hand turned by two right angles.

    (c) Here, the hour hand moves from 5 to 11. It starts from 5 and covers digits 6, 7, 8, 9, 10 and 11. So, hour hand turned by two right angles.

    (d) Here, the hour hand moves from 10 to 1. It starts from 10 and covers digits 11, 12 and 1. So, hour hand turned by one right angle.

    (e) Here, the hour hand moves from 12 to 9. It starts from 12 and covers digits 1 to 9. So, hour hand turned by three right angles.

(f) Here, the hour hand move from 12 to 6. It starts from 12 and covers digits 1, 2, 3, 4, 5 and 6. So, hour hand turned by two right angles.

Que 6. How many right angles do you make, if you start facing
- (a) South and turn clockwise to West?
- (b) North and turn anti-clockwise to East?
- (c) West and turn to West?
- (d) South and turn to North?

Sol. We know that, angle between two adjacent directions is a right angle.

(a) We have,

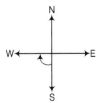

If we start turning clockwise from South to West, we make one right angle.

(b) We have,

If we start turning anti-clockwise from North to East, we make three right angles.

(c) We have,

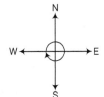

If we start turning anti-clockwise or clockwise from West to West, we make four right angles.

(d) We have,

If we start turning clockwise from South to North, we make two right angles.

Que 7. Where will the hour hand of a clock stop, if it starts

(a) from 6 and turns through 1 right angle?

(b) from 8 and turns through 2 right angles?

(c) from 10 and turns through 3 right angles?

(d) from 7 and turns through 2 straight angles?

Sol. (a) It is clear from the figure, that the hour hand starts from 6 and turns through 1 right angle. Hence, it will be reach at 9.

(b) It is clear from the figure, that the hour hand starts from 8 and turns through 2 right angles. Hence, it will be reach at 2.

(c) It is clear from the figure, that the hour hand starts from 10 and turns through 3 right angles. Hence, it will be reach at 7.

(d) It is clear from the figure, that the hour hand starts from 7 and turns through 2 straight angles. Hence, it will be reach at 7 because 2 straight angles is equal to 4 right angles.

Try These (Page 93)

Que 1. The hour hand of a clock moves from 12 to 5. Is the revolution of the hour hand more than 1 right angle?

Sol. Yes, it is clear from the figure that, hour hand makes one right angle from 12 to 3 and since 5 lies between 3 and 6. So, rsevolution of the hour hand is more than 1 right angle.

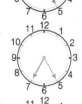

Que 2. What does the angle made by the hour hand of the clock look like, when it moves from 5 to 7. Is the angle moved more than 1 right angle?

Sol. We know that, hour hand of a clock makes a right angle to cover three digits as from 12 to 3, it makes a right angle (∵ it covers three digits 1, 2 and 3). Here, hour hand moves from 5 to 7 (covers only two digits 6 and 7). So, the angle moved by hour hand is less than 1 right angle.

Que 3. Draw the following and check the angle with your RA (right angle) tester going

    (a) from 12 to 2   (b) from 6 to 7

    (c) from 4 to 8   (d) from 2 to 5

Sol. (a) On checking the angle moved by an hour hand, while going from 12 to 2 by RA (right angle) tester, it is clear that it is less than 1 right angle.

    (b) On checking the angle moved by an hour hand, while going from 6 to 7 by RA (right angle) tester, it is clear that it is less than 1 right angle.

    (c) On checking the angle moved by an hour hand, while going from 4 to 8 by RA (right angle) tester, it is clear that it is more than 1 right angle.

(d) On checking the angle moved by an hour hand, while going from 2 to 5 by RA (right angle) tester, it is clear that it is equal to 1 right angle.

Exercise 5.3

Que 1. Match the following :

(i)	Straight angle	(a)	Less than one-fourth of a revolution
(ii)	Right angle	(b)	More than half of a revolution
(iii)	Acute angle	(c)	Half of a revolution
(iv)	Obtuse angle	(d)	One-fourth of a revolution
(v)	Reflex angle	(e)	Between $\frac{1}{4}$ and $\frac{1}{2}$ of a revolution
		(f)	One complete revolution

Sol. (i) Straight angle is half of a revolution.

(ii) Right angle is one-fourth of a revolution.

(iii) Acute angle is less than one-fourth of a revolution.

(iv) Obtuse angle is between 1/4 and 1/2 of a revolution.

(v) Reflex angle is more than half of a revolution.

So, after matching, we find

(i)	Straight angle	(c)	Half of a revolution
(ii)	Right angle	(d)	One-fourth of a revolution
(iii)	Acute angle	(a)	Less than one-fouth of a revolution
(iv)	Obtuse angle	(e)	Between 1/4 and 1/2 of a revolution
(v)	Reflex angle	(b)	More than half of a revolution

Que 2. Classify each one of the following angles as right, straight, acute, obtuse or reflex.

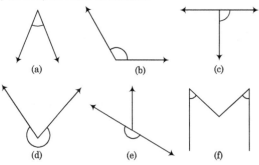

       (a)   (b)   (c)

       (d)   (e)   (f)

Sol. We know that,

An angle which is smaller than a right angle is called an acute angle.

An angle with measure 90° is called a right angle.

An angle which is greater than a right angle but smaller than a straight angle is called an obtuse angle.

An angle with measure 180° is called a straight angle.

An angle which is greater than a straight angle but smaller than a complete angle is called a reflex angle.

Now, from these results

   (a) Given angle is smaller than a right angle, so it is an acute angle.

   (b) Given angle is more than a right angle, so it is an obtuse angle.

   (c) Given angle is a right angle.

   (d) Given angle is more than a straight angle, so it is a reflex angle.

   (e) Given angle is a straight angle.

   (f) Both angles are smaller than a right angle, so both these are acute angles.

Exercise 5.4

Que 1. What is the measure of

   (a) a right angle?   (b) a straight angle?

Sol. (a) The measure of a right angle $= 90°$

   (b) The measure of a straight angle $= 2 \times$ right angles
$$= 2 \times 90° = 180°$$

Que 2. Say true or false.

   (a) The measure of an acute angle $< 90°$.

   (b) The measure of an obtuse angle $< 90°$.

   (c) The measure of a reflex angle $> 180°$.

   (d) The measure of one complete revolution $= 360°$.

   (e) If $m\angle A = 53°$ and $m\angle B = 35°$, then $m\angle A > m\angle B$.

Sol. (a) True, because the measure of an acute angle is always less than 90°.

   (b) False, because the measure of an obtuse angle is always greater than 90°.

   (c) True, because the measure of a reflex angle is always greater than 180° and less than 360°.

   (d) True, because the measure of one complete revolution is equal to 360°.

   (e) True, because the measure of angle A is greater than angle B.

Que 3. Write down the measures of

    (a) some acute angles.

    (b) some obtuse angles.   (give atleast two examples of each)

Sol. (a) We know that, the measure of an acute angle is always less than 90°.

      So, 45°, 50°, 55°, 60°, 65° all are acute angles.

    (b) We know that the measure of an obtuse angle is always greater than 90° but less than 180°.

      So, 120°, 125°, 135°, 140° all are obtuse angles.

Que 4. Measure the angles given below using the protractor and write down the measure.

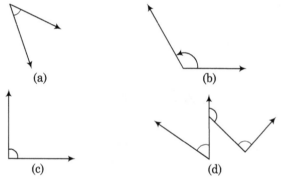

Sol. On measuring the given angles using protractor, we find that

    (a) angle in figure (a) is 45°.

    (b) angle in figure (b) is 125°.

    (c) angle in figure (c) is 90°.

    (d) angles in figure (d) are 60°, 125° and 90°, respectively.

Que 5. Which angle has a large measure?

    First estimate and then measure.

    Measure of angle $A =$

    Measure of angle $B =$

Sol. Observing the given angles, we find that $\angle B > \angle A$
   On measuring, we find that
   Measure of angle $A = 40°$
   Measure of angle $B = 65°$
∴ $\angle B > \angle A$

Que 6. From these two angles which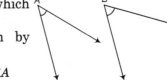
has larger measure?
Estimate and then confirm by
measuring them.

Sol. On observing, we find that $\angle B > \angle A$
   On measuring, we find that
                       $\angle A = 45°$ and $\angle B = 60°$
   Thus, $\angle B > \angle A$

Que 7. Fill in the blanks with acute, obtuse, right or straight
   angle.
   (a) An angle whose measure is less than that of a right
       angle is _____.
   (b) An angle whose measure is greater than that of a right
       angle is _____ .
   (c) An angle whose measure is the sum of the measures of
       two right angles is _____.
   (d) When the sum of the measures of two angles is that of a
       right angle, then each one of them is _____.
   (e) When the sum of the measures of two angles is that of a
       straight angle and if one of them is acute, then the other
       should be _____.

Sol. (a) acute angle   (b) obtuse angle   (c) straight angle
       (d) acute angle   (e) obtuse angle

Que 8. Find the measure of the angle shown in each figure.
   (First estimate with your eyes and then find the actual
   measure with a protractor)

   (a)   (b)   (c)   (d)

Sol. On estimating with eyes, the measure of angle shown in figure are as follows :

(a) 45°   (b) 125°   (c) 60°   (d) 135°

Now, on measuring with the protractor, measure of angle shown in figure are as follows :

(a) 40°   (b) 130°   (c) 65°   (d) 135°

Que 9. Find the angle measure between the hands of the clock in each figure.

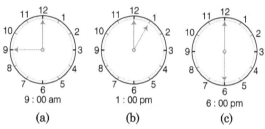

(a)   (b)   (c)

Sol. (a) Number of divisions between 9 to 12 = 3

We know that,   12 divisions = 360°

$$1 \text{ division} = \frac{360°}{12}$$

∴ $$3 \text{ divisions} = \frac{360°}{12} \times 3 = 90°$$

(b) Number of divisions between 12 to 1 = 1

We know that,   12 divisions = 360°

∴ $$1 \text{ division} = \frac{360°}{12} = 30°$$

(c) Now, number of divisions between 12 to 6 = 6

We know that,   12 divisions = 360°

∴ $$1 \text{ division} = \frac{360°}{12}$$

∴ $$6 \text{ divisions} = \frac{360°}{12} \times 6 = 180°$$

Hence, angle between the hands of the clock in each figure is 90°, 30° and 180°, respectively.

Alternate Solution

Here, we will use the protractor to find measure of required angle.

Firstly, place the protractor so that the mid-point of its straight edge lies on the centre of clock (i.e. vertex of angle) and greater hand of the clock (i.e. on side of angle) along the straight edge of the protractor, then mark shown by smaller hand of the clock (i.e. second side of angle) on the curved edge gives the degree measure of angle formed at 9 : 00 am.

Thus, at 9 : 00 am, angle measure is 90°.

Similarly, angle measure between the hands of the clock at 1 : 00 pm is 30° and at 6 : 00 pm is 180°.

Que 10. **Investigate**

In the given figure, the angle measures 30°. Look at the same figure through a magnifying glass. Does the angle becomes larger? Does the size of the angle change?

Sol. No, looking through a magnifying glass does not make the angle larger. Also, the size of angle does not change.

Que 11. Measure and classify each angle.

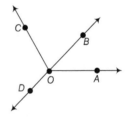

Angle	Measure	Type
∠AOB		
∠AOC		
∠BOC		
∠DOC		
∠DOA		
∠DOB		

Sol. The measure of angle (by using the protractor) and its classification are shown as below

Angle	Measure	Type
∠AOB	40°	Acute angle
∠AOC	125°	Obtuse angle
∠BOC	85°	Acute angle
∠DOC	95°	Obtuse angle
∠DOA	140°	Obtuse angle
∠DOB	180°	Straight angle

Exercise 5.5

Que 1. Which of the following are models for perpendicular lines :

(a) The adjacent edges of a table top.

(b) The lines of a railway track.

(c) The line segments forming the letter 'L'.

(d) The letter 'V'.

TIPS

When two lines intersect and the angle between them is a right angle, then the lines are said to be perpendicular.

Sol. (a) Yes, the adjacent edges of a table top make a model of perpendicular lines.

(b) No, the lines of a railway track does not make a model of perpendicular lines.

(c) Yes, the line segments forming the letter 'L' makes a model of perpendicular lines.

(d) No, the letter 'V' does not make a model of perpendicular lines.

Que 2. Let $\overline{PQ}$ be the perpendicular to the line segment $\overline{XY}$. Let $\overline{PQ}$ and $\overline{XY}$ intersect in the point A. What is the measure of $\angle PAY$?

Sol. Given, $\overline{PQ}$ is perpendicular to the line segment $\overline{XY}$ and $\overline{PQ}$ and $\overline{XY}$ intersect in the point A.

So, it is clear from the above figure that

$$\angle PAY = 90°$$

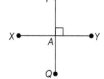

Que 3. There are two set-squares in your box. What are the measures of the angles that are formed at their corners? Do they have any angle measure that is common?

Sol. We have, two set-squares in our box. In one of them, angles are of 30°, 60°, 90° and in the others, angles are of 45°, 45°, 90°.

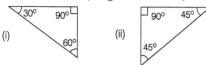

Clearly, they have one angle measure in common, which is 90°.

Que 4. Study the diagram. The line l is perpendicular to line m

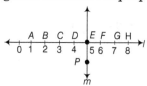

(a) Is $CE = EG$?

(b) Does PE bisect CG?

(c) Identify any two line segments for which *PE* is the perpendicular bisector.

(d) Are these true?

(i) $AC > FG$ (ii) $CD = GH$ (iii) $BC < EH$

Sol. (a) From given figure,

$$CE = CD + DE \qquad [CD = DE = 1 \text{ unit}]$$
$$= 1 + 1 = 2 \text{ units}$$

and $$EG = EF + FG \qquad [EF = FG = 1 \text{ unit}]$$
$$= 1 + 1 = 2 \text{ units}$$

∴ $$CE = EG = 2 \text{ units}$$

(b) Since, $CE = EG$

So, *E* is the mid-point of *CG*.

Thus, *PE* bisects *CG*

(c) In the given figure, we can see that *PE* is perpendicular to the given line segment.

Since, $DE = EF$ [each = 1 unit]

So, *PE* is the perpendicular bisector of *DF*.

Again, $\qquad CE = EG \qquad$ [each = 2 units]

So, *PE* is the perpendicular bisector of *CG*.

(d) (i) Here, $\quad AC = AB + BC = 1 + 1 = 2 \text{ units} \qquad [AB = BC = 1 \text{unit}]$

and $\qquad FG = 1 \text{ unit}$

∴ $\qquad AC > FG$ is true.

(ii) Here, $CD = 1 \text{ unit}$ and $\quad GH = 1 \text{ unit}$

∴ $\qquad CD = GH$ is true.

(iii) Here, $\qquad BC = 1 \text{ unit}$

and $\qquad EH = EF + FG + GH = 1 + 1 + 1 = 3 \text{ units}$

∴ $\qquad BC < EH$ is true.

Exercise 5.6

Que 1. Name the types of following triangles.

(a) Triangle with lengths of sides 7 cm, 8 cm and 9 cm.

(b) $\triangle ABC$ with $AB = 8.7$ cm, $AC = 7$ cm and $BC = 6$ cm.

(c) $\triangle PQR$ such that $PQ = QR = PR = 5$ cm.

(d) $\triangle DEF$ with $m\angle D = 90°$.

(e) $\triangle XYZ$ with $m\angle Y = 90°$ and $XY = YZ$.

(f) $\triangle LMN$ with $m\angle L = 30°$, $m\angle M = 70°$ and $m\angle N = 80°$.

Sol. (a) Given, first side = 7 cm; second side = 8 cm and third side = 9 cm
where,   7 cm ≠ 8 cm ≠ 9 cm
i.e. all the sides are of different length. So, it is a scalene triangle.

(b) Given, $AB = 8.7$ cm, $AC = 7$ cm and $BC = 6$ cm
where, $AB \neq BC \neq CA$
i.e. all the sides are of different length.
So, it is a scalene triangle.

(c) Given, $PQ = QR = PR = 5$ cm
i.e. all the sides are equal. So, it is an equilateral triangle.

(d) Given, $m\angle D = 90°$
i.e. measure of $\angle D$ is 90°. So, it is a right angled triangle.

(e) Given, $m\angle Y = 90°$ i.e. measure of $\angle Y = 90°$ and $XY = YZ$
Here, one angle is right angle and two sides are equal.
So, it is an isosceles right angled triangle.

(f) Given, $m\angle L = 30°$ i.e. measure of $\angle L = 30°$ (acute angle),
$m\angle M = 70°$ i.e. measure of $\angle M = 70°$ (acute angle)
and $m\angle N = 80°$ i.e. measure of $\angle N = 80°$ (acute angle)
Thus, all the angles are different and less than 90°.
So, it is an acute angled triangle.

Que 2. Match the following:

	Measures of Triangle		Types of Triangle
(i)	3 sides of equal length	(a)	Scalene
(ii)	2 sides of equal length	(b)	Isosceles right angled
(iii)	All sides are of different length	(c)	Obtuse angled
(iv)	3 acute angles	(d)	Right angled
(v)	1 right angle	(e)	Equilateral
(vi)	1 obtuse angle	(f)	Acute angled
(vii)	1 right angle with two sides of equal length	(g)	Isosceles

Sol. We know that,
A triangle having three equal sides is called an equilateral triangle.
A triangle having two equal sides is called an isosceles triangle.
A triangle having all sides unequal is called a scalene triangle
In a triangle, if each angle is acute angle then triangle is called an acute angled triangle.
If a triangle has a right angle, then it is called a right angled triangle.
If a triangle has an obtuse angle, then it is an obtuse angled triangle.
If a triangle has a right angle and two equal sides is called an isosceles right angled triangle.

So, required matching is shown as below :

Measures of Triangle		Types of Triangle	
(i)	3 sides of equal length	(e)	Equilateral
(ii)	2 sides of equal length	(g)	Isosceles
(iii)	All sides are of different length	(a)	Scalene
(iv)	3 acute angles	(f)	Acute angled
(v)	1 right angle	(d)	Right angled
(vi)	1 obtuse angle	(c)	Obtuse angled
(vii)	1 right angle with two sides of equal length	(b)	Isosceles right angled

Que. 3. Name each of the following triangles in two different ways: (you may judge the nature of the angle by observation)

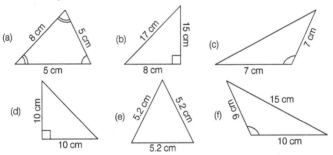

Sol. By observing the given triangles in two different ways, name of each triangle is as given below

(a) In the given triangle, two sides are equal, so it is an isosceles triangle and all the angles are acute angles. So, it is an acute angled triangle also.

(b) In the given triangle, all the sides are different, so it is a scalene triangle and one angle is right angle. So, it is a right angled triangle also.

(c) In the given triangle, two sides are equal, so it is an isosceles triangle and one angle is an obtuse angle. So, it is an obtuse angled triangle also.

(d) In the given triangle, two sides are equal, so it is an isosceles triangle and one angle is right angle. So, it is a right angled triangle also.

(e) In the given triangle, all the sides are equal, so it is an equilateral triangle and all the angles are acute. So, it is an acute angled triangle also.

(f) In the given triangle, all the sides are different, so it is a scalene triangle and one angle is an obtuse angle. So, it is an obtuse angled triangle also.

Que 4. Try to construct triangles using matchsticks. Some are shown here.

Can you make a triangle with
(a) 3 matchsticks?　　　　　(b) 4 matchsticks?
(c) 5 matchsticks?　　　　　(d) 6 matchsticks?
(Remember you have to use all the available matchsticks in each case)
Name the type of triangle in each case.
If you cannot make a triangle, think of reasons for it.

Sol. (a) With the help of 3 matchsticks, we can make an equilateral triangle. Since, all three matchsticks are of equal length.

Equilateral triangle

(b) With the help of 4 matchsticks, we cannot make any triangle because in this case, sum of two sides is equal to third side and we know that the sum of the lengths of any two sides of a triangle is always greater than the length of the third side.

(c) With the help of 5 matchsticks, we can make an isosceles triangle. Since, we get two sides equal in this case.

Isosceles triangle

(d) With the help of 6 matchsticks, we can make an equilateral triangle. Since, we get three sides equal in this case.

Equilateral triangle

Exercise 5.7

Que 1. Say true or false :
(a) Each angle of a rectangle is a right angle.
(b) The opposite sides of a rectangle are equal in length.
(c) The diagonals of a square are perpendicular to one another.

    (d) All the sides of a rhombus are of equal length.

    (e) All the sides of a parallelogram are of equal length.

    (f) The opposite sides of a trapezium are parallel.

Sol. (a) True   (b) True   (c) True   (d) True

    (e) False, because opposite sides of a parallelogram are of equal length and parallel.

    (f) False, because a pair of opposite sides of trapezium are parallel and other pair of opposite sides are non-parallel.

Que 2. Give reasons for the following :

    (a) A square can be thought of as a special rectangle.

    (b) A rectangle can be thought of as a special parallelogram.

    (c) A square can be thought of as a special rhombus.

    (d) Squares, rectangles, parallelograms are all quadrilaterals.

    (e) Square is also a parallelogram.

Sol. (a) We know that in a rectangle, opposite sides are equal and each angle is a right angle. If all its side are equal, then it becomes square.

    So, a square can be thought of as a special rectangle.

    (b) We know that in a parallelogram, opposite sides are parallel as well as equal and opposite angles are equal. If its opposite angles are right angles, then it becomes a rectangle. So, a rectangle can be thought of as a special parallelogram.

    (c) We know that in a rhombus, all four sides are equal and opposite sides are parallel. If its all angles are right angles, then it become a square. So, a square can be thought of as a special rhombus.

    (d) We know that a polygon, which has four sides is called a quadrilateral. Square, rectangle and parallelogram also have four sides. So, these all are quadrilaterals.

    (e) We know that in a parallelogram, opposite sides are parallel as well as equal and opposite angles are equal. In a square, opposite sides are parallel as well as equal and opposite angles are equal to right angle. So, a square is also a parallelogram.

Que 3. A figure is said to be regular, if its sides are equal in length and angles are equal in measure. Can you identify the regular quadrilateral?

Sol. Yes, a square is a regular quadrilateral because all sides and angles of a square are equal.

Exercise 5.8

Que 1. Examine whether the following are polygons. If any one among them is not, say why?

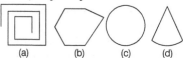

(a)　　(b)　　(c)　　(d)

Sol. (a) It is an open figure. So, it is not a polygon.

(b) It is closed figure. So, it is a polygon with six sides i.e. hexagon.

(c) It is not made by line segments. So, it is not a polygon.

(d) It is made by line segments and curved line also. So, it is not a polygon.

Que 2. Name each polygon.

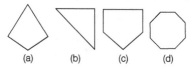

(a)　　(b)　　(c)　　(d)

Make two more examples of each of these.

Sol. (a) This polygon has four sides, so it is a quadrilateral. e.g.

(b) This polygon has three sides, so it is a triangle. e.g.

(c) This polygon has five sides, so it is a pentagon. e.g.

(d) This polygon has eight sides, so it is an octagon. e.g.

Que 3. Draw a rough sketch of a regular hexagon. Connecting any three of its vertices, draw a triangle. Identify the type of the triangle you have drawn.

Sol. Here, *PQRSTU* is a regular hexagon.
Joining its alternate vertices *P*, *R* and *T*.
We get, Δ*TPR*, which is a regular triangle (since, all sides are equal).
Thus, the triangle so formed is an equilateral triangle.

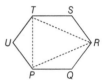

Que 4. Draw a rough sketch of a regular octagon. (Use squared paper if you wish).
Draw a rectangle by joining exactly four of the vertices of the octagon.

Sol. Here, *ABCDEFGH* is a regular octagon. Joining vertices *G* and *D*, we get $\overline{GD}$. Again, joining *H* and *C*, we get $\overline{HC}$.

Thus, we get a rectangle *HCDG*.
Again, by joining *A*, *F* and *B*, *E*, we can get another rectangle *ABEF*.

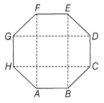

Que 5. A diagonal is a line segment that joins any two vertices of the polygon and is not a side of the polygon. Draw a rough sketch of a pentagon and draw its diagonals.

Sol. Rough sketch is shown below

Here, *ABCDE* is a pentagon.
By joining any two vertices, we get diagonals as $\overline{AC}$, $\overline{AD}$, $\overline{BD}$, $\overline{BE}$ and $\overline{CE}$.

Exercise 5.9

Question 1. Match the following:

(a)	Cone	(i)	
(b)	Sphere	(ii)	
(c)	Cylinder	(iii)	
(d)	Cuboid	(iv)	
(e)	Pyramid	(v)	

Give two new examples of each shape.

Sol. (a) **Cone** A cone is a solid figure with a circular base. It has a flat surface at the base. A cone has no straight edge and its other face is curved.

(b) **Sphere** A solid sphere has curved surface only, it has no flat surface and no straight edge.

(c) **Cylinder** A cylinder is a solid figure, having two circular bases and a curved surface. It has no straight edge. A cylinder has two flat surfaces.

(d) **Cuboid** A solid bounded by six rectangular plane faces is called cuboid. e.g. A box, a match box, a book, a brick.

(e) **Pyramid** Pyramid is a solid shape with a polygonal base and having other faces as triangle meeting at a point.

The matching is as under

(a) → (ii), (b) → (iv), (c) → (v), (d) → (iii), (e) → (i)

Other examples are as follows:
(a) Cone → (i) An ice-cream cone (ii) A birthday cap
(b) Sphere → (i) A cricket ball (ii) A tennis ball
(c) Cylinder → (i) A lawn-roller (ii) A road-roller
(d) Cuboid → (i) A brick (ii) A book
(e) Pyramid → (i) Pyramids of Egypt (ii) A diamond

Que 2. What shape is
    (a) your instrument box?   (b) a brick?
    (c) a match box?   (d) a road-roller?
    (e) a sweet laddu?

Sol. (a) Shape of instrument box is cuboid.
    (b) Shape of a brick is cuboid.
    (c) Shape of a match box is cuboid.
    (d) Shape of a road-roller is cylinder.
    (e) Shape of a sweet laddu is sphere.

Selected **NCERT Exemplar Problems**

Directions *In questions 1 to 6 only one of the four options is correct.*

Que 1. The number of triangles in figure is
    (a) 10   (b) 12   (c) 13   (d) 14

Sol. In the given figure, total 13 triangles are formed.
    i.e. $\triangle AEG$, $\triangle AGD$, $\triangle EFG$, $\triangle DFG$, $\triangle AED$, $\triangle EDF$,
$\triangle BFF$, $\triangle DFC$,
    $\triangle AEF$, $\triangle ADF$, $\triangle ABF$, $\triangle ACF$, and $\triangle ABC$.
    Hence, option (c) is correct.

Que 2. If the sum of two angles is equal to an obtuse angle, then which of the following is not possible?
    (a) One obtuse angle and one acute angle
    (b) One right angle and one acute angle
    (c) Two acute angles
    (d) Two right angles

Sol. (a) The sum of one obtuse angle and one acute angle is always an obtuse angle, which is possible

(b) The sum of one right angle and one acute angle is always an obtuse angle, which is possible.

(c) The sum of two acute angle may or may not be obtuse angles, which may or may not be possible.

(d) The sum of two right angle is equal to 180°, so it is not an obtuse angle which is not possible.

Hence, option (d) is correct.

Que 3. In the given figure, $AB = BC$ and $AD = BD = DC$. The number of isosceles triangles in the figure is/are

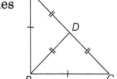

(a) 1   (b) 2

(c) 3   (d) 4

Sol. Given, in $\triangle ABC$, $AB = BC$ and $AD = BD = DC$

Isosceles triangles in the figure are $\triangle ABC$, $\triangle ABD$ and $\triangle BCD$.

So, the number of isosceles triangles in the figure are 3.

Hence, the option (c) is correct.

Que 4. In the given figure, $\angle BAC = 90°$ and $AD \perp BC$. The number of right triangles in the figure is/are

(a) 1   (b) 2

(c) 3   (d) 4

Sol. Given, $\triangle ABC$ is a right angled triangle in which $\angle BAC = 90°$ and $AD \perp BC$.

Right triangles in the figure are $\triangle BAC$, $\triangle ADB$ and $\triangle ADC$.

So, the number of right triangles in the figure are 3.

Hence, option (c) is correct

Que 5. In the given figure, $PQ \perp QR$, $PQ = 5$ cm and $QR = 5$ cm. Then, $\triangle PQR$ is

(a) a right triangle but not isosceles

(b) an isosceles right triangle

(c) isosceles but not a right triangle

(d) neither isosceles nor right triangle

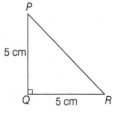

Sol. (b) In $\triangle PQR$, $\qquad PQ \perp QR$,

$\qquad\qquad\qquad PQ = 5$ cm and $QR = 5$ cm

i.e. $\qquad\qquad\qquad PQ = QR$

So, $\triangle PQR$ is an isosceles right triangle.

Hence, option (b) is correct.

Que 6. The number of triangles in Fig. 2.10 is

   (a) 10   (b) 12   (c) 13   (d) 14

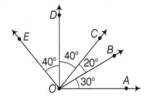

Sol. (a) $\angle AOD$ is a right angle.

   Hint $\angle AOD = \angle AOD + \angle BOC + \angle COD = 30°+20°+40° = 90°$

   Hence, $\angle AOD$ is a right angle.

  (b) $\angle COA$ is a an acute angle

   Hint $\angle COA = \angle AOB + \angle BOC = 30°+20° = 50°$

   which is less then 90°

   Hence, $\angle COA$ is an acute angle

  (c) $\angle AOE$ is an obtuse angle.

   Hint $\angle AOE = \angle AOB + \angle BOC + \angle COD + \angle DOF$

      $= 30° + 20° + 40° + 40°$

      $= 130°$, which is greater 90° but less than 180°

   Hence, $\angle AOE$ is an obtuse angle.

Que 7. Number of angles less than 180° in is ———— and their names are ————.

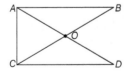

Sol. Number of angle is less than angle of figure is 12 and their names are $\angle OAB, \angle OBA, \angle AOB, \angle OAC, \angle OCA, \angle AOC, \angle BOD, \angle OCD, \angle ODC,$ $\angle COD, \angle BAC, \angle ACD,$

Que 8. If the sum of two angles is equal to an obtuse angle, then which of the following is not possible?
    (a) One obtuse angle and one acute angle
    (b) One right angle and one acute angle
    (c) Two acute angles
    (d) Two right angles

Sol. If the sum of two angles is equal to an obtuse angle, then two right angles is not possible. Hence, option (d) is correct

Que 9. A horizontal line and a vertical line always intersect at right angles.

Sol. True, because horizontal line and a vertical line make only right angle between them.

Que 10. Name the line segments shown in the given figure:

Sol. The line segments are $\overline{AB}, \overline{BC}, \overline{CD}, \overline{DE}$ and $\overline{EA}$

Que 11. State the mid-points of all the sides of the given figure:

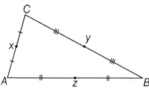

Sol. From the given figure, x, y and z are the mid-points of CA, CB and AB, respectively.

Que 12. Name the following angles of figure using three letters:
    (a) $\angle 1$ (b) $\angle 2$
    (c) $\angle 3$ (d) $\angle 1 + \angle 2$
    (e) $\angle 2 + \angle 3$ (f) $\angle 1 + \angle 2 + \angle 3$
    (g) $\angle CBA - \angle 1$

Sol. Name of the angles are as follows:
    (a) $\angle 1 = \angle CBD$ (b) $\angle 2 = \angle DBE$
    (c) $\angle 3 = \angle EBA$ (d) $\angle 1 + \angle 2 = \angle CBE$

(e) $\angle 2 + \angle 3 = \angle DBA$ (f) $\angle 1 + \angle 2 + \angle 3 = \angle CBA$

(g) $\angle CBA = \angle 1 =$ In the given figure $[\because \angle CBA = \angle 1 + \angle 2 + \angle 3]$

Put the value of $\angle CBA = \angle 1 + \angle 2 + \angle 3 - \angle 1$

$$= \angle 2 + \angle 3$$

$$= \angle DBA \qquad [\because \angle DBA = \angle 2 + \angle 3]$$

Que 13. Name the vetices and the line segments in figure

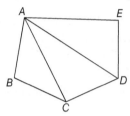

Sol. From the given figure,

(a) The name of vertices of the figure is A, B, C, D and E.

(b) The name of line segments are $\overline{AB}$, $\overline{AC}$, $\overline{AD}$, $\overline{AE}$, $\overline{BC}$, $\overline{CD}$, and $\overline{DE}$.

Que 14. In which of the following figures

(a) Perpendicular bisector is shown?

(b) bisector is shown ?

(c) only bisector is shown?

(d) only perpendicular is shown?

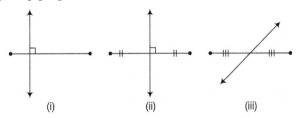

(i)   (ii)   (iii)

Sol. (a) Perpendicular bisector means, a line is perpendicular to the another line and divides in equal parts.

Here fig. (ii) is the perpendicular bisector.

(b) Bisector means, a line divides the another line equal parts.

Here figures (ii) and (iii) are bisectors.

(c) Only bisector is shown it means we do not consider perpendicular bisector which is shown in figure (iii).

(d) Only perpendiculars is shown in figure (i).

Que 15. Write down fifteen angles (less than 180°) involved in the given figure,

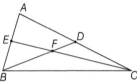

Sol. Fifteen angles (less than 180°) in the given figure are as follows:

∠EAD, ∠AEF, ∠EFD, ∠ADF, ∠DFC, ∠DCF, ∠CDF, ∠BEF, ∠BFE, ∠EBF, ∠FBC, ∠FCB, ∠BFC, ∠ABC, ∠ACB.

Que 16. In the given figure,

(a) Name any four angles that appear to be acute angle.

(b) Name any two angles that appear to be obtuse angle.

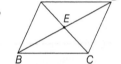

Sol. (a) From the given figure, any four angles that appear to be acute angle are ∠AEB, ∠ADE, ∠BAE and ∠BCE .

(b) Any two angles that appear to be obtuse angle are ∠BCD and ∠BAD.

Que 17. In the given figure,

(a) What is $AE + EC$?

(b) What is $AC - EC$?

(c) What is $BD - BE$?

(d) What is $BD - DE$?

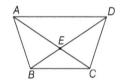

Sol. From the given figure,

(a) $AE + EC = AC$ (b) $AC - EC = AE$

(c) $BD - BE = ED$ (d) $BD - DE = BE$

Que 18. Using the information given, name the right angles in each part of Fig. 2.40:

(a) BA ⊥ BD   (b) RT ⊥ ST

(c) AC ⊥ BD

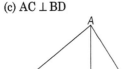

(d) RT ⊥ SW

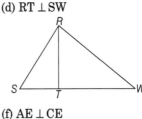

(e) AC ⊥ BD

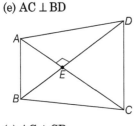

(f) AE ⊥ CE

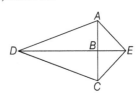

(g) AC ⊥ CD

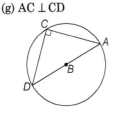

(h) OP ⊥ AB

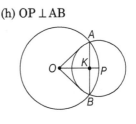

Sol. (a) Since *BA* ⊥ *BD*, it means ∠*B* = 90°

     ∴ ∠*ABD* is a right angle.

(b) Since, *RT* ⊥ *ST*, it means ∠*T* = 90°

     ∴ ∠*RTS* is a right angle.

(c) Since, *AC* ⊥ *BD*, it means, ∠*C* = 90°

     ∴ ∠*ACD* and ∠*ACB* are right angle.

(d) Since, *RT* ⊥ *SW*, it means ∠*T* = 90°

     ∴ ∠*RTS* and ∠*RTW* are right angles.

(e) Since, *AC* ⊥ *BD*, it means ∠*E* = 90°.

     ∴ ∠*AEB*, ∠*BEC*, ∠*CED* and ∠*AED* are right angles.

(f) Since, *AE* ⊥ *CE*, it means ∠*E* = 90°

     ∴ ∠*AEC* is a right angle.

(g) Since, *AC* ⊥ *CD*, it means ∠*C* = 90°

     ∴ ∠*ACD* is a right angle.

(h) Since, *OP* ⊥ *AB*, it means ∠*K* = 90°

     ∴ ∠*AKO*, ∠*OKB*, ∠*BKP* and ∠*AKP* and right angle

Que 19. What conclusion can be drawn each part of figure
   (a) DB is the bisector of $\angle ADC$?

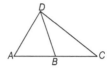

   (b) BD bisects $\angle ABC$?

   (c) DC is the bisector of $\angle ADB$, CA $\perp$ DA and CB $\perp$ DB?

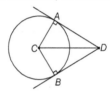

Sol. We know that bisector line divide that angle into two equal angles.
   (a) Since, BD is the bisector of $\angle ADC$,
   ∴ $\angle ADB = \angle BDC$
   (b) Since, BD bisector $\angle ABC$,
   ∴ $\angle ABD = \angle CBD$
   (c) Since, DC is the bisector of $\angle ADB$ and $CA \perp DA$ and $CB \perp DB$
   ∴ $\angle ADC = \angle BDC$ and $\angle CAD = 90°$, $\angle CBD = 90°$

Que 20. Write the name of
   (a) vertices.   (b) edges.
   (c) faces of the prism shown in the given figure.

Sol. From the given figure,
   (a) The name of vertices of the prism are A, B, C, D, E and F.
   (b) The name of edges of the prism are AB, AC, BC, BD, DF, FC, EF, ED and AE.
   (c) The name of the faces of the prism are ABC, DEF, $AEFC$, $AEDB$ and $BDFC$.

Que 21. How many edges, faces and vertices are there in a sphere?

Sol. There are no edges, no faces and no vertices in a sphere.

Chapter **6**

Integers

Important Points

- **Natural numbers** are counting numbers such as 1, 2, 3...,. If we include 0 (zero) with natural numbers, then they are called as **whole numbers**.

- **Number line** When we represent a number on a line, then it is called a number line. On the number line, numbers to the right of zero are represented by '+' (positive) sign and to the left of zero are represented by '−' (negative) sign.

  Note One more than given number gives a **successor** and one less than that of given number gives a **predecessor**.

- **Integers** If we put the whole numbers and the negative numbers together, the new collection of numbers will look like ... −5, −4, −3, −2, −1, −1, 0, 1, 2, 3, 4, 5, ... and this collection of numbers is known as integers. Here, 1, 2, 3, ... are said to be positive integers and − 1, − 2, − 3, ... are said to be negative integers. Zero is an integer which is neither positive nor negative.

- **Representation of integers on a number line** To represent integers on a number line, draw a line and mark some points at equal distance on it as shown in the figure given below. Mark a point as zero on it. Points to the right of zero are positive integers and are marked as +1, +2, +3 etc or simply 1, 2, 3 etc. Points to the left of zero are negative integers and are marked as −1, −2, −3, etc.

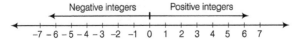

▪ **Ordering of integers** On the number line, the number increases as we move to the right and decreases as we move to the left.

Therefore, $-4 < -3 < -2 < -1 < 0 < 1 < 2 < 3 < 4$ and so on.

▪ **Addition of integers**

(i) To add two positive integers, we simply add them and to add two negative integers, we firstly add them by taking negative sign common and then put negative sign before the sum.

e.g. $(+3) + (+2) = +5$ and $(-2) + (-3) = -(2+3) = -5$

Thus, sum of two positive integers is a positive integer and sum of two negative integers is a negative integer.

(ii) When we have one positive and one negative integer, then we must subtract but answer will take the sign of the bigger integer. (To find bigger integer, we ignore their sign and then decide, which is bigger).

(iii) When a positive integer is added to an integer, then the resulting integer becomes greater than the given integer. When a negative integer is added to an integer, then the resulting integer becomes less then the given integer.

▪ **Addition of integers on a number line** Firstly, draw the number line and represent first number on it. Then, to add second number in first number, we move right to the first number.

e.g. To add 6 and 2, we start from 6 and go to 2 steps to the right of 6 and reach at 8.

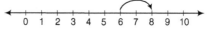

So, $6 + 2 = 8$

> **Note** If two numbers, when added to each other give the sum zero, then they are called **additive inverse** of each other. e.g. $3 + (-3) = 0$. So, 3 is additive inverse of –3 and –3 is additive inverse of 3.

▪ **Subtraction of integers** To subtract an integer from another integer, we add the additive inverse of the integer that is being subtracted to the other integer.

e.g. $(-10) - (-4) = (-10) + (\text{additive inverse of} -4)$
$$= -10 + 4 = -6$$

i.e. subtraction of an integer is the same as the addition of its additive inverse.

■ **Subtraction of integers on a number line** Firstly, draw the number line and represent first number (which have positive sign) on it. Then, to subtract second number from first number, we move left to the first number.

e.g. To subtract 3 from 5, we move 3 steps to the left of 5 and reach at 2.

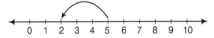

0 1 2 3 4 5 6 7 8 9 10

So, $5 - 3 = 2$

Do this (Page 114-115)

Que 1. Suppose David and Mohan have started walking from zero position in opposite directions. Let the steps to the right of zero be represented by '+' sign and to the left of zero be represented by '−' sign. If Mohan moves 5 steps to the right of zero, it can be represented as + 5 and if David moves 5 steps to the left of zero, it can be represented as − 5. Now, represent the following positions with + sign or − sign.

(a) 8 steps to the left of zero.   (b) 7 steps to the right of zero.

(c) 11 steps to the right of zero. (d) 6 steps to the left of zero.

Sol. We know that, on the number line, all numbers to the right of 0 are positive integers and all numbers to the left of 0 are negative integers. Thus, representation of numbers on number line is as follows:

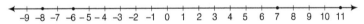

−9 −8 −7 −6 −5 −4 −3 −2 −1 0 1 2 3 4 5 6 7 8 9 10 11

(a) 8 steps to the left of zero is represented by − 8.
(b) 7 steps to the right of zero is represented by + 7.
(c) 11 steps to the right of zero is represented by + 11.
(d) 6 steps to the left of zero is represented by − 6.

Que 2. Write the succeeding number of the following:

Number	Successor
10	
8	
−5	
−3	
0	

Sol. We know that, one more than given number gives a successor. So, the succeeding numbers of given numbers are given as below

Number	Successor
10	$10 + 1 = 11$
8	$8 + 1 = 9$
– 5	$-5 + 1 = -4$
– 3	$-3 + 1 = -2$
0	$0 + 1 = 1$

Que 3. Write the preceding number of the following:

Number	Predecessor
10	
8	
5	
3	
0	

Sol. We know that, one less than given number gives a predecessor. So, the preceding numbers of the given numbers are given as below:

Number	Predecessor
10	$10 - 1 = 9$
8	$8 - 1 = 7$
5	$5 - 1 = 4$
3	$3 - 1 = 2$
0	$0 - 1 = -1$

Try These (Page 116)

Que 4. Write the following numbers with appropriate signs.
  (a) 100 m below sea level
  (b) 25°C above 0°C temperature
  (c) 15°C below 0°C temperature
  (d) Any five numbers less than 0

Sol. (a) We can write 100 m below sea level as –100 m because below sea level represents '–' sign and above sea level represents '+' sign.

  (b) We can write 25°C above 0°C temperature as +25°C because temperature above 0° C is denoted by '+' sign and temperature below 0°C is denoted by '–' sign.

(c) We can write 15°C below 0°C temperature as −15°C because temperature above 0°C is denoted by '+' sign and temperature below 0°C is denoted by '−' sign.

(d) Every negative integer is less than zero and every positive integer is greater than zero.

∴ Numbers less than 0 are −1, −2, −3, −4, −5...

Try These (Page 118)

Que 5. Mark −3, 7, −4, −8, −1 and 3 on the number line.

TIPS
If an integer has positive (+) sign, then it will lies to the right of zero on the number line and if an integer has negative (−) sign, then it will lies to the left of zero on the number line.

Sol. Draw a line and mark some points at equal distance on it as shown in the figure given below. Mark a point on it as zero. Points to the right of zero are positive integers and marked by +1, +2, +3 etc., or simply 1, 2, 3 etc and points to the left of zero are negative integers and marked by −1, −2, −3 etc.

Now, −3 is a negative integer (since, −3 has negative sign). So, move 3 points to the left of zero and represent it by point C.

7 is a positive integer (since +7 has positive sign). So, move 7 points to the right of zero and represent it by point F.

To mark −4 on this line, move 4 points to the left of zero and represent it by point B.

To mark −8, on this line, move 8 points to the left of zero and represent it by point A.

To mark −1 on this line, move 1 point to the left of zero and represent it by point D.

To mark 3 on this line, move 3 points to the right of zero and represent it by point E.

Thus, we get the following representation of these integers on number line.

```
     A              B  C    D            E              F
 ←—+—+—○—+—+—+—○—○—+—○—+—+—+—○—+—+—+—○—+—+—→
  −10 −9 −8 −7 −6 −5 −4 −3 −2 −1  0  1  2  3  4  5  6  7  8  9 10
```

Try These (Page 119)

Que 6. Compare the following pairs of numbers using > or <.

(i) 0 ☐ −8   (ii) −1 ☐ −15   (iii) 5 ☐ −5

(iv) 11 ☐ 15   (v) 0 ☐ 6   (vi) −20 ☐ 2

From the above exercise, Rohini arrived at the following conclusions:

(a) Every positive integer is larger than every negative integer.

(b) Zero is less than every positive integer.

(c) Zero is larger than every negative integer.

(d) Zero is neither a negative integer nor a positive integer.

(e) Farther a number from zero on the right, larger is its value.

(f) Farther a number from zero on the left, smaller is its value.

Do you agree with her? Give examples.

TIPS

> We know that, the number increases as we move to the right and decreases as we move to the left. So, if first number is to the right of second number, then use < and if first number is to the left of second number then use > .

Sol. (i) We have, $0 \boxed{} -8$
    Since, 0 is to the right of – 8.   ∴ $0 \boxed{>} -8$

(ii) We have, $-1 \boxed{} -15$
    Since, – 1 is to the right of – 15.   ∴ $-1 \boxed{>} -15$

(iii) We have, $5 \boxed{} -5$
    Since, 5 is to the right of – 5.   ∴ $5 \boxed{>} -5$

(iv) We have, $11 \boxed{\phantom{<}} 15$
    Since, 11 is to the left of 15.   ∴ $11 \boxed{<} 15$

(v) We have, $0 \boxed{\phantom{<}} 6$
    Since, 0 is to the left of 6.   ∴ $0 \boxed{<} 6$

(vi) We have, $-20 \boxed{\phantom{<}} 2$
    Since, – 20 is to the left of 2.   ∴ $-20 \boxed{<} 2$

Yes, I agree with Rohini. Some examples are as follows:

(a) Every positive integer is larger than every negative integer, e. g. $5 > -2$

(b) Zero is less than every positive integer, e. g. $0 < 3$.

(c) Zero is larger than every negative integer, e. g. $0 > -4$.

(d) Zero is neither a negative integer nor a positive integer, because 0 has neither '+' sign nor '–' sign.

(e) Farther a number from zero, on the right side, larger is its value because on number line, every integer on the right from zero is greater than zero, e. g. $5 > 0$.

(f) Farther a number from zero, on the left side, smaller is its value because on number line, every integer on the left from zero is smaller than zero, e. g. $-8 < 0$.

Exercise 6.1

Que 1. Write opposites of the following:
   (a) Increase in weight   (b) 30 km North
   (c) 326 BC   (d) Loss of ₹ 700
   (e) 100 m above sea level

Sol. (a) Opposite of increase in weight is **decrease in weight**.
   (b) Opposite of 30 km North is **30 km South**.
   (c) Opposite of 326 BC is **326 AD**.
   (d) Opposite of loss of ₹ 700 is **profit of ₹ 700**.
   (e) Opposite of 100 m above sea level is **100 m below** sea level.

Que 2. Represent the following numbers as integers with appropriate signs.
   (a) An aeroplane is flying at a height of two thousand metre above the ground.
   (b) A submarine is moving at a depth, eight hundred metre below the sea level.
   (c) A deposit of rupees two hundred.
   (d) Withdrawal of rupees seven hundred.

Sol. (a) An aeroplane is flying at a height of two thousand metre above the ground can be written as + 2000 m because height above the ground is taken as positive.
   (b) A submarine is moving at a depth eight hundred metre below the sea level can be written as –800 m because depth below the sea level is taken as negative.
   (c) A deposit of rupees two hundred can be written as + ₹ 200 because deposit is represented with + sign.
   (d) Withdrawal of rupees seven hundred can be written as – ₹ 700 because withdrawal is represented with – sign.

Que 3. Represent the following numbers on a number line:

(a) $+5$ (b) -10 (c) $+8$ (d) -1 (e) -6

TIPS Firstly, draw a number line, then represent a negative integer on the left of zero on the number line and a positive integer on the right of zero on the number line.

Sol. Draw a line and mark some points at equal distance on it. Mark a point as zero on it. Points to the right of zero are positive integers and are marked by $+1, +2, +3$ or simply by 1, 2, 3, etc. Points to the left of zero are negative integers and are marked by $-1, -2, -3$, etc.

(a) **Representation of $+5$** To mark $+5$ on number line, we move 5 points to the right of zero as shown in the figure.

In the above figure, point A represents $+5$.

(b) **Representation of -10** To mark -10 on number line, we move 10 points to the left of zero as shown in the figure.

In the above figure, point A represents -10.

(c) **Representation of $+8$** To mark $+8$ on number line, we move 8 points to the right of zero as shown in the figure.

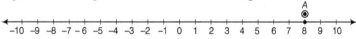

In the above figure, point A represents $+8$.

(d) **Representation of -1** To mark -1 on number line, we move 1 point to the left of zero as shown in the figure.

In the above figure, point A represents -1.

(e) **Representation of -6** To mark -6 on number line, we move 6 points to the left of zero as shown in the figure.

In the above figure, point A represents -6.

Que 4. Adjacent figure is a vertical number line, representing integers. Observe it and locate the following points.

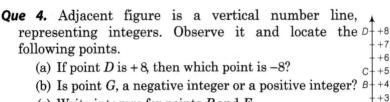

(a) If point D is $+8$, then which point is -8?

(b) Is point G, a negative integer or a positive integer?

(c) Write integers for points B and E.

(d) Which point marked on this number line has the least value?

(e) Arrange all the points in decreasing order of value?

TIPS

Positive integers are represented on the right of zero and negative integers are represented on the left of zero on a number line but here vertical line is given. So, positive integers will be represented above zero and negative integers will be represented below zero on vertical number line.

Sol. (a) Now, from figure, it is clear that $+8$ is on point D, then for getting -8, we should move below to 0.

After moving 8 steps below 0, we reach at point F.

So, point F represents -8.

(b) We know that, points lie above zero are positive integers and lie below zero are negative integers.

Here, we see that point G lies below zero.

So, G is a negative integer.

(c) On given number line, point B lies above zero and point E lies below zero.

So, it is clear that point B is a positive integer and point E is a negative integer. Now, counting from 0, the distance of $B = +4$ units because it is on right of zero and counting from 0, the distance of $E = -10$ units because it is on left of zero.

∴ Integer $B = +4$ and Integer $E = -10$

(d) Here, we see that the distance of point E is far from 0 and below from 0 and we know that on vertical number line below from 0 the value of integers are negative.

Hence, point E has the least value.

(e) We know that, on a number line the number decreases as we move to left. Here, vertical number line is given to us, so the number decreases as we move to down. So, decreasing order of values of all points is given here.

$$D, C, B, A, O, H, G, F, E$$

Que 5. Following is the list of temperatures of five places in India on a particular day of the year:

Place	Temperature	
Siachin	10°C below 0°C	....
Shimla	2°C below 0°C	....
Ahmedabad	30°C above 0°C	....
Delhi	20°C above 0°C	....
Srinagar	5°C below 0°C	....

(a) Write the temperatures of these places in the form of integers in the blank column.

(b) Following is the number line representing the temperature in degree Celsius.

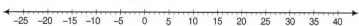

Plot the name of the city against its temperature.

(c) Which is the coolest place?

(d) Write the names of the places, where temperature are above 10°C.

 TIPS

Temperature below 0°C is denoted with negative (–) sign and temperature above 0°C is denoted with positive (+) sign.

Sol. (a)

Place	Temperature	Form of integers
Siachin	10°C below 0°C	–10° C
Shimla	2°C below 0°C	–2° C
Ahmedabad	30°C above 0°C	+ 30° C
Delhi	20°C above 0°C	+20° C
Srinagar	5°C below 0°C	–5° C

(b) The name of city against its temperature on the number line is given below

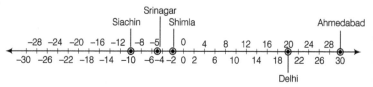

(c) After checking the temperature of all places, we can say that the Siachin (–10°) is the coolest place.

(d) Delhi (+20°C) and Ahmedabad (+30°C) are the places, where temperature is above 10°C.

Que 6. In each of the following pairs, which number is to the right of the other on the number line?

(a) 2, 9   (b) −3, − 8   (c) 0, − 1

(d) − 11, 10   (e) − 6, 6   (f) 1, − 100

Sol. (a)

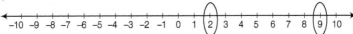

Here, 2 and 9 both are on the right of zero but 9 is farther from zero in comparison of 2. So, number 9 is right of number 2.

(b)

Here, −3 and −8 both are on the left of zero but −3 is near to the zero in comparison of −8. So, −3 is to the right of −8.

(c)

Here, −1 is on the left of zero, so we can say that 0 is to the right of −1.

(d)

Here, − 11 is to the left of zero and 10 is on the right of zero. So, 10 is to the right of − 11.

(e)

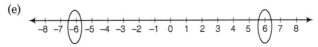

Here, −6 is to the left of zero and 6 is to the right of zero. So, we can say that 6 is to the right of −6.

(f)

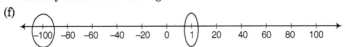

Here, −100 is to the left of zero and 1 is to the right of zero. So, we can say that 1 is to the right of −100.

Que 7. Write all the integers between the given pair (write them in the increasing order).

(a) 0 and –7   (b) –4 and 4   (c) –8 and –15 (d) –30 and –23

TIPS

We know that on a number line, the number increases as we move to the right and decreases as we move to the left. Here, for increasing order of integers, we will move to the right on number line.

Sol. (a)   Integer 0 and –7 are on number line are shown as below

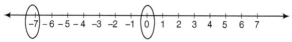

From the above figure, it is clear that integers between 0 and –7 are –1, –2, –3, –4, –5 and –6.

Now, increasing order of these integers is
–6 < –5 < –4 < –3 < –2 < –1, because we are moving to the right from –7 to 0.

(b)   Integers –4 and 4 on number line are shown as below

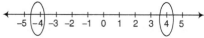

From the above figure, it is clear that integers between –4 and 4 are –3, –2 , –1, 0, 1, 2 and 3.

Now, increasing order of these integers is
– 3 < – 2 < – 1 < 0 < 1 < 2 < 3 because we are moving to the right from – 4 to 4.

(c)   Integers –8 and –15 on the number line are shown as below

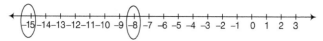

From the above figure, it is clear that integers between –8 and –15 are –9, –10, –11, –12, –13 and –14

Now, increasing order of these integers is
$$-14 < -13 < -12 < -11 < -10 < -9,$$
because we are moving to the right from – 15 to – 8.

(d)   Integers –30 and –23 on the number line are shown as below

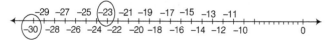

From figure, it is clear that integers between –30 and –23 are
–24, –25 –26, –27, –28 and – 29.

Now, increasing order of these integers is
$$-29 < -28 < -27 < -26 < -25 < -24,$$
because we are moving to the right from – 30 to – 23.

Que 8. (a) Write four negative integers greater than –20.

(b) Write four negative integers less than –10.

Sol. (a) Negative integers greater than –20 on number line are shown as below

When we move on number line to the right, then the value of integer increases.

So, it is clear from figure that when we move right of –20, we will get integers greater than –20. So, four negative integers greater than –20 are –19, –18, –17 and –16.

(b) Negative integers which are less than –10 on number line are shown as below

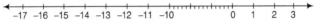

When we move on number line to the left , then the value of integer decreases.

So, it is clear from the above figure that when we move left of –10, we will get integers less than of –10.

So, four negative integers less than–10 are –11, –12, –13 and –14.

Que 9. For the following statements, write True (T) or False (F). If the statement is false, correct the statement.

(a) –8 is to the right of –10 on a number line.

(b) –100 is to the right of –50 on a number line.

(c) Smallest negative integer is –1.

(d) –26 is greater than –25.

Sol. (a) True, because on number line going to the right, value of integer is increases. Here, –8 is greater to –10, so –8 is to the right of –10 on number line.

(b) False, because on number line going to the left, value of integer is decreases. Here, –100 is less than –50. So, –100 is to the left of –50 on number line.

(c) False, because on number line –1 is situated on the right of all negative integers. So, it is the greatest negative integer.

(d) False, because on number line –25 is on the right of –26. So, –25 is greater than –26.

Que 10. Draw a number line and answer the following:

(a) Which number will we reach if we move 4 numbers to the right of –2 .

(b) Which number will we reach if we move 5 numbers to the left of 1.

(c) If we are at –8 on the number line, in which direction should we move to reach –13 ?

(d) If we are at –6 on the number line, in which direction should we move to reach –1 ?

Sol. (a) On number line, starting from –2 and moving 4 points towards right (each step being equal to 1 unit), we will reach at 2.

(b) On number line, starting from 1 and moving 5 points towards left (each step being equal to 1 unit), we will reach at – 4.

(c)

Here, –8 > –13. So, –13 is on the left of –8. Hence, if we are at –8 on number line, then move to the left from –8 to reach at –13.

(d)

Here, –1 > –6. So, –1 is on the right of –6. Hence, if we are at –6 on the number line, then move to the right from –6 to reach at –1.

Try These (Page 125)

Que 1. Find the answers of the following additions:

(a) (–11) + (–12)   (b) (+10) + (+4)

(c) (–32) + (–25)   (d) (+23) + (+40)

> **TIPS**
> To add two positive integers, we simply add them and to add two negative integers we firstly add them by taking negative sign common and then put negative sign before the sum.

Sol. (a) $(-11) + (-12) = -(11 + 12) = -23$

(b) $(+10) + (+4) = +(10 + 4) = +14$

(c) $(-32) + (-25) = -(32 + 25) = -57$

(d) $(+23) + (+40) = +(23 + 40) = +63$

Que 2. Find the solution of the following:

    (a) $(-7) + (+8)$ (b) $(-9) + (+13)$

    (c) $(+7) + (-10)$ (d) $(+12) + (-7)$

TIPS When we have one positive and one negative integer, we must subtract but answer will take the sign of the bigger integer (to find bigger integer we ignore their sign and then decide which is bigger).

Sol. (a) $(-7) + (+8) = (-7) + (+7) + (+1)$ $[\because 7 + 1 = 8]$

               $= 0 + (+1) = +1$ $[\because (-7) + (+7) = 0]$

    (b) $(-9) + (+13) = (-9) + (+9) + (+4)$ $[\because 9 + 4 = 13]$

               $= 0 + (+4) = +4$ $[\because (-9) + (+9) = 0]$

    (c) $(+7) + (-10) = (+7) + (-7) + (-3)$ $[\because -10 = 7 + 3 - 7 = 3]$

               $= 0 + (-3) = -3$ $[\because (+7) + (-7) = 0]$

    (d) $(+12) + (-7) = (+5) + (+7) + (-7)$ $[\because 12 = 5 + 7]$

               $= (+5) + 0 = +5$ $[\because (+7) + (-7) = 0]$

Try These (Page 127)

Que 3. Find the solution of the following additions using a number line:

    (a) $(-2) + 6$ (b) $(-6) + 2$

Make two such questions and solve them using the number line.

Sol. (a)

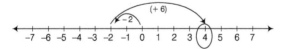

Firstly, draw a number line. Here, -2 is a negative integer and 6 is a positive integer. Then, we first move 2 steps to the left of 0 reaching at -2, then we move 6 steps to the right of -2 and reach at 4. Thus, $(-2) + 6 = +4$

    (b)

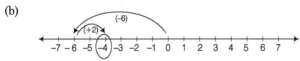

Firstly, draw a number line. Here, -6 is a negative integer and 2 is a positive integer. Then, we first move 6 steps to the left of 0 reaching at -6, then we move 2 steps to the right of -6 and reach at -4. Thus, $(-6) + 2 = -4$

Two such questions are as follows:

(a) $(-3) + 5$ (b) $5 + (-1)$

(a) We have, $(-3) + 5$

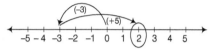

Here, we first move 3 steps to the left of 0 reaching at –3, then we move 5 steps to the right of –3 and reach at 2.

Thus, $(-3) + 5 = +2$

(b) We have, $5 + (-1)$

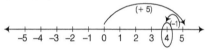

Here, we first move 5 steps to the right of zero (0) reaching at 5, then we move 1 step to the left of 5 and reach at 4.

Thus, $5 + (-1) = 4$

Que 4. Find the solution of the following without using number line:

(a) $(+7) + (-11)$ (b) $(-13) + (+10)$
(c) $(-7) + (+9)$ (d) $(+10) + (-5)$

Make five such questions and solve them.

Sol. (a) $(+7) + (-11) = (+7) + (-7) + (-4)$ $[\because 11 = 7 + 4 \Rightarrow -11 = (-7) + (-4)]$
$= 0 + (-4) = -4$ $[\because (+7) + (-7) = 0]$

(b) $(-13) + (+10) = (-10) + (-3) + (+10)$
$[\because 13 = 10 + 3 \Rightarrow -13 = -10 + (-3)]$
$= (-10) + (+10) + (-3) = 0 + (-3) = -3$
$[\because (-10) + (+10) = 0]$

(c) $(-7) + (+9) = (-7) + (+7) + (+2)$ $[\because 9 = 7 + 2]$
$= 0 + (+2) = +2$ $[\because (-7) + (+7) = 0]$

(d) $(+10) + (-5) = (+5) + (+5) + (-5)$ $[\because 10 = 5 + 5]$
$= (+5) + 0 = +5$ $[\because (+5) + (-5) = 0]$

Five such other questions are as follows:

(a) $(+7) + (-9)$ (b) $(+5) + (-2)$ (c) $(-6) + (+2)$
(d) $(-8) + (+5)$ (e) $(+12) + (-8)$
(a) We have, $(+7) + (-9) = (+7) + (-7) + (-2)$
$[\because 9 = 7 + 2 \Rightarrow -9 = -7 + (-2)]$
$= 0 + (-2) = (-2)$ $[\because (+7) + (-7) = 0]$

(b) We have, $(+5) + (-2) = (+3) + (+2) + (-2)$ $[\because 5 = 3 + 2]$

$\qquad\qquad\qquad = (+3) + 0 = +3$ $[\because (-2) + (+2) = 0]$

(c) We have, $(-6) + (+2) = (-4) + (-2) + (+2)$

$\qquad\qquad\qquad\qquad [\because 6 = 4 + 2 \Rightarrow -6 = -4 + (-2)]$

$\qquad\qquad\qquad = (-4) + 0 = -4$ $[\because (-2) + (+2) = 0]$

(d) We have, $(-8) + (+5) = (-5) + (-3) + (+5)$

$\qquad\qquad\qquad\qquad [\because 8 = 5 + 3 \Rightarrow -8 = -5 + (-3)]$

$\qquad\qquad\qquad = (-5) + (+5) + (-3)$

$\qquad\qquad\qquad = 0 + (-3) = (-3)$ $[\because (-5) + (+5) = 0]$

(e) We have, $(+12) + (-8) = (+8) + (+4) + (-8)$ $[\because 12 = 8 + 4]$

$\qquad\qquad\qquad = (+8) + (-8) + (+4)$

$\qquad\qquad\qquad = 0 + (+4) = +4$ $[\because (+8) + (-8) = 0]$

Exercise 6.2

Que 1. Using the number line write the integer which is

    (a) 3 more than 5   (b) 5 more than −5

    (c) 6 less than 2   (d) 3 less than −2

TIPS To find a number more than given number, we move to right of that given number and to find a number less than given number, we move to left of that number.

Sol. (a) To get the integer 3 more than 5, we start from 5 and move 3 steps to the right of 5 and reach at 8, as shown in the figure given below

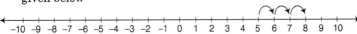

      Hence, 3 more than 5 is 8.

  (b) To get the integer 5 more than −5, we start from −5 and move 5 steps to the right of −5 and reach at 0, as shown in the figure given below

      Hence, 5 more than −5 is 0.

  (c) To get the integer 6 less than 2, we start from 2 and move 6 steps to the left of 2 and reach at −4, as shown in the figure given below

      Hence, 6 less than 2 is −4.

(d) To get the integer 3 less than –2, we start from –2 and moves 3 steps to the left of –2 and reach at –5, as shown in the figure given below

Hence, 3 less than –2 is –5.

Que 2. Use number line and add the following integers

(a) $9 + (-6)$ (b) $5 + (-11)$ (c) $(-1) + (-7)$

(d) $(-5) + 10$ (e) $(-1) + (-2) + (-3)$ (f) $(-2) + 8 + (-4)$

Firstly, draw the number line and represent first number on it. Now, to add second number in first number, we move right to the first number, if second number is positive and move left to the first number, if second number is negative.

Sol. (a) We have, $9 + (-6)$

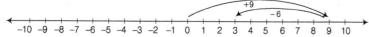

Firstly, draw a number line, then, we move 9 steps to the right of 0 and reach at 9. Now, we move 6 steps to the left of 9 [∵ –6 is a negative integer] and reach at 3, as shown in the above figure. Hence, $9 + (-6) = 3$

(b) We have, $5 + (-11)$

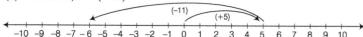

Firstly, draw the number line, then we move 5 steps to the right of 0 and reach at 5. Now, we move 11 steps to the left of 5 [∵ –11 is a negative integer] and reach at –6, as shown in the above figure. Hence, $5 + (-11) = -6$

(c) We have, $(-1) + (-7)$

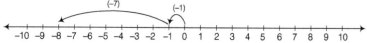

Firstly, draw the number line, then we move one step to the left of 0 (zero) and reach at –1. Now, we move 7 steps to the left of –1 [∵ – 7 is a negative integer] and reach –8, as shown in the above figure. Hence, $(-1) + (-7) = -8$

(d) We have, $(-5) + 10$

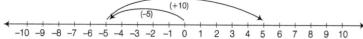

Firstly, draw the number line, then we move 5 steps to the left of 0 and reach at –5. Then, we move 10 steps to the right of –5 [∵ 10 is a positive integer] and reach at 5, as shown in the above figure. Hence, (–5) + (+10) = 5

(e) We have, (– 1) + (– 2) + (– 3)

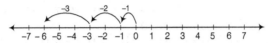

Firstly, draw the number line, then we move one step to the left of 0 and reach at –1. Now, we move 2 steps to the left of –1 [∵ – 2 is a negative integer] and reach at –3. Then, we move 3 steps to the left of –3 [∵ – 3 is a negative integer] and reach at –6, as shown in the above figure.

Hence, (–1) + (–2) + (–3) = (–6)

(f) We have, (– 2) + 8 + (– 4)

Firstly, draw the number line, then we move 2 steps to the left of 0 and reach at –2. Now, we move 8 steps to the right of –2 [∵ 8 is a positive integer] and reach at 6. Again, from 6, we move 4 steps to the left of 6 [∵ – 4 is a negative integer] and reach at 2, as shown in the above figure. Hence, (–2) + (8) + (–4) = 2

Que 3. Add without using number line:

(a) $11 + (-7)$ (b) $(-13) + (+18)$

(c) $(-10) + (+19)$ (d) $(-250) + (+150)$

(e) $(-380) + (-270)$ (f) $(-217) + (-100)$

Sol. (a) We have, $11 + (-7) = (+4) + (+7) + (-7)$ [∵ $11 = 4 + 7$]

$= (+4) + (0) = 4$ [∵ $(+7) + (-7) = 0$]

(b) We have, $(-13) + (+18) = (-13) + (+13) + (5)$ [∵ $18 = 13 + 5$]

$= 0 + (+5) = 5$ [∵ $(-13) + (+13) = 0$]

(c) We have, $(-10) + (+19) = (-10) + (+10) + (9)$ [∵ $19 = 10 + 9$]

$= 0 + (+9) = 9$ [∵ $(-10) + (+10) = 0$]

(d) We have, $(-250) + (+150) = (-150) + (-100) + (+150)$

[∵ $250 = 150 + 100 \Rightarrow -250 = -150 + (-100)$]

$= (-150) + (+150) + (-100)$

$= 0 + (-100) = -100$ [∵ $(-150) + (+150) = 0$]

(e) We have, $(-380) + (-270) = -(380 + 270) = -650$

(f) We have, $(-217) + (-100) = -(217 + 100) = -317$

Que 4. Find the sum of

    (a) 137 and –354   (b) –52 and 52

    (c) –312, 39 and 192   (d) –50, –200 and 300

Sol. (a) We have, $137 + (-354) = 137 + (-137) + (-217)$

$$[\because 354 = 137 + 217 \Rightarrow -354 = -137 + (-217)]$$
$$= 0 + (-217) = -217 \quad [\because 137 + (-137) = 0]$$

(b) We have, $-52 + (+52) = 0$

(c) We have, $-312 + 39 + 192 = -312 + 231 = (-231) + (-81) + 231$

$$[\because 312 = 231 + 81 \Rightarrow -312 = -231 + (-81)]$$
$$= (-231) + 231 + (-81)$$
$$= 0 + (-81) = -81 \quad [\because (-231) + 231 = 0]$$

(d) We have, $(-50) + (-200) + (300) = -(50 + 200) + 300$

$$= (-250) + (300) \quad [\because 300 = 250 + 50]$$
$$= (-250) + (250) + (50)$$
$$= 0 + 50 = 50 \quad [\because (-250) + (250) = 0]$$

Que 5. Find the sum:

    (a) $(-7) + (-9) + 4 + 16$ (b) $(37) + (-2) + (-65) + (-8)$

 Firstly, add the numbers having same sign and get new number. Now, add the numbers having opposite signs.

Sol. (a) We have, $(-7) + (-9) + 4 + 16 = -(7 + 9) + 4 + 16 \quad [\because 20 = 16 + 4]$

$$= -16 + 20 = -16 + 16 + 4$$
$$= 0 + 4 = 4 \quad [\because -16 + 16 = 0]$$

(b) We have, $(37) + (-2) + (-65) + (-8) = 37 - (2 + 65 + 8)$

$$= 37 - 75 = 37 - 37 - 38$$
$$[\because 75 = 37 + 38 \Rightarrow -75 = -37 - 38]$$
$$= 0 - 38 = -38 \quad [\because -37 + 37 = 0]$$

Exercise 6.3

Que 1. Find

    (a) $35 - (20)$ (b) $72 - (90)$ (c) $(-15) - (-18)$

    (d) $(-20) - (13)$ (e) $23 - (-12)$ (f) $(-32) - (-40)$

 To subtract an integer from another integer, we add additive inverse of the integer that is being subtracted to the other integer.

Sol. (a) We have, $35 - (20) = 35 + ($Additive inverse of $20) = 35 + (-20)$

$$= 15 + 20 + (-20) \quad [\because 35 = 20 + 15]$$
$$= 15 + 0 = 15 \quad [\because 20 + (-20) = 0]$$

(b) We have, $72 - 90 = 72 +$ (Additive inverse of 90)
$$= 72 + (-90) = 72 + (-72) + (-18)$$
$$[\because 90 = 72 + 18 \Rightarrow -90 = -72 + (-18)]$$
$$= 0 + (-18) = -18 \qquad [\because 72 + (-72) = 0]$$

(c) We have, $(-15) - (-18) = -15 +$ (Additive inverse of -18)
$$= -15 + 18$$
$$= (-15) + (15) + (3) \qquad [\because 18 = 15 + 3]$$
$$= 0 + 3 = 3 \qquad [\because (-15) + (15) = 0]$$

(d) We have, $(-20) - (13) = (-20) +$ (Additive inverse of 13)
$$= (-20) + (-13) = -(20 + 13) = -33$$

(e) We have, $23 - (-12) = 23 +$ (Additive inverse of -12)
$$= 23 + 12 = 35$$

(f) We have, $(-32) - (-40) = (-32) +$ (Additive inverse of -40)
$$= (-32) + 40 = (-32) + (32) + (8) \quad [\because 40 = 32 + 8]$$
$$= 0 + 8 = 8 \qquad [\because (-32) + (32) = 0]$$

Que 2. Fill in the blanks with >, < or = sign.

    (a) $(-3) + (-6)$ ___ $(-3) - (-6)$

    (b) $(-21) - (-10)$ ___ $(-31) + (-11)$

    (c) $45 - (-11)$ ___ $57 + (-4)$

    (d) $(-25) - (-42)$ ___ $(-42) - (-25)$

TIPS

> Firstly, find the value of LHS (left hand side) and RHS (right hand side). Then, put the sign > (greater than), < (less than) or = (equal to) by using these rules
>
>   (i) Every positive integer > 0 then negative integer.
>
> (ii) Every negative integer < 0 then positive integer.
>
> (iii) If LHS and RHS give same value, then use equal to (=)

Sol. (a) We have, $(-3) + (-6)$ ___ $(-3) - (-6)$
$$\text{LHS} = (-3) + (-6) = -9$$
$$\text{RHS} = (-3) - (-6) = (-3) + (\text{Additive inverse of } -6)$$
$$= -3 + 6 = 3$$

Since, -9 is a negative integer and 3 is a positive integer.

$$\therefore \qquad\qquad -9 \boxed{<} 3$$

(b) We have, $(-21) - (-10)$ ___ $(-31) + (-11)$
$$\text{LHS} = (-21) - (-10) = -21 + (\text{Additive inverse of } -10)$$
$$= -21 + 10 = -11$$
$$\text{RHS} = (-31) + (-11) = -42$$

Here, both are negative integers but -42 is to the left of -11.

$$\therefore \qquad\qquad -11 \boxed{>} -42$$

(c) We have, $45 - (-11)\underline{\quad}57 + (-4)$

LHS $= 45 - (-11) = 45 + 11$ [∵ Additive inverse of -11 is 11]

$\qquad = 56$

RHS $= 57 + (-4) = 53 + 4 + (-4) = 53 + 0 = 53$

Here, both are positive integers but 56 is to the right of 53.

∴ $56 \boxed{>} 53$

(d) We have, $(-25) - (-42)\underline{\quad}(-42) - (-25)$

LHS $= (-25) - (-42) = -25 + ($Additive inverse of $-42)$

$\qquad = -25 + 42 = 17$

RHS $= (-42) - (-25) = -42 + ($Additive inverse of $-25)$

$\qquad = -42 + 25 = -17$

Here, 17 is a positive integer and -17 is a negative integer.

∴ $17 \boxed{>} -17$

Que 3. Fill in the blanks.

(a) $(-8) + \underline{\quad} = 0$ (b) $13 + \underline{\quad} = 0$

(c) $12 + (-12) = \underline{\quad}$ (d) $(-4) + \underline{\quad} = -12$

(e) $\underline{\quad} -15 = -10$

TIPS   We know that, if sum of two integers is zero, then these number are called additive inverse of each other. So, to find the additive inverse of a number reverse its sign i.e. if number is positive, then its additive inverse is negative and *vice-versa*.

Sol. (a) We have, $(-8) + \underline{\quad} = 0$

$\qquad (-8) + \mathbf{8} = 0$ [∵ Additive inverse of -8 is 8]

(b) We have, $13 + \underline{\quad} = 0$

$\qquad 13 + (-\mathbf{13}) = 0$ [∵ Additive inverse of -13 is 13]

(c) We have, $12 + (-12) = \underline{\quad}\ 12 + (-12) = \mathbf{0}$

$\qquad$ [∵ 12 and -12 are additive inverse of each other]

(d) We have, $(-4) + \underline{\quad} = -12$

Here, sum of two integers is not zero, so here we cannot write additive inverse of -4.

$\qquad -4 + \underline{\quad} = -12 \Rightarrow -4 + \underline{\quad} = -(4+8)$

$\Rightarrow \qquad -4 + \underline{\quad} = (-4) + (-8)$

So, on comparing both sides, we get -8 to fill the blank space.

Thus, $(-4) + (-\mathbf{8}) = -12$

(e) We have, $\underline{\quad} 15 = -10 \Rightarrow \underline{\quad} - (10+5) = -10$

$\Rightarrow \qquad \underline{\quad} -10 - 5 = -10$

To get RHS = –10, we need to add additive inverse of – 5, i.e. 5 in RHS. So, + 5 – 10 – 5 = – 10

Hence, + **5** – 15 = – 10

Que 4. Find

(a) $(-7) - 8 - (-25)$ (b) $(-13) + 32 - 8 - 1$

(c) $(-7) + (-8) + (-90)$ (d) $50 - (-40) - (-2)$

Sol. (a) $(-7) - 8 - (-25) = (-7) + (-8) + 25$

[∵ Additive inverse of –25 is 25]

$$= -15 + 25 = -15 + 15 + 10 \qquad [\because 25 = 15 + 10]$$
$$= 0 + 10 = 10 \qquad [\because -15 + 15 = 0]$$

(b) $(-13) + 32 - 8 - 1 = (-13) + 32 - 9$

$$= -13 + 32 + (\text{Additive inverse of } 9)$$
$$= (-13) + 32 + (-9)$$
$$= -13 - 9 + 32 = -22 + 32 \; [\because 32 = 22 + 10]$$
$$= -22 + 22 + 10$$
$$= 0 + 10 = 10 \qquad [\because -22 + 22 = 0]$$

(c) $(-7) + (-8) + (-90) = -15 + (-90) = -105$

(d) $50 - (-40) - (-2) = 50 + (\text{Additive inverse of } - 40)$

$$+ (\text{Additive inverse of } - 2)$$
$$= 50 + 40 + 2 = 92$$

Selected **NCERT Exemplar Problems**

Directions *In Questions 1 to 8, only one of the four options is correct. Write the correct one.*

Que 1. The predecessor of the integer –1 is

(a) 1   (b) 2   (c) –2   (d) 1

Sol. We know that, one less than a given integer, gives a predecessor.

∴ The predecessor of the integer $-1 = -1 - 1 = -2$

Hence, the option (c) is correct.

Que 2. The least integer lying between –10 and –15 is

(a) –10   (b) –11   (c) –15   (d) –14

Sol. ∵ The integers between –10 and –15 are –11, –12, –13 and –14.

∴ The integer –11 is the largest and –14 is the smallest.

Hence, the option (d) is correct.

Que 3. The integer with negative sign (–) is always less than

    (a) 0   (b) –3   (c) –1   (d) –2

Sol. We know that, negative integer is always less than zero.

    Hence, the option (a) is correct.

Que 4. The successor of the predecessor of –50 is

    (a) –48   (b) –49   (c) –50   (d) –51

Sol. We know that, one less than given number gives a predecessor and one more than given number gives a successor.

    $\therefore$ The predecessor of $-50 = -50 - 1 = -51$

    and the successor of $-51 = -51 + 1 = -50$

    Hence, the option (c) is correct.

Que 5. The additive inverse of a negative integer

    (a) is always negative   (b) is always positive

    (c) is the same integer   (d) zero

Sol. We know that, additive inverse of an integer is obtained by changing the sign of the integer.

    $\therefore$ The additive inverse of a negative integer is always positive.

    e.g. Let a negative integer be –5.

    $\therefore$ The additive inverse of $-3 = -(-3) = 3$

    Hence, the option (b) is correct.

Que 6. Amulya and Amar visited two places A and B, respectively in Kashmir and recorded the minimum tempera- tures on a particular day as –4°C at A and –1°C at B. Which of the following statement is true?

    (a) A is cooler than B

    (b) B is cooler than A

    (c) There is a difference of 2°C in the temperature

    (d) The temperature at A is 4°C higher than that at B

Sol. We know that, as the temperature decrease the cooling increases.

    For place A, minimum temperature on a particular day is –4°C

    and for place B, it is –1°C

    Here, $-4°C < -1°C$

    $\therefore$ A is cooler than B. Hence, the option (a) is correct.

Que 7. When a negative integer is subtracted from another negative integer, the sign of the result

    (a) is always negative

(b) is always positive

(c) is never negative

(d) depends on the numerical value of the integers

Sol. Let two negative integers be –7 and –11.

We subtract (–7) from –11 and give a minus sign to the result.

i.e. $-11 - (-7) = -11 + 7 = -4$

Again, we subtract –11 from –7 and give a plus sign to the result.

i.e. $-7 - (-11) = -7 + 11 = 4$

Hence, a negative integer is subtracted from another negative integer, the sign of the result depends on the numerical value of the integers. Hence, the option (d) is correct.

Que 8. Which of the following shows the maximum rise in temperature?

(a) 0°C to 10°C   (b) –4°C to 8°C

(c) –15°C to –8°C   (d) –7°C to 0°C

Sol. We know that, the maximum rise in the temperature is equal to the maximum value of difference of two temperatures.

(a) Difference of 0°C and 10°C $= (10°\text{C} - 0°\text{C}) = (10 - 0)°\text{C} = 9°\text{C}$

(b) Difference of –4°C and 8°C $= 8°\text{C} - (-4°\text{C}) = (8 + 4)°\text{C} = 12°\text{C}$

(c) Difference of –15°C and –8°C $= -8°\text{C} - (-15°\text{C}) = -8°\text{C} + 15°\text{C}$

$$= 15°\text{C} - 8°\text{C} = (15 - 8)°\text{C} = 7°\text{C}$$

(d) Difference of –7°C and 0°C $= 0°\text{C} - (-7°\text{C}) = 0°\text{C} + 7°\text{C}$

$$= (0 + 7)°\text{C} = 7°\text{C}$$

Hence, the option (b) is correct.

Directions *In Questions 9 to 12, state whether the given statements are true (T) or false (F).*

Que 9. The sum of all the integers between –5 and –1 is –6.

Sol. False, the integers between –5 and –1 are –4, –3, –2, –1.

∴ Sum of integers –4, –3, –2 and –1

$= -4 + (-3) + (-2) + (-1) = -4 - 3 - 2 - 1 = -10$

Que 10. The sum of any two negative integers is always greater than both the integers.

Sol. False, let two negative integers be –3 and –5.

Now, sum of –3 and –5 $= -3 + (-5) = -3 - 5 = -8$

Here, $-8 < -3$ and $-8 < -5$.

Que 11. The difference between an integer and its additive inverse is always even.

Sol. True, let a integer be –3 and additive inverse of –3 is 3.

Now, the difference between 3 and –3 = 3 – (–3) = 3 + 3 = 6

Hence, the difference between an integer and its additive inverse is always even.

Que 12. The sum of three different integers can never be zero.

Sol. False, let the three integers be 2, 3, and –5.

Sum of 2, 3 and –5 = 2 + 3 + (–5) = 2 + 3 – 5 = 5 – 5 = 0

Directions *In questions 13 and 14, fill in the blanks using* $<, =$ *or* $>$

Que 13. $-11 + (-15)$____$11 + 15$

Sol. LHS = –11 + (–15) = –11 – 15 = –26; RHS = 11 + 15 = 26

Here,   –26 < 26   [$\because$ –26 is to the left of 26]

$\therefore$ –11 + (–15) < 11 + 15

Que 14. $(-2) + (-5) + (-6)$____$(-3) + (-4) + (-6)$

Sol. LHS = (–2) + (–5) + (–6) = –2 – 5 – 6 = –13

RHS = (–3) + (–4) + (–6) = –3 – 4 – 6 = –13

Here,   –13 = –13

$\therefore$ (–2) + (–5) + (–6) = (–3) + (–4) + (–6)

Que 15. Match the items of Column I with that of Column II.

	Column I		Column II
(i)	The additive inverse of +2	(a)	0
(ii)	The greatest negative integer	(b)	–2
(iii)	The greatest negative even integer	(c)	2
(iv)	The smallest integer than every negative integer	(d)	1
(v)	Sum of predecessor and successor of –1	(e)	–1

Sol. (i) The additive inverse of +2 = –2

(ii) The greatest negative integer = –1

(iii) The greatest negative even integer = –2

(iv) The smallest integer greater than every negative integer = 0

(v) The predecessor of –1 = –1 –1 = –2 and the successor of
–1 = –1 + 1 = 0

$\therefore$ Sum of predecessor and successor of –1 = –2 + 0 = –2

(i) $\to b$ (ii) $\to e$ (iii) $\to b$ (iv) $\to a$ (v) $\to b$

Que 16. If we denote the height of a place above sea level by a positive integer and depth below the sea level by a negative integer, write the following using integers with the appropriate signs

    (a) 200 m above sea level   (b) 100 m below sea level

    (c) 10 m above sea level   (d) sea level

Sol. Given, the height of a place above sea level is denoted by (+) sign and depth below the sea level by is denoted by (–) sign.

    (a) We can write 200 m above sea level as + 200 m because above sea level represent + sign.

    (b) We can write 100 m below sea level as – 100 m because below sea level represent – sign.

    (c) We can write 10 m above sea level as +100 m because above sea level represent + sign.

    (d) We can write sea level as 0 m because sea level is neither above nor below.

Que 17. Write two integers, whose sum is 6 and difference is also 6.

Sol. We know that, 0 is an integer such that if we add any integer to it then we get same integer and if we subtract it from any integer, then also we get same integer. So, possible two integers are 6 and 0.

    i.e. $6 + 0 = 6$ and $6 - 0 = 6$

Que 18. Observe the following :

$$1 + 2 - 3 + 4 + 5 - 6 - 7 + 8 - 9 = -5$$

Change one '–' sign as '+' sign to get the sum 9.

Sol. Given, $1 + 2 - 3 + 4 + 5 - 6 - 7 + 8 - 9 = -5$

Now, add 14 both sides, because we have to get the sum of 9.

$$1 + 2 - 3 + 4 + 5 - 6 - 7 + 8 - 9 + 14 = -5 + 14$$

Now, we can arrange the integer so that the positive integers and negative integers are grouped together.

$\therefore$ $1 + 2 + 4 + 5 + 8 + 14 + (-3) + (-6) + (-7) + (-9)$

$$= 1 + 2 + 4 + 5 + 8 + 14 - 3 - 6 - 7 - 9 = 34 - 25 = 9$$

As we add 14 on left hand side, we see that $(-7 + 14) = + 7$, it means that we have to change the sign of 7.

Que 19. The sum of two integers is 30. If one of the integers is −42, then find the other.

Sol. Given, the sum of two integers = 30 and one of the integer = −42

Now, the other integer is obtained by subtracting −42 from 30.

∴ The required integer = 30 − (−42) = 30 + 42 = 72

Hence, the second integer is 72.

Que 20. Arrange the following integers in the ascending order.
$$-2, 1, 0, -3, +4, -5$$

Sol. Integers −2, 1, 0, −3, +4, and −5 are on number line are shown as below

Now, increasing (ascending) order of these integers is
$$-5 < -3 < -2 < 0 < 1 < 4$$

Que 21. Write six distinct integers whose sum is 7.

Sol. Let the six integers be 1, 2, −2, 3, −3 and 6.

Now, sum of above integers = 1 + 2 + (−2) + 3 + (−3) + 6

We can arrange the numbers so that the positive integers and the negative integers are grouped together.

We have, i.e. = 1 + 2 + 3 + 6 + (−2) + (−3) = 12 − 2 − 3 = 12 − 5 = 7

Hence, required integers are 1, 2, −2, 3, −3 and 6.

> **Note** There are infinite combination exist.

Que 22. Write the integer, which is 4 more than its additive inverse.

Sol. Firstly, draw a number line.

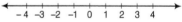

Let +1 be an integer and its additive inverse is −1. From the number line, we see that 2 more than its additive inverse. So, we reject this integer.

Again, let +2 be an integer and its additive inverse is −2. From the number line, we see that 4 more than its additive inverse.

Hence, the required integer is 2.

Que 23. Temperature of a place at 12 :00 noon was +5°C. Temperature increased by 3°C in first hour and decreased by 1°C in the second hour. What was the temperature at 2:00 pm?

Sol. Given, initial temperature at 12:00 noon was +5°C. Since, the temperature increased by 3°C in first hour.

∴Temperature at 1: 00 pm = 5°C + 3°C = 8°C

Also, the temperature decreased by 1°C in the second hour.

∴Temperature at 2:00 pm = 8°C – 1°C = 7°C

Hence, the temperature at 2:00 pm is 7°C.

Que 24. Write the digits 0, 1, 2, 3, ..., 9 in this order and insert '+' or '–' between them to get the result 3.

Sol. Arrange the given digit in given order, we have
$$0 - 1 - 2 - 3 - 4 - 5 - 6 + 7 + 8 + 9 = -21 + 24 = 3$$

Que 25. Subtract –5308 from the sum [(–2100) + (–2001)].

Sol. Firstly, we find the sum [(–2100) + (–2001)]

Sum of –2100 and –2001 = –2100 + (–2001) = –2100 – 2001 = –4101

Now, subtract –5308 from –4101.
$$-4101 - (-5308) = -4101 + 5308 = +1207$$

Que 26. Compute each of the following :

    (a) 30 + (– 25) + (– 10)   (b) (– 20) + (– 5)

    (c) 70 + (– 20) + (– 30)   (d) – 50 + (– 60) + 50

    (e) 1 + (– 2) + (– 3) + (– 4)   (f) 0 + (– 5) + (– 2)

    (g) 0 – (– 6) – (+ 6)   (h) 0 – 2 – (– 2)

Sol. (a) 30 + (– 25) + (– 10) = 30 – (25 + 10) = 30 – 35 = 30 + (– 30) + (– 5)

                      = 0 + (– 5) = – 5   [∵ + 30 – 30 = 0]

    (b) (– 20) + (– 5) = – (20 + 5) = – 25

    (c) 70 + (– 20) + (– 30) = 70 – (20 + 30) = 70 – 50

                      = (+ 20) + (+ 50) + (– 50)   [∵ 70 = 20 + 50]

                      = + 20 + 0 = 20

    (d) – 50 + (– 60) + 50 = – 50 + (– 10) + (– 50) + 50   [∵ 60 = 10 + 50]

                    = – 50 + (– 10) + 0 = – (50 + 10) = – 60

    (e) 1 + (– 2) + (– 3) + (– 4) = 1 – (2 + 3 + 4) = 1 – (9) = – 8

    (f) 0 + (– 5) + (– 2) = (– 5) + (– 2) = – (5 + 2) = – 7

    (g) 0 – (– 6) – (+ 6) = 0 – (– 6 + 6) = – (0) = 0

    (h) 0 – 2 – (– 2) = – 2 – (– 2) = – (2 – 2) = – (0) = 0

Que 27. Using number line, how do you compare

  (a) two negative integers?

  (b) two positive integers?

  (c) one positive and one negative integer?

Sol. We know that on the number line points to the right of zero are positive integers and points to the left of zero are negative integers. Also if move from left to the right on the number line, then number increases and if we move from right to the left on the number line, the number decreases.

  (a) If we compare two negative integers on the number line, then the number which is on right of the other number will be greater if

  e.g.

  Here, we see that – 2 is on the right of – 3, so – 2 is greater and – 3 is smaller.

  (b) If we compare two positive integers on the number line, then the number which is on right of the other number will be greater

  e.g.

  Here, we see that 3 is on right of the 1, so 3 is greater and 1 is smaller.

  (c) If we compare one positive and one negative integers on the number line, then the number which is on right of the other number will be greater.

  e.g.

  Here, we see that 2 is on right of the – 1, so 2 is greater and – 1 is smaller.

Chapter 7

Fractions

Important Points

- **Fraction** A fraction is a number representing part of a whole. The whole may be a single object or a group of objects.

  e.g. $\dfrac{7}{12}$ is a fraction and it reads as seven-twelfths, which means that 7 parts out of 12 equal parts in which the whole is divided. Also, here 7 is called the **numerator** and 12 is called the **denominator**.

- While expressing a situation of counting parts to write a fraction, it must be ensured that all parts are equal.

- Fractions can be shown on a number line. Every fraction has a point associated with it on the number line.

- **Proper fraction** A fraction whose numerator is always less than the denominator is called a proper fraction. It is always less than 1. So, if we represent a proper fraction on a number line, it always lies to the left of 1.

  e.g. $\dfrac{9}{10}, \dfrac{5}{8}$ are proper fractions.

- **Improper fraction** A fraction whose numerator is always greater than the denominator is called an improper fraction.

  e.g. $\dfrac{3}{2}, \dfrac{18}{5}$ are improper fractions.

  It is always greater than 1. So, if we represent an improper fraction on a number line, it always lies to the right of 1.

- **Mixed fraction** A combination of a whole number and a proper fraction (or part) is called a mixed fraction.

e.g. $1\frac{1}{4}$ is a mixed fraction. Here, 1 is a whole number and $\frac{1}{4}$ is a proper fraction.

■ To express an improper fraction as a mixed fraction, firstly divide the numerator by denominator to obtain the quotient and the remainder. Then,

$$\text{Mixed fraction} = \text{Quotient} \frac{\text{Remainder}}{\text{Divisor}}$$

e.g. Consider an improper fraction $= \frac{17}{4}$

Now, dividing numerator by denominator i.e. 17 by 4.

$$\begin{array}{r} 4\overline{)17}(4 \\ \underline{16} \\ 1 \end{array}$$

Hence, mixed fraction $= 4\frac{1}{4}$

■ We can also express a mixed fraction as an improper fraction as

$$\frac{(\text{Whole} \times \text{Denominator}) + \text{Numerator}}{\text{Denominator}}$$

e.g. Consider the mixed fraction $= 4\frac{5}{6}$

Now, improper fraction $= \frac{(4 \times 6) + 5}{6}$

$$= \frac{24 + 5}{6} = \frac{29}{6}$$

■ **Equivalent fractions** Fractions having the same values are called equivalent fractions. An equivalent fraction of a given fraction can be obtained by multiplying its numerator and denominator by the same number (other than zero).

e.g. Equivalent fractions of $\frac{1}{3}$ are $\frac{2}{6}$ (multiply by 2), $\frac{3}{9}$ (multiply by 3), $\frac{4}{12}$ (multiply by 4) and many more.

- We can check whether two fractions are equivalent or not by cross product i.e. we multiply the numerator of first fraction with the denominator of second fraction and the denominator of first fraction with the numerator of second fraction. If the two products are equal, then the given fractions are equivalent, otherwise not.

  e.g. Two fractions are $\dfrac{4}{5}$ and $\dfrac{28}{35}$.

  Here, numerator of first $\times$ denominator of second $= 4 \times 35 = 140$
  and denominator of first $\times$ numerator of second $= 5 \times 28 = 140$

  Since, the two products are same, so given fractions are equivalent.

- **Simplest form of a fraction** A fraction is said to be in the simplest (or lowest) form, if its numerator and denominator have no common factor except 1.

  To find the equivalent fraction in the simplest form, we find the HCF of the numerator and denominator and then divide both of them by the HCF. e.g. Consider the equivalent fraction $12 / 8$

  The HCF of 12 and 8 is 4.

  Therefore, $\qquad \dfrac{12}{8} = \dfrac{12 \div 4}{8 \div 4} = \dfrac{3}{2}$

  Thus, $\dfrac{3}{2}$ is the simplest form of a equivalent fraction.

- **Like fractions and unlike fractions** Fractions with same denominators are called like fractions. If their denominators are different, then they are called unlike fractions.

  e.g. $\dfrac{1}{14}, \dfrac{2}{14}, \dfrac{3}{14}$ are all like fractions and $\dfrac{1}{15}, \dfrac{7}{27}$ are unlike fractions.

- **Comparing fractions** To compare fractions, we use the following results.

  (i) **Comparing like fractions** If two fractions with the same denominator, then fraction with the greater numerator is greater.

  e.g. Between $\dfrac{11}{20}$ and $\dfrac{13}{20}, \dfrac{13}{20}$ is greater.

(ii) **Comparing unlike fractions** If the numerator is the same in two fractions, then the fraction with the smaller denominator is greater of the two.

e.g. between $\dfrac{2}{3}$ and $\dfrac{2}{5}, \dfrac{2}{3}$ is greater.

(iii) **Comparing unlike fractions with different numerators** If numerator and denominator both are different of given two fractions, then for comparing, we use the method of equivalent fractions i.e. we change the denominator of a fraction without changing its value. e.g. to compare $\dfrac{2}{3}$ and $\dfrac{3}{4}$. We get equivalent fractions of these as $\dfrac{8}{12}$ and $\dfrac{9}{12}$, respectively with the same denominator 12.

Now, $\dfrac{9}{12} > \dfrac{8}{12}$, so $\dfrac{3}{4} > \dfrac{2}{3}$

Note Here, the LCM of the denominators of the fractions is preferred as the common denominator.

■ **Addition and subtraction of like fractions** To add like fractions, we add their numerators keeping denominator unchanged and then write in simplest form. To subtract like fractions, we subtract the smaller numerator from the greater numerator, keeping denominator unchanged and then write in simplest form.

e.g. $\dfrac{5}{27} + \dfrac{4}{27} = \dfrac{5+4}{27} = \dfrac{9}{27}$ and $\dfrac{7}{12} - \dfrac{3}{12} = \dfrac{7-3}{12} = \dfrac{4}{12}$

$$= \dfrac{1}{3} \qquad\qquad \text{[simplest form]}$$

■ **Addition and subtraction of unlike fractions** To add or subtract unlike fractions, we first convert them into equivalent fractions with the same denominator (which is LCM of denominators) and then add or subtract them as like fractions.

e.g. $\dfrac{2}{5} + \dfrac{1}{3} = \dfrac{2 \times 3}{5 \times 3} + \dfrac{1 \times 5}{3 \times 5}$ [∵ LCM of 5 and 3 is 15]

$$= \dfrac{6}{15} + \dfrac{5}{15} = \dfrac{11}{15}$$

- **Addition and subtraction of mixed fractions** To add mixed fractions, we add whole part of first fraction to second fraction and fractional part of first fraction to second fraction.

or

First, we convert both mixed fractions into improper fractions and then add them by converting into equivalent fractions with the same denominator.

To subtract mixed fractions, we subtract smaller whole part from greater whole part and subtract corresponding fractional parts.

Exercises 7.1

Que 1. Write the fraction representing the shaded portion.

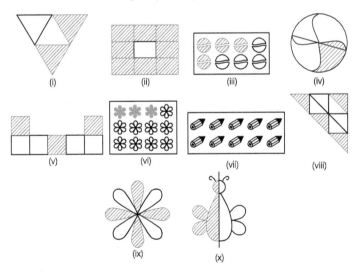

Sol. From the above figure,

(i) Total number of equal parts = 4; Shaded parts = 2

∴ Fraction representing the shaded portion

$$= \frac{\text{Number of shaded parts}}{\text{Total number of equal parts}} = \frac{2}{4}$$

(ii) Total number of equal parts = 9; Shaded parts = 8

∴ Fraction representing the shaded portion $= \dfrac{8}{9}$

(iii) Total number of equal parts = 8; Shaded parts = 4

∴ Fraction representing the shaded portion = $\dfrac{4}{8}$

(iv) Total number of equal parts = 4; Shaded part = 1

∴ Fraction representing the shaded portion = $\dfrac{1}{4}$

(v) Total number of equal parts = 7; Shaded parts = 3

∴ Fraction representing the shaded portion = $\dfrac{3}{7}$

(vi) Total number of equal parts = 12; Shaded parts = 3

∴ Fraction representing the shaded portion = $\dfrac{3}{12}$

(vii) Total number of equal parts = 10; Shaded parts = 10

∴ Fraction representing the shaded portion = $\dfrac{10}{10}$

(viii) Total number of equal parts = 9; Shaded parts = 4

∴ Fraction representing the shaded portion = $\dfrac{4}{9}$

(ix) Total number of equal parts = 8; Shaded parts = 4

∴ Fraction representing the shaded portion = $\dfrac{4}{8}$

(x) Total number of equal parts = 2; Shaded part = 1

∴ Fraction representing the shaded portion = $\dfrac{1}{2}$

Que 2. Colour the part according to the given fraction.

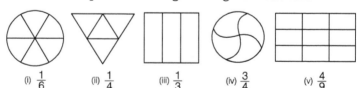

(i) $\dfrac{1}{6}$ (ii) $\dfrac{1}{4}$ (iii) $\dfrac{1}{3}$ (iv) $\dfrac{3}{4}$ (v) $\dfrac{4}{9}$

Sol.   (i) Here, fraction 1/6 shows that out of 6 equal parts 1 part is shaded. So, the required figure is

(ii) Here, fraction 1/4 shows that out of 4 equal parts 1 part is shaded. So, the required figure is

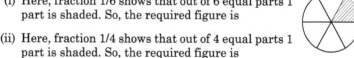

Sol. (i) Here, fraction $\dfrac{1}{6}$ shows that out of 6 equal parts 1 part is shaded. So, the required figure is

  (ii) Here, fraction $\dfrac{1}{4}$ shows that out of 4 equal parts 1 part is shaded. So, the required figure is

  (iii) Here, fraction $\dfrac{1}{3}$ shows that out of 3 equal parts 1 part is shaded. So, the required figure is

  (iv) Here, fraction $\dfrac{3}{4}$ shows that out of 4 equal parts 3 parts are shaded. So, the required figure is

  (v) Here, fraction $\dfrac{4}{9}$ shows that out of 9 equal parts 4 parts are shaded. So, the required figure is

Que 3. Identify the error, if any.

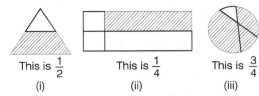

This is $\dfrac{1}{2}$	This is $\dfrac{1}{4}$	This is $\dfrac{3}{4}$
(i)	(ii)	(iii)

Sol. (i) In the given figure, shaded portion is not equal to unshaded portion. So, fraction is not equal to 1/2.

  (ii) In the given figure, four parts are not equal.

    ∴ Fraction is not equal to 1/4.

Que 6. Arya, Abhimanyu and Vivek shared lunch. Arya has brought two sandwiches, one made of vegetable and one of jam. The other two boys forgot to bring their lunch. Arya agreed to share his sandwiches so that each person will have an equal share of each sandwich.

(a) How can Arya divide his sandwiches so that each person has an equal share?

(b) What part of a sandwich will each boy receive?

Sol. Total number of sandwiches = 2; Total number of boys = 3

(a) Here, Arya has to divide 2 sandwiches into 3 persons. So, he will divide each sandwich into three equal parts and give one part of each sandwich to each of them. Thus, each person gets 2/3 sandwiches.

(b) One sandwich is to be divided among three boys.
∴ Each boy will get = 1/3 part of a sandwich.

Que 7. Kanchan dyes dresses. She had to dye 30 dresses. She has so far finished 20 dresses. What fraction of dresses has she finished?

Sol. Total number of dresses to be dyed = 30

Number of dresses finished = 20

∴ Required fraction of finished dresses $= \dfrac{20}{30} = \dfrac{2}{3}$

Que 8. Write the natural numbers from 2 to 12. What fraction of them are prime numbers?

Sol. Natural numbers from 2 to 12 = 2, 3, 4, 5, 6, 7, 8, 9, 10, 11, 12

Total natural numbers = 11

Prime numbers from 2 to 12 = 2, 3, 5, 7, 11

Total prime numbers = 5

∴   Required fraction $= \dfrac{\text{Total prime numbers}}{\text{Total natural numbers}} = \dfrac{5}{11}$

Que 9. Write the natural numbers from 102 to 113. What fraction of them are prime numbers?

Sol. Natural numbers from 102 to 113 = 102, 103, 104, 105, 106, 107, 108, 109, 110, 111, 112 and 113.

Total natural numbers = 12

Prime numbers from 102 to 113 = 103, 107, 109, 113

Total prime numbers = 4

∴   Required fraction $= \dfrac{\text{Total prime numbers}}{\text{Total natural numbers}} = \dfrac{4}{12} = \dfrac{1}{3}$

Que 10. What fraction of these circles have X's in them?

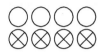

Sol. Total number of circles = 8; Number of circles having X's = 4

∴ Required fraction $= \dfrac{4}{8}$

Que 11. Kristin received a CD player for her birthday. She bought 3 CDs and received 5 others as gifts. What fraction of her total CDs did she buy and what fraction did she receive as gifts?

Sol. Number of CDs bought by Kristin = 3

Number of CDs received as gifts = 5

∴ Total number of CDs = 3 + 5 = 8

Hence, fraction of CDs bought by Kristin $= \dfrac{3}{8}$

and fraction of CDs, she received as gifts $= \dfrac{5}{8}$

Try These (Page 137)

Que 1. Show 3/5 on a number line.

Sol. We know that, 3/5 is greater than zero but less than 1. So, it will lie between 0 and 1.

Since, we have to show 3/5, so we have to divide the gap between 0 and 1 into five equal parts. Then, each part shows 1/5 and 3 parts will show 3/5.

$$\underset{\substack{\dfrac{0}{5} \quad \dfrac{1}{5} \quad \dfrac{2}{5} \quad \dfrac{3}{5} \quad \dfrac{4}{5} \quad \dfrac{5}{5}=1}}{\xleftarrow{\qquad\overset{A}{\underset{}{}}\qquad\xrightarrow{\quad}}} \qquad \left[\text{also } \dfrac{0}{5}=0\right]$$

Hence, point A represents 3/5.

Que 2. Show $\dfrac{1}{10}, \dfrac{0}{10}, \dfrac{5}{10}$ and $\dfrac{10}{10}$ on a number line.

Sol. We know that, all given fractions are greater than zero but less than or equal to 1. So, they will lie between 0 and 1.

So, we have to divide the gap between 0 and 1 into ten equal parts, then each part shows $\dfrac{1}{10}$ and 5 parts show $\dfrac{5}{10}$, 10 parts show $\dfrac{10}{10}$. Also, 0 shows $\dfrac{0}{10}$. $\left[\text{also } \dfrac{0}{5} = 0\right]$

Hence, points A, B, C and D respectively represent the fractions $\dfrac{0}{10}$, $\dfrac{1}{10}$, $\dfrac{5}{10}$ and $\dfrac{10}{10}$.

Que 3. Can you show any other fraction between 0 and 1?

Write five more fractions that you can show and depict them on the number line.

Sol. Yes, we can show many other fractions which are greater than 0 and less than 1 i.e. between 0 and 1.

Five other fractions are $\dfrac{1}{8}, \dfrac{2}{8}, \dfrac{3}{8}, \dfrac{4}{8}$ and $\dfrac{5}{8}$.

These fractions are shown on a number line as given below

Here, points A, B, C, D and E represent $\dfrac{1}{8}, \dfrac{2}{8}, \dfrac{3}{8}, \dfrac{4}{8}$ and $\dfrac{5}{8}$ respectively.

Que 4. How many fractions lie between 0 and 1? Think, discuss and write your answer?

Sol. There are infinite number of points between 0 and 1 on the number line. So, there are infinite number of fractions between 0 and 1.

Try These (Page 138)

Que 5. Give a proper fraction,

(a) whose numerator is 5 and denominator is 7.

(b) whose denominator is 9 and numerator is 5.

(c) whose numerator and denominator add upto 10. How many fractions of this kind can you make?

(d) whose denominator is 4 more than the numerator.

Give any five. How many more can you make?

Sol. (a) Numerator = 5 and Denominator = 7

∴ Required fraction = $\dfrac{5}{7}$

(b) Numerator = 5 and Denominator = 9

∴ Required fraction = $\dfrac{5}{9}$

(c) Possible pairs of numerator and denominator which add upto 10 are (0,10), (1, 9), (2, 8), (3, 7) and (4, 6).

Now, proper fractions = $\dfrac{0}{10}, \dfrac{1}{9}, \dfrac{2}{8}, \dfrac{3}{7}$ and $\dfrac{4}{6}$.

There are five fractions. So, we can make five such fractions.

(d) There can be infinite number of fractions whose denominator is 4 more than the numerator. Some of them are $\dfrac{0}{4}, \dfrac{1}{5}, \dfrac{2}{6}, \dfrac{3}{7}$ and $\dfrac{4}{8}$.

Que 6. A fraction is given.

How will you decide, by just looking at it, whether the fraction is

(a) less than 1?   (b) equal to 1?

Sol. (a) In a fraction, if numerator is less than denominator, then the fraction is less than 1.

(b) In a fraction, if numerator is equal to denominator, then the fraction is equal to 1.

Que 7. Fill up using one of these : '>', '<' or '='

(a) $\dfrac{1}{2} \,\square\, 1$ (b) $\dfrac{3}{5} \,\square\, 1$ (c) $1 \,\square\, \dfrac{7}{8}$

(d) $\dfrac{4}{4} \,\square\, 1$ (e) $\dfrac{2005}{2005} \,\square\, 1$

TIPS

If LHS (left hand side) is greater than RHS (right hand side), then put > (greater than), If LHS is less than RHS, then put < (less than) and if LHS equals RHS, then put = (equal to).

Sol. (a) $\dfrac{1}{2} \,\boxed{<}\, 1$ (b) $\dfrac{3}{5} \,\boxed{<}\, 1$ (c) $1 \,\boxed{>}\, \dfrac{7}{8}$

(d) $\dfrac{4}{4} \,\boxed{=}\, 1$ (e) $\dfrac{2005}{2005} \,\boxed{=}\, 1$

Exercise 7.2

Que 1. Draw number lines and locate the points on them.

(a) $\dfrac{1}{2}, \dfrac{1}{4}, \dfrac{3}{4}, \dfrac{4}{4}$ (b) $\dfrac{1}{8}, \dfrac{2}{8}, \dfrac{3}{8}, \dfrac{7}{8}$ (c) $\dfrac{2}{5}, \dfrac{3}{5}, \dfrac{8}{5}, \dfrac{4}{5}$

Sol. (a) Here, fractions are $\dfrac{1}{2}, \dfrac{1}{4}, \dfrac{3}{4}, \dfrac{4}{4}$ Also, $\dfrac{1}{2} = \dfrac{1 \times 2}{2 \times 2} = \dfrac{2}{4}$

Now, draw a number line, mark two points 0 and 1 on it. Divide the gap between 0 and 1 into four equal parts because denominator is 4, then each part will show $\dfrac{1}{4}$. Also, 2 parts show $\dfrac{2}{4}$, 3 parts show $\dfrac{3}{4}$ and 4 parts show $\dfrac{4}{4}$.

$$\begin{array}{ccccc} & A & B & C & D \\ 0 & \frac{1}{4} & \frac{2}{4} & \frac{3}{4} & \frac{4}{4}=1 \end{array}$$

Here, A, B, C and D represent $\dfrac{1}{4}, \dfrac{2}{4}, \dfrac{3}{4}$ and $\dfrac{4}{4}$ respectively.

(b) Here, fractions are $\dfrac{1}{8}, \dfrac{2}{8}, \dfrac{3}{8}$ and $\dfrac{7}{8}$.

Now, draw a number line, mark two points 0 and 1 on it. Divide the gap between 0 and 1 into eight equal parts because denominator is 8, then each part will show $\dfrac{1}{8}$. Also, 2 parts show $\dfrac{2}{8}$, 3 parts show $\dfrac{3}{8}$ and 7 parts show $\dfrac{7}{8}$.

$$\begin{array}{ccccccccc} & A & B & C & & & & D & \\ 0 & \frac{1}{8} & \frac{2}{8} & \frac{3}{8} & \frac{4}{8} & \frac{5}{8} & \frac{6}{8} & \frac{7}{8} & \frac{8}{8}=1 \end{array}$$

Hence, A, B, C and D represent $\dfrac{1}{8}, \dfrac{2}{8}, \dfrac{3}{8}$ and $\dfrac{7}{8}$ respectively.

(c) Here, fractions are $\dfrac{2}{5}, \dfrac{3}{5}, \dfrac{8}{5}$ and $\dfrac{4}{5}$.

Now, draw a number line, mark two points 0 and 1 on it. Divide the gap between 0 and 1 into five equal parts because

denominator is 5, then each part will show $\dfrac{1}{5}$. Also, 2 parts show $\dfrac{2}{5}$, 3 parts show $\dfrac{3}{5}$ and 4 parts show $\dfrac{4}{5}$.

denominator is 8, then each part will show $\frac{1}{8}$. Also, 2 parts show $\frac{2}{8}$, 3 parts show $\frac{3}{8}$ and 7 parts show $\frac{7}{8}$.

Hence, A, B, C and D represent $\frac{1}{8}, \frac{2}{8}, \frac{3}{8}$ and $\frac{7}{8}$ respectively.

(c) Here, fractions are $\frac{2}{5}, \frac{3}{5}, \frac{8}{5}$ and $\frac{4}{5}$.

Now, draw a number line, mark two points 0 and 1 on it. Divide the gap between 0 and 1 into five equal parts because denominator is 5, then each part will show $\frac{1}{5}$. Also, 2 parts show $\frac{2}{5}$, 3 parts show $\frac{3}{5}$ and 4 parts show $\frac{4}{5}$.

Here, A, B and C represent $\frac{2}{5}, \frac{3}{5}$ and $\frac{4}{5}$ respectively.

For representation of $\frac{8}{5}$,

Draw a number line. Take a point 0 on it. Let it represents O.

Here, $\qquad \frac{8}{5} = 1\frac{3}{5} = 1 + \frac{3}{5}$

Mark point A on the number line at unit distance from 0 to the right and mark point B at unit distance from 1 to the right. Let these segments be OA and AB. Then, clearly points A and B represent 1 and 2 respectively which is shown below

Take 1 unit length to the right of 0. Divide the 2nd unit AB into five equal parts, here each part will represent $\frac{1}{5}$. Take 3 parts out of 5 parts to reach at M. Then, M represents $\frac{8}{5}$.

Que 2. Express the following as mixed fractions.

(a) $\dfrac{20}{3}$ (b) $\dfrac{11}{5}$ (c) $\dfrac{17}{7}$

(d) $\dfrac{28}{5}$ (e) $\dfrac{19}{6}$ (f) $\dfrac{35}{9}$

To express an improper fraction as a mixed fraction, firstly divide the numerator by denominator to obtain the quotient and the remainder. Then,

$$\text{Mixed fraction} = \text{Quotient} \dfrac{\text{Remainder}}{\text{Divisor}}$$

Sol. (a) We have, $\dfrac{20}{3}$

$$3\overline{)20}(6$$
$$\underline{18}$$
$$2$$

On dividing 20 by 3, we get quotient $= 6$, remainder $= 2$

$\therefore \qquad \dfrac{20}{3} = 6\dfrac{2}{3}$ i.e. 6 whole and $\dfrac{2}{3}$ more

(b) We have, $\dfrac{11}{5}$

$$5\overline{)11}(2$$
$$\underline{10}$$
$$1$$

On dividing 11 by 5, we get quotient $= 2$, remainder $= 1$

$\therefore \dfrac{11}{5} = 2\dfrac{1}{5}$ i.e. 2 whole and $\dfrac{1}{5}$ more

(c) We have, $\dfrac{17}{7}$

$$7\overline{)17}(2$$
$$\underline{14}$$
$$3$$

On dividing 17 by 7, we get quotient $= 2$, remainder $= 3$

$\therefore \qquad \dfrac{17}{7} = 2\dfrac{3}{7}$ i.e. 2 whole and $\dfrac{3}{7}$ more

(d) We have, $\dfrac{28}{5}$

$$5\overline{)28}(5$$
$$\underline{25}$$
$$3$$

On dividing 28 by 5, we get quotient $= 5$, remainder $= 3$

$\therefore \qquad \dfrac{28}{5} = 5\dfrac{3}{5}$ i.e. 5 whole and $\dfrac{3}{5}$ more

(e) We have, $\dfrac{19}{6}$

$$6\overline{)19}(3$$
$$\underline{18}$$
$$1$$

On dividing 19 by 6, we get quotient $= 3$, remainder $= 1$

$\therefore \qquad \dfrac{19}{6} = 3\dfrac{1}{6}$ i.e. 3 whole and $\dfrac{1}{6}$ more

(f) We have, $\dfrac{35}{9}$

$9\overline{)35}(3$
27
$\overline{8}$

On dividing 35 by 9, we get quotient = 3, remainder = 8

$\therefore \dfrac{35}{9} = 3\dfrac{8}{9}$ i.e. 3 whole and $\dfrac{8}{9}$ more

Que 3. Express the following as improper fractions.

(a) $7\dfrac{3}{4}$ (b) $5\dfrac{6}{7}$ (c) $2\dfrac{5}{6}$

(d) $10\dfrac{3}{5}$ (e) $9\dfrac{3}{7}$ (f) $8\dfrac{4}{9}$

 TIPS

> We can express a mixed fraction as an improper fraction as
> $$\dfrac{(\text{Whole} \times \text{Denominator}) + \text{Numerator}}{\text{Denominator}}$$

Sol. (a) $7\dfrac{3}{4} = 7 + \dfrac{3}{4} = \dfrac{7 \times 4 + 3}{4} = \dfrac{31}{4}$ (b) $5\dfrac{6}{7} = 5 + \dfrac{6}{7} = \dfrac{5 \times 7 + 6}{7} = \dfrac{41}{7}$

(c) $2\dfrac{5}{6} = 2 + \dfrac{5}{6} = \dfrac{2 \times 6 + 5}{6} = \dfrac{17}{6}$ (d) $10\dfrac{3}{5} = 10 + \dfrac{3}{5} = \dfrac{10 \times 5 + 3}{5} = \dfrac{53}{5}$

(e) $9\dfrac{3}{7} = 9 + \dfrac{3}{7} = \dfrac{9 \times 7 + 3}{7} = \dfrac{66}{7}$ (f) $8\dfrac{4}{9} = 8 + \dfrac{4}{9} = \dfrac{8 \times 9 + 4}{9} = \dfrac{76}{9}$

Try These (Page 142)

Que 1. Are $\dfrac{1}{3}$ and $\dfrac{2}{7}$; $\dfrac{2}{5}$ and $\dfrac{2}{7}$; $\dfrac{2}{9}$ and $\dfrac{6}{27}$ equivalent? Give reason.

 TIPS

> Firstly, multiply the numerator of first fraction by denominator of
> second fraction and multiply the denominator of first fraction by
> numerator of second fraction. If both products are same, then given
> fractions are equivalent and if both products are not same, then given
> fractions are not equivalent.

Sol. (i) $\dfrac{1}{3}$ and $\dfrac{2}{7}$

Here, $1 \times 7 = 7$ and $3 \times 2 = 6$

$\because$ $7 \neq 6$, so $\dfrac{1}{3}$ and $\dfrac{2}{7}$ are not equivalent fractions.

(ii) $\dfrac{2}{5}$ and $\dfrac{2}{7}$

Here, $2 \times 7 = 14$ and $5 \times 2 = 10$

∵ $14 \neq 10$, so $\dfrac{2}{5}$ and $\dfrac{2}{7}$ are not equivalent fractions.

(iii) $\dfrac{2}{9}$ and $\dfrac{6}{27}$

Here, $2 \times 27 = 54$ and $9 \times 6 = 54$

∵ $54 = 54$, so $\dfrac{2}{9}$ and $\dfrac{6}{27}$ are equivalent fractions.

Que 2. Give examples of four equivalent fractions.

Sol. Four equivalent fractions are $\dfrac{1}{2}, \dfrac{2}{4}, \dfrac{3}{6}, \dfrac{4}{8}$, etc.

Que 3. Identify the fractions in each. Are these fractions equivalent?

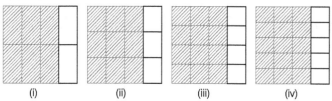

    (i)   (ii)   (iii)   (iv)

Sol. (i) Here, total parts are 8, out of which 6 parts are shaded.

So, required fraction $= \dfrac{6}{8}$

(ii) Here, total parts are 12, out of which 9 parts are shaded.

So, required fraction $= \dfrac{9}{12}$

(iii) Here, total parts are 16, out of which 12 parts are shaded.

So, required fraction $= \dfrac{12}{16}$

(iv) Here, total parts are 20, out of which 15 parts are shaded.

So, required fraction $= \dfrac{15}{20}$

Now, take $\dfrac{6}{8}$ and $\dfrac{9}{12}$

Here, $6 \times 12 = 72$ and $8 \times 9 = 72$

∵ $72 = 72$, so $\dfrac{6}{8}$ and $\dfrac{9}{12}$ are equivalent.

Now, take $\dfrac{9}{12}$ and $\dfrac{12}{16}$

Here, $9 \times 16 = 144$ and $12 \times 12 = 144$

$\because \qquad 144 = 144$, so $\dfrac{9}{12}$ and $\dfrac{12}{16}$ are equivalent.

Now, take $\dfrac{12}{16}$ and $\dfrac{15}{20}$

Here, $12 \times 20 = 240$ and $16 \times 15 = 240$

$\because \qquad 240 = 240$, so $\dfrac{12}{16}$ and $\dfrac{15}{20}$ are equivalent.

Hence, all these fractions are equivalent because they represent same parts of whole.

Try These (Page 143)

Que 4. Find five equivalent fractions of each of the following :

(i) $\dfrac{2}{3}$ (ii) $\dfrac{1}{5}$ (iii) $\dfrac{3}{5}$ (iv) $\dfrac{5}{9}$

> **TIPS**
> To find an equivalent fraction of a given fraction, we will multiply both numerator and denominator of the given fraction by the same number.

Sol. (i) Five equivalent fractions of $\dfrac{2}{3}$ are as follows:

$$\dfrac{2}{3} = \dfrac{2 \times 2}{3 \times 2} = \dfrac{4}{6}; \qquad \dfrac{2}{3} = \dfrac{2 \times 3}{3 \times 3} = \dfrac{6}{9}; \qquad \dfrac{2}{3} = \dfrac{2 \times 4}{3 \times 4} = \dfrac{8}{12}$$

$$\dfrac{2}{3} = \dfrac{2 \times 5}{3 \times 5} = \dfrac{10}{15}; \qquad \dfrac{2}{3} = \dfrac{2 \times 6}{3 \times 6} = \dfrac{12}{18}$$

Thus, five equivalent fractions of $\dfrac{2}{3}$ are $\dfrac{4}{6}, \dfrac{6}{9}, \dfrac{8}{12}, \dfrac{10}{15}$ and $\dfrac{12}{18}$.

(ii) Five equivalent fractions of $\dfrac{1}{5}$ are as follows:

$$\dfrac{1}{5} = \dfrac{1 \times 2}{5 \times 2} = \dfrac{2}{10}; \qquad \dfrac{1}{5} = \dfrac{1 \times 3}{5 \times 3} = \dfrac{3}{15}; \qquad \dfrac{1}{5} = \dfrac{1 \times 4}{5 \times 4} = \dfrac{4}{20}$$

$$\dfrac{1}{5} = \dfrac{1 \times 5}{5 \times 5} = \dfrac{5}{25}; \qquad \dfrac{1}{5} = \dfrac{1 \times 6}{5 \times 6} = \dfrac{6}{30}$$

Thus, five equivalent fractions of $\dfrac{1}{5}$ are $\dfrac{2}{10}, \dfrac{3}{15}, \dfrac{4}{20}, \dfrac{5}{25}$ and $\dfrac{6}{30}$.

(iii) Five equivalent fractions of $\dfrac{3}{5}$ are as follows:

$$\dfrac{3}{5} = \dfrac{3 \times 2}{5 \times 2} = \dfrac{6}{10}; \qquad \dfrac{3}{5} = \dfrac{3 \times 3}{5 \times 3} = \dfrac{9}{15}; \qquad \dfrac{3}{5} = \dfrac{3 \times 4}{5 \times 4} = \dfrac{12}{20}$$

$$\dfrac{3}{5} = \dfrac{3 \times 5}{5 \times 5} = \dfrac{15}{25}; \qquad \dfrac{3}{5} = \dfrac{3 \times 6}{5 \times 6} = \dfrac{18}{30}$$

Thus, five equivalent fractions of $\dfrac{3}{5}$ are $\dfrac{6}{10}, \dfrac{9}{15}, \dfrac{12}{20}, \dfrac{15}{25}$ and $\dfrac{18}{30}$.

(iv) Five equivalent fractions of $\dfrac{5}{9}$ are as follows:

$$\dfrac{5}{9} = \dfrac{5 \times 2}{9 \times 2} = \dfrac{10}{18}; \qquad \dfrac{5}{9} = \dfrac{5 \times 3}{9 \times 3} = \dfrac{15}{27}; \qquad \dfrac{5}{9} = \dfrac{5 \times 4}{9 \times 4} = \dfrac{20}{36}$$

$$\dfrac{5}{9} = \dfrac{5 \times 5}{9 \times 5} = \dfrac{25}{45}; \qquad \dfrac{5}{9} = \dfrac{5 \times 6}{9 \times 6} = \dfrac{30}{54}$$

Thus, five equivalent fractions of $\dfrac{5}{9}$ are $\dfrac{10}{18}, \dfrac{15}{27}, \dfrac{20}{36}, \dfrac{25}{45}$ and $\dfrac{30}{54}$.

Try These (Page 146)

Que 5. Write the simplest form of

(i) $\dfrac{15}{75}$ (ii) $\dfrac{16}{72}$ (iii) $\dfrac{17}{51}$

(iv) $\dfrac{42}{28}$ (v) $\dfrac{80}{24}$

TIPS
A fraction is said to be in the simplest form, (lowest form) if its numerator and denominator have no common factor except 1. So, to convert in simplest form, divide numerator and denominator both by their HCF.

Sol. (i) We have, $\dfrac{15}{75}$

Now,   factors of $15 = \boxed{3} \times \boxed{5}$

and   factors of $75 = \boxed{3} \times \boxed{5} \times 5$

Common factors = 3 and 5

∴   HCF of 15 and 75 $= 3 \times 5 = 15$

Then, $\dfrac{15}{75} = \dfrac{15 \div 15}{75 \div 15} = \dfrac{1}{5}$

Hence, fraction 1/5 is the simplest form of given fraction.

(ii) We have, $\dfrac{16}{72}$

Now,   factors of $16 = \boxed{2} \times \boxed{2} \times \boxed{2} \times 2$

and   factors of $72 = \boxed{2} \times \boxed{2} \times \boxed{2} \times 3 \times 3$

Common factors = 2, 2 and 2

∴   HCF of 16 and 72 $= 2 \times 2 \times 2 = 8$

Then, $\dfrac{16}{72} = \dfrac{16 \div 8}{72 \div 8} = \dfrac{2}{9}$

Hence, fraction $\dfrac{2}{9}$ is the simplest form of given fraction.

(iii) We have, $\dfrac{17}{51}$

     Now,   factors of $17 = \boxed{17}$

     and   factors of $51 = \underline{17} \times 3$

     Common factor $= 17$

     $\therefore$ HCF of 17 and $51 = 17$

     Then, $\dfrac{17}{51} = \dfrac{17 \div 17}{51 \div 17} = \dfrac{1}{3}$

     Hence, fraction $\dfrac{1}{3}$ is the simplest form of given fraction.

(iv) We have, $\dfrac{42}{28}$

     Now,   factors of $42 = \boxed{2} \times 3 \times \boxed{7}$

     and   factors of $28 = \boxed{2} \times 2 \times \boxed{7}$

     Common factors $= 2$ and 7

     $\therefore$ HCF of 42 and $28 = 2 \times 7 = 14$

     Then, $\dfrac{42}{28} = \dfrac{42 \div 14}{28 \div 14} = \dfrac{3}{2}$

     Hence, fraction $\dfrac{3}{2}$ is the simplest form of given fraction.

(v) We have, $\dfrac{80}{24}$

     Now,   factors of $80 = \boxed{2} \times \boxed{2} \times \boxed{2} \times 2 \times 5$

     and   factors of $24 = \boxed{2} \times \boxed{2} \times \boxed{2} \times 3$

     Common factors $= 2, 2$ and 2

     $\therefore$ HCF of 80 and $24 = 2 \times 2 \times 2 = 8$

     Then, $\dfrac{80}{24} = \dfrac{80 \div 8}{24 \div 8} = \dfrac{10}{3}$

     Hence, fraction $\dfrac{10}{3}$ is the simplest form of given fraction.

Que 6. Is $\dfrac{49}{64}$ in its simplest form?

Sol. Here, factors of $49 = 7 \times 7$ and   factors of $64 = 8 \times 8$

    $\therefore$ 49 and 64 have no common factor except 1.

    Hence, fraction $\dfrac{49}{64}$ is in simplest form.

Exercise 7.3

Que 1. Write the fractions. Are all these fractions equivalent?

(a)

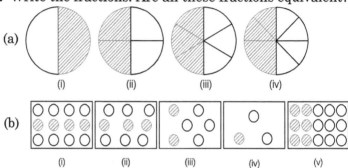

(i) (ii) (iii) (iv)

(b)

(i) (ii) (iii) (iv) (v)

TIPS

To write the fractions, firstly find number of equal parts and number of shaded parts, then

$$\text{Fraction} = \frac{\text{Number of shaded parts}}{\text{Total number of equal parts}}$$

Now, convert all these fractions in simplest form. If simplest form is same, then these fractions will be equivalent otherwise not.

Sol. (a) (i) Total number of equal parts = 2; Number of shaded parts = 1

∴ Fraction for shaded portion = $\dfrac{\text{Number of shaded parts}}{\text{Total number of equal paarts}} = \dfrac{1}{2}$

(ii) Total number of equal parts = 4; Number of shaded parts = 2

∴ Fraction for shaded portion = 2/4

(iii) Total number of equal parts = 6; Number of shaded parts = 3

∴ Fraction for shaded portion = 3/6

(iv) Total number of equal parts = 8; Number of shaded parts = 4

∴ Fraction for shaded portion = 4/8

Now,

$$\frac{2}{4} = \frac{2 \div 2}{4 \div 2} = \frac{1}{2} \qquad [\because \text{HCF of 2 and 4 is 2}]$$

$$\frac{3}{6} = \frac{3 \div 3}{6 \div 3} = \frac{1}{2} \qquad [\because \text{HCF of 3 and 6 is 3}]$$

$$\frac{4}{8} = \frac{4 \div 4}{8 \div 4} = \frac{1}{2} \qquad [\because \text{HCF of 4 and 8 is 4}]$$

Since, all fractions in simplest form are same.

∴ $\dfrac{1}{2} = \dfrac{2}{4} = \dfrac{3}{6} = \dfrac{4}{8}$ i.e. the fractions are equivalent.

(b) (i) Total number of equal parts $= 12$
   Number of shaded parts $= 4$
   $\therefore$ Fraction for shaded portion $= \dfrac{4}{12}$

(ii) Total number of equal parts $= 9$
   Number of shaded parts $= 3$
   $\therefore$ Fraction for shaded portion $= 3/9$

(iii) Total number of equal parts $= 6$; Number of shaded parts $= 2$
   $\because$ Fraction for shaded portion $= 2/6$

(iv) Total number of equal parts $= 3$; Number of shaded parts $= 1$
   $\therefore$ Fraction for shaded portion $= 1/3$

(v) Total number of equal parts $= 15$; Number of shaded parts $= 6$
   $\therefore$ Fraction for shaded portion $= \dfrac{6}{15}$

Now, $\quad \dfrac{4}{12} = \dfrac{4 \div 4}{12 \div 4} = \dfrac{1}{3}$ $\qquad$ [$\because$ HCF of 4 and 12 is 4]

$\qquad\quad \dfrac{3}{9} = \dfrac{3 \div 3}{9 \div 3} = \dfrac{1}{3}$ $\qquad$ [$\because$ HCF of 3 and 9 is 3]

$\qquad\quad \dfrac{2}{6} = \dfrac{2 \div 2}{6 \div 2} = \dfrac{1}{3}$ $\qquad$ [$\because$ HCF of 2 and 6 is 2]

$\qquad\quad \dfrac{6}{15} = \dfrac{6 \div 3}{15 \div 3} = \dfrac{2}{5}$ $\qquad$ [$\because$ HCF of 6 and 15 is 3]

Here, except $\dfrac{6}{15}$ all the fractions in simplest form are same.

So, $\qquad \dfrac{4}{12} = \dfrac{3}{9} = \dfrac{2}{6} = \dfrac{1}{3} \neq \dfrac{2}{5}$

Hence, these fraction are not equivalent.

Que 2. Write the fractions and pair up the equivalent fractions from each row.

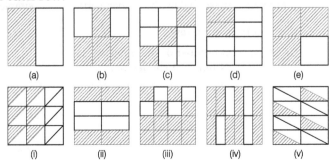

Sol. (a) Here, total number of equal parts = 2; Number of shaded parts = 1

$\therefore$ Fraction represented by the shaded portion $= \dfrac{1}{2}$ [simplest form]

(b) Here, total number of equal parts = 6
Number of shaded parts = 4

$\therefore$ Fraction represented by the shaded portion $= \dfrac{4}{6}$

$$= \dfrac{4 \div 2}{6 \div 2} \qquad \text{[}\because \text{ HCF of 4 and 6 is 2]}$$

$$= \dfrac{2}{3} \qquad \text{[simplest form]}$$

(c) Here, total number of equal parts = 9
Number of shaded parts = 3

$\therefore$ Fraction represented by the shaded portion $= \dfrac{3}{9}$

$$= \dfrac{3 \div 3}{9 \div 3} \qquad \text{[}\because \text{ HCF of 3 and 9 is 3]}$$

$$= \dfrac{1}{3} \qquad \text{[simplest form]}$$

(d) Here, total number of equal parts = 8
Number of shaded parts = 2

$\therefore$ Fraction represented by the shaded portion $= \dfrac{2}{8}$

$$= \dfrac{2 \div 2}{8 \div 2} \qquad \text{[}\because \text{ HCF of 2 and 8 is 2]}$$

$$= \dfrac{1}{4} \qquad \text{[simplest form]}$$

(e) Here, total number of equal parts = 4
Number of shaded parts = 3

$\therefore$ Fraction represented by the shaded portion $= \dfrac{3}{4}$ [simplest form]

Now, taking second row

(i) Here, total number of equal parts = 18
Number of shaded parts = 6

$\therefore$ Fraction represented by the shaded portion $= \dfrac{6}{18}$

$$= \dfrac{6 \div 6}{18 \div 6} \qquad \text{[}\because \text{ HCF of 6 and 18 is 6]}$$

$$= \dfrac{1}{3} \qquad \text{[simplest form]}$$

(ii) Here, total number of equal parts = 8

Number of shaded parts = 4

∴ Fraction represented by the shaded portion $= \dfrac{4}{8}$

$$= \dfrac{4 \div 4}{8 \div 4} \qquad [\because \text{HCF of 4 and 8 is 4}]$$

$$= \dfrac{1}{2} \qquad \text{[simplest form]}$$

(iii) Here, total number of equal parts = 16

Number of shaded parts = 12

∴ Fraction represented by the shaded portion $= \dfrac{12}{16}$

$$= \dfrac{12 \div 4}{16 \div 4} \qquad [\because \text{HCF of 12 and 16 is 4}]$$

$$= \dfrac{3}{4} \qquad \text{[simplest form]}$$

(iv) Here, total number of equal parts = 12

Number of shaded parts = 8

∴ Fraction represented by the shaded portion $= \dfrac{8}{12}$

$$= \dfrac{8 \div 4}{12 \div 4} \qquad [\because \text{HCF of 8 and 12 is 4}]$$

$$= \dfrac{2}{3} \qquad \text{[simplest form]}$$

(v) Here, total number of equal parts = 16

Number of shaded parts = 4

∴ Fraction represented by the shaded portion $= \dfrac{4}{16}$

$$= \dfrac{4 \div 4}{16 \div 4} \qquad [\because \text{HCF of 4 and 16 is 4}]$$

$$= \dfrac{1}{4} \qquad \text{[simplest form]}$$

Now, the equivalent fractions are

(a) → (ii) $\left[\because \dfrac{1}{2} = \dfrac{1}{2}\right];$ (b) → (iv) $\left[\because \dfrac{2}{3} = \dfrac{2}{3}\right]$

(c) → (i) $\left[\because \dfrac{1}{3} = \dfrac{1}{3}\right];$ (d) → (v) $\left[\because \dfrac{1}{4} = \dfrac{1}{4}\right]$

(e) → (iii) $\left[\because \dfrac{3}{4} = \dfrac{3}{4}\right]$

Que 3. Replace ☐ in each of the following by the correct number.

(a) $\dfrac{2}{7} = \dfrac{8}{\square}$ (b) $\dfrac{5}{8} = \dfrac{10}{\square}$ (c) $\dfrac{3}{5} = \dfrac{\square}{20}$

(d) $\dfrac{45}{60} = \dfrac{15}{\square}$ (e) $\dfrac{18}{24} = \dfrac{\square}{4}$

Sol. (a) We have, $\dfrac{2}{7} = \dfrac{8}{\square}$

∴ $2 \times \square = 7 \times 8$

So, $2 \times \square = 7 \times 2 \times 4 = 28 \times 2$ [∵ $8 = 2 \times 4$]

or $2 \times \square = 2 \times 28$

On comparing, we get ☐ $= 28$

Hence, $\dfrac{2}{7} = \dfrac{8}{\boxed{28}}$

(b) We have, $\dfrac{5}{8} = \dfrac{10}{\square}$

∴ $5 \times \square = 8 \times 10$

So, $5 \times \square = 8 \times 2 \times 5 = 16 \times 5$ [∵ $10 = 2 \times 5$]

or $5 \times \square = 5 \times 16$

On comparing, we get ☐ $= 16$

Hence, $\dfrac{5}{8} = \dfrac{10}{\boxed{16}}$

(c) We have, $\dfrac{3}{5} = \dfrac{\square}{20}$

∴ $3 \times 20 = 5 \times \square$

So, $3 \times 5 \times 4 = 5 \times \square$ [∵ $20 = 5 \times 4$]

or $5 \times 12 = 5 \times \square$

On comparing, we get ☐ $= 12$

Hence, $\dfrac{3}{5} = \dfrac{\boxed{12}}{20}$

(d) We have, $\dfrac{45}{60} = \dfrac{15}{\square}$

∴ $45 \times \square = 15 \times 60$

So, $45 \times \square = 15 \times 20 \times 3$ [∵ $60 = 20 \times 3$]

or $45 \times \square = 45 \times 20$

On comparing, we get ☐ $= 20$

Hence, $\dfrac{45}{60} = \dfrac{15}{\boxed{20}}$

(e) We have, $\dfrac{18}{24} = \dfrac{\square}{4}$

∴ $24 \times \square = 18 \times 4$

So, $6 \times 4 \times \square = 6 \times 3 \times 4$ [∵ $24 = 6 \times 4$ and $18 = 6 \times 3$]

$24 \times \square = 24 \times 3$

On comparing, we get $\square = 3$

Hence, $\dfrac{18}{24} = \dfrac{\boxed{3}}{4}$

Que 4. Find the equivalent fraction of $\dfrac{3}{5}$ having

(a) denominator 20   (b) numerator 9
(c) denominator 30   (d) numerator 27

Sol. Let N stands for the numerator and D stands for the denominator.

(a) Given, denominator of an equivalent fraction $= 20$

∴ $\dfrac{N}{20} = \dfrac{3}{5} \Rightarrow N \times 5 = 20 \times 3$

So, $N \times 5 = 4 \times 5 \times 3$ [but $20 = 4 \times 5$]
⇒ $N \times 5 = 12 \times 5$

On comparing, we get $N = 12$

∴ Required equivalent fraction of $\dfrac{3}{5} = \dfrac{N}{D} = \dfrac{12}{20}$

(b) Given, numerator of an equivalent fraction $= 9$

∴ $\dfrac{9}{D} = \dfrac{3}{5}$

⇒ $D \times 3 = 9 \times 5$
So, $D \times 3 = 3 \times 3 \times 5$ [but $9 = 3 \times 3$]
⇒ $D \times 3 = 15 \times 3$

On comparing, we get $D = 15$

∴ Required equivalent fraction of $\dfrac{3}{5} = \dfrac{N}{D} = \dfrac{9}{15}$

(c) Given, denominator of an equivalent fraction $= 30$

∴ $\dfrac{N}{30} = \dfrac{3}{5} \Rightarrow N \times 5 = 30 \times 3$

So, $N \times 5 = 6 \times 5 \times 3$ [but $30 = 6 \times 5$]
⇒ $N \times 5 = 18 \times 5$

On comparing, we get $N = 18$

∴ Required equivalent fraction of $\dfrac{3}{5} = \dfrac{N}{D} = \dfrac{18}{30}$

(d) Given, numerator of an equivalent fraction $= 27$

$$\therefore \qquad \frac{27}{D} = \frac{3}{5}$$

$\Rightarrow \qquad D \times 3 = 27 \times 5$

So, $\qquad D \times 3 = 3 \times 9 \times 5 \qquad \qquad$ [but $27 = 3 \times 9$]

$\Rightarrow \qquad D \times 3 = 45 \times 3$

On comparing, we get $D = 45$

$\therefore$ Required equivalent fraction of $\dfrac{3}{5} = \dfrac{N}{D} = \dfrac{27}{45}$

Que 5. Find the equivalent fraction of $\dfrac{36}{48}$ with

(a) numerator 9 (b) denominator 4

Sol. Let N stands for the numerator and D stands for the denominator.

(a) Given, numerator of an equivalent fraction $= 9$

$$\therefore \qquad \frac{9}{D} = \frac{36}{48}$$

$\Rightarrow \qquad 9 \times 48 = D \times 36 \qquad \qquad$ [by cross product]

$\Rightarrow \qquad D = \dfrac{9 \times 48}{36} = 12 \Rightarrow D = 12$

$\therefore$ Required equivalent fraction of $\dfrac{36}{48} = \dfrac{N}{D} = \dfrac{9}{12}$

(b) Given, denominator of an equivalent fraction $= 4$

$$\therefore \qquad \frac{N}{4} = \frac{36}{48}$$

$\Rightarrow \qquad N \times 48 = 4 \times 36 \qquad \qquad$ [by cross product]

$\Rightarrow \qquad N = \dfrac{4 \times 36}{48} = 3 \Rightarrow N = 3$

$\therefore$ Required equivalent fraction of $\dfrac{36}{48} = \dfrac{N}{D} = \dfrac{3}{4}$

Que 6. Check whether the given fractions are equivalent.

(a) $\dfrac{5}{9}, \dfrac{30}{54}$ (b) $\dfrac{3}{10}, \dfrac{12}{50}$ (c) $\dfrac{7}{13}, \dfrac{5}{11}$

TIPS

If the product of numerator of first fraction and denominator of second fraction is equal to the product of denominator of first fraction and numerator of second fraction, then given fractions will be equivalent otherwise not.

Sol. (a) We have, $\dfrac{5}{9}$ and $\dfrac{30}{54}$

Now, $5 \times 54 = 270$

$9 \times 30 = 270$

$\because$ $270 = 270$ [by cross product]

$\therefore$ $\dfrac{5}{9}$ and $\dfrac{30}{54}$ are equivalent fractions.

(b) We have, $\dfrac{3}{10}$ and $\dfrac{12}{50}$

Now, $3 \times 50 = 150$

$10 \times 12 = 120$

But $150 \neq 120$ [by cross product]

$\therefore$ $\dfrac{3}{10}$ and $\dfrac{12}{50}$ are not equivalent fractions.

(c) We have, $\dfrac{7}{13}$ and $\dfrac{5}{11}$

Now, $7 \times 11 = 77$

$13 \times 5 = 65$

But $77 \neq 65$ [by cross product]

$\therefore$ $\dfrac{7}{13}$ and $\dfrac{5}{11}$ are not equivalent fractions.

Que 7. Reduce the following fractions to simplest form.

(a) $\dfrac{48}{60}$ (b) $\dfrac{150}{60}$ (c) $\dfrac{84}{98}$ (d) $\dfrac{12}{52}$ (e) $\dfrac{7}{28}$

Sol. (a) We have, $\dfrac{48}{60}$

Now, factors of $48 = \boxed{2} \times \boxed{2} \times \boxed{3} \times 2 \times 2$

and factors of $60 = \boxed{2} \times \boxed{2} \times \boxed{3} \times 5$

Common factors $= 2, 2$ and 3

HCF of 48 and 60 $= 2 \times 2 \times 3 = 12$

$\therefore$ $\dfrac{48}{60} = \dfrac{48 \div 12}{60 \div 12} = \dfrac{4}{5}$

Hence, simplest form of the fraction $\dfrac{48}{60}$ is $\dfrac{4}{5}$.

(b) We have, $\dfrac{150}{60}$

Now, factors of $150 = \boxed{2} \times \boxed{3} \times \boxed{5} \times 5$

and factors of 60 $= \boxed{2} \times \boxed{3} \times \boxed{5} \times 2$

Common factors = 2, 3 and 5

HCF of 150 and 60 = $2 \times 3 \times 5 = 30$

$\therefore \qquad \dfrac{150}{60} = \dfrac{150 \div 30}{60 \div 30} = \dfrac{5}{2}$

Hence, simplest form of the fraction $\dfrac{150}{60}$ is $\dfrac{5}{2}$.

(c) We have, $\dfrac{84}{98}$

Now, factors of $84 = \boxed{2} \times \boxed{7} \times 3 \times 2$

and factors of $98 = \boxed{2} \times \boxed{7} \times 7$

Common factors = 2 and 7

HCF of 84 and 98 = $2 \times 7 = 14$

$\therefore \qquad \dfrac{84}{98} = \dfrac{84 \div 14}{98 \div 14} = \dfrac{6}{7}$

Hence, simplest form of the fraction $\dfrac{84}{98}$ is $\dfrac{6}{7}$.

(d) We have, $\dfrac{12}{52}$

Now, factors of $12 = \boxed{2} \times \boxed{2} \times 3$

and factors of $52 = \boxed{2} \times \boxed{2} \times 13$

Common factors = 2 and 2

HCF of 12 and 52 = $2 \times 2 = 4$

$\therefore \qquad \dfrac{12}{52} = \dfrac{12 \div 4}{52 \div 4} = \dfrac{3}{13}$

Hence, simplest form of the fraction $\dfrac{12}{52}$ is $\dfrac{3}{13}$.

(e) We have, $\dfrac{7}{28}$

Now, factors of $7 = \boxed{7}$

and factors of $28 = \boxed{7} \times 2 \times 2$

Common factor = 7

HCF of 7 and 28 = 7

$\therefore \qquad \dfrac{7}{28} = \dfrac{7 \div 7}{28 \div 7} = \dfrac{1}{4}$

Hence, simplest form of the fraction $\dfrac{7}{28}$ is $\dfrac{1}{4}$.

Que 8. Ramesh had 20 pencils, Sheelu had 50 pencils and Jamaal had 80 pencils. After 4 months, Ramesh used up 10 pencils, Sheelu used up 25 pencils and Jamaal used up 40 pencils. What fraction did each use up? Check if each has used up an equal fraction of her/his pencils?

Sol. Here, fraction of pencils used by Ramesh $= \dfrac{10}{20}$

Fraction of pencils used by Sheelu $= \dfrac{25}{50}$

and fraction of pencils used by Jamaal $= \dfrac{40}{80}$

Now, $\dfrac{10}{20} = \dfrac{10 \div 10}{20 \div 10} = \dfrac{1}{2}$ [∵ HCF of 10 and 20 is 10]

$\dfrac{25}{50} = \dfrac{25 \div 25}{50 \div 25} = \dfrac{1}{2}$ [∵ HCF of 25 and 50 is 25]

and $\dfrac{40}{80} = \dfrac{40 \div 40}{80 \div 40} = \dfrac{1}{2}$ [∵ HCF of 40 and 80 is 40]

Thus, $\dfrac{10}{20} = \dfrac{25}{50} = \dfrac{40}{80} = \dfrac{1}{2}$

Hence, each has used up an equal fraction of his/her pencils.

Que 9. Match the equivalent fractions and write two more for each.

	Column I		Column II
(i)	$\dfrac{250}{400}$	(a)	$\dfrac{2}{3}$
(ii)	$\dfrac{180}{200}$	(b)	$\dfrac{2}{5}$
(iii)	$\dfrac{660}{990}$	(c)	$\dfrac{1}{2}$
(iv)	$\dfrac{180}{360}$	(d)	$\dfrac{5}{8}$
(v)	$\dfrac{220}{550}$	(e)	$\dfrac{9}{10}$

TIPS
Firstly, reduce (i), (ii), (iii), (iv) and (v) into simplest form. Then, match the equivalent fractions. To write more equivalent fractions, multiply numerator and denominator both by same number.

Sol.   (i) We have, $\dfrac{250}{400}$

Now,   factors of $250 = \boxed{2} \times \boxed{5} \times \boxed{5} \times 5$

and   factors of $400 = \boxed{2} \times \boxed{5} \times \boxed{5} \times 2 \times 2 \times 2$

Common factors are 2, 5 and 5

HCF of 250 and 400 $= 2 \times 5 \times 5 = 50$

$\therefore$ $\dfrac{250}{400} = \dfrac{250 \div 50}{400 \div 50} = \dfrac{5}{8}$

So, $\dfrac{250}{400}$ is equivalent to $\dfrac{5}{8}$ i.e. (i) $\rightarrow$ *(d)*

Two more equivalent fractions are

$$\dfrac{5 \times 2}{8 \times 2} = \dfrac{10}{16} \quad \text{and} \quad \dfrac{5 \times 3}{8 \times 3} = \dfrac{15}{24}$$

(ii) We have, $\dfrac{180}{200}$

Now,   factors of $180 = \boxed{2} \times \boxed{2} \times \boxed{5} \times 3 \times 3$

and   factors of $200 = \boxed{2} \times \boxed{2} \times \boxed{5} \times 5 \times 2$

Common factors $= 2, 2$ and 5

HCF of 180 and 200 $= 2 \times 5 \times 2 = 20$

$\therefore$ $\dfrac{180}{200} = \dfrac{180 \div 20}{200 \div 20} = \dfrac{9}{10}$

So, $\dfrac{180}{200}$ is equivalent to $\dfrac{9}{10}$ i.e. (ii) $\rightarrow$ *(e)*

Two more equivalent fractions are

$$\dfrac{9 \times 2}{10 \times 2} = \dfrac{18}{20} \quad \text{and} \quad \dfrac{9 \times 3}{10 \times 3} = \dfrac{27}{30}$$

(iii) We have, $\dfrac{660}{990}$

Now,   factors of $660 = \boxed{2} \times 2 \times \boxed{3} \times \boxed{5} \times \boxed{11}$

and   factors of $990 = \boxed{2} \times 3 \times \boxed{3} \times \boxed{5} \times \boxed{11}$

Common factors $= 2, 3, 5$ and 11

HCF of 660 and 990 $= 2 \times 3 \times 5 \times 11 = 330$

$\therefore$ $\dfrac{660}{990} = \dfrac{660 \div 330}{990 \div 330} = \dfrac{2}{3}$

So, $\dfrac{660}{990}$ is equivalent to $\dfrac{2}{3}$ i.e. (iii) $\rightarrow$ *(a)*

Two more equivalent fractions are

$$\dfrac{2 \times 2}{3 \times 2} = \dfrac{4}{6} \quad \text{and} \quad \dfrac{2 \times 3}{3 \times 3} = \dfrac{6}{9}$$

(iv) We have, $\dfrac{180}{360}$

Now, factors of $180 = \boxed{2} \times \boxed{2} \times \boxed{3} \times \boxed{3} \times \boxed{5}$

and factors of $360 = \boxed{2} \times \boxed{2} \times \boxed{3} \times \boxed{3} \times \boxed{5} \times 2$

Common factors $= 2, 2, 3, 3$ and 5

HCF of 180 and 360 $= 2 \times 2 \times 3 \times 3 \times 5 = 180$

∴ $\dfrac{180}{360} = \dfrac{180 \div 180}{360 \div 180} = \dfrac{1}{2}$

So, $\dfrac{180}{360}$ is equivalent to $\dfrac{1}{2}$ i.e. (iv) → (c)

Two more equivalent fractions are

$$\dfrac{1 \times 2}{2 \times 2} = \dfrac{2}{4} \qquad \text{and} \qquad \dfrac{1 \times 3}{2 \times 3} = \dfrac{3}{6}$$

(v) We have, $\dfrac{220}{550}$

Now, factors of $220 = \boxed{2} \times 2 \times \boxed{5} \times \boxed{11}$

Factors of $550 = \boxed{2} \times 5 \times \boxed{5} \times \boxed{11}$

Common factors $= 2, 5$ and 11

HCF of 220 and 550 $= 2 \times 5 \times 11 = 110$

∴ $\dfrac{220}{550} = \dfrac{220 \div 110}{550 \div 110} = \dfrac{2}{5}$

So, $\dfrac{220}{530}$ is equivalent to $\dfrac{2}{5}$ i.e. (v) → (b)

Two more equivalent fractions are

$$\dfrac{2 \times 2}{5 \times 2} = \dfrac{4}{10} \text{ and } \dfrac{2 \times 3}{5 \times 3} = \dfrac{6}{15}$$

Try These (Page 148)

Que 1. You get one-fifth of a bottle of juice and your sister gets one-third of a bottle of juice. Who gets more?

Sol. Here, we will compare one-fifth i.e. 1/5 and one-third i.e. 1/3.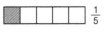

Let us divide a rectangle into 5 equal parts and shade one of them. i.e. one-fifth part is shaded.

Now, divide the same rectangle into 3 equal parts and shade one of them i.e. one-third part is shaded, obviously one-third is greater.

Also, since $\dfrac{1}{5}$ and $\dfrac{1}{3}$ have same numerator, so the fraction with smaller denominator is greater. Thus, $\dfrac{1}{3} > \dfrac{1}{5}$

Thus, your sister gets more juice.

Try These (Page 149)

Que 2. Which is the larger fraction?

    (i) $\dfrac{7}{10}$ or $\dfrac{8}{10}$ (ii) $\dfrac{11}{24}$ or $\dfrac{13}{24}$ (iii) $\dfrac{17}{102}$ or $\dfrac{12}{102}$

    why one these comparisions easy to make?

> **TIPS**
> If two fractions have the same denominator, then the fraction with the greater numberator will be greater.

Sol.   (i) We have, $\dfrac{7}{10}$ or $\dfrac{8}{10}$

    Here, denominator of both fractions are same and $8 > 7$.

    ∴ $\dfrac{8}{10} > \dfrac{7}{10}$ i.e. $\dfrac{8}{10}$ is larger.

  (ii) We have, $\dfrac{11}{24}$ or $\dfrac{13}{24}$

    Here, denominator of both fractions are same and $13 > 11$.

    ∴ $\dfrac{13}{24} > \dfrac{11}{24}$ i.e. $\dfrac{13}{24}$ is larger.

  (iii) We have, $\dfrac{17}{102}$ or $\dfrac{12}{102}$

    Here, denominator of both fractions are same and $17 > 12$.

    ∴ $\dfrac{17}{102} > \dfrac{12}{102}$ i.e. $\dfrac{17}{102}$ is larger.

    These comparisions are easy to make because they are like fractions. So, only their numerators are to be compared.

Que 3. Write these in ascending and also in descending order.

    (a) $\dfrac{1}{8}, \dfrac{5}{8}, \dfrac{3}{8}$ (b) $\dfrac{1}{5}, \dfrac{11}{5}, \dfrac{4}{5}, \dfrac{3}{5}, \dfrac{7}{5}$ (c) $\dfrac{1}{7}, \dfrac{3}{7}, \dfrac{13}{7}, \dfrac{11}{7}, \dfrac{7}{7}$

> **TIPS**
> Like fractions can be written in ascending or in descending order according to their numerators, since their denominators are same.

Sol. (a) We have, $\dfrac{1}{8}, \dfrac{5}{8}, \dfrac{3}{8}$

Here, denominators of all fractions are same.

∴   Ascending order of numerators $= 1 < 3 < 5$

and descending order of numerators $= 5 > 3 > 1$

∴   Ascending order of fractions $= \dfrac{1}{8} < \dfrac{3}{8} < \dfrac{5}{8}$

and   descending order of fractions $= \dfrac{5}{8} > \dfrac{3}{8} > \dfrac{1}{8}$

(b) We have, $\dfrac{1}{5}, \dfrac{11}{5}, \dfrac{4}{5}, \dfrac{3}{5}, \dfrac{7}{5}$

Here, denominators of all fractions are same.

∴   Ascending order of numerators $= 1 < 3 < 4 < 7 < 11$

and descending order of numerators $= 11 > 7 > 4 > 3 > 1$

∴   Ascending order of fractions $= \dfrac{1}{5} < \dfrac{3}{5} < \dfrac{4}{5} < \dfrac{7}{5} < \dfrac{11}{5}$

and   descending order of fractions $= \dfrac{11}{5} > \dfrac{7}{5} > \dfrac{4}{5} > \dfrac{3}{5} > \dfrac{1}{5}$

(c) We have, $\dfrac{1}{7}, \dfrac{3}{7}, \dfrac{13}{7}, \dfrac{11}{7}, \dfrac{7}{7}$

Here, denominators of all fractions are same.

∴   Ascending order of numerators $= 1 < 3 < 7 < 11 < 13$

and descending order of numerators $= 13 > 11 > 7 > 3 > 1$

∴   Ascending order of fractions $= \dfrac{1}{7} < \dfrac{3}{7} < \dfrac{7}{7} < \dfrac{11}{7} < \dfrac{13}{7}$

and   descending order of fractions $= \dfrac{13}{7} > \dfrac{11}{7} > \dfrac{7}{7} > \dfrac{3}{7} > \dfrac{1}{7}$

Try These (Page 151)

Que 4. Arrange the following in ascending and descending order.

(a) $\dfrac{1}{12}, \dfrac{1}{23}, \dfrac{1}{5}, \dfrac{1}{7}, \dfrac{1}{50}, \dfrac{1}{9}, \dfrac{1}{17}$ (b) $\dfrac{3}{7}, \dfrac{3}{11}, \dfrac{3}{5}, \dfrac{3}{2}, \dfrac{3}{13}, \dfrac{3}{4}, \dfrac{3}{17}$

(c) Write 3 more similar examples and arrange them in ascending and descending order.

TIPS

If numerator of given fractions are same, then the fraction having large denominator will be the smaller fraction and fraction having smaller denominator will be the large fraction.

Sol. (a) Here, numerators of all fractions are same.

Descending order of denominators $= 50 > 23 > 17 > 12 > 9 > 7 > 5$

$\therefore$ Ascending order of fractions $= \dfrac{1}{50}, \dfrac{1}{23}, \dfrac{1}{17}, \dfrac{1}{12}, \dfrac{1}{9}, \dfrac{1}{7}, \dfrac{1}{5}$

$$\left[\because \dfrac{1}{50} \text{ has larger denominator, so it is smallest fraction} \right]$$

and descending order of fractions $= \dfrac{1}{5}, \dfrac{1}{7}, \dfrac{1}{9}, \dfrac{1}{12}, \dfrac{1}{17}, \dfrac{1}{23}, \dfrac{1}{50}$

(b) Here, numerators of all fractions are same.

Descending order of denominators $= 17 > 13 > 11 > 7 > 5 > 4 > 2$

$\therefore$ Ascending order of fractions $= \dfrac{3}{17}, \dfrac{3}{13}, \dfrac{3}{11}, \dfrac{3}{7}, \dfrac{3}{5}, \dfrac{3}{4}, \dfrac{3}{2}$

and   descending order of fractions $= \dfrac{3}{2}, \dfrac{3}{4}, \dfrac{3}{5}, \dfrac{3}{7}, \dfrac{3}{11}, \dfrac{3}{13}, \dfrac{3}{17}$

(c) Three more similar examples can be taken as

(i) $\dfrac{2}{11}, \dfrac{2}{21}, \dfrac{2}{9}, \dfrac{2}{7}, \dfrac{2}{8}, \dfrac{2}{15}$

Here, descending order of denominators $= 21 > 15 > 11 > 9 > 8 > 7$

$\therefore$ Ascending order of fractions $= \dfrac{2}{21}, \dfrac{2}{15}, \dfrac{2}{11}, \dfrac{2}{9}, \dfrac{2}{8}, \dfrac{2}{7}$

and   descending order of fractions $= \dfrac{2}{7}, \dfrac{2}{8}, \dfrac{2}{9}, \dfrac{2}{11}, \dfrac{2}{15}, \dfrac{2}{21}$

(ii) $\dfrac{4}{5}, \dfrac{4}{6}, \dfrac{4}{13}, \dfrac{4}{2}, \dfrac{4}{9}, \dfrac{4}{11}$

Here, descending order of denominators $= 13 > 11 > 9 > 6 > 5 > 2$

$\therefore$ Ascending order of fractions $= \dfrac{4}{13}, \dfrac{4}{11}, \dfrac{4}{9}, \dfrac{4}{6}, \dfrac{4}{5}, \dfrac{4}{2}$

and   descending order of fractions $= \dfrac{4}{2}, \dfrac{4}{5}, \dfrac{4}{6}, \dfrac{4}{9}, \dfrac{4}{11}, \dfrac{4}{13}$

(iii) $\dfrac{7}{11}, \dfrac{7}{13}, \dfrac{7}{5}, \dfrac{7}{2}, \dfrac{7}{3}, \dfrac{7}{4}$

Here, descending order of denominators $= 13 > 11 > 5 > 4 > 3 > 2$

$\therefore$ Ascending order of fractions $= \dfrac{7}{13}, \dfrac{7}{11}, \dfrac{7}{5}, \dfrac{7}{4}, \dfrac{7}{3}, \dfrac{7}{2}$

and   descending order of fractions $= \dfrac{7}{2}, \dfrac{7}{3}, \dfrac{7}{4}, \dfrac{7}{5}, \dfrac{7}{11}, \dfrac{7}{13}$

Exercise 7.4

Que 1. Write shaded portion as fraction. Arrange them in ascending and descending order using correct sign '<', '=', '>' between the fractions.

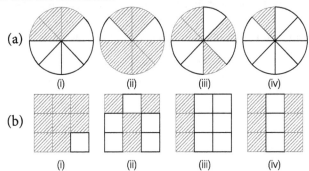

(a)

(i)   (ii)   (iii)   (iv)

(b)

(i)   (ii)   (iii)   (iv)

(c) (i) Show $\dfrac{2}{6}, \dfrac{4}{6}, \dfrac{8}{6}$ and $\dfrac{6}{6}$ on the number line.

    (ii) Put appropriate signs between the fractions given.

$$\dfrac{5}{6} \square \dfrac{2}{6}, \qquad \dfrac{3}{6} \square 0, \qquad \dfrac{1}{6} \square \dfrac{6}{6}, \qquad \dfrac{8}{6} \square \dfrac{5}{6}$$

Sol. (a) Here, total number of equal parts in all figures $= 8$

Shaded portion of figure (i) represents fraction $= \dfrac{3}{8}$

Shaded portion of figure (ii) represents fraction $= \dfrac{6}{8}$

Shaded portion of figure (iii) represents fraction $= \dfrac{4}{8}$

Shaded portion of figure (iv) represents fraction $= \dfrac{1}{8}$

∴ Denominators of all fractions are same. So, we arrange them in ascending and descending order according to their numerators.

∴ Ascending order of fractions $= \dfrac{1}{8} < \dfrac{3}{8} < \dfrac{4}{8} < \dfrac{6}{8}$

[∵ fraction having small numerator will be smaller]

and descending order of fractions $= \dfrac{6}{8} > \dfrac{4}{8} > \dfrac{3}{8} > \dfrac{1}{8}$

[∵ fraction having greatest numerator will be greatest]

(b) Here, total number of equal parts in all figures = 9

Shaded portion of figure (i) represents fraction = $\dfrac{8}{9}$

Shaded portion of figure (ii) represents fraction = $\dfrac{4}{9}$

Shaded portion of figure (iii) represents fraction = $\dfrac{3}{9}$

Shaded portion of figure (iv) represents fraction = $\dfrac{6}{9}$

∴ Denominators of all fractions are same. So, we arrange them in ascending and descending order according to their numerators.

∴ Ascending order of fractions = $\dfrac{3}{9} < \dfrac{4}{9} < \dfrac{6}{9} < \dfrac{8}{9}$

and descending order of fractions = $\dfrac{8}{9} > \dfrac{6}{9} > \dfrac{4}{9} > \dfrac{3}{9}$

(c) (i) Given, fractions are $\dfrac{2}{6}, \dfrac{4}{6}, \dfrac{8}{6}$ and $\dfrac{6}{6}$. These fractions lie between 0 to 1. To show these fractions on a number line, divide the number line into 6 equal parts, where each part represents $\dfrac{1}{6}$ part.

So, on the number line these fractions can be shown as below

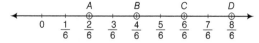

Points A, B, C and D represent the fractions $\dfrac{2}{6}, \dfrac{4}{6}, \dfrac{6}{6}$ and $\dfrac{8}{6}$ on the number line respectively.

(ii) Since, all fractions have same denominator, so fraction having larger numerator will be larger and fraction having smaller numerator will be smaller.

∴ $\dfrac{5}{6} \boxed{>} \dfrac{2}{6}$, $\dfrac{3}{6} \boxed{>} 0$, $\dfrac{1}{6} \boxed{<} \dfrac{6}{6}$, $\dfrac{8}{6} \boxed{>} \dfrac{5}{6}$

Que 2. Compare the fractions and put an appropriate sign.

(a) $\dfrac{3}{6} \square \dfrac{5}{6}$ (b) $\dfrac{1}{7} \square \dfrac{1}{4}$

(c) $\dfrac{4}{5} \square \dfrac{5}{5}$ (d) $\dfrac{3}{5} \square \dfrac{3}{7}$

Sol. (a) We have, $\dfrac{3}{6}\,\square\,\dfrac{5}{6}$

Here, denominators are same of both fractions. So, fraction having smaller numerator will be smaller.

∴ $\dfrac{3}{6}\,\boxed{<}\,\dfrac{5}{6}$

(b) We have, $\dfrac{1}{7}\,\square\,\dfrac{1}{4}$

Here, numerators are same of both fractions. So, fraction having smaller denominator will be greater.

∴ $\dfrac{1}{7}\,\boxed{<}\,\dfrac{1}{4}$

(c) We have, $\dfrac{4}{5}\,\square\,\dfrac{5}{5}$

Here, denominators are same of both fractions. So, fraction having smaller numerator will be smaller.

∴ $\dfrac{4}{5}\,\boxed{<}\,\dfrac{5}{5}$

(d) We have, $\dfrac{3}{5}\,\square\,\dfrac{3}{7}$

Here, numerators are same of both fractions. So, fraction having smaller denominator will be greater.

∴ $\dfrac{3}{5}\,\boxed{>}\,\dfrac{3}{7}$

Que 3. Make five more such pairs and put appropriate signs.

Sol. Five more such pairs may be taken us under

(i) $\dfrac{3}{7}\,\square\,\dfrac{5}{7}$ (ii) $\dfrac{1}{9}\,\square\,\dfrac{1}{5}$ (iii) $\dfrac{3}{8}\,\square\,\dfrac{0}{8}$

(iv) $\dfrac{5}{18}\,\square\,\dfrac{7}{18}$ (v) $\dfrac{2}{11}\,\square\,\dfrac{1}{11}$

After putting the appropriate signs, we have

(i) $\dfrac{3}{7}\,\boxed{<}\,\dfrac{5}{7}$ (ii) $\dfrac{1}{9}\,\boxed{<}\,\dfrac{1}{5}$ (iii) $\dfrac{3}{8}\,\boxed{>}\,\dfrac{0}{8}$

(iv) $\dfrac{5}{18}\,\boxed{<}\,\dfrac{7}{18}$ (v) $\dfrac{2}{11}\,\boxed{>}\,\dfrac{1}{11}$

Que 4. Look at the figures and write '<' or '>', '=' between the given pairs of fractions.

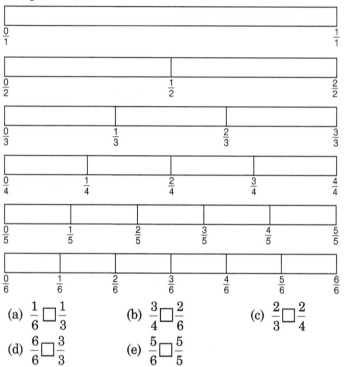

(a) $\dfrac{1}{6} \square \dfrac{1}{3}$ (b) $\dfrac{3}{4} \square \dfrac{2}{6}$ (c) $\dfrac{2}{3} \square \dfrac{2}{4}$

(d) $\dfrac{6}{6} \square \dfrac{3}{3}$ (e) $\dfrac{5}{6} \square \dfrac{5}{5}$

Make five more such problems and solve them with your friends.

Sol.   (a) From the given figures, $\dfrac{1}{6} \boxed{<} \dfrac{1}{3}$ because $\dfrac{1}{6}$ lies on the left of $\dfrac{1}{3}$.

(b) $\dfrac{3}{4} \boxed{>} \dfrac{2}{6}$ because $\dfrac{3}{4}$ is on the right side of $\dfrac{2}{6}$.

(c) $\dfrac{2}{3} \boxed{>} \dfrac{2}{4}$ because $\dfrac{2}{3}$ is on the right side of $\dfrac{2}{4}$.

(d) $\dfrac{6}{6} \boxed{=} \dfrac{3}{3}$ because $\dfrac{6}{6}$ and $\dfrac{3}{3}$ lies on the same point.

(e) $\dfrac{5}{6} \boxed{<} \dfrac{5}{5}$ because $\dfrac{5}{6}$ is on the left side of $\dfrac{5}{5}$.

Five more such examples can be taken as under

(i) $\dfrac{1}{5} \square \dfrac{1}{2}$ (ii) $\dfrac{3}{5} \square \dfrac{2}{6}$ (iii) $\dfrac{2}{4} \square \dfrac{2}{5}$

(iv) $\dfrac{5}{5} \square \dfrac{4}{4}$ (v) $\dfrac{0}{2} \square \dfrac{0}{3}$

Sol. (i) $\dfrac{1}{5}\boxed{<}\dfrac{1}{2}$ because $\dfrac{1}{5}$ lies on the left side of $\dfrac{1}{2}$.

(ii) $\dfrac{3}{5}\boxed{>}\dfrac{2}{6}$ because $\dfrac{3}{5}$ lies on the right side of $\dfrac{2}{6}$.

(iii) $\dfrac{2}{4}\boxed{>}\dfrac{2}{5}$ because $\dfrac{2}{4}$ lies on the right side of $\dfrac{2}{5}$.

(iv) $\dfrac{5}{5}\boxed{=}\dfrac{4}{4}$ because they lies on the same point.

(v) $\dfrac{0}{2}\boxed{=}\dfrac{0}{3}$ because they lies on the same point.

Que 5. How quickly can you do this? Fill appropriate sign. ('<', '=', '>').

(a) $\dfrac{1}{2}\ \square\ \dfrac{1}{5}$ (b) $\dfrac{2}{4}\ \square\ \dfrac{3}{6}$ (c) $\dfrac{3}{5}\ \square\ \dfrac{2}{3}$ (d) $\dfrac{3}{4}\ \square\ \dfrac{2}{8}$

(e) $\dfrac{3}{5}\ \square\ \dfrac{6}{5}$ (f) $\dfrac{7}{9}\ \square\ \dfrac{3}{9}$ (g) $\dfrac{1}{4}\ \square\ \dfrac{2}{8}$ (h) $\dfrac{6}{10}\ \square\ \dfrac{4}{5}$

(i) $\dfrac{3}{4}\ \square\ \dfrac{7}{8}$ (j) $\dfrac{5}{7}\ \square\ \dfrac{15}{21}$

TIPS
We have to use cross-product method for quicker calculation. According to this method, firstly find the products of numerator of first fraction with denominator of second fraction and denominator of first fraction with numerator of second fraction. Then, the fraction having that numerator which gives greater product will be greater.

Sol. (a) We have, $\dfrac{1}{2}$ and $\dfrac{1}{5}$

Here, $\qquad 1\times 5 = 5$ and $2\times 1 = 2$

$\because \qquad\qquad 5 > 2$

$\therefore \qquad\qquad \dfrac{1}{2}\ \boxed{>}\ \dfrac{1}{5}$

(b) We have, $\dfrac{2}{4}$ and $\dfrac{3}{6}$

Here, $\qquad 2\times 6 = 12$ and $4\times 3 = 12$

$\because \qquad\qquad 12 = 12$

$\therefore \qquad\qquad \dfrac{2}{4}\ \boxed{=}\ \dfrac{3}{6}$

(c) We have, $\dfrac{3}{5}$ and $\dfrac{2}{3}$

Here, $\qquad 3\times 3 = 9$ and $5\times 2 = 10$

$\because \qquad\qquad 9 < 10$

$\therefore \qquad\qquad \dfrac{3}{5}\ \boxed{<}\ \dfrac{2}{3}$

(d) We have, $\dfrac{3}{4}$ and $\dfrac{2}{8}$

Here, $3 \times 8 = 24$ and $4 \times 2 = 8$

$\because$ $24 > 8$

$\therefore$ $\dfrac{3}{4} \boxed{>} \dfrac{2}{8}$

(e) We have, $\dfrac{3}{5}$ and $\dfrac{6}{5}$

Here, $3 \times 5 = 15$ and $5 \times 6 = 30$

$\because$ $15 < 30$

$\therefore$ $\dfrac{3}{5} \boxed{<} \dfrac{6}{5}$

(f) We have, $\dfrac{7}{9}$ and $\dfrac{3}{9}$

Here, $7 \times 9 = 63$ and $9 \times 3 = 27$

$\because$ $63 > 27$

$\therefore$ $\dfrac{7}{9} \boxed{>} \dfrac{3}{9}$

(g) We have, $\dfrac{1}{4}$ and $\dfrac{2}{8}$

Here, $1 \times 8 = 8$ and $4 \times 2 = 8$

$\because$ $8 = 8$

$\therefore$ $\dfrac{1}{4} \boxed{=} \dfrac{2}{8}$

(h) We have, $\dfrac{6}{10}$ and $\dfrac{4}{5}$

Here, $6 \times 5 = 30$ and $10 \times 4 = 40$

$\because$ $30 < 40$

$\therefore$ $\dfrac{6}{10} \boxed{<} \dfrac{4}{5}$

(i) We have, $\dfrac{3}{4}$ and $\dfrac{7}{8}$

Here, $3 \times 8 = 24$ and $4 \times 7 = 28$

$\because$ $24 < 28$

$\therefore$ $\dfrac{3}{4} \boxed{<} \dfrac{7}{8}$

(j) We have, $\dfrac{5}{7}$ and $\dfrac{15}{21}$

Here, $5 \times 21 = 105$ and $7 \times 15 = 105$

$\because$ $105 = 105$

$\therefore$ $\dfrac{5}{7} \boxed{=} \dfrac{15}{21}$

Que 6. The following fractions represent just three different numbers. Separate them into three groups of equivalent fractions, by changing each one in its simplest form.

(a) $\dfrac{2}{12}$ (b) $\dfrac{3}{15}$ (c) $\dfrac{8}{50}$ (d) $\dfrac{16}{100}$

(e) $\dfrac{10}{60}$ (f) $\dfrac{15}{75}$ (g) $\dfrac{12}{60}$ (h) $\dfrac{16}{96}$

(i) $\dfrac{12}{75}$ (j) $\dfrac{12}{72}$ (k) $\dfrac{3}{18}$ (l) $\dfrac{4}{25}$

TIPS To convert the given fraction into its simplest form, divide numerator and denominator both by their HCF.

Sol. First, we have to convert all the fractions in the simplest form.

(a) We have, $\dfrac{2}{12} \Rightarrow \dfrac{2 \div 2}{12 \div 2} = \dfrac{1}{6}$ [$\because$ HCF of 2 and 12 = 2]

(b) We have, $\dfrac{3}{15} \Rightarrow \dfrac{3 \div 3}{15 \div 3} = \dfrac{1}{5}$ [$\because$ HCF of 3 and 15 = 3]

(c) We have, $\dfrac{8}{50} \Rightarrow \dfrac{8 \div 2}{50 \div 2} = \dfrac{4}{25}$ [$\because$ HCF of 8 and 50 = 2]

(d) We have, $\dfrac{16}{100} \Rightarrow \dfrac{16 \div 4}{100 \div 4} = \dfrac{4}{25}$ [$\because$ HCF of 16 and 100 = 4]

(e) We have, $\dfrac{10}{60} \Rightarrow \dfrac{10 \div 10}{60 \div 10} = \dfrac{1}{6}$ [$\because$ HCF of 10 and 60 = 10]

(f) We have, $\dfrac{15}{75} \Rightarrow \dfrac{15 \div 15}{75 \div 15} = \dfrac{1}{5}$ [$\because$ HCF of 15 and 75 = 15]

(g) We have, $\dfrac{12}{60} \Rightarrow \dfrac{12 \div 12}{60 \div 12} = \dfrac{1}{5}$ [$\because$ HCF of 12 and 60 = 12]

(h) We have, $\dfrac{16}{96} \Rightarrow \dfrac{16 \div 16}{96 \div 16} = \dfrac{1}{6}$ [$\because$ HCF of 16 and 96 = 16]

(i) We have, $\dfrac{12}{75} \Rightarrow \dfrac{12 \div 3}{75 \div 3} = \dfrac{4}{25}$ [$\because$ HCF of 12 and 75 = 3]

(j) We have, $\dfrac{12}{72} \Rightarrow \dfrac{12 \div 12}{72 \div 12} = \dfrac{1}{6}$ [$\because$ HCF of 12 and 72 = 12]

(k) We have, $\dfrac{3}{18} \Rightarrow \dfrac{3 \div 3}{18 \div 3} = \dfrac{1}{6}$ [$\because$ HCF of 3 and 18 = 3]

(l) We have, $\dfrac{4}{25} \Rightarrow \dfrac{4 \div 1}{25 \div 1} = \dfrac{4}{25}$ [$\because$ HCF of 4 and 25 = 1]

Now, on grouping into three groups of equivalent fractions with the help of simplest form of fractions, we get

(i) $\dfrac{2}{12} = \dfrac{10}{60} = \dfrac{16}{96} = \dfrac{12}{72} = \dfrac{3}{18}$ $\left[\text{simplest form of each fraction} = \dfrac{1}{6}\right]$

(ii) $\dfrac{3}{15} = \dfrac{15}{75} = \dfrac{12}{60}$ $\left[\text{simplest form of each fraction} = \dfrac{1}{5}\right]$

(iii) $\dfrac{8}{50} = \dfrac{16}{100} = \dfrac{12}{75} = \dfrac{4}{25}$ $\left[\text{simplest form of each fraction} = \dfrac{4}{25}\right]$

Que 7. Find answers to the following. Write and indicate how you solved them.

(a) Is $\dfrac{5}{9}$ equal to $\dfrac{4}{5}$? (b) Is $\dfrac{9}{16}$ equal to $\dfrac{5}{9}$?

(c) Is $\dfrac{4}{5}$ equal to $\dfrac{16}{20}$? (d) Is $\dfrac{1}{15}$ equal to $\dfrac{4}{30}$?

TIPS

To show that given fractions are equal or not. Firstly, we convert them into like fractions by multiplying numerator and denominator with same number and then compare.

Sol. (a) LCM of 9 and 5 = 45

Now, $\dfrac{5}{9} = \dfrac{5 \times 5}{9 \times 5} = \dfrac{25}{45}$ and $\dfrac{4}{5} = \dfrac{4 \times 9}{5 \times 9} = \dfrac{36}{45}$

Thus, both fractions are like fractions but $\dfrac{25}{45} \neq \dfrac{36}{45}$

∴ $\dfrac{5}{9} \neq \dfrac{4}{5}$

(b) LCM of 16 and 9 = 144

Now, $\dfrac{9}{16} = \dfrac{9 \times 9}{16 \times 9} = \dfrac{81}{144}$ and $\dfrac{5}{9} = \dfrac{5 \times 16}{9 \times 16} = \dfrac{80}{144}$

Thus, both fractions are like fractions but $\dfrac{81}{144} \neq \dfrac{80}{144}$

∴ $\dfrac{9}{16} \neq \dfrac{5}{9}$

(c) LCM of 5 and 20 = 20

Now, $\dfrac{4}{5} = \dfrac{4 \times 4}{5 \times 4} = \dfrac{16}{20}$ and $\dfrac{16}{20} = \dfrac{16}{20}$

Thus, both fractions are like fractions and $\dfrac{16}{20} = \dfrac{16}{20}$

∴ $\dfrac{4}{5} = \dfrac{16}{20}$

(d) LCM of 15 and 30 = 30

Now, $\dfrac{1}{15} = \dfrac{1 \times 2}{15 \times 2} = \dfrac{2}{30}$ and $\dfrac{2}{30} \neq \dfrac{4}{30}$

Thus, both fractions are like fractions but $\dfrac{2}{30} \neq \dfrac{4}{30}$

∴ $\dfrac{1}{15} \neq \dfrac{4}{30}$

Que 8. Ila reads 25 pages of a book containing 100 pages. Lalita reads $\dfrac{2}{5}$ of the same book. Who read less?

Sol. Fraction of book read by Ila $= \dfrac{25}{100} = \dfrac{25 \div 25}{100 \div 25} = \dfrac{1}{4}$

[∵ HCF of 25 and 100 = 25]

Fraction of book read by Lalita $= \dfrac{2}{5}$

For comparing $\dfrac{1}{4}$ and $\dfrac{2}{5}$

We have, $1 \times 5 = 5$ and $4 \times 2 = 8$ [by cross-product]

∵ $5 < 8;$ ∴ $\dfrac{1}{4} < \dfrac{2}{5}$

Hence, Ila reads less pages of a book.

Que 9. Rafiq exercised for $\dfrac{3}{6}$ of an hour while Rohit exercised for $\dfrac{3}{4}$ of an hour. Who exercised for a longer time?

Sol. Rafiq exercised for $\dfrac{3}{6}$ h. Rohit exercised for $\dfrac{3}{4}$ h.

Now, we have to compare $\dfrac{3}{6}$ and $\dfrac{3}{4}$.

Here, numerator of both fractions are same.

We know that, if two fractions have same numerator, then the fraction having less denominator will be greater.

∴ $\dfrac{3}{4} > \dfrac{3}{6}$

Hence, Rohit exercised for a longer time.

Que 10. In a class *A* of 25 students, 20 passed in first class; in another class *B* of 30 students, 24 passed in first class. In which class, was a greater fraction of students getting first class?

Sol. Fraction of students, who got first class in class A

$$= \frac{20}{25} = \frac{20 \div 5}{25 \div 5} \qquad [\because \text{HCF of 20 and 25} = 5]$$

$$= \frac{4}{5}$$

Fraction of students, who got first class in class B

$$= \frac{24}{30} = \frac{24 \div 6}{30 \div 6} \qquad [\because \text{HCF of 24 and 30} = 6]$$

$$= \frac{4}{5}$$

$$\because \qquad \frac{20}{25} = \frac{24}{30} = \frac{4}{5}$$

So, it is clear that an equal number of students got first class in both the classes.

Try These (Page 155)

Que 1. My mother divided an apple into 4 equal parts. She gave me two parts and to my brother one part. How much apple did she give to both of us together?

Sol. Here, mother divided an apple into 4 equal parts, so each part will represents $\frac{1}{4}$. She gave me two parts i.e. $\frac{2}{4}$ apple and she gave to my brother one part i.e. $\frac{1}{4}$ part.

Part of apple she gave to both of us $= \frac{2}{4} + \frac{1}{4}$

$\because$ Here, denominators of both fractions are same, so we add numerator to find their sum.

i.e. $\qquad \frac{2+1}{4} = \frac{3}{4}$

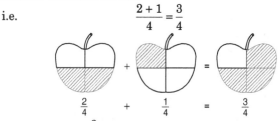

$$\frac{2}{4} \qquad + \qquad \frac{1}{4} \qquad = \qquad \frac{3}{4}$$

Hence, she gave $\frac{3}{4}$ apple to both of us.

Que 2. Mother asked Neelu and her brother to pick stones from the wheat. Neelu picked one-fourth of the total stones from it and her brother also picked up one-fourth of the stones. What fraction of the stones did both pick up together?

Sol. Neelu and her brother picked up $\frac{1}{4}$th of stones each from the wheat.

∴ Total stones picked up by both of them $= \frac{1}{4} + \frac{1}{4} = \frac{1+1}{4} = \frac{2}{4} = \frac{1}{2}$

Hence, both together picked up $\frac{1}{2}$ fraction of the stones.

Que 3. Sohan was putting covers on his notebooks. He put one-fourth of the covers on Monday. He put another one-fourth on Tuesday and the remaining on Wednesday. What fraction of the covers did he put on Wednesday?

Sol. Covers putting by Sohan on Monday $= \frac{1}{4}$

Covers putting by him on Tuesday $= \frac{1}{4}$

∴ Covers putting by him on Wednesday $= 1 - \frac{1}{4} - \frac{1}{4} = \frac{4}{4} - \frac{1}{4} - \frac{1}{4}$

$$\left[\because 1 \text{ and } \frac{4}{4} \text{ are equivalent fractions}\right]$$

$$= \frac{4-1-1}{4} = \frac{2}{4} = \frac{1}{2}$$

Hence, he put one-half of the covers on Wednesday.

Try These (Page 156)

Que 4. Add with the help of a diagram.

(i) $\frac{1}{8} + \frac{1}{8}$ (ii) $\frac{2}{5} + \frac{3}{5}$ (iii) $\frac{1}{6} + \frac{1}{6} + \frac{1}{6}$

Sol. (i) Here, draw two rectangles and divide them into 8 equal parts out of which 1 part is shaded. On adding them, we get 2 parts shaded out of 8 equal parts. Thus,

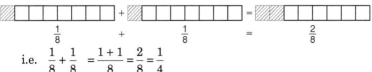

$$\frac{1}{8} \qquad + \qquad \frac{1}{8} \qquad = \qquad \frac{2}{8}$$

i.e. $\frac{1}{8} + \frac{1}{8} = \frac{1+1}{8} = \frac{2}{8} = \frac{1}{4}$

(ii) Here, draw two rectangles and divide them into 5 equal parts separately. In first rectangle, 2 parts out of 5 parts are shaded and in second rectangle, 3 parts out of 5 parts are shaded. On adding them, we get all 5 parts shaded. Thus,

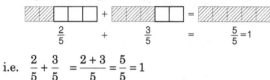

$$\frac{2}{5} \qquad + \qquad \frac{3}{5} \qquad = \qquad \frac{5}{5}=1$$

i.e. $\dfrac{2}{5} + \dfrac{3}{5} = \dfrac{2+3}{5} = \dfrac{5}{5} = 1$

(iii) Here, draw three rectangles and divide them into 6 equal parts separately and shade 1 part out of 6 parts of each rectangle. On adding them, we get 3 parts shade out of 6 parts i.e. one-half rectangle shaded. Thus,

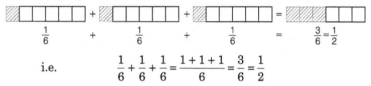

$$\frac{1}{6} \quad + \quad \frac{1}{6} \quad + \quad \frac{1}{6} \quad = \quad \frac{3}{6}=\frac{1}{2}$$

i.e. $\qquad \dfrac{1}{6} + \dfrac{1}{6} + \dfrac{1}{6} = \dfrac{1+1+1}{6} = \dfrac{3}{6} = \dfrac{1}{2}$

Que 5. Add $\dfrac{1}{12} + \dfrac{1}{12}$. How will we show this pictorially? Using paper folding?

Sol. We have, $\qquad \dfrac{1}{12} + \dfrac{1}{12} = \dfrac{1+1}{12} = \dfrac{2}{12} = \dfrac{1}{6}$

Pictorially, it can be shown as

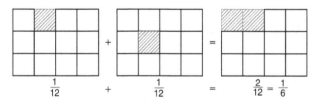

$$\frac{1}{12} \qquad + \qquad \frac{1}{12} \qquad = \qquad \frac{2}{12} = \frac{1}{6}$$

By folding paper, it can be shown in the following way

Take a square piece of paper say *ABCD* [figure (i)].

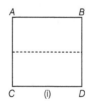

Fold it by overlapping its edge *AB* and *CD* to get figure (ii).

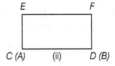

Again, refold it by taking *EF* over *C*(*A*) *D*(*B*) to get figure (iii).

Now, reopen it, then we get the following figure (iv)

Now, fold it vertically at two places to obtain three equal vertical portion as shown in figure (v).

Shaded $\dfrac{1}{12}$ portion twice,

We see that, $\quad \dfrac{1}{12} + \dfrac{1}{12} = \dfrac{1+1}{12} = \dfrac{2}{12} = \dfrac{1}{6}$

Try These (Page 157)

Que 6. Find the difference between $\dfrac{7}{8}$ and $\dfrac{3}{8}$.

 TIPS

Here, both fractions are like fractions, so difference is obtained by subtracting smaller numerator from greater numerator.

Sol. Given, $\dfrac{7}{8}$ and $\dfrac{3}{8}$

∴ $\qquad$ Difference $= \dfrac{7}{8} - \dfrac{3}{8} = \dfrac{7-3}{8} = \dfrac{4}{8} = \dfrac{1}{2}$

Que 7. Mother made a gud patti in a round shape. She divided it into 5 parts. Seema ate one piece from it. If I eat another piece, then how much would be left?

Sol. Total number of equal parts of gud patti = 5

Gud patti eaten by Seema = $\dfrac{1}{5}$; Gud patti eaten by me = $\dfrac{1}{5}$

Fraction of gud patti eaten by Seema and me = $\dfrac{1}{5} + \dfrac{1}{5}$

$$= \dfrac{1+1}{5} = \dfrac{2}{5}$$

∴ Fraction of gud patti left out = $\dfrac{1}{1} - \dfrac{2}{5} = \dfrac{5-2}{5} = \dfrac{3}{5}$

Hence, $\dfrac{3}{5}$th of the gud patti would be left.

Que 8. My elder sister divided the watermelon into 16 parts. I ate 7 out of them. My friend ate 4. How much did we eat between us? How much more of the watermelon did I eat than my friend? What portion of the watermelon remained?

Sol. Here, a watermelon is divided into 16 parts.

∴   Each part = $\dfrac{1}{16}$

I ate 7 parts out of 16 parts i.e. $\dfrac{7}{16}$ part

My friend ate 4 parts out of 16 parts i.e. $\dfrac{4}{16}$ part

Now, the part which we eat together = $\dfrac{7}{16} + \dfrac{4}{16}$

$$= \dfrac{7+4}{16} = \dfrac{11}{16} \text{ part}$$

Now, difference between our parts = $\dfrac{7}{16} - \dfrac{4}{16} = \dfrac{7-4}{16} = \dfrac{3}{16}$

So, I ate $\dfrac{3}{16}$ part of watermelon more than my friend.

Now, remaining part of the watermelon = $1 - \dfrac{11}{16} = \dfrac{16}{16} - \dfrac{11}{16}$

$$\left[\because \dfrac{16}{16} \text{ and 1 are equivalent fractions}\right]$$

$$= \dfrac{16-11}{16} = \dfrac{5}{16}$$

Exercise 7.5

Que 1. Write these fractions appropriately as additions or subtractions

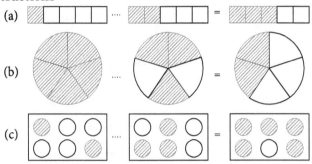

(a)

(b)

(c)

Sol. (a) In first figure, fraction for shaded portion $= \dfrac{1}{5}$

In second figure, fraction for shaded portion $= \dfrac{2}{5}$

and in third figure, fraction for shaded portion $= \dfrac{3}{5}$

Here, third figure represents more shaded portion than first and second figures.

So, $\qquad \dfrac{1}{5} + \dfrac{2}{5} = \dfrac{1+2}{5} = \dfrac{3}{5}$

$\therefore$ The given figure will be as follows:

$$\dfrac{1}{5} \qquad + \qquad \dfrac{2}{5} \qquad = \qquad \dfrac{3}{5}$$

(b) In first figure, fraction for shaded portion $= 1$ or $\dfrac{5}{5}$

In second figure, fraction for shaded portion $= \dfrac{3}{5}$

and in third figure, fraction for shaded portion $= \dfrac{2}{5}$

Here, third figure represents less shaded portion than first and second figure.

So, $\qquad 1 - \dfrac{3}{5} = \dfrac{5-3}{5} = \dfrac{2}{5}$

∴ The given figure is represented as follows :

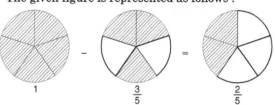

(c) In first figure, fraction for shaded portion $= \dfrac{2}{6}$

In second figure, fraction for shaded portion $= \dfrac{3}{6}$

and in third figure, fraction for shaded portion $= \dfrac{5}{6}$

Here, third figure represents more shaded portion than first and second figures.

So, $\dfrac{2}{6} + \dfrac{3}{6} = \dfrac{2+3}{6} = \dfrac{5}{6}$

∴ The given figure is represented as follows:

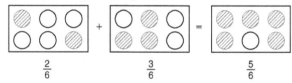

Que 2. Solve :

(a) $\dfrac{1}{18} + \dfrac{1}{18}$ (b) $\dfrac{8}{15} + \dfrac{3}{15}$ (c) $\dfrac{7}{7} - \dfrac{5}{7}$

(d) $\dfrac{1}{22} + \dfrac{21}{22}$ (e) $\dfrac{12}{15} - \dfrac{7}{15}$ (f) $\dfrac{5}{8} + \dfrac{3}{8}$

(g) $1 - \dfrac{2}{3}$ (h) $\dfrac{1}{4} + \dfrac{0}{4}$ (i) $3 - \dfrac{12}{5}$

TIPS
To add or subtract like fractions, we add the numerators or subtract the smaller numerator from greater numerator keeping denominator unchanged and then write in simplest form.

Sol. (a) We have, $\dfrac{1}{18} + \dfrac{1}{18} = \dfrac{1+1}{18} = \dfrac{2}{18} = \dfrac{1}{9}$ [simplest form]

(b) We have, $\dfrac{8}{15} + \dfrac{3}{15} = \dfrac{8+3}{15} = \dfrac{11}{15}$ [simplest form]

(c) We have, $\dfrac{7}{7} - \dfrac{5}{7} = \dfrac{7-5}{7} = \dfrac{2}{7}$ [simplest form]

(d) We have, $\dfrac{1}{22} + \dfrac{21}{22} = \dfrac{1+21}{22} = \dfrac{22}{22} = 1$ [simplest form]

(e) We have, $\dfrac{12}{15} - \dfrac{7}{15} = \dfrac{12-7}{15} = \dfrac{5}{15} = \dfrac{1}{3}$ [simplest form]

(f) We have, $\dfrac{5}{8} + \dfrac{3}{8} = \dfrac{5+3}{8} = \dfrac{8}{8} = 1$ [simplest form]

(g) We have, $1 - \dfrac{2}{3} = \dfrac{3}{3} - \dfrac{2}{3} = \dfrac{3-2}{3} = \dfrac{1}{3}$

$$\left[\because\; 1 \text{ and } \dfrac{3}{3} \text{ are [simplest form]}\atop \text{equivalent fractions}\right]$$

(h) We have, $\dfrac{1}{4} + \dfrac{0}{4} = \dfrac{1+0}{4} = \dfrac{1}{4}$ [simplest form]

(i) We have, $3 - \dfrac{12}{5} = \dfrac{3}{1} - \dfrac{12}{5}$

$$\left[\text{converting } \dfrac{3}{1} \text{ into like fraction}\atop \text{by multiplying numerator and denominator by 5}\right]$$

$= \dfrac{3 \times 5}{1 \times 5} - \dfrac{12}{5}$

$= \dfrac{15}{5} - \dfrac{12}{5} = \dfrac{15-12}{5} = \dfrac{3}{5}$ [simplest form]

Que 3. Shubham painted 2/3 of the wall space in his room. His sister Madhavi helped and painted 1/3 of the wall space. How much did they paint together?

Sol. Portion of the wall painted by Shubham $= \dfrac{2}{3}$

Portion of the wall painted by Madhavi $= \dfrac{1}{3}$

Portion of the wall painted by both $= \dfrac{2}{3} + \dfrac{1}{3} = \dfrac{2+1}{3} = \dfrac{3}{3} = 1$

Hence, they painted complete wall together.

Que 4. Fill in the missing fractions.

(a) $\dfrac{7}{10} - \square = \dfrac{3}{10}$ (b) $\square - \dfrac{3}{21} = \dfrac{5}{21}$

(c) $\square - \dfrac{3}{6} = \dfrac{3}{6}$ (d) $\square + \dfrac{5}{27} = \dfrac{12}{27}$

Sol. (a) We have, $\dfrac{7}{10} - \square = \dfrac{3}{10}$

Here, missing fraction is subtracted from $\dfrac{7}{10}$ to get $\dfrac{3}{10}$. This means on adding missing term to $\dfrac{3}{10}$, we get $\dfrac{7}{10}$. So, we subtract $\dfrac{3}{10}$ from $\dfrac{7}{10}$ to get missing fraction.

∴ Missing fraction $= \dfrac{7}{10} - \dfrac{3}{10} = \dfrac{7-3}{10} = \dfrac{4}{10}$ or $\dfrac{2}{5}$ [simplest form]

Thus, $\dfrac{7}{10} - \boxed{\dfrac{2}{5}} = \dfrac{3}{10}$

(b) We have, $\square - \dfrac{3}{21} = \dfrac{5}{21}$

Here, $\dfrac{3}{21}$ is subtracted from missing fraction to get $\dfrac{5}{21}$. So, we add $\dfrac{3}{21}$ to $\dfrac{5}{21}$ to get missing fraction.

∴ Missing fraction $= \dfrac{3}{21} + \dfrac{5}{21} = \dfrac{3+5}{21} = \dfrac{8}{21}$

Thus, $\dfrac{8}{21} - \dfrac{3}{21} = \dfrac{5}{21}$

(c) We have, $\square - \dfrac{3}{6} = \dfrac{3}{6}$

Here, $\dfrac{3}{6}$ is subtracted from missing fraction to get $\dfrac{3}{6}$. So, we add $\dfrac{3}{6}$ to $\dfrac{3}{6}$, to get missing fraction.

∴ Missing fraction $= \dfrac{3}{6} + \dfrac{3}{6} = \dfrac{3+3}{6} = \dfrac{6}{6} = 1$

Thus, $\boxed{\dfrac{6}{6}} - \dfrac{3}{6} = \dfrac{3}{6}$

(d) We have, $\square + \dfrac{5}{27} = \dfrac{12}{27}$

Here, $\dfrac{5}{27}$ is added to missing fraction to get $\dfrac{12}{27}$. So, we subtract $\dfrac{5}{27}$ from $\dfrac{12}{27}$ to get missing fraction.

∴ Missing fraction $= \dfrac{12}{27} - \dfrac{5}{27} = \dfrac{12-5}{27} = \dfrac{7}{27}$

Thus, $\boxed{\dfrac{7}{27}} + \dfrac{5}{27} = \dfrac{12}{27}$

Que 5. Javed was given 5/7 of a basket of oranges. What fraction of oranges was left in the basket?

Sol. Let full basket of oranges $= 1 = \dfrac{7}{7}$

Part of oranges given to Javed $= \dfrac{5}{7}$

∴ Part of oranges left in the basket $= \dfrac{7}{7} - \dfrac{5}{7} = \dfrac{7-5}{7} = \dfrac{2}{7}$

Hence, $\dfrac{2}{7}$ part of oranges was left in the basket.

Try These (Page 159)

Que 1. Add $\dfrac{2}{5}$ and $\dfrac{3}{7}$.

> **TIPS**
> To add unlike fractions, firstly convert them into equivalent fractions with same denominator which is LCM of denominators of given fractions and then add same as like fractions.

Sol. We have, $\dfrac{2}{5} + \dfrac{3}{7}$

LCM of 5 and 7 = 35

∴ $\dfrac{2}{5} + \dfrac{3}{7} = \dfrac{2 \times 7}{5 \times 7} + \dfrac{3 \times 5}{7 \times 5} = \dfrac{14}{35} + \dfrac{15}{35} = \dfrac{14+15}{35} = \dfrac{29}{35}$

Hence, $\dfrac{2}{5} + \dfrac{3}{7} = \dfrac{29}{35}$

Que 2. Subtract $\dfrac{2}{5}$ from $\dfrac{5}{7}$.

> **TIPS**
> To subtract unlike fractions, firstly convert them into equivalent fractions with same denominator which is LCM of denominators of given fractions and then subtract smaller numerator from greater numerator.

Sol. We have, $\dfrac{5}{7} - \dfrac{2}{5}$

LCM of 5 and 7 = 35

∴ $\dfrac{5}{7} - \dfrac{2}{5} = \dfrac{5 \times 5}{7 \times 5} - \dfrac{2 \times 7}{5 \times 7} = \dfrac{25}{35} - \dfrac{14}{35} = \dfrac{25-14}{35} = \dfrac{11}{35}$

Hence, $\dfrac{5}{7} - \dfrac{2}{5} = \dfrac{11}{35}$

Exercise 7.6

Que 1. Solve

(a) $\dfrac{2}{3} + \dfrac{1}{7}$

(b) $\dfrac{3}{10} + \dfrac{7}{15}$

(c) $\dfrac{4}{9} + \dfrac{2}{7}$

(d) $\dfrac{5}{7} + \dfrac{1}{3}$

(e) $\dfrac{2}{5} + \dfrac{1}{6}$

(f) $\dfrac{4}{5} + \dfrac{2}{3}$

(g) $\dfrac{3}{4} - \dfrac{1}{3}$

(h) $\dfrac{5}{6} - \dfrac{1}{3}$

(i) $\dfrac{2}{3} + \dfrac{3}{4} + \dfrac{1}{2}$

(j) $\dfrac{1}{2} + \dfrac{1}{3} + \dfrac{1}{6}$

(k) $1\dfrac{1}{3} + 3\dfrac{2}{3}$

(l) $4\dfrac{2}{3} + 3\dfrac{1}{4}$

(m) $\dfrac{16}{5} - \dfrac{7}{5}$

(n) $\dfrac{4}{3} - \dfrac{1}{2}$

TIPS

To add mixed fraction, we add whole part of first fraction to second fraction and fractional part of first fraction to second fraction.

Sol. (a) We have, $\dfrac{2}{3} + \dfrac{1}{7}$

LCM of 3 and 7 = 21

∴ $\dfrac{2}{3} + \dfrac{1}{7} = \dfrac{2 \times 7}{3 \times 7} + \dfrac{1 \times 3}{7 \times 3} = \dfrac{14}{21} + \dfrac{3}{21} = \dfrac{14 + 3}{21} = \dfrac{17}{21}$

Hence, $\dfrac{2}{3} + \dfrac{1}{7} = \dfrac{17}{21}$

(b) We have, $\dfrac{3}{10} + \dfrac{7}{15}$

LCM of 10 and 15 = 30

∴ $\dfrac{3}{10} + \dfrac{7}{15} = \dfrac{3 \times 3}{10 \times 3} + \dfrac{7 \times 2}{15 \times 2} = \dfrac{9}{30} + \dfrac{14}{30} = \dfrac{9 + 14}{30} = \dfrac{23}{30}$

Hence, $\dfrac{3}{10} + \dfrac{7}{15} = \dfrac{23}{30}$

(c) We have, $\dfrac{4}{9} + \dfrac{2}{7}$

LCM of 9 and 7 = 63

∴ $\dfrac{4}{9} + \dfrac{2}{7} = \dfrac{4 \times 7}{9 \times 7} + \dfrac{2 \times 9}{7 \times 9} = \dfrac{28}{63} + \dfrac{18}{63} = \dfrac{28 + 18}{63} = \dfrac{46}{63}$

Hence, $\dfrac{4}{9} + \dfrac{2}{7} = \dfrac{46}{63}$

(d) We have, $\dfrac{5}{7} + \dfrac{1}{3}$

     LCM of 3 and 7 = 21

$\therefore$ $\dfrac{5}{7} + \dfrac{1}{3} = \dfrac{5 \times 3}{7 \times 3} + \dfrac{1 \times 7}{3 \times 7} = \dfrac{15}{21} + \dfrac{7}{21} = \dfrac{15 + 7}{21} = \dfrac{22}{21}$

Hence, $\dfrac{5}{7} + \dfrac{1}{3} = \dfrac{22}{21}$

(e) We have, $\dfrac{2}{5} + \dfrac{1}{6}$

     LCM of 5 and 6 = 30

$\therefore$ $\dfrac{2}{5} + \dfrac{1}{6} = \dfrac{2 \times 6}{5 \times 6} + \dfrac{1 \times 5}{6 \times 5} = \dfrac{12}{30} + \dfrac{5}{30} = \dfrac{12 + 5}{30} = \dfrac{17}{30}$

Hence, $\dfrac{2}{5} + \dfrac{1}{6} = \dfrac{17}{30}$

(f) We have, $\dfrac{4}{5} + \dfrac{2}{3}$

     LCM of 5 and 3 = 15

$\therefore$ $\dfrac{4}{5} + \dfrac{2}{3} = \dfrac{4 \times 3}{5 \times 3} + \dfrac{2 \times 5}{3 \times 5} = \dfrac{12}{15} + \dfrac{10}{15} = \dfrac{12 + 10}{15} = \dfrac{22}{15}$

Hence, $\dfrac{4}{5} + \dfrac{2}{3} = \dfrac{22}{15}$

(g) We have, $\dfrac{3}{4} - \dfrac{1}{3}$

     LCM of 4 and 3 = 12

$\therefore$ $\dfrac{3}{4} - \dfrac{1}{3} = \dfrac{3 \times 3}{4 \times 3} - \dfrac{1 \times 4}{3 \times 4} = \dfrac{9}{12} - \dfrac{4}{12} = \dfrac{9 - 4}{12} = \dfrac{5}{12}$

Hence, $\dfrac{3}{4} - \dfrac{1}{3} = \dfrac{5}{12}$

(h) We have, $\dfrac{5}{6} - \dfrac{1}{3}$

     LCM of 6 and 3 = 6

$\therefore$ $\dfrac{5}{6} - \dfrac{1}{3} = \dfrac{5 \times 1}{6 \times 1} - \dfrac{1 \times 2}{3 \times 2} = \dfrac{5}{6} - \dfrac{2}{6} = \dfrac{5 - 2}{6} = \dfrac{3}{6} = \dfrac{1}{2}$

Hence, $\dfrac{5}{6} - \dfrac{1}{3} = \dfrac{1}{2}$

(i) We have, $\dfrac{2}{3} + \dfrac{3}{4} + \dfrac{1}{2}$

LCM of 3, 4 and 2 = 12

$\therefore \qquad \dfrac{2}{3} + \dfrac{3}{4} + \dfrac{1}{2} = \dfrac{2 \times 4}{3 \times 4} + \dfrac{3 \times 3}{4 \times 3} + \dfrac{1 \times 6}{2 \times 6}$

$$= \dfrac{8}{12} + \dfrac{9}{12} + \dfrac{6}{12} = \dfrac{8 + 9 + 6}{12} = \dfrac{23}{12}$$

Hence, $\qquad \dfrac{2}{3} + \dfrac{3}{4} + \dfrac{1}{2} = \dfrac{23}{12}$

(j) We have, $\dfrac{1}{2} + \dfrac{1}{3} + \dfrac{1}{6}$

LCM of 2, 3 and 6 = 6

$\therefore \qquad \dfrac{1}{2} + \dfrac{1}{3} + \dfrac{1}{6} = \dfrac{1 \times 3}{2 \times 3} + \dfrac{1 \times 2}{3 \times 2} + \dfrac{1 \times 1}{6 \times 1}$

$$= \dfrac{3}{6} + \dfrac{2}{6} + \dfrac{1}{6} = \dfrac{3 + 2 + 1}{6} = \dfrac{6}{6} = 1$$

Hence, $\qquad \dfrac{1}{2} + \dfrac{1}{3} + \dfrac{1}{6} = 1$

(k) We have, $1\dfrac{1}{3} + 3\dfrac{2}{3} = 1 + \dfrac{1}{3} + 3 + \dfrac{2}{3}$

$$= (1 + 3) + \left(\dfrac{1}{3} + \dfrac{2}{3}\right) = 4 + \dfrac{1}{3} + \dfrac{2}{3}$$

Now, $\qquad \dfrac{1}{3} + \dfrac{2}{3} = \dfrac{1 + 2}{3} = \dfrac{3}{3} = 1$

$\therefore \qquad 4 + \dfrac{1}{3} + \dfrac{2}{3} = 4 + 1 = 5$

Hence, $\qquad 1\dfrac{1}{3} + 3\dfrac{2}{3} = 5$

(l) We have, $4\dfrac{2}{3} + 3\dfrac{1}{4} = 4 + \dfrac{2}{3} + 3 + \dfrac{1}{4}$

$$= (4 + 3) + \left(\dfrac{2}{3} + \dfrac{1}{4}\right) = 7 + \dfrac{2}{3} + \dfrac{1}{4}$$

Now, $\qquad \dfrac{2}{3} + \dfrac{1}{4} = \dfrac{2 \times 4}{3 \times 4} + \dfrac{1 \times 3}{4 \times 3}$ $\qquad$ [$\because$ LCM of 3 and 4 is 12]

$$= \dfrac{8}{12} + \dfrac{3}{12} = \dfrac{8 + 3}{12} = \dfrac{11}{12}$$

$\therefore \qquad 7 + \dfrac{2}{3} + \dfrac{1}{4} = 7 + \dfrac{11}{12} = 7\dfrac{11}{12}$ or $\dfrac{7 \times 12 + 11}{12} = \dfrac{95}{12}$

Hence, $\qquad 4\dfrac{2}{3} + 3\dfrac{1}{4} = 7\dfrac{11}{12}$ or $\dfrac{95}{12}$

(m) We have, $\dfrac{16}{5} - \dfrac{7}{5} = \dfrac{16-7}{5} = \dfrac{9}{5}$

Hence, $\dfrac{16}{5} - \dfrac{7}{5} = \dfrac{9}{5}$

(n) We have, $\dfrac{4}{3} - \dfrac{1}{2}$

LCM of 3 and 2 = 6

$\therefore$ $\dfrac{4}{3} - \dfrac{1}{2} = \dfrac{4\times2}{3\times2} - \dfrac{1\times3}{2\times3} = \dfrac{8}{6} - \dfrac{3}{6} = \dfrac{8-3}{6} = \dfrac{5}{6}$

Hence, $\dfrac{4}{3} - \dfrac{1}{2} = \dfrac{5}{6}$

Que 2. Sarita bought $\dfrac{2}{5}$ metre of ribbon and Lalita bought $\dfrac{3}{4}$ metre of ribbon. What is the total length of the ribbon they bought?

Sol. Given, ribbon bought by Sarita $= \dfrac{2}{5}$ m

and ribbon bought by Lalita $= \dfrac{3}{4}$ m

$\therefore$ Total length of the ribbon bought by them $= \dfrac{2}{5} + \dfrac{3}{4}$

Now, LCM of 5 and 4 = 20

$\therefore$ $\dfrac{2}{5} + \dfrac{3}{4} = \dfrac{2\times4}{5\times4} + \dfrac{3\times5}{4\times5} = \dfrac{8}{20} + \dfrac{15}{20} = \dfrac{8+15}{20} = \dfrac{23}{20}$

Hence, total length of the ribbon bought by them is $\dfrac{23}{20}$ m.

Que 3. Naina was given $1\dfrac{1}{2}$ piece of cake and Najma was given $1\dfrac{1}{3}$ piece of cake. Find the total amount of cake was given to both of them.

TIPS

To add two mixed fractions, firstly we convert them into improper fractions and then add them by converting into equivalent fractions with the same denominator.

Sol. Cake given to Naina $= 1\dfrac{1}{2}$ piece;

Cake given to Najma $= 1\dfrac{1}{3}$ piece

Total cake given to both of them $= 1\dfrac{1}{2} + 1\dfrac{1}{3}$

$$= \dfrac{1 \times 2 + 1}{2} + \dfrac{1 \times 3 + 1}{3} = \dfrac{3}{2} + \dfrac{4}{3}$$

LCM of 2 and 3 $= 6$

$\therefore \qquad \dfrac{3}{2} + \dfrac{4}{3} = \dfrac{3 \times 3}{2 \times 3} + \dfrac{4 \times 2}{3 \times 2} = \dfrac{9}{6} + \dfrac{8}{6} = \dfrac{9 + 8}{6} = \dfrac{17}{6}$

Hence, total cake given to both of them $= \dfrac{17}{6}$ piece.

Que 4. Fill in the boxes

(a) $\Box - \dfrac{5}{8} = \dfrac{1}{4}$ (b) $\Box - \dfrac{1}{5} = \dfrac{1}{2}$ (c) $\dfrac{1}{2} - \Box = \dfrac{1}{6}$

Sol. (a) We have, $\Box - \dfrac{5}{8} = \dfrac{1}{4}$

Here, $\dfrac{5}{8}$ is subtracted from missing fraction to get $\dfrac{1}{4}$. This means addition of $\dfrac{5}{8}$ and $\dfrac{1}{4}$ givens the missing fraction.

$\therefore$ Missing fraction $= \dfrac{1}{4} + \dfrac{5}{8}$

$$\dfrac{1}{4} = \dfrac{1 \times 2}{4 \times 2} = \dfrac{2}{8}$$

Now, $\dfrac{1}{4} + \dfrac{5}{8} = \dfrac{2}{8} + \dfrac{5}{8} = \dfrac{2 + 5}{8} = \dfrac{7}{8}$

Hence, $\boxed{\dfrac{7}{8}} - \dfrac{5}{8} = \dfrac{1}{4}$

(b) We have, $\Box - \dfrac{1}{5} = \dfrac{1}{2}$

Here, $\dfrac{1}{5}$ is subtracted from missing fraction to get $\dfrac{1}{2}$. This means addition of $\dfrac{1}{2}$ and $\dfrac{1}{5}$ givens the missing fraction.

$\therefore$ Missing fraction $= \dfrac{1}{2} + \dfrac{1}{5}$

$$= \left[\dfrac{1 \times 5}{2 \times 5}\right] + \left[\dfrac{1 \times 2}{5 \times 2}\right] \qquad [\because \text{LCM of 2 and 5} = 10]$$

$$= \dfrac{5}{10} + \dfrac{2}{10} = \dfrac{5 + 2}{10} \text{ or } \dfrac{7}{10}$$

Hence, $\boxed{\dfrac{7}{10}} - \dfrac{1}{5} = \dfrac{1}{2}$

(c) We have, $\dfrac{1}{2} - \square = \dfrac{1}{6}$

Here, missing fraction is subtracted from $\dfrac{1}{2}$ to get $\dfrac{1}{6}$. This means addition of $\dfrac{1}{6}$ and missing fraction gives $\dfrac{1}{2}$. So, we subtract $\dfrac{1}{6}$ from $\dfrac{1}{2}$ to get missing fraction.

$\therefore$ Missing fraction $= \dfrac{1}{2} - \dfrac{1}{6}$

We have, $\qquad \dfrac{1}{2} = \dfrac{1 \times 3}{2 \times 3} = \dfrac{3}{6}$

$\therefore$ Missing fraction $= \dfrac{1}{2} - \dfrac{1}{6} = \dfrac{3}{6} - \dfrac{1}{6} = \dfrac{3-1}{6} = \dfrac{2}{6} = \dfrac{1}{3}$

Hence, $\qquad \dfrac{1}{2} - \boxed{\dfrac{1}{3}} = \dfrac{1}{6}$

Que 5. Complete the addition-subtraction box.

Sol. (a) Here, $\dfrac{2}{3} + \dfrac{4}{3} = \dfrac{2+4}{3} = \dfrac{6}{3} = 2$ and $\dfrac{1}{3} + \dfrac{2}{3} = \dfrac{1+2}{3} = \dfrac{3}{3} = 1$

Now, $\dfrac{2}{3} - \dfrac{1}{3} = \dfrac{2-1}{3} = \dfrac{1}{3}$

and $\qquad \dfrac{4}{3} - \dfrac{2}{3} = \dfrac{4-2}{3} = \dfrac{2}{3}$

Also, we have $2 - 1 = 1$ and $\dfrac{1}{3} + \dfrac{2}{3} = \dfrac{1+2}{3} = \dfrac{3}{3} = 1$

Hence, the required complete box is

(b) Here, $\dfrac{1}{2} + \dfrac{1}{3} = \dfrac{1 \times 3}{2 \times 3} + \dfrac{1 \times 2}{3 \times 2}$ [∵ LCM of 2 and 3 = 6]

$$= \dfrac{3}{6} + \dfrac{2}{6} = \dfrac{3+2}{6} = \dfrac{5}{6}$$

and $\dfrac{1}{3} + \dfrac{1}{4} = \dfrac{1 \times 4}{3 \times 4} + \dfrac{1 \times 3}{4 \times 3}$ [∵ LCM of 3 and 4 = 12]

$$= \dfrac{4}{12} + \dfrac{3}{12} = \dfrac{4+3}{12} = \dfrac{7}{12}$$

Now, $\dfrac{1}{2} - \dfrac{1}{3} = \dfrac{1 \times 3}{2 \times 3} - \dfrac{1 \times 2}{3 \times 2}$ [∵ LCM of 2 and 3 = 6]

$$= \dfrac{3}{6} - \dfrac{2}{6} = \dfrac{3-2}{6} = \dfrac{1}{6}$$

and $\dfrac{1}{3} - \dfrac{1}{4} = \dfrac{1 \times 4}{3 \times 4} - \dfrac{1 \times 3}{4 \times 3}$ [∵ LCM of 3 and 4 = 12]

$$= \dfrac{4}{12} - \dfrac{3}{12} = \dfrac{4-3}{12} = \dfrac{1}{12}$$

Also, we have $\dfrac{5}{6} - \dfrac{7}{12} = \dfrac{5 \times 2}{6 \times 2} - \dfrac{7 \times 1}{12 \times 1}$ [∵ LCM of 6 and 12 = 12]

$$= \dfrac{10}{12} - \dfrac{7}{12} = \dfrac{10-7}{12} = \dfrac{3}{12} = \dfrac{1}{4}$$

[dividing numerator and denominator by 3]

and $\dfrac{1}{6} + \dfrac{1}{12} = \dfrac{1 \times 2}{6 \times 2} + \dfrac{1 \times 1}{12 \times 1}$ [∵ LCM of 6 and 12 = 12]

$$= \dfrac{2}{12} + \dfrac{1}{12} = \dfrac{2+1}{12} = \dfrac{3}{12} = \dfrac{1}{4}$$

[dividing numerator and denominator by 3]

Hence, the required complete box is

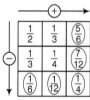

Que 6. A piece of wire $\dfrac{7}{8}$ metre long broke into two pieces. One piece was $\dfrac{1}{4}$ metre long. How long is the other piece?

Sol. Given, total length of a piece of wire $= \dfrac{7}{8}$ m

Length of one piece of wire $= \dfrac{1}{4}$ m

∴ Length of another piece $= \left(\dfrac{7}{8} - \dfrac{1}{4}\right)$ m

LCM of 8 and 4 = 8

∴ $\dfrac{7}{8} - \dfrac{1}{4} = \dfrac{7 \times 1}{8 \times 1} - \dfrac{1 \times 2}{4 \times 2} = \dfrac{7}{8} - \dfrac{2}{8} = \dfrac{7-2}{8} = \dfrac{5}{8}$

Hence, length of another piece of wire is $\dfrac{5}{8}$ m.

Que 7. Nandini's house is $\dfrac{9}{10}$ km from her school. She walked some distance and then took a bus for $\dfrac{1}{2}$ km to reach the school. How far did she walk?

Sol. Given, distance of school from Nandini's house $= \dfrac{9}{10}$ km

Distance covered by Nandini by bus $= \dfrac{1}{2}$ km

∴ Distance covered by Nandini by walking $= \dfrac{9}{10} - \dfrac{1}{2}$

LCM of 10 and 2 = 10

$\dfrac{9}{10} - \dfrac{1}{2} = \dfrac{9 \times 1}{10 \times 1} - \dfrac{1 \times 5}{2 \times 5} = \dfrac{9}{10} - \dfrac{5}{10} = \dfrac{9-5}{10} = \dfrac{4}{10} = \dfrac{2}{5}$ km

Hence, she walked $\dfrac{2}{5}$ km.

Que 8. Asha and Samuel have bookshelves of the same size partly filled with books. Asha's shelf is $\dfrac{5}{6}$th full and Samuel's shelf is $\dfrac{2}{5}$th full. Whose bookshelf is more full? By what fraction?

Sol. The portion of Asha's shelf filled by books $= \dfrac{5}{6}$ part

and the portion of Samuel's shelf filled by books $= \dfrac{2}{5}$ part

Now, LCM of 6 and 5 = 30

Equivalent fractions of $\dfrac{5}{6}$ are $\dfrac{5 \times 2}{6 \times 2}, \dfrac{5 \times 3}{6 \times 3}, \dfrac{5 \times 4}{6 \times 4}, \dfrac{5 \times 5}{6 \times 5}, \dots$

i.e. $\dfrac{10}{12}, \dfrac{15}{18}, \dfrac{20}{24}, \dfrac{25}{30}, \dots$

and equivalent fractions of $\dfrac{2}{5}$ are $\dfrac{2 \times 2}{5 \times 2}, \dfrac{2 \times 3}{5 \times 3}, \dfrac{2 \times 4}{5 \times 4}, \dfrac{2 \times 5}{5 \times 5}, \dfrac{2 \times 6}{5 \times 6}, \cdots$

i.e. $\qquad\qquad \dfrac{4}{10}, \dfrac{6}{15}, \dfrac{8}{20}, \dfrac{10}{25}, \dfrac{12}{30}, \cdots$

Here, equivalent fractions $\dfrac{12}{30}$ and $\dfrac{25}{30}$ have same denominator.

$\because \qquad\qquad\qquad 25 > 12$

$\therefore \qquad\qquad\qquad \dfrac{25}{30} > \dfrac{12}{30}$ i.e. $\dfrac{5}{6} > \dfrac{2}{5}$

Now, $\qquad\qquad \dfrac{5}{6} - \dfrac{2}{5} = \dfrac{25}{30} - \dfrac{12}{30} = \dfrac{25 - 12}{30} = \dfrac{13}{30}$

Hence, Asha's book shelf is more full by fraction $\dfrac{13}{30}$.

Que 9. Jaidev takes $2\dfrac{1}{5}$ minutes to walk across the school ground. Rahul takes $\dfrac{7}{4}$ minutes to do the same. Who takes less time and by what fraction?

Sol. Time taken by Jaidev to walk across the school ground

$$= 2\dfrac{1}{5} \text{ min} = \dfrac{11}{5} \text{ min}$$

and time taken by Rahul to walk across the school ground $= \dfrac{7}{4}$ min

Now, equivalent fractions of $\dfrac{11}{5}$ are $\dfrac{11 \times 2}{5 \times 2}, \dfrac{11 \times 3}{5 \times 3}, \dfrac{11 \times 4}{5 \times 4}, \dfrac{11 \times 5}{5 \times 5}, \cdots$

i.e. $\qquad\qquad \dfrac{22}{10}, \dfrac{33}{15}, \dfrac{44}{20}, \dfrac{55}{25}, \cdots$

and equivalent fractions of $\dfrac{7}{4}$ are $\dfrac{7 \times 2}{4 \times 2}, \dfrac{7 \times 3}{4 \times 3}, \dfrac{7 \times 4}{4 \times 4}, \dfrac{7 \times 5}{4 \times 5}, \cdots$

i.e. $\qquad\qquad \dfrac{14}{8}, \dfrac{21}{12}, \dfrac{28}{16}, \dfrac{35}{20}, \cdots$

Here, equivalent fractions $\dfrac{44}{20}$ and $\dfrac{35}{20}$ have same denominators.

$\because \qquad\qquad\qquad 44 > 35$

$\therefore \qquad\qquad\qquad \dfrac{44}{20} > \dfrac{35}{20}$ i.e. $\dfrac{11}{5} > \dfrac{7}{4}$

Now, $\qquad\qquad \dfrac{11}{5} - \dfrac{7}{4} = \dfrac{44}{20} - \dfrac{35}{20} = \dfrac{44 - 35}{20} = \dfrac{9}{20}$

Hence, Rahul takes less time by $\dfrac{9}{20}$ min.

Selected **NCERT Exemplar Problems**

Directions *In Questions 1 to 5, out of the four options, only one answer is correct. Choose the correct answer.*

Que 1. The fraction which is not equal to $\dfrac{4}{5}$ is

  (a) $\dfrac{40}{50}$ (b) $\dfrac{12}{15}$ (c) $\dfrac{16}{20}$ (d) $\dfrac{9}{15}$

Sol. (a) We have, $\dfrac{40}{50}$

Now,   factors of $40 = \boxed{2} \times \boxed{5} \times 2 \times 2$

Factors of $50 = \boxed{2} \times \boxed{5} \times 5$

Common factors $= 2$ and 5

$\therefore$ HCF of 40 and 50 $= 2 \times 5 = 10$

Then, $\dfrac{40}{50} = \dfrac{40 \div 10}{50 \div 10} = \dfrac{4}{5}$

Hence, the fraction $\dfrac{40}{50}$ is equal to $\dfrac{4}{5}$.

(b) We have, $\dfrac{12}{15}$

Now,   factors of $12 = \boxed{3} \times 2 \times 2$

Factors of $15 = \boxed{3} \times 5$

Common factor $= 3$

$\therefore$ HCF of 12 and 15 $= 3$

Then, $\dfrac{12}{15} = \dfrac{12 \div 3}{15 \div 3} = \dfrac{4}{5}$

Hence, the fraction $\dfrac{12}{15}$ is equal to $\dfrac{4}{5}$.

(c) We have, $\dfrac{16}{20}$

Now,   factors of $16 = 2 \times 2 \times 2 \times 2$

Factors of $20 = 2 \times 2 \times 5$

Common factors of 16 and 20 $= 2$ and 2

$\therefore$ HCF of 16 and 20 $= 2 \times 2 = 4$

Then, $\dfrac{16}{20} = \dfrac{16 \div 4}{20 \div 4} = \dfrac{4}{5}$

Hence, fraction $\dfrac{16}{20}$ is equal to $\dfrac{4}{5}$.

(d) We have, $\dfrac{9}{15}$

Now,   factors of $9 = 3 \times 3$

Factors of $15 = 3 \times 5$

Common factor $= 3$

$\therefore$ HCF of 9 and 15 $= 3$

Then, $\dfrac{9}{15} = \dfrac{9 \div 3}{15 \div 3} = \dfrac{3}{5}$

Hence, fraction $\dfrac{9}{15}$ is not equal to $\dfrac{4}{5}$. Hence, option (d) is correct.

Que 2. Sum of $\dfrac{4}{17}$ and $\dfrac{15}{17}$ is

(a) $\dfrac{19}{17}$ (b) $\dfrac{11}{17}$ (c) $\dfrac{19}{34}$ (d) $\dfrac{2}{17}$

Sol. We have, $\dfrac{4}{17} + \dfrac{15}{17} = \dfrac{4+15}{17} = \dfrac{19}{17}$

Hence, option (a) is correct.

Que 3. On subtracting $\dfrac{5}{9}$ from $\dfrac{19}{9}$, the result is

(a) $\dfrac{24}{9}$ (b) $\dfrac{14}{9}$ (c) $\dfrac{14}{18}$ (d) $\dfrac{14}{0}$

Sol. We have, $\dfrac{19}{9} - \dfrac{5}{9} = \dfrac{19-5}{9} = \dfrac{14}{9}$

Hence, option (b) is correct.

Que 4. When $\dfrac{1}{4}$ is written with denominator as 12, its numerator is

(a) 3   (b) 8

(c) 24   (d) 12

Sol. Let N stands for numerator and D stands for the denominator.

Given, denominator of an fraction $= 12$

$\therefore$ $\dfrac{N}{D} = \dfrac{1}{4}$ $\Rightarrow$ $\dfrac{N}{12} = \dfrac{1}{4}$

$\Rightarrow$ $N \times 4 = 12 \times 1$ [by cross product]

$\Rightarrow$ $N = \dfrac{12 \times 1}{4}$ $\Rightarrow$ $N = 3$

Hence, option (a) is correct.

Que 5. If $\dfrac{5}{8} = \dfrac{20}{p}$, then value of p is

    (a) 23   (b) 2   (c) 32   (d) 16

Sol. We have, $\dfrac{5}{8} = \dfrac{20}{p}$

$\Rightarrow$ $5 \times p = 20 \times 8$ [by cross product]

$\Rightarrow$ $p = \dfrac{20 \times 8}{5}$

$\Rightarrow$ $p = 4 \times 8 = 32$

Hence, option (c) is correct.

Directions *In Questions 6 to 11, fill in the blanks to make the statements true.*

Que 6. A number representing a part of a _____ is called a fraction.

Sol. A number representing a part of a **whole** is called a fraction.

Que 7. A fraction with denominator greater than the numerator is called a _____ fraction.

Sol. A fraction with denominator greater than the numerator is called a **proper** fraction.

Que 8. Fractions with the same denominators are called _____ fractions.

Sol Fractions with the same denominators are called **like** fractions.

Que 9. $13\dfrac{5}{18}$ is a _____ fraction.

Sol. $13\dfrac{5}{18}$ is a **mixed** fraction.

Because it is combination of a whole number and a proper fraction.

Here, $13\dfrac{5}{18}$, 13 is a whole number and $\dfrac{5}{18}$ is a proper fraction.

Que 10. $\dfrac{5}{8}$ and $\dfrac{3}{8}$ are _____ proper fractions.

Sol. $\dfrac{5}{8}$ and $\dfrac{3}{8}$ are **like** proper fractions.

Because these fractions have same denominators.

Que 11. $\dfrac{6}{11}$ and $\dfrac{6}{13}$ are _____ proper fractions.

Sol. $\dfrac{6}{11}$ and $\dfrac{6}{13}$ are **unlike** proper fractions.

Because these fractions have different denominators

Directions *In questions 12 to 15, state whether the statement is true or false*

Que 12. Fractions $\dfrac{15}{39}$ and $\dfrac{45}{117}$ are equivalent fractions.

Sol. True, because product of 15 and $117 = 15 \times 117 = 1755$
and product of 39 and $45 = 39 \times 45 = 1755$

Hence, $\dfrac{15}{39}$ and $\dfrac{45}{117}$ are equivalent fractions.

Que 13. The sum of two fractions is always a fraction.

Sol. False, e.g. let two fractions be 3/2 and 5/2.

Now, sum of $\dfrac{3}{2}$ and $\dfrac{5}{2} = \dfrac{3}{2} + \dfrac{5}{2} = \dfrac{8}{2} = 4$, which is a whole number but not

a fraction.

Que 14. The result obtained by subtracting a fraction from another fraction is necessarily a fraction.

Sol. False, e.g. let two fractions be $\dfrac{5}{3}$ and $\dfrac{11}{3}$.

Now, subtract $\dfrac{5}{3}$ from $\dfrac{11}{3} = \dfrac{11}{3} - \dfrac{5}{3} = \dfrac{6}{3} = 2$,

which is a whole number but not a fraction.

Que 15. If a whole or an object is divided into a number of equal parts, then each part represents a fraction.

Sol. True, Let a whole number be 4 and equal part of $4 = 2, 2$

Total number of equal parts $= 2$

$\therefore$ Required fraction $= \dfrac{2}{4} = \dfrac{1}{2}$

Que 16. Ali divided one fruit cake equally among six persons. What part of the cake he gave to each person?

Sol. Given, total number of fruit cake $= 1$

Here, Ali divided one fruit cake equally among six persons.

$\therefore$ The part of cake given to one person $= 1/6$.

Hence, the required part is 1/6.

Que 17. Convert 2009 paise to rupees and express the result as a mixed fraction.

Sol. We know that, 1 paise $= \dfrac{1}{100}$ rupees

∴ 2009 paise $= \dfrac{2009}{100}$ rupees $= ₹\,20.09$

Now,
$$100)\,2009\,(20$$
$$\underline{2000}$$
$$9$$

When, we divide 2009 by 100, we get

Quotient $= 20$ and Remainder $= 9$

∴ $\dfrac{2009}{100} = 20\dfrac{9}{100}$

Que 18. Convert 1537 cm to m and express the result as an improper fraction.

Sol. We know that, 1 cm $= \dfrac{1}{100}$ m

∴ $1537 \text{ cm} = \dfrac{1537}{100} \text{ m} = 15.37 \text{ m}$

Now,
$$100)\,1537\,(15$$
$$\underline{100}$$
$$537$$
$$\underline{500}$$
$$37$$

When we divide 1537 by 100, we get

Quotient $= 15$ and Remainder $= 37$

∴ $\dfrac{1537}{100} = 15\dfrac{37}{100}.$

Que 19. Convert 2435m to km and express the result as mixed fraction.

Sol. We know that, $1 \text{ m} = \dfrac{1}{1000} \text{ km}$

∴ $2435 \text{ m} = \dfrac{2435}{1000} \text{ km} = 2.435 \text{ km}$

Now,
$$1000\,)\,2435\,(2$$
$$\underline{2000}$$
$$435$$

When we divide 2435 by 1000, we get

Quotient $= 2$ and Remainder $= 435$

∴ $\dfrac{2435}{1000} = 2\dfrac{435}{1000}$

Que 20. A rectangle is divided into certain number of equal parts. If 16 of the parts , so formed represent the fraction 1/4, find the number of parts in which the rectangle has been divided.

Sol. We know that, a part represents by fraction as 1/4.

$\therefore$ Fraction of their part $= \dfrac{\text{Number of parts}}{\text{Total number of parts}}$

$$\dfrac{1}{4} = \dfrac{16}{\text{Total number of parts}}$$

$\Rightarrow$ Total number of parts $= 4 \times 16 = 64$ [by cross product]

Hence, the total number of parts is 64.

Que 21. On an average, 1/10 of the food eaten is turned into organism's own body and is available for the next level of consumer in a food chain. What fraction of the food eaten is not available for the next level?

Sol. Let the complete eaten food be 1.

Part of eaten food which is available for next level $= 1/10$

$\therefore$ Remaining part of eaten food $= \dfrac{1}{1} - \dfrac{1}{10}$

Here, LCM of 1 and 10 $= 10$

$\therefore$ $\dfrac{1}{1} = \dfrac{1 \times 10}{1 \times 10} = \dfrac{10}{10}$

Now, $\dfrac{1}{1} - \dfrac{1}{10} = \dfrac{10}{10} - \dfrac{1}{10} = \dfrac{10-1}{10} = \dfrac{9}{10}$

Que 22. Mr Rajan got a job at the age of 24 years and he got retired from the job at the age of 60 years. What fraction of his age till retirement was he in the job?

Sol. Given, Rajan age on the joining $= 24$ yr

and retirement age $= 60$ yr

The number of years, he did the job $=$ Retirement age $-$ Joining age
$$= 60 - 24 = 36 \text{ yr}$$

$\therefore$ The fraction of his age till retirement, when he was in the job
$$= \dfrac{\text{Total years he did the job}}{\text{Retirement age}} = \dfrac{36}{60}$$

Now, HCF of 36 and 60 $= 12$

$\therefore$ $\dfrac{36}{60} = \dfrac{36 \div 12}{60 \div 12} = \dfrac{3}{5}$. Hence, the required fraction is $\dfrac{3}{5}$.

Que 23. It was estimated that because of people switching to Metro trains, about 33000 tonnes of CNG, 3300 tonnes of diesel and 21000 tonnes of petrol was saved by the end of year 2007. Find the fraction of

    (i) the quantity of diesel saved to the quantity of petrol saved.

    (ii) the quantity of diesel saved to the quantity of CNG saved.

Sol. Given, quantity of CNG saved = 33000 tonnes

    Quantity of diesel saved = 3300 tonnes

    and quantity of petrol saved = 21000 tonnes

(i) Required fraction $= \dfrac{\text{Quantity of diesel saved}}{\text{Quantity of petrol saved}} = \dfrac{3300}{21000} = \dfrac{33}{210}$

HCF of 33 and $210 = 3$ $\therefore$ $\dfrac{33}{210} = \dfrac{33 \div 3}{210 \div 3} = \dfrac{11}{70}$

(ii) Required fraction $= \dfrac{\text{Quantity of diesel saved}}{\text{Quantity of CNG saved}} = \dfrac{3300}{33000} = \dfrac{33}{330}$

HCF of 33 and $330 = 33$ $\therefore$ $\dfrac{33}{330} = \dfrac{33 \div 33}{330 \div 33} = \dfrac{1}{10}$

Que 24. Energy content of different foods are as follows

Food	Energy content per kg (in Joules)
Wheat	3.2 J
Rice	5.3 J
Potatoes (Cooked)	3.7 J
Milk	3.0 J

Which food provides the least energy and which provides the maximum?

Express the least energy as a fraction of the maximum energy.

Sol. In the given table, we see that the minimum value is 3.0 J and maximum value is 5.3 J

Now, least energy provide by food = 3.0 J

Food maximum energy provide by food = 5.3 J

$\therefore$ Required fraction $= \dfrac{\text{Least energy}}{\text{Maximum energy}} = \dfrac{3.0}{5.3} = \dfrac{30}{53}$

Que 25. Sunil purchased $12\dfrac{1}{2}$ litres of juice on Monday and $14\dfrac{3}{4}$ litres of juice on Tuesday. How many litres of juice did he purchase together in two days?

Sol. Sunil purchased juice on Monday $= 12\dfrac{1}{2}$ L $= \dfrac{25}{2}$ L

Sunil purchased juice on Tuesday $= 14\dfrac{3}{4}$ L $= \dfrac{59}{4}$ L

Total purchased juice in two days $= \dfrac{25}{2} + \dfrac{59}{4}$

LCM of 2 and 4 $= 4$ $\therefore$ $\dfrac{25 \times 2}{2 \times 2} + \dfrac{59}{4} = \dfrac{50}{4} + \dfrac{59}{4} = \dfrac{109}{4}$ L

Hence, the required juice is $\dfrac{109}{4}$ L

Que 26. Roma gave a wooden board of length $150\dfrac{1}{4}$ cm to a carpenter for making a shelf. The carpenter sawed off a piece of $40\dfrac{1}{5}$ cm from it. What is the length of the remaining piece?

Sol. Given, length of a wooden board $= 150\dfrac{1}{4}$ cm $= \dfrac{601}{4}$ cm

Carpenter sawed off a piece of wooden board $= 40\dfrac{1}{5}$ cm $= \dfrac{201}{5}$ cm

Length of the remaining piece $= \dfrac{601}{4} - \dfrac{201}{5}$

LCM of 4 and 5 $= 20$

$\therefore$ $\dfrac{601 \times 5}{4 \times 5} - \dfrac{201 \times 4}{5 \times 4} = \dfrac{3005}{20} - \dfrac{804}{20} = \dfrac{3005 - 804}{20} = \dfrac{2201}{20}$ m

Hence, the length of remaining piece is $\dfrac{2201}{20}$ m.

Que 27. Nasir travelled $3\dfrac{1}{2}$ km in a bus and then walked $1\dfrac{1}{8}$ km to reach a town. How much did he travel to reach the town?

Sol. Given, distance travelled by a bus $= 3\dfrac{1}{2}$ km $= \dfrac{7}{2}$ km

and distance travelled on foot $= 1\dfrac{1}{8}$ km $= \dfrac{9}{8}$ km

Total distance travelled by Nasir $= \dfrac{7}{2} + \dfrac{9}{8} = \dfrac{7 \times 4}{2 \times 4} + \dfrac{9}{8}$

[$\because$ LCM of 2 and 8 $= 8$]

$= \dfrac{28}{8} + \dfrac{9}{8} = \dfrac{28 + 9}{8} = \dfrac{37}{8}$ km

Hence, the distance travelled by Nasir is $\dfrac{37}{8}$ km.

Que 28. The fish caught by Neetu was of weight $3\frac{3}{4}$ kg and the fish caught by Narendra was of weight $2\frac{1}{2}$ kg. How much more did Neetu's fish weigh than that of Narendra?

Sol. Given, weight of fish caught by Neetu $= 3\frac{3}{4}$ kg $= \frac{15}{4}$ kg.

and weight of fish caught by Narendra $= 2\frac{1}{2}$ kg $= \frac{5}{2}$ kg.

By comparing $\frac{15}{4}$ and $\frac{5}{2}$, we get $15 \times 2 = 30$ and $4 \times 5 = 20$

Clearly, $30 > 20$ $\therefore$ $\frac{15}{4} > \frac{5}{2}$

$\therefore$ Difference between their weight $= \frac{15}{4} - \frac{5}{2} = \frac{15}{4} - \frac{5 \times 2}{2 \times 2}$

$$[\because \text{LCM of 2 and 4}]$$

$$= \frac{15}{4} - \frac{10}{4} = \frac{15 - 10}{4} = \frac{5}{4} \text{ km}$$

Que 29. Neelam's father needs $1\frac{3}{4}$ m of cloth for the skirt of Neelam's new dress and $\frac{1}{2}$ m for the scarf. How much cloth must he buy in all?

Sol. Given, need of cloth for the skirt of Neelam $= 1\frac{3}{4}$ m $= \frac{7}{4}$ m

Need of cloth for the scarf of Neelam $= \frac{1}{2}$ m

$\therefore$ Required cloths of skirt and scarf $= \frac{7}{4} + \frac{1}{2} = \frac{7}{4} + \frac{2 \times 1}{2 \times 2}$

$$[\because \text{LCM of 4 and 2} = 2]$$

$$= \frac{7}{4} + \frac{2}{4} = \frac{7 + 2}{4} = \frac{9}{4} \text{ m}$$

Hence, the required cloths is $\frac{9}{4}$ m.

Que 30. Write the fraction representing the total number of natural numbers in the collecting of numbers $-3, -2, -1, 0, 1, 2, 3$. What fraction will it be for whole numbers? What fraction will it be for integers?

Sol. Given, the collection of numbers are $-3, -2, -1, 0, 1, 2, 3$.

Total integer numbers = 7, Total natural numbers = 3

∴ Required fraction $= \dfrac{\text{Total natural numbers}}{\text{Total integer numbers}} = \dfrac{3}{7}$

Now, in the given numbers, total whole numbers = 4

∴ Required fraction $= \dfrac{\text{Total whole numbers}}{\text{Total integer numbers}} = \dfrac{4}{7}$

Again, fraction will be for integers

∴ Required fraction $= \dfrac{\text{Total integer numbers}}{\text{Total integer numbers}} = \dfrac{7}{7}$

Que 31. Put the right card in the right bag.

Cards	Bags
	Bag I
(i) $\dfrac{3}{7}$	
(ii) $\dfrac{4}{4}$	Fraction less than 1
(iii) $\dfrac{9}{8}$	
(iv) $\dfrac{8}{9}$	Bag II
(v) $\dfrac{5}{6}$	
(vi) $\dfrac{6}{11}$	Fraction equal to 1
(vii) $\dfrac{18}{18}$	
(viii) $\dfrac{19}{25}$	Bag III
(ix) $\dfrac{2}{3}$	
(x) $\dfrac{13}{17}$	Fraction greater than 1

TIPS

We know that, if numerator and denominator are equal, then this fraction is equal to 1.

If numerator is greater than denominator, then this fraction is greater than 1.

If numerator is less than denominator, then this fraction is less than 1.

Sol. (i) We have $\dfrac{3}{7}$, here 3 < 7

Given fraction is less than 1. So, we put this card in the bag I.

(ii) We have $\dfrac{4}{4}$, here 4 = 4

Given fraction is equal to 1. So, we put this card in the bag II.

(iii) We have $\dfrac{9}{8}$, here 9 > 8

Given fraction is greater than 1. So, we put this card in the bag III.

(iv) We have $\dfrac{8}{9}$, here 8 < 9

Given fraction is less than 1. So, we put this card in the bag I.

(v) We have $\dfrac{5}{6}$, here 5 < 6

Given fraction is less than 1. So, we put this card in the bag I.

(vi) We have $\dfrac{6}{11}$, here 6 < 11

Given fraction is less than 1. So, we put this card in the bag I.

(vii) We have $\dfrac{18}{18}$, here 18 = 18

Given fraction is equal to 1. So, we put this card in the bag II.

(viii) We have $\dfrac{19}{25}$, here 19 > 25

Given fraction is loss than 1. So, we put this card in the bag I.

(ix) We have $\dfrac{2}{3}$, here 2 < 3

Given fraction is less than 1. So, we put this card in the bag I.

(x) We have $\dfrac{13}{17}$, here 13 < 17

Given fraction is less than 1. So, we put this card in the bag I.

Chapter **8**

Decimals

Important Points

- Every decimal has two parts: whole part (or number) and decimal part.
  e.g. in 23.55, whole part = 23 and decimal part = .55
- **Tenths** If a whole is divided into 10 equal parts, then each part is $\frac{1}{10}$ (one-tenth) of a unit. In decimal notation, it is written as 0.1 and read as 'zero point one'. The 'dot' represents the decimal point and it comes between the units place and the tenths place.
- **Fractions as decimals** Every fraction with denominator 10 or 100 can be written in decimal notation and *vice-versa*. So, for writing the fraction in decimal notation upto tenths or hundredths place, we make denominator 10 or 100 by multiplying numerator and denominator of fraction with a suitable number.

  e.g.
  $$\frac{11}{5} = \frac{11 \times 2}{5 \times 2}$$
  $$= \frac{22}{10} = 2.2 \qquad \text{[in decimal notation]}$$

- **Decimals as fractions** To write a decimals as fractions, firstly we write the given decimal into fraction with denominator 10 or 100 and then simplify to write in lowest form.

  e.g. $1.2 = \frac{12}{10} = \frac{6}{5}$ [dividing numerator and denominator by 2]

  Note Decimal numbers having the same number of decimal places are called **like decimals** and decimal numbers having the different number of decimal places are called **unlike decimals**.

- **Hundredths** If a one block (or whole) is divided into 100 equal parts, then each part is $\dfrac{1}{100}$ (one-hundredth) of a unit. In decimal notation, it is written as 0.01 and read as 'zero point zero one'.

- The place value table can be further extended from hundredths to $\dfrac{1}{10}$ of hundredths i.e. thousandths $\left(\dfrac{1}{1000}\right)$. In decimal notation , it is written as 0.001 and read as ' zero point zero zero one'.

- **Comparing decimals** For comparing decimals, we first compare the whole part and decimal having greater whole part will be greater.
   (i) If whole part is same for both, then compare the tenths part and decimal having greater tenths part will be greater.
   (ii) If tenths part is also same, then compare the hundredths part and decimal having greater hundredth part will be greater.
   (iii) If hundredths part is same, then compare the thousandths part and find greater decimal number and so on.

   e.g. In 1.09 and 1.093, the whole part, tenths part, hundredths part are same and thousandths part of 1.093 is greater, so 1.093 is greater than 1.09.

- The place value table for a decimal is as follows:

Hundreds	Tens	Ones	Tenths	Hundredths	Thousandths
100	10	1	1/10	1/100	1/1000

Note In the place value table, if we go from left to right, then multiplying factor becomes 1/10 of the previous factor.

- All decimals can also be represented on a number line.

   Draw a number line and divide the unit length between two whole numbers into 10 equal parts each of these equal parts represents 0.1 or $\dfrac{1}{10}$.

   Now, we locate the given decimals on this line.

Important points to be remembered

- Decimals are used in many ways in our life.
  e.g. In representing units of money, length and weight.
- We know that, 100 paise = ₹ 1

$$\therefore \qquad 1 \text{ paise} = ₹\frac{1}{100} = ₹\,0.01$$

So, to convert paise (money) into rupee, multiply paise by $\frac{1}{100}$.

- We know that, 100 cm = 1m

$$\therefore \qquad 1 \text{ cm} = \frac{1}{100}\text{ m} = 0.01\,\text{m}$$

So, to convert cm into m, multiply cm by 1/100 .

Also,   1000 m = 1 km

$$\therefore \qquad 1 \text{ m} = \frac{1}{1000}\text{ km}$$

So, to convert m into km, multiply m by 1/1000.

and   10 mm = 1 cm

$$\therefore \qquad 1 \text{ mm} = \frac{1}{10}\text{ cm}$$

So, to convert mm into cm, multiply mm by 1/10.

- We know that, 1000 g = 1 kg

$$\therefore \qquad 1 \text{ g} = \frac{1}{1000}\text{ kg} = 0.001 \text{ kg}$$

So, to convert g into kg, multiply g by $\frac{1}{1000}$ (i.e. thousandths).

- To add or subtract decimals, firstly write the given decimals with like terms (i.e. tens, ones, tenths, hundredths, thousandths) one below the other and then add or subtract same as whole numbers.
  e.g. (i) Add 0.35 and 0.42

	Ones	Tenths	Hundredths
	0	3	5
+	0	4	2
	0	7	7

Thus, $0.35 + 0.42 = 0.77$

(ii) Subtract 1.32 from 2.58

Ones	Tenths	Hundredths
2	5	8
− 1	3	2
1	2	6

Thus, $2.58 - 1.32 = 1.26$

▪ **Lowest form** Numerator and denominator have no common factor other than1.

Try These (Page 165)

Que 1. Can you now write the following as decimals?

Hundreds (100)	Tens (10)	Ones (1)	Tenths $\left(\dfrac{1}{10}\right)$
5	3	8	1
2	7	3	4
3	5	4	6

Sol. Given numbers can be written in decimals as follows:

(i) 5 hundreds + 3 tens + 8 ones +1tenth

$$= 5 \times 100 + 3 \times 10 + 8 \times 1 + 1 \times \frac{1}{10}$$

$$= 500 + 30 + 8 + \frac{1}{10} = 538 + 0.1 = 538.1$$

(ii) 2 hundreds + 7 tens + 3 ones + 4 tenths

$$= 2 \times 100 + 7 \times 10 + 3 \times 1 + 4 \times \frac{1}{10}$$

$$= 200 + 70 + 3 + \frac{4}{10} = 273 + 0.4 = 273.4$$

(iii) 3 hundreds + 5 tens + 4 ones + 6 tenths

$$= 3 \times 100 + 5 \times 10 + 4 \times 1 + 6 \times \frac{1}{10}$$

$$= 300 + 50 + 4 + \frac{6}{10} = 354 + 0.6 = 354.6$$

Que 2. Ravi and Raju measured the length of their pencils. Ravi's pencil was 7 cm and 5 mm long and Raju's pencil was 8 cm and 3 mm long. Write the length of Ravi's and Raju's pencil in 'cm' using decimals.

Sol. Given, length of Ravi's pencil = 7 cm 5 mm
and length of Raju's pencil = 8 cm 3 mm

We know that, 10 mm = 1cm

$\therefore$ 1 mm = $\dfrac{1}{10}$ cm or one-tenth cm = 0. 1 cm

Now, length of Ravi's pencil = 7 cm 5 mm

$\qquad$ = 7 cm and 5 tenths cm

$\qquad$ = 7 cm + $\dfrac{5}{10}$ cm = 7 cm + 0.5 cm = 7. 5 cm

and length of Raju's pencil = 8 cm 3 mm

$\qquad$ = 8 cm and 3 tenths cm

$\qquad$ = 8 cm + $\dfrac{3}{10}$ cm = 8 cm + 0.3 cm = 8.3 cm

Que 3. Make three more examples similar to the one given in Que 1 and solve them.

Sol. Three more examples are as follows:

Hundreds	Tens	Ones	Tenths
(100)	(10)	(1)	(1/10)
2	1	6	3
4	5	4	2
7	3	2	1

Given numbers can be represented in decimals as follows:

(i) 2 × hundreds + 1 × ten + 6 × ones + 3 × tenths

$\qquad = 2 \times 100 + 1 \times 10 + 6 \times 1 + 3 \times \dfrac{1}{10}$

$\qquad = 200 + 10 + 6 + \dfrac{3}{10} = 216 + 0.3 = 216.3$

(ii) 4 × hundreds + 5 × tens + 4 × ones + 2 × tenths

$\qquad = 4 \times 100 + 5 \times 10 + 4 \times 1 + 2 \times \dfrac{1}{10}$

$\qquad = 400 + 50 + 4 + \dfrac{2}{10} = 454 + 0.2 = 454.2$

(iii) 7 × hundreds + 3 × tens + 2 × ones + 1 × tenths

$\qquad = 7 \times 100 + 3 \times 10 + 2 \times 1 + 1 \times \dfrac{1}{10}$

$\qquad = 700 + 30 + 2 + \dfrac{1}{10} = 732 + 0. 1 = 732.1$

In Text (Page 166)

Que 4. Write five numbers between 0 and 1 and show them on the number line.

Sol. Let five numbers between 0 and 1 be 0.1, 0.3, 0.5, 0.7 and 0.9. Now, we will represent them on the number line.

We know that, all these numbers are greater than 0 but less than 1. So, divide a unit length between 0 and 1 into 10 equal parts and each part represents 0.1 (one-tenths).

Now, take 1 part, 3 parts, 5 parts, 7 parts and 9 parts, respectively. Thus, 0.1, 0.3, 0.5, 0.7 and 0.9 are shown by *A*, *B*, *C*, *D* and *E* respectively on the number line.

Que 5. Can you now represent 2.3 on a number line? Check, how many ones and tenths are there in 2.3. Where will it lie on the number line?

Sol. Yes, we can represent all decimals on the number line.

We know that, 2.3 is greater than 2 but less than 3. So, divide the unit length between 2 and 3 into 10 equal parts and take 3 parts as shown below:

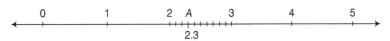

Thus, A represents 2.3 on the number line. There are 2 ones and 3 tenths in 2.3 and it will lie between 2 and 3 on the number line.

Que 6. Show 1.4 on the number line.

Sol. We know that, 1.4 is greater than 1 but less than 2. So, divide the unit length between 1 and 2 into 10 equal parts.

Here, each part represents 0.1 (one-tenths). So, take 4 parts from 1 as shown below:

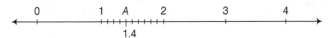

Thus, *A* represents 1.4 on the number line.

Try These (Page 167)

Que 7. Write $\dfrac{3}{2}, \dfrac{4}{5}$ and $\dfrac{8}{5}$ in decimal notation.

 TIPS

> For writing the fraction in decimal notation upto tenth place, we make denominator 10 by multiplying numerator and denominator of fraction with a suitable number.

Sol. (i) $\dfrac{3}{2} = \dfrac{3 \times 5}{2 \times 5}$ [multiplying numerator and denominator by 5 to make denominator 10]

$$= \dfrac{15}{10} = 1\dfrac{5}{10} = 1 + \dfrac{5}{10} = 1 + 0.5 = 1.5$$

Therefore, $\dfrac{3}{2}$ is 1.5 in decimal notation.

(ii) $\dfrac{4}{5} = \dfrac{4 \times 2}{5 \times 2}$ [multiplying numerator and denominator by 2 to make denominator 10]

$$= \dfrac{8}{10} = 0.8$$

Therefore, $\dfrac{4}{5}$ is 0.8 in decimal notation.

(iii) $\dfrac{8}{5} = \dfrac{8 \times 2}{5 \times 2}$ [multiplying numerator and denominator by 2 to make denominator 10]

$$= \dfrac{16}{10} = 1\dfrac{6}{10} = 1 + \dfrac{6}{10} = 1 + 0.6 = 1.6$$

Therefore, $\dfrac{8}{5}$ is 1.6 in decimal notation.

Exercise 8.1

Que 1. Write the following as numbers in the given table.

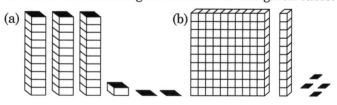

(a)

Tens   Ones   Tenths

(b)

Hundreds   Tens   Tenths

Hundreds (100)	Tens (10)	Ones (1)	Tenths (1/10)

Sol. (a) In figure (a), there are 3 towers (each of tens units), one block of 1 unit and 2 small parts (each equal to ones-tenths).
So, in table these can be written as

Hundreds (100)	Tens (10)	Ones (1)	Tenths (1/10)
0	3	1	2

(b) In figure (b), there is 1 tower (each of hundreds units), 1 tower (each of tens units) and no block (each of one unit) but 4 parts (each of ones-tenths).
So, in table these can be written as

Hundreds (100)	Tens (10)	Ones (1)	Tenths (1/10)
1	1	0	4

Que 2. Write the following decimals in the place value table.

    (a) 19.4   (b) 0.3   (c) 10.6   (d) 205.9

Sol. We can write the given decimals as follows:

(a) We have, $19.4 = \boxed{1} \times 10 + \boxed{9} \times 1 + \boxed{4} \times \dfrac{1}{10}$

Now, putting these values in place value table, we get

Hundreds (100)	Tens (10)	Ones (1)	Tenths (1/10)
0	1	9	4

(b) We have, $0.3 = \boxed{0} \times 10 + \boxed{0} \times 1 + \boxed{3} \times \dfrac{1}{10}$

Now, putting these values in place value table, we get

Hundreds (100)	Tens (10)	Ones (1)	Tenths (1/10)
0	0	0	3

(c) We have, $10.6 = \boxed{1} \times 10 + \boxed{0} \times 1 + \boxed{6} \times \dfrac{1}{10}$

Now, putting these values in place value table, we get

Hundreds (100)	Tens (10)	Ones (1)	Tenths (1/10)
0	1	0	6

(d) We have, $205.\,9 = \boxed{2} \times 100 + \boxed{0} \times 10 + \boxed{5} \times 1 + \boxed{9} \times \dfrac{1}{10}$

Now, putting these values in place value table, we get

Hundreds (100)	Tens (10)	Ones (1)	Tenths (1/10)
2	0	5	9

Que 3. Write each of the following as decimals.

   (a) Seven-tenths   (b) Two-tens and nine-tenths

   (c) Fourteen point six   (d) One hundred and two ones

   (e) Six hundred point eight

Sol. (a) Seven-tenths $= 7 \times \dfrac{1}{10} = \dfrac{7}{10} = 0.7$

   (b) Two-tens and nine-tenths $= 2 \times 10 + 9 \times \dfrac{1}{10}$

$$= 20 + \dfrac{9}{10} = 20 + 0.9 = 20.9$$

   (c) Fourteen point six $= 14.6$

   (d) One hundred and two ones $= 1 \times 100 + 0 \times 10 + 2 \times 1$

$$= 100 + 0 + 2 = 102$$

   (e) Six hundred point eight $= 600.8$

Que 4. Write each of the following as decimals.

   (a) $\dfrac{5}{10}$ (b) $3 + \dfrac{7}{10}$ (c) $200 + 60 + 5 + \dfrac{1}{10}$

   (d) $70 + \dfrac{8}{10}$ (e) $\dfrac{88}{10}$ (f) $\dfrac{2}{10}$ (g) $\dfrac{3}{2}$

   (h) $\dfrac{2}{5}$ (i) $\dfrac{12}{5}$ (j) $3\dfrac{3}{5}$ (k) $4\dfrac{1}{2}$

Sol. (a) We have, $\dfrac{5}{10}$

   Here, it has 5 tenths.

   i.e. $\qquad\qquad\qquad\qquad 5 \times \dfrac{1}{10} = \dfrac{5}{10} = 0.5$

   (b) We have, $3 + \dfrac{7}{10}$

   Here, it has 3 ones and 7 tenths.

   i.e. $\qquad\qquad\qquad\qquad 3 + \dfrac{7}{10} = 3 + 0.7 = 3.7$

(c) We have, $200 + 60 + 5 + \dfrac{1}{10}$

Here, it has 2 hundreds, 6 tens, 5 ones and one-tenths.

i.e. $2 \times 100 + 6 \times 10 + 5 \times 1 + 1 \times \dfrac{1}{10}$

$$= 200 + 60 + 5 + \dfrac{1}{10} = 265 + 0.1 = 265.1$$

(d) We have, $70 + \dfrac{8}{10}$

Here, it has 7 tens, 0 ones and 8 tenths.

i.e. $7 \times 10 + 0 \times 1 + 8 \times \dfrac{1}{10} = 70 + \dfrac{8}{10} = 70 + 0.8 = 70.8$

(e) We have, $\dfrac{88}{10} = 8\dfrac{8}{10} = 8 + \dfrac{8}{10}$

Here, it has 8 ones and 8 tenths.

i.e. $8 \times 1 + 8 \times \dfrac{1}{10} = 8 + 0.8 = 8.8$

(f) We have, $\dfrac{2}{10}$

Here, it has only 2 tenths.

i.e. $2 \times \dfrac{1}{10} = \dfrac{2}{10} = 0.2$

(g) We have, $\dfrac{3}{2} = 1\dfrac{1}{2} = 1 + \dfrac{1}{2}$

Here, it has one ones but tenths is not complete.

On multiplying by 5 in its numerator and denominator of $\dfrac{1}{2}$,

we get $1 + \dfrac{1}{2} = 1 + \dfrac{1 \times 5}{2 \times 5} = 1 + \dfrac{5}{10}$

Here, it has 1 ones and 5 tenths.

i.e. $1 \times 1 + 5 \times \dfrac{1}{10} = 1 + 0.5 = 1.5$

(h) We have, $\dfrac{2}{5}$. To make this fraction in tenths, we have to multiply

by 2 in its numerator and denominator both.

$\therefore$ $\dfrac{2}{5} = \dfrac{2 \times 2}{5 \times 2} = \dfrac{4}{10}$

Here, it has 4 tenths.

i.e. $\dfrac{4}{10} = 0.4$

(i) We have, $\dfrac{12}{5}$. To make this fraction in tenths, we have to multiply by 2 in ts numerator and denominator both.

$$\therefore \qquad \dfrac{12}{5} = \dfrac{12 \times 2}{5 \times 2} = \dfrac{24}{10} = 2\dfrac{4}{10} = 2 + \dfrac{4}{10}$$

Here, it has 2 ones and 4 tenths.

i.e. $\qquad 2 \times 1 + 4 \times \dfrac{1}{10} = 2 + \dfrac{4}{10} = 2 + 0.4 = 2.4$

(j) We have, $3\dfrac{3}{5} = 3 + \dfrac{3}{5}$. To make this fraction in tenths, we have to multiply by 2 in its numerator and denominator of 3/5.

$$\therefore \qquad 3 + \dfrac{3 \times 2}{5 \times 2} = 3 + \dfrac{6}{10}$$

Here, it has 3 ones and 6 tenths.

i.e. $\qquad 3 \times 1 + 6 \times \dfrac{1}{10} = 3 + \dfrac{6}{10} = 3 + 0.6 = 3.6$

(k) We have, $4\dfrac{1}{2} = 4 + \dfrac{1}{2}$. To make this fraction in tenths, we have to multiply by 5 in its numerator and denominator of 1/2.

$$\therefore \qquad 4 + \dfrac{1 \times 5}{2 \times 5} = 4 + \dfrac{5}{10}$$

Here, it has 4 ones and 5 tenths.

i.e. $\qquad 4 \times 1 + 5 \times \dfrac{1}{10} = 4 + \dfrac{5}{10} = 4 + 0.5 = 4.5$

Que 5. Write the following decimals as fractions. Reduce the fractions to lowest form.

(a) 0.6   (b) 2.5   (c) 1.0   (d) 3.8

(e) 13.7   (f) 21.2   (g) 6.4

TIPS

Firstly, write the given decimal into fraction with denominator 10 and then simplify fraction to write in lowest form i.e. numerator and denominator have no common factor other than 1.

Sol. (a) We have, $0.6 = 0 + \dfrac{6}{10} = \dfrac{6}{10}$

Lowest form $= \dfrac{6 \div 2}{10 \div 2} = \dfrac{3}{5}$ [$\because$ HCF of 6 and 10 = 2]

$\therefore$ Fraction of $0.6 = \dfrac{6}{10}$ and lowest form $= \dfrac{3}{5}$

(b) We have, $2.5 = 2 + \dfrac{5}{10} = \dfrac{2 \times 10}{1 \times 10} + \dfrac{5}{10}$

[multiplying by 10 in numerator and denominator of 2]

$$= \dfrac{20}{10} + \dfrac{5}{10} = \dfrac{20 + 5}{10} = \dfrac{25}{10}$$

Lowest form $= \dfrac{25 \div 5}{10 \div 5} = \dfrac{5}{2}$ [∵ HCF of 25 and 10 = 5]

∴Fraction of $2.5 = \dfrac{25}{10}$ and lowest form $= \dfrac{5}{2}$

(c) We have, $1.0 = 1 + \dfrac{0}{10} = 1 + 0 = 1$

∴ Fraction of 1.0 as well as lowest form = 1

(d) We have, $3.8 = 3 + \dfrac{8}{10} = \dfrac{3 \times 10}{1 \times 10} + \dfrac{8}{10}$

[multiplying by 10 in numerator and denominator of 3]

$$= \dfrac{30}{10} + \dfrac{8}{10} = \dfrac{30 + 8}{10} = \dfrac{38}{10}$$

Lowest form $= \dfrac{38 \div 2}{10 \div 2} = \dfrac{19}{5}$ [∵ HCF of 38 and 10 = 2]

∴Fraction of $3.8 = \dfrac{38}{10}$ and lowest form $= \dfrac{19}{5}$

(e) We have, $13.7 = 13 + \dfrac{7}{10} = \dfrac{13 \times 10}{1 \times 10} + \dfrac{7}{10}$

[multiplying by 10 in numerator and denominator of 13]

$$= \dfrac{130}{10} + \dfrac{7}{10} = \dfrac{130 + 7}{10} = \dfrac{137}{10}$$

Lowest form $= \dfrac{137 \div 1}{10 \div 1} = \dfrac{137}{10}$ [∵ HCF of 137 and 10 = 1]

∴Fraction of $13.7 = \dfrac{137}{10}$ and lowest form $= \dfrac{137}{10}$

(f) We have, $21.2 = 21 + \dfrac{2}{10} = \dfrac{21 \times 10}{1 \times 10} + \dfrac{2}{10}$

[multiplying by 10 in numerator and denominator of 21]

$$= \dfrac{210}{10} + \dfrac{2}{10} = \dfrac{210 + 2}{10} = \dfrac{212}{10}$$

Lowest form $= \dfrac{212 \div 2}{10 \div 2} = \dfrac{106}{5}$ [∵ HCF of 212 and 10 = 2]

∴Fraction of $21.2 = \dfrac{212}{10}$ and lowest form $= \dfrac{106}{5}$

(g) We have, $6.4 = 6 + \dfrac{4}{10} = \dfrac{6 \times 10}{1 \times 10} + \dfrac{4}{10}$

[multiplying by 10 in numerator and denominator of 6]

$$= \dfrac{60}{10} + \dfrac{4}{10} = \dfrac{60+4}{10} = \dfrac{64}{10}$$

Lowest form $= \dfrac{64 \div 2}{10 \div 2} = \dfrac{32}{5}$ [∵ HCF of 64 and 10 = 2]

∴ Fraction of $6.4 = \dfrac{64}{10}$ and lowest form $= \dfrac{32}{5}$

Que 6. Express the following as cm using decimals.

    (a) 2 mm   (b) 30 mm   (c) 116 mm

    (d) 4 cm 2 mm   (e) 162 mm   (f) 83 mm

TIPS

As we know that, $10 \text{ mm} = 1 \text{ cm} \Rightarrow 1 \text{ mm} = \dfrac{1}{10} \text{ cm}$

To convert mm into cm, we use tenths i.e. multiply given mm by 1/10 cm.

Sol. (a) We know that, $10 \text{ mm} = 1 \text{ cm} \Rightarrow 1 \text{ mm} = 1/10 \text{ cm}$

∴ $2 \text{ mm} = 2 \times \dfrac{1}{10} \text{ cm} = \dfrac{2}{10} \text{ cm} = 0.2 \text{ cm}$

(b) We know that, $10 \text{ mm} = 1 \text{ cm} \Rightarrow 1 \text{ mm} = \dfrac{1}{10} \text{ cm}$

∴ $30 \text{ mm} = 30 \times \dfrac{1}{10} \text{ cm} = \dfrac{30}{10} \text{ cm} = 3 \text{ cm}$

(c) We know that, $10 \text{ mm} = 1 \text{ cm} \Rightarrow 1 \text{ mm} = \dfrac{1}{10} \text{ cm}$

∴ $116 \text{ mm} = 116 \times \dfrac{1}{10} \text{ cm}$

$$= \dfrac{116}{10} \text{ cm} = 11\dfrac{6}{10} \text{ cm} = \left(11 + \dfrac{6}{10}\right) \text{ cm}$$

$$= (11 + 0.6) \text{ cm} = 11.6 \text{ cm}$$

(d) We know that, $10 \text{ mm} = 1 \text{ cm} \Rightarrow 1 \text{ mm} = \dfrac{1}{10} \text{ cm}$

∴ $4 \text{ cm } 2 \text{ mm} = 4 \text{ cm} + 2 \text{ mm}$

$$= 4 \text{ cm} + 2 \times \dfrac{1}{10} \text{ cm} = 4 \text{ cm} + \dfrac{2}{10} \text{ cm}$$

$$= (4 + 0.2) \text{ cm} = 4.2 \text{ cm}$$

(e) We know that, $10 \text{ mm} = 1 \text{ cm} \Rightarrow 1 \text{ mm} = \dfrac{1}{10} \text{ cm}$

$\therefore 162 \text{ mm} = 162 \times \dfrac{1}{10} \text{ cm} = \dfrac{162}{10} \text{ cm} = 16\dfrac{2}{10} \text{ cm} = \left(16 + \dfrac{2}{10}\right) \text{ cm}$

$= (16 + 0.2) \text{ cm} = 16.2 \text{ cm}$

(f) We know that, $10 \text{ mm} = 1 \text{ cm} \Rightarrow 1 \text{ mm} = 1 \text{ cm}$

$\therefore \quad 83 \text{ mm} = 83 \times \dfrac{1}{10} \text{ cm} = \dfrac{83}{10} \text{ cm} = 8\dfrac{3}{10} \text{ cm} = \left(8 + \dfrac{3}{10}\right) \text{ cm}$

$= (8 + 0.3) \text{ cm} = 8.3 \text{ cm}$

Que 7. Between which two whole numbers on the number line are the given numbers lie? Which of these whole numbers is nearer the number?

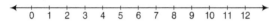

(a) 0.8   (b) 5.1   (c) 2.6

(d) 6.4   (e) 9.1   (f) 4.9

Sol. Firstly, draw the number line and divide the unit length between two whole numbers into 10 equal parts, each of these equal parts represents 0.1 or 1/10. Now, locate the given decimals on this line.

(a) We have, 0.8.

From the above figure, it is clear that number 0.8 lies between the whole numbers 0 and 1.

Hence, number 0.8 is nearer to number 1.

(b) We have, 5.1.

From the above figure, it is clear that number 5.1 lies between the whole numbers 5 and 6.

Hence, number 5.1 is nearer to number 5.

(c) We have, 2.6.

From the above figure, it is clear that number 2.6 lies between the whole numbers 2 and 3.

Hence, number 2.6 is nearer to number 3.

(d) We have, 6.4.

From the above figure, it is clear that number 6.4 lies between the whole numbers 6 and 7.

Hence, number 6.4 is nearer to number 6.

(e) We have, 9.1.

From the above figure, it is clear that number 9.1 lies between the whole numbers 9 and 10.

Hence, number 9.1 is nearer to number 9.

(f) We have, 4.9

From the above figure, it is clear that number 4.9 lies between the whole numbers 4 and 5.

Hence, number 4.9 is nearer to number 5.

Note A decimal will be nearer to that number from, which it has minimum distance, e.g. 6.4 lies between 6 and 7 and its distance from 6 (distance 4 parts) is minimum than 7 (distance 6 parts).

Que 8. Show the following numbers on the number line.

   (a) 0.2   (b) 1.9   (c) 1.1   (d) 2.5

Sol. (a) We know that, 0.2 is more than 0 but less than 1. There are 2 tenths in it. Divide the unit length between 0 and 1 on the number line into 10 equal parts and take 2 parts, which represent 0.2 as shown below on the number line.

In the figure, point A shows 0.2.

(b) We know that, 1.9 is more than 1 but less than 2. There are one ones and 9 tenths in it. Divide the unit length between 0 and 1, 1 and 2 on the number line into 10 equal parts and take 9 parts, which represents $1.9 = (1 + 0.9)$ as shown below on the number line.

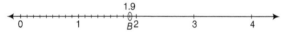

In the figure, point B shows 1.9.

(c) We know that, 1.1 is more than 1 but less than 2. There are one ones and one-tenths in it. Divide the unit length between 0 and 1, 1 and 2 on the number line into 10 equal parts, and take 1 part which represents $1.1 = (1 + 0.1)$ as shown below on the number line.

In the figure, point C shows 1.1.

(d) We know that, 2.5 is more than 2 but less than 3. There are 2 ones and 5 tenths in it. Divide the unit length between 0 and 1, 1 and 2, 2 and 3 into 10 equal parts and take 5 parts, which represents $2.5 = (2 + 0.5)$ as shown below on the number line.

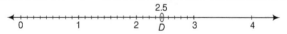

In the figure, point D shows 2.5.

Que 9. Write the decimal number represented by the points
A, B, C and *D* on the given number line.

 To write the decimal numbers represented by given points on the number line, we count their distance from 0. Here, each part represents 0.1.

Sol. Given number line is as follows

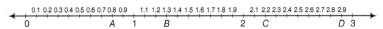

(i) From the figure, it is clear that $A = 0.8$ as the unit length between 0 and 1 has been divided into 10 equal parts and 8 parts from 0 have been taken.

(ii) From the figure, it is clear that $B = 1.3$ as the unit length between 1 and 2 has been divided into 10 equal parts and unit length between 0 to 1 and then 3 parts have been taken.

(iii) From the figure, it is clear that $C = 2.2$ as the unit length between 2 and 3 has been divided into 10 equal parts and unit length between 0 to 1, 1 to 2 and then 2 parts have been taken.

(iv) From the figure, it is clear that $D = 2.9$ as the unit length between 2 and 3 has been divided into 10 equal parts and unit length between 0 to 1, 1 to 2 and then 9 parts have been taken.

Que 10. (a) The length of Ramesh's notebook is 9 cm 5 mm. What will be its length in cm?

(b) The length of a young gram plant is 65 mm. Express its length in cm.

Sol. (a) Given, length of Ramesh's notebook = 9 cm 5 mm

We know that, $10 \text{ mm} = 1 \text{ cm} \Rightarrow 1 \text{ mm} = \dfrac{1}{10} \text{ cm}$

∴ Length of Ramesh's notebook = 9 cm 5 mm

$$= 9 \text{ cm} + 5 \times \dfrac{1}{10} \text{ cm} = 9 \text{ cm} + \dfrac{5}{10} \text{ cm}$$

$$= 9 \text{ cm} + 0.5 \text{ cm} = (9 + 0.5) \text{ cm} = 9.5 \text{ cm}$$

(b) Given, length of young gram plant = 65 mm

We know that, $10 \text{ mm} = 1 \text{ cm} \Rightarrow 1 \text{ mm} = 1/10 \text{ cm}$

∴ Length of young gram plant $= 65 \times \dfrac{1}{10} \text{ cm} = \dfrac{65}{10} \text{ cm}$

$$= 6\dfrac{5}{10} \text{ cm} = \left(6 + \dfrac{5}{10}\right) \text{ cm} = (6 + 0.5) \text{ cm} = 6.5 \text{ cm}$$

In Text (Page 169)

Que 1. What part of the whole square is the shaded portion, if we shade 8 squares, 15 squares, 50 squares, 92 squares of the whole square?

Sol. (i) If we shade 8 squares, then whole square with shaded portion is given.

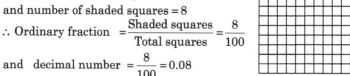

Here, total number of squares = 100

and number of shaded squares = 8

∴ Ordinary fraction $= \dfrac{\text{Shaded squares}}{\text{Total squares}} = \dfrac{8}{100}$

and decimal number $= \dfrac{8}{100} = 0.08$

(ii) If we shade 15 squares, then whole square with shaded portion is given.

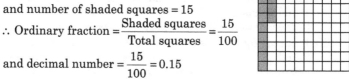

Here, total number of squares = 100

and number of shaded squares = 15

∴ Ordinary fraction $= \dfrac{\text{Shaded squares}}{\text{Total squares}} = \dfrac{15}{100}$

and decimal number $= \dfrac{15}{100} = 0.15$

(iii) If we shade 50 squares, then whole square with shaded portion is given.

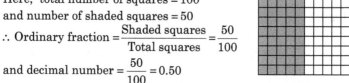

Here, total number of squares = 100

and number of shaded squares = 50

∴ Ordinary fraction $= \dfrac{\text{Shaded squares}}{\text{Total squares}} = \dfrac{50}{100}$

and decimal number $= \dfrac{50}{100} = 0.50$

(iv) If we shade 92 squares, then whole squares with shaded portion is given.

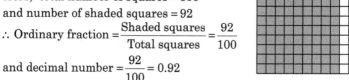

Here, total number of squares = 100

and number of shaded squares = 92

∴ Ordinary fraction $= \dfrac{\text{Shaded squares}}{\text{Total squares}} = \dfrac{92}{100}$

and decimal number $= \dfrac{92}{100} = 0.92$

Now, we can write it in the form of table as shown below:

Shaded portions	Ordinary fraction	Decimal number
8 squares	$\frac{8}{100}$	0.08
15 squares	$\frac{15}{100}$	0.15
50 squares	$\boxed{\frac{50}{100}}$	$\boxed{0.50}$
92 squares	$\boxed{\frac{92}{100}}$	$\boxed{0.92}$

Exercise 8.2

Que 1. Complete the table with the help of these boxes and use decimals to write the number.

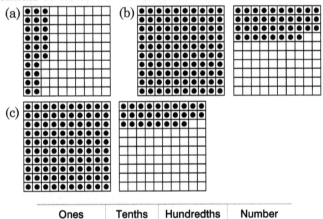

	Ones	Tenths	Hundredths	Number
(a)				
(b)				
(c)				

Sol. Here, in each figure, boxes which are given, are is divided into 10 rectangles. Each rectangle is divided into 10 small squares. Thus, given box is divided into 100 equal parts.

Here, each rectangle shows 1/10 or one-tenth and each small square shows 1/100 or one-hundredth.

(a) Here, 2 rectangle and 6 small squares are shaded (or having dark circles).

So, in decimal it can be written as $2 \times \dfrac{1}{10} + 6 \times \dfrac{1}{100} = 0.26$

(b) Here, 1 box, 3 rectangles and 8 small squares are shaded.

So, in decimal it can be written as $1 \times 1 + 3 \times \dfrac{1}{10} + 8 \times \dfrac{1}{100} = 1.38$

(c) Here, 1 box, 2 rectangles and 8 small squares are shaded.

So, in decimal it clan be written as $1 \times 1 + 2 \times \dfrac{1}{10} + 8 \times \dfrac{1}{100} = 1.28$

Thus, the complete table is given below:

	Ones (1)	Tenths (1/10)	Hundredths (1/100)	Number
(a)	0	2	6	0.26
(b)	1	3	8	1.38
(c)	1	2	8	1.28

Que 2. Write the numbers given in the following place value table in decimal form.

	Hundreds (100)	Tens (10)	Ones (1)	Tenths (1/10)	Hundredths (1/100)	Thousandths (1/1000)
(a)	0	0	3	2	5	0
(b)	1	0	2	6	3	0
(c)	0	3	0	0	2	5
(d)	2	1	1	9	0	2
(e)	0	1	2	2	4	1

Sol. (a) Here, $0 \times 100 + 0 \times 10 + 3 \times 1 + 2 \times \dfrac{1}{10} + 5 \times \dfrac{1}{100} + 0 \times \dfrac{1}{1000}$

$$= 0 + 0 + 3 + \dfrac{2}{10} + \dfrac{5}{100} + 0$$

$$= 3 + \dfrac{2}{10} + \dfrac{5}{100} = 3 + 0.2 + 0.05 = 3.25$$

(b) Here, $1 \times 100 + 0 \times 10 + 2 \times 1 + 6 \times \dfrac{1}{10} + 3 \times \dfrac{1}{100} + 0 \times \dfrac{1}{1000}$

$$= 100 + 0 + 2 + \dfrac{6}{10} + \dfrac{3}{100} + 0 = 102 + \dfrac{6}{10} + \dfrac{3}{100}$$

$$= 102 + 0.6 + 0.03 = 102.63$$

(c) Here, $0 \times 100 + 3 \times 10 + 0 \times 1 + 0 \times \dfrac{1}{10} + 2 \times \dfrac{1}{100} + 5 \times \dfrac{1}{1000}$

$$= 0 + 30 + 0 + 0 + \dfrac{2}{100} + \dfrac{5}{1000}$$

$$= 30 + \dfrac{2}{100} + \dfrac{5}{1000} = 30 + 0.02 + 0.005 = 30.025$$

(d) Here, $2 \times 100 + 1 \times 10 + 1 \times 1 + 9 \times \dfrac{1}{10} + 0 \times \dfrac{1}{100} + 2 \times \dfrac{1}{1000}$

$= 200 + 10 + 1 + \dfrac{9}{10} + 0 + \dfrac{2}{1000} = 211 + \dfrac{9}{10} + \dfrac{2}{1000}$

$= 211 + 0.9 + 0.002 = 211.902$

(e) Here, $0 \times 100 + 1 \times 10 + 2 \times 1 + 2 \times \dfrac{1}{10} + 4 \times \dfrac{1}{100} + 1 \times \dfrac{1}{1000}$

$= 0 + 10 + 2 + \dfrac{2}{10} + \dfrac{4}{100} + \dfrac{1}{1000} = 12 + \dfrac{2}{10} + \dfrac{4}{100} + \dfrac{1}{1000}$

$= 12 + 0.2 + 0.04 + 0.001 = 12.241$

Que 3. Write the following decimals in the place value table.

(a) 0.29   (b) 2.08   (c) 19.60

(d) 148.32   (e) 200.812

Sol. The given decimals can be written as

(a) $0.29 = 0 + \dfrac{2}{10} + \dfrac{9}{100}$ (b) $2.08 = 2 + \dfrac{0}{10} + \dfrac{8}{100}$

(c) $19.60 = 10 + 9 + \dfrac{6}{10} + \dfrac{0}{100}$ (d) $148.32 = 100 + 40 + 8 + \dfrac{3}{10} + \dfrac{2}{100}$

(e) $200.812 = 200 + 00 + 0 + \dfrac{8}{10} + \dfrac{1}{100} + \dfrac{2}{1000}$

Now, the place value table is given below:

Decimal number	Hundreds (100)	Tens (10)	Ones (1)	Tenths (1/10)	Hundredths (1/100)	Thousandths (1/1000)
(a) 0.29	0	0	0	2	9	0
(b) 2.08	0	0	2	0	8	0
(c) 19.60	0	1	9	6	0	0
(d) 148.32	1	4	8	3	2	0
(e) 200.812	2	0	0	8	1	2

Que 4. Write each of the following as decimals.

(a) $20 + 9 + \dfrac{4}{10} + \dfrac{1}{100}$ (b) $137 + \dfrac{5}{100}$

(c) $\dfrac{7}{10} + \dfrac{6}{100} + \dfrac{4}{1000}$ (d) $23 + \dfrac{2}{10} + \dfrac{6}{1000}$

(e) $700 + 20 + 5 + \dfrac{9}{100}$

Sol. (a) We have, $20 + 9 + \dfrac{4}{10} + \dfrac{1}{100} = 29 + 4 \times \dfrac{1}{10} + 1 \times \dfrac{1}{100}$

$= 29 + 0.4 + 0.01 = 29.41$

(b) We have, $137 + \dfrac{5}{100}$

$$= 137 + 0 \times \dfrac{1}{10} + 5 \times \dfrac{1}{100} = 137 + 0 + 0.05 = 137.05$$

(c) We have, $\dfrac{7}{10} + \dfrac{6}{100} + \dfrac{4}{1000}$

$$= 7 \times \dfrac{1}{10} + 6 \times \dfrac{1}{100} + 4 \times \dfrac{1}{1000}$$

$$= 0.7 + 0.06 + 0.004 = 0.764$$

(d) We have, $23 + \dfrac{2}{10} + \dfrac{6}{1000} = 23 + 2 \times \dfrac{1}{10} + 0 \times \dfrac{1}{100} + 6 \times \dfrac{1}{1000}$

$$= 23 + 0.2 + 0 + 0.006 = 23.206$$

(e) We have, $700 + 20 + 5 + \dfrac{9}{100}$

$$= 725 + 0 \times \dfrac{1}{10} + 9 \times \dfrac{1}{100} = 725 + 0 + 0.09 = 725.09$$

Que 5. Write each of the following decimals in words.

    (a) 0.03   (b) 1.20   (c) 108.56

    (d) 10.07   (e) 0.032   (f) 5.008

Sol. Decimals in words are given below:

    (a) We have, 0.03   = Zero point zero three

    (b) We have, 1.20   = One point two zero

    (c) We have, 108.56 = One hundred eight point five six

    (d) We have, 10.07 = Ten point zero seven

    (e) We have, 0.032 = Zero point zero three two

    (f) We have, 5.008 = Five point zero zero eight

Que 6. Between which two numbers in tenths place on the number line does each of the given number lie?

    (a) 0.06   (b) 0.45   (c) 0.19

    (d) 0.66   (e) 0.92   (f) 0.57

TIPS   Firstly, draw a number line and divide the unit length between 0 and 1 into 10 equal parts. Each part out of these parts represents 0.1 or one tenths. Again, we divide unit length between two-tenths into 10 equal parts. Each of these part will represent one-hundredths. Then, represent each decimal on number line to find two numbers between on which it lies.

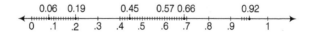

Sol. Given numbers can be represented on number line as given below:
(a) Here, 0.06 is more than 0 but less than 0.1.
   So, it lies between 0 and 0.1.
(b) Here, 0.45 is more than 0.4 but less than 0.5.
   So, it lies between 0.4 and 0.5.
(c) Here, 0.19 is more than 0.1 but less than 0.2.
   So, it lies between 0.1 and 0.2.
(d) Here, 0.66 is more than 0.6 but less than 0.7.
   So, it lies between 0.6 and 0.7.
(e) Here, 0.92 is more than 0.9 but less than 1.
   So, it lies between 0.9 and 1.
(f) Here, 0.57 is more than 0.5 but less than 0.6.
   So, it lies between 0.5 and 0.6.

Que 7. Write as fractions in lowest terms.
   (a) 0.60   (b) 0.05   (c) 0.75   (d) 0.18
   (e) 0.25   (f) 0.125   (g) 0.066

> **TIPS**
> Firstly, write the given decimal as a fraction with denominator 10, 100
> or 1000 (10 for tenths, 100 for hundredths and 1000 for thousandths)
> and then divide numerator and denominator by their HCF to write in
> lowest form.

Sol. (a) We have, $0.60 = \dfrac{60}{100} = \dfrac{60 \div 20}{100 \div 20} = \dfrac{3}{5}$ [∵ HCF of 60 and 100 = 20]

(b) We have, $0.05 = \dfrac{5}{100} = \dfrac{5 \div 5}{100 \div 5} = \dfrac{1}{20}$ [∵ HCF of 5 and 100 = 5]

(c) We have, $0.75 = \dfrac{75}{100} = \dfrac{75 \div 25}{100 \div 25} = \dfrac{3}{4}$ [∵ HCF of 75 and 100 = 25]

(d) We have, $0.18 = \dfrac{18}{100} = \dfrac{18 \div 2}{100 \div 2} = \dfrac{9}{50}$ [∵ HCF of 18 and 100 = 2]

(e) We have, $0.25 = \dfrac{25}{100} = \dfrac{25 \div 25}{100 \div 25} = \dfrac{1}{4}$ [∵ HCF of 25 and 100 = 25]

(f) We have, $0.125 = \dfrac{125}{1000} = \dfrac{125 \div 125}{1000 \div 125} = \dfrac{1}{8}$

[∵ HCF of 125 and 1000 = 125]

(g) We have, $0.066 = \dfrac{66}{1000} = \dfrac{66 \div 2}{1000 \div 2} = \dfrac{33}{500}$

[∵ HCF of 66 and 1000 = 2]

Exercise 8.3

Que 1. Which is greater?

    (a) 0.3 or 0.4   (b) 0.07 or 0.02   (c) 3 or 0.8

    (d) 0.5 or 0.05   (e) 1.23 or 1.2   (f) 0.099 or 0.19

    (g) 1.5 or 1.50   (h) 1.431 or 1.490   (i) 3.3 or 3.300

    (j) 5.64 or 5.603

TIPS

Firstly, write the given decimal in place value term to know about greater in given two decimals. We first compare the whole part and decimal having greater whole part will be greater.

If whole part is same for both, then compare the tenths part and decimal having greater tenths part will be greater. If tenths part is also same, then compare the hundredths part and decimal having greater hundredths part will be greater.

If hundredths part is same, then compare the thousandths part and find greater decimal number.

Sol. (a) We have, 0.3 or 0.4

$$\therefore \qquad 0.3 = 0 + \frac{3}{10} \text{ and } 0.4 = 0 + \frac{4}{10}$$

Here, whole part of both numbers are same.

Now, tenths part of $0.3 = \frac{3}{10}$ and tenths part of $0.4 = \frac{4}{10}$

Here, 4 is greater than 3.

$$\therefore \qquad \frac{4}{10} > \frac{3}{10}$$

Hence, 0.4 is greater than 0.3.

(b) We have, 0.07 or 0.02

$$\therefore \ 0.07 = 0 + 0 \times \frac{1}{10} + 7 \times \frac{1}{100} \text{ and } 0.02 = 0 + 0 \times \frac{1}{10} + 2 \times \frac{1}{100}$$

Here, whole parts as well as tenths parts of both numbers are same i.e. 0.

Now, hundredths part of $0.07 = \frac{7}{100}$

and hundredths part of $0.02 = \frac{2}{100}$

Here, 7 is greater than 2. $\therefore \ \dfrac{7}{100} > \dfrac{2}{100}$

Hence, 0.07 is greater than 0.02.

(c) We have, 3 or 0.8

∴ $\qquad 3 = 3 + \dfrac{0}{10} + \dfrac{0}{100}$ and $0.8 = 0 + \dfrac{8}{10} + \dfrac{0}{100}$

Here, whole part of number $3 = 3$

and whole part of number $0.8 = 0$

∵ $\qquad\qquad\qquad 3 > 0$

Hence, 3 is greater than 0.8.

(d) We have, 0.5 or 0.05

∴ $\qquad 0.5 = 0 + \dfrac{5}{10}$ and $0.05 = 0 + 0 \times \dfrac{1}{10} + \dfrac{5}{100}$

Here, whole parts of both numbers are same i.e. 0.

Now, tenths part of $0.5 = \dfrac{5}{10}$ and tenths part of $0.05 = \dfrac{0}{10}$

∴ $\qquad\qquad\qquad \dfrac{5}{10} > \dfrac{0}{10}$

Hence, 0.5 is greater than 0.05.

(e) We have, 1.23 or 1.2

∴ $\qquad 1.23 = 1 + \dfrac{2}{10} + \dfrac{3}{100}$ and $1.2 = 1 + \dfrac{2}{10} + \dfrac{0}{100}$

Here, whole parts and tenths parts of both numbers are same.

Now, hundredths part of $1.23 = \dfrac{3}{100}$

and hundredths part of $1.2 = \dfrac{0}{100}$

∴ $\qquad\qquad\qquad \dfrac{3}{100} > \dfrac{0}{100}$

Hence, 1.23 is greater than 1.2.

(f) We have, 0.099 or 0.19

∴ $0.099 = 0 + \dfrac{0}{10} + \dfrac{9}{100} + \dfrac{9}{1000}$ and $0.19 = 0 + \dfrac{1}{10} + \dfrac{9}{100} + \dfrac{0}{1000}$

Here, whole parts of both numbers are same.

Now, tenths part of $0.099 = \dfrac{0}{10}$ and tenths part of $0.19 = \dfrac{1}{10}$

∴ $\qquad\qquad\qquad \dfrac{1}{10} > \dfrac{0}{10}$

Hence, 0.19 is greater than 0.099.

(g) We have, 1.5 or 1.50

∴ $\qquad 1.5 = 1 + \dfrac{5}{10} + \dfrac{0}{100}$ and $1.50 = 1 + \dfrac{5}{10} + \dfrac{0}{100}$

Here, whole parts, tenths parts as well as hundredths parts of both numbers are same.

∴ $1.5 = 1.50$

Hence, both numbers are equal.

(h) We have, 1.431 or 1.490

∴$1.431 = 1 + \dfrac{4}{10} + \dfrac{3}{100} + \dfrac{1}{1000}$ and $1.490 = 1 + \dfrac{4}{10} + \dfrac{9}{100} + \dfrac{0}{1000}$

Here, whole parts and tenths parts of both numbers are same.

Now, hundredths part of $1.431 = \dfrac{3}{100}$

and hundredths part of $1.490 = \dfrac{9}{100}$

∴ $\dfrac{9}{100} > \dfrac{3}{100}$

Hence, 1.490 is greater than 1.431.

(i) We have, 3.3 or 3.300

∴ $3.3 = 3 + \dfrac{3}{10} + \dfrac{0}{100} + \dfrac{0}{1000}$ and $3.300 = 3 + \dfrac{3}{10} + \dfrac{0}{100} + \dfrac{0}{1000}$

Here, whole parts, tenths parts, hundredths part as well as thousandths parts of both numbers are same.

∴ $3.3 = 3.300$

Hence, both numbers are equal.

(j) We have, 5.64 or 5.603

∴ $5.64 = 5 + \dfrac{6}{10} + \dfrac{4}{100} + \dfrac{0}{1000}$ and $5.603 = 5 + \dfrac{6}{10} + \dfrac{0}{100} + \dfrac{3}{1000}$

Here, whole parts and tenths parts of both numbers are same.

Now, hundredths part of $5.64 = \dfrac{4}{100}$

and hundredths part of $5.603 = \dfrac{0}{100}$

∴ $\dfrac{4}{100} > \dfrac{0}{100}$

Hence, 5.64 is greater than 5.603.

Que 2. Make five more examples and find the greater number from them.

Sol. (i) Let 0.3 or 0.8

∴ $0.3 = 0 + \dfrac{3}{10}$ and $0.8 = 0 + \dfrac{8}{10}$

Here, whole parts of both numbers are same.

Now, tenths part of $0.3 = \dfrac{3}{10}$ and tenths part of $= 0.8 = \dfrac{8}{10}$

$\therefore \qquad\qquad \dfrac{8}{10} > \dfrac{3}{10}$

Hence, 0.8 is greater than 0.3.

(ii) Let 0.063 or 0.22

$\therefore \quad 0.063 = 0 + \dfrac{0}{10} + \dfrac{6}{100} + \dfrac{3}{1000}$ and $0.22 = 0 + \dfrac{2}{10} + \dfrac{2}{100} + \dfrac{0}{1000}$

Here, whole parts of both numbers are same.

Now, tenths part of $\quad 0.063 = \dfrac{0}{10}$ and tenths part of $0.22 = \dfrac{2}{10}$

$\therefore \qquad\qquad \dfrac{2}{10} > \dfrac{0}{10}$

Hence, 0.22 is greater than 0.063.

(iii) Let 3.012 or 2.99

$\therefore \quad 3.012 = 3 + \dfrac{0}{10} + \dfrac{1}{100} + \dfrac{2}{1000}$ and $2.99 = 2 + \dfrac{9}{10} + \dfrac{9}{100} + \dfrac{0}{1000}$

Here, whole part of $3.012 = 3$ and whole part of $2.99 = 2$

$\because \qquad\qquad\qquad 3 > 2$

Hence, 3.012 is greater than 2.99.

(iv) Let 1.34 or 1.39

$\therefore \qquad\quad 1.34 = 1 + \dfrac{3}{10} + \dfrac{4}{100}$ and $1.39 = 1 + \dfrac{3}{10} + \dfrac{9}{100}$

Here, whole parts and tenths parts of both numbers are same.

Now, hundredths part of $1.34 = \dfrac{4}{100}$

and hundredths part of $\quad 1.39 = \dfrac{9}{100}$

$\therefore \qquad\qquad \dfrac{9}{100} > \dfrac{4}{100}$

Hence, 1.39 is greater than 1.34.

(v) Let 1.52 and 2.05

$\therefore \qquad\qquad 1.52 = 1 + \dfrac{5}{10} + \dfrac{2}{100}$

and $\qquad\qquad 2.05 = 2 + \dfrac{0}{10} + \dfrac{5}{100}$

Here, whole part of $1.52 = 1$ and whole part of $2.05 = 2$

$\because \qquad\qquad\qquad 2 > 1$

Hence, 2.05 is greater than 1.52.

Try These (Page 175)

Que 1. Write 2 rupees 5 paise and 2 rupees 50 paise in decimals.

As we know that, 100 paise = ₹ 1 ∴ 1 paise = ₹ $\dfrac{1}{100}$ = ₹ 0.01

So, to convert paise into rupee multiply paise by $\dfrac{1}{100}$.

Sol. We have, 2 rupees 5 paise = 2 rupees + 5 paise

$= 2$ rupees $+ 5 \times \dfrac{1}{100}$ rupees $= (2 + 0.05)$ rupees $= 2.05$ rupees

and 2 rupees 50 paise = 2 rupees + 50 paise

$= 2$ rupees $+ 50 \times \dfrac{1}{100}$ rupees $= (2 + 0.50)$ rupees $= 2.50$ rupees

Que 2. Write 20 rupees 7 paise and 21 rupees 75 paise in decimals.

Sol. We have, 20 rupees 7 paise = 20 rupees + 7 paise

$= 20$ rupees $+ 7 \times \dfrac{1}{100}$ rupees $= (20 + 0.07)$ rupees $= 20.07$ rupees

and 21 rupees 75 paise = 21 rupees + 75 paise

$= 21$ rupees $+ 75 \times \dfrac{1}{100}$ rupees $= (21 + 0.75)$ rupees $= 21.75$ rupees

Try These (Page 176)

Que 3. Can you write 4 mm in 'cm' using decimals?

Sol. Yes, we can write 4 mm in cm using decimals as follows.

We know that, 10 mm = 1 cm $\Rightarrow$ 1 mm $= \dfrac{1}{10}$ cm

∴   4 mm $= 4 \times \dfrac{1}{10}$ cm $= \dfrac{4}{10}$ cm $= 0.4$ cm

Que 4. How will you write 7 cm 5 mm in 'cm' using decimals?

Sol. We know that,   10 mm = 1 cm $\Rightarrow$ 1 mm $= \dfrac{1}{10}$ cm

∴   7 cm 5 mm = 7 cm + 5 mm

$= 7$ cm $+ 5 \times \dfrac{1}{10}$ cm $\left[\because 1 \text{ mm} = \dfrac{1}{10} \text{ cm} \right]$

$= 7$ cm $+ \dfrac{5}{10}$ cm $= \left(7 + \dfrac{5}{10} \right)$ cm

$= (7 + 0.5)$ cm $= 7.5$ cm

Que 5. Can you now write 52 m as ' km' using decimals? How will you write 340 m as 'km' using decimals? How will you write 2008 m in 'km'?

Sol. Yes, we can write 52 m as 'km' using decimals as follows.

we know that, 1000 m $\Rightarrow$ 1km

$\Rightarrow$ $$1\,m = \frac{1}{1000}\,km$$

$\therefore$ $$52\,m = 52 \times \frac{1}{1000}\,km = \frac{52}{1000}\,km = 0.052\,km$$

To write 340 m as km.

We know that, $1\,m = \frac{1}{1000}\,km$

$\therefore$ $$340\,m = 340 \times \frac{1}{1000}\,km = \frac{340}{1000}\,km = 0.340\,km$$

To write 2008 m as km.

We know that, $1\,m = \frac{1}{1000}\,km$

$\therefore$ $$2008\,m = 2008 \times \frac{1}{1000}\,km = \frac{2008}{1000}\,km = 2.008\,km$$

Try These (Page 176)

Que 6. Can you now write 456 g as 'kg' using decimals?

Sol. We know that, 1000 g = 1 kg

$\Rightarrow$ $$1\,g = \frac{1}{1000}\,kg$$

$\therefore$ $$456\,g = 456 \times \frac{1}{1000}\,kg = \frac{456}{1000}\,kg = 0.456\,kg$$

Que 7. How will you write 2 kg 9 g in 'kg' using decimals?

Sol. We have, $2\,kg\,9\,g = 2\,kg + 9\,g$

$$= 2\,kg + 9 \times \frac{1}{1000}\,kg \qquad \left[\because 1\,g = \frac{1}{1000}\,kg\right]$$

$$= 2\,kg + \frac{9}{1000}\,kg = 2\,kg + 0.009\,kg$$

$$= (2 + 0.009)\,kg = 2.009\,kg$$

Exercise 8.4

Que 1. Express as rupees using decimals.

    (a) 5 paise   (b) 75 paise   (c) 20 paise

    (d) 50 rupees 90 paise   (e) 725 paise

TIPS

As we know that, 100 paise = ₹1 ∴1 paise = ₹ $\dfrac{1}{100}$ = ₹ 0.01

So, to express paise as rupees, multiply paise by $\dfrac{1}{100}$

(i.e. hundredths).

Sol. (a) We know that, 1 paise = ₹ $\dfrac{1}{100}$

∴   5 paise = ₹ $5 \times \dfrac{1}{100}$ = ₹ $\dfrac{5}{100}$ = ₹ 0.05

  (b) We know that, 1 paise = ₹ $\dfrac{1}{100}$

∴   75 paise = ₹ $75 \times \dfrac{1}{100}$ = ₹ $\dfrac{75}{100}$ = ₹ 0.75

  (c) We know that, 1 paise = ₹ $\dfrac{1}{100}$

∴ 20 paise = ₹ $20 \times \dfrac{1}{100}$ = ₹ $\dfrac{20}{100}$ = ₹ 0.20

  (d) We know that, 1 paise = ₹ $\dfrac{1}{100}$

∴   50 rupees 90 paise = ₹ 50 + 90 paise

                     = ₹ 50 + ₹ $90 \times \dfrac{1}{100}$ = ₹ 50 + ₹ $\dfrac{90}{100}$

                     = ₹ 50 + ₹ 0.90 = ₹ (50 + 0.90) = ₹ 50.90

  (e) We know that, 1 paise = ₹ $\dfrac{1}{100}$

∴   725 paise = ₹ $725 \times \dfrac{1}{100}$ = ₹ $\dfrac{725}{100}$ = ₹ 7.25

Que 2. Express as metres using decimals.

    (a) 15 cm   (b) 6 cm   (c) 2 m 45 cm   (d) 9 m 7 cm   (e) 419 cm

TIPS

As we know that, 100 cm = 1 m ∴ 1 cm = $\dfrac{1}{100}$ m = 0.01 m

So, to express cm as m, multiply cm by $\dfrac{1}{100}$ (i.e. hundredths).

Sol. (a) We know that, $100 \text{ cm} = 1\text{m} \Rightarrow 1 \text{ cm} = \dfrac{1}{100} \text{ m}$

∴　　　　$15 \text{ cm} = 15 \times \dfrac{1}{100} \text{ m} = \dfrac{15}{100} \text{ m} = 0.15 \text{ m}$

(b) We know that, $1 \text{ cm} = \dfrac{1}{100} \text{ m}$

∴　　　　$6 \text{ cm} = 6 \times \dfrac{1}{100} \text{ m} = \dfrac{6}{100} \text{ m} = 0.06 \text{ m}$

(c) We know that, $1 \text{ cm} = \dfrac{1}{100} \text{ m}$

∴ $2 \text{ m } 45 \text{ cm} = 2 \text{ m} + 45 \text{ cm} = 2 \text{ m} + 45 \times \dfrac{1}{100} \text{ m}$

$= 2 \text{ m} + \dfrac{45}{100} \text{ m} = 2 \text{ m} + 0.45 \text{ m} = (2 + 0.45) \text{ m} = 2.45 \text{ m}$

(d) We know that, $1 \text{ cm} = \dfrac{1}{100} \text{ m}$

∴　　　　$9 \text{ m } 7 \text{ cm} = 9 \text{ m} + 7 \text{ cm} = 9 \text{ m} + 7 \times \dfrac{1}{100} \text{ m}$

$= 9 \text{ m} + \dfrac{7}{100} \text{ m} = (9 + 0.07) \text{ m} = 9.07 \text{ m}$

(e) We know that, $1 \text{ cm} = \dfrac{1}{100} \text{ m}$

∴　　　　$419 \text{ cm} = 419 \times \dfrac{1}{100} \text{ m} = \dfrac{419}{100} \text{ m} = 4.19 \text{ m}$

Que 3. Express as cm using decimals.

(a) 5 mm　　　　(b) 60 mm　　　　(c) 164 mm
(d) 9 cm 8 mm　　(e) 93 mm

TIPS

As we know that, $10 \text{ mm} = 1 \text{ cm}$ ∴ $1 \text{ mm} = \dfrac{1}{10} \text{ cm}$

So, to express mm as cm, multiply mm by $\dfrac{1}{10}$ (i.e. tenths)

Sol. (a) We know that, $1 \text{ mm} = \dfrac{1}{10} \text{ cm}$

∴　$5 \text{ mm} = 5 \times \dfrac{1}{10} \text{ cm} = \dfrac{5}{10} \text{ cm} = 0.5 \text{ cm}$

(b) We know that, $1 \text{ mm} = \dfrac{1}{10} \text{ cm}$

∴　　　　$60 \text{ mm} = 60 \times \dfrac{1}{10} \text{ cm} = \dfrac{60}{10} \text{ cm} = 6.0 \text{ cm}$

(c) We know that, 1 mm $= \dfrac{1}{10}$ cm

∴ $\qquad$ 164 mm $= 164 \times \dfrac{1}{10}$ cm $= \dfrac{164}{10}$ cm $= 16.4$ cm

(d) We know that, 1mm $= \dfrac{1}{10}$ cm

∴ 9 cm 8 mm $= 9$ cm $+ 8$ mm $= 9$ cm $+ 8 \times \dfrac{1}{10}$ cm

$\qquad = 9$ cm $+ \dfrac{8}{10}$ cm $= \left(9 + \dfrac{8}{10}\right)$ cm $= (9 + 0.8)$ cm $= 9.8$ cm

(e) We know that, 1mm $= \dfrac{1}{10}$ cm

∴ $\qquad$ 93 mm $= 93 \times \dfrac{1}{10}$ cm $= \dfrac{93}{10}$ cm $= 9.3$ cm

Que 4. Express as km using decimals.

$\qquad$ (a) 8 m $\qquad$ (b) 88 m $\qquad$ (c) 8888 m $\qquad$ (d) 70 km 5 m

TIPS

As we know that, 1000 m = 1 km ∴ 1 m $= \dfrac{1}{1000}$ km $= 0.001$ km

So, to express m as, km multiply m by $\dfrac{1}{1000}$ (i.e. thousandths).

Sol. (a) We know that, 1000 m $= 1$km $\Rightarrow 1$ m $= \dfrac{1}{1000}$ km

∴ $\qquad$ 8 m $= 8 \times \dfrac{1}{1000}$ km $= \dfrac{8}{1000}$ km $= 0.008$ km

(b) We know that, 1 m $= \dfrac{1}{1000}$ km

∴ $\qquad$ 88 m $= 88 \times \dfrac{1}{1000}$ km $= \dfrac{88}{1000}$ km $= 0.088$ km

(c) We know that, 1 m $= \dfrac{1}{1000}$ km

∴ $\qquad$ 8888 m $= 8888 \times \dfrac{1}{1000}$ km $= \dfrac{8888}{1000}$ km $= 8.888$ km

(d) We know that, 1 m $= \dfrac{1}{1000}$ km

∴ 70 km 5 m $= 70$ km $+ 5$ m $= 70$ km $+ 5 \times \dfrac{1}{1000}$ km

$\qquad = 70$ km $+ \dfrac{5}{1000}$ km $= (70 + 0.005)$ km $= 70.005$ km

Que 5. Express as kg using decimals.

    (a) 2 g   (b) 100 g   (c) 3750 g   (d) 5 kg 8 g

    (e) 26 kg 50 g

Sol. (a) We know that, $1000 \text{ g} = 1 \text{ kg} \Rightarrow 1 \text{ g} = \dfrac{1}{1000} \text{ kg}$

$\therefore \qquad\qquad 2 \text{ g} = 2 \times \dfrac{1}{1000} \text{ kg} = \dfrac{2}{1000} \text{ kg} = 0.002 \text{ kg}$

(b) We know that, $\qquad 1 \text{ g} = \dfrac{1}{1000} \text{ kg}$

$\therefore \qquad\qquad 100 \text{ g} = 100 \times \dfrac{1}{1000} \text{ kg} = \dfrac{100}{1000} \text{ kg} = 0.1 \text{ kg}$

(c) We know that, $\quad 1 \text{ g} = \dfrac{1}{1000} \text{ kg}$

$\therefore \qquad\qquad 3750 \text{ g} = 3750 \times \dfrac{1}{1000} \text{ kg} = \dfrac{3750}{1000} \text{ kg} = 3.750 \text{ kg}$

(d) We know that, $\quad 1 \text{ g} = \dfrac{1}{1000} \text{ kg}$

$\therefore \qquad\qquad 5 \text{ kg } 8 \text{ g} = 5 \text{ kg} + 8 \text{ g} = 5 \text{ kg} + 8 \times \dfrac{1}{1000} \text{ kg}$

$$= 5 \text{ kg} + \dfrac{8}{1000} \text{ kg} = (5 + 0.008) \text{ kg} = 5.008 \text{ kg}$$

(e) We know that, $\quad 1 \text{ g} = \dfrac{1}{1000} \text{ kg}$

$\therefore \qquad 26 \text{ kg } 50 \text{ g} = 26 \text{ kg} + 50 \text{ g} = 26 \text{ kg} + 50 \times \dfrac{1}{1000} \text{ kg}$

$$= 26 \text{ kg} + \dfrac{50}{1000} \text{ kg} = 26 \text{ kg} + 0.050 \text{ kg}$$

$$= (26 + 0.050) \text{ kg} = 26.050 \text{ kg}$$

Try These (Page 178)

Que 1. Find

    (a) $0.29 + 0.36$ (b) $0.7 + 0.08$

    (c) $1.54 + 1.80$ (d) $2.66 + 1.85$

Sol. (a) $0.29 + 0.36$

	Ones	Tenths	Hundredths
	0	2	9
+	0	3	6
	0	6	5

$\therefore \qquad 0.29 + 0.36 = 0.65$

(b) 0.7 + 0.08

	Ones	Tenths	Hundredths
	0	7	0
+	0	0	8
	0	7	8

∴   0.7 + 0.08 = 0.78

(c) 1.54 + 1.80

	Ones	Tenths	Hundredths
	1	5	4
+	1	8	0
	3	3	4

∴   1.54 + 1.80 = 3.34

(d) 2.66 + 1.85

	Ones	Tenths	Hundredths
	2	6	6
+	1	8	5
	4	5	1

∴   2.66 + 1.85 = 4.51

Exercise 8.5

Que 1. Find the sum in each of the following.

(a) 0.007 + 8.5 + 30.08   (b) 15 + 0.632 + 13.8

(c) 27.076 + 0.55 + 0.004   (d) 25.65 + 9.005 + 3.7

(e) 0.75 + 10.425 + 2   (f) 280.69 + 25.2 + 38

> **TIPS**
> Firstly, write the given decimals with like terms (i.e. tens, ones, tenths, hundredths, thousandths) one below the other and then, add same as whole numbers.

Sol. (a) We have, 0.007 + 8.5 + 30.08

	Tens	Ones	Tenths	Hundredths	Thousandths
	0	0	0	0	7
	0	8	5	0	0
+	3	0	0	8	0
	3	8	5	8	7

∴   0.007 + 8.5 + 30.08 = 38.587

(b) We have, $15 + 0.632 + 13.8$

	Tens	Ones	Tenths	Hundredths	Thousandths
	1	5	0	0	0
	0	0	6	3	2
+	1	3	8	0	0
	2	9	4	3	2

$\therefore \qquad 15 + 0.632 + 13.8 = 29.432$

(c) We have, $27.076 + 0.55 + 0.004$

	Tens	Ones	Tenths	Hundredths	Thousandths
	2	7	0	7	6
	0	0	5	5	0
+	0	0	0	0	4
	2	7	6	3	0

$\therefore \qquad 27.076 + 0.55 + 0.004 = 27.630$

(d) We have, $25.65 + 9.005 + 3.7$

	Tens	Ones	Tenths	Hundredths	Thousandths
	2	5	6	5	0
	0	9	0	0	5
+	0	3	7	0	0
	3	8	3	5	5

$\therefore \qquad 25.65 + 9.005 + 3.7 = 38.355$

(e) We have, $0.75 + 10.425 + 2$

	Tens	Ones	Tenths	Hundredths	Thousandths
	0	0	7	5	0
	1	0	4	2	5
+	0	2	0	0	0
	1	3	1	7	5

$\therefore \qquad 0.75 + 10.425 + 2 = 13.175$

(f) We have, $280.69 + 25.2 + 38$

	Hundreds	Tens	Ones	Tenths	Hundredths
	2	8	0	6	9
	0	2	5	2	0
+	0	3	8	0	0
	3	4	3	8	9

$\therefore \qquad 280.69 + 25.2 + 38 = 343.89$

Que 2. Rashid spent ₹ 35.75 for Maths book and ₹ 32.60 for Science book. Then, find the total amount spent by Rashid.

Sol. ∵ Money spent by Rashid for Maths book = ₹ 35.75

and money spent by Rashid for Science book = ₹ 32.60

∴ Total money spent

$$\begin{array}{r} 35.75 \\ + \ 32.60 \\ \hline 68.35 \\ \hline \end{array}$$

Hence, total money spent by Rashid is ₹ 68.35.

Que 3. Radhika's mother gave her ₹ 10.50 and her father gave her ₹ 15.80, then find the total amount given to Radhika by the parents.

Sol. ∴ Money given to Radhika by her mother = ₹ 10.50

and money given to Radhika by her father = ₹ 15.80

∴ Total money

$$\begin{array}{r} 10.50 \\ + \ 15.80 \\ \hline 26.30 \\ \hline \end{array}$$

Hence, total money given to Radhika by her parents is ₹ 26.30.

Que 4. Nasreen bought 3 m 20 cm cloth for her shirt and 2 m 5 cm cloth for her trouser. Then, find the total length of cloth bought by her.

 TIPS Firstly, write the given length in metre using decimal and then add by putting one below other same as whole numbers.

Sol. Cloth bought by Nasreen for her shirt = 3 m 20 cm

$$= 3 \text{ m} + 20 \text{ cm}$$

$$= 3 \text{ m} + 20 \times \frac{1}{100} \text{ m} \qquad \left[\because 1 \text{ cm} = \frac{1}{100} \text{ m} \right]$$

$$= 3 \text{ m} + 0.20 \text{ m} = (3 + 0.20) \text{ m} = 3.20 \text{ m}$$

Cloth bought by Nasreen for her trouser

$$= 2 \text{ m } 5 \text{ cm} = 2 \text{ m} + 5 \text{ cm}$$

$$= 2 \text{ m} + 5 \times \frac{1}{100} \text{ m} \qquad \left[\because 1 \text{ cm} = \frac{1}{100} \text{ m} \right]$$

$$= 2 \text{ m} + 0.05 \text{ m} = (2 + 0.05) \text{ m} = 2.05 \text{ m}$$

∴ Total cloths

$$3.20$$
$$+\ 2.05$$
$$\overline{5.25}$$

Hence, total cloths bought by Nasreen is 5.25 m.

Que 5. Naresh walked 2 km 35 m in the morning and 1 km 7 m in the evening. How much distance did he walk in all?

TIPS Firstly, write the given distance into km using decimals and then add by putting one below other same as whole numbers.

Sol. Naresh walked in morning

$$= 2 \text{ km } 35 \text{ m} = 2 \text{ km} + 35 \text{ m}$$
$$= 2 \text{ km} + 35 \times \frac{1}{1000} \text{ km} \qquad \left[\because 1 \text{ m} = \frac{1}{1000} \text{ km} \right]$$
$$= 2 \text{ km} + \frac{35}{1000} \text{ km} = (2 + 0.035) \text{ km} = 2.035 \text{ km}$$

Naresh walked in evening

$$= 1 \text{ km } 7 \text{ m} = 1 \text{ km} + 7 \text{ m}$$
$$= 1 \text{ km} + 7 \times \frac{1}{1000} \text{ km} \qquad \left[\because 1 \text{ m} = \frac{1}{1000} \text{ km} \right]$$
$$= 1 \text{ km} + \frac{7}{1000} \text{ km} = (1 + 0.007) \text{ km} = 1.007 \text{ km}$$

∴ Total distance

$$2.035$$
$$+\ 1.007$$
$$\overline{3.042}$$

Hence, total distance walked by Naresh is 3.042 km.

Que 6. Sunita travelled 15 km 268 m by bus, 7 km 7 m by car and 500 m on foot in order to reach her school. How far is her school from her residence?

Sol. Distance travelled by bus

$$= 15 \text{ km } 268 \text{ m} = 15 \text{ km} + 268 \text{ m}$$
$$= 15 \text{ km} + 268 \times \frac{1}{1000} \text{ km} \qquad \left[\because 1 \text{ m} = \frac{1}{1000} \text{ km} \right]$$
$$= 15 \text{ km} + \frac{268}{1000} \text{ km} = (15 + 0.268) \text{ km} = 15.268 \text{ km}$$

Distance travelled by car

$$= 7 \text{ km } 7 \text{ m} = 7 \text{ km} + 7 \text{ m}$$

$$= 7 \text{ km} + 7 \times \frac{1}{1000} \text{ km} \qquad \left[\because 1 \text{ m} = \frac{1}{1000} \text{ km} \right]$$

$$= 7 \text{ km} + \frac{7}{1000} \text{ km} = 7 \text{ km} + 0.007 \text{ km}$$

$$= (7 + 0.007) \text{ km} = 7.007 \text{ km}$$

Distance travelled by foot

$$= 500 \text{ m} = 500 \times \frac{1}{1000} \text{ km} \qquad \left[\because 1 \text{ m} = \frac{1}{1000} \text{ km} \right]$$

$$= \frac{500}{1000} \text{ km} = 0.500 \text{ km}$$

∴ Total distance travelled by Sunita

$$\begin{array}{r} 15.268 \\ 7.007 \\ + \ 0.500 \\ \hline 22.775 \end{array}$$

Hence, total distance travelled by Sunita is 22.775 km.

Que 7. Ravi purchased 5 kg 400 g rice, 2 kg 20 g sugar and 10 kg 850 g flour. Find the total weight of his purchases.

TIPS

Firstly, write the weight in kg using decimals and then add by putting one below other same as whole numbers.

Sol. Weight of rice purchased by Ravi

$$= 5 \text{ kg } 400 \text{ g} = 5 \text{ kg} + 400 \text{g}$$

$$= 5 \text{ kg} + 400 \times \frac{1}{1000} \text{ kg} \qquad \left[\because 1 \text{ g} = \frac{1}{1000} \text{ kg} \right]$$

$$= 5 \text{ kg} + \frac{400}{1000} \text{ kg} = (5 + 0.400) \text{ kg} = 5.400 \text{ kg}$$

Weight of sugar purchased by Ravi

$$= 2 \text{ kg } 20 \text{ g} = 2 \text{ kg} + 20 \text{ g}$$

$$= 2 \text{ kg} + 20 \times \frac{1}{1000} \text{ kg} \qquad \left[\because 1 \text{ g} = \frac{1}{1000} \text{ kg} \right]$$

$$= 2 \text{ kg} + \frac{20}{1000} \text{ kg} = (2 + 0.020) \text{ kg} = 2.020 \text{ kg}$$

Weight of flour purchased by Ravi

$$= 10 \text{ kg } 850 \text{ g} = 10 \text{ kg} + 850 \text{ g}$$

$$= 10 \text{ kg} + 850 \times \frac{1}{1000} \text{ kg} \qquad \left[\because 1 \text{ g} = \frac{1}{1000} \text{ kg} \right]$$

$$= 10 \text{ kg} + \frac{850}{1000} \text{ kg} = (10 + 0.850) \text{ kg} = 10.850 \text{ kg}$$

∴ Total weight of his purchases

$$\begin{array}{r} 5.400 \\ 2.020 \\ + \; 10.850 \\ \hline 18.270 \end{array}$$

Hence, total weight of all his purchases is 18.270 kg.

Try These (Page 180)

Que 1. Subtract 1.85 from 5.46.

TIPS Firstly, write the decimals in columns one below the other and then subtract as whole numbers i.e. subtracting hundredths from hundredths, tenths from tenths, ones from ones and so on.

Sol. We have, 5.46 – 1.85

Now,

	Ones	Tenths	Hundredths
	5	4	6
−	1	8	5
	3	6	1

∴ $5.46 - 1.85 = 3.61$

Que 2. Subtract 5.25 from 8.28

Sol. We have, 8.28 – 5.25

Now,

	Ones	Tenths	Hundredths
	8	2	8
−	5	2	5
	3	0	3

∴ $8.28 - 5.25 = 3.03$

Que 3. Subtract 0.95 from 2.29.

Sol. We have, 2.29 – 0.95

Now,

	Ones	Tenths	Hundredths
	2	2	9
−	0	9	5
	1	3	4

∴ $2.29 - 0.95 = 1.34$

Note Sometimes we have to subtract a greater digit from smaller digit, then we regroup it to subtract as i.e. do in above question. 9 cannot be subtract from 2, so we regroup 2 as 12 and 2 at ones place at 1.

Que 4. Subtract 2.25 from 5.68.

Sol. We have, 5.68 – 2.25

Now,

	Ones	Tenths	Hundredths
	5	6	8
−	2	2	5
	3	4	3

∴ $5.68 - 2.25 = 3.43$

Exercise 8.6

Que 1. Subtract.

(a) ₹ 18.25 from ₹ 20.75   (b) 202.54 m from 250 m

(c) ₹ 5.36 from ₹ 8.40   (d) 2.051 km from 5.206 km

(e) 0.314 kg from 2.107 kg

Sol. (a) We have, ₹ 20.75 – ₹ 18.25

Now,

	Tens	Ones	Tenths	Hundredths
	2	0	7	5
−	1	8	2	5
		2	5	0

∴   ₹ 20.75 – ₹ 18.25 = ₹ (20.75 – 18.25) = ₹ 2.50

(b) We have, 250 m – 202.54m

Now,

	Hundreds	Tens	Ones	Tenths	Hundredths
	2	5	0	0	0
−	2	0	2	5	4
		4	7	4	6

∴   250 m – 202.54 m = (250 – 202.54) m = 47.46 m

(c) We have, ₹ 8.40 – ₹ 5.36

Now,

	Ones	Tenths	Hundredths
	8	4	0
−	5	3	6
	3	0	4

∴   ₹ 8.40 – ₹ 5.36 = ₹ (8.40 – 5.36) = ₹ 3.04

(d) We have, 5.206 km – 2.051 km

Now,	Ones	Tenths	Hundredths	Thousandths
	5	2	0	6
–	2	0	5	1
	3	1	5	5

∴ 5.206 km – 2.051 km = (5.206 – 2.051) km = 3.155 km

(e) We have, 2.107 kg – 0.314 kg

Now,	Ones	Tenths	Hundredths	Thousandths
	2	1	0	7
–	0	3	1	4
	1	7	9	3

∴ 2.107 kg – 0.314 kg = (2.107 – 0.314) kg = 1.793 kg

Que 2. Find the value of

    (a) 9.756 – 6.28   (b) 21.05 – 15.27

    (c) 18.5 – 6.79   (d) 11.6 – 9.847

TIPS

Firstly, write the decimals in columns with decimal points directly below each other, then subtract same as whole numbers.

Sol. (a) We have, 9.756 – 6.28

Now,
$$9.756$$
$$-\ 6.280$$
$$\overline{3.476}$$

∴   9.756 – 6.28 = 3.476

(b) We have, 21.05 – 15.27

Now,
$$21.05$$
$$-\ 15.27$$
$$\overline{5.78}$$

∴   21.05 – 15.27 = 5.78

(c) We have, 18.5 – 6.79

Now,
$$18.50$$
$$-\ 6.79$$
$$\overline{11.71}$$

∴   18.50 – 6.79 = 11.71

(d) We have, $11.6 - 9.847$

Now,

$$11.600$$
$$-\ 9.847$$
$$\overline{\ \ \ 1.753}$$

$\therefore$ $11.6 - 9.847 = 1.753$

Que 3. Raju bought a book for ₹ 35.65. He gave ₹ 50 to the shopkeeper. How much money did he get back from the shopkeeper?

Sol. $\therefore$ Book bought by Raju = ₹ 35.65

and money gave to shopkeeper = ₹ 50

$\therefore$ Money get back from shopkeeper = ₹ (50 − 35.65) = ₹ 14.35

Hence, money get book from shopkeeper is ₹ 14.35.

Que 4. Rani had ₹ 18.50. She bought one ice-cream for ₹ 11.75. How much money does she have now?

Sol. $\therefore$ Total money Rani had = ₹ 18.50 and cost of ice-cream = ₹ 11.75

$\therefore$ Remaining money = ₹ (18.50 − 11.75) = ₹ 6.75

Hence, she have ₹ 6.75.

Que 5. Tina had 20 m 5 cm long cloth. She cuts 4 m 50 cm length of cloth from this for making a curtain. How much cloth is left with her?

Sol. $\because$ Tina had length of cloth = 20 m 5 cm = 20 m + 5 cm

$$= 20 \text{ m} + 5 \times \frac{1}{100} \text{ m} \qquad \left[\because 1 \text{ cm} = \frac{1}{100} \text{ m} \right]$$

$$= 20 \text{ m} + \frac{5}{100} \text{ m} = (20 + 0.05) \text{ m} = 20.05 \text{ m}$$

and length of cloth cut by her = 4 m 50 cm = 4 m + 50 cm

$$= 4 \text{ m} + 50 \times \frac{1}{100} \text{ m} \qquad \left[\because 1 \text{ cm} = \frac{1}{100} \text{ m} \right]$$

$$= 4 \text{ m} + \frac{50}{100} \text{ m} = (4 + 0.50) \text{ m} = 4.50 \text{ m}$$

$\therefore$ Length of cloth left with Tina

$$= 20.05 \text{ m} - 4.50 \text{ m} = (20.05 - 4.50) \text{ m} = 15.55 \text{ m}$$

Hence, 15.55 m cloth is left with her.

Que 6. Namita travels 20 km 50 m everyday. Out of this she travels 10 km 200 m by bus and the rest by auto. How much distance does she travel by auto?

TIPS
Firstly, write the distance travelled by Namita in km using decimals. To find the distance travelled by auto, subtract distance travelled by bus from total distance travelled by Namita.

Sol. ∵ Total distance travelled by Namita

$$= 20 \text{ km } 50 \text{ m} = 20 \text{ km} + 50 \text{ m}$$

$$= 20 \text{ km} + 50 \times \frac{1}{1000} \text{ km} \qquad \left[\because 1 \text{ m} = \frac{1}{1000} \text{ km} \right]$$

$$= 20 \text{ km} + \frac{50}{1000} \text{ km} = (20 + 0.050) \text{ km} = 20.050 \text{ km}$$

and distance travelled by Namita by bus

$$= 10 \text{ km } 200 \text{ m} = 10 \text{ km} + 200 \text{ m}$$

$$= 10 \text{ km} + 200 \times \frac{1}{1000} \text{ km} \qquad \left[\because 1 \text{ m} = \frac{1}{1000} \text{ km} \right]$$

$$= 10 \text{ km} + \frac{200}{1000} \text{ km}$$

$$= 10 \text{ km} + 0.200 \text{ km} = (10 + 0.200) \text{ km} = 10.200 \text{ km}$$

∴ Distance travelled by auto

$$= 20.050 \text{ km} - 10.200 \text{ km} = (20.050 - 10.200) \text{ km} = 9.850 \text{ km}$$

Hence, she travels 9.850 km by auto.

Que 7. Aakash bought vegetables weighing 10 kg. Out of this, 3 kg 500 g is onions, 2 kg 75 g is tomatoes and the rest is potatoes. What is the weight of the potatoes?

TIPS
Firstly, write the weight of all vegetables in kg using decimals, then add the weight of onions and tomatoes. To find the weight of potatoes, subtract this sum from total weight of vegetables.

Sol. Given, total weight of vegetables = 10 kg

Weight of onions = 3 kg 500 g = 3 kg + 500 g

$$= 3 \text{ kg} + 500 \times \frac{1}{1000} \text{ kg} \qquad \left[\because 1 \text{ g} = \frac{1}{1000} \text{ kg} \right]$$

$$= 3 \text{ kg} + \frac{500}{1000} \text{ kg} = 3 \text{ kg} + 0.500 \text{ kg}$$

$$= (3 + 0.500) \text{ kg} = 3.500 \text{ kg}$$

Weight of tomatoes $= 2$ kg 75 g $= 2$ kg $+ 75$ g

$$= 2 \text{ kg} + 75 \times \frac{1}{1000} \text{ kg} \qquad \left[\because 1 \text{ g} = \frac{1}{1000} \text{ kg} \right]$$

$$= 2 \text{ kg} + \frac{75}{1000} \text{ kg} = 2 \text{ kg} + 0.075 \text{ kg}$$

$$= (2 + 0.075) \text{ kg} = 2.075 \text{ kg}$$

∴ Total weight of onions and tomatoes

$$= 3.500 \text{ kg} + 2.075 \text{ kg} = (3.500 + 2.075) \text{ kg} = 5.575 \text{ kg}$$

Now, weight of potatoes

$$= \text{Total weight of vegetables}$$
$$- \text{Weight of onions and tomatoes}$$
$$= 10 \text{ kg} - 5.575 \text{ kg} = (10 - 5.575) \text{ kg} = 4.425 \text{ kg}$$

Hence, the weight of potatoes is 4.425 kg.

Selected **NCERT Exemplar Problems**

Que 1. 0.7499 lies between

    (a) 0.7 and 0.74   (b) 0.75 and 0.79

    (c) 0.749 and 0.75   (d) 0.74992 and 0.75

Sol. Firstly, we convert the given two decimals of each option into like decimals and then check the given decimal lies between two decimals.

    (a) Convert the given decimals into like decimals

        we get, 0.7000 and 0.7400.

        Here, 0.7499 is more than 0.7400

        So, it is not lies between 0.7000 and 0.7400.

    (b) Convert the given decimals into like decimals

        we get, 0.7500 and 0.7900.

        Here, 0.7499 is less than 0.7500.

        So, it is not lies between 0.7500 and 0.7900

    (c) Convert the given decimals into like decimals

        we get, 0.7490 and 0.7500.

        Here, 0.7499 is more than 0.7490 but less than 0.7500.

        So, it lies between 0.7490 and 0.7500.

    (d) Convert the given decimals into like decimals

        we get, 0.74992 and 0.75000.

        Here, 0.7499 is less than 0.74992.

        So, it is not lies between 0.74992 and 0.75000.

        Hence, option (c) is correct.

Que 2. The decimal 0.238 is equal to the fraction

(a) $\dfrac{119}{500}$ (b) $\dfrac{238}{25}$ (c) $\dfrac{119}{25}$ (d) $\dfrac{119}{50}$

Sol. Firstly, write the given decimal as a fraction with denominator 1000 and then divide numerator and denominator by their HCF to write in lowest term.

We have, $\qquad 0.238 = 0 + \dfrac{238}{1000}$

Now, HCF of 238 and 1000 = 2

$\therefore \qquad \dfrac{238}{1000} = \dfrac{238 \div 2}{1000 \div 2} = \dfrac{119}{500}$

[dividing numerator and denominator both by 2]

The fraction of 0.238 is $\dfrac{119}{500}$.

Hence, option (a) is correct.

Que 3. The value of 50 coins of 50 paise = ₹ ....

Sol. Given, number of coins of 50 paise = 50

Total amount of 50 coins = $50 \times 50 = 2500$ paise

We know that, 1 paise $= ₹\dfrac{1}{100}$ $\therefore$ 2500 paise $= ₹\dfrac{2500}{100} = ₹25.0$

Que 4. 3 hundredths + 3 tenths = ...

Sol. We have, 3 hundredths + 3 tenths

$$= 3 \times \dfrac{1}{100} + 3 \times \dfrac{1}{10} = \dfrac{3}{100} + \dfrac{3}{10}$$

Now, LCM of 100 and 10 = 100

$\therefore \qquad \dfrac{3}{100} + \dfrac{3}{10} = \dfrac{3}{100} + \dfrac{3 \times 10}{10 \times 10} = \dfrac{3}{100} + \dfrac{30}{100} = \dfrac{33}{100} = 0.33$

$\therefore$ 3 hundredths + 3 tenths = 0.33

Que 5. The place value of a digit at the tenths place is 10 times the same digit at the ones place.

Sol. False, because the place value of a digit at the tenths place is 1/10 times the same digit at the ones place,

e.g. Let a number be 23.37.

Here, place value of 3 at ones place = 3

and place value of 3 at tenths place

$$= \dfrac{3}{10} = 3 \times \dfrac{1}{10} = \dfrac{1}{10} \times \text{Place value of 3 at ones place.}$$

Que 6. The place value of a digit at the hundredths place is 1/10 times the same digit at the tenths place.

Sol. True, because the place value of a digit at the hundredths place is 1/10 times the same digit at the tenths place. e.g. Let a number be 5.77
Here, place value of 7 at tenths place = 7/10
and place value of 7 at hundredths place

$$= \frac{7}{100} = \frac{7}{10} \times \frac{1}{10} = \frac{1}{10} \times \text{Place value of 7 at tenths place.}$$

Que 7. Arrange 12.142, 12.124, 12.104, 12.401 and 12.214 in ascending order.

Sol. Given numbers are 12.142, 12.124, 12.104, 12.401 and 12.214.

$$\therefore \qquad 12.142 = 12 + \frac{1}{10} + \frac{4}{100} + \frac{2}{1000}$$

$$12.124 = 12 + \frac{1}{10} + \frac{2}{100} + \frac{4}{1000}$$

$$12.104 = 12 + \frac{1}{10} + \frac{0}{100} + \frac{4}{1000}$$

$$12.401 = 12 + \frac{4}{10} + \frac{0}{100} + \frac{1}{1000}$$

$$12.214 = 12 + \frac{2}{10} + \frac{1}{100} + \frac{4}{1000}$$

Here, whole part of all numbers are same and tenths part of 12.142, 12.124 and 12.104 are same.

Now, tenths part of $12.401 = 4/10$ and tenths part of $12.214 = \frac{2}{10}$

$$\therefore \qquad \frac{4}{10} > \frac{2}{10}$$

∴ Hence, $\qquad 12.401 > 12.214$

Again, hundredths part of $12.142 = \frac{4}{100}$

$$\therefore \qquad \text{Hundredths part of } 12.124 = \frac{2}{100}$$

and hundredths part of $12.104 = \frac{0}{100}$

$$\therefore \qquad \frac{4}{100} > \frac{2}{100} > \frac{0}{100} \quad \therefore \ 12.142 > 12.124 > 12.104$$

Hence, the ascending order of given numbers are

$$12.104 < 12.124 < 12.142 < 12.214 < 12.401.$$

Que 8. Write the largest four digit decimal number less than 1 using the digits 1, 5, 3 and 8 once.

Sol. Here, largest four digit number by using 1, 5, 3 and 8 is 8531.

For four digit decimal number less than 1, we divided 8531 by 10000.

i.e. $\dfrac{8531}{10000} = 0.8531$

Hence, the required decimal number is 0.8531.

Que 9. Using the digits 2, 4, 5 and 3 once, write the smallest four digit decimal number.

Sol. Here, smallest four digit number by using 2, 4, 5 and 3 is 2345.

For four digit decimal number, we divided 2345 by 10000.

i.e. $\dfrac{2345}{10000} = 0.2345$

Hence, the required decimal number is 0.2345.

Que 10. Round off 20.83 to nearest tenths.

Sol. For rounding off to tenths place, we look at the hundredths place. Here, the digit is 3.

So, the digit at the tenths place (8) will not be increased by 1.

i.e. it will be equal to 0.

Hence, rounding off 20.83 to nearest tenths, we get 20.80.

Que 11. Round off 75.195 to nearest hundredths.

Sol. For rounding off to hundredths place, we look at the thousandths place. Here, the digit is 5.

So, the digit at the hundredths place (9) will be increased by 1 (i.e. it will becomes 9 + 1).

Hence, the rounding off 75.195 to hundredths place, we get 75.200.

Que 12. Round off 27.981 to nearest tenths.

Sol. For rounding off to tenths place, we look at the hundredths place, here the digit is 8.

So, the digit of the tenths place (9) will be increased by 1. (i.e. it will becomes 9 + 1 = 10)

∴ $27.0 = 27 + 10 = 28.0$

Hence, the round off 27.981, we get 28.0

Que 13. What should be added to 25.5 to get 50?

Sol. Here, we want to fill in the box in 25.5 +......= 50

For this we will have to find 50 – 25.5.

We perform this operation as follows by written the two numbers having equal number of decimal places. i.e. 50 = 50.0

Subtract 25.5 from 50.0 = 50.0 – 25.5 = 24.5

Hence, the required number to be added to 25.5 is 24.5.

Que 14. Alok purchased 1 kg 200 g potatoes, 250 g dhania, 5 kg 300 g onion, 500 g palak and 2 kg 600 g tomatoes. Find the total weight of his purchases in kilograms.

Sol. Firstly, we convert all the weight in the same unit i.e. gram into kilogram by divide 1000 and then find the total weight.

Given, weight of potatoes = 1 kg + 200 g = 1 kg + 200 g

$$= 1 \text{ kg} + \frac{200}{1000} \text{ kg} = 1 \text{ kg} + 0.200 \text{ kg} = 1.200 \text{ kg} \left[\because 1 \text{ g} = \frac{1}{1000} \text{ kg} \right]$$

Weight of dhania $= 250 \text{ g} = \frac{250}{1000} \text{ kg} = 0.250 \text{ kg}$

Weight of onion = 5 kg 300 g = 5 kg + 300 g

$$= 5 \text{ kg} + \frac{300}{1000} \text{ kg} = 5 \text{ kg} + 0.300 \text{ kg} = 5.300 \text{ kg}$$

Weight of palak $= 500 \text{ g} = \frac{500}{1000} \text{ kg} = 0.500 \text{ kg}$

Weight of tomatoes = 2 kg 600 g = 2 kg + 600 g

$$= 2 \text{ kg} + \frac{600}{1000} \text{ kg} \qquad \left[\because 1 \text{ g} = \frac{1}{1000} \text{ kg} \right]$$

$$= 2 \text{ kg} + 0.600 \text{ kg} = 2.600 \text{ kg}$$

∴ Total weight of his purchases in kilograms

= Weight of potatoes + Weight of dhania + Weight of onion

+ Weight of palak + Weight of tomatoes

= 1.200 kg + 0.250 kg + 5.300 kg + 0.500 kg + 2.600 kg

= [1.200 + 0.250 + 5.300 + 0.500 + 2.600] kg = 9·850 kg

Hence, the total weight is 9.850 kg.

Que 15. Which one is greater? 1 m 40 cm + 60 cm or 2.6 m.

Sol. Given, 1 m 40 cm + 60 cm. ⇒ 1 m + 40 cm + 60 cm = 1 m + 100 cm

We know that, $1 \text{ cm} = \frac{1}{100} \text{ m}$

∴ $1 \text{ m } 40 \text{ cm} + 60 \text{ cm} = 1 \text{ m} + \frac{100}{100} \text{ m} = 1 \text{ m} + 1 \text{ m} = 2.0 \text{ m}$

On comparing 2.0 m and 2.6 m.

We have, $2.0 = 2 + \frac{0}{10}$ and $2.6 = 2 + \frac{6}{10}$

Here, whole part of both numbers are same i.e. 2.

Now, tenths part of $2 = \frac{0}{10}$ and tenths part of $2.6 = \frac{6}{10}$ ∴ $\frac{6}{10} > \frac{0}{10}$

Hence, 2.6 is greater than 2.

Chapter 9

Data Handling

Important Points

- **Data** A collection of numbers (values) gathered to give some information is called data. There are two types of data:

  (i) Primary data   (ii) Secondary data

  Primary data If the data is collected directly from the sources, it is called primary data.

  Secondary data If the data is collected from secondary sources (i.e. newspapers, magazines, TV, internet, etc.), then it is called secondary data.

- **Recording and organisation of data** To get particular information from the given data quickly, the data can be arranged in a tabular form using tally marks. In other words, we can say that tally marks are used for recording and organisation of data. Counting of data is done in a group of five, which is shown by symbol 𝖭𝖭, thus 𝖭𝖭 ||| shows five plus three i.e. 8 and 𝖭𝖭 𝖭𝖭 shows five plus five i.e. 10.

- **Pictograph** Pictograph is the way of representing data using image/picture of objects. Each picture (image) stands for a certain number of objects. It helps us to answer the questions on the data at a glance.

- **Interpretation of a pictograph** Interpretation of a pictograph means find some conclusions from it. The first step in interpretation of a pictograph is to know what is represent or what information is given by it. It is also important to know the number of units represented by one picture symbol.

- **Drawing a pictograph** In drawing a pictograph, sometimes a symbol may represent multiple units and it may be difficult to draw. So, we use simpler symbol as ☥ .

  If ☥ represents 5 students/persons, then we can assume that

  ☥ represents 4 students/persons

  ☥ represents 3 students/persons

  ☥ represents 2 students/persons

  ☥ represents 1 student/person

- **Bargraph (or bar diagram)** A bar graph is a pictorial representation of numerical data in the form of rectangles (or bars) of equal width and varying (different) heights.

  Bars of uniform width can be drawn horizontally or vertically with equal spacing between them and the length of each bar represents the given number.

- **Interpretation of a bar graph** The first step in reading a bar graph is to know what it represents or what information is given by it. For this, we read the **captions** which are generally written just below the horizontal line (X-axis) and adjacent to vertical line (Y-axis). After knowing that, we read the scale and find some conclusions from a given bar graph which is interpretation of the bar graph.

- **Drawing a bar graph** For drawing a bar graph, we use the following steps.

  Step I   Firstly, draw two lines perpendicular to each other, i.e. Horizontal line and a vertical line.

  Step II   Along the horizontal line, mark the information given in the data as weeks, months, years, places, objects, etc., at uniform gaps and along vertical line, mark corresponding numerical values as number of students, number of objects, etc.

  Step III   Choose a suitable scale (as 1 unit = 100 students) to determine the heights of the bars and then mark the heights on the vertical axis.

  Step IV   Draw bars of equal width and of height calculated in step (iii) on horizontal line and get required bar graph.

Exercise 9.1

Que 1. In a Mathematics test, the following marks were obtained by 40 students. Arrange these marks in a table using tally marks.

8	1	3	7	6	5	5	4	4	2
4	9	5	3	7	1	6	5	2	7
7	3	8	4	2	8	9	5	8	6
7	4	5	6	9	6	4	4	6	6

(a) Find how many students obtained marks equal to or more than 7.

(b) How many students obtained marks below 4?

Sol. The table with tally marks is shown below

Marks	Tally marks	Number of students
1	||	2
2	|||	3
3	|||	3
4	꤅| ||	7
5	꤅| |	6
6	꤅| ||	7
7	꤅|	5
8	꤅||	4
9	|||	3
Total		40

(a) Here, we have to find out the students who obtained marks equal to 7 or more than 7. So, we have to add the number of students who obtained marks equal to 7 or more than 7 i.e. 7, 8 and 9.
∴ Number of those students = 5 + 4 + 3 = 12
Hence, 12 students obtained marks equal to 7 or more than 7.

(b) Here, we have to find out the students who obtained marks below 4.
So, we have to add the number of students who obtained marks below 4 i.e. 1, 2 and 3.
∴ Number of those students = 3 + 3 + 2 = 8
Hence, 8 students obtained marks below 4.

Que 2. Following is the choice of sweets for 30 students of class VI. Ladoo, Barfi, Ladoo, Jalebi, Ladoo, Rasgulla, Jalebi, Ladoo, Barfi, Rasgulla, Ladoo, Jalebi, Jalebi, Rasgulla, Ladoo, Rasgulla, Jalebi, Ladoo, Rasgulla, Ladoo, Ladoo, Barfi, Rasgulla, Rasgulla, Jalebi, Rasgulla, Ladoo, Rasgulla, Jalebi, and Ladoo.

(a) Arrange the names of sweets in a table using tally marks.

(b) Which sweet is preferred by most of the students?

 TIPS Write the name of sweets in first column, then in second column use tally marks to represent number of students like corresponding sweet and in third column write the number of students.

Sol. (a) The table with tally marks is shown below below.

Sweets	Tally marks	Number of students
Ladoo	ⅢⅢ Ⅲ	11
Barfi	|||	3
Jalebi	ⅢⅡ	7
Rasgulla	ⅢⅢ	9
Total		30

(b) By examine the above table, we see that Ladoo is preferred by most of the students. i.e. 11 students.

Que 3. Catherine threw a dice 40 times and noted the number appearing each time as shown below

1	3	5	6	6	3	5	4	1	6
2	5	3	4	6	1	5	5	6	1
1	2	2	3	5	2	4	5	5	6
5	1	6	2	3	5	2	4	1	5

Make a table and enter the data using tally marks. Find the number that appeared.

(a) the minimum number of times.

(b) the maximum number of times.

(c) Find those numbers that appear an equal number of times.

Sol. On arranging the given data in a table using tally marks, we get the following table.

Numbers	Tally marks	Number of times
1	ⅢⅡ	7
2	ⅢⅠ	6
3	Ⅲ	5
4	‖‖	4
5	Ⅲ ⅢⅠ	11
6	ⅢⅡ	7
Total		40

(a) From table, we can say that the number that appeared minimum number of times, is 4 i.e. 4 times.

(b) From table, we can say that the number that appeared maximum number of times, is 5 i.e.11 times.

(c) From table, we can say that the number that appeared an equal number of times, are 1 and 6 i.e. 7 times.

Que 4. Following pictograph shows the number of tractors in five villages.

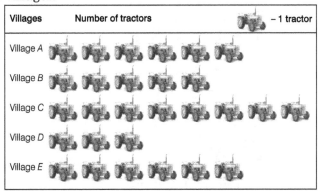

Observe the pictograph and answer the following questions.

(i) Which village has the minimum number of tractors?

(ii) Which village has the maximum number of tractors?

(iii) How many more tractors village *C* has as compared to village *B?*

(iv) What is the total number of tractors in all the five villages?

Sol. We know that, a pictograph represents data through pictures of objects.

  (i) Observing the pictograph, it is clear that village D has the minimum number of tractors i.e. only 3 tractors.

 (ii) Observing the pictograph, it is clear that village C has the maximum number of tractors i.e. 8 tractors.

(iii) Observing the pictograph, it is clear that village C has 8 tractors and village B has 5 tractors.

   So, village C has $8 - 5 = 3$ more tractors as compared to village B.

 (iv) Total number of tractors in all the five villages = Sum of all tractors in villages A, B, C, D and E $= 6 + 5 + 8 + 3 + 6 = 28$

   Hence, there are 28 tractors in all the five villages.

Que 5. The number of girl students in each class of a co-educational middle school is depicted by the pictograph.

Observe this pictograph and answer the following questions.

  (a) Which class has the minimum number of girl students?

  (b) Is the number of girls in Class VI less than the number of girls in Class V?

  (c) How many girls are there in Class VII?

Sol. In the given pictograph, 1 picture = 4 girls, half picture = 2 girls

  (a) Observing the pictograph, it is clear that the minimum number of girl students are in class VIII

   i. e. $4 + 2 = 6$

(b) Observing the pictograph, it is clear that
Number of girls in class VI = $4 \times 4 = 16$
and number of girls in class V = $2 \times 4 + 1 \times 2 = 8 + 2 = 10$
∵ $\quad\quad\quad\quad\quad\quad\quad 10 < 16$
So, it is clear that number of girls in class VI is not less than the number of girls in class V.

(c) Observing the pictograph, number of girls in class VII = $3 \times 4 = 12$

Que 6. The sale of electric bulbs on different days of a week is shown below

Observe the pictograph and answer the following questions.
(a) How many bulbs were sold on Friday?
(b) On which day were the maximum number of bulbs sold?
(c) On which of the days same number of bulbs were sold?
(d) On which of the days minimum number of bulbs were sold?
(e) If one big carton can hold 9 bulbs. How many cartons were needed in the given week?

Sol. In the given pictograph, 1 picture = 2 bulbs

Now, number of bulbs sold on Monday = 6 pictures = $6 \times 2 = 12$ bulbs
Number of bulbs sold on Tuesday = $8 \times 2 = 16$ bulbs
Number of bulbs sold on Wednesday = $4 \times 2 = 8$ bulbs
Number of bulbs sold on Thursday = $5 \times 2 = 10$ bulbs
Number of bulbs sold on Friday = $7 \times 2 = 14$ bulbs
Number of bulbs sold on Saturday = $4 \times 2 = 8$ bulbs
Number of bulbs sold on Sunday = $9 \times 2 = 18$ bulbs

(a) Number of bulbs sold on Friday = $7 \times 2 = 14$ bulbs

(b) Maximum number of bulbs were sold on Sunday i.e. 18 bulbs.

(c) The same number of bulbs were sold on Wednesday and Saturday i.e. 8 bulbs.

(d) The minimum number of bulbs were sold on Wednesday and Saturday i.e. 8 bulbs.

(e) Total number of bulbs sold in a week

$$= 12 + 16 + 8 + 10 + 14 + 8 + 18 = 86$$

Now, number of cartons which can hold 9 bulbs $= 1$

and number of carton which can hold 1 bulb $= \dfrac{1}{9}$

$\therefore$ Number of cartons which can hold 86 bulbs $= \dfrac{1 \times 86}{9}$

$$= \dfrac{86}{9} = 9\dfrac{5}{9} \approx 10$$

Hence, 10 cartons were needed in the given week.

Que 7. In a village six fruit merchants sold the following number of fruit baskets in a particular season.

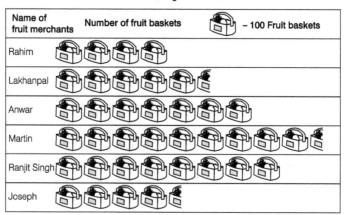

Observe this pictograph and answer the following questions.

(a) Which merchant sold the maximum number of baskets?

(b) How many fruit baskets were sold by Anwar?

(c) The merchants who have sold 600 or more number of baskets are planning to buy a godown for the next season. Can you name them?

Sol. (a) Given, 1 picture $= 100$ baskets

$\therefore$ Half picture $= 50$ baskets

From the pictograph, we have

Number of baskets sold by Rahim $= 4 \times 100 = 400$

Number of baskets sold by Lakhanpal $= 5$ full 1 half

$$= 5 \times 100 + 1 \times 50 = 550$$

Number of baskets sold by Anwar $= 7 \times 100 = 700$

Number of baskets sold by Martin $= 9$ full 1 half

$$= 9 \times 100 + 1 \times 50 = 950$$

Number of baskets sold by Ranjit Singh $= 8 \times 100 = 800$

and number of baskets sold by Joseph $= 4$ full 1 half

$$= 4 \times 100 + 1 \times 50 = 450$$

Hence, Martin sold the maximum number of baskets i.e. 950.

(b) From (a), Anwar sold 700 fruit baskets.

(c) Yes, after observing the pictograph, we can say that Anwar, Martin and Ranjit Singh have sold 600 or more number of baskets and they are planning to buy a godown for the next season.

Exercise 9.2

Que 1. Total number of animals in five villages are as follows:

Villages	Number of animals
Village A	80
Village B	120
Village C	90
Village D	40
Village E	60

Prepare a pictograph of these animals using one symbol ⊗ to represent 10 animals and answer the following questions.

(a) How many symbols represent animals of village E?

(b) Which village has the maximum number of animals?

(c) Which village has more animals : village A or village C?

Sol. Given, 10 animals are represented by 1 symbol ⊗.

∴ 1 animal is represented by 1/10 symbol ⊗

For village A,

80 animals are represented by $\dfrac{80 \times 1}{10} = 8$ symbols ⊗

For village B,

120 animals are represented by $\dfrac{120 \times 1}{10} = 12$ symbols ⊗

For village C,

90 animals are represented by $\dfrac{90 \times 1}{10} = 9$ symbols ⊗

For village D,

40 animals are represented by $\dfrac{40 \times 1}{10} = 4$ symbols ⊗

For village E,

60 animals are represented by $\dfrac{60 \times 1}{10} = 6$ symbols ⊗

Then, we have the following pictograph.

Villages	Number of animals	⊗ – 10 animals
Village A	⊗ ⊗ ⊗ ⊗ ⊗ ⊗ ⊗ ⊗	
Village B	⊗ ⊗ ⊗ ⊗ ⊗ ⊗ ⊗ ⊗ ⊗ ⊗ ⊗ ⊗	
Village C	⊗ ⊗ ⊗ ⊗ ⊗ ⊗ ⊗ ⊗ ⊗	
Village D	⊗ ⊗ ⊗ ⊗	
Village E	⊗ ⊗ ⊗ ⊗ ⊗ ⊗	

(a) It is clear from the pictograph, that 6 symbols represent animals of village E.

(b) It is clear from the pictograph, that village B has the maximum number of animals i.e.120 animals.

(c) Form the pictograph, number of animals in village A = 80
Number of animals in village = 90

∵   90 > 80

∴ Village C has more animals.

Que 2. Total number of students of a school in different years is shown in the following table.

Years	Number of students
1996	400
1998	535
2000	472
2002	600
2004	623

A. Prepare a pictograph of students using one symbol ☺ to represent 100 students and answer the following questions.

      (a) How many symbols represent total number of students in the year 2002?

      (b) How many symbols represent total number of students in the year 1998?

   B. Prepare another pictograph of students using any other symbol each representing 50 students. Which pictograph do you find more informative?

Sol. (A) According to the question, 100 students can be represented by

      = 1 symbol ♀

$\therefore$ 1 student can be represented by $\dfrac{1}{100}$ symbols

Now, for year 1996,

400 students can be represented by $\dfrac{400 \times 1}{100} = 4$ symbols

For year 1998,

535 students can be represented by $\dfrac{535 \times 1}{100} = 5$ symbols

+ 35 students = 5 complete symbols and 1 incomplete symbol

For year 2000,

472 students can be represented by $\dfrac{472 \times 1}{100}$

      = 4 complete symbols + 72 students

      = 4 complete symbols and 1 incomplete symbol

For year 2002,

600 students can be represented by $\dfrac{600 \times 1}{100}$

      = 6 complete symbols

For year 2004,

623 students can be represented by $\dfrac{623 \times 1}{600}$

6 complete symbol +23 students

      = 6 complete symbols and 1 incomplete symbol

Hence, the required pictograph of given data is shown below

Years	Number of students	♀ – 100 Students
1996	♀ ♀ ♀ ♀	
1998	♀ ♀ ♀ ♀ ♀ ſ	
2000	♀ ♀ ♀ ♀ ♀	
2002	♀ ♀ ♀ ♀ ♀ ♀	
2004	♀ ♀ ♀ ♀ ♀ ♀ ſ	

(a) 6 symbols represent total number of students in the year 2002.

(b) 5 complete symbols and 1 incomplete symbol represent total number of students for the year 1998.

(B) According to the question, 50 students can be represented by 1 symbol

∴ 1 student can be represented by $\dfrac{1}{50}$ symbols

Now, for year 1996,

400 students can be represented by $\dfrac{400 \times 1}{50}$ symbols

$$= \dfrac{400}{50} = 8 \text{ complete symbols}$$

For year 1998,

535 students can be represented by $\dfrac{535 \times 1}{50} = \dfrac{535}{50}$ symbols

$= 10$ complete symbols + 1 incomplete symbol

For year 2000,

472 students can be represented by $\dfrac{472 \times 1}{50}$ symbols

$= \dfrac{472}{50} = 9$ complete symbols + 1 incomplete symbol

For year 2002,

600 students can be represented by $\dfrac{600 \times 1}{50}$ symbols

$$= \dfrac{600}{50} = 12 \text{ complete symbols}$$

For year 2004,

623 students can be represented by $\dfrac{623 \times 1}{50}$ symbols

$= \dfrac{623}{50} = 12$ complete symbols + 1 incomplete symbol

Hence, the required pictograph of given data is shown below

Years	Number of students	⊗ – 50 Students
1996	⊗ ⊗ ⊗ ⊗ ⊗ ⊗ ⊗ ⊗	
1998	⊗ ⊗ ⊗ ⊗ ⊗ ⊗ ⊗ ⊗ ⊗ ⊗ ✕	
2000	⊗ ⊗ ⊗ ⊗ ⊗ ⊗ ⊗ ⊗ ⊗ ✕	
2002	⊗ ⊗ ⊗ ⊗ ⊗ ⊗ ⊗ ⊗ ⊗ ⊗ ⊗ ⊗	
2004	⊗ ⊗ ⊗ ⊗ ⊗ ⊗ ⊗ ⊗ ⊗ ⊗ ⊗ ⊗ ✕	

Therefore, we observe that pictograph *B* is more informative because it gives better approximation.

Exercise 9.3

Que 1. The bar graph given below shows the amount of wheat purchased by government during the year 1998-2002.

Read the bar graph and write down your observations. In which year was

(a) the wheat production maximum?

(b) the wheat production minimum?

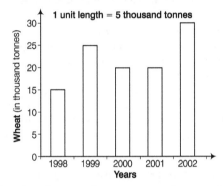

Sol. (a) From the given bar graph, we can say that maximum production is shown by largest bar (i.e. 30 thousand tonnes) for the year 2002.

(b) From the given bar graph, we can say that minimum production is shown by the smallest bar (i.e. 15 thousand tonnes) for the year 1998.

Que 2. Observe this bar graph, which is showing the sale of shirts in a ready made shop from Monday to Saturday.

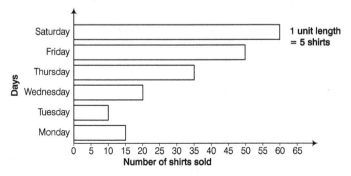

Now, answer the following questions.

(a) What information does the above bar graph give?

(b) What is the scale chosen on the horizontal line representing number of shirts?

(c) On which day were the maximum number of shirts sold? How many shirts were sold on that day?

(d) On which day were the minimum number of shirts sold?

(e) How many shirts were sold on Thursday?

Sol. (a) Given bar graph shows the number of shirts sold from Monday to Saturday.

(b) Scale on horizontal line is 1 unit = 5 shirts.

(c) From given bar graph, it is clear that maximum number of shirts sold is shown by the largest bar (i.e. on Saturday). Hence, on Saturday 60 shirts were sold.

(d) From given bar graph, it is clear that smallest bar shows the minimum number of sold shirts (i.e. on Tuesday.) Hence, the minimum number of shirts were sold on Tuesday.

(e) From given bar graph, it is clear that on Thursday, 35 shirts were sold.

Que 3. Observe this bar graph which shows the marks obtained by Aziz in half-yearly examination in different subjects.

Answer the given questions.

(a) What information does the bar graph give?

(b) Name the subject, in which Aziz scored maximum marks.

(c) Name the subject, in which he has scored minimum marks.

(d) State the name of subjects and marks obtained in each of them.

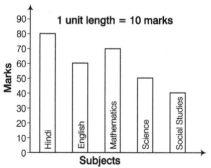

Sol. (a) Given bar graph represents the marks obtained by Aziz in half-yearly examination in different subjects.

(b) From the bar graph, it is clear that maximum marks are shown by the largest bar. So, Aziz scored maximum marks (i.e. 80 marks) in Hindi.

(c) From the bar graph, it is clear that minimum marks are shown by the smallest bar. So, Aziz has scored minimum marks (i.e. 40 marks) in Social Studies.

(d) From the bar graph, Aziz's subjects and marks obtained in corresponding subject are as follows :

Subjects	Marks
Hindi	80
English	60
Mathematics	70
Science	50
Social Studies	40

Exercise 9.4

Que 1. A survey of 120 school students was done to find which activity they prefer to do in their free time.

Preferred activity	Number of students
Playing	45
Reading story books	30
Watching TV	20
Listening to music	10
Painting	15

Draw a bar graph to illustrate the above data taking scale of 1 unit length = 5 students.

Which activity is preferred by most of the students other than playing?

Sol. To draw a bar graph of given data, we use the following steps.

(i) Firstly, draw two perpendicular lines, one is horizontal and one is vertical. Along the horizontal line, mark the preferred activity and along the vertical line, mark the corresponding number of students.

(ii) Now, take scale of 1 unit length = 5 students along the vertical line and then mark the corresponding values.

Also, the height of the bars for various activities are as follows:

Playing	$\dfrac{45}{5}$ = 9 units
Reading story books	$\dfrac{30}{5}$ = 6 units
Watching TV	$\dfrac{20}{5}$ = 4 units
Listening to music	$\dfrac{10}{5}$ = 2 units
Painting	$\dfrac{15}{5}$ = 3 units

(iii) Draw bar of equal width and of height calculated in Step (ii) on horizontal line with equal spacing between them.

Thus, we get the following bar graph

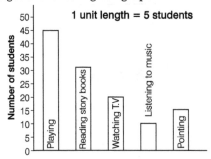

From the above bar graph, it is clear that the activity 'reading story books' is preferred by most of the students other than playing. Because the second larger bar is for reading story books.

Que 2. The number of Mathematics books sold by a shopkeeper on six consecutive days is shown below

Days	Sunday	Monday	Tuesday	Wednesday	Thursday	Friday
Number of books sold	65	40	30	50	20	70

Draw a bar graph to represent the above information choosing the scale of your choice.

Sol. To draw a bar graph, we will use the following steps.

(i) Firstly, draw two perpendicular lines, one is horizontal and one is vertical. Along the horizontal line, mark 'days' and along the vertical line mark 'number of books sold'.

(ii) Now, take scale of 1 unit length = 5 books, along the vertical line and then mark the corresponding values.

Also, the heights of the bars for various days are as follows:

Sunday	$\dfrac{65}{5} = 13$ units
Monday	$\dfrac{40}{5} = 8$ units
Tuesday	$\dfrac{30}{5} = 6$ units
Wednesday	$\dfrac{50}{5} = 10$ units
Thursday	$\dfrac{20}{5} = 4$ units
Friday	$\dfrac{70}{5} = 14$ units

(iii) Draw bars of equal width and of height calculated in Step (ii) on the horizontal line with equal spacing (or gap) between them. Thus, we get the following bar graph.

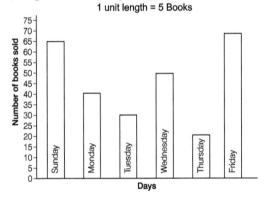

Que 3. Following table shows the number of bicycles manufactured in a factory during the years 1998 to 2002. Illustrate this data using a bar graph. Choose a scale of your choice.

Years	Number of bicycles manufactured
1998	800
1999	600
2000	900
2001	1100
2002	1200

(a) In which year were the maximum number of bicycles manufactured?

(b) In which year were the minimum number of bicycles manufactured?

Sol. To draw the bar graph, we will use the following steps

   (i) Firstly, draw two perpendicular lines, one is horizontal and one is vertical. Along the horizontal line mark 'years' and along vertical line mark 'number of bicycles manufactured'.

  (ii) Now, take scale of 1 units length = 100 bicycles along the vertical line and then mark the corresponding values.

     Also, the heights of the bars for various years are as follows:

1998	$\dfrac{800}{100} = 8$ units
1999	$\dfrac{600}{100} = 6$ units
2000	$\dfrac{900}{100} = 9$ units
2001	$\dfrac{1100}{100} = 11$ units
2002	$\dfrac{1200}{100} = 12$ units

 (iii) Draw bar of equal width and of heights calculated in Step (ii) on the horizontal line with uniform gap between them.

     Thus we get the following bar graph

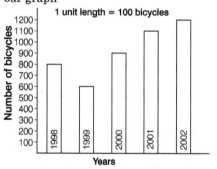

1 unit length = 100 bicycles

  (a) The maximum number of bicycles were manufactured in the year 2002 (because the bar is largest for 2002).

  (b) The minimum number of bicycles were manufactured in the year 1999 (because the bar is smallest for 1999).

Que 4. Number of persons in various age groups in a town is given in the following table

Age group	Number of persons
1-14	2 lakh
15-29	1 lakh 60 thousands
30-44	1 lakh 20 thousands
45-59	1 lakh 20 thousands
60-74	80 thousands
75 and above	40 thousands

    Draw a bar graph to represent the above information and answer the following questions. (take 1 unit length = 20 thousands)

(a) Which two age groups have same population?

(b) All persons in the age group of 60 and above are called senior citizens. How many senior citizens are there in the town?

Sol. To draw the bar graph, we will use the following steps.

(i) Firstly, draw two perpendicular lines, one is horizontal and one is vertical. Along the horizontal line mark 'age–group' and along vertical line mark 'number of persons'.

(ii) Now, take scale of 1 unit length = 20000 along the vertical line and then mark the corresponding values.

Also, the heights of bars for various groups are as follows:

1-14	$\dfrac{200000}{20000} = 10$ units
15-29	$\dfrac{160000}{20000} = 8$ units
30-44	$\dfrac{120000}{20000} = 6$ units
45-59	$\dfrac{120000}{20000} = 6$ units
60-74	$\dfrac{80000}{20000} = 4$ units
75 and above	$\dfrac{40000}{20000} = 2$ units

(iii) Draw bar of equal width and of height calculated in Step (ii) on the horizontal line with equal gap between them.

Thus, we get the following bar graph

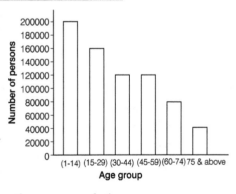

(a) From bar graph, we see that the lengths of bars for age group 30-44 and 45-59 are same, so age group (30-44) and (45-59) have the same population.

(b) ∵ persons having age 60 or above are called senior citizens.

∴ Number of senior citizens in the town

= Number of persons of age group (60-74) + Number of persons of age 75 and above = 80000 + 40000 = 120000

Selected **NCERT Exemplar Problems**

Directions *In questions 1 to 2, out of the four options, only one is correct, Write the correct answer.*

Que 1. Using tally marks, which one of the following represents the number eight

(a) 〔|||||〕||| (b) ᴺ ᴺ

(c) ᴺ||| (d) ᴺ|||

Sol. We know that, $8 = 5 + 3$

Here, 5 is represented by ᴺ and 3 is represented by |||

∴ 8 is represented by ᴺ |||

Hence, the option (d) is correct.

Que 2. The choices of the fruits of 42 students in a class are as follows:

A, O, B, M, A, G, B, G, A, G,
B, M, A, G, M, A, B, G, M, B,
A, O, M, O, G, B, O, M, G, A,
A, B, M, O, M, G, B, A, M, O, M, O,

Where A, B, G and O stand for the fruits apple, banana, grapes, mango, and orange, respectively.

Which two fruits are liked by an equal number of students?

(a) A and M   (b) M and B   (c) B and O   (d) B and G

Sol. The table with tally marks is shown as below

Fruits name	Tally marks	Number of students
A (Apple)	ᴺ ᴺ	9
B (Banana)	ᴺ |||	8
G (Grapes)	ᴺ |||	8
M (Mango)	ᴺ ᴺ	10
O (Orange)	ᴺ ||	7
Total		42

Here, by examine the above table, we see that banana and grapes are liked by an equal number of students (i.e. 8). hence option (d) is correct.

Directions *In questions 3 and 4, State whether the given statement is true ar false.*

Que 3. In a bar graph, bars of uniform width are drawn vertically only.

Sol. **False** since the bars of uniform width can be drawn horizontally as well as vertically.

Que 4. An observation occurring five times in a data is recorded as ⌐HⲎ | , using tally marks.

Sol. **False** the fifth mark in a group of five marks should be used as across, as shown by ⌐HⲎ.

Directions *In questions 7 to 9, fill in the blank to make a statement true.*

Que 5. The data can be arranged in a tabular form using .... marks.

Sol. The data can be arranged in a tabular form using **tally** marks.

Que 6. A..........represents data through pictures of objects.

Sol. A **pictograph** represents data through pictures of objects.

Que 7. In a pictograph, if a symbol ✿ represents 20 flowers in a basket, then ✿✿✿ stands for .... flowers.

Sol. In the given pictograph, 1 symbol represents 20 flowers
(i.e. 1 ✿ = 20 flowers)
∴ 3 symbols represent = $3 \times 20 = 60$ flowers

Que 8. The lengths in centimetres (to the nearest centimetre) of 30 carrots are given as follows:
15, 22, 21, 20, 22, 15, 15, 20, 20, 15, 20, 18, 20, 22, 21,
20, 21, 18, 21, 18, 20, 18, 21, 18, 22, 20, 15, 21, 18, 20
Arrange the data given above in a table using tally marks and answer the following questions.
  (a) What is the number of carrots which have length more than 20 cm?
  (b) Which length of the carrots occur maximum number of times and minimum number of times?

Sol. On arranging the given data in a table using tally marks, we get the following table.

Carrots (length in cm)	Tally marks	Number of times
15	𝍸	5
18	𝍸 |	6
20	𝍸 ||||	9
21	𝍸 |	6
22	||||	4

(a) Here we have to find the length of the carrots having more than 20 cm. So we have to add the carrots having lengths 21 cm and 22 cm.

$\therefore$ Number of such carrots $= 6 + 4 = 10$

(b) From the table, we can say that length of carrots 20 cm occurs the maximum number of times i.e. 9 times and the length of carrots 22 cm occurs the minimum number of times i.e. 4 times.

Que 9. Following are the choices of games of 40 students of Class VI. Football, cricket, football, kho-kho, hockey, cricket, hockey, kho-kho, tennis, tennis, cricket, football, football, hockey, kho-kho, football, cricket, tennis, football, hockey, kho-kho, football, cricket, cricket, football, hockey, kho-kho, tennis, football, hockey, cricket, football, hockey, cricket, football, kho-kho, football, cricket, hockey, football.

(a) Arrange the choices of games in a table using tally marks.

(b) Which game is liked by most of the students?

(c) Which game is liked by minimum number of students?

Sol. (a) Firstly, write the name of games in first column, then in second column use tally marks to represent number of students like corresponding games and in the third column write the number of students. Thus, we get the following table.

Games	Tally marks	Number of students
Football	𝍸 𝍸 |||	13
Cricket	𝍸 𝍸	9
Kho-kho	𝍸 |	6
Hockey	𝍸 |||	8
Tennis	𝍸	4
Total		**40**

(b) By examine the above table, we see that the football is liked by most of the students, (i.e. 13 students).

(c) By examine the above table, we see that the tennis is liked by minimum number of students (i.e. 4 students).

Que 10. Fill in the blanks in the following table which represents shirt size of 40 students of a school.

Shirt size	Tally marks	Number of students
30					3
32	||||\	—
34	—	8
36	||||\	—
38	||||—	10
40	—	7

Sol. (ii) ⊮, shows four vertical lines and one intersect line.

∴ Its count to be four plus one (i.e. 5).

(iii) We know that, 8 = 5 + 3

Here, 5 is represented by ⊮ and 3 is represented by |||

∴ 8 is represented by ⊮ |||.

(iv) ⊮ || means 5+2 i.e. 7

(v) We know that, 10 = 5 + 5

Here, 5 is represented by ⊮

∴ 10 is represented by ⊮ ⊮

(vi) We know that, 7 = 5 + 2

Here, 5 is represented by ⊮ and 2 is represented by ||

∴ 7 is represented by ⊮ ||

Thus, the complete table is shown as

Shirt size	Tally marks	Number of students
30					3
32						5
34	⊮ |||	8
36	⊮ ||	7
38	⊮ ⊮	10
40	⊮ ||	7

Que 11. Following pictograph represents some surnames of people listed in the telephone directory of a city

Surname	Number of people	= 100 people
Khan		
Patel		
Rao		
Roy		
Saikia		
Singh		

Observe the pictograph and answer the following questions:

(a) How many people have surname 'Roy'?

(b) Which surname appears the maximum number of times in the telephone directory?

(c) Which surname appears the least number of times in the directory?

(d) Which two surnames appear an equal number of times?

Sol. In the given pictograph, 1 palm = 100 people

(a) The total number of plam having surname Roy = 4

∴ The total number of people having surname Roy = 4 × 100
= 400 people

(b) From the given table, we see that the patel appears the maximum number of times in the telephone directory i.e. 5 times.

(c) From the given table, we see that the saikia appears the minimum number of times in the telephone directory i.e. 2 times

(d) From the given table, we see that the Rao and Roy has appears the same number of times in the telephone directory i.e. 4 times.

Que 12. The following table gives information about the circulation of newspapers (dailies) in a town in five languages.

Language	English	Hindi	Tamil	Punjabi	Gujarati
Number of newspapers	5000	8500	500	2500	1000

Prepare a pictograph of the above data, using a symbol of your choice, each representing 1000 newspapers.

Sol. Given, 1000 newspapers can be represented by = 1 symbol ⊞

$\therefore$ 1 newspaper can be represented by $= \dfrac{1}{1000}$ symbol ⊞

For English language,

5000 newspapers can be represented by $\dfrac{5000 \times 1}{1000}$

$= 5$ complete symbols

For Hindi language,

8500 newspapers can be represented by $\dfrac{8500 \times 1}{1000}$

$= 8$ complete symbols + 1 incomplete symbol

For Tamil language,

500 newspapers can be represented by $\dfrac{500 \times 1}{1000} = 0.5$ newspapers

$= 0$ complete symbol + 1 incomplete symbol

For Punjabi language,

2500 newspapers can be represented by $\dfrac{2500 \times 1}{1000}$

$= 2$ complete symbols + 1 incomplete symbol

For Gujarati language,

1000 newspapers can be represented by $\dfrac{1000 \times 1}{1000}$

$= 1$ complete symbol

Hence, the required pictograph of given data is shown below

Language	Numbers of newspapers	⊞ = newspapers
English	⊞⊞⊞⊞⊞	
Hindi	⊞⊞⊞⊞⊞⊞⊞⊞▢	
Tamil	▢	
Punjabi	⊞⊞▢	
Gujrati	⊞	

Que 13. The following graph gives the information about the number of railway tickets sold for different cities on a railway ticket counter between 6.00 am 10.00 am. Read the bar graph and answer the following questions.

(a) How many tickets were sold in all?

(b) For which city were the maximum number of tickets sold?

(c) For which city were the minimum number of tickets sold?

(d) Name the cities for which the number of tickets sold is more than 20.

(e) Fill in the blank.

Number of tickets sold for Delhi and Jaipur together exceeds the total number of tickets sold for Patna and Chennai by

Graph

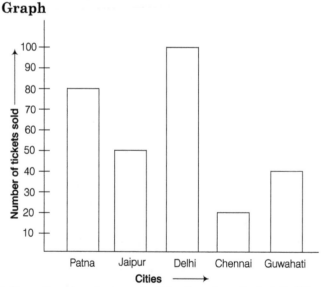

Sol. (a) From the given bar graph, it is clear that the height of bar graph is represented by the number of tickets sold.

∴Number of tickets sold for Patna = 80

Number of tickets sold for Jaipur = 50

Number of tickets sold for Delhi = 100

Number of tickets sold for Chennai = 20

and number of tickets sold for Guwahati = 45

Now, total number of tickets sold for all cities

$$= 80 + 50 + 100 + 20 + 45 = 295$$

(b) From the given bar graph, it is clear that maximum number of tickets sold is shown by largest bar (i.e.100). Hence, the maximum number of tickets sold for Delhi.

(c) From the given bar graph, it is clear that minimum number of tickets sold is shown by smallest bar (i.e. 20). Hence, the minimum number of tickets were sold for Chennai.

(d) From the given bar graph, it is clear that tickets sold for cities Patna, Jaipur, Delhi and Guwahati is more than 20.

(e) From the given bar graph, number of tickets sold for Delhi and Jaipur $= 100 + 50 = 150$

and number of tickets sold for Patna and Chennai $= 80 + 20 = 100$

$\therefore$ Number of tickets sold for Delhi and Jaipur together exceeds the total number of tickets sold for Patna and Chennai by 50 (i. e. $150 - 100 = 50$).

Que 14. The following pictograph depicts the information about the areas in sqkm (to nearest hundred) of some districts of Chhattisgarh State:

(a) What is the area of Koria district?

(b) Which two districts have the same area?

(c) How many districts have area more than 5000 square kilometres?

Sol. In the given pictograph 1 picture $= 1000$ sqkm

(a) In a Koria district, their are 6 pictures given.

$\therefore$ Area of Koria district $= 6 \times 1000 = 6000$ sq km

(b) From the ta1ble, we see that the districts Raigarh and Jashpur has same number of areas, because both has same number of pictures.

(c) The district having more than 5000 sqkm is equal to the district having more than 5 pictures (∵ 1 picture = 1000 sqkm). It is clear from the table that, districts Raigarh, Rajnandgaon, Koria and Jashpur have more than 5 picture (i.e. more than 5000 sqkm)

Hence, number of districts having more than 5000 sqkm is four.

Que 15. The length in km (rounded off to nearest hundred) of some major rivers of India is given below

River	Length (in km)
Narmada	1300
Mahanadi	900
Brahmaputra	2900
Ganga	2500
Kaveri	800
Krishna	1300

Draw a bar graph to represent the above information.

Sol. To draw a bar graph, we will use the following steps.

(i) Firstly, draw two perpendicular lines, one is horizontal and other is vertical. Along the horizontal line, mark rivers and along the vertical line mark length (in km).

(ii) Now, take scale of 1 unit length = 100 km, along the vertical line and then mark the corresponding values.

Also, the height of the bars for various rivers are as follows:

Narmada	$\dfrac{1300}{100} = 13$ units
Mahanadi	$\dfrac{900}{100} = 9$ units
Brahmaputra	$\dfrac{2900}{100} = 29$ units
Ganga	$\dfrac{2500}{100} = 25$ units
Kaveri	$\dfrac{800}{100} = 8$ units
Krishna	$\dfrac{1300}{100} = 13$ units

(iii) Draw bars of equal width and the height calculated in Step (ii) on the horizontal line with equal spacing or gap between them. Thus, we get the following bar graph.

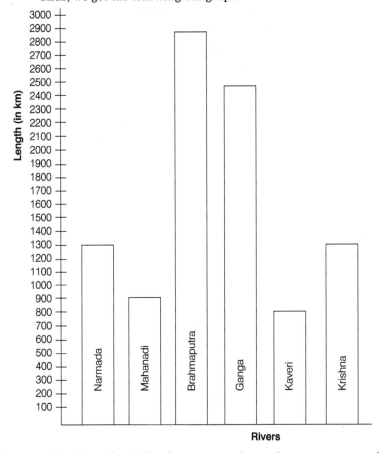

Que 16. Number of mobile phone users in various age groups in a city is listed below:

Age group (in years)	Number of mobile users
1-20	25000
21-40	40000
41-60	35000
61-80	10000

Draw a bar graph to represent the above information.

Sol. To draw a bar graph, we will use the following steps.

   (i) Firstly, draw two perpendicular lines, one is horizontal and one is vertical. Along the horizontal line, mark 'Age group' and along the vertical line mark 'Number of mobile users'

  (ii) Now, take scale of 1 unit length = 5000 mobile users, along the vertical line and then mark the corresponding values.

Also, the heights of the bars for various age group are as follows.

Age group (in yrs) heights of bar group

1-20	$\dfrac{25000}{5000} = 5$
21-40	$\dfrac{40000}{5000} = 8$
41-60	$\dfrac{35000}{5000} = 7$
61-80	$\dfrac{10000}{5000} = 2$

 (iii) Draw bars of equal width and of height calculated in step (ii) on the horizontal line with equal spacing (or gap)

Thus we get the following bar graph.

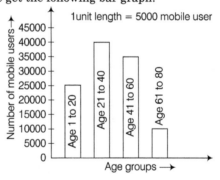

Que 17. In a botanical garden, the number of different types of plants are found as follows:

Type of the plant	Number of plants
Herb	50
Shrub	60
Creeper	20
Climber	45
Tree	95

Draw a bar graph to represent the above information and answer the following questions:

(a) Which type of plant is maximum in number in the garden?

(b) Which type of plant is minimum in number in the garden?

Sol. To draw a bar graph, we will use the following steps

(i) Firstly, draw two perpendicular lines, one is horizontal and one is vertical. Along the horizontal line, mark 'type of the plant' and along the vertical line mark 'Number of plants'

(ii) Now, take scale of 1 unit length = 10 plants along the vertical line and then mark the corresponding values

Also, the heights of the bars for various type of the plant are an follows :

Type of the plant	Height of bar group
Herb	$\dfrac{50}{10} = 5$
Shrub	$\dfrac{60}{10} = 6$
Creeper	$\dfrac{20}{10} = 2$
Climber	$\dfrac{45}{10} = 4.5$
Tree	$\dfrac{95}{10} = 9.5$

(iii) Draw bars of equal width and of heights calculated in step (ii) on the horizontal line with equal spacing (or gap)

Thus, we get the following bar graph

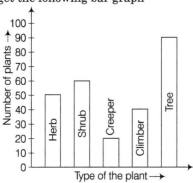

Chapter **10**

Mensuration

Important Points

- **Perimeter** The distance covered along the boundary forming a closed figure, when we go round the figure once is called perimeter. So, to find perimeter, add the lengths of all sides (which are line segments of given figure).

  e.g. Perimeter of a rectangle $= 2 \times$ (Length + Breadth)

  Note In calculating the perimeter of a rectangle, we must express the length and breadth in the same unit.

- **Regular closed figures** Figures in which all sides are of equal length and all angles are of equal measure are called regular closed figures. e.g. square, equilateral triangle, regular hexagon etc.

- **Perimeter of regular shapes** In regular shapes, all sides are of equal length and all angles are of equal measure.

  Formulae related to perimeter of regular shapes
  - (i) Perimeter of an equilateral triangle $= 3 \times$ Length of one side
  - (ii) Perimeter of a square (or regular quadrilateral)
    $$= 4 \times \text{Length of one side}$$
  - (iii) Perimeter of a regular pentagon $= 5 \times$ Length of one side
  - (iv) Perimeter of a regular hexagon $= 6 \times$ Length of one side
  - (v) Perimeter of a regular octagon $= 8 \times$ Length of one side

- **Area** The amount of surface (the measurement of the region) enclosed by a closed figure is called the **area** of that figure. The standard unit of area is square unit (i.e. sq unit)

  Formulae related to area of regular figures
  - (i) Area of a rectangle $=$ Length $\times$ Breadth
  - (ii) Area of a square $=$ Side $\times$ Side or $(\text{Side})^2$

- To calculate the area of a figure using a squared paper, the following conventions are adopted:

    (i) The area of one full square is taken as 1 sq unit.

    (ii) The area of the portion, which is less than half a square is ignored.

    (iii) The area of the portion, which is exactly half of the square is counted as $\frac{1}{2}$ sq unit.

    (iv) The area of the portion which is more than half of a square is counted as 1 sq unit.

Try These (Page 206-207)

Que 1. Measure and write the length of the four sides of the top of your study table.

$AB = \underline{\quad}$ cm

$BC = \underline{\quad}$ cm

$CD = \underline{\quad}$ cm

$DA = \underline{\quad}$ cm

Now, the sum of the lengths of the four sides
$$= AB + BC + CD + DA$$
$$= \underline{\quad} \text{cm} + \underline{\quad}\text{cm} + \underline{\quad}\text{cm} + \underline{\quad}\text{cm} = \underline{\quad} \text{cm}$$

What is the perimeter?

TIPS

Perimeter is the distance covered along the boundary forming a closed figure, when we go round the figure once. So, the perimeter of table is equal to sum of length of the four sides.

Sol. Here, AB and CD are equal and DA and BC are equal.

On measuring, we get $AB = CD = 60$ cm and $DA = BC = 30$ cm

Now, the sum of the lengths of the four sides
$$= AB + BC + CD + DA$$
$$= 60 \text{ cm} + 30 \text{ cm} + 60 \text{ cm} + 30 \text{ cm}$$
$$= (60 + 30 + 60 + 30) \text{ cm} = 80 \text{ cm}$$

∴ Perimeter of the table = Sum of the lengths of the four sides = 180 cm

Hence, the perimeter of the study table is 180 cm.

Que 2. Measure and write the lengths of the four sides of a page of your notebook. The sum of the lengths of the four sides
$$= AB + BC + CD + DA$$
$$= \_\_\_cm + \_\_\_cm + \_\_\_cm + \_\_\_cm = \_\_\_cm$$

What is the perimeter of the page?

Sol. Let $ABCD$ be the page of a notebook.

On measuring , $AB = CD = 15$ cm, and $BC = DA = 20$ cm

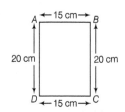

Then, the sum of the lengths of four sides
$$= AB + BC + CD + DA$$
$$= 15 \text{ cm} + 20 \text{ cm} + 15 \text{ cm} + 20 \text{ cm}$$
$$= (15 + 20 + 15 + 20) \text{ cm} = 70 \text{ cm}$$

Hence, the sum of the four sides is 70 cm.

Now, perimeter of the page = Sum of the lengths of four sides = 70 cm

Que 3. Meera went to a park 150 m long and 80 m wide. She took one complete round on its boundary. What is the distance covered by her?

Sol. Let $ABCD$ is a park whose lengths are BC, AD and widths are AB, CD respectively.

Here, $AB = CD = 80$ m and $BC = DA = 150$ m

Now, the sum of the lengths of four sides
$$= AB + BC + CD + DA$$
$$= 80 \text{ m} + 150 \text{ m} + 80 \text{ m} + 150 \text{ m}$$
$$= (80 + 150 + 80 + 150) \text{ m} = 460 \text{ m}$$

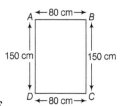

∴ Perimeter of the park = Sum of the lengths of four sides of the park = 460 m

Hence, the distance covered by Meera is 460 m.

Que 4. Find the perimeter of the following figures.

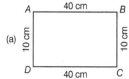

(a)

Perimeter $= AB + BC + CD + DA$
$$= \_\_\_ + \_\_\_ + \_\_\_ + \_\_\_ = \_\_\_$$

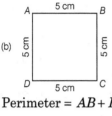

(b)

Perimeter = $AB + BC + CD + DA$

= ___ + ___ + ___ + ___ = ____

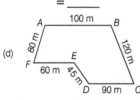

(c)

Perimeter = $AB + BC + CD + DE + EF + FG + GH$

$+ HI + IJ + JK + KL + LA$

= ___ + ___ + ___ + ___ + ___ + ___ + ___ + ___

+ ___ + ___ + ___ + ___

= _____

(d)

Perimeter = $AB + BC + CD + DE + EF + FA$

= ___ + ___ + ___ + ___ + ___ + ___ = _____

Sol. (a) From the given figure, we have

$AB = 40$ cm, $BC = 10$ cm, $CD = 40$ cm and $DA = 10$ cm

Now, the sum of the lengths of the four sides

$= AB + BC + CD + DA$

$= 40$ cm $+ 10$ cm $+ 40$ cm $+ 10$ cm

$= (40 + 10 + 40 + 10)$ cm $= 100$ cm

∴ Perimeter of the given figure = Sum of the lengths of four sides

$= 100$ cm

Hence, the perimeter of the given figure is 100 cm.

(b) From the given figure, we have $AB = BC = CD = DA = 5$ cm
i.e. each side of the given figure is 5 cm.
Now, the sum of the lengths of the four sides
$$= AB + BC + CD + DA = 5 \text{ cm} + 5 \text{ cm} + 5 \text{ cm} + 5 \text{ cm}$$
$$= (5 + 5 + 5 + 5) \text{ cm} = 20 \text{ cm}$$
∴ Perimeter of the given figure = Sum of the lengths of four sides
$$= 20 \text{ cm}$$
Hence, the perimeter of the given figure is 20 cm.

(c) From given figure, we have $AB = DE = GH = JK = 1$ cm
and $BC = CD = EF = FG = HI = IJ = KL = LA = 3$ cm
Sum of the lengths of all sides
$$= AB + BC + CD + DE + EF + FG + GH$$
$$+ HI + IJ + JK + KL + LA$$
$$= 1 \text{ cm} + 3 \text{ cm} + 3 \text{ cm} + 1 \text{ cm} + 3 \text{ cm} + 3 \text{ cm}$$
$$+ 1 \text{ cm} + 3 \text{ cm} + 3 \text{ cm} + 1 \text{ cm} + 3 \text{ cm} + 3 \text{ cm}$$
$$= (1 + 3 + 3 + 1 + 3 + 3 + 1 + 3 + 3 + 1 + 3 + 3) \text{ cm} = 28 \text{ cm}$$
∴ Perimeter of the given figure = Sum of the lengths of four sides
$$= 28 \text{ cm}$$
Hence, the perimeter of the given figure is 28 cm.

(d) From the given figure,
We have, $AB = 100$ m, $BC = 120$ m, $CD = 90$ m,
$$DE = 45 \text{ m}, EF = 60 \text{ m and } FA = 80 \text{ m}$$
Now, the sum of the lengths of all sides
$$= AB + BC + CD + DE + EF + FA$$
$$= 100 \text{ m} + 120 \text{ m} + 90 \text{ m} + 45 \text{ m} + 60 \text{ m} + 80 \text{ m}$$
$$= (100 + 120 + 90 + 45 + 60 + 80) \text{ m} = 495 \text{ m}$$
∴ Perimeter of the given figure = Sum of the lengths of all sides
$$= 495 \text{ m}$$
Hence, the perimeter of the given figure is 495 m.

Try These (Page 208)

Que 5. Find the perimeter of the following rectangles.

	Length of rectangle	Breadth of rectangle	Perimeter by adding all the sides	Perimeter by × (Length + Breadth)
(i)	25 cm	12 cm	= 25 cm + 12 cm + 25 cm + 12 cm = 74 cm	= 2 × (25 cm + 12 cm) = 2 × (37 cm) = 74 cm
(ii)	0.5 m	0.25 m		
(iii)	18 cm	15 cm		
(iv)	10.5 cm	8.5 cm		

Sol. (ii) Perimeter by adding all the sides
$$= 0.5 \text{ m} + 0.25 \text{ m} + 0.5 \text{ m} + 0.25 \text{ m} = 1.5 \text{ m}$$
Now, perimeter by 2 × (length + breadth)
$$= 2 \times (0.5 \text{ m} + 0.25 \text{ m}) = 2 \times 0.75 \text{ m} = 1.5 \text{ m}$$

(iii) Perimeter by adding all the sides $= 18 \text{ cm} + 15 \text{ cm} + 18 \text{ cm} + 15 \text{ cm}$
$$= 66 \text{ cm}$$
Now, perimeter by 2 × (length + breadth)
$$= 2 \times (18 \text{ cm} + 15 \text{ cm}) = 2 \times 33 \text{ cm} = 66 \text{ cm}$$

(iv) Perimeter by adding all the sides
$$= 10.5 \text{ cm} + 8.5 \text{ cm} + 10.5 \text{ cm} + 8.5 \text{ cm} = 38 \text{ cm}$$
Now, perimeter by 2 × (length + breadth)
$$= 2 \times (10.5 \text{ cm} + 8.5 \text{ cm})$$
$$= 2 \times 19 \text{ cm} = 38 \text{ cm}$$

Exercise 10.1

Que 1. Find the perimeter of each of the following figures.

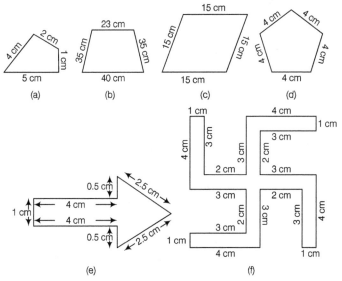

 TIPS

Perimeter is the distance covered along the boundary forming a closed figure when we go round the figure once. So, to find perimeter, add the length of all sides (which are line segments) of the given figure.

Sol. (a) Let the given figure be *ABCD*.

Here, *AB* = 5 cm, *BC* = 1 cm, *CD* = 2 cm and *DA* = 4 cm

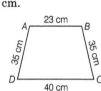

∴ Perimeter of the given figure = Sum of the lengths of all sides

= *AB* + *BC* + *CD* + *DA*

= 5 cm + 1 cm + 2 cm + 4 cm = (5 + 1 + 2 + 4) cm = 12 cm

Hence, the perimeter of the given figure is 12 cm.

(b) Let the given figure be *ABCD*.

Here, *AB* = 23 cm, *BC* = 35 cm, *CD* = 40 cm and *DA* = 35 cm

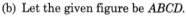

∴ Perimeter of the given figure
= Sum of the lengths of all sides
= *AB* + *BC* + *CD* + *DA*

= 23 cm + 35 cm + 40 cm + 35 cm

= (23 + 35 + 40 + 35) cm = 133 cm

Hence, the perimeter of the given figure is 133 cm.

(c) Let the given figure be *ABCD*.

Here, *AB* = *BC* = *CD* = *DA* = 15 cm

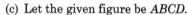

∴ Perimeter of the given figure
= Sum of the lengths of all sides
= *AB* + *BC* + *CD* + *DA*

= 15 cm + 15 cm + 15 cm + 15cm

= (15 + 15 + 15 + 15) cm = 60 cm

Hence, the perimeter of the given figure is 60 cm.

(d) Let the given figure be *ABCDE*.

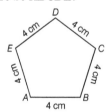

Here, *AB* = *BC* = *CD* = *DE* = *EA* = 4 cm

∴ Perimeter of the given figure = Sum of the lengths of all sides
= *AB* + *BC* + *CD* + *DE* + *EA*

= 4 cm + 4 cm + 4 cm + 4 cm + 4 cm

= (4 + 4 + 4 + 4 + 4) cm = 20 cm

Hence, the perimeter of the given figure is 20 cm.

(e) Let the given figure be *ABCDEFG.*

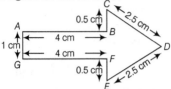

Here, $AB = 4$ cm, $BC = 0.5$ cm, $CD = 2.5$ cm, $DE = 2.5$ cm,
$\quad$ $EF = 0.5$ cm, $FG = 4$ cm and $GA = 1$ cm

∴ Perimeter of the given figure = Sum of the lengths of all sides
$\quad = AB + BC + CD + DE + EF + FG + GA$
$\quad = 4$ cm $+ 0.5$ cm $+ 2.5$ cm $+ 2.5$ cm $+ 0.5$ cm $+ 4$ cm+1cm
$\quad = (4 + 0.5 + 2.5 + 2.5 + 0.5 + 4 + 1)$ cm = 15 cm

Hence, the perimeter of the given figure is 15 cm.

(f) Let the given figure be named as shown below

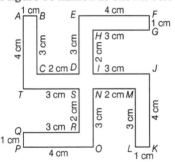

Here, $AB = FG = KL = PQ = 1$ cm
$\quad BC = DE = GH = IJ = LM = NO = QR = ST = 3$ cm
$\quad CD = HI = MN = RS = 2$ cm
$\quad EF = JK = OP = TA = 4$ cm

∴ Perimeter of the given figure = Sum of the lengths of all sides
$\quad = AB + BC + CD + DE + EF + FG + GH + HI + IJ + JK$
$\quad + KL + LM + MN + NO + OP + PQ + QR + RS + ST + TA$
$\quad = (1 + 3 + 2 + 3 + 4 + 1 + 3 + 2 + 3 + 4 + 1$
$\qquad\qquad\qquad + 3 + 2 + 3 + 4 + 1 + 3 + 2 + 3 + 4)$ cm
$\quad = 52$ cm

Hence, the perimeter of the given figure is 52 cm.

Que 2. The lid of a rectangular box of sid 40 cm by 10 cm is sealed all round with tape. What is the length of tape required?

Sol. Given, length of lid of a rectangular box = 40 cm

and breadth of the lid of a rectangular box = 10 cm

Length of the tape required = Perimeter of the lid of the rectangular box

= 2× (Length + Breadth)

= 2 ×(40 cm + 10 cm) = 2 × 50 cm = 100 cm or 1 m

$$[\because 1 \text{ cm} = \frac{1}{100} \text{ m or } 100 \text{ cm} = 1 \text{ m}]$$

Hence, the length of tape required is 100 cm or 1 m.

Que 3. A table-top measures 2 m 25 cm by 1 m 50 cm. What is the perimeter of the table-top?

 TIPS Firstly, change all the units in same unit and then find perimeter by using 2 (length + breadth).

Sol. Given,   length of table-top = 2 m 25 cm

$$= 2 \text{ m} + 25 \times \frac{1}{100} \text{ m} \qquad [\because 1 \text{ cm} = \frac{1}{100} \text{ m}]$$

$$= 2 \text{ m} + \frac{25}{100} \text{ m} = 2 \text{ m} + 0.25 \text{ m}$$

$$= (2 + 0.25) \text{ m} = 2.25 \text{ m}$$

Breadth of table-top = 1 m 50 cm = 1 m + 50 cm

$$= 1 \text{ m} + 50 \times \frac{1}{100} \text{ m} \qquad [\because 1 \text{ cm} = \frac{1}{100} \text{ m}]$$

$$= 1 \text{ m} + \frac{50}{100} \text{ m} = 1\text{m} + 0.50 \text{ m}$$

$$= (1 + 0.50) \text{ m} = 1.50 \text{ m}$$

∴ Perimeter of table top = 2 × (Length + Breadth)

= 2× (2.25 m + 1.50 m) = 2 × 3.75 m = 7.50 m

Hence, the perimeter of the table– top is 7.50 m.

Que 4. What is the length of the wooden strip required to frame a photograph of length and breadth 32 cm and 21 cm respectively?

Sol. Given, length of the wooden strip = 32 cm

and breadth of the wooden strip = 21 cm

Now, wooden strip required = Perimeter of the photograph

= 2 × (Length + Breadth)

= 2 × (32 cm + 21 cm)

= 2 × 53cm = 106 cm

Hence, the required length of wooden strip is 106 cm.

Que 5. A rectangular piece of land measures 0.7 km by 0.5 km. Each side is to be fenced with 4 rows of wires. What is the length of the wire needed?

 TIPS
> Firstly, find the perimeter of rectangular piece of land and then multiply by 4 to find the length of wire.

Sol. Given length of piece of land = 0.7 km
and breadth of piece of land = 0.5 km

∴ Perimeter of the rectangular piece of land

$$= 2 \times (\text{Length} + \text{Breadth}) = 2 \times (0.7 + 0.5) \text{ km}$$
$$= 2 \times 1.2 \text{ km} = 2.4 \text{ km}$$

Then, length of wire fencing for 1 row

$$= \text{Perimeter of rectangular piece of land} = 2.4 \text{ km}$$

∴ Length of wire fencing for 4 rows = 4×2.4 km = 9.6 km

Hence, the wire of length 9.6 km is needed.

Que 6. Find the perimeter of each of the following shapes.
- (a) A triangle of sides 3 cm, 4 cm and 5 cm.
- (b) An equilateral triangle of side 9 cm.
- (c) An isosceles triangle with equal sides 8 cm each and third side 6 cm.

Sol. (a) Let the given triangle be ABC.

Here, $AB = 3$ cm, $BC = 4$ cm and $CA = 5$ cm.

∴ Perimeter of a triangle = Sum of lengths of all
side $= AB + BC + CA$
$= (3 \text{ cm} + 4 \text{ cm} + 5 \text{ cm})$
$= (3 + 4 + 5) \text{ cm} = 12 \text{ cm}$

Hence, the perimeter of a triangle is 12 cm.

(b) Let the given triangle be ABC.

Here, $AB = 9$ cm, $BC = 9$ cm and $CA = 9$ cm

∴ Perimeter of an equilateral triangle
$= \text{Sum of lengths of all sides}$
$= AB + BC + CA$

$= (9 \text{ cm} + 9 \text{ cm} + 9 \text{ cm}) = (9 + 9 + 9) \text{ cm} = 27 \text{ cm}$

Hence, the perimeter of a triangle is 27 cm.

(c) Let the given isosceles triangle is *ABC*.

∴ Here, *AB* = 8 cm, *BC* = 6 cm and *CA* = 8 cm

Perimeter of an isosceles triangle
   = Sum of lengths of all sides
   = *AB* + *BC* + *CA* = (8 cm + 6 cm + 8 cm)
   = (8 + 6 + 8) cm = 22 cm

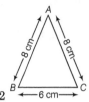

Hence, the perimeter of an isosceles triangle is 22 cm.

Que 7. Find the perimeter of a triangle with sides measuring 10 cm, 14 cm and 15 cm.

Sol. Given, first side of triangle = 10 cm

   Second side of triangle = 14 cm

and third side of triangle = 15 cm

∴ Perimeter of a triangle = Sum of all sides of triangle
      = 10 cm + 14 cm + 15 cm = (10 + 14 + 15) cm = 39 cm

Hence, the perimeter of a triangle is 39 cm.

Que 8. Find the perimeter of a regular hexagon with each side measuring 8 m.

Sol. A regular hexagon has 6 sides and each side is of 8 cm.

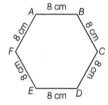

∴ Perimeter of a regular hexagon = 6 × Length of one side
      = 6 × 8 m = 48 m

Hence, the perimeter of a regular hexagon is 48 cm.

Que 9. Find the side of the square whose perimeter is 20 m.

Sol. Given, the perimeter of a square = 20 m

∴ Perimeter of a square = 4 × length of a side

We know that a square has 4 equal .

So, we can divide given perimeter by 4 to get the side of a square.

∴   One side of the square $= \dfrac{\text{Perimeter of a square}}{4} = \dfrac{20}{4}$ m $= 5$ m

Hence, the side of a square is 5 m.

Que 10. The perimeter of a regular pentagon is 100 cm. How long is its each side?

Sol. Given, perimeter of a regular pentagon = 100 cm

We know that, a regular pentagon has 5 equal sides.

∴ Perimeter of a regular pentagon = 5 × Length of a side

So, we can divide given perimeter by 5 to get the one side of a regular pentagon.

$$\therefore \text{ Length of one side} = \frac{\text{Perimeter of a regular pentagon}}{5}$$

$$= \frac{100}{5} \text{ cm} = 20 \text{ cm}$$

Hence, all the sides of a regular pentagon is of 20 cm.

Que 11. A piece of string is 30 cm long. What will be the length of each side, if the string is used to form

    (a) a square?   (b) an equilateral triangle?

    (c) a regular hexagon?

TIPS

Here, perimeter of each figure will be equal to length of string i.e. 30 cm. Also, perimeter = Sum of all sides of a figure, since each figure has all sides equal, so to find a side of a figure, divide its perimeter by number of sides.

Sol. (a) Here, length of string will be the perimeter of square.

    ∴ Perimeter of square = 30 cm

    We know that, a square has 4 equal sides.

    ∴ Perimeter of a square = 4 × Length of a side

    Now, Length of one side $= \dfrac{\text{Perimeter of a square}}{4} = \dfrac{30}{4} \text{ cm} = 7.5 \text{ cm}$

    Hence, length of each side of a square is 7.5 cm.

    (b) Here, length of string will be the perimeter of an equilateral triangle.

    ∴ Perimeter of equilateral triangle = 30 cm

    We know that, an equilateral triangle has 3 equal sides.

    Perimeter of an equilatesal triangle = 3 × Length of a Side

$$\therefore \text{ Length of a side} = \frac{\text{Perimeter of an equilateral triangle}}{3}$$

$$= \frac{30}{3} \text{ cm} = 10 \text{ cm}$$

    Hence, the length of each side of an equilateral triangle is 10 cm.

(c) Here, length of string will be the perimeter of regular hexagon.

∴ Perimeter of regular hexagon = 30 cm

We know that, a regular hexagon has 6 equal sides

∴ Perimeter of a regular hexagon = 6 ×Length of one side

∴ Length of a side $= \dfrac{\text{Perimeter of a regular hexagon}}{6}$

$$= \dfrac{30}{6} \text{ cm} = 5 \text{ cm}$$

Hence, the length of each side of a regular hexagon is 5 cm.

Que 12. Two sides of a triangle are 12 cm and 14 cm. The perimeter of the triangle is 36 cm. What is its third side?

Sol. Let *ABC* be the given triangle and its sides

$$AB = 12 \text{ cm and } BC = 14 \text{ cm.}$$

Also perimeter of triangle = 36 cm

We know that,

Perimeter of a triangle = Sum of all its sides

i.e. $AB + BC + CA = 36$ cm

     12 cm + 14 cm + CA = 36 cm

⇒   (12 + 14) cm + CA = 36 cm ⇒ 26 cm + CA = 36 cm

⇒ CA = (36 − 26) cm = 10 cm

Hence, the third side of the triangle is 10 cm.

Que 13. Find the cost of fencing a square park of side 250 m at the rate of ₹ 20 per metre.

TIPS

> To find the cost of fencing, multiply the perimeter of square (4 × length of side) by rate of fencing.

Sol. Given, side of square park = 250 m

Then, the perimeter of square park = 4 × Length of side of park

$$= 4 \times 250 \text{ m} = 1000 \text{ m}$$

Cost of fencing per metre = ₹ 20

∴ Cost of fencing 2000m = 1000 × 20 = ₹ 20000

Hence, the cost of fencing a square park is ₹ 20000.

Que 14. Find the cost of fencing a rectangular park of length 175 m and breadth 125 m at the rate of ₹ 12 per metre.

TIPS

> To find the cost of fencing a rectangular park, multiply its perimeter [2 (length + Breadth)] by rate of fencing.

Sol. Given, length of rectangular park = 175 m

and breadth of rectangular park = 125 m

Then, the perimeter of rectangular park = 2 (Length + Breadth)

= 2 (175 + 125) m = 2 × 300 cm = 600 m

Cost of fencing per metre = ₹ 12

∴ Cost of fencing 600m = 600 × 12 = ₹ 7200

Hence, the cost of fencing a rectangular park is ₹ 7200.

Que 15. Sweety runs around a square park of side 75 m. Bulbul runs around a rectangular park with length 60 m and breadth 45 m. Who covers less distance?

Sol. Now, distance covered by in one round = Perimeter of park

∴ Perimeter of square park = 4 × Length of a side = 4 × 75 m = 300 m

and distance covered by Bulbul in one round

= Perimeter of rectangle = 2× (Length + Breadth)

= 2 × (60 + 45) m = 2 × 105 m = 210 m

Since, 300 m > 210 m

Hence, Bulbul covers less distance.

Que 16. What is the perimeter of each of the following figures? What do you infer from the answers?

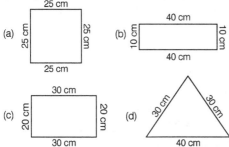

Sol. (a) Given, the figure is a square whose side is 25 cm.

∴ Perimeter of square = 4 × Length of a Side = 4 × 25 cm = 100 cm

(b) Given, the figure is a rectangle whose length = 40 cm

and breadth = 10 cm

∴ Perimeter of rectangle = 2× (Length + Breadth)

= 2 × (40 + 10) cm = 2 × 50 cm = 100 cm

(c) Given, the figure is a rectangle whose length = 30 cm

and breadth = 20 cm

∴ Perimeter of rectangle = 2× (Length + Breadth)

= 2 × (30 + 20) cm = 2 × 50 cm = 100 cm

(d) Given, the figure is an isosceles triangle whose sides are 30 cm, 30 cm and 40 cm respectively.

∴ Perimeter of triangle = Sum of all sides of a triangle

$$= (30 + 30 + 40)\,cm = 100\,cm$$

Here, we observe that the perimeter of each figure is 100 cm i.e. they have equal perimeters.

Que 17. Avneet buys 9 square paving slabs, each with a side of $\frac{1}{2}$ m. He lays them in the form of a square.

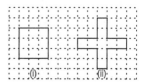

(a) What is the perimeter of his arrangement in the figure(i)?

(b) Shari does not like his arrangement. She gets him to lay them out like a cross. What is the perimeter of her arrangement in the figure (ii)?

(c) Which has greater perimeter?

(d) Avneet wonders, if there is a way of getting an even greater perimeter. Can you find a way of doing this? (The paving slabs must meet along complete edges i.e. they cannot be broken.)

Sol. (a) Avneet lays 9 squares in the form of a square as shown in the figure, then side of the square

$$= \left(\frac{1}{2} + \frac{1}{2} + \frac{1}{2}\right) m = \frac{1+1+1}{2} = \frac{3}{2}\,m$$

∴ Perimeter of Avneet's arrangement

= 4 × Length of a side

$$= 4 \times \frac{3}{2}\,m = 6\,m$$

Hence, the perimeter of Avneet's arrangement is 6 m.

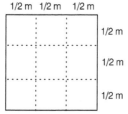

(b) Shari lays 9 squares in the form of a cross as shown in figure, then perimeter of Shari's arrangement = Sum of all sides

= AB + BC + CD + DE + EF + FG

+ GH + HI + IJ + JK + KL + LA

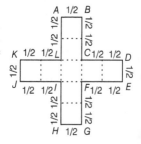

$$= \frac{1}{2} + \left(\frac{1}{2} + \frac{1}{2}\right) + \left(\frac{1}{2} + \frac{1}{2}\right) + \frac{1}{2} + \left(\frac{1}{2} + \frac{1}{2}\right) + \left(\frac{1}{2} + \frac{1}{2}\right)$$

$$+ \frac{1}{2} + \left(\frac{1}{2} + \frac{1}{2}\right) + \left(\frac{1}{2} + \frac{1}{2}\right) + \frac{1}{2} + \left(\frac{1}{2} + \frac{1}{2}\right) + \left(\frac{1}{2} + \frac{1}{2}\right)$$

$$= \left(\frac{1}{2} + 1 + 1 + \frac{1}{2} + 1 + 1 + \frac{1}{2} + 1 + 1 + \frac{1}{2} + 1 + 1\right) m$$

$$= \left(\frac{1}{2} + \frac{1}{2} + \frac{1}{2} + \frac{1}{2} + 8\right) m = (1 + 1 + 8) \, m = 10 \, m$$

Hence, the perimeter of Shari's arrangement is 10 m.

(c) From above, it is clear that Shari's arrangement i.e. a cross has greater perimeter.

(d) Yes, there is a way shown alongside in which we get a greater perimeter. Here. we have arrange the 9 squares in the form of a rectangle Now, length of rectangle

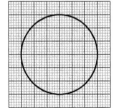

$$= \left(\frac{1}{2} + \frac{1}{2} + \frac{1}{2} + \frac{1}{2} + \frac{1}{2} + \frac{1}{2} + \frac{1}{2} + \frac{1}{2} + \frac{1}{2}\right) m = \frac{9}{2} \, m$$

and breadth of rectangle $= 1/2$ m

∴ Perimeter of this rectangle $= 2 \times$ (Length + Breadth)

$$= 2 \times \left(\frac{9}{2} + \frac{1}{2}\right) = 2 \times \left(\frac{9+1}{2}\right) = 2 \times \frac{10}{2} = 10 \, m$$

It is clear that, it has the perimeter equal to cross.

So, we can say that cross has greater perimeter in comparison to square.

Try These (Page 215)

Que 1. Draw any circle on a graph sheet. Count the squares and use them to estimate the area of the circular region.

Sol. First make a circle of any suitable radius, on the graph paper. Then, count full, half and more than half or less than half squares come under the circle.

    In the figure,

    Fully filled squares = 16

    Half filled squares = 8

    More than half filled squares = 8

∴ Total area $= 16 \times 1 + 8 \times \dfrac{1}{2} + 8 \times 1 = 16 + 4 + 8 = 28$ sq units

Exercise 10.2

Que 1. Find the areas of the following figures by counting square.

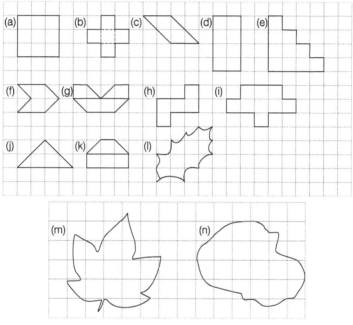

Sol. (a) Given figure is covered by 9 full squares.

∴ Area $= 9 \times 1$ sq unit $= 9$ sq units

(b) Given figure is covered by 5 full squares.

∴ Area $= 5 \times 1$ sq unit $= 5$ sq units

(c) Given figure is covered by 2 full squares and 4 half squares.

∴ Area $= \left(2 \times 1 + 4 \times \dfrac{1}{2} \right)$ sq units $= (2 + 2)$ sq units $= 4$ sq units

(d) Given figure is covered by 8 full squares.

∴ Area $= 8 \times 1 = 8$ sq units

(e) Given figure is covered by 10 full squares.

∴ Area $= 10 \times 1$ sq unit $= 10$ sq units

(f) Given figure is covered by 2 full squares and 4 half squares.

∴ Area $= \left(2 \times 1 + 4 \times \dfrac{1}{2} \right)$ sq units $= (2 + 2)$ sq units $= 4$ sq units

(g) Given figure is covered by 4 full squares and 4 half squares.

∴ Area $= \left(4 \times 1 + 4 \times \dfrac{1}{2} \right)$ sq units $= (4 + 2)$ sq units $= 6$ sq units

(h) Given figure is covered by 5 full squares.

∴ Area $= (5 \times 1)$ sq units $= 5$ sq units

(i) Given figure is covered by 9 full squares.

∴ Area $= (9 \times 1)$ sq units $= 9$ sq units

(j) Given figure is covered by 2 full squares and 4 half squares.

∴ Area $= \left(2 \times 1 + 4 \times \dfrac{1}{2}\right)$ sq units $= (2 + 2)$ sq units $= 4$ sq units

(k) Given figure is covered by 4 full squares and 2 half squares.

∴ Area $= \left(4 \times 1 + 2 \times \dfrac{1}{2}\right)$ sq units $= (4 + 1)$ sq units $= 5$ sq units

(l) Given figure is covered by 3 full squares, 4 half squares, 3 more than half squares and 1 less than half square.

∴ $= \left(3 \times 1 + 4 \times \dfrac{1}{2} + 3 \times 1 + 1 \times 0\right)$ sq units

$= (3 + 2 + 3 + 0)$ sq unit $= 8$ sq units

(m) Given figure is covered by 7 full squares, 8 half squares, 3 more than half squares and 3 less than half squares

∴ Area $= \left(7 \times 1 + 8 \times \dfrac{1}{2} + 3 \times 1 + 3 \times 0\right)$ sq units

$= (7 + 4 + 3 + 0)$ sq unit $= 14$ sq units

(n) Given figure is covered by 9 full squares, 6 half squares, 6 more than half squares and 4 less than half squares.

∴ Area $= \left(9 \times 1 + 6 \times \dfrac{1}{2} + 6 \times 1 + 4 \times 0\right)$ sq units

$= (9 + 3 + 6 + 0)$ sq units $= 18$ sq units

Exercise 10.3

Que 1. Find the areas of the rectangles whose sides are

    (a) 3 cm and 4 cm   (b) 2 m and 21 m

    (c) 2 km and 3 km   (d) 2 m and 70 cm

TIPS

If the length and breadth of a rectangle are given, then Area of rectangle = Length × Breadth.

Sol. (a) Here, length of the rectangle $= 4$ cm

      and breadth of the rectangle $= 3$ cm

      ∴Area of rectangle = Length × Breadth $= 4$ cm $\times 3$ cm $= 12$ sq cm

      Hence, the area of the rectangle is 12 sq cm.

(b) Here, length of the rectangle = 21 m
and breadth of the rectangle = 12 m
∴ Area of rectangle = Length × Breadth = 21 m × 12 m = 252 sq m
Hence, the area of the rectangle is 252 sq m.

(c) Here, length of the rectangle = 3 km
and breadth of the rectangle = 2 km
∴ Area of rectangle = Length × Breadth = 3 km × 2 km = 6 sq km
Hence, the area of the rectangle is 6 sq km.

(d) Here, length of the rectangle = 2 m
and breadth of the rectangle = 70 cm

$$= 70 \times \frac{1}{100} \text{ m} \qquad \left[\because 1 \text{ cm} = \frac{1}{100} \text{ m} \right]$$

$$= \frac{70}{100} \text{ m} = 0.70 \text{ m}$$

∴ Area of rectangle = Length × Breadth = 2 m × 0.70 m = 1.40 sq m
Hence, the area of the rectangle is 1.40 sq m.

Que 2. Find the areas of the squares whose sides are

(a) 10 cm   (b) 14 cm   (c) 5 cm

 TIPS
If the side of a square is given, then Area of a square = Side × Side.

Sol. (a) Here, side of the square = 10 cm
∴ Area of square = Side × Side = 10 cm × 10 cm = 100 sq cm
Hence, the area of the square is 100 sq cm.

(b) Here, side of the square = 14 cm
∴ Area of square = Side × Side = 14 cm × 14 cm = 196 sq cm
Hence, the area of the square is 196 sq cm.

(c) Here, side of the square = 5 cm
∴ Area of square = Side × Side = 5 cm × 5 cm = 25 sq cm
Hence, the area of the square is 25 sq cm.

Que 3. The length and breadth of three rectangles are as given below

(a) 9 m and 6 m   (b) 17 m and 3 m   (c) 4 m and 14 m

Which one has the largest area and which one has the smallest?

Sol. (a) Here, length of the rectangle = 9 m
and breadth of the rectangle = 6 m
∴ Area of the rectangle = Length × Breadth = 54 sq m
Hence, the area of the rectangle is 54 sq m.

(b) Here, length of the rectangle = 17 m
and breadth of the rectangle = 3 m
∴ Area of the rectangle = Length × Breadth = 17m × 3m = 51 sq m
Hence, the area of the rectangle is 51 sq m.

(c) Here, length of the rectangle = 14 m
and breadth of the rectangle = 4 m
∴ Area of the rectangle = Length × Breadth = 14 m × 4 m = 56 sq m
Hence, the area of the rectangle is 56 sq m.
Now, we have   56 > 54 > 51
Hence, the rectangle having sides 4 m and 14 m has the largest area and the rectangle having sides 17 m and 3 m has the smallest area.

Que 4. The area of a rectangular garden 50 m long is 300 sq m. Find the width of the garden.

Sol. Given, area of the rectangular garden = 300 sq m
and length of the rectangular garden = 50 m
We know that,
∴ Area of the rectangular garden = Length × Breadth
⇒   300 sq m = 50 m × Breadth
⇒   Breadth $= \dfrac{300 \text{ sq m}}{50 \text{ m}} = 6$ m

Hence, the breadth or width of the garden is 6 m.

Que 5. What is the cost of tiling a rectangular plot of land 500 m long and 200 m wide at the rate of ₹ 8 per hundred sq m?

TIPS

Firstly, find the area of a rectangular plot. Then, to find the required cost, multiply the area by rate of tiling i.e. $\dfrac{8}{100}$.
[∵ rate = ₹ 8 per hundred sq m]

Sol. Given, length of a rectangular plot = 500 m
and breadth of a rectangular plot = 200 m
∴ Area of the rectangular plot = Length × Breadth
                          = 500 m × 200 m = 100000 sq m
∵ Cost of tiling per hundred square metres = ₹ 8
∴ Cost of one sq metre $= ₹ \dfrac{8}{100}$

Now, cost of 100000 sq metre $= ₹\ 100000 \times \dfrac{8}{100} = ₹\ 8000$
Hence, the cost of tiling rectangular plot is ₹ 8000.

Que 6. A table-top measures 2 m by 1m 50 cm. What is its area in square metres?

TIPS

Firstly, convert the measures in same unit say *m* using decimals. Then, Area of table-top = Length × Breadth.

Sol. Given, length of the table-top = 2 m

and breadth of the table-top = 1m 50 cm = 1m + 50 cm

$$= 1m + 50 \times \frac{1}{100} m \qquad \left[\because 1 \text{ cm} = \frac{1}{100} m \right]$$

$$= 1m + \frac{50}{100} m = 1m + 0.50 \text{ m} = 1.50 m$$

∴Area of the table-top = Length × Breadth = 2 m × 1.50 m = 3 sq m

Hence, the area of the table-top is 3 sq m.

Que 7. A room is 4 m long and 3 m 50 cm wide. How many square metres of carpet is needed to cover the floor of the room?

Sol. Given, length of the room = 4 m

and breadth of the room = 3 m 50 cm = 3 m + 50 cm

$$= 3 \text{ m} + 50 \times \frac{1}{100} \text{ m} \qquad \left[\because 1 \text{ cm} = \frac{1}{100} \text{ m} \right]$$

$$= 3 \text{ m} + \frac{50}{100} \text{ m} = 3 \text{ m} + 0.50 \text{ m} = 3.50 \text{ m}$$

∵ Carpet needed to cover the floor of the room = Area of the floor

= Length × Breadth = 4 m × 3.50 m = 14 sq m

Hence, the carpet needed to cover the floor of the room is 14 sq m.

Que 8. A floor is 5 m long and 4 m wide. A square carpet of sides 3 m is laid on the floor. Find the area of the floor that is not carpeted.

TIPS

Firstly, find the area of rectangular floor and square carpet separately. Then, the area of required floor will be obtained by subtracting area of carpet from area of floor.

Sol. Given, length of the floor = 5 m

and breadth of the floor = 4 m

Then, area of the floor = Length × Breadth

= 5 m × 4 m = 20 sq m

Side of the square carpet = 3 m

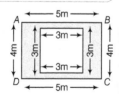

∴ Area of the carpet = Side × Side = 3 m × 3 m = 9 sq m

Now, area of the floor that is not carpeted

$$= \text{Area of the floor} - \text{Area of the carpet}$$
$$= (20 - 9) \text{ sq m} = 11 \text{ sq m}$$

Hence, 11 sq m area of the floor is not carpeted.

Que 9. Five square flower beds each of sides 1 m are dug on a piece of land 5 m long and 4 m wide. What is the area of the remaining part of the land?

 TIPS Firstly, find the area of five square flower beds and piece of land separately. Then, area of the remaining part of the land will be obtained by subtracting the area of five beds from area of land.

Sol. Given, length of the piece of land = 5 m and breadth of the piece of land = 4 m

Area of the piece of land = Length × Breadth = 5 m × 4 m = 20 sq m

Given, side of one square flower bed = 1 m

∴ Area of one square flower bed = Side × Side = (1 m × 1 m) = 1 sq m

Then, area of 5 such flower beds = 5 × Area of one square flower bed
$$= 5 \times 1 \text{ sq m} = 5 \text{ sq m}$$

Now, area of the remaining part of land

$$= \text{Area of the piece of land} - \text{Area of 5 square flower beds}$$
$$= (20 - 5) \text{ sq m} = 15 \text{ sq m}$$

Hence, the area of the remaining part of the land is 15 sq m.

Que 10. By splitting the following figures into rectangles, find their areas (the measures are given in centimetres).

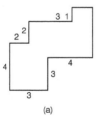

(a)

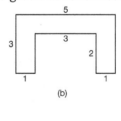

(b)

Sol. (a) Let the given figure be divided into rectangles A, B, C and D and their length and breadth be written on the figure.

For rectangle A,

Length = 4 cm and breadth = 2 cm

Now, area of the rectangle A = Length × Breadth
$$= 4 \text{ cm} \times 2 \text{ cm} = 8 \text{ sq cm}$$

For rectangle B,

Length = 3 cm and breadth = 3 cm

Area of the rectangle B = Length × Breadth
$$= 3 \text{ cm} \times 3 \text{ cm} = 9 \text{ sq cm}$$

For rectangle C,

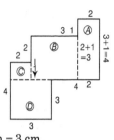

Length = 2 cm and breadth = 1 cm

Area of the rectangle C = Length × Breadth
$$= 2 \text{ cm} \times 1 \text{ cm} = 2 \text{ sq cm}$$

For rectangle D, Length = 3 cm and Breadth = 3 cm

∴Area of the rectangle D = Length × Breadth
$$= 3 \text{ sq cm} \times 3 \text{ sq cm} = 9 \text{ sq cm}$$

Now, total area of the given figure = Area of the rectangle A
+ Area of the rectangle B + Area of the rectangle C
+ Area of the rectangle D
$$= (8 + 9 + 2 + 9) \text{ sq cm} = 28 \text{ sq cm}$$

Hence, the required area is 28 sq cm.

(b) Let the given figure is divided into rectangles A, B and C and their length and breadth are written on the figure.

For rectangle A,

Length = 2 cm and breadth = 1 cm

∴Area of the rectangle A = Length × Breadth = $2 \times 1 = 2$ sq cm

For rectangle B,

Length = 5 cm and breadth = 1 cm

∴Area of the rectangle B
$$= \text{Length} \times \text{Breadth} = 5 \times 1 = 5 \text{ sq cm}$$

For rectangle C,

Length = 2 cm and breadth = 1 cm

∴Area of the rectangle C = Length × Breadth = $2 \times 1 = 2$ sq cm

Now, total area of the given figure = Area of rectangle A
+ Area of rectangle B + Area of rectangle C
$$= (2 + 5 + 2) \text{ sq cm} = 9 \text{ sq cm}$$

Hence, the area of the given figure is 9 sq cm.

Que 11. Split the following shapes into rectangles and find their areas (The measures are given in centimetres).

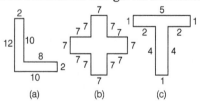

(a)   (b)   (c)

Sol. (a) Let the given figure is divided into two rectangles A, B and their length and breadth are written on the figure.

For rectangle A,
Length = 12 cm and breadth = 2 cm
∴ Area of the rectangle A = Length × Breadth
   = 12 cm × 2 cm = 24 sq cm

For rectangle B,
Length = 8 cm and breadth = 2cm
∴ Area of the rectangle B = Length × Breadth
   = 8 cm × 2 cm = 16 sq cm

Now, total area of given figure

= Area of rectangle A + Area of rectangle B

= (24 + 16) sq cm = 40 sq cm

Hence, required area is 40 sq cm.

(b) Let the given figure is divided into 5 squares and their length are written on the figure

∴ Side of the one square = 7 cm

∴ Area of the one square = Side × Side = 7 cm × 7 cm = 49 sq cm

Since, all squares have equal sides i.e. 7 cm.

So, all five square have same area i.e. 49 sq cm.

Now, total area of given figure 5 × Area of one square

= (5 × 49) sq cm = 245 sq cm

Hence, required area is 245 sq cm.

(c) Let the given figure is divided into rectangles A, B and their length and breadth are written on the figure.

For rectangle A,

Length = 5 cm and breadth = 1 cm

∴ Area of the rectangle A = Length × Breadth
   = 5 × 1 cm = 5 sq cm

For rectangle B,

Length = 4 cm and breadth = 1 cm

∴ Area of the rectangle B = Length × Breadth
   = 4 cm × 1 cm = 4 sq cm

Now, area of given figure = Area of rectangle A
                         + Area of rectangle B
= (5 + 4) sq cm = 9 sq cm

Hence, the area of the given figure is 9 sq cm.

Que 12. How many tiles whose length and breadth are 12 cm and 5 cm respectively will be needed to fit in a rectangular region whose length and breadth are respectively.

    (a) 100 cm and 144 cm   (b) 70 cm and 36 cm

> Firstly, find the area of one tile and rectangular region separately. Then,
>
> Required number of tiles = $\dfrac{\text{Area of rectangular region}}{\text{Area of one tile}}$

Sol. Given, length of a tile = 12 cm and breadth of a tile = 5 cm

∴ Area of one tile = Length × Breadth = 12 cm × 5 cm = 60 sq cm

    (a) Here, length of the rectangular region = 100 cm
and breadth of the rectangular region = 144 cm
∴Area of the rectangular region = Length × Breadth
                  = 100 cm × 144 cm = 14400 sq cm

    Now, number of required tiles = $\dfrac{\text{Area of the rectangular region}}{\text{Area of the one tile}}$

                        = $\dfrac{14400}{60} = 240$

    Hence, the number of required tiles is 240.

    (b) Given, length of the rectangular region = 70 cm
and breadth of the rectangular region = 36 cm
∴Area of the rectangular region = Length × Breadth
                       = 70 cm × 36 cm = 2520 sq cm

    Now, number of the required tiles = $\dfrac{\text{Area of the rectangular region}}{\text{Area of the one tile}}$

                        = $\dfrac{2520}{60} = 42$

    Hence, the number of the required tiles is 42.

A challenge! (Page 220)

Que 13. On a centimetre squared paper, make as many rectangles as you can, such that the area of the rectangle is 16 sq cm (consider only natural number lengths).

    (a) Which rectangle has the greatest perimeter?
    (b) Which rectangle has the least perimeter?

If you take a rectangle of area 24 sq cm, what will be your answers? Given any area, is it possible to predict the shape of the rectangle with the greatest perimeter? With the least perimeter? Give example and reason.

Sol. We know that,

Area of the rectangle = Length × Breadth

Here, the area of the rectangle is 16 sq cm.

So, for getting the area 16 sq cm, there are three cases.

Case I When length of the rectangle = 16 cm

and   breadth of the rectangle = 1 cm

∴   Area of the rectangle = Length × Breadth

$$= 16\,cm \times 1\,cm = 16\,sq\,cm$$

and   perimeter of the rectangle $= 2 \times$ (Length + Breadth)

$$= 2 \times (16\,cm + 1\,cm) = (2 \times 17)\,cm$$

$$= 34\,cm$$

Case II When length of the rectangle = 4 cm

and   breadth of the rectangle = 4 cm

∴ Area of the rectangle = Length × Breadth $= 4\,cm \times 4\,cm = 16\,sq\,cm$

and   perimeter of the rectangle $= 2 \times$ (Length + Breadth)

$$= 2 \times (4\,cm + 4\,cm) = (2 \times 8)\,cm = 16\,cm$$

Case III When length of the rectangle = 8 cm

and   breadth of the rectangle = 2 cm

∴   Area of the rectangle = Length × Breadth

$$= 8\,cm \times 2\,cm = 16\,sq\,cm$$

and perimeter of the rectangle $= 2 \times$ (Length + Breadth)

$$= 2 \times (8\,cm + 2\,cm) = (2 \times 10)\,cm = 20\,cm$$

(a) The rectangle which made in Case I has the greatest perimeter.

(b) The rectangle which made in Case II has the least perimeter.

Now, given that the area of the rectangle is 24 sq cm.

Again, for getting the area 24 sq cm, there are three cases.

Case I When length of the rectangle = 24 cm

and   breadth of the rectangle = 1 cm

∴ Area of the rectangle = Length × Breadth $= 24\,cm \times 1\,cm = 24\,sq\,cm$

and   perimeter of the rectangle $= 2 \times$ (Length + Breadth)

$$= 2 \times (24\,cm + 1\,cm) = (2 \times 25)\,cm = 50\,cm$$

Case II When length of the rectangle = 12 cm

and   breadth of the rectangle = 2 cm

∴ Area of the rectangle = Length × Breadth $= 12\,cm \times 2\,cm = 24\,sq\,cm$

and   perimeter of the rectangle $= 2 \times$ (Length + Breadth)

$$= 2 \times (12\,cm + 2\,cm) = (2 \times 14)\,cm = 28\,cm$$

Case III When length of the rectangle = 6 cm

and   breadth of the rectangle = 4 cm

∴ Area of the rectangle = Length × Breadth = 6 cm × 4 cm = 24 sq cm
and   perimeter of the rectangle = 2 × (Length + Breadth)

$$= 2 \times (6\,cm + 4\,cm) = 2 \times 10 \ cm = 20 \ cm$$

(a) The rectangle which made in Case I has the greatest perimeter.

(b) The rectangle which made in Case III has the least perimeter.

Yes, it is possible to predict the shape of the rectangle with greatest perimeter and with least perimeter e.g. A rectangle having area 16 sq cm and greatest perimeter 34 cm is of the shape 16 cm × 1 cm   (i.e. length = 16 cm and breadth = 1 cm), also a rectangle having area 24 sq cm and least perimeter 20 cm is of the shape 6 cm × 4 cm (i.e. length = 6 cm and breadth = 4 cm)

Reason The rectangle with the greatest length has the maximum perimeter and the rectangle with the smallest length has the least perimeter.

Selected **NCERT Exemplar Problems**

Directions *In questions 1 and 2, out of the four options, only one is correct. Write the correct answer.*

Que 1. The side of a square is 10 cm. How many times will the new perimeter become, if the side of the square is doubled?

   (a) 2 times   (b) 4 times   (c) 6 times   (d) 8 times

Sol. Given, the side of a square = 10 cm

We know that, the perimeter of a square = 4 × Length of one side

∴   Initial perimeter of a square = 4 × 10 = 40 cm

According to the question, if the side of the square is doubled.

Then, new side of a square = 2 × 10 = 20 cm

∴ Perimeter of new square = 4 × New length of one side

= 4 × 20 = 80 cm = 2 × 40 cm = 2 × Perimeter of initial square

Hence, option (a) is correct.

Que 2. Two regular hexagons of perimeter 30 cm each are joined as shown in figure. The perimeter of the new figure is

   (a) 65 cm   (b) 60 cm   (c) 55 cm   (d) 50 cm

TIPS   Firstly, find the one side of a regular hexagon. Divide the given perimeter by 6 and then to find the perimeter, add all the outer sides of the join figure.

Sol. Given, the perimeter of a regular hexagon = 30 cm

We know that, a regular hexagon has 6 sides, so we can divide the perimeter by 6 to get the length of one side.

$\therefore$ Perimeter of a regular hexagon = 6 × Length of one side

Now, $30 = 6 \times$ Length of one side

$\therefore$ Length of one side $= \dfrac{30}{6} = 5$ cm

$\because$ Two regular hexagons are joined, then each side of join figure is 5 cm.

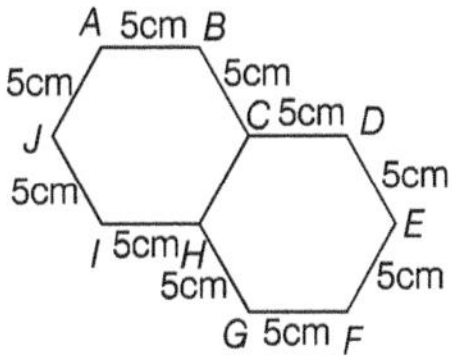

$\therefore$ Let the given figure be $ABCDEFGHIJ$.

Here, $AB = BC = CD = DE = EF = FG = GH = HI = IJ = JA = 5$ cm

Now, perimeter of the join figure

$$= \text{Sum of all outer sides of the join figure}$$
$$= AB + BC + CD + DE + EF + FG + GH + HI + IJ + JA$$
$$= 5\text{ cm} + 5\text{ cm} + 5\text{ cm} + 5\text{ cm} + 5\text{ cm} + 5\text{ cm} + 5\text{ cm} + 5\text{ cm} + 5\text{ cm} + 5\text{ cm}$$
$$= 50\text{ cm}$$

Hence, the option (d) is correct.

Que 3. Match the shapes (each sides measures 2cm) in column I with the corresponding perimeters in column II.

Column I		Column II	
(a)		(i)	16 cm
(b)		(ii)	20 cm

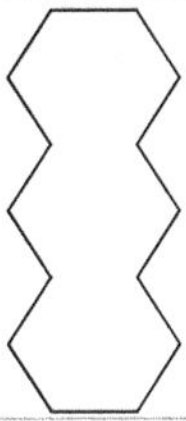

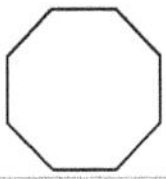

Column I		Column II
(c)	(iii)	24 cm
(d)	(iv)	28 cm
	(v)	32 cm

TIPS

Perimeter is the distance covered along the boundary forming a closed figure, when we go round the figure once. So, to find perimeter, add the lengths of all sides which are line segments of the given figure.

Sol. (a) –(iv) Let the given figure be *ABCDEFGHIJKLMN.*

Here, $AB = BC = CD = DE = EF = FG = GH$
$= HI = IJ = JK = KL = LM = MN = NA = 2$ cm

∴ Perimeter of the given figure = Sum of the lengths of all sides
$= AB + BC + CD + DE + EF + FG + GH + HI + IJ$
$+ JK + KL + LM + MN + NA$
$= 2$ cm $+ 2$ cm $+ 2$ cm $+ 2$ cm $+ 2$ cm $+ 2$ cm $+ 2$ cm
$+ 2$ cm $+ 2$ cm $+ 2$ cm $+ 2$ cm $+ 2$ cm $+ 2$ cm $+ 2$ cm $= 28$ cm

Hence, the perimeter of the given figure is 28 cm.

(b)–(i) Let the given figure is *ABCDEFGH.*

Here, $AB = BC = CD = DE = EF = FG = GH = HA$
∴ Perimeter of the given figure
= Sum of the lengths of all sides
$= AB + BC + CD + DE + EF + FG + GH + HA$
$= 2$ cm $+ 2$ cm $+ 2$ cm $+ 2$ cm $+ 2$ cm $+2$ cm $+ 2$ cm $+ 2$ cm $= 16$ cm

Hence, the perimeter of the given figure is 16 cm.

(c)–(ii) Let the given figure be *ABCDEFGHIJ*.

Here, $AB = BC = CD = DE = EF = FG = GH$
$= HI = IJ = JA = 2$ cm

∴ Perimeter of the given figure
= Sum of the lengths of all sides
$= AB + BC + CD + DE + EF + FG + GH + HI + IJ + JA$
$= 2$ cm $+ 2$ cm $+ 2$ cm $+ 2$ cm $+ 2$ cm $+ 2$ cm $+ 2$ cm $+ 2$ cm
$+ 2$ cm $+ 2$cm $= 20$ cm

Hence, the perimeter of the given figure is 20 cm.

(d)–(iii) Let the given figure be *ABCDEFGHIJKL*.

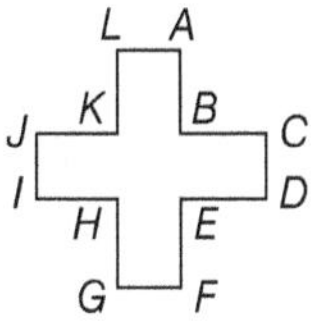

Here, $AB = BC = CD = DE = EF = FG = GH$
$= HI = IJ = JK = KL = LA$

∴ Perimeter of the given figure
= Sum of lengths of all sides
$= AB + BC + CD + DE + EF + FG$
$+ GH + HI + IJ + JK + KL + LA$
$= 2$ cm $+ 2$ cm $+ 2$ cm $+ 2$ cm $+ 2$ cm $+ 2$ cm $+ 2$ cm
$+ 2$ cm $+ 2$ cm $+ 2$cm $+ 2$ cm $+ 2$ cm $= 24$ cm

Hence, the perimeter of the given is 24 cm.

Que 4. Match the following.

	Shapes		Perimeter
(a) 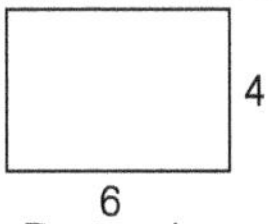	Rectangle (6 × 4)	(i)	10
(b) 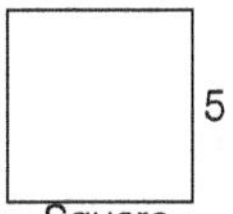	Square (5)	(ii)	18
(c) 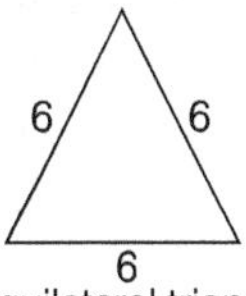	Equilateral triangle (6, 6, 6)	(iii)	20
(d) 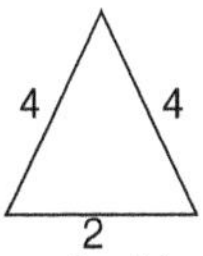	Isosceles triangle (4, 4, 2)	(iv)	25

Sol. (a) – (iii) In the given figure, length of a rectangle = 6 units and breadth of a rectangle = 4 units

∴ Perimeter of a rectangle = 2 × (Length + Breadth)
$$= 2 \times (6 + 4) = 2 \times 10 = 20 \text{ units}$$

(b) – (iii) In the given figure, length of a square = 5 units

∴ Perimeter of a square = 4 × Length of a side
$$= 4 \times 5 = 20 \text{ units}$$

(c) –(ii) Given figure is an equilateral triangle, each sides equal to 6 units.

∴ Perimeter of an equilateral triangle = 3 × Length of a side
$$= 3 \times 6 = 18 \text{ units}$$

(d) –(i) Given figure is an isosceles triangle whose sides are 4 units, 4 units and 2 units respectively.

∴ Perimeter of an isosceles triangle
$$= \text{Sum of all sides of a triangle} = 4 + 4 + 2 = 10 \text{ units}$$

Direction *In question 5, fill in the blanks to make the statements true.*

Que 5. A rectangle and a square have the same perimeter as shown in figure given below:

(a) The area of the rectangle is _____.

(b) The area of the square is _____.

Sol. In the given figure,

Length of a rectangle = 6 units
and breadth of a rectangle = 2 units
We know that,

Perimeter of a rectangle = 2 × (Length + Breadth)
$$= 2 \times (6 + 2) = 2 \times 8 = 16 \text{ units}$$

Given, a rectangle and a square have the same perimeter.

∴ Perimeter of a square = Perimeter of a rectangle
4 × Length of one side = 16 units

$$\Rightarrow \text{Length of one side} = \frac{16}{4} = 4 \text{ units}$$

(a) Now, the area of the rectangle = Length × Breadth
$$= 6 \times 2 = 12 \text{ sq units}$$

(b) The area of the square = Side × Side = 4 × 4 = 16 sq units

Hence, the area of the rectangle is12 sq units and area of the square is 16 sq units.

Directions *In questions 6 and 7, state which of the statements are true and which are false.*

Que 6. If length of a rectangle is halved and breadth is doubled, then the area of the rectangle obtained remains same.

Sol. True, let the length and breadth of a rectangle be l and b respectively.

We know that,

Area of the initial rectangle = Length × Breadth

$= l \times b$ sq units

If length of a rectangle is havled and breadth is doubled.

i.e. new length $= \dfrac{l}{2}$ units and new breadth $= 2b$ units

Then, area of the new rectangle = New Length × New breadth

$$= \frac{l}{2} \times 2b = lb \text{ sq units}$$

Que 7. Area of a square is doubled, if the side of the square is doubled.

Sol. False, if the side of the square is doubled, then area of a square becomes 4 times.

e.g. Let the length of a side of a square be x units.

We know that a square has 4 equal sides.

∴ Initial area of a square = Side × Side = $x \times x$ sq units = x^2 sq units

Now, if the side of the square is doubled.

Then, New side of a square = $2x$ units

∴ New area of a square = New side × New side

$$= 2x \times 2x = 4x^2 \text{ sq units}$$

$$= 4 \times \text{Initial area of a square}$$

Que 8. Four regular hexagons are drawn, so as to form the design as shown in figure. If the perimeter of the design is 28 cm. Then, find the length of each side of the hexagon.

TIPS

Firstly, count the outer sides of the given design and then to find the one side of a hexagon, divide the given perimeter by total number of outer sides of the design.

Sol. Given, four regular hexagons so as form the design as shown in the figure:

Perimeter of the design = 28 cm

∵ Perimeter of the given design = Sum of all outer sides of the four hexagon

Here, this figure has 14 outer equal sides.

∴ Perimeter of the design = 14 × Length of one side of hexagon

28 = 14 × Length of one side of hexagon

Length of one side of hexagon = $\dfrac{28}{14}$ = 2 cm

Hence, the length of each side of the hexagon is 2 cm.

Que 9. There is a rectangular lawn 10 m long and 4 m wide in front of Meena's house. It is fenced along the two smaller sides and one longer side leaving a gap of 1 m for the entrance. Find the length of fencing.

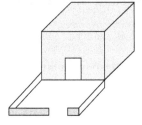 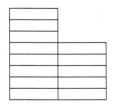

Ans. Given width of the lawn $AB = EF = 4$ m and length of the lawn, $BE = 10$ m

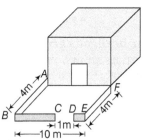

Also, Given length of gap, $CD = 1$ m

Total length of fencing $= AB + (BC + DE) + EF$
$$= AB + (BE - CD) + EF$$
[∵ Here we subtract the length gap (CD) from]
$$= 4 \text{ cm} + (10 - 1) \text{ cm} + 4 \text{ cm}$$
$$= (4 + 9 + 4) \text{ cm} = 17 \text{ m}$$

Hence, the length of fencing the lawn in 17.

Que 10 Tahir measured the distance around a square field as 200 rods (*lathi*). Later, he found that the length of this rod was 140cm. Find the side of this field in metres.

Sol. Given, Tahir measured the distance around a square field as 200 rods(*lathi*).

Distance covered by Tahir in one round = Perimeter of the square field

i.e. Perimeter of a square field = 200 rods

Later on, Tahir found that the length of this rod was 140 cm.

∴ Perimeter of a square field (in cm) $= 200 \times 140 \text{ cm}$

and perimeter of a square field in metres $= \dfrac{200 \times 140}{100}$ m

$$\left[\because 1 \text{ cm} = \dfrac{1}{100} \text{ m} \right]$$

$$= 2 \times 140 \text{ m} = 280 \text{ m}$$

We know that, Perimeter of a square field $= 4 \times$ Length of one side

$$280 = 4 \times \text{Length of one side}$$

∴ Length of one side $= \dfrac{280}{4} = 70 \text{ m}$

Hence, the side of a square field is 70 m.

Que 11. The length of a rectangular field is twice its breadth. Jamal jogged around it four times and covered a distance of 6 km. What is the length of the field?

Sol. Let breadth of a rectangular field be x m and length of a rectangular field be $2x$ m.

Given, distance covered by Jamal in four round $= 6$ km

$$= 6 \times 1000 \text{ m} \qquad [\because 1 \text{ km} = 1000 \text{ m}]$$

Now, distance covered by Jamal in one round $= \dfrac{6000}{4}$ m

We know that,

Distance covered by Jamal in one round

$$= \text{Perimeter of the rectangular field}$$

$$\Rightarrow \qquad \dfrac{6000}{4} = 2 \times (\text{Length} + \text{Breadth})$$

$$\therefore \qquad 2 \times [2x + x] = \frac{6000}{4} \Rightarrow 2 \times 3x = \frac{6000}{4} \Rightarrow 6x = \frac{6000}{4}$$

$$\Rightarrow \qquad x = \frac{6000}{6 \times 4} \Rightarrow x = \frac{1000}{4} = 250 \text{ m}$$

$\therefore$ Length of the rectangular field is $2x = 2 \times 250 = 500$ m

Hence, the length of a rectangular field is 500 m.

Que 12. In the given figure, all triangles are equilateral and $AB = 8$ units. Other triangles have been formed by taking the mid-points of the sides. What is the perimeter of the figure?

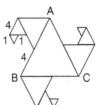

TIPS Firstly, find the all outer sides of the given triangles and then find the perimeter by using sum of all outer sides of the triangles.

Sol. Given, $\triangle ABC$ is an equilateral triangle.

Here, $AB = 8$ units

$\therefore AB = BC = CA = 8$ units

Thus, $\triangle ADE$ is an equilateral triangle.

Here, E is the mid-point of AB

$$\therefore \qquad AE = BE = \frac{AB}{2} = \frac{8}{2} = 4 \text{ units}$$

Now, in $\triangle ADE$,

$$AD = DE = EA = 4 \text{ units}$$

Similarly, equilateral triangles are $\triangle BOT$ and $\triangle UPC$, having each sides i.e. $BO = OT = BT = UC = PC = PU = 4$ units.

It is also clear that $OC = PA = 40$ units

Also, $\triangle DIF$ is an equilateral triangle.

Here, F is the mid-point of DE.

$$\therefore \quad DF = FE = \frac{DE}{2} = \frac{4}{2} = 2 \text{ units}$$

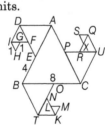

Now, in $\triangle DIF$, $DI = IF = DF = 2$ units

Similarly, in $\triangle TKN$ and $\triangle RQU$,

$$TK = KN = TN = RQ = UQ = UR = 2 \text{ units}$$

It is also clear that $NO = RP = 22$ units

Also, $\triangle HIG$ is an equilateral triangle.

Here, G is the mid-point of IF.

$\therefore \qquad IG = GF = \dfrac{IF}{2} = \dfrac{2}{2} = 1$ unit

Now, in $\triangle HIG, HG = HI = GI = 1$ unit

Similarly, in $\triangle MLK$ and $\triangle XQS$,

$$ML = MK = SQ = XS = QX = 1 \text{ unit}$$

It is also clear that $LN = XR = 1$ unit

Now, the perimeter of the given figure

$\qquad\qquad$ = Sum of all outer sides of the given figure

$\qquad\qquad = AD + DI + IH + HG + GF + FE + EB + BT$

$\qquad\qquad\qquad + TK + KM + LM + LN + NO + OC$

$\qquad\qquad\qquad + CU + UQ + QS + XS + XR + PR + PA$

$\qquad\qquad = 4 + 2 + 1 + 1 + 1 + 2 + 4 + 4 + 2 + 1 + 1 + 1 + 2$

$\qquad\qquad\qquad + 4 + 4 + 2 + 1 + 1 + 1 + 2 + 4$

$\qquad\qquad = 45 \text{ cm}$

Hence, the perimeter of the given figure is 45 cm.

Que 13. The perimeter of a triangle is 28 cm. One of it's sides is 8 cm. Write all the sides of the possible isosceles triangles with these measurements.

Sol. Let an isosceles triangle with equal sides be x cm.

$\qquad$ Given, one side of an isosceles triangle = 8 cm

$\qquad$ and perimeter of a triangle = 28 cm

$\qquad$ We know that, Perimeter of a triangle = Sum of lengths of all sides

$\Rightarrow \qquad\qquad 28 = x + x + 8 \Rightarrow 28 = 2x + 8 \Rightarrow 2x = 28 - 8 \Rightarrow 2x = 20$

$\therefore \qquad\qquad x = \dfrac{20}{2} = 10 \text{ cm}$

$\qquad$ Hence, the isosceles triangle with equal sides are 10 cm, 10 cm and third side is 8 cm.

Que 14. What is the length of outer boundary of the park shown in figure? What will be the total cost of fencing it at the rate of ₹ 20 per metre? There is a rectangular flower bed in the centre of the park. Find the cost of manuring the flower bed at the rate of ₹ 50 per square metre.

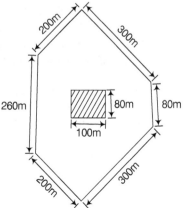

TIPS
Firstly, find the perimeter of the given park by using sum of lengths of all sides. Then, to find the required cost, multiply the perimeter by rate of fencing. Similarly, find the area of rectangular bed byusing formula length × breadth, then to find the required cost, multiply the area by rate of manuring.

Sol.

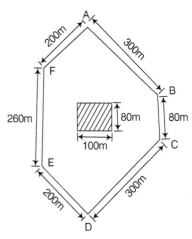

Let the part be *ABCDEF*.
Here, *AB* = 300 m, *BC* = 80 m, *CD* = 300 m, *DE* = 200 m,
        EF = 260 m and *FA* =200 m.
The total length of outer boundary of the park or perimeter of the park = Sum of outer length of all sides
                = *AB* + *BC* + *CD* + *DE* + *EF* + *FA*
                = 300 m + 80 m + 300 m + 200 m + 260 m + 200 m
                = (300 + 80 + 300 + 200 + 260 + 200)m = 1340 m
Hence, the total length of outer boundary of the park is 1340m.
Given, cost of fencing per metre =₹20
∴ Cost of fencing a park =₹20 × Perimeter of the park
                = 20 × 1340 = ₹ 26800
  Given, a rectangular flower bed in the centre of the park.
  Length of rectangular flower bed = 100 m
and breadth of rectangular of flower bed = 80 m
We know that,
Area of the rectangle flower bed = Length × Breadth
                = 100 m × 80 m = 8000 sq m
∵ Cost of manuring the flower bed per sq metre =₹50
∴ Cost of manuring the flower bed = 8000 × 50 =₹400000

Que 15. Total cost of fencing the park shown in Figure is Rs 55000. Find the cost of fencing per metre.

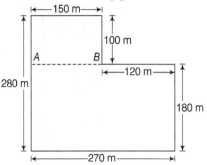

Ans. Total perimeter for fencing the park

$$= FE + ED + DC + CB + BG + GF$$

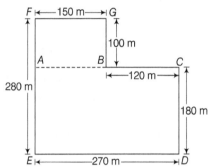

$$= 280 \text{ cm} + 270 \text{ cm} + 180 \text{ cm} + 120 \text{ cm} + 100 \text{ cm} + 150 \text{ cm}$$

$$= 1100 \text{ m}$$

But it is given, the total cost of fencing the park = ₹ 55000.

∴ Cost of fencing the park for 1100 m = ₹ 55000

∴ Cost of fencing the park for per meter = $\dfrac{₹\, 55000}{1100}$ = ₹ 50

Hence, the cost of fencing per meter is ₹ 50.

Que 16. In figure each square is of unit length

    (a) What is the perimeter of the rectangle *ABCD*?

    (b) What is the area of the rectangle *ABCD*?

    (c) Divide this rectangle into ten parts of equal area by shading squares.

        (Two parts of equal area are shown here)

(d) Find the perimeter of each part which you have divided. Are they all equal?

Ans. Given length of each square is of unit length. In a figure contain height of 10 squares and width of 6 squares.

Now, length of rectangle $AD = BC$

= height of 10 squares of unit length = $10 \times 1 = 10$ units

and breadth of rectangle, $AB = DC$

= width of 6 squares = $6 \times 1 = 6$ units

(a) The perimeter of the rectangle $ABCD$
= $AB + BC + CD + DA = 6 + 10 + 6 + 10 = 32$ units

(b) The area of the rectangle $ABCD$ = length × breadth
= $AD \times AB = 10 \times 6 = 60$ units

(c) The total area of rectangle = 60 units.

Now, we have to divide the rectangle into 10 equal parts i.e. $\dfrac{60}{10} = 6$ square units i.e. we have to take a group of 6-6 square blocks which is shown in the

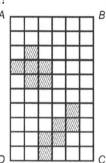

(d) Now, we find the perimeter of part I.

We know that perimeter of a figure is the total length of its boundary

∴Perimeter of part I = $1 + 1 + 1 + 1 + 1 + 1 + 1 + 1 + 1 + 1 + 1 + 1$

= 12 unit.

Similarly, we can find the perimeters of remaining 9 parts, all the parts have some perimeter i.e. 12 units.

Yes, all the parts have some perimeter.

Que 17. Rectangular wall *MNOP* of a kitchen is covered with square tiles of 15cm length (Fig. 6.19). Find the area of the wall.

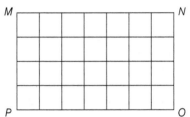

Sol. Let us denote some points of a rectangular wall *MNOP* of a kitchen is

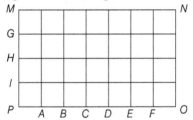

Now, $PA = AB = BC = CD = DE$
$\qquad = EF = FO = PI = HI = HG = GM = 15$ cm

given, length of a square tiles $= 15$ cm

∴ Length of a rectangular wall $MNOP = PO$
$\qquad = PA + AB + BC + CD + DE + EF + FO$
$\qquad = 15$ cm $+ 15$ cm $+ 15$ cm $+ 15$ cm $+ 15$ cm
$\qquad\qquad\qquad\qquad\qquad\qquad + 15$ cm $+15$ cm
$\qquad = 105$ cm

and breadth of rectangular wall $MNOP = PM$
$\qquad = PI + IH + HG + GM$
$\qquad = 15$ cm $+ 15$ cm $+ 15$ cm $+ 15$ cm
$\qquad = 60$ cm

Now, area of the wall $(MNOP) =$ Length $(PO) \times$ Breadth (PM)
$\qquad = PO \times PM$
$\qquad = 105 \times 60 = 6300$ sq cm

Hence, the area of the wall is 6300 sq cm.

Que 18. A magazine charges ₹ 300 per 10 sq cm area for advertising. A company decided to order a half page advertisment. If each page of the magazine is 15cm × 24cm, what amount will the company has to pay for it?

Sol. Firstly, find the area of full page of a magazine by using length × breadth. Also, find area of half page and to get required cost, we multiply the area of half page by rate of advertising i.e. $\dfrac{300}{10}$

$$[\because \text{rate} = ₹\ 300 \text{ per } 10 \text{ sq cm}]$$

Given, length of each page of the magazine = 24 cm

and breadth of each page of the magazine = 15 cm

∴Area of the full page of the magazine

$$= \text{Length} \times \text{Breadth} = 24\text{ cm} \times 15\text{ cm} = 360\text{ sq cm}$$

∵ Company decided to order of half page advertisment.

∴Area of half page of the magazine $= \dfrac{360}{2} = 180$ sq cm

Given, cost of per 10 sq m = ₹ 300

Cost of 1 sq m = ₹ $\dfrac{300}{10}$

Cost of 180 sq m = $\dfrac{300}{10} \times 180 = 300 \times 18 = ₹\ 5400$

Hence, the company will pay ₹ 5400 for it.

Que 19. The perimeter of a square garden is 48m. A small flower bed covers 18 sqm area inside this garden. What is the area of the garden that is not covered by the flower bed? What fractional part of the garden is covered by flower bed? Find the ratio of the area covered by the flower bed and the remaining area.

Ans. Let side of s square garden be x m.

Given that, perimeter of a square garden = 48 m

∴ 4 × side of a square = 48

$$\Rightarrow \qquad\qquad 4x = 48 \ \Rightarrow\ x = \dfrac{48}{4} = 12\text{ m}$$

Now, area of the square garden = $(x)^2$

$$= (12)^2 = 144\text{ m}^2$$

Also given, area of small flower bed cover in side the garden = $18\,\text{m}^2$

∴Area of the garden not covered the flower bed

$$= \text{Area of square garden} - \text{Area of flower bed}$$

$$= 144\,\text{m}^2 - 18\,\text{m}^2 = 126\,\text{m}^2$$

The fractional part of the garden covered by flower bed

$$= \dfrac{\text{Area covered by the flower}}{\text{Area of a square garden}} = \dfrac{18}{144} = \dfrac{1}{8}$$

The ratio of the area covered by the flower bed and the remaining area = 1 : (8-1) = 1 : 2

Que 20. Perimeter of a square and a rectangle is same. If a side of the square is 15cm and one side of the rectangle is 18 cm. Find the area of the rectangle.

Sol. Given, a side of a square = 15 cm

We know that, the perimeter of a square
$$= 4 \times \text{Side of a square}$$
$$= 4 \times 15 \text{ cm} = 60 \text{ m}$$

Here, length of a rectangle = 18 cm

$\therefore$ Perimeter of a rectangle $= 2 \times (\text{Length} + \text{Breadth})$
$$= 2 (18 + \text{Breadth})$$

According to the question,

Perimeter of a square = Perimeter of a rectangle

$\therefore$ $60 = 2 (18 + \text{Breadth})$

$$\frac{60}{2} = (18 + \text{Breadth})$$

$\Rightarrow$ $18 + \text{Breadth} = 30$

$\therefore$ $\text{Breadth} = 30 - 18 = 12 \text{ cm}$

Now, area of the rectangle = Length × Breadth
$$= 18 \times 12 = 216 \text{ sq cm}$$

Hence, the area of the rectangle is 216 sq cm

Que 21. The area of each square on a chess board is 4sqcm. Find the area of the board.

(a) At the beginning of game when all the chess men are put on the board, write area of the squares left unoccupied.

(b) Find the area of the squares occupied by chess men.

Ans. We know that, their are 64 square in a class board.

Given area of each square class board = 4 m^2

$\therefore$ Area of the board = Number of square in a board
$$\times \text{Area of one square}$$
$$= 64 \times 4 \text{ m}^2 = 256 \text{ m}^2$$

(a) We know that in a game of Chess, then are two players each of how. 16 Chess men.

Now, total number of squares occupied by the chess men in the board = $16 \times 2 = 32$

$\because$ Total number of squares are by the chess men in the occupied by the chess men in the board
$$= \text{Total number of squares in a chess board}$$
$$- \text{Number of squares occupied by the chess men}$$
$$= 64 - 32 = 32.$$

∴ The area of the squares left in occupied = Number of squares left unoccupied by the chess men × area of one square
$$= 32 \times 4 \text{ m}^2 = 128 \text{ m}^2$$

(b) The area of the squares occupied by chess men = Number of square occupied by chess board × Area of one square
$$= 32 \times 4 \text{ m}^2 = 128 \text{ m}^2$$

Que 22. (a) Find all the possible dimensions (in natural numbers) of a rectangle with a perimeter 36cm and find their areas.

(b) Find all the possible dimensions (in natural numbers) of a rectangle with an area of 36 sq cm and find their perimeters.

Sol. Let length and breadth of a rectangle be l and b respectively.

(a) Given, perimeter of a rectangle = 36 cm
$$2 \times [l + b] = 36 \text{ cm}$$
$$l + b = \frac{36}{2} \Rightarrow l + b = 18 \text{ cm}$$

and area of the rectangle = $l \times b$ sq cm

Now, put different dimensions of l and b, we get different areas of rectangle.

Dimensions in cm	Area in sq cm i.e. ×
$l = 1$ and $b = 17$	$1 \times 17 = 17$
$l = 2$ and $b = 16$	$2 \times 16 = 32$
$l = 3$ and $b = 15$	$3 \times 15 = 45$
$l = 4$ and $b = 14$	$4 \times 14 = 56$
$l = 5$ and $b = 13$	$5 \times 13 = 65$
$l = 6$ and $b = 12$	$6 \times 12 = 72$
$l = 7$ and $b = 11$	$7 \times 11 = 77$
$l = 8$ and $b = 10$	$8 \times 10 = 80$
$l = 9$ and $b = 9$	$9 \times 9 = 81$
$l = 17$ and $b = 1$	$17 \times 1 = 17$

(b) Given, the area of the rectangle = 36 sq cm
i.e. $l \times b = 36$ sq cm

Now, perimeter of the rectangle = $2 [l + b]$ cm

Now, put different dimensions of l and b, we get different perimeters of the rectangle.

Dimensions in cm	Perimeter in cm [i.e. +]
$l = 1$ and $b = 36$	$2(1 + 36) = 2 \times 37 = 74$
$l = 2$ and $b = 18$	$2(2 + 18) = 2 \times 20 = 40$
$l = 3$ and $b = 12$	$2(3 + 12) = 2 \times 15 = 30$
$l = 4$ and $b = 9$	$2(4 + 9) = 2 \times 13 = 26$
$l = 6$ and $b = 6$	$2(6 + 6) = 2 \times 12 = 24$

Chapter 11

Algebra

Important Points

- **Arithmetic** The branch of mathematics dealing with the properties and manipulation of number.
- **Geometry** The branch of mathematics concerned with the properties and relations of points, time, surface, solids and higher dimensional analogues.
- **Algebra** Arithmetic is a branch of mathematics which is known as **algebra**.

  In the algebra, we studied about variables, equations and solutions of numbers. In this branch of mathematics, we study the use of letters. Use of letters allow us to write rules and formulae in a general way. Here letters stand for unknown quantities.
- **Variables** The word variable means something that can vary i.e. change. The value of a variable is not fixed. It can take different values. e.g. The length of a square can have any values, so it is a variable but the number of angles of a square has a fixed value 4, so it is not a variable. We use a variable to represent a number and denote it by any letter such as l, m, n, p, x, y, z, etc.

  e.g.

Number of Ls formed	1	2	3	4	5	6	7	8	...	...
Number of matchsticks required	2	4	6	8	10	12	14	16	...	...

In the above example, we found a rule to give the number of matchsticks required to make a pattern of Ls. The rule was.

[Number of matchsticks required = $2n$]

Here, n is the number of Ls in the pattern and n takes values 1 , 2, 3, 4,.... Let us look at above table once again. In the table, the value of n goes on changing (increasing). As a result, the number of matchsticks required also goes on changing (increasing).

n is an example of a variable. Its value is not fixed, it can take any value 1, 2, 3, 4, ... We wrote the rule for the number of matchsticks required using the variable n.

- **Use of variables in common rules** Let us now see how certain common rules in mathematics that we have already learnt are expressed using variables.

  Some of them are following :

  (i) Rules for geometry

  (a) **Perimeter of a square** We know that, perimeter of any polygon (a closed figure made up of 3 or more line segments) is the sum of the lengths of its sides.

    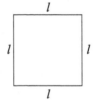

    A square has 4 sides and they are equal in length .

    Therefore,

    The perimeter of a square = Sum of the lengths of the sides of the square

    $\qquad$ = 4 times the length of a side of the square

    $\qquad P = 4 \times l = 4l$

    Thus, we get the rule for the perimeter of a square. The use of the variable l allows us to write the general rule in a way that is concise and easy to remember.

  (b) **Perimeter of a rectangle** We know that, a rectangle has four sides.

    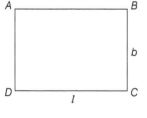

    e.g. The rectangle $ABCD$ has four sides AB, BC, CD and DA. The opposite sides of any rectangle are always equal in length. Thus, in the rectangle $ABCD$, let us denote by l, the length of the sides *AB* or *CD* and by *b*, the length of the sides *AD* or *BC*. Therefore,

Perimeter of a rectangle = Length of *AB* + Length of *BC*

$$+ \text{Length of } CD + \text{ Length of } AD$$

$$= 2 \times \text{Length of } CD + 2 \times \text{Length of } BC$$

$$= 2l + 2b$$

Therefore, the perimeter of a rectangle = $2l + 2b$

where, *l* and *b* are respectively the length and breadth of the rectangle.

If we denote the perimeter of the rectangle by the variable *P*, the rule for perimeter of a rectangle becomes

$$P = 2l + 2b = 2(l + b)$$

where, *l* and *b* are variables. They take values independent of each other.

(ii) **Rules for arithmetic**

(a) **Commutativity of addition of two numbers**

We know that, $4 + 3 = 7$ and $3 + 4 = 7$ i.e. $4 + 3 = 3 + 4$

As we have seen in the chapter on whole numbers, this is true for any two numbers. This property of numbers is known as the commutativity of   addition of numbers. Commuting means interchanging. Commuting the order of numbers in addition does not change the sum. The use of variables allows us to express the generality of this property in a concise way.

Let *a* and *b* be two variables, which can take any number value. Then, $\qquad a + b = b + a$

Once, we write the rule this way, all special cases are included in it.

e.g. If $a = 37$ and $b = 73$, then we get $37 + 73 = 73 + 37$ and so on.

(b) **Commutativity of multiplication of two numbers**

We have seen in the chapter on whole numbers that for multiplication of two numbers, the order of the two numbers being multiplied does not matter.

e.g. $\qquad$ $4 \times 3 = 12, \ 3 \times 4 = 12$

Hence, $\qquad$ $4 \times 3 = 3 \times 4$

This property of numbers is known as commutativity of multiplication of numbers. Commuting (interchanging) the order of numbers in multiplication does not change the product. Using variables a and b as in the case of addition , we can express the commutativity of multiplication of two numbers as $\qquad$ $a \times b = b \times a$

Note a and b can take any number value, since they are variables. All the special cases like $4 \times 3 = 3 \times 4$ or $37 \times 73 = 73 \times 37$ follow from the general rule.

(c) **Distributivity of numbers**

Suppose, we are asked to calculate 7×38. We obviously do not know, the table of 38. So, we do the following.

$7 \times 38 = 7 \times (30 + 8) = 7 \times 30 + 7 \times 8 = 210 + 56 = 266$

This is always true for any three numbers like 7, 30 and 8. This property is known as distributivity of multiplication over addition of numbers.

By using variables, we can write this property of numbers also in a general and concise way. Let a, b and c be three variables, each of which can take any number.

Then, $\qquad$ $a \times (b + c) = a \times b + a \times c$

Note A number expression like $(2 \times 4) + 2$ can be immediately evaluated as $(2 \times 4) + 2 = 8 + 2 = 10$

But an expression like $(2x + 5)$, which contain the variable x, cannat be evaluated unless x is given some value

e.g. if $x = 2$, then $2x + 5 = 2 \times 2 + 5 = 4 + 5 = 9$

■ **Important points about variable**

(i) A variable allows us to express relations in any practical situation.

(ii) Variables are numbers, although there value is not fixed. We can do operations of addition, subtraction, multiplication and division on per part as in the case of fixed numbers.

(iii) A variable allows us to express many common rules in both geometry and arithmetic in a general way.

■ **Equation** An expression with a variable, constants and the sign of equality (=) is called equation.

e.g. Balu is 3 yr younger than Raju. Taking Raju's age to be x yr, Balu's age is $(x - 3)$ yr. Suppose, Balu is 11 yr old. Then, let us see how our method gives Raju's age.

We have, Balu's age, $x - 3 = 11$

This is an equation in the variable x. We shall prepare a table of values of $(x - 3)$ for various values of x.

x	3	4	5	6	7	8	9	10	11	12	13	14	15	16	17	18
$x-3$	0	1	–	–	–	–	–	–	–	9	10	11	12	13	–	–

Complete the entries which are left blank. From the table, we find that only for $x = 14$, the condition $x - 3 = 11$ is satisfied. For other values, e.g. for $x = 16$ or for $x = 12$, the condition is not satisfied. Therefore, Raju's age is 14 yr. The equation $x - 3 = 11$, is satisfied only by the value 14 for the variable x.

Note If the LHS and RHS are not equal, then we do not get an equation.
If an equation has an equal sign (=) between its two sides. The equation says that the value of the left hand side (LHS) is equal to the value of the right hand side (RHS).

e.g. The statement $2n$ is greater than 10, i.e. $2n > 10$ is not an equation. Similarly, the statement $2n$ is smaller than 10, i.e. $2n < 10$ is not an equation.

■ **Solution of an equation** The value of the variable in an equation, which satisfies the equation is called a solution of the equation.
e.g. Let us take the equation $x - 3 = 11$.

This equation is satisfied by $x = 14$ because for $x = 14$,

LHS of the equation $= 14 - 3 = 11 =$ RHS of the equation.

It is not satisfied by $x = 16$, because for $x = 16$,

LHS of the equation $= 16 - 3 = 13$, which is not equal to RHS.

Thus, $x = 14$ is a solution to the equation $x - 3 = 11$ and $x = 16$ is not a solution to the equation. Also, $x = 12$ is not a solution to the equation.

We can also make a table for getting solution by putting the values of variable in given equation. If it gives real value, then solution exist. i.e. Yes, otherwise not i.e. No.

	Equation	Value of the variable	Solution (Yes/No)
1.	$x + 10 = 30$	$x = 10$	No
2.	$x + 10 = 30$	$x = 30$	No
3.	$x + 10 = 30$	$x = 20$	Yes
4.	$p - 3 = 7$	$p = 5$	No
5.	$p - 3 = 7$	$p = 15$	No
6.	$p - 3 = 7$	$p = 10$	Yes

Exercise 11.1

Que 1. Find the rule which gives the number of matchsticks required to make the following matchstick patterns. Use a variable to write the rule.

  (a) A pattern of letter T as **T**   (b) A pattern of letter Z as Z

  (c) A pattern of letter U as ∪   (d) A pattern of letter V as V

  (e) A pattern of letter E as E   (f) A pattern of letter S as 5

  (g) A pattern of letter A as A

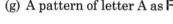

TIPS

Firstly, form the given letter by matchsticks and then form the pattern. Since, number of letter is increasing in this pattern, so let the number of letter is a variable. Put the different values 1, 2, 3, ... *n*, of variable, find number of matchsticks and then get the required rule.

Sol. (a) One T can be formed by 2 matchsticks and 2T can be formed by 4 matchsticks. Thus, we get the following patterns of letter T.

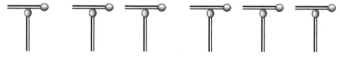

Here, the number of Ts is increasing.

So, let variable n denotes the number of Ts.

Now, number of matchsticks required to make pattern of 'T' are given below :

For $n = 1$, the number of matchsticks required $= 2 \times 1 = 2$

For $n = 2$, the number of matchsticks required $= 2 \times 2 = 4$

For $n = 3$, the number of matchsticks required $= 2 \times 3 = 6$

For $n = n$, the number of matchsticks required $= 2 \times n = 2n$

Hence, the required rule for a pattern of letter T is $2n$.

(b) One Z can be formed by 3 matchsticks and 2Z can be formed by 6 matchsticks. Thus, we get the following patterns of letter Z.

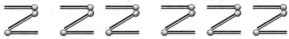

Here, the number of Zs is increasing.

So, let variable n denotes the number of Zs.

Now, the number of matchsticks required to make pattern of 'Z' are given below :

For $n = 1$, the number of matchsticks required $= 3 \times 1 = 3$

For $n = 2$, the number of matchsticks required $= 3 \times 2 = 6$

For $n = 3$, the number of matchsticks required $= 3 \times 3 = 9$

For $n = n$, the number of matchsticks required $= 3 \times n = 3n$

Hence, the required rule for a pattern of letter Z is $3n$.

(c) One U can be formed by 3 matchsticks and 2U can be formed by 6 matchsticks. Thus, we get the following pattern of letter U.

Here, the number of Us is increasing.

Let variable n denotes the number of Us.

Now, the number of matchsticks required to make pattern of 'U' are given below :

For $n = 1$, the number of matchsticks required $= 3 \times 1 = 3$

For $n = 2$, the number of matchsticks required $= 3 \times 2 = 6$

For $n = 3$, the number of matchsticks required $= 3 \times 3 = 9$

For $n = n$, the number of matchsticks required $= 3 \times n = 3n$

Hence, the required rule for a pattern of letter U is $3n$.

(d) One V can be formed by 2 matchsticks and 2V can be formed by 4 matchsticks. Thus, we get the following pattern of letter V.

Here, the number of Vs is increasing.

Let variable n denotes the number of Vs.

Now, the number of matchsticks required to make pattern of 'V' are given below :

For $n = 1$, the number of matchsticks required $= 2 \times 1 = 2$

For $n = 2$, the number of matchsticks required $= 2 \times 2 = 4$

For $n = 3$, the number of matchsticks required $= 2 \times 3 = 6$

For $n = n$, the number of matchsticks required $= 2 \times n = 2n$

Hence, the required rule for a pattern of letter V is $2n$.

(e) One E can be formed by 5 matchsticks and 2E can be formed by 10 matchsticks. Thus, we get the following pattern of letter E.

Let variable n denotes the number of Es.

Now, the number of matchsticks required to make pattern of 'E' are given below :

For $n = 1$, the number of matchsticks required $= 5 \times 1 = 5$

For $n = 2$, the number of matchsticks required $= 5 \times 2 = 10$

For $n = 3$, the number of matchsticks required $= 5 \times 3 = 15$

For $n = n$, the number of matchsticks required $= 5 \times n = 5n$

Hence, the required rule for a pattern of letter E is $5n$.

(f) One S can be formed by 5 matchsticks and 2S can be formed by 10 matchsticks. Thus, we get the following pattern of letter S.

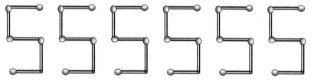

Let variable n denotes the number of Ss.

Now, number of matchsticks required to make pattern 'S' is

For $n = 1$, number of matchsticks $= 5 \times 1 = 5$

For $n = 2$, number of matchsticks $= 5 \times 2 = 10$

For $n = 3$, number of matchsticks $= 5 \times 3 = 15$

For $n = n$, number of matchsticks $= 5 \times n = 5n$

Thus, the required rule for a pattern of letter S is $5n$.

(g) One A can be formed by 6 matchsticks and 2A can be formed by 12 matchsticks. Thus, we get the following pattern of letter A.

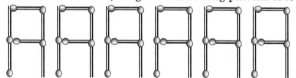

Here, the number of As is increasing.

Let variable n denotes the number of As.

Now, the number of matchsticks required to make pattern 'A' is

For $n = 1$, the number of matchsticks required $= 6 \times 1 = 6$

For $n = 2$, the number of matchsticks required $= 6 \times 2 = 12$

For $n = 3$, the number of matchsticks required $= 6 \times 3 = 18$

For $n = n$, the number of matchsticks required $= 6 \times n = 6n$

Hence, the required rule for a pattern of letter 'A' is $6n$.

Que 2. We already know the rule for the pattern of letters L, C and F. Some of the letters from question 1 (given above) give us the same rule as that given by 'L'. Which are these? Why does this happen?

Sol. Rules for the pattern of letters L, C and F are as follow :

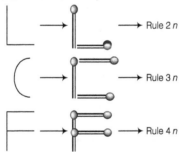

In question 1, letter T and V have same rule as that given by L. This happens because the number of matchsticks required in each of them is 2.

Que 3. Cadets are marching in a parade. There are 5 cadets in a row. What is the rule which gives the number of cadets, given the number of rows? (Use n for the number of rows.)

Sol. Let the number of rows $= n$

Given, the number of cadets in each row $= 5$

∴ Total number of cadets $= 5n$

Here, $\bullet = 1$ cadet

Hence, rule to find the number of cadets in 'n' rows is $5n$.

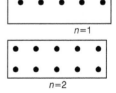

Que 4. If there are 50 mangoes in a box, how will you write the total number of mangoes in terms of the number of boxes? (Use b for the number of boxes).

Sol. Given, b is the number of boxes and, the number of mangoes in a box $= 50$

When there is one box i.e. $b = 1$, then the number of mangoes $= 50 \times 1$ i.e. 50.

When there are two boxes i.e. $b = 2$, then the number of mangoes $= 50 \times 2$ i.e. 100

When there are three boxes i.e. $b = 3$, then the number of mangoes $= 50 \times 3$ i.e. 150

When there are b boxes i.e. $b = b$, then the number of mangoes $= 50 \times b = 50\,b$

Hence, total number of mangoes in terms of number of boxes can be written as $50\,b$.

Que 5. The teacher distributes 5 pencils per student. Can you tell how many pencils are needed, given the number of students? (Use s for the number of students).

Sol. Let number of students $= s$

Given, number of pencils distributed to each student $= 5$

When there is one student i.e. $s = 1$, then number of pencils $= 5 \times 1$ i.e. 5

When there are two students i.e. $s = 2$, then number of pencils $= 5 \times 2$ i.e. 10

When there are three students i.e. $s = 3$, then number of pencils $= 5 \times 3$ i.e. 15

When there are s students i.e. $s = s$, then number of pencils $= 5 \times s$ i.e. $5s$

Hence, $5s$ pencils are needed for s students.

Que 6. A bird flies 1 kilometer in one minute. Can you express the distance covered by the bird in terms of its flying time in minutes? (Use t for flying time in minutes).

Sol. Let flying time of bird $= t$ min.

Then, bird flies in one min $= 1$ km

$\therefore$ Bird flies in t min $= t \times 1$ km $= t$ km

Hence, the distance covered by the bird in its flying time i.e. in t min is t km.

Que 7. Radha is drawing a dot Rangoli (a beautiful pattern of lines joining dots with chalk powder). She has 9 dots in a row. How many dots will her Rangoli have for r rows? How many dots are there, if there are 8 rows? If there are 10 rows?

Sol. Given, the number of rows = r

and the number of dots in one row i.e. $r = 1$ is $9 \times 1 = 9$

∴the number of dots in 2 rows i.e. $r = 2$ is $9 \times 2 = 18$

the number of dots in 3 rows i.e. $r = 3$ is $9 \times 3 = 27$

∴ Total number of dots in r rows is $= 9 \times r = 9r$

Now, if there are 8 rows i.e. $r = 8$, then the number of dots
$$= 9 \times 8 = 72 \text{ dots}$$
and for $r = 10$, the number of dots $= 9 \times 10 = 90$ dots.

Que 8. Leela is Radha's younger sister. Leela is 4 years younger than Radha. Can you write Leela's age in terms of Radha's age? Take Radha's age to be x years.

Sol. Let Radha's age be $= x$ yr

Given, the Leela is 4 yr younger than Radha.

So, age of Leela = (Age of Radha) – 4 yr

$\Rightarrow$ Age of Leela $= (x - 4)$ yr

Thus, yes we can write Leela's age in terms of Radha's age.

Que 9. Mother has made laddus. She gives some laddus to guests and family members; still 5 laddus remain. If the number of laddus mother gave away is l, how many laddus did she make?

Sol. Given, the number of laddus given away by mother $= l$

and the number of laddus left over $= 5$

∴ Total number of laddus made by mother

= Number of laddus given away + Number of laddus left over $= l + 5$

Hence, the number of laddus made by mother is $l + 5$.

Que 10. Oranges are to be transferred from larger boxes into smaller boxes. When a large box is emptied, the oranges from it fill two smaller boxes and still 10 oranges remain outside. If the number of oranges in a small box are taken to be x, what is the number of oranges in the larger box?

Sol. Given, the number of oranges in a smaller box $= x$

Since, one larger box is emptied to fill two smaller boxes.

So, the number of oranges in two smaller boxes $= 2 \times$ The number of oranges in one box $= 2 \times x = 2x$

Also, 10 oranges remain outside, when large box is emptied to fill two smaller boxes.

So, number of oranges in the larger box = Number of oranges in two smaller boxes + Oranges left over $= 2x + 10$

Hence, the number of oranges in the larger box is $(2x + 10)$.

Que 11. (i) Look at the following matchstick pattern of squares. The squares are not separate. Two neighbouring squares have a common matchstick. Observe the patterns and find the rule that gives the number of matchsticks in terms of the number of squares.

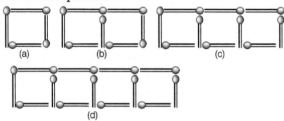

(a)   (b)   (c)

(d)

(**Hint** If you remove the vertical stick at the end, you will get a pattern of Cs.)

(ii) Figure depict below gives a matchstick pattern of triangles. As in Exercise 11 (A) above, find the general rule that gives the number of matchsticks in terms of the number of triangles.

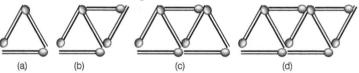

(a)   (b)   (c)   (d)

Sol. (i) In figures,

(a) Number of squares = 1
and number of matchsticks $= 4 = 3 \times 1 + 1$
$= 3 \times$ Number of square $+ 1$

(b) Number of squares = 2
and number of matchsticks $= 7 = 3 \times 2 + 1$
$= 3 \times$ Number of squares $+ 1$

(c) Number of squares = 3
and number of matchsticks $= 10 = 3 \times 3 + 1$
$= 3 \times$ Number of squares $+ 1$

(d) Number of squares = 4
and number of matchsticks $= 13 = 3 \times 4 + 1$
$= 3 \times$ Number of squares $+ 1$

Thus, if number of squares $= x$

Then, number of matchsticks $= 3 \times$ Number of squares $+ 1$
$= 3x + 1$

Hence, the required rule that gives the number of matchsticks is $3x + 1$, where x is number of squares.

(ii) In figures,
   (a) Number of triangles = 1
      and number of matchsticks = $3 = 2 \times 1 + 1$
      $$= 2 \times \text{Number of triangle} + 1$$
   (b) Number of triangles = 2
      and number of matchsticks = $5 = 2 \times 2 + 1$
      $$= 2 \times \text{Number of triangles} + 1$$
   (c) Number of triangles = 3
      and number of matchsticks = $7 = 2 \times 3 + 1$
      $$= 2 \times \text{Number of triangles} + 1$$
   (d) Number of triangles = 4
      and number of matchsticks = $9 = 2 \times 4 + 1$
      $$= 2 \times \text{Number of triangles} + 1$$
Thus, if number of triangles = x
Then, number of matchsticks = $2 \times \text{Number of triangles} + 1 = 2x + 1$
Hence, the required rule that gives the number of matchsticks is $2x + 1$, where x is number of triangles.

Exercise 11.2

Que 1. The side of an equilateral triangle is shown by l. Express the perimeter of the equilateral triangle using l.

Sol. Let $\triangle ABC$ is an equilateral triangle, where each side is denoted by l.
   i.e. $\qquad AB = BC = CA = l$
   We know that, the perimeter of a triangle
   $$= \text{Sum of all the sides of a triangle}$$
   $\therefore$ Perimeter of an equilateral triangle
   $$= AB + BC + CA = l + l + l = 3\,l$$
Thus, the perimeter of an equilateral triangle using l can be expresed as $3\,l$.

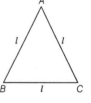

Que 2. The side of a regular hexagon is denoted by l. Express the perimeter of the hexagon using l.

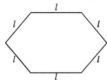

(**Hint** A regular hexagon has all its six sides equal in length).

Sol. Let *ABCDEF* is the given regular hexagon whose each side is denoted by *l*.

i.e. $AB = BC = CD = DE = EF = FA = l$

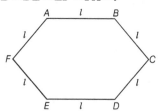

We know that, perimeter of a regular hexagon

= Sum of all the sides of hexagon

∴ Perimeter of a regular hexagon = $AB + BC + CD + DE + EF + FA$

$$= l + l + l + l + l + l = 6l$$

Hence, perimeter of a hexagon using *l* can be expressed as $6l$.

Que 3. A cube is a three-dimensional figure as shown in figure. It has six faces and all of them are identical squares. The length of an edge of the cube is given by *l*. Find the formula for the total length of the edges of a cube.

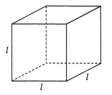

Sol. We know that, a cube is a three-dimensional figure which has six faces and 12 edges.

Given, that all edges are equal in length

and length of edge = *l*

Now, total length of the edges of a cube = Sum of all 12 edges of a cube

$$= l + l + l + l + l + l + l + l + l + l + l + l$$

$$= 12l$$

Hence, the required formula for the total length of the edges of a cube is $12l$, where *l* = length of an edge.

Que 4. The diameter of a circle is a line, which joins two points on the circle and also passes through the centre of the circle. (In the figure given below, *AB* is a diameter of the circle, *C* is its centre). Express the diameter of the circle (*d*) in terms of its radius (*r*).

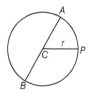

Sol. Given, *AB* is diameter of the circle. Also, *C* is the centre of the circle and *PC* is the radius.

We know that, diameter of a circle $= 2 \times$ radius $= 2 \times PC$

$\Rightarrow$ $\qquad d = 2 \times r$ $\qquad \Rightarrow$ $\qquad d = 2r$

Hence, the diameter of the circle in terms of its radius can be expressed as $d = 2r$.

Que. 5. To find sum of three numbers 14, 27 and 13, we can have two ways

    (a) We may first add 14 and 27 to get 41 and then add 13 to it to get the total sum 54

or

    (b) We may add 27 and 13 to get 40 and then add 14 to get the sum 54. Thus, $(14 + 27) + 13 = 14 + (27 + 13)$

    This can be done for any three numbers. This property is known as the associativity of addition of numbers. Express this property which we have already studied in the chapter on Whole Numbers, in a general way, by using variables a, b and c.

Sol. According to the question,

Sum of three numbers 14, 27 and 13 can be found in two ways,

(a) $(14 + 27) + 13 = 41 + 13 = 54$

(b) $(27 + 13) + 14 = 40 + 14 = 54$ or $14 + (27 + 13) = 54$

    Thus, $(14 + 27) + 13 = 14 + (27 + 13) = 54$

By using variables, we can write this property of numbers also in general way. Let a, b and c be three numbers each of which can take any numerical value. Then, $(a + b) + c = a + (b + c)$

This property is called an **associativity of addition** of numbers.

Exercise 11.3

Que 1. Make up as many expressions with numbers (no variables) as you can from three numbers 5, 7 and 8. Every number should be used not more than once. Use only addition, subtraction and multiplication.

(**Hints** Three possible expressions are $5 + (8 - 7)$, $5 - (8 - 7)$, $(5 \times 8) + 7$, make the other expressions.)

Sol. The possible expressions formed by three numbers 5, 7 and 8 are

$$5 + (8 - 7), 5 - (8 - 7), (5 \times 8) + 7, (5 + 8) + 7,$$
$$5 - (8 \times 7), (5 + 8) - 7, (5 \times 8) - 7, 8 \times (7 + 5) \text{ etc.}$$

Que 2. Which out of the following are expressions with numbers only?

(a) $y + 3$ (b) $(7 \times 20) - 8z$

(c) $5(21 - 7) + 7 \times 2$ (d) 5

(e) $3x$ (f) $5 - 5n$

(g) $(7 \times 20) - (5 \times 10) - 45 + p$

Sol. (a) $y + 3$, Here, variable y is present. So, it is not an expression with numbers only.

(b) $(7 \times 20) - 8z$, Here, variable z is present. So, it is not an expression with numbers only.

(c) $5(21 - 7) + 7 \times 2$, Here, no variable is present. So, it is an expression with numbers only.

(d) 5, Here, no variable is present. So, it is an expression with number only.

(e) $3x$, Here, variable x is present. So, it is not an expression with numbers only.

(f) $5 - 5n$, Here, variable n is present. So, it is not an expression with numbers only.

(g) $(7 \times 20) - (5 \times 10) - 45 + p$, Here, variable p is present. So, it is not an expression with numbers only.

From above it is clear that (c) and (d) are expressions with numbers only.

Que 3. Identify the operations (addition, subtraction, division, multiplication) in forming the following expressions and tell how the expressions have been formed.

(a) $z + 1, z - 1, y + 17, y - 17$ (b) $17y, \dfrac{y}{17}, 5z$

(c) $2y + 17, 2y - 17$ (d) $7m, -7m + 3, -7m - 3$

Sol. (a) (i) $z + 1$, Here, operation is addition and expression is formed by adding 1 to z.

(ii) $z - 1$, Here, operation is subtraction and expression is formed by subtracting 1 from z.

(iii) $y + 17$, Here, operation is addition and expression is formed by adding 17 to y.

(iv) $y - 17$, Here, operation is subtraction and expression is formed by subtracting 17 from y.

(b) (i) $17y$, Here, operation is multiplication and expression is formed by multiplying y by 17.

(ii) $\dfrac{y}{17}$, Here, operation is division and expression is formed by dividing y by 17.

(iii) $5z$, Here, operation is multiplication and expression is formed by multiplying z by 5.

(c) (i) $2y + 17$, Here, operation is multiplication and addition and to form an expression firstly 2 is multiplied by y and then 17 is added to $2y$.

(ii) $2y - 17$, Here, operation is multiplication and subtraction and to form an expression, firstly y is multiplied by 2 and then 17 is subtracted from $2y$.

(d) (i) $7m$, Here, operation is multiplication and expression is formed on multiplying m by 7.

(ii) $-7m + 3$, Here, operation is multiplication and addition and, to form an expression, firstly m is multiplied by (-7) and then 3 is added to $-7m$.

(iii) $-7m - 3$, Here, operation is multiplication and subtraction and to form an expression, firstly m is multiplied by (-7) and then is 3 subtracted from $-7m$.

Que 4. Give expressions for the following cases.

(a) 7 added to p

(b) 7 subtracted from p

(c) p multiplied by 7

(d) p divided by 7

(e) 7 subtracted from $-m$

(f) $-p$ multiplied by 5

(g) $-p$ divided by 5

(h) p multiplied by -5

Sol. (a) When 7 is added to p, then expression is $p + 7$.

(b) When 7 is subtracted from p, then expression is $p - 7$.

(c) When p is multiplied by 7, then expression is $7 \times p = 7p$

(d) When p is divided by 7, then expression is $\dfrac{p}{7}$.

(e) When 7 is subtracted from $-m$, then expression is $-m - 7$.

(f) When $-p$ is multiplied by 5, then expression is $-p \times 5 = -5p$.

(g) When $-p$ is divided by 5, then expression is $\dfrac{-p}{5}$.

(h) When p is multiplied by -5, then expression is $p \times -5 = -5p$.

Que 5. Give expressions in the following cases.

(a) 11 added to $2m$

(b) 11 subtracted from $2m$

(c) 5 times y to which 3 is added

(d) 5 times y from which 3 is subtracted

(e) y is multiplied by -8

(f) y is multiplied by -8 and then 5 is added to the result

(g) y is multiplied by 5 and the result is subtracted from 16

(h) y is multiplied by -5 and the result is added to 16.

Sol (a) When 11 is added to $2m$, then expression is $2m + 11$.

   (b) When 11 is subtracted from $2m$, then expression is $2m - 11$.

   (c) 5 times of y is $5y$, when 3 added to $5y$, then expression is $5y + 3$.

   (d) 5 times of y is $5y$, when 3 is subtracted from $5y$, then expression is $5y - 3$.

   (e) When y is multiplied by -8, then expression is $-8y$.

   (f) When y is multiplied by -8, then result is $-8y$ and then 5 is added to it, then expression will be $-8y + 5$.

   (g) When y is multiplied by 5, then result is $5y$ and then this result is subtracted from 16, then expression will be $16 - 5y$.

   (h) When y is multiplied by -5, then result is $-5y$ and then this result is added to 16, then expression will be $-5y + 16$.

Que 6. (a) Form expressions using t and 4. Use not more than one number operation. Every expression must have t in it.

   (b) Form expression using y, 2 and 7. Every expression must have y in it. Use only two number operations. These should be different.

Sol. (a) By using only one number operation, we can form the following expressions $t + 4$, $t - 4$, $4t$, $\dfrac{t}{4}$, $\dfrac{4}{t}$, $4 - t$, $4 + t$, etc.

   (b) By using only two number operations, we can form following expressions by using y, 2 and 7

$$2y + 7, 2y - 7, 7y + 2, 7y - 2,$$
$$\dfrac{y}{2} + 7, \dfrac{y}{2} - 7, \dfrac{y}{7} + 2, \dfrac{y}{7} - 2, \text{ etc.}$$

All these expressions are different.

Exercise 11.4

Answer the following.

Que 1. (a) Take Sarita's present age to be y years.

   (i) What will be her age 5 years from now?

   (ii) What was her age 3 years back?

   (iii) Sarita's grandfather is 6 times her age. What is the age of her grandfather?

   (iv) Grandmother is 2 years younger than grandfather. What is grandmother's age?

   (v) Sarita's father's age is 5 years more than 3 times Sarita's age. What is her father's age?

Sol. Let Sarita's present age = y yr

   (i) Sarita's age after 5 yr from now = $(y + 5)$ yr

  (ii) Sarita's age 3 yr back = $(y - 3)$ yr

 (iii) Given, Sarita's grandfather is 6 times of her age

     So, Sarita's grandfather age = 6 × Sarita's present age

$$= 6 \times y = 6y \text{ yr}$$

 (iv) Given, grandmother is 2 yr younger than grandfather.

     Age of grandfather = $6y$ yr   [from (iii)]

     ∴ Age of grandmother = [Grandfather's age – 2] yr

$$= (6y - 2) \text{ yr}$$

  (v) Given, Sarita's father's age is 5 yr more than 3 times Sarita's age.

     Sarita's present age = y yr

     3 times of Sarita's age = $3y$ yr

     ∴ Sarita's father age = 3 × Sarita's age + 5

$$= (3y + 5) \text{ yr}$$

Que 1. (b) The length of a rectangular hall is 4 meters less than 3 times the breadth of the hall. What is the length, if the breadth is b meters?

Sol. Given, the breadth of the hall = b m

   Now, according to the question,

   Length of hall = 4 m less than 3 times the breadth of the hall

$$= (3 \times \text{breadth of hall}) - 4$$
$$= (3 \times b - 4) \text{ m}$$
$$= (3b - 4) \text{ m}$$

   Hence, if breadth is b m, then length of hall is $(3b - 4)$ m.

Que 1. (c) A rectangular box has height h cm. Its length is 5 times the height and breadth is 10 cm less than the length. Express the length and the breadth of the box in terms of the height.

Sol. Given, the height of a rectangular box = h cm

   According to the question,

        Length of the box = 5 times the height

$$= 5h \text{ cm}$$

  and breadth of the box = 10 cm less than the length

$$= 10 \text{ cm less than } 5h$$
$$= (5h - 10) \text{ cm}$$

Que 1. (d) Meena, Beena and Leena are climbing the steps to the hill top. Meena is at step s, Beena is 8 steps ahead and Leena 7 steps behind. Where are Beena and Meena? The total number of steps to the hill top is 10 less than 4 times what Meena has reached. Express the total number of steps using s.

Sol. Given, the Meena is at step $= s$

Also, Beena is 8 steps ahead.

∴ Beena is at step $= s + 8$

and Leena is 7 steps behind

∴Leena is at step $= s - 7$

Now, total number of steps $= 10$ less than 4 times Meena's steps
$$= 4 \times \text{Meena's steps} - 10 = 4s - 10$$

Hence, total number of steps using s can be expressed as $(4s - 10)$.

Que 1. (e) A bus travels at v km per hour. It is going from Daspur to Beespur. After the bus has travelled 5 hours, Beespur is still 20 km away. What is the distance from Daspur to Beespur? Express it using v.

Sol. Given, speed of the bus $= v$ km/h

i.e. Distance travelled by bus in 1 h $= v$ km

∴Distance travelled by bus is 5 h from Daspur $= 5v$ km

After travelling 5 hours, Beespur is still 20 km away.

So, total distance from Daspur to Beespur $= (5v + 20)$ km.

Hence, distance from Daspur to Beespur in terms of v can be expressed as $(5v + 20)$ km.

Que 2. Change the following statements using expressions into statements in ordinary language.

(For Example, Given Salim scores r runs in a cricket match, Nalin scores $(r + 15)$ runs. In ordinary language–Nalin scores 15 runs more than Salim).

(a) A notebook costs ₹ p. A book costs ₹ $3p$.

(b) Tony puts q marbles on the table. He has $8q$ marbles in his box.

(c) Our class has n students. The school has $20n$ students.

(d) Jaggu is z years old. His uncle is $4z$ years old and his aunt is $(4z - 3)$ years old.

(e) In an arrangement of dots, there are r rows. Each row contains 5 dots.

Sol. (a) A book costs three times the cost of a notebook.

(b) Tony's box contains 8 times the marbles on the table.

(c) Total number of students in the school is 20 times that of our class.

(d) Jaggu's uncle is 4 times older than Jaggu and Jaggu's aunt is 3 yr younger than his uncle.

(e) The total number of dots in an arrangement is 5 times the number of rows.

Que 3. Answer the following.

(a) Given Munnu's age to be x years, can you guess what $(x - 2)$ may show?

(**Hint** Think of Munnu's younger brother).

Can you guess what $(x + 4)$ may show? What $(3x + 7)$ may show?

(b) Given Sara's age today to be y years. Think of her age in the future or in the past. What will the following expression indicate?

$$y + 7,\ y - 3,\ y + 4\frac{1}{2},\ y - 2\frac{1}{2}$$

(c) Given n students in the class like football, what may $2n$ show? What may $n/2$ show?

(**Hint** Think of games other than football).

Sol. (a) Given, Munnu's age $= x$ yr

Then, $(x - 2)$ may Munnu's younger brother or sister's age.

$(x + 4)$ may show Munnu's elder brother or sister's age and $(3x + 7)$ may show the age of Munnu's father or mother.

(b) Given, Sara's present age $= y$ yr.

Then, $(y + 7)$ shows Sara's age after 7 yr from now,

$(y - 3)$ shows Sara's age 3 yr back.

$\left(y + 4\dfrac{1}{2}\right)$ shows Sara's age after $4\dfrac{1}{2}$ yr from now,

$\left(y - 2\dfrac{1}{2}\right)$, shows Sara's age $2\dfrac{1}{2}$ yr back.

(c) Given, number of students like football $= n$

Now, $2n$ may show the number of students who like cricket

and $\dfrac{n}{2}$ may show the number of students who like hockey.

Exercise 11.5

Que 1. State which of the following are equations (with a variable). Give reason for your answer. Identify the variable from the equations with a variable.

(a) $17 = x + 7$

(b) $(t - 7) > 5$

(c) $\dfrac{4}{2} = 2$

(d) $(7 \times 3) - 19 = 8$

(e) $5 \times 4 - 8 = 2x$

(f) $x - 2 = 0$

(g) $2m < 30$

(h) $2n + 1 = 11$

(i) $7 = (11 \times 5) - (12 \times 4)$

(j) $7 = (11 \times 2) + p$

(k) $20 = 5y$

(l) $\dfrac{3q}{2} < 5$

(m) $z + 12 > 24$

(n) $20 - (10 - 5) = 3 \times 5$

(o) $7 - x = 5$

Sol. (a) $17 = x + 7$, It is an equation with variable x, since it has an equal sign.

(b) $(t - 7) > 5$, It is not an equation because it has greater than sign (>).

(c) $\dfrac{4}{2} = 2$, It is an equation with numbers, since it has an equal sign and has no variable.

(d) $(7 \times 3) - 19 = 8$, It is an equation with numbers, since it has an equal sign and has no variable.

(e) $5 \times 4 - 8 = 2x$, It is an equation with variable x, since it has an equal sign.

(f) $x - 2 = 0$, It is an equation with variable x, since it has an equal sign.

(g) $2m < 30$, It is not an equation because it has less than sign (<).

(h) $2n + 1 = 11$, It is an equation with variable n, since it has an equal sign.

(i) $7 = (11 \times 5) - (12 \times 4)$, It is an equation with numbers, since it has an equal sign.

(j) $7 = (11 \times 2) + p$, It is an equation with variable p, since it has an equal sign.

(k) $20 = 5y$, It is an equation with variable y, since it has an equal sign.

(l) $\dfrac{3q}{2} < 5$, It is not an equation because it has less than sign (<).

(m) $z + 12 > 24$, It is not an equation because it has greater than sign (>).

(n) $20 - (10 - 5) = 3 \times 5$, It is an equation with numbers, since it has an equal sign.

(o) $7 - x = 5$, It is an equation with variable x, since it has an equal sign.

Que 2. Complete the entries in the third column of the table.

S. No.	Equation	Value of variable	Equation satisfied Yes/No
(a)	$10y = 80$	$y = 10$	
(b)	$10y = 80$	$y = 8$	
(c)	$10y = 80$	$y = 5$	
(d)	$4l = 20$	$l = 20$	
(e)	$4l = 20$	$l = 80$	
(f)	$4l = 20$	$l = 5$	
(g)	$b + 5 = 9$	$b = 5$	
(h)	$b + 5 = 9$	$b = 9$	
(i)	$b + 5 = 9$	$b = 4$	
(j)	$h - 8 = 5$	$h = 13$	
(k)	$h - 8 = 5$	$h = 8$	
(l)	$h - 8 = 5$	$h = 0$	
(m)	$p + 3 = 1$	$p = 3$	
(n)	$p + 3 = 1$	$p = 1$	
(o)	$p + 3 = 1$	$p = 0$	
(p)	$p + 3 = 1$	$p = -1$	
(q)	$p + 3 = 1$	$p = -2$	

TIPS

Firstly, put the given value of variable in LHS of given equation and simplify. If value of LHS is equal to RHS, then that value of variable will satisfy the equation otherwise not.

Sol.

S. No.	Equation	Value of variable	Equation satisfied Yes/No
(a)	$10y = 80$	$y = 10$	No, on putting $y = 10$ in LHS of equation $10y = 80$, we get LHS $= 10 \times 10 = 100 \neq 80$ i.e. LHS $\neq$ RHS
(b)	$10y = 80$	$y = 8$	Yes, on putting $y = 8$ in LHS of equation $10y = 80$, we get LHS $= 10 \times 8 = 80 = 80$ i.e. LHS $=$ RHS

S. No.	Equation	Value of variable	Equation satisfied Yes/No
(c)	$10y = 80$	$y = 5$	No, on putting $y = 5$ in LHS of equation $10y = 80$, we get LHS $= 10 \times 5 = 50 \neq 80$ i.e. LHS $\neq$ RHS
(d)	$4l = 20$	$l = 20$	No, on putting $l = 20$ in LHS of equation $4l = 20$, we get LHS $= 4 \times 20 = 80 \neq 20$ i.e. LHS $\neq$ RHS
(e)	$4l = 20$	$l = 80$	No, on putting $l = 80$ in LHS of equation $4l = 20$, we get LHS $= 4 \times 80 = 320 \neq 20$ i.e. LHS = RHS
(f)	$4l = 20$	$l = 5$	Yes, on putting $l = 5$ in LHS of equation $4l = 20$, we get LHS $= 4 \times 5 = 20 = 20$ i.e. LHS = RHS
(g)	$b + 5 = 9$	$b = 5$	No, on putting $b = 5$ in LHS of equation $b + 5 = 9$, we get LHS $= 5 + 5 = 10 \neq 9$ i.e. LHS = RHS
(h)	$b + 5 = 9$	$b = 9$	No, on putting $b = 9$ in LHS of equation $b + 5 = 9$, we get LHS $= 9 + 5 = 14 \neq 9$ i.e. LHS $\neq$ RHS
(i)	$b + 5 = 9$	$b = 4$	Yes, on putting $b = 4$ in LHS of equation $b + 5 = 9$, we get LHS $= 4 + 5 = 9 = 9$ i.e. LHS = RHS
(j)	$h - 8 = 5$	$h = 13$	Yes, on putting $h = 13$ in LHS of equation $h - 8 = 5$, we get LHS $= 13 - 8 = 5 = 5$ i.e. LHS = RHS
(k)	$h - 8 = 5$	$h = 8$	No, on putting $h = 8$ in LHS of equation $h - 8 = 5$, we get LHS $= 8 - 8 = 0 \neq 5$ i.e. LHS $\neq$ RHS
(l)	$h - 8 = 5$	$h = 0$	No, on putting $h = 0$ in LHS of equation $h - 8 = 5$, we get LHS $= 0 - 8 = -8 - 8 \neq 5$ i.e. LHS $\neq$ RHS
(m)	$p + 3 = 1$	$p = 3$	No, on putting $p = 3$ in LHS of equation $p + 3 = 1$, we get LHS $= 3 + 3 = 6 \neq 1$ i.e. LHS $\neq$ RHS
(n)	$p + 3 = 1$	$p = 1$	No, on putting $p = 1$ in LHS of equation $p + 3 = 1$, we get LHS $= 1 + 3 = 4 \neq 1$ i.e. LHS $\neq$ RHS
(o)	$p + 3 = 1$	$p = 0$	No, on putting $p = 0$ in LHS of equation $p + 3 = 1$, we get LHS $= 0 + 3 = 3 \neq 1$ i.e. LHS $\neq$ RHS

S. No.	Equation	Value of variable	Equation satisfied Yes/No
(p)	$p + 3 = 1$	$p = -1$	No, on putting $p = -1$ in LHS of equation $p + 3 = 1$, we get LHS $= -1 + 3 = 2 \neq 1$ i.e. LHS $\neq$ RHS
(q)	$p + 3 = 1$	$p = -2$	Yes, on putting $p = -2$ in LHS of equation $p + 3 = 1$, we get LHS $= -2 + 3 = 1$ i.e. LHS $\neq$ RHS

Que 3. Pick out the solution from the values given in the bracket next to each equation. Show that the other values do not satisfy the equation.

(a) $5m = 60$ (10, 5, 12, 15)
(b) $n + 12 = 20$ (12, 8, 20, 0)
(c) $p - 5 = 5$ (0, 10, 5, − 5)
(d) $\dfrac{q}{2} = 7$ (7, 2, 10, 14)
(e) $r - 4 = 0$ (4, − 4, 8, 0)
(f) $x + 4 = 2$ (−2, 0, 2, 4)

TIPS

Firstly, write the LHS and RHS of given equation. Then, put given values one by one in LHS. If value of LHS is equal to RHS, then that value of variable is the solution of given equation otherwise not.

Sol. (a) Given, equation is $5m = 60$
     Here,   LHS $= 5\,m$ and RHS $= 60$
     Now, for $m = 10$,   LHS $= 5 \times 10 = 50 \neq$ RHS
     So, $m = 10$ does not satisfy the equation.
     For $m = 5$,
                      LHS $= 5 \times 5 = 25 \neq$ RHS
     So, $m = 5$ does not satisfy the equation.
     For $m = 12$ LHS $= 5 \times 12 = 60 =$ RHS
     So, $m = 12$ is the solution of given equation.
     For $m = 15$,   LHS $= 5 \times 15 = 75 \neq$ RHS
     So, $m = 15$ does not satisfy the equation.
     Hence, 12 is a solution of equation $5m = 60$.
  (b) Given, equation is $n + 12 = 20$
     Here,   LHS $= n + 12$ and RHS $= 20$
     Now, for $n = 12$ LHS $= 12 + 12 = 24 \neq$ RHS
     So, $n = 12$ does not satisfy the equation.
     For $n = 8$,   LHS $= 8 + 12 = 20 =$ RHS

So, $n = 8$ is the solution of given equation.

Now, for $n = 20$,   LHS $= 20 + 12 = 32 \neq$ RHS

So, $n = 20$ does not satisfy the equation.

For $n = 0$,   LHS $= 0 + 12 = 12 \neq$ RHS

So, $n = 0$ does not satisfy the equation.

Hence, $n = 8$ is a solution of equation $n + 12 = 20$.

(c) Given, equation is $p - 5 = 5$

Here, LHS $= p - 5$ and RHS $= 5$

Now, for $p = 0$,   LHS $= 0 - 5 = -5 \neq$ RHS

So, $p = 0$ does not satisfy the equation.

For $p = 10$,   LHS $= 10 - 5 = 5 =$ RHS

So, $p = 10$ is the solution of given equation.

Now, for $p = 5$,   LHS $= 5 - 5 = 0 \neq$ RHS

So, $p = 5$ does not satisfy the equation.

Now, for $p = -5$,   LHS $= -5 - 5 = -10 \neq$ RHS

So, $p = -5$ does not satisfy the equation.

Hence, $p = 10$ is a solution of equation $p - 5 = 5$.

(d) Given equation is $\dfrac{q}{2} = 7$.

Here,   LHS $= \dfrac{q}{2}$ and RHS $= 7$

Now, for $q = 7$,   LHS $= \dfrac{7}{2} = 3\dfrac{1}{2} \neq$ RHS

So, $q = 7$ does not satisfy the equation.

Now, for $q = 2$,   LHS $= \dfrac{2}{2} = 1 \neq$ RHS

So, $q = 2$ does not satisfy the equation.

Now, for $q = 10$,   LHS $= \dfrac{10}{2} = 5 \neq$ RHS

So, $q = 10$ does not satisfy the equation.

For $q = 14$,   LHS $= \dfrac{14}{2} = 7 =$ RHS

So, $q = 14$ is the solution of given equation.

Hence, $q = 14$ is a solution of equation $\dfrac{q}{2} = 7$.

(e) Given equation is $r - 4 = 0$

Here,   LHS $= r - 4$ and RHS $= 0$

Now, for $r = 4$,   LHS $= 4 - 4 = 0 =$ RHS

So, $r = 4$ is the solution of given equation.

Now, for $r = -4$,   LHS $= -4 - 4 = -8 \neq$ RHS

So, $r = -4$ does not satisfy the equation.

Now, for $r = 8$, LHS $= 8 - 4 = 4 \neq$ RHS

So, $r = 8$ does not satisfy the equation.

Now, for $r = 0$, LHS $= 0 - 4 = -4 \neq$ RHS

So, $r = 0$ does not satisfy the equation.

Hence, $r = 4$ is a solution of equation $r - 4 = 0$.

(f) Given equation is $x + 4 = 2$

Here, LHS $= x + 4$ and RHS $= 2$

Now, for $x = -2$, LHS $= -2 + 4 = 2 =$ RHS

So, $x = -2$ is the solution of given equation.

Now, for $x = 0$, LHS $= 0 + 4 = 4 \neq$ RHS

So, does not satisfy the equation.

Now, for $x = 2$, LHS $= 2 + 4 = 6 \neq$ RHS

So, does not satisfy the equation.

Now, for $x = 4$, LHS $= 4 + 4 = 8 \neq$ RHS

So, $x = 4$ does not satisfy the equation.

Hence, $x = -2$ is a solution of equation $x + 4 = 2$.

Que 4. (a) Complete the table and by inspection of the table, find the solution to the equation $m + 10 = 16$.

m	1	2	3	4	5	6	7	8	9	10	—	—	—	—
$m + 10$	—	—	—	—	—	—	—	—	—	—	—	—	—	—

(b) Complete the table and by inspection of the table, find the solution to the equation $5t = 35$.

t	3	4	5	6	7	8	9	10	11	—	—	—	—	—
$5t$	—	—	—	—	—	—	—	—	—	—	—	—	—	—

(c) Complete the table and find the solution of the equation $z/3 = 4$ using the table.

z	8	9	10	11	12	13	14	15	16	—	—	—	—
$\dfrac{z}{3}$	$2\dfrac{2}{3}$	3	$3\dfrac{1}{3}$	—	—	—	—	—	—	—	—	—	—

(d) Complete the table and find the solution to the equation $m - 7 = 3$.

m	5	6	7	8	9	10	11	12	13	—	—
$m - 7$	—	—	—	—	—	—	—	—	—	—	—

Sol. (a) The complete table is shown below

m	$m + 10$
1	$1 + 10 = 11$
2	$2 + 10 = 12$
3	$3 + 10 = 13$
4	$4 + 10 = 14$
5	$5 + 10 = 15$
6	$6 + 10 = 16$
7	$7 + 10 = 17$
8	$8 + 10 = 18$
9	$9 + 10 = 19$
10	$10 + 10 = 20$
11	$11 + 10 = 21$
12	$12 + 10 = 22$
13	$13 + 10 = 23$

By inspection of the above table, we see that $m = 6$ satisfies the equation $m + 10 = 16$.   [$\because$ at $m = 6$, LHS = RHS]

Hence, $m = 6$ is its solution.

(b) The complete table is shown below

t	$5t$
3	$5 \times 3 = 15$
4	$5 \times 4 = 20$
5	$5 \times 5 = 25$
6	$5 \times 6 = 30$
7	$5 \times 7 = 35$
8	$5 \times 8 = 40$
9	$5 \times 9 = 45$
10	$5 \times 10 = 50$
11	$5 \times 11 = 55$
12	$5 \times 12 = 60$
13	$5 \times 13 = 65$
14	$5 \times 14 = 70$
15	$5 \times 15 = 75$
16	$5 \times 16 = 80$

By inspection of the above table, we find that $t = 7$ satisfies the equation $5t = 35$.   [$\because$ at $t = 7$, LHS = RHS]

Hence, $t = 7$ is its solution.

(c) The complete table is shown below

z	$\dfrac{z}{3}$
8	$\dfrac{8}{3} = 2\dfrac{2}{3}$
9	$\dfrac{9}{3} = 3$
10	$\dfrac{10}{3} = 3\dfrac{1}{3}$
11	$\dfrac{11}{3} = 3\dfrac{2}{3}$
12	$\dfrac{12}{3} = 4$
13	$\dfrac{13}{3} = 4\dfrac{1}{3}$
14	$\dfrac{14}{3} = 4\dfrac{2}{3}$
15	$\dfrac{15}{3} = 5$
16	$\dfrac{16}{3} = 5\dfrac{1}{3}$
17	$\dfrac{17}{3} = 5\dfrac{2}{3}$
18	$\dfrac{18}{3} = 6$
19	$\dfrac{19}{3} = 6\dfrac{1}{3}$
20	$\dfrac{20}{3} = 6\dfrac{2}{3}$

By inspection of the above table, we find that $t = 12$ satisfies the equation $\dfrac{z}{3} = 4$. 　　　　　[$\because$ at $t = 12$, LHS = RHS]

Hence, $z = 12$ is its solution.

(d) The complete table is shown below

m	$m - 7$
5	$5 - 7 = -2$
6	$6 - 7 = -1$
7	$7 - 7 = 0$
8	$8 - 7 = 1$
9	$9 - 7 = 2$
10	$10 - 7 = 3$
11	$11 - 7 = 4$
12	$12 - 7 = 5$
13	$13 - 7 = 6$
14	$14 - 7 = 7$
15	$15 - 7 = 8$

By inspection of the above table, we find that $m = 10$ satisfies the equation $m - 7 = 3$. 　　　　　　　[∵ at $m = 10$, LHS = RHS]

Hence, $m = 10$ is its solution.

Que 5. Solve the following riddles, you may yourself construct such riddles.

Who am I ?

  (i) Go round a square

     Counting every corner

     Thrice and no more!

     Add the count to me

     To get exactly thirty four!

 (ii) For each day of the week

     make an upcount from me

     If you make no mistake

     You will get twenty three!

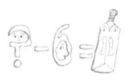

(iii) I am a special number

     Take away from me a six!

     A whole cricket team

     You will still be able to fix!

 (iv) Tell me who I am

     I shall give a pretty clue!

     You will get me back

     If you take me out of twenty two!

Sol. (i) Let I be denoted by x.

We know that a square has 4 corners and each corner is counted thrice.

∴ Total number of corners $= 4 \times 3 = 12$

By given condition, my self + total number of corners

$\Rightarrow$ 　　　　　　　　　$x + 12 = 34$

Now, 　　　　　　　$x = 34 - 12 = 22$ 　　$\Rightarrow$ 　　$x = 22$

By inspection, we have 　$22 + 12 = 34$

Thus, I am 22.

(ii) Let I be denoted by x. There are 7 days in a week.

By given condition upcounting from x for 7, we get the sum $= 23$

i.e. 　　　　　　　$x + 7 = 23$

Now, 　　　　　　　$x = 23 - 7 = 16$ 　$\Rightarrow$ 　　$x = 16$

By inspection, we have $16 + 7 = 23$

Thus, I am 16.

(iii) Let the special number = x

Then, as per given condition take away 6 from x = whole cricket team i.e. $x - 6 = 11$

In cricket team, number of players = 11

Now, $x = 11 + 6 = 17$ $\Rightarrow$ $x = 17$

By inspection, we have $17 - 6 = 11$

Thus, the special number is 17.

(iv) Let I be denoted by x.

By given condition, take x out of $22 = x$

$\Rightarrow$ $22 - x = x$ $\Rightarrow x + x = 22$

$\Rightarrow$ $2x = 22$ $\Rightarrow$ $x = 11$

By inspection, we have $2 \times 11 = 22$

Thus, I am 11.

Selected **NCERT Exemplar Problems**

Directions *In questions 1 to 10, out of the four options, only one is correct. Write the correct answer.*

Que 1. If each match box contains 50 matchsticks, the number of matchsticks required to fill n such boxes is

(a) $50 + n$ (b) $50n$ (c) $50 \div n$ (d) $50 - n$

Sol. $\because$ One match box contains 50 matchsticks,

Then, required matchsticks to fill match box = $50 \times n = 50n$

Hence, option (b) is correct answer.

Que 2. Amulya is x yr of age now. 5 yr ago her age was

(a) $(5 - x)$ yr   (b) $(5 + x)$ yr

(c) $(x - 5)$ yr   (d) $(5 \div x)$ yr

Sol. Amulya's age now = x yr

$\therefore$ 5 yr ago her age was = $(x - 5)$ yr

[$\because$ 5 yr ago age was given by subtracting age now to 5 yr ago age]

Hence, option (c) is correct answer.

Que 3. In algebra, $a\ b$ means ab, but in arithmetic 3 5 is

(a) 35   (b) 53   (c) 15   (d) 8

Sol. By algebra, $a\ b$ means ab [multiplying a by b is ab]

By multiplication rule in arithmetic,

$35 = 3 \times 5$ [here, $a = 3$ and $b = 5$, then applying $a\ b = ab$]

$= 15$

Hence, option (c) is correct answer.

Que 4. Which of the following equation has $x = 2$ as a solution?

    (a) $x + 2 = 5$ (b) $x - 2 = 0$

    (c) $2x + 1 = 0$ (d) $x + 3 = 6$

Sol. To get solution as $x = 2$, solve each equation

    (a) $x + 2 = 5$ $\Rightarrow$ $x = 5 - 2 = 3$

    (b) $x - 2 = 0$ $\Rightarrow$ $x = 0 + 2$ $\Rightarrow$ $x = 2$

    (c) $2x + 1 = 0$ $\Rightarrow$ $2x = -1$ $\Rightarrow$ $x = -\dfrac{1}{2}$

    (d) $x + 3 = 6$ $\Rightarrow$ $x = 6 - 3 = 3$

    Therefore, we get $x = 2$ in option (b).

    Hence, option (b) is correct answer.

Que 5. Savitri has a sum of ₹x. She spent ₹1000 on grocery, ₹500 on clothes and ₹400 on education, and received ₹200 as a gift. How much money (in ₹) is left with her?

    (a) $x - 1700$ (b) $x - 1900$

    (c) $x + 200$ (d) $x - 2100$

Sol. Savitri has a total sum $= ₹\,x$

    Total money spents = [Grocery + Clothes + Education]

                    $= ₹\,(1000 + 500 + 400) = ₹\,1900$

    After that she received a gift $= ₹\,200$

    Then, money left with her = [Sum of money + Received gift

                                           – total spent money]

                   $= (x + 200 - 1900)$

                   $= (x - 1700)$

    Hence, option (a) is correct answer.

Que 6. If the perimeter of a regular hexagon is x m, then the length of each of its sides is

    (a) $(x + 6)$ m   (b) $(x \div 6)$ m

    (c) $(x - 6)$ m   (d) $(6 \div x)$ m

Sol. Given, perimeter of regular hexagon $= x$ m

    Sides in a regular hexagon $= 6$

    $\because$ Perimeter of regular hexagon $= 6 \times$ Each side of regular hexagon

    i.e. $x = 6 \times$ Each side of regular hexagon

    $\therefore$ Each side of regular hexagon $= \dfrac{x}{6}$ or $x \div 6$

    Hence, option (b) is correct answer.

Que 7. $\dfrac{4}{2}$ denotes a

    (a) numerical equation   (b) algebraic expression
    (c) equation with a variable   (d) false statement

Sol. $\dfrac{4}{2} = 2$ denotes a numerical equation,

Hence, option (a) is correct.

Que 8. I think of a number and on adding 13 to it, I get 27. The equation for this is

    (a) $x - 27 = 13$ (b) $x - 13 = 27$
    (c) $x + 27 = 13$ (d) $x + 13 = 27$

Sol. Let the number be x.

According to the question,
13 is added to the number $= x + 13$
After adding that equation is equals to 27.
Hence, $x + 13 = 27$
Hence, option (d) is correct answer.

Que 9. Kanta has p pencils in her box. She puts q more pencils in the box. The total number of pencils with her are

    (a) $p + q$ (b) pq (c) $p - q$ (d) $\dfrac{p}{q}$

Sol. Given,

Kanta's box has pencils $= p$
Then, she puts some pencils in the box $= q$
Hence, total number of pencils in the box will be given by adding property $=$ [before putting pencil + after putting pencils] $= p + q$
Hence, option (a) is correct answer.

Que 10. The two digit number whose ten's digit is 't' and units's digit is 'u' is _____.

Sol. Given, unit place digit $= u$ and ten's place digit $= t$

So, the two digit number $= 10t + 4$

Que 11. $x = 5$ is the solution of the equation $3x + 2 = 20$ is true or false?

Sol. Given equation, $3x + 2 = 20$ $\Rightarrow$ $3x = 20 - 2$

                             $3x = 18$ $\Rightarrow$ $x = \dfrac{18}{3}$ [by deviation rule]

                             $x = 6$

Hence, solution of x is false.

Que 12. The equations $x + 1 = 0$ and $2x + 2 = 0$ have the same solution is true or false.

Sol. For getting answer, we have to solve both equations.

Given, equations are $x + 1 = 0$ and $2x + 2 = 0$

$$x + 1 = 0 \quad \Rightarrow \quad x = -1 \qquad \text{[by transposing rule]}$$

$$\text{and} \quad 2x + 2 = 0 \quad \Rightarrow \quad 2x = -2 \qquad \text{[by transposing rule]}$$

$$x = -\frac{2}{2} = -1 \qquad \text{[by dividation rule]}$$

Hence, it is true that both equations have same solution.

Que 13. The additive inverse of an integer x is $2x$ is true or false.

Sol. Given, integer $= x$

Let 2 is added to the given integer

Then, the expression $= x + 2$

But in equation additive property gives $2x$.

Hence, the equation is false.

Que 14. One third of a number added to itself gives 8, can be expressed as $\frac{x}{3} + 8 = x$ is true or false.

Sol. Let the number be x.

According to the question,

One-third of the number $= \frac{x}{3}$

After that it is added to itself, i.e. $x + \frac{x}{3}$

And this equation is equal to 8.

Hence, the equation is $x + \frac{x}{3} = 8$

But the given equation is $\frac{x}{3} + 8 = x$

So, the given equation is false.

Que 15. One more than twice the number. Give corresponding expression.

Sol. Let the number be x.

Twice of the number $= 2x$ [given]

After that, $2x$ is add by 1 to get another number, which is more than that number.

Then, expression $= 2x + 1$

Que 16. Area of the rectangle with length k units and breadth n units. Give corresponding expressions.

Sol. Given, the length of rectangle = k units

and breadth of the rectangle = n units

∵ Area of the rectangle = Length × Breadth = $k \times n$ = kn

Hence, the expression is kn.

Que 17. Write two equations for which 2 is the solution. Give corresponding expressions.

Sol. Let the two numbers be x and y, which has solution 2 in equation.

(i) For getting first equation, the number x is multiplied by 2, then the number is $2x$. After that it, 3 is subtracted from it which results into 1.

Hence, we have $2x - 3 = 1$

On solving $2x = 3 + 1 \quad \Rightarrow \quad 2x = 4 \Rightarrow x = 2$

(ii) For getting second equation, the number y is multiplied by 3, then the number is $3y$. After that it will be added by 4 and equal to 10.

Hence, we have, $3y + 4 = 10$

On solving, $\quad 3y = 10 - 4 \quad \Rightarrow \quad 3y = 6 \quad \Rightarrow \quad y = 2$

Hence, both equations are $2x - 3 = 1$ and $3y + 4 = 10$.

Que 18. On my last birthday. I weighed 40 kg. If I put on m kg of weight after a year, what is my present weight?

Sol. According to the question,

Weight on last birthday = 40 kg

After a year, putting weight = m kg

Then, present weight = [weight on last birthday + after a year weight]

$$= (40 + m) \text{ kg}$$

Que 19. If m is a whole number less than 5, complete the table and by inspection of the table, find the solution of the equation $2m - 5 = -1$.

m				
$2m - 5$				

Sol. Given, m is a whole number which is less than 5, then solution of the equation is given by putting value of m in the table.

When $m = 0$, $\quad 2m - 5 = 2(0) - 5 = -5 \quad \Rightarrow \quad m = -5$

When $m = 1$ $\quad 2m - 5 = 2(1) - 5 = 2 - 5 = -3 \quad \Rightarrow \quad m = -3$

When $m = 2$, $\quad 2m - 5 = 2(2) - 5 = 4 - 5 = -1 \quad \Rightarrow \quad m = -1$

When $m = 3$, $2m - 5 = 2 \times (3) - 5 = 6 - 5 = 1 \Rightarrow m = 1$

When $m = 4$, $2m - 5 = 2 \times 4 - 5 = 8 - 5$ $\Rightarrow m = 3$

m	0	1	2	3	4
$2m - 5$	-5	-3	-1	1	3

Hence, solution of the equation is given by $m = 2$.

Que 20. What is the area of a square, whose side is m cm?

Sol. Given, side of the square $= m$ cm

∴   Area of square $=$ Side $\times$ Side $= m \times m = m^2$ sq cm

Que 21. A class with p students has planned a picnic. ₹ 50 per student is collected, out of which ₹ 1800 is paid in advance for transport. How much money is left with them to spend on other items?

Sol. According to the question,

Total students in the class $= p$

Collected money from per student $= ₹ 50$

Then, total money collected $= ₹ 50p$

Advance paid for transport $= ₹ 1800$ [given]

∴ Left money for spend on other items

     $=$ [Total money collected $-$ Advance paid money] $= ₹ (50p - 1800)$

Que 22. In a village, there are 8 water tanks to collect rain water. On a particular day, x L of rain water is collected per tank. If 100 L of water was already there in one of the tanks, what is the total amount of water in the tanks on that day?

Sol. According to the question,

Tanks to collect rain water $= 8$

Rain water is collected per tank (in L) $= x$

Then, total rain water in tanks (in L)

               $=$ Number of tanks $\times$ Per tank collected rain water

               $= 8 \times x = 8x$

But in the one tank, already 100 L of water exist, then

Total amount of water is given by $= 100 +$ [total rain water in L]

                         $= 100 + 8x$ or $8x + 100$ L

Que 23. Sunita is half the age of her mother Geeta. Find their ages

     (i) after 4 yr?   (ii) before 3 yr?

Sol. Let the age of Sunita's mother $= 2x$ yr

Then, according to the question

$$\text{Geeta age} = \frac{2x}{2} = x \qquad \text{[half of her mother's age]}$$

  (i) Since, in the after years, present age is added in given years.

      $\therefore$ Sunita's age $= (x + 4)$ yr

      Her mother's age $= (2x + 4)$ yr

 (ii) Since, in the before years, given year is subtracted from present age.

      $\therefore$ Sunita's age $= (x - 3)$ yr and her mother's age $= (2x - 3)$ yr

Que 24. Perimeter of a triangle is found by using the formula $P = a + b + c$, where a, b and c are the sides of the triangle. Write the rule that is expressed by this formula in words.

Sol. In this question, given formula for getting perimeter of triangle is

$$P = a + b + c$$

Here a, b and c are sides of the triangle.

Hence, the perimeter of the triangle is given by the sum of sides of triangle.

Que 25. Match the items of Column I with that of Column II.

	Column I		Column II
(i)	The number of corners of a quadrilateral	(A)	$=$
(ii)	The variable in the equation $2p + 3 = 5$	(B)	constant
(iii)	The solution of the equation $x + 2 = 3$	(C)	$+ 1$
(iv)	Solution of the equation $2p + 3 = 5$	(D)	$- 1$
(v)	A sign used in an equation	(E)	p
		(F)	x

Sol. (i) In a quadrilateral, numbers of corners are constant

      $\therefore$ (i) $\rightarrow$ (B)

 (ii) In the equation $2p + 3 = 5$

      p is variable. $\therefore$ (ii) $\rightarrow$ (E)

(iii) Given equation, $x + 2 = 3$

      For solving equation use transposing rule, $x + 2 = 3$

$$x = 3 - 2 \Rightarrow x = 1$$

      On solving equation, we get $x = 1$,

      $\therefore$ (iii) $\rightarrow$ (C)

 (iv) Given equation, $2p + 3 = 5$

      For solving equation use transposing rule, $2p + 3 = 5$

$$2p = 5 - 3, \quad \Rightarrow \quad 2p = 2 \quad \Rightarrow \quad p = 1$$

      On solving equation, we get $p = 1$, $\therefore$ (iv) $\rightarrow$ (C)

  (v) The sign used for equation is $(=)$.

      e.g. $2x + y = 3$, $\therefore$ (v) $\rightarrow$ (A)

Chapter **12**

Ratio and Proportion

Important Points

- **Ratio** The comparison of two numbers or quantities by division is known as the ratio of numbers and it is denoted by symbol ':'.

  e.g. Let two numbers are a and b where $(b \neq 0)$, then the ratio of a and b is $a : b$.

- **Term of a ratio** In the ratio form $a : b$, a is known as the first term or **antecedent** and b is known as the second term or **consequent**.

  e.g. In the ratio $7 : 5$, the first term or antecedent is 7 and the second term or consequent is 5.

- **Properties of ratio** A ratio may be treated as a fraction.

- Two ratio of quantities are equal, if the fractions corresponding quantities are equal.

  e.g. Two ratios $a : b$ and $c : d$ are equal, if $\dfrac{a}{b} = \dfrac{c}{d}$.

  Note (i) Two quantities can be compared only if they are in the same unit.

  (ii) We can get equivalent ratios by multiplying on dividing the numerator and denominator by the same number.

- **Proportion** If the ratio of the first and second quantities is equal to the ratio of the third and fourth quantities, then the quantities are in proportion and it is denoted by symbol '::' or '='.

  e.g. 5, 7, 35 and 49 are in proportion as $5 : 7 :: 35 : 49$ but 3, 8, 64 and 24 are not in proportion.

Note (i) First and fourth terms are called extreme terms or extremes. Second and third terms are called the middle terms or means.

    (ii) If two ratios are not equal, then they are not in proportion.

        e.g. Let a, b, c and d be in proportion. If $ad \neq bc$, then a, b, c and d are not in proportion.

    (iii) In the proportion, four quantities involved when taken in order are known as respective terms.

- **Unitary method** A method in which the value of unit quantity is first obtained to find the value of any required quantity, then it is called unitary method.

- In the solving of unitary method, we see that two types of variations:

   (i) Direct variation or direct proportion

   (ii) Inverse variation or inverse proportion

- Two quantities a and b are said to be direct proportion, if the ratio of both a and b, $\left(\dfrac{a}{b}\right)$ remains constant.

e.g. The cost of articles varies or increase directly as the number of articles.

(More articles, more cost) and (Less articles, less cost)

Try These (Page 245)

Que 1. In a class, there are 20 boys and 40 girls. What is the ratio of the number of boys to the number of girls?

    If we compare the two quantities in terms of division, then this comparison is known as the ratio.

Sol. Here, number of boys $= 20$

      and number of girls $= 40$

$\therefore$ Ratio of number of boys to the number of girls

$$= \frac{\text{Number of boys}}{\text{Number of girls}} = \frac{20}{40} = \frac{2}{4}$$

        [dividing numerator and denominator by 10]

$$= \frac{1}{2} = 1 : 2$$

Hence, the required ratio is 1 : 2.

Que 2. Ravi walks 6 km in an hour while Roshan walks 4 km in an hour. What is the ratio of the distance covered by Ravi to the distance covered by Roshan?

Sol. Given, Ravi walks 6 km in an hour i.e. distance covered by Ravi in one hour = 6 km

Roshan walks 4 km in an hour i.e. distance covered by Roshan in one hour = 4 km

∴ Ratio of distance covered by Ravi to the distance covered by Roshan

$$= \frac{\text{Distance covered by Ravi in one hour}}{\text{Distance covered by Roshan in one hour}} = \frac{6 \text{ km}}{4 \text{ km}} = \frac{6}{4} = \frac{3}{2} = 3:2$$

Hence, the required ratio is 3 : 2.

Try These (Page 246)

Que 3. Saurabh takes 15 minutes to reach school from his house and Sachin takes one hour to reach school from his house. Find the ratio of the time taken by Saurabh to the time taken by Sachin.

Sol. Here, time taken by Saurabh is in minutes and time taken by Sachin is in hours. So, we have to convert time taken by both into the same unit.

∴ Time taken by Sachin = 1 hr = 1 × 60 min = 60 min [∵ 1 hr = 60 min]

and time taken by Saurabh = 15 min

∴ Ratio of time taken by Saurabh to the time taken by Sachin

$$= \frac{\text{Time taken by Saurabh}}{\text{Time taken by Sachin}} = \frac{15}{60}$$

$$= \frac{15 \div 15}{60 \div 15} = \frac{1}{4} = 1:4 \qquad [\because \text{HCF of 15 and 60} = 15]$$

Hence, the required ratio is 1 : 4.

Que 4. Cost of a toffee is 50 paise and cost of a chocolate is ₹10. Find the ratio of the cost of a toffee to the cost of a chocolate.

Sol. Here, cost of a toffee and a chocolate are not in the same unit. So, we have to convert both into the same unit.

∴ Cost of a toffee = 50 paise

and cost of a chocolate = ₹ 10 = 10 × 100 paise [∵ ₹1 = 100 paise]

= 1000 paise

∴ Ratio of the cost of a toffee to the cost of a chocolate

$$= \frac{\text{Cost of a toffee}}{\text{Cost of a chocolate}} = \frac{50}{1000}$$

$$= \frac{50 \div 50}{1000 \div 50} = \frac{1}{20} = 1:20 \qquad [\because \text{ HCF of 50 and 1000} = 50]$$

Hence, the required ratio is 1 : 20.

Que 5. In a school, there were 73 holidays in one year. What is the ratio of the number of holidays to the number of days in one year?

Sol. Given, number of holidays in one year = 73

We know that, number of days in one year = 365

∴ Ratio of number of holidays to the number of days in one year

$$= \frac{\text{Number of holidays}}{\text{Total number of days}} = \frac{73}{365} = \frac{73 \div 73}{365 \div 73} = \frac{1}{5} = 1:5$$

$$[\because \text{ HCF of 73 and 365} = 73]$$

Hence, the required ratio is 1 : 5.

Exercise 12.1

Que 1. There are 20 girls and 15 boys in a class.

(a) What is the ratio of number of girls to the number of boys?

(b) What is the ratio of number of girls to the total number of students in the class?

Sol. Given, number of girls = 20 and number of boys = 15

∴ Total number of students in the class = 20 + 15 = 35

(a) Ratio of number of girls to the number of boys

$$= \frac{\text{Number of girls}}{\text{Number of boys}} = \frac{20}{15}$$

$$= \frac{20 \div 5}{15 \div 5} = \frac{4}{3} = 4:3 \qquad [\because \text{ HCF of 20 and 15} = 5]$$

(b) Ratio of number of girls to the total number of students in the class

$$= \frac{\text{Number of girls}}{\text{Total number of students}} = \frac{20}{35}$$

$$= \frac{20 \div 5}{35 \div 5} = \frac{4}{7} = 4:7 \qquad [\because \text{ HCF of 20 and 35} = 5]$$

Que 2. Out of 30 students in a class, 6 like football, 12 like cricket and remaining like tennis. Find the ratio of

(a) Number of students liking football to number of students liking tennis.

(b) Number of students liking cricket to total number of students.

 TIPS　Firstly, find the number of students like tennis by subtracting number of students like football and cricket from total number of students and then find the required ratio.

Sol. Given, total number of students in a class $= 30$

Number of students who like football $= 6$

Number of students who like cricket $= 12$

Then, number of students who like tennis

$$= \text{Total number of students} - (\text{Number of students who like football} + \text{Number of students who like cricket})$$

$$= 30 - (6 + 12) = 30 - 18 = 12$$

(a) Ratio of number of students liking football to number of students

liking tennis $= \dfrac{\text{Number of students who like football}}{\text{Number of students who like tennis}} = \dfrac{6}{12}$

$$= \dfrac{6 \div 6}{12 \div 6} = \dfrac{1}{2} = 1 : 2 \qquad [\because \text{HCF of 6 and 12} = 6]$$

(b) Ratio of number of students liking cricket to total number of students

$$= \dfrac{\text{Number of students who like cricket}}{\text{Total number of students}} = \dfrac{12}{30}$$

$$= \dfrac{12 \div 6}{30 \div 6} = \dfrac{2}{5} \qquad [\because \text{HCF of 12 and 30} = 6]$$

Que 3. See the figure and find the ratio of

(a) Number of triangles to the number of circles inside the rectangle.

(b) Number of squares to all the figures inside the rectangle.

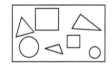

(c) Number of circles to all the figures inside the rectangle.

 TIPS　Firstly, find the number of triangles, squares and circles from given figure, then find the required ratio.

Sol. In the given figure,

Number of triangles = 3; Number of squares = 2

Number of circles = 2

∴ Total number of figures = 3 + 2 + 2 = 7

(a) Required ratio of number of triangles to the number of circles

$$= \frac{\text{Number of triangles}}{\text{Number of circles}} = \frac{3}{2} = 3:2$$

(b) Required ratio of number of squares to all the figures

$$= \frac{\text{Number of squares}}{\text{Total number of figures}} = \frac{2}{7} = 2:7$$

(c) Required ratio of number of circles to all tha figures

$$= \frac{\text{Number of circles}}{\text{Total number of figures}} = \frac{2}{7} = 2:7$$

Que 4. Distances travelled by Hamid and Akhtar in an hour are 9 km and 12 km. Find the ratio of speed of Hamid to the speed of Akhtar.

TIPS

Firstly, find the speed of Hamid and Akhtar separately by using the formula, $\text{Speed} = \frac{\text{Distance}}{\text{Time}}$, then find required ratio by dividing speed of Hamid by speed of Akhtar.

Sol. Given, speed of Hamid $= \dfrac{\text{Distance}}{\text{Time}} = \dfrac{9}{1} = 9$ km/h

and distance travelled by Akhtar in one hour = 12 km

∴ Speed of Akhtar $= \dfrac{12}{1} = 12$ km/h

∴ Ratio of speed of Hamid to speed of Akhtar

$$= \frac{\text{Speed of Hamid}}{\text{Speed of Akhtar}} = \frac{9}{12} = \frac{9 \div 3}{12 \div 3} = \frac{3}{4} = 3:4 \quad [\because \text{HCF of 9 and 12} = 3]$$

Que 5. Fill in the following blanks.

$$\frac{15}{18} = \frac{\Box}{6} = \frac{10}{\Box} = \frac{\Box}{30}$$

[Are these equivalent ratios?]

TIPS

We can get equivalent ratios by multiplying or dividing the numerator and denominator by the same number.

Sol. In order to get the missing number, we consider the fact that $18 = 6 \times 3$ i.e. when we divide 18 by 3, we get 6.

So, to get the missing number of second ratio, 15 must also be divided by 3.

Then, we have $\qquad\qquad 15 \div 3 = 5$

Hence, the second ratio is $\dfrac{\boxed{5}}{6}$

i.e. $\qquad\qquad\qquad \dfrac{15}{18} = \dfrac{\boxed{5}}{6}$ $\qquad\qquad$ ... (i)

Similarly, to get third ratio, we multiply both terms of second ratio by 2. $\qquad\qquad\qquad\qquad\qquad\qquad$ $[\because 5 \times 2 = 10]$

i.e. $\qquad\qquad \dfrac{\boxed{5}}{6} = \dfrac{5 \times 2}{6 \times 2} = \dfrac{10}{12} = 10 : 12$

$\qquad\qquad\qquad$ [multiplying numerator and denominator by 2]

$\therefore \qquad\qquad\qquad\qquad \dfrac{5}{6} = \dfrac{10}{12}$ $\qquad\qquad$ ... (ii)

Hence, the third ratio is 10/12.

Now, to get the fourth ratio, we consider the fact that $30 = 6 \times 5$ i.e. when we divide 30 by 6, we get 5.

So, in second ratio we multiply by 5, i.e. $\dfrac{5}{6} = \dfrac{5 \times 5}{6 \times 5} = \dfrac{25}{30}$

$\therefore \qquad\qquad\qquad\qquad \dfrac{5}{6} = \dfrac{\boxed{25}}{30}$ $\qquad\qquad$ ... (iii)

From Eqs. (i), (ii) and (iii), we have $\dfrac{15}{18} = \dfrac{\boxed{5}}{6} = \dfrac{10}{\boxed{12}} = \dfrac{\boxed{25}}{30}$

Here, from above relation, we can say that all these are equivalent ratios.

Que 6. Find the ratio of the following.

$\qquad$ (a) 81 to 108 $\qquad\qquad\qquad$ (b) 98 to 63

$\qquad$ (c) 33 km to 121 km $\qquad\quad$ (d) 30 min to 45 min

Sol. (a) Required ratio $= \dfrac{81}{108}$

$\qquad\quad \because 81 = 3 \times 3 \times 3 \times 3$ and $108 = 3 \times 3 \times 3 \times 2 \times 2$

$\qquad\quad \therefore \qquad$ HCF of 81 and 108 $= 27$

$\qquad\qquad\qquad\qquad$ Ratio $= \dfrac{81 \div 27}{108 \div 27} = \dfrac{3}{4} = 3 : 4$

$\qquad$ (b) Required ratio $= \dfrac{98}{63}$

$\qquad\qquad \therefore 98 = 2 \times 7 \times 7$ and $63 = 3 \times 3 \times 7$ $\therefore$ HCF of 98 and 63 $= 7$

$\qquad\qquad\qquad\qquad$ Ratio $= \dfrac{98 \div 7}{63 \div 7} = \dfrac{14}{9} = 14 : 9$

(c) Required ratio $= \dfrac{33 \text{ km}}{121 \text{ km}} = \dfrac{33}{121}$

$\therefore$ $\qquad 33 = 3 \times 11$ and $121 = 11 \times 11$

$\therefore$ $\qquad$ HCF of 33 and 121 = 11

$\qquad$ Ratio $= \dfrac{33 + 11}{121 \div 11} = \dfrac{3}{11} = 3 : 11$

(d) Required ratio $= \dfrac{30 \text{ min}}{45 \text{ min}} = \dfrac{30}{45}$

$\therefore$ $\qquad 45 = 3 \times 5 \times 3$ and $30 = 3 \times 5 \times 2$

$\therefore$ $\qquad$ HCF of 30 and 45 = 15

Ratio $= \dfrac{30 \div 15}{45 \div 15} = \dfrac{2}{3} = 2 : 3$

Que 7. Find the ratio of the following.

(a) 30 min to 1.5 h $\qquad\qquad$ (b) 40 cm to 1.5 m

(c) 55 paise to ₹ 1 $\qquad\qquad$ (d) 500 mL to 2 L

TIPS

Firstly, convert both the quantities in same unit and then find required ratio.

Sol. (a) Here, we have to convert 1.5 h into min.

$\qquad$ We know that, $\qquad$ 1 h = 60 min

$\qquad \therefore$ $\qquad\qquad$ 1.5 h = 1.5 × 60 min = 90 min

$\qquad \therefore$ $\qquad$ Required ratio $= \dfrac{30 \text{ min}}{90 \text{ min}} = \dfrac{30}{90}$

$\qquad \because 30 = 2 \times 3 \times 5$ and $90 = 2 \times 3 \times 5 \times 3$

$\qquad \therefore$ $\qquad$ HCF of 30 and 90 = $2 \times 3 \times 5 = 30$

$\qquad\qquad\qquad$ Ratio $= \dfrac{30 \div 30}{90 \div 30} = \dfrac{1}{3} = 1 : 3$

(b) Here, we have to convert 1.5 m into cm. We know that,

$\qquad\qquad\qquad$ 1 m = 100 cm

$\qquad \therefore$ $\qquad\qquad$ 1.5 m = 1.5 × 100 cm = 150 cm

$\qquad \therefore$ $\qquad$ Required ratio $= \dfrac{40 \text{ cm}}{150 \text{ cm}} = \dfrac{40}{150}$

$\qquad \because$ $\qquad\qquad 40 = 2 \times 2 \times 2 \times 5$ and $150 = 5 \times 3 \times 2 \times 5$

$\qquad \therefore$ $\qquad$ HCF of 40 and 150 = $2 \times 5 = 10$

$\qquad\qquad\qquad$ Ratio $= \dfrac{40 \div 10}{150 \div 10} = \dfrac{4}{15} = 4 : 15$

(c) Here, we have to convert ₹ 1 into paise.

$\qquad$ We know that, $\qquad$ ₹ 1 = 100 paise

$\therefore$ $\qquad$ Required ratio $= \dfrac{55 \text{ paise}}{100 \text{ paise}} = \dfrac{55}{100}$

$\because$ $\qquad\qquad$ $55 = 5 \times 11$ and $100 = 5 \times 2 \times 2 \times 5$

$\therefore$ $\quad$ HCF of 55 and $100 = 5 = \dfrac{55 \div 5}{100 \div 5} = \dfrac{11}{20} = 11 : 20$

(d) Here, we have to convert Litre into mL.
We know that, $\qquad$ $1\text{L} = 1000 \text{ mL}$

$\therefore$ $\qquad\qquad$ $2\text{ L} = 2 \times 1000 \text{ mL} = 2000 \text{ mL}$

$\therefore$ $\qquad$ Required ratio $= \dfrac{500 \text{ mL}}{2000 \text{ mL}} = \dfrac{500}{2000} = \dfrac{5}{20}$

$\qquad\qquad$ [dividing numerator and denominator by 100]

$\qquad$ Ratio $= 1/4 = 1 : 4$

Que 8. In a year, Seema earns ₹ 150000 and saves ₹ 50000. Find the ratio of

$\qquad$ (a) Money that Seema earns to the money she saves.

$\qquad$ (b) Money that she saves to the money she spends.

TIPS

For part (a), divide earn money by save money to get required ratio and for part (b), firstly find spend money, which is obtained on subtracting save money from earn money and then divide save money by spend money to get required ratio.

Sol. Given, money earned by Seema = ₹ 150000
and money saved by Seema = ₹ 50000

$\qquad$ (a) Required ratio $= \dfrac{\text{Money earned by Seema}}{\text{Money saved by Seema}}$

$\qquad\qquad = \dfrac{₹\,150000}{₹\,50000} = \dfrac{15000 \div 50000}{50000 \div 50000} = \dfrac{3}{1} = 3 : 1$

$\qquad\qquad$ [$\because$ HCF of 150000 and 50000 = 50000]

$\qquad$ (b) $\because$ Money spend by Seema = Earned money $-$ Saved money

$\qquad\qquad\qquad = (150000 - 50000) = ₹\,100000$

$\therefore$ $\qquad$ Required ratio $= \dfrac{\text{Money saved by Seema}}{\text{Money spend by Seema}} = ₹\dfrac{50000}{100000}$

$\qquad\qquad = \dfrac{50000 \div 50000}{100000 \div 50000} = \dfrac{1}{2} = 1 : 2$

$\qquad\qquad$ [$\because$ HCF of 50000 and 100000 = 50000]

Que 9. There are 102 teachers in a school of 3300 students. Find the ratio of the number of teachers to the number of students.

Sol. Given, number of teachers = 102 and number of students = 3300

∴ Required ratio of teachers to the number of students

$$= \frac{\text{Number of teachers}}{\text{Number of students}} = \frac{102}{3300}$$

∵ $102 = 2 \times 3 \times 17$ and $3300 = 2 \times 3 \times 2 \times 5 \times 5 \times 11$

∴ HCF of 102 and 3300 $= 2 \times 3 = 6 = \dfrac{102 \div 6}{3300 \div 6} = \dfrac{17}{550} = 17 : 550$

Que 10. In a college, out of 4320 students, 2300 are girls. Find the ratio of
 (a) number of girls to the total number of students.
 (b) number of boys to the number of girls.
 (c) number of boys to the total number of students.

TIPS Firstly, find the number of boys, which is obtained on subtracting the number of girls from total number of students and then find the required ratios.

Sol. Given, number of girls = 2300 and total number of students = 4320

∴ Number of boys = Total number of students – Number of girls
$$= 4320 - 2300 = 2020$$

(a) Required ratio $= \dfrac{\text{Number of girls}}{\text{Total number of students}} = \dfrac{2300}{4320}$

∵ $2300 = 2 \times 2 \times 5 \times 5 \times 23$ and $4320 = 2 \times 2 \times 5 \times 2 \times 2 \times 2 \times 3 \times 3 \times 3$

∴ HCF of 2300 and 4320 $= 2 \times 2 \times 5 = 20$

$$= \frac{2300 \div 20}{4320 \div 20} = \frac{115}{216} = 115 : 216$$

(b) Required ratio $= \dfrac{\text{Number of boys}}{\text{Number of girls}} = \dfrac{2020}{2300}$

∵ $2020 = 2 \times 2 \times 5 \times 101$ and $2300 = 2 \times 2 \times 5 \times 5 \times 23$

∴ HCF of 2020 and 2300 $= 2 \times 2 \times 5 = 20$

$$= \frac{2020 \div 20}{2300 \div 20} = \frac{101}{115} = 101 : 115$$

(c) Required ratio $= \dfrac{\text{Number of boys}}{\text{Total number of students}} = \dfrac{2020}{4320}$

∵ $2020 = 2 \times 2 \times 5 \times 101$ and $4320 = 2 \times 2 \times 5 \times 2 \times 2 \times 2 \times 3 \times 3 \times 3$

∴ HCF of 2020 and 4320 $= 2 \times 2 \times 5 = 20$

$$= \frac{2020 \div 20}{4320 \div 20} = \frac{101}{216} = 101 : 216$$

Que 11. Out of 1800 students in a school, 750 opted basketball, 800 opted cricket and remaining opted table tennis. If a student can opted only one game, find the ratio of

    (a) number of students, who opted basketball to the number of students who opted table tennis.

    (b) number of students, who opted cricket to the number of students opting basketball.

    (c) number of students, who opted basketball to the total number of students.

Sol. Given, total number of students = 1800

Number of students who opted basketball = 750

Number of students who opted cricket = 800

> **TIPS**
>
> ∴ Number of students who opted table tennis
> = Total number of students – Number of students, who opted
> (basketball + cricket)
> = 1800 – (750 + 800) = 1800 – 1550 = 250

(a) Required ratio = $\dfrac{\text{Number of students who opted basketball}}{\text{Number of students who opted table tennis}}$

$= \dfrac{750}{250} = \dfrac{75}{25}$

              [dividing numerator and denominator by 10]

$= \dfrac{75}{25} = \dfrac{75 \div 25}{75 \div 25} = \dfrac{3}{1} = 3:1$ [∵ HCF of 75 and 25 = 25]

(b) Required ratio = $\dfrac{\text{Number of students who opted cricket}}{\text{Number of students who opted basketball}}$

$= \dfrac{800}{750} = \dfrac{80}{75}$

              [dividing numerator and denominator by 10]

$= \dfrac{80 \div 5}{75 \div 5} = \dfrac{16}{15} = 16:15$ $\begin{bmatrix} ∵ \quad 80 = 2 \times 2 \times 5 \times 2 \times 2 \\ \text{and} \quad 75 = 3 \times 5 \times 5 \\ ∴ \text{ HCF of 80 and 75} = 5 \end{bmatrix}$

(c) Required ratio = $\dfrac{\text{Number of students who opted basketball}}{\text{Total number of students}}$

$= \dfrac{750}{1800} = \dfrac{75}{180}$ [dividing numerator and denominator by 10]

$= \dfrac{75 \div 15}{180 \div 15} = \dfrac{5}{12} = 5:12$ $\begin{bmatrix} ∵ \; 75 = 3 \times 5 \times 5 \text{ and } 180 = 3 \times 5 \times 3 \times 2 \times 2 \\ ∴ \text{ HCF of 75 and 180} = 3 \times 5 = 15 \end{bmatrix}$

Que 12. Cost of a dozen pens is ₹ 180 and cost of 8 ball pens is ₹ 56. Find the ratio of the cost of a pen to the cost of a ball pen.

Sol. Given, cost of 12 pens = ₹ 180

∴ Cost of 1 pen = $\dfrac{\text{Total cost of pens}}{\text{Number of pens}}$ = ₹ $\dfrac{180}{12}$ = ₹ 15 [∵ 1 dozen = 12 unit]

Also given, cost of 8 ball pens = ₹ 56

∴ Cost of 1 ball pen = $\dfrac{\text{Total cost of ball pens}}{\text{Number of ball pens}}$ = ₹ $\dfrac{56}{8}$ = ₹ 7

Now, required ratio = $\dfrac{\text{Cost of 1 pen}}{\text{Cost of 1 ball pen}}$ = $\dfrac{₹\,15}{₹\,7}$ = $\dfrac{15}{7}$ = 15 : 7

Que 13. Consider the statement : Ratio of breadth and length of a hall is 2 : 5. Complete the following table that shows some possible breadths and lengths of the hall.

Breadth of the hall (in m)	10	☐	40
Length of the hall (in m)	25	50	☐

TIPS Firstly, check that ratio of given breadth and length of hall is equal to given ratio or not. Then, for missing term multiply by same number in given value of length and breadth both.

Sol. Given, ratio of breadth and length of a hall = 2 : 5

Also given, breadth of the hall = 10 and length of the hall = 25

Then, the ratio of breadth and length = $\dfrac{10}{25}$ = $\dfrac{2}{5}$ = 2 : 5

Now, for finding first missing number, we have 25 × 2 = 50
i.e. when we multiply 25 by 2 we get 50.

So, to get first missing term, we multiply 10 by 2.

∴   10 × 2 = 20

Hence, second breadth of the hall = 20 and length of the hall = 50

For finding second missing number, we have 40 = 10 × 4
i.e. when we multiply 10 by 4 we get 40.

So, to get second missing term, we multiply 25 by 4.

∴   25 × 4 = 100

Hence, third breadth of hall = 40 and length = 100

Thus, the complete table is

Breadth of the hall (in m)	10	20	40
Length of the hall (in m)	25	50	100

Que 14. Divide 20 pens between Sheela and Sangeeta in the ratio of 3 : 2.

Sol. Given, ratio is 3 : 2 whose two parts are 3 and 2.

∴   Sum of two parts = 3 + 2 = 5

This means, if there are 5 pens, Sheela gets 3 pens and Sangeeta gets 2 pens.

We can say that, Sheela gets 3 parts and Sangeeta gets 2 parts out of every 5 parts.

Now,   total number of pens = 20

∴   Number of pens for Sheela = $\dfrac{3}{5} \times 20 = 12$

and number of pens for Sangeeta = $\dfrac{2}{5} \times 20 = 8$

Hence, out of 20 pens Sheela gets 12 pens and Sangeeta gets 8 pens.

Que 15. Mother wants to divide ₹ 36 between her daughters Shreya and Bhoomika in the ratio of their ages. If age of Shreya is 15 yr and age of Bhoomika is 12 yr find, how much Shreya and Bhoomika will get.

Mother wants to divide the money between Shreya and Bhoomika, according to their age. So, firstly we find the ratio of their ages and then divide ₹ 36 between them in that ratio.

Sol. Given, Shreya's age = 15 yr

and Bhoomika's age = 12 yr

∴   Ratio of their ages = $\dfrac{\text{Shreya's age}}{\text{Bhoomika's age}} = \dfrac{15 \text{ yr}}{12 \text{ yr}} = \dfrac{15}{12}$

$= \dfrac{15 \div 3}{12 \div 3} = \dfrac{5}{4} = 5 : 4$ [∵ HCF of 15 and 12 = 3]

Now, mother wants to divide ₹ 36 between her daughters in the ratio of their ages.

∴ Sum of the parts of ratios = 5 + 4 = 9

Amount which has to be divided = ₹ 36

Here, we can say that Shreya gets 5 parts and Bhoomika gets 4 parts out of every 9 parts.

∴ Shreya's share = $\dfrac{5}{9} \times 36 = ₹ 20$ and Bhoomika's share = $\dfrac{4}{9} \times 36 = ₹ 16$

Hence, Shreya gets ₹ 20 and Bhoomika gets ₹ 16.

Que 16. Present age of father is 42 yr and that of his son is 14 yr. Find the ratio of

    (a) present age of father to the present age of son.

    (b) age of the father to the age of son, when son was 12 yr old.

    (c) age of father after 10 yr to the age of son after 10 yr.

    (d) age of father to the age of son when father was 30 yr old.

Sol.   Given, present age of father = 42 yr and present age of son = 14 yr

    (a) Required ratio $= \dfrac{\text{Present age of father}}{\text{Present age of son}} = \dfrac{42 \text{ yr}}{14 \text{ yr}} = \dfrac{42}{14}$

$$= \dfrac{42 \div 14}{14 \div 14} = \dfrac{3}{1} = 3:1 \qquad [\because \text{HCF of 42 and 14} = 14]$$

    (b) When son's age was 12 yr i.e. 2 yr back (because son's present age is 14 yr), then father's age = (42 − 2) = 40 yr

       $\therefore$ Required ratio $= \dfrac{\text{2 yr back father's age}}{\text{2 yr back son's age}} = \dfrac{40 \text{ yr}}{12 \text{ yr}} = \dfrac{40}{12} = \dfrac{40 \div 4}{12 \div 4}$

       $\because 40 = 2 \times 2 \times 2 \times 5$ and $12 = 2 \times 2 \times 3$

       $\therefore$ HCF of 40 and $12 = 2 \times 2 = 4 = \dfrac{10}{3} = 10:3$

    (c) After 10 yr father and son's age will be (42 + 10) yr and (14 + 10) yr respectively i.e. 52 yr and 24 yr.

       $\therefore$ Required ratio $= \dfrac{\text{After 10 yr father's age}}{\text{After 10 yr son's age}} = \dfrac{52 \text{ yr}}{24 \text{ yr}} = \dfrac{52 \div 4}{24 \div 4}$

       $\because \quad 52 = 2 \times 2 \times 13$ and $24 = 2 \times 2 \times 2 \times 3$

       $\therefore$ HCF of 52 and $24 = 4 = \dfrac{13}{6} = 13:6$

    (d) When father's age was 30 yr i.e. 12 yr back (because father's present age is 42 yr and (42 − 12) = 30 yr.

       Then, son's age = (14 − 12) = 2 yr

       $\therefore$ Required ratio $= \dfrac{\text{12 yr back father's age}}{\text{12 yr back son's age}} = \dfrac{30 \text{ yr}}{2 \text{ yr}} = \dfrac{30}{2}$

$$= \dfrac{30 \div 2}{2 \div 2} = \dfrac{15}{1} = 15:1 \qquad [\because \text{HCF of 30 and 2} = 2]$$

Try These (Page 254)

    Check whether the given ratios are equal, i.e. they are in proportion.

    If yes, then write them in the proper form.

Que 1. $1 : 5$ and $3 : 15$

 TIPS If two ratios are equal, then we can say that they are in proportion and use the symbol '::' or '=' to equate the two ratios.

Sol. We have, $1 : 5$ and $3 : 15$

Here, $$3 : 15 = \frac{3}{15} = \frac{3 \div 3}{15 \div 3} = \frac{1}{5} = 1 : 5$$

[dividing numerator and denominator both by 3]

i.e. $1 : 5$ and $3 : 15$ are in proportion.

Thus, the proper form is $1 : 5 :: 3 : 15$.

Que 2. $2 : 9$ and $18 : 81$

Sol. We have, $2 : 9$ and $18 : 81$

Here, $$18 : 81 = \frac{18}{81} = \frac{18 \div 9}{81 \div 9}$$

$\because\ 18 = 2 \times 3 \times 3 \quad$ and $\quad 81 = 3 \times 3 \times 3 \times 3$

$\therefore$ HCF of 18 and 81 $= 3 \times 3 = 9 = \dfrac{2}{9} = 2 : 9$

i.e. $2 : 9$ and $18 : 81$ are in proportion.

Thus, the proper form is $2 : 9 :: 18 : 81$.

Que 3. $15 : 45$ and $5 : 25$

Sol. We have, $15 : 45$ and $5 : 25$

Here, $$15 : 45 = \frac{15}{45} = \frac{15 \div 15}{45 \div 15}$$

[dividing numerator and denominator both by 15]

$$= \frac{1}{3} = 1 : 3 \text{ and } 5 : 25 = \frac{5}{25} = \frac{5 \div 5}{25 \div 5} = \frac{1}{5} = 1 : 5$$

[dividing numerator and denominator both by 5]

Here, $\qquad 15 : 45 \neq 5 : 25$

Thus, $15 : 45$ and $5 : 25$ are not in proportion.

Que 4. $4 : 12$ and $9 : 27$

Sol. We have, $4 : 12$ and $9 : 27$

Here, $$4 : 12 = \frac{4}{12} = \frac{4 \div 4}{12 \div 4} = \frac{1}{3} = 1 : 3$$

[dividing numerator and denominator both by 4]

Now, $\qquad 9:27 = \dfrac{9}{27} = \dfrac{9 \div 9}{27 \div 9} = \dfrac{1}{3} = 1:3$

[dividing numerator and denominator both by 9]

Hence, $4:12 = 9:27 = 1:3$ i.e. $4:12$ and $9:27$ are in proportion.

Thus, the proper form is $4:12::9:27$.

Que 5. ₹ 10 to ₹ 15 and 4 to 6

Sol. We have, ₹ 10 : ₹ 15 = 10 : 15 and 4 : 6

Now, $\qquad 10:15 = \dfrac{10}{15} = \dfrac{10 \div 5}{15 \div 5}$

∵ $\qquad\qquad 10 = 2 \times 5 \quad$ and $\quad 15 = 3 \times 5$

∴ HCF of 10 and 15 $= 5 = \dfrac{2}{3} = 2:3$ and $4:6 = \dfrac{4}{6} = \dfrac{4 \div 2}{6 \div 2} = \dfrac{2}{3} = 2:3$

[dividing numerator and denominator by 2]

Here, $10:15 = 4:6 = 2:3$ i.e. $10:15$ and $4:6$ are in proportion.

Thus, the proper form is $10:15::4:6$.

Exercise 12.2

Que 1. Determine, if the following are in proportion.

    (a) 15, 45, 40, 120 (b) 33, 121, 9, 96   (c) 24, 28, 36, 48

    (d) 32, 48, 70, 210 (e) 4, 6, 8, 12   (f) 33, 44, 75, 100

 Firstly, find the ratio between two terms of each pair. If the ratio of both pairs is same, then they are in proportion, otherwise not.

Sol. (a) We have, 15, 45, 40, 120

∴ $\qquad$ Ratio of 15 to 45 $= \dfrac{15}{45} = \dfrac{15 \div 15}{45 \div 15}$ [∵ HCF of 15 and 45 = 15]

$$= \dfrac{1}{3} = 1:3$$

and $\quad$ ratio of 40 to 120 $= \dfrac{40}{120} = \dfrac{40 \div 40}{120 \div 40} = \dfrac{1}{3} = 1:3$

$$\left[\because \text{HCF of 40 and 120} = \dfrac{1}{3} = 1:3 \right]$$

Here, $\quad 15:45 = 40:120 = 1:3$

Therefore, 15, 45, 40, and 120 are in proportion.

(b) We have, 33, 121, 9, 96

$\therefore$ Ratio of 33 to $121 = \dfrac{33}{121} = \dfrac{33 \div 11}{121 \div 11}$ [$\because$ HCF of 33 and $121 = 11$]

$$= \dfrac{3}{11} = 3:11$$

and   ratio of 9 to $96 = \dfrac{9}{96} = \dfrac{9 \div 3}{96 \div 3}$ [$\because$ HCF of 9 and $96 = 3$]

$$= \dfrac{3}{32} = 3:32$$

Here, $3 : 11 \neq 3 : 32$ i.e. $33 : 121 \neq 9 : 96$

Therefore, 33, 121, 9 and 96 are not in proportion.

(c) We have, 24, 28, 36, 48

$\therefore$ Ratio of 24 to $28 = \dfrac{24}{28} = \dfrac{24 \div 4}{28 \div 4}$ [$\because$ HCF of 24 and $28 = 2 \times 2 = 4$]

$$= \dfrac{6}{7} = 6:7$$

and ratio of 36 to $48 = \dfrac{36}{48} = \dfrac{36 \div 12}{48 \div 12} = \dfrac{3}{4} = 3:4$

[$\because$ HCF of 36 and $48 = 2 \times 2 \times 3 = 12$]

Here, $6 : 7 \neq 3 : 4$ i.e. $24 : 28 \neq 36 : 48$

Therefore, 24, 28, 36 and 48 are not in proportion.

(d) We have, 32, 48, 70, 210

$\therefore$ Ratio of 32 to $48 = \dfrac{32}{48} = \dfrac{32 \div 16}{48 \div 16} = \dfrac{2}{3} = 2:3$

[$\because$ HCF of 32 and $48 = 2 \times 2 \times 2 \times 2 = 16$]

and ratio of 70 to $210 = \dfrac{70}{210} = \dfrac{70 \div 70}{210 \div 70} = \dfrac{1}{3} = 1:3$

[$\because$ HCF of 70 and $210 = 2 \times 5 \times 7 = 70$]

Here, $2:3 \neq 1:3$ i.e. $32:48 \neq 70:210$

Therefore, 32, 48, 70 and 210 are not in proportion.

(e) We have, 4, 6, 8, 12

$\therefore$ Ratio of 4 to $6 = \dfrac{4}{6} = \dfrac{4 \div 2}{6 \div 2} = \dfrac{2}{3} = 2:3$

[dividing numerator and denominator both by 2]

and   ratio of 8 to $12 = \dfrac{8}{12} = \dfrac{8 \div 4}{12 \div 4} = \dfrac{2}{3} = 2:3$

[dividing numerator and denominator both by 4]

Here, $4 : 6 = 8 : 12 = 2 : 3$

Therefore, 4, 6, 8 and 12 are in proportion.

(f) We have 33, 44, 75, 100

∴ Ratio of 33 to 44 = $\dfrac{33}{44} = \dfrac{33 \div 11}{44 \div 11}$ [∵ HCF of 33 and 44 = 11]

$= \dfrac{3}{4} = 3 : 4$

and   ratio of 75 to 100 = $\dfrac{75}{100} = \dfrac{75 \div 25}{100 \div 25} = \dfrac{3}{4} = 3 : 4$

[∵ HCF of 75 and 100 = 5 × 5 = 25]

Here, 33 : 44 = 75 : 100 = 3 : 4

Therefore, 33, 44, 75 and 100 are in proportion.

Que 2. Write true (T) or false (F) against each of the following statements:

    (a) 16 : 24 : : 20 : 30   (b) 21 : 6 : : 35 : 10

    (c) 12 : 18 : : 28 : 12   (d) 8 : 9 : : 24 : 27

    (e) 5.2 : 3.9 : : 3 : 4   (f) 0.9 : 0.36 : : 10 : 4

 TIPS

Firstly, write the given ratios in lowest form. If lowest form of both ratios are same, then they will be in proportion and given statement will be true, otherwise given statement will be false.

Sol. (a) We have, 16 : 24 : : 20 : 30

∴   Ratio of 16 to 24 = $\dfrac{16}{24} = \dfrac{16 \div 8}{24 \div 8} = \dfrac{2}{3} = 2 : 3$

[∵ HCF of 16 and 24 = 2 × 2 × 2 = 8]

and   ratio of 20 to 30 = $\dfrac{20}{30} = \dfrac{20 \div 10}{30 \div 10} = \dfrac{2}{3} = 2 : 3$

[dividing numerator and denominator both by 10]

Here, 16 : 24 = 20 : 30 = 2 : 3, so 16 : 24 : : 20 : 30

Hence, given statement is true.

(b) We have, 21 : 6 : : 35 : 10

Ratio of 21 to 6 = $\dfrac{21}{6} = \dfrac{21 \div 3}{6 \div 3} = \dfrac{7}{2} = 7 : 2$

[dividing numerator and denominator both by 3]

and   ratio of 35 to 10 = $\dfrac{35}{10} = \dfrac{35 \div 5}{10 \div 5} = \dfrac{7}{2} = 7 : 2$

[dividing numerator and denominator both by 5]

Here, 21 : 6 = 35 : 10 = 7 : 2, so 21 : 6 : : 35 : 10

Hence, given statement is true.

(c) We have, $12 : 18 : : 28 : 12$

$\therefore$ Ratio of 12 to 18 $= \dfrac{12}{18} = \dfrac{12 \div 6}{18 \div 6} = \dfrac{2}{3} = 2 : 3$

[dividing numerator and denominator both by 6]

and   ratio of 28 to 12 $= \dfrac{28}{12} = \dfrac{28 \div 4}{12 \div 4} = \dfrac{7}{3} = 7 : 3$

[dividing numerator and denominator both by 4]

Here, $2 : 3 \neq 7 : 3$ i.e. $12 : 18 \neq 28 : 12$

Hence, given statement is false.

(d) We have, $8 : 9 : : 24 : 27$

$\therefore$ Ratio of 8 to 9 $= \dfrac{8}{9} = 8 : 9$

and   ratio of 24 to 27 $= \dfrac{24}{27} = \dfrac{24 \div 3}{27 \div 3} = \dfrac{8}{9} = 8 : 9$

[dividing numerator and denominator both by 3]

Here, $8 : 9 = 24 : 27$, so $8 : 9 : : 24 : 27$

Hence, given statement is true.

(e) We have, $5.2 : 3.9 : : 3 : 4$

$\therefore$ Ratio of 5.2 to 3.9 $= \dfrac{5.2}{3.9} = \dfrac{52}{39}$

[multiplying numerator and denominator both by 10]

$= \dfrac{52 \div 13}{39 \div 13} = \dfrac{4}{3} = 4 : 3$ [$\because$ HCF of 52 and 39 $= 13$]

and   ratio of 3 to 4 $= \dfrac{3}{4} = 3 : 4$

Here, $4 : 3 \neq 3 : 4$ i.e. $5.2 : 3.9 \neq 3 : 4$

Hence, given statement is false.

(f) We have, $0.9 : 0.36 : : 10 : 4$

$\therefore$ Ratio of 0.9 to 0.36 $= \dfrac{0.9}{0.36} = \dfrac{90}{36}$

[multiplying numerator and denominator both by 100]

$= \dfrac{90 \div 18}{36 \div 18} = \dfrac{5}{2} = 5 : 2$ [$\because$ HCF of 36 and 90 $= 2 \times 3 \times 3 = 18$]

and   ratio of 10 to 4 $= \dfrac{10}{4} = \dfrac{10 \div 2}{4 \div 2} = \dfrac{5}{2} = 5 : 2$

[dividing numerator and denominator both by 2]

Here, $0.9 : 0.36 = 10 : 4 = 5 : 2$, so $0.9 : 0.36 : : 10 : 4$

Hence, given statement is true.

Que 3. Are the following statements true?

    (a) 40 persons : 200 persons = ₹ 15 : ₹ 75

    (b) 7.5 L : 15 L = 5 kg : 10 kg

    (c) 99 kg : 45 kg = ₹ 44 : ₹ 20

    (d) 32 m : 64 m = 6 s : 12 s

    (e) 45 km : 60 km = 12 h : 15 h

Sol. (a) 40 persons : 200 persons $= \dfrac{40}{200} = \dfrac{40 \div 10}{200 \div 10} = \dfrac{4}{20} = \dfrac{1}{5} = 1 : 5$

[dividing numerator and denominator both by 10]

and   ₹ 15 : ₹ 75 $= \dfrac{15}{75} = \dfrac{15 \div 15}{75 \div 15} = \dfrac{1}{5} = 1 : 5$

[dividing numerator and denominator both by 15]

Here, $1 : 5 = 1 : 5$. So, given statement is true.

(b) 7.5 L : 15 L $= \dfrac{7.5}{15} = \dfrac{75}{150}$

[multiply numerator and denominator both by 10]

$= \dfrac{75 \div 75}{150 \div 75} = \dfrac{1}{2} = 1 : 2$ [∵ HCF of 75 and 150 = 75]

and 5 kg : 10 kg $= \dfrac{5}{10} = \dfrac{5 \div 5}{5 \div 10} = \dfrac{1}{2} = 1 : 2$ [∵ HCF of 5 and 10 = 5]

Here, $1 : 2 = 1 : 2$. So, given statement is true.

(c) 99 kg : 45 kg $= \dfrac{99}{45} = \dfrac{99 \div 9}{45 \div 9} = \dfrac{11}{5} = 11 : 5$ [∵ HCF of 99 and 45 = 9]

and ₹ 44 : ₹ 20 $= \dfrac{44}{20} = \dfrac{44 \div 4}{20 \div 4} = \dfrac{11}{5} = 11 : 5$ [∵ HCF of 44 and 20 = 4]

Here, $11 : 5 = 11 : 5$. So, given statement is true.

(d) 32 m : 64 m $= \dfrac{32}{64} = \dfrac{32 \div 32}{64 \div 32} = \dfrac{1}{2} = 1 : 2$

[∵ HCF of 32 and 64 = $2 \times 2 \times 2 \times 2 \times 2 = 32$]

and 6 s : 12 s $= \dfrac{6}{12} = \dfrac{6 \div 6}{12 \div 6} = \dfrac{1}{2} = 1 : 2$

[dividing numerator and denominator both by 6]

Here, $1 : 2 = 1 : 2$. So, given statement is true.

(e) 45 km : 60 km $= \dfrac{45}{60} = \dfrac{45 \div 15}{60 \div 15} = \dfrac{3}{4} = 3 : 4$ [∵ HCF of 45 and 60 = 15]

and 12 h : 15 h $= \dfrac{12}{15} = \dfrac{12 \div 3}{15 \div 3} = \dfrac{4}{5} = 4 : 5$ [∵ HCF of 12 and 15 = 3]

Here, $3 : 4 \neq 4 : 5$. So, given statement is false.

Que 4. Determine, if the following ratios form a proportion. Also, write the middle term and extreme terms, where the ratios form a proportion.

(a) 25 cm : 1 m and ₹ 40 : ₹ 160

(b) 39 L : 65 L and 6 bottles : 10 bottles

(c) 2 kg : 80 kg and 25 g : 625 g

(d) 200 mL : 2.5 L and ₹ 4 : ₹ 50

TIPS

Firstly, convert the terms of a ratio in same unit, then write the given ratios in their lowest form. If lowest form of both ratios are same, then they will be in proportion and their first and fourth terms are known as extreme terms, second and third terms are known as middle terms.

Sol. (a) Here, $2\,5$ cm : 1 m = 25 cm : 1 × 100 cm   [∵ 1 m = 100 cm]

$$= 25 \text{ cm} : 100 \text{ cm}$$

$$= 25 : 100 = \frac{25}{100} = \frac{25 \div 25}{100 \div 25} = \frac{1}{4} = 1 : 4$$

[dividing numerator and denominator both by 25]

and   ₹ 40 : ₹ 160 = 40 : 160 = $\frac{40}{160} = \frac{4}{16} = \frac{1}{4} = 1 : 4$

[dividing numerator and denominator both by 10]

Here, 1 : 4 = 1 : 4 i.e. 25 cm : 1 m = ₹ 40 : ₹ 160

So, the ratios of 25 cm : 1 m and ₹ 40 : ₹ 160 are in proportion.

i.e. 25 cm : 1 m : : ₹ 40 : ₹ 160

Now, middle terms are 1 m and ₹ 40 and extreme terms are 25 cm and ₹ 160.

(b) Here, 39 L : 65 L = 39 : 65 = $\frac{39}{65} = \frac{39 \div 13}{65 \div 13}$ [∵ HCF of 39 and 65 = 13]

$$= \frac{3}{5} = 3 : 5$$

and 6 bottles : 10 bottles = 6 : 10 = $\frac{6}{10} = \frac{6 \div 2}{10 \div 2} = \frac{3}{5} = 3 : 5$

[dividing numerator and denominator both by 2]

Here, 3 : 5 = 3 : 5 i.e. 39 L : 65 L = 6 bottles : 10 bottles

So, the ratio of 39 L : 65 L and 6 bottles : 10 bottles are in proportion.

i.e. 39 L : 65 L : : 6 bottles : 10 bottles

Now, middle terms of ratios are 65 L and 6 bottles and extreme terms of ratios are 39 L and 10 bottles.

(c) Here, $2 \text{ kg} : 80 \text{ kg} = 2 : 80 = \dfrac{2}{80} = \dfrac{2 \div 2}{80 \div 2} = \dfrac{1}{40} = 1 : 40$

[dividing numerator and denominator both by 2]

and $25 \text{ g} : 625 \text{ g} = 25 : 625 = \dfrac{25}{625} = \dfrac{25 \div 25}{625 \div 25} = \dfrac{1}{25} = 1 : 25$

[∵ HCF of 25 and 625 $= 5 \times 5 = 25$]

Since, both ratios are not equal.

∴ $2 \text{ kg} : 80 \text{ kg} \neq 25 \text{ g} : 625 \text{ g}$

Hence, the given ratios are not in proportion.

(d) Here, $200 \text{ mL} : 2.5 \text{ L} = 200 \times \dfrac{1}{1000} \text{ L} : 2.5 \text{ L}$ $\left[\because 1 \text{ mL} = \dfrac{1}{1000} \text{ L} \right]$

$= \dfrac{200}{1000} \text{ L} : 2.5 \text{ L} = 0.200 \text{ L} : 2.5 \text{ L}$

$= 0.200 : 2.5 = \dfrac{0.200}{2.5} = \dfrac{2}{25} = 2 : 25$

[multiplying numerator and denominator both by 10]

and   ₹ $4 : ₹ 50 = 4 : 50 = \dfrac{4}{50} = \dfrac{4 \div 2}{50 \div 2} = \dfrac{2}{25} = 2 : 25$

[dividing numerator and denominator both by 2]

Here, $2 : 25 = 2 : 25$ i.e. $200 \text{ mL} : 2.5 \text{ L} = ₹ 4 : ₹ 50$

So, the ratios of $200 \text{ mL} : 2.5 \text{ L}$ and ₹ $4 : ₹ 50$ are in proportion.

i.e. $200 \text{ mL} : 2.5 \text{ L} :: ₹ 4 : ₹ 50$

Now, middle terms of ratios are 2.5 L and ₹ 4 and extreme terms of ratios are 200 mL and ₹ 50.

Try These (Page 257)

Que 1. Read the table and fill in the boxes.

Time	Distance travelled by Karan	Distance travelled by Kriti
2 h	8 km	6 km
1 h	4 km	☐
4 h	☐	☐

Sol. From the above table,

Distance travelled by Kriti in 2 h $= 6$ km

∴ Distance travelled by Kriti in 1 h $= \dfrac{6}{2} = \boxed{3 \text{ km}}$

Now, distance travelled by Kriti in 4 h $= 3 \times 4 = \boxed{12 \text{ km}}$

Also, distance travelled by Karan in 1 h $= \boxed{4 \text{ km}}$

∴ Distance travelled by Karan in 4 h $= 4 \times 4 = \boxed{16 \text{ km}}$

On completing the boxes, we get the following table:

Time	Distance travelled by Karan	Distance travelled by Kriti
2 h	8 km	6 km
1 h	4 km	3 km
4 h	16 km	12 km

Exercise 12.3

Que 1. If the cost of 7 m of cloth is ₹ 294, find the cost of 5 m of cloth.

Sol. Given,   Cost of 7 m of cloth = ₹ 294

∴   Cost of 1 m of cloth = $₹\dfrac{294}{7}$ = ₹ 42

∴   Cost of 5 m of cloth = ₹ 42 × 5 = ₹ 210

Hence, the cost of 5 m of cloth is ₹ 210.

Que 2. Ekta earns ₹ 1500 in 10 days. How much will she earn in 30 days?

Sol. Here, the number of days is known and money earns is unknown. Given, Ekta earns in 10 days = ₹ 1500

∴   Ekta earns in 1 day = $₹\dfrac{1500}{10}$ = ₹ 150

∴   Ekta earns in 30 days = ₹ 150 × 30 = ₹ 4500

Hence, Ekta earns ₹ 4500 in 30 days.

Que 3. If it has rained 276 mm in the last 3 days, how many centimetre of rain will fall in one full week (7 days)? Assume that the rain continues to fall at the same rate.

Sol. Here, the number of days is known and rain fall is unknown. Given, rainfall in 3 days = 276 mm

∴ Rainfall in 1 day = $\dfrac{276}{3}$ = 92 mm

∴ Rainfall in one full week i.e. 7 days = 92 × 7 = 644 mm

In centimetre, rainfall in one full week

$$= 644 \times \frac{1}{10} \text{ cm} = 64.4 \text{ cm} \qquad \left[\because 1\,\text{mm} = \frac{1}{10}\,\text{cm} \right]$$

Hence, 644 mm or 64.4 cm rain will fall in 7 days or one full week.

Que 4. Cost of 5 kg of wheat is ₹ 30.50.

(a) What will be the cost of 8 kg of wheat?

(b) What quantity of wheat can be purchased in ₹ 61?

Sol. (a) Here, the quantity of wheat is known and cost is unknown.

Given, cost of 5 kg of wheat = ₹ 30.50

∴　　Cost of 1 kg of wheat = ₹ $\dfrac{30.50}{5}$ = ₹ 6.10

∴　　Cost of 8 kg of wheat = ₹ 6.10 × 8 = ₹ 48.80

Hence, the Cost of 8 kg of wheat is ₹ 48.80.

(b) Here, the cost of wheat is known and quantity of wheat is unknown.

Given, in ₹ 30.50 quantity of wheat that can be purchased = 5 kg

∴ In ₹ 1, quantity of wheat that can be purchased

$$= \dfrac{5}{30.50} \text{ kg} = \dfrac{5 \times 10}{305} \text{ kg} = \dfrac{50}{305} \text{ kg}$$

[multiplying numerator and denominator both by 10]

∴　In ₹ 61, quantity of wheat that can be purchased

$$= \dfrac{50}{305} \times 61 = \dfrac{50}{5} \text{ kg} = 10 \text{ kg}$$

Hence, 10 kg wheat can be purchased in ₹ 61.

Que 5. The temperature dropped 15 degree celsius in the last 30 days. If the rate of temperature drop remains the same, how many degrees will the temperature drop in the next 10 days?

Sol. Given, in last 30 days, temperature drop = 15 degree

∴ In 1 day, temperature drop = $\dfrac{15}{30}$ degree = $\dfrac{15 \div 15}{30 \div 15} = \dfrac{1}{2}$ degree

[∵ HCF of 15 and 30 = 15]

∴　In next 10 days, temperature drop = $\dfrac{1}{2} \times 10$ degree = 5 degree

Hence, temperature dropped 5 degree in the next 10 days.

Que 6. Shaina pays ₹ 7500 as rent for 3 months. How much does she has to pay for a whole year, if the rent per month remains same?

Sol. Given, rent paid for 3 months = ₹ 7500

∴ Rent paid for 1 month = ₹ $\dfrac{7500}{3}$ = ₹ 2500

∴ Rent paid for a whole year i.e. 12 months = ₹(2500 × 12) = ₹ 30000

Hence, she has to pay ₹ 30000 for a whole year.

Que 7. Cost of 4 dozens bananas is ₹ 60. How many bananas can be purchased for ₹ 12.50?

Sol. We know that, 1 dozen = 12 units

Given, in ₹ 60, number of bananas that can be purchased = 4 dozens

$$= 4 \times 12 = 48 \qquad [\because 1 \text{ dozen} = 12 \text{ units}]$$

∴ In ₹ 1, number of bananas that can be purchased

$$= \frac{48}{60} = \frac{48 \div 12}{60 \div 12} = \frac{4}{5}$$

$$[\because \text{HCF of } 48 \text{ and } 60 = 2 \times 2 \times 3 = 12]$$

∴ In ₹ 12.50, number of bananas that can be purchased

$$= \frac{4}{5} \times 12.50 = \frac{50}{5} = 10$$

Hence, 10 bananas can be purchased for ₹ 12.50.

Que 8. The weight of 72 books is 9 kg. What is the weight of 40 such books?

Sol. Given, weight of 72 books = 9 kg

∴ Weight of 1 book $= \dfrac{9}{72}$ kg

∴ Weight of 40 books $= \dfrac{9}{72} \times 40$ kg $= \dfrac{360}{72}$ kg $= \dfrac{360 \div 72}{72 \div 72} = 5$ kg

$$[\because \text{HCF of } 360 \text{ and } 72 = 2 \times 2 \times 2 \times 3 \times 3 = 72]$$

Hence, the weight of 40 books is 5 kg.

Que 9. A truck requires 108 L of diesel for covering a distance of 594 km. How much diesel will be required by the truck to cover a distance of 1650 km?

sol. Given, diesel required for 594 km = 108 L

∴ Diesel required for 1 km $= \dfrac{108}{594}$ L $= \dfrac{108 \div 54}{594 \div 54} = \dfrac{2}{11}$ L

$$[\because \text{HCF of } 108 \text{ and } 594 = 3 \times 3 \times 3 \times 2 = 54]$$

∴ Diesel required for 1650 km $= \dfrac{2}{11} \times 1650$ L $= 2 \times 150 = 300$ L

```
11) 1650 (150
      11
      ──
      55
      55
      ──
       ×
```

Hence, 300 L diesel required by the truck to cover 1650 km.

Que 10. Raju purchases 10 pens for ₹ 150 and Manish buys 7 pens for ₹ 84. Can you say who got the pens cheaper?

 TIPS Firstly, find the cost of 1 pen for both Raju and Manish by unitary method, then compare who got the pens cheaper.

Sol. For Raju, Cost of 10 pens = ₹ 150 ∴ Cost of 1 pen = ₹ $\dfrac{150}{10}$ = ₹ 15

For Manish, Cost of 7 pens = ₹ 84 ∴ Cost of 1 pen = ₹ $\dfrac{84}{7}$ = ₹ 12

Here, ₹ 12 < ₹15

Hence, Manish got the pens cheaper.

Que 11. Anish made 42 runs in 6 overs and Anup made 63 runs in 7 overs. Who made more runs per over?

 TIPS Firstly, find the runs made by them in one over separately and then compare who made more runs.

Sol. For Anish, Runs made by Anish in 6 overs = 42

∴ Runs made by Anish in 1 over = $\dfrac{42}{6}$ = 7

For Anup, Runs made by Anup in 7 overs = 63

∴ Runs made by Anup in 1 over = $\dfrac{63}{7}$ = 9

∵ 9 > 7

Hence, Anup made more runs per over.

Selected **NCERT Exemplar Problems**

Que 1. Mathematics textbook for Class VI has 320 pages. The chapter 'symmetry' runs from page 261 to page 272. The ratio of the number of pages of this chapter to the total number of pages of the book is

(a) 11 : 320   (b) 3 : 40   (c) 3 : 80   (d) 272 : 320

Sol. ∴ Total pages of textbook for Class VI = 320 pages and total pages this chapter (symmetry) = (261 to 272) = 12 pages

Rato of the number of pages = $\dfrac{\text{Total pages of this chapter}}{\text{Total pages of textbook}}$

$= \dfrac{12}{320} = \dfrac{12 \div 4}{320 \div 4} = \dfrac{3}{80}$ [∴ HCF of 12 and 320 = 4]

Hence, option (c) is correct.

Que 2. Neelam's annnual income is ₹ 288000. Her annual savings amount to ₹ 36000. The ratio of her savings to her expenditure is

    (a) 1 : 8   (b) 1 : 7   (c) 1 : 6   (d) 1 : 5

Sol.   Given, Neelam's annual income = ₹ 288000

      Her annual savings amount = ₹ 36000

∴ Total expenditure of Neelam = (Neelam's annual income

$$- \text{ Her annual savings amount)}$$

$$= (288000 - 36000) = ₹ \ 252000$$

∴ Ratio of her savings to her expenditure

$$= \text{Her savings amount : Her expenditure}$$

$$= 36000 : 252000 = \frac{36000}{252000} = \frac{36}{252}$$

[on dividing numerator and denominator both by 1000]

$$= \frac{36 \div 36}{252 \div 36} = \frac{1}{7} = 1 : 7 \qquad [\because \text{HCF of 36 and } 252 = 36]$$

Hence, option (b) is correct

Que 3. If a bus travels 160 km in 4 h and a train travels 320 km in 5 h at uniform speeds. Then, the ratio of the distances travelled by them in one hour is

    (a) 1 : 2   (b) 4 : 5   (c) 5 : 8   (d) 8 : 5

Sol. Given, total distance travelled by bus in 4 h = 160 km

Then, bus travels in 1 h $= \dfrac{\text{Total distance}}{\text{Total hours}} = \dfrac{160}{4} = 40 \text{ km}$

and total distance travel by train in 5 h = 320 km

Then, the train travels in 1 h $= \dfrac{\text{Total distance}}{\text{Total hours}} = \dfrac{320}{5} = 64 \text{ km}$

∴ Ratio of the distance travelled by them in 1 h

$$= \text{Distance travels by bus in 1 h : Distance travels by train in 1 h}$$

$$= 40 : 64 = \frac{40}{64} = \frac{40 \div 8}{64 \div 8} = \frac{5}{8} = 5 : 8 \qquad [\because \text{HCF of 40 and 64} = 8]$$

Que 4. There are '*b*' boys and '*g*' girls in a class. The ratio of the number of boys to the total number of students in the class is

    (a) $\dfrac{b}{b+g}$ (b) $\dfrac{g}{b+g}$ (c) $\dfrac{b}{g}$ (d) $\dfrac{b+g}{b}$

Sol. Given, number of boys in the class = *b*

      and number of girls in the class = *g*

∴ Total number of students = Numbers of boys in class

+ Number of girls in class

$$= b + g$$

Ratio of boys to the total number of students

= Number of boys in class : Total number of students

$$= b : b + g = \frac{b}{b+g}$$

Hence, option (a) is correct.

Que 5. On a shelf, books with green cover and that with brown cover are in the ratio 2 : 3. If there are 18 books with green cover. Then, the number of books with brown cover is

(a) 12   (b) 24   (c) 27   (d) 36

Sol. Given, ratio of books with green cover to brown cover $= 2:3$

and number of books with green cover $= 18$

Let the number of books $= 2x : 3x$ [where, x is a multiple of books]

∴ Number of the brown cover $= \dfrac{2x}{3x} = \dfrac{18}{\text{Brown cover books}}$

⇒ $2x \times$ Brown cover books $= 18 \times 3x$ [by interchanging property]

∴ Brown cover books $= \dfrac{18 \times 3x}{2x} = 27$

So, the number of books with brown cover is 27.

Hence, option (c) is correct.

Que 6. In a box, the ratio of red marbles to blue marbles is 7 : 4. Which of the following could be the total number of marbles in the box?

(a) 18   (b) 19   (c) 21   (d) 22

Sol. Given, ratio of red marbles to blue marbles $= 7:4$

Let the number of marbles in the box $= 7x : 4x$

[where, x is a multiple of marbles]

Then, total number of marbles in the box

= Number of red marbles+ Number of blue marbles

$$= 7x + 4x = 11x$$

Now, the number of marbles can be calculated by putting the multiple values of x.

When $x = 1$, then number of marbles $= 11 \times 1 = 11$

When $x = 2$, then number of marbles $= 11 \times 2 = 22$

So, the number of marbles is 22. Hence, option (d) is correct.

Que 7. The marked price of a table is ₹ 625 and its sale price is ₹ 500. What is the ratio of the sale price to the marked price?

Sol. Given, marked price of a table = ₹ 625

and   sale price of a table = ₹ 500

∴   Ratio of the sale price to the marked price

       = Sale price of the table : Marked price of the table

       = 500 : 625 = 4 : 5   [dividing by 125 in both ratios]

Hence, the ratio of sale price to marked price is 4 : 5.

Que 8. The number of milk teeth in human beings is 20 and the number of permanent teeth is 32. Find the ratio of the number of milk teeth to the number of permanent teeth.

Sol. Given, number of milk teeth = 20

and number of permanent teeth = 32

∴   Ratio of the number of milk teeth to the number of permanent teeth

         = Number of milk teeth : Number of permanent teeth

         = 20 : 32 = 5 : 8   [dividing by 4 in both ratios]

Hence, the required ratio is 5 : 8

Que 9. In a year, Ravi earns ₹ 360000 and paid ₹ 24000 as income tax. Find the ratio of his

     (a) income to income tax.

     (b) income tax to income after paying income tax.

Sol. Given, Ravi earns in a year = ₹360000

and Ravi paid income tax in a year = ₹ 24000

     (a) Ratio of income to the income tax = 360000 : 24000

                       = 360 : 24   [dividing by 1000 in both ratios]

                       = 15 : 1   [dividing by 24 in both ratios]

     Hence, the ratio of income to income tax is 15 : 1.

     (b) After income tax paying remaining income

                      = Total income – Income tax

                      = 360000 – 24000 = ₹ 336000

∴ Ratio of income tax to after paying income tax

                      = Income tax   after paying income tax

                      = 24000 : 336000

                      = 24 : 336   [dividing by 1000 in both ratios]

                      = 1 : 14   [dividing by 14 in both ratios]

Hence, the ratio of income tax to afer paying income tax is 1 : 14.

Que 10. Ramesh earns ₹ 28000 per month. His wife Rama earns ₹ 36000 per month. Find the ratio of

    (a) Ramesh's earnings to their total earnings.

    (b) Rama's earnings to their total earnings.

Sol. Given, Ramesh earns per month = ₹ 28000

and Rama earns per month = ₹ 36000

∴   Total earnings = (Ramesh earns per month

+ Rama earns per month)

$$= ₹ (28000 + 36000) = ₹ 64000$$

(a) Ratio of Ramesh's earnings to their total earnings

= Ramesh's earnings : Total earnings

$$= 28000 : 64000$$

$$= 28 : 64 \qquad \text{[dividing by 1000 in both ratios]}$$

$$= 7 : 16 \qquad \text{[dividing by 4 in both ratios]}$$

Hence, the ratio of Ramesh's earnings to total earnings is 7 : 16.

(b) Rama's earning's to their total earnings

= Rama's earnings : Total earnings

$$= 36000 : 64000$$

$$= 36 : 64 \qquad \text{[dividing by 1000 in both ratios]}$$

$$= 9 : 16 \qquad \text{[dividing by 4 in both ratios]}$$

Hence, the ratio of Rama's earnings to their total earnings is 9 : 16.

Que 11. Reshma prepared 18 kg of burfi by mixing khoya with sugar in the ratio of 7 : 2. How much khoya did she use?

Sol. Given, total burfi prepared by Reshma = 18 kg

and ratio of khoya and sugar in the burfi = 7 : 2

Let the quantity of khoya and sugar in the burfi= $7x : 2x$

[where, x is a multiple of quantity]

Then, total quantity of khoya and sugar = $7x + 2x = 9x$

But the total amount of burfi = 18 kg

Hence, $9x = 18$ kg   [since, both quantities are same]

⇒ $x = \dfrac{18}{9} \Rightarrow x = 2$

Therefore, she used khoya in burfi = $7x$ [∵ $x = 2$, by solving]

$$= 7 \times 2 = 14 \text{ kg}$$

Hence she used khaya in burfi is 14 by.

Que 12. A line segment 56 cm long is to be divided into two parts in the ratio of $2:5$. Find the length of each part.

Sol. Given, total length of line segment $= 56$ cm

and ratio of divided parts $= 2:5$

Let the length of line segment $= 2x : 5x$

[where, x is a multiple of quantify]

Then, total length of line segment $= 2x + 5x = 7x$

[since, divided length ratio is equals to length of line segment]

$$7x = 56 \quad \Rightarrow \quad x = \frac{56}{7} \quad \Rightarrow \quad x = 8$$

On putting the value af x in both parts, we get length of each part.

$\therefore$ First part $= 2x = 2 \times 8 = 16$ [$x = 8$, by solving]

and   second part $= 5x = 5 \times 8 = 40$ [$x = 8$, by solving]

Hence, first part 16 cm and second part is 40 cm.

Que 13. The shadow of a 3 m long stick is 4 m long. At the same time of the day, if the shadow of a flagstaff is 24 m long, how tall is the flagstaff?

Sol. Given, length of long stick $= 3$ m

and length of shadow of long stick $= 4$ m

Then, the ratio of long stick to shadaw of long stick $= 3:4$

and shadow of a flagstaff $= 24$ m   [given]

since, according to the question, ratio of long stick to shadow of long stick is equal to the ratio of flagstaff to shadow of flagstaff]

Let the length of flagstaff $= x$ m

According to the question, $3:4 = x:24$

$\Rightarrow$ $\dfrac{3}{4} = \dfrac{x}{24} \Rightarrow 4 \times x = 24 \times 3$

$\Rightarrow$ $x = \dfrac{24 \times 3}{4} \Rightarrow x = 18$

Hence, the length of flagstaff is 18 m.

Que 14. In a school, the ratio of the number of large classrooms to small classrooms is $3:4$. If the number of small rooms is 20, then find the number of large rooms.

Sol. Given, ratio of number of large classrooms to small classrooms $= 3:4$

and number of small rooms $= 20$

According to the ratio property, ratio of large classrooms to small classrooms is equal to the number of large classrooms to small classrooms.

Let the number of large rooms = x

Then, number of large classrooms, $3 : 4 = x : 20$

$\Rightarrow \qquad \dfrac{3}{4} = \dfrac{x}{20} \qquad \Rightarrow \qquad 3 \times 20 = 4x$

$\Rightarrow \qquad 4x = 3 \times 20 \qquad \qquad$ [by interchanging property]

$\Rightarrow \qquad 4x = 3 \times 20 \quad \Rightarrow x = \dfrac{3 \times 20}{4} \Rightarrow x = 15$

Hence, the number of large rooms is 15.

Que 15. A recipe calls for 1 cup of milk for every $2\dfrac{1}{2}$ cups of flour to make a cake that would feed 6 persons. How many cups of both flour and milk will be needed to make a similar cake for 8 peoples?

Sol. Given, milk needed for making cake = 1 cup

and flour needed for making cake $= 2\dfrac{1}{2}$ cups $= \dfrac{5}{2}$ cups

Then, total amount needed = (Milk + Flour) $= \left(1 + \dfrac{5}{2}\right)$ cups $= \dfrac{7}{2}$ cups

So, $\dfrac{7}{2}$ cups of milk and flour needed to making cake for 6 persons.

Let the needed amount of cups = x $\qquad$ [where, x is a multiple of cups]

Then, by ratio and proportional law $\dfrac{\frac{7}{2}}{6} = \dfrac{x}{8}$

$\Rightarrow \qquad \dfrac{7}{2} \times 8 = 6 \times x \qquad \qquad$ [by interchanging property]

$\Rightarrow \qquad x = \dfrac{28}{6} \Rightarrow x = \dfrac{14}{3} \qquad$ [dividing by 2 in both ratios]

Hence, the cups needed for 8 persons is $\dfrac{14}{3}$ [milk + flour].

Que 16. An office opens at 9 am and closes at 5:30 pm with a lunch break of 30 min. What is the ratio of lunch break to the total period in the office?

Sol. Total time period in the office = Time of office closed

$-$ Time of office opens

$= 5 : 30 - 9 : 00 = 8 : 30\,\text{h} = 8\dfrac{1}{2}\,\text{h} = \dfrac{17}{2}\,\text{h}$

$\therefore$ Time of lunch break $= 30\,\text{min} = \dfrac{1}{2}\,\text{h} \qquad\qquad$ [given]

∴ Ratio of lunch break to the total period in the office

$$= \frac{1}{2} : \frac{17}{2} = \frac{\frac{1}{2}}{\frac{17}{22}} = 1 : 17$$

Hence, the ratio of lunch break to the total period is 1 : 17.

Que 17. Samira sells newspapers at Janpath crossing daily. On a particular day, she had 312 newspapers out of which 216 are in English and remaining in Hindi. Find the ratio of the

(a) number of English newspapers to the number of Hindi newspapers.

(b) number of Hindi newspapers to the total number of newspapers.

Sol. Given, total number of newspapers sells = 312

and number of English newspapers sells = 216

∴ Numbers of Hindi newspapers sells

= Total numbers of newspapers

     − Number of English newspapers

= 312 − 216 = 96

(a) Ratio of English newspapers to the numbers of Hindi newspapers

     = 216 : 96 = 9 : 4   [dividing by 24 in both ratios]

Hence, the ratio of number of English newspapers to the numbers of Hindi newspapers is 9 : 4.

(b) Ratio of Hindi newspapers to the total number of newspapers

     = 96 : 312 = 4 : 13   [divided by 24 in both ratios]

Hence, the ratio of number of Hindi newspapers to the total number of newspapers is 4 : 13.

Que 18. A scooter travels 120 km in 3 h and a train travels 120 km in 2 h. Find the ratio of their speeds.

$$\left[\textbf{Hint } \text{Speed} = \frac{\text{Distance travelled}}{\text{Time taken}} \right]$$

Sol. Given, distance travels by a scooter = 120 km

Time taken by a scooter = 3 h

$$\text{Speed} = \frac{\text{Distance travelled}}{\text{Time taken}} = \frac{120 \text{km}}{3 \text{ h}} = 40 \text{ km/h}$$

Distance travels by train = 120 km and time taken by a train = 2 h

$$\text{Speed of the train} = \frac{\text{Distance travelled}}{\text{Time taken}} = \frac{120 \text{km}}{2 \text{ h}} = 60 \text{ km/h}$$

∴ Ratio of their speeds = Speed of the scooter : Speed of the train

= 40 : 60 = 2 : 3   [dividing by 20 in both ratios]

Hence , the ratio of their speeds is 2 : 3.

Que 19. The ratio of 8 books to 20 books is

(a) 2 : 5   (b) 5 : 2   (c) 4 : 5   (d) 5 : 4

Sol. Given, ratio of given books = 8 : 20 = 2 : 5 [dividing by 4 in both ratios]

Que 20. A picture is 60 cm wide and 1.8 m long The ratio of its width to its perimeter in lowest form is

(a) 1 : 2   (b) 1 : 3   (c) 1 : 4   (d) 1 : 8

Sol. Given,   wide of picture = 60 cm

and   length of picture = 1.8 m = 180 cm   [∵ 1 m = 100 cm]

∴   Perimeter of picture = 2 (Width + Length)

[by formula of rectangular's perimeter]

= 2 (60 + 180) = 2 (240) = 480 cm   [given]

∴ Ratio of width of picture to perimeter of picture is

= 60 : 480 = 1 : 8   [dividing by 60 in both ratios]

Que 21. A rectangular sheet of paper is of length 1.2 m and width 21 cm. Find the ratio of width of the paper to its length.

Sol. Given, length of rectangular sheet =1. 2 m = 120 cm   [∵ 1 m = 100 cm]

and   width of rectangular sheet = 21 cm

∴   Ratio of width to its length = 21 : 120 = 7 : 40

[dividing by 3 in both ratios]

Hence, the required ratio is 7 : 40.

Que 22. Which ratio is larger 10 : 21 or 21 : 93?

Sol. For getting larger ratio, compare both ratios 10 : 21 and 21 : 93.

(a) $10 : 21 = \dfrac{10}{21} = 0.476$ [by dividation]

(b) $21 : 93 = \dfrac{21}{93} = 0.225$ [by dividation]

Here, 0·476 > 0·225

So, the value of 10 : 21 is larger than ratio of 21 : 93. Hence, the ratio 10 : 21 is larger.

Que 23. Of the 288 persons working in a company, 112 are men and the remaining are women. Find the ratio of the number of

(a) men to that of women.

(b) men to the total number of persons.

(c) women to the total number of persons.

Sol. Given, total number of persons working in a company = 288

and number of men working in a company = 112

∴ Remaining persons, which are women in a company

= Total persons working in a company

– Men working in a company

= 288 – 112 = 176

(a) Ratio of the number of men to that of women = 112 : 176

= 7 : 11   [both ratios divided by 16]

Hence, the ratio of the number of men of that to women is 7 : 11.

(b) Ratio of the number of men to the total number of persons

= 112 : 288 = 7 : 18   [both ratios divided by 16]

Hence, the ratio of the number of men to the total number of persons is 7 : 18.

(c) Ratio of the number of women to the total number of persons

= 176 : 288 = 11 : 18   [both ratios divided by 16]

Hence, the ratio of the number of women to the total number of persons is 11 : 18.

Que 24. At the parking stand of Ramleela ground, Kartik counted that there are 115 cycles, 75 scooters and 45 bikes. Find the ratio of the number of cycles to the total number of vehicles.

Sol. Given, counted cycles at ground = 115

Counted scooters at ground = 75

Counted bikes at ground = 45

∴ Total vehicles at ground = (Number of cycles

+ Number of scooter + Number of bikes)

= (115 + 75 + 45) = 235

∴ Ratio of number of cycles to the total number of vehicles

= Number of cycles : Total number of vehicles

= 115 : 235 = 23 : 47   [both ratios divided by 5]

Hence, the required ratio is 23 : 47.

Que 25. A train takes 2 h to travel from Ajmer to Jaipur, which are 130 km apart. How much time will it take to travel from Delhi to Bhopal which are 780 km apart, if the train is travelling the uniform speed?

Sol. Given, distance travel by train = 130 km

and time taken by train = 2 h

∴ Speed of train = $\dfrac{130 \text{ km}}{2 \text{ h}}$ = 65 km/h

and distance between Delhi to Bhopal = 780 km

Let time taken by train = x h

Then, speed of train = $\dfrac{\text{Distance between Bhopal to Delhi}}{\text{Time taken by train}}$

⇒ $65 = \dfrac{780}{x} \Rightarrow x = \dfrac{780}{65} \Rightarrow x = 12$ h   [by interchanging property]

Hence, the required time is 12 h for distance 780 km.

Que 26. When Chinmay visted chowpati at Mumbai on a holiday, he observed that the ratio of North Indian food stalls to South Indian food stalls is 5 : 4. If the total number of food stalls is 117, find the number of each type of food stalls.

Sol. Given, ratio of North Indian food stalls to South Indian food stalls

$= 5:4$

and total number of food stalls = 117

Let the number of stalls = $5x:4x$

[where, x is a multiple of food stalls]

∴ Total number of ratios of stalls = $5x + 4x = 9x$

If total number of ratios is equal to the total number of food stalls, then

$$9x = 117 \Rightarrow x = \dfrac{117}{9} = 13$$

∴ Number of food stalls of North Indian = $5x = 5 \times 13 = 65$

and number of food stalls of South Indian = $4x = 4 \times 13 = 52$

Hence, North Indian stalls is 65 and South Indian stalls is 52.

Que 27. An alloy contains only zinc and copper and they are in the ratio of 7 : 9. If the weight of the alloy is 8 kg, then find the weight of copper in the alloy.

Sol. Given, the ratio of zinc and copper in alloy $= 7:9$

and total weight of alloy = 8 kg

Let the weight of zinc and copper in alloy $= 7x : 9x$

[where, x is a multiple of weight]

Then, total weight of both ratios $= 7x + 9x = 16x$

If total weight of alloy is equal to the total weight of both ratios, then

$$16x = 8\,\text{kg} \Rightarrow x = \frac{8}{16} \Rightarrow x = \frac{1}{2}$$

$\therefore$ Weight of copper in alloy $= 9x = 9 \times \dfrac{1}{2}$

$$= \frac{9}{2}\,\text{kg} = 4\frac{1}{2}\,\text{kg}$$

Hence, the weight of copper is $4\dfrac{1}{2}\,\text{kg}$.

Que 28. Find two numbers, whose sum is 100 and whose ratio is 9 : 16.

Sol. Let the ratio of two numbers $= 9x : 16x$

[where, x is multiple of two numbers]

Sum of two numbers $= 9x + 16x = 25x$

Here, sum of two numbers $= 100$ [given]

If the sum of two numbers is equal to the sum of two numbers's ratio, then

$$25x = 100 \Rightarrow x = \frac{100}{25} \Rightarrow x = 4$$

On putting the value of x in both ratios, we get

First number $= 9x = 9 \times 4 = 36$ and second number $= 16x = 16 \times 4 = 64$

Hence, two numbers are 36 and 64, respectively.

Chapter 13

Symmetry

Important Points

- **Line of symmetry** A figure is said to be line of symmetry, if by folding the figure along a line, the left and right parts of it coincide exactly. This line is called the line (or axis) of symmetry of the figure.

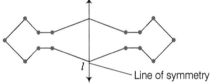

Line of symmetry

In the given figure, *l* is line of symmetry because it divides the left and right parts of figure equally.

A figure contains many types of line of symmetry, such as, no line of symmetry one line of symmetry, two lines of symmetry and multiple (or more than two) lines of symmetry.

(i) **No line of symmetry** No line of symmetry means that there is no line segment in figure which can divides figure in two equal parts.

e.g.

S ⟶ No line of symmetry

In the letter 'S', there is no line of symmetry.

(ii) **One line of symmetry** One line of symmetry means that there is only one line segment in figure which divides the figure in two equal parts of figure.

e.g.

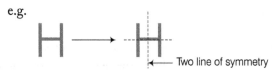

—— One line of symmetry

In the letter 'T', there is one line of symmetry which divides the alphabet 'T' in two equal parts.

(iii) **Two lines of symmetry** Two lines of symmetry means that there is two lines segment which divides the figure in equal parts.

e.g.

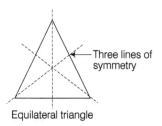

—— Two line of symmetry

In the letter 'H', there is two lines of symmetry which divides the alphabet 'H' in equal parts.

(iv) **Three lines of symmetry** Three lines of symmetry means there is three lines segment which divides the figure in equal parts.

e.g.

—— Three lines of symmetry

Equilateral triangle

In an equilateral triangle, there are three medians in triangle which divides the triangle in equal parts.

Hence, the line of symmetry of equilateral triangle is three.

■ **Reflection and symmetry** Line symmetry is closely related to mirror reflection. The distance of the image of a point from the line of symmetry is the same as that of the point from that line of symmetry.

A figure is said to be symmetrical about a line *l*, if it is identical an either side of *l*, where *l* is called the line of axis of symmetry.

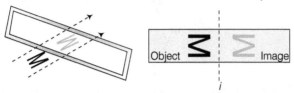

■ **Points to be Remembered**

(i) A line segment is symmetrical about its perpendicular bisector.

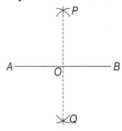

(ii) A given angle having equal arms is symmetrical about the bisector of the angle.

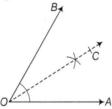

(iii) An isosceles triangle is symmetrical about the bisector of the angle included between the equal sides.

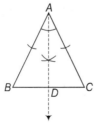

(iv) A kite is symmetrical about the bisector of the angles between the sides.

(v) A rectangle has two lines of symmetry, each one of which is the line joining the mid-points of opposite sides.

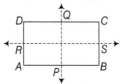

(vi) A rhombus is symmetrical about each one of its diagonals.

(vii) A square has 4 lines of symmetry namely the diagonals and the lines joining the mid-points of its opposite sides.

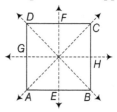

(viii) An equilateral triangle is symmetrical about each one of the bisectors of its interior angles.

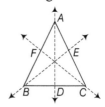

(ix) A circle is symmetrical about each one of its diameters.

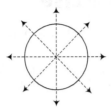

(x) Each of the following capital letters of the English alphabet is symmetrical about the dotted line or lines as shown given below.

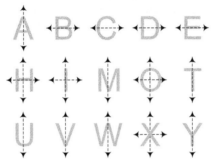

Try These (Page 262)

Que 1. You have two set-squares in your 'mathematical instruments box'. Are they symmetric?

Sol. There are two types of set-square in the instruments box which are given below:

    (i) 30°, 60° and 90° set-square
    (ii) 45°, 45° and 90° set-square

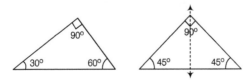

From these two set-squares, first one is not symmetric, whereas second is symmetric.

Exercise 13.1

Que 1. List any four symmetrical objects from your home or school.

Sol. There are many symmetrical objects which found in our school or home. Some of these are blackboard, table top, wall clock, bucket, photoframe, etc.

Que 2. For the given figure, which one is the mirror line, l_1 or l_2?

Sol. We know that, if we fold a picture in half, such that the left and right halves match exactly, then the picture is said to have line of symmetry or mirror line. Here, if we fold the picture about l_2, then the left and right halves match exactly. So, l_2 is the mirror line.

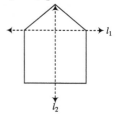

Que 3. Identify the shapes given below. Check whether, they are symmetric or not. Draw the line of symmetry as well.

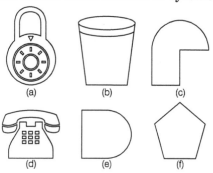

(a)　　(b)　　(c)

(d)　　(e)　　(f)

 TIPS

We know that, if we place a mirror on the fold, then the image of one side of picture will fall exactly on the other side of the picture, then the fold, which is the mirror line, is a line of symmetry for the picture.

Sol. (a) It is a symmetrical figure and its line of symmetry is shown below:

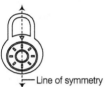

(b) It is a symmetrical figure and its line of symmetry is shown below:

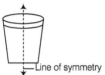

(c) This is not a symmetrical figure because if we fold, then we cannot get the image of one side exactly fall on the other side.

(d) The given figure is symmetric and its line of symmetry is shown below:

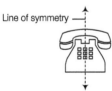

(e) The given figure is symmetric and its line of symmetry is shown below:

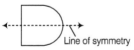

(f) The given figure is symmetric and its line of symmetry is shown below:

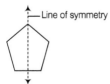

Que 4. Copy the following on a squared paper. A square paper is what you would have used in your arithmetic notebook in earlier classes. Then, complete them such that the dotted line is the line of symmetry.

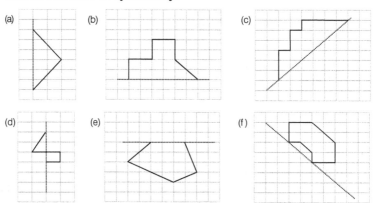

Sol. On completing the given figure considering the dotted lines as the line of symmetry, we get the following figure which are shown as below:

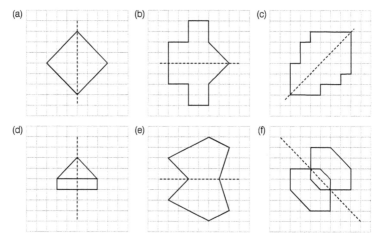

Que 5. In the figure, *l* is the line of symmetry. Complete the diagram to make it symmetric.

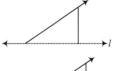

Sol. On completing the diagram, we get the following figure which is symmetrical about the line *l*, where *l* is the line of symmetry.

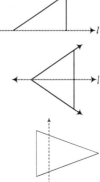

Que 6. In the figure, *l* is the line of symmetry. Draw the image of the triangle and complete the diagram, so that it becomes symmetric.

Sol. On drawing the image of the triangle and completing the diagram, we get the following figure which is symmetrical about the line of symmetry *l*.

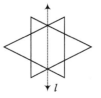

Try These (Page 264)

Que 1. Form as many shapes as you can by combining two or more set-squares. Draw them on squared paper and note their line of symmetry.

Sol. (i) On combining two identical set-squares which have angles of measure 30°, 60° and 90°, we get the following shapes.

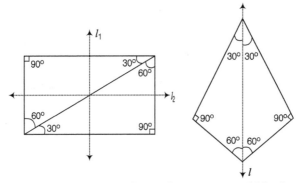

Here, rectangle has 2 lines of symmetry and kite has 1 line of symmetry which are shown by dotted lines in above figures.

(ii) On combining two identical set-squares which have angles of measure 45°, 45° and 90°, we get the following shapes.

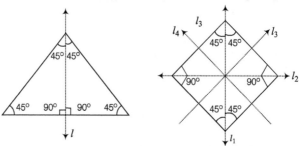

Here, right angled isosceles triangle has 1 line of symmetry, square has 4 line of symmetry, which are shown by dotted lines in above figures.

(iii) On combining three identical set-squares which have angles of measure 45°, 90° and 45°, we get the following shape.

Here, isosceles trapizium has 1 line of symmetry which is shown by dotted line in the above figure.

Exercise 13.2

Que 1. Find the number of lines of symmetry for each of the following shapes.

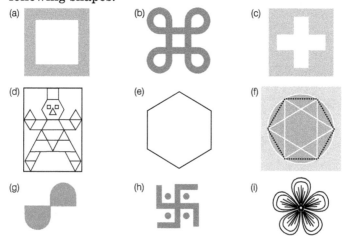

Sol. (a) Given figure is

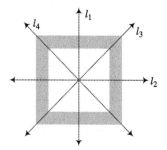

Here, l_1, l_2, l_3 and l_4 are four lines of symmetry.

(b) Given figure is

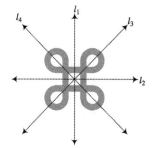

Here, l_1, l_2, l_3 and l_4 are four lines of symmetry.

(c) Given figure is

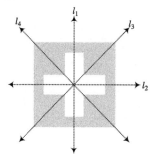

Here, l_1, l_2, l_3 and l_4 are four lines of symmetry.

(d) Given figure is

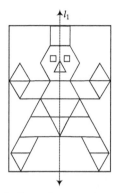

Here, l_1 is the only line of symmetry.

(e) Given figure is

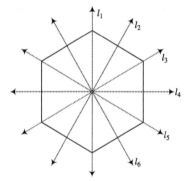

Here, l_1, l_2, l_3, l_4, l_5 and l_6 are six lines of symmetry.

(f) Given figure is

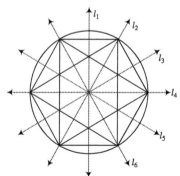

Here, l_1, l_2, l_3, l_4, l_5 and l_6 are six lines of symmetry.

(g) Given figure is

No line of symmetry is here.

(h) Given figure is

No line of symmetry is here.

(i) Given figure is

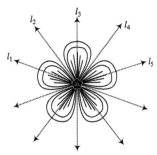

Here, l_1, l_2, l_3, l_4 and l_5 are five lines of symmetry.

Que 2. Copy the triangle in each of the following figures on squared paper. In each case, draw the line(s) of symmetry, if any and identify the type of triangle.

(a)

(b)

(c)

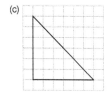

(d)

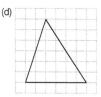

Sol. On copying the triangles on squared paper, we get the following figures:

(a) Here, the given triangle is an isosceles right angled triangle and one angle is 90° and its line of symmetry is l_1.

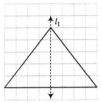

(b) Here, the given triangle is an isosceles triangle and its line of symmetry is l_1.

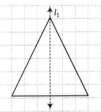

(c) Here, the given triangle is an isosceles right angled triangle and one angle is 90° and its line of symmetry is l_1.

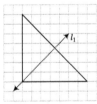

(d) Here, the given triangle is scalene triangle. So, this is not the symmetrical figure. Therefore, there is no line of symmetry.

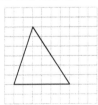

Que 3. Complete the following table.

Shape	Rough figure	Number of lines of symmetry
Equilateral triangle	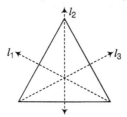	3
Square		
Rectangle		
Isosceles triangle		
Rhombus		
Circle		

Sol. First, we draw rough figure of each shape.

(i) A rough figure of an equilateral triangle is given below :

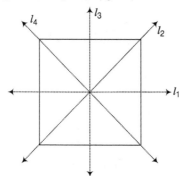

In equilateral triangle, l_1, l_2 and l_3 are three lines of symmetry.

(ii) A rough figure of a square is given below:

In square, l_1, l_2, l_3 and l_4 are four lines of symmetry.

(iii) A rough figure of a rectangle is given below :

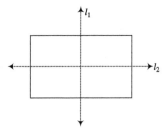

In rectangle, l_1 and l_2 are two lines of symmetry.

(iv) A rough figure of an isosceles triangle is given below :

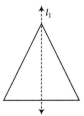

In isosceles triangle, l_1 is the only line of symmetry.

(v) A rough figure of a rhombus is given below

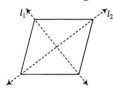

In rhombus, l_1 and l_2 are two lines of symmetry.

(vi) A rough figure of a circle is given below:

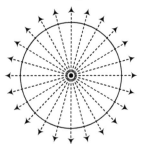

In circle, there are infinite lines of symmetry.

Now, the complete table is given below:

Shape	Rough figure	Number of lines of symmetry
Equilateral triangle		3
Square		4
Rectangle		2
Isosceles triangle		1
Rhombus		2
Circle		Infinite

Que 4. Can you draw a triangle which has
   (a) exactly one line of symmetry?
   (b) exactly two lines of symmetry?
   (c) exactly three lines of symmetry?
   (d) no lines of symmetry?

Sol. (a) Yes, we can draw an isosceles triangle which has exactly one line of symmetry, as shown below :

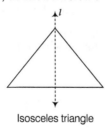

Isosceles triangle

   (b) No, we cannot draw a triangle which has exactly two lines of symmetry.

(c) Yes, we can draw an equilateral triangle which has exactly three lines of symmetry, as shown below :

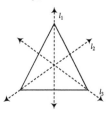

Equilateral triangle

(d) Yes, we can draw a scalene triangle which has no lines of symmetry, as shown below:

Scalene triangle

Question 5. On a squared paper, sketch the following.

(a) A triangle with a horizontal line of symmetry but no vertical line of symmetry.

(b) A quadrilateral with both horizontal and vertical lines of symmetry.

(c) A quadrilateral with a horizontal line of symmetry but no vertical line of symmetry.

(d) A hexagon with exactly two lines of symmetry.

(e) A hexagon with six lines of symmetry.

(**Hint** : It will be helpful, if you first draw the lines of symmetry and then complete the figures.)

Sol. (a) An isosceles triangle has only one line of symmetry. On a squared paper, its figure with a horizontal line of symmetry is given below :

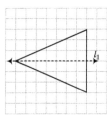

(b) A square is also a quadrilateral and a square has both horizontal and vertical lines of symmetry. On a squared paper, its figure with both horizontal and vertical lines of symmetry, is given below:

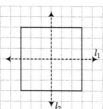

(c) A quadrilateral with a horizontal line of symmetry but no vertical line of symmetry on a squared paper, is shown below:

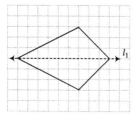

(d) A hexagon has two lines of symmetry on a squared paper, is shown below:

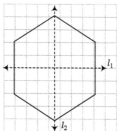

(e) A hexagon with six lines of symmetry on a squared paper, is shown below:

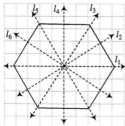

Que 6. Trace each figure and draw the lines of symmetry, if any.

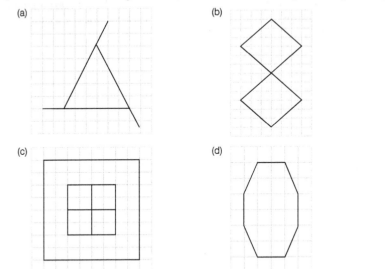

Sol. On tracing given figures, we get the following figures.

    (a) There is no line of symmetry.

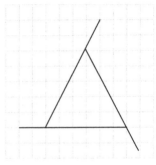

(b) There are two lines of symmetry.

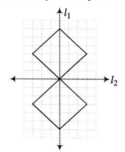

(c) There are four lines of symmetry.

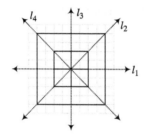

(d) There are two lines of symmetry.

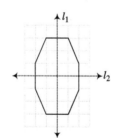

(e) There is one line of symmetry.

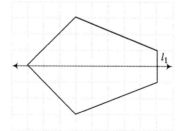

(f) There are four lines of symmetry.

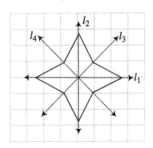

Que 7. Consider the letters of English alphabets A to Z. List among them the letters which have

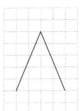

    (a) vertical lines of symmetry (like A).

    (b) horizontal lines of symmetry (like B).

    (c) no lines of symmetry (like Q).

Sol. (a) The letters of English alphabet which have vertical lines of symmetry (like A), are

A, H, I, M, O, T, U, V, W, X, Y

    (b) The letters of English alphabet which have horizontal lines of symmetry (like B), are

B, C, D, E, H, I, K, O, X

    (c) The letters of English alphabet which have no lines of symmetry (like Q), are

F, G, J, L, N, P, Q, R, S, Z

Que 8. Given, here are figures of a few folded sheets and designs drawn about the fold. In each case, draw a rough diagram of the complete figure that would be seen, when the design is cut off.

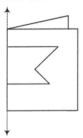 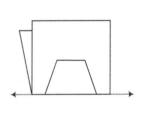

Sol. The rough diagram of the complete figure that would be seen when the design is cut off, are given below:

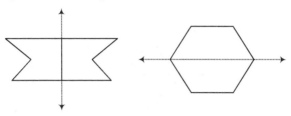

Try These (Page 270)

Que 1. If you are 100 cm in front of a mirror, where does your image appear to be? If you towards the mirror, how does your image move?

Sol. We know that, the object and its image are symmetrical with reference to the mirror line. If we are 100 cm in front of a mirror, then our image appears to be 100 cm behind the mirror. If we move towards the mirror, then our image also appears to come closer.

Exercise 13.3

Que 1. Find the number of lines of symmetry in each of the following shapes. How will you check your answers?

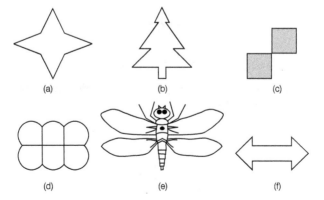

(a)   (b)   (c)

(d)   (e)   (f)

Sol. (a) The number of lines of symmetry for this figure are 4, which are shown below:

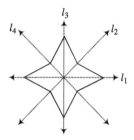

(b) The number of lines of symmetry for this figure is 1, which is shown below:

(c) The number of lines of symmetry for this figure are 2, which are shown below:

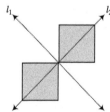

(d) The number of lines of symmetry for this figure are 2, which are shown below:

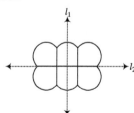

(e) The number of lines of symmetry for this figure is 1, which is shown below:

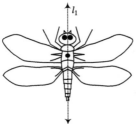

(f) The number of lines of symmetry for this figure are 2, which are shown below:

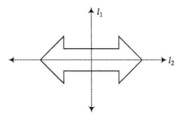

For checking, we fold the figure about line of symmetry. If one side of the picture fall exactly on the other side of the picture, then our line of symmetry is correct, otherwise line of symmetry is not correct.

Que 2. Copy the following drawing on squared paper. Complete each one of them such that the resulting figure has two dotted lines as two lines of symmetry.

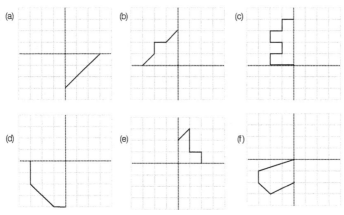

How did you go about completing the picture?

Sol. The complete figures with two dotted lines as two lines of symmetry, are given below:

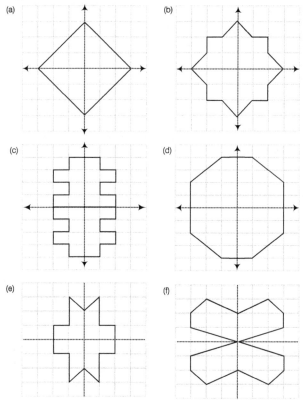

By using the given line of symmetry, we go about completing the picture.

Que 3. In each figure alongside, a letter of the alphabet is shown along with a vertical line. Take the mirror image of the letter in the given line. Find which letters look the same after reflection (i.e. which letters look the same in the image) and which do not? Can you guess, why?
[Try of OEMNPHLTSVX]

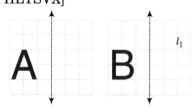

Sol. Taking the mirror image of the letters A and B in the given line. These will look as shown below:

It is clear that, A look the same after reflection and B do not look the same because A has reflection symmetry but B do not have.

Now, the mirror image of other letters are shown below:

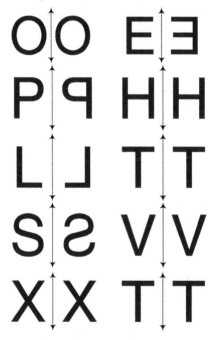

From above, we can say that A, O, M, H, T, V and X look the same after reflection because these letters are symmetrical.

Also, we see that B, E, N, P, L and S do not look the same after reflection because these letters are not symmetrical.

Selected **NCERT Exemplar Problems**

Directions *In Questions 1 to 5, out of the four options, only one options is correct. Give the correct answer.*

Que 1. In the following figures, the figure that is not symmetric with respect to any line, is

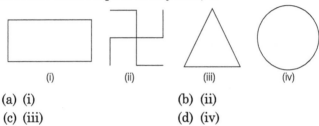

(i)   (ii)   (iii)   (iv)

(a) (i)   (b) (ii)
(c) (iii)   (d) (iv)

Sol. In the figure (ii), there is no line segment.

So, the figure is not symmetric.

Hence, option (b) is correct

Que 2. The number of lines of symmetry in a scalene triangle is

(a) 0   (b) 1   (c) 2   (d) 3

Sol. Triangle shown in figure is a scalene triangle and in this triangle, there is no line segment to divide into equal parts.

Hence, option (a) is correct

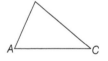

Que 3. The number of lines of symmetry in a circle is

(a) 0   (b) 2
(c) 4   (d) more than 4

Sol. In the figure, we can draw many diameter to cut in symmetrical parts of a circle.

Hence, option (d) is correct

circle

Que 4. Which of the following letters have both horizontal and vertical lines of symmetry?

(a) X   (b) E   (c) M   (d) K

Sol. In the figure X, we can draw both horizontal and vertical lines for symmetry.

Hence, option (a) is correct.

Que 5. Which of the following letters has only one line of symmetry?

    (a) H   (b) X   (c) Z   (d) T

Sol. By checking one by one all figures, we observe that in figure T, we can draw only one line segment for symmetry.

Hence, option (d) is correct.

Que 6. Write the number of lines of symmetry in each letter of the word 'SYMMETRY'.

Sol. For defining the lines of symmetry in the word 'SYMMETRY', check one by one line at segment.

    (a) S → In the letter S, there is no line segment for dividing equal parts, hence lines of symmetry in S is zero.

    (b) Y → In the letter Y, there is one line segment for dividing equal parts, hence lines of symmetry of Y letter is one.

    (c) M → In the letter M, there is one line segment for dividing equal parts, hence lines of symmetry of M letter is one.

    (d) E → In the letter E, there is one line segment for dividing equal parts, hence lines of symmetry of E letter is one.

    (e) T → In the letter T, there is one line segment for dividing equal parts, hence lines of symmetry of T letter is one.

    (f) R → In the letter R, there is no line of segment for dividing equal parts, hence lines of symmetry of R letter is zero.

Que 7. Write the letters of the word 'MATHEMATICS' which have no line of symmetry.

Sol. For finding the no line of symmetry in the word 'MATHEMATICS', check all the letters one by one.

Then,

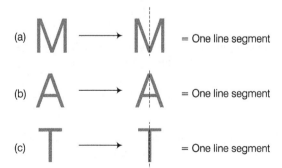

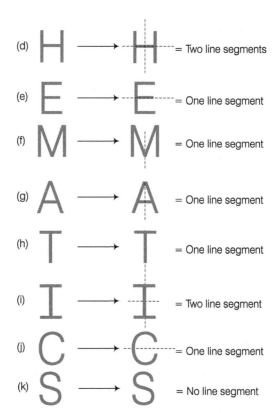

(d) H ⟶ H = Two line segments

(e) E ⟶ E = One line segment

(f) M ⟶ M = One line segment

(g) A ⟶ A = One line segment

(h) T ⟶ T = One line segment

(i) I ⟶ I = Two line segment

(j) C ⟶ C = One line segment

(k) S ⟶ S = No line segment

Hence, in the word 'MATHEMATICS', S letter has no line of symmetry

Que 8. The number of lines of symmetry in figure is _____.

Sol. In the given figure of circle, we can draw 5 lines of segment to bisect the figure in equal parts.

Hence, the line of symmetry of given circle is 5.

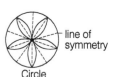
line of symmetry
Circle

Que 9. Is there any line of symmetry in the figure? If yes, draw all the lines of symmetry.

Sol. Yes, in the given figure, we can draw only one line of symmetry as shown in figure that divides the figure into two equal parts.

Que 10. In figure, *PQRS* is a rectangle. State the lines of symmetry of the rectangle.

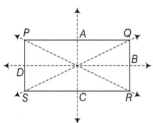

Sol. In the given figure, *AC* and *BD* are bisectors of rectangle which divides the rectangle in two equal parts.

Hence, the line of symmetry of given rectangular figure is two.

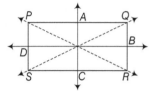

Que 11. A circle has only 16 lines of symmetry, is true or false.

Sol.

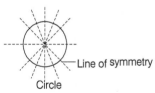

It is false, because the line of symmetry of circle is infinite.

Que 12. The number of lines of symmetry in a ruler is

(a) 0   (b) 1

(c) 2   (d) 4

Sol. In the figure of ruler, we can draw both horizontal and vertical lines to bisect into equal parts.

Hence, the line of symmetry of ruler is 2.

Que 13. Open your geometry box. There are some drawing tools. Observe them and complete the following table:

	Name of the tool	Number of lines of symmetry
(i)	Ruler	_____
(ii)	Divider	_____
(iii)	Compasses	_____
(iv)	Protractor	_____
(v)	Triangular piece with two equal sides	_____
(vi)	Triangular piece with unequal sides	_____

Sol. By observing the geometry tools, we find some important results.

(i) In the ruler, we can draw both horizontal and vertical lines. Hence, in the ruler, number of lines of symmetry is 2.

(ii) In the divider, we can draw only one line of segment for dividing. So, in the divider, number of lines of symmetry is 1.

(iii) In the compass, we can not draw any line of segment for dividing in each part. So, in the divider, number of lines of symmetry is 0.

(iv) In the protector, we can draw only one line of segment for dividing in each part. So, in the protractor, number of lines of symmetry is 1.

(v) In the triangular piece with two equal sides, we can draw only one line of segment because there are two equal sides of triangle. Hence, the line of symmetry is 1.

(vi) In the triangular piece with unequal sides, we can't draw any line of segment because there is no equal sides of triangular. Hence, the line of symmetry is 0.

	Name of the tool	Number of lines of symmetry
(i)	Ruler	2
(ii)	Divider	1
(iii)	Compasses	0
(iv)	Protractor	1
(v)	Triangular piece with two equal sides	1
(vi)	Triangular piece with unequal sides	0

Que 14. Write all the capital letters of the English alphabets which have more than one lines of symmetry.

Sol. For solution of this question, observe all English alphabets A to Z.

(i)

In the letter H, we can draw two lines of segment. Hence, the lines of symmetry is 2.

(ii) I ⟶ I ⟍ Line of symmetry

In the letter I, we can draw two lines of segment. Hence, the lines of symmetry is 2.

(iii) O ⟶ O ⟍ Line of symmetry

In the letter O, we can draw two lines of segment. Hence, the lines of symmetry is 2.

(iv) X ⟶ X ⟍ Line of symmetry

In the letter X, we can draw two lines of segment. Hence, the lines of symmetry is 2.

Que 15. Match the following.

Shapes		Number of lines of symmetry
(i) Isosceles triangle	(a)	6
(ii) Square	(b)	5
(iii) Kite	(c)	4
(iv) Equilateral triangle	(d)	3
(v) Rectangle	(e)	2
(vi) Regular hexagon	(f)	1
(vii) Scalene triangle	(g)	0

Sol. (i) **Isosceles triangle**

In an isosceles triangle, there are two equal sides of the triangle, then in an isosceles triangle, only one line of segment which divides into equal parts. Hence, the line of symmetry is 1 and option is (f).

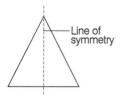

(ii) **Square**

In the square, there are four equal sides, then in the square, we can draw four lines of segment, which divides square in equal parts. Hence, the line of symmetry is 4 and option is (c).

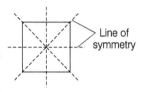

(iii) **Kite**

In the kite, there is only one line of segment which bisect the kite into equal parts. Hence, the lines of symmetry in kite is 1 and option is (f).

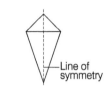

(iv) **Equilateral triangle**

In an equilateral triangle, there are three equal sides and medians of equilateral triangle bisect the triangle in three equal parts. Hence, the lines of symmetry in equilateral triangle is 3 and option is (d).

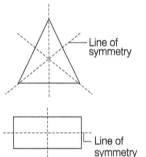

(v) **Rectangle**

In the rectangle, there are two equal sides, then there are two lines of segment which divides into equal parts. Hence, in the rectangle, the lines of symmetry in the rectangle is 2 and option is (e).

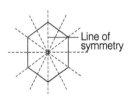

(vi) **Regular hexagon**

In the regular hexagon, there are six equal sides, then the lines of segment in hexagon is six, which bisect the regular hexagon in equal parts. Hence, the lines of symmetry in regular hexagon is 6 and option is (a).

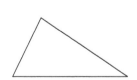

(vii) **Scalene triangle**

In the scalene triangle, there is no equal sides. Hence, we can't draw any line of segment. Hence, there is no line of symmetry and option is (g).

Chapter 14
Practical Geometry

Important Points

■ In this chapter, we will learn about different types of shapes with which we are familiar. We have learnt about some of these shapes in earlier chapters as well. In making of these shapes, we need to use some tools. Some of these tools are given below in table.

S.No.	Name and Figure	Description	Use
1.	The Ruler [or the straight edge]	A ruler ideally has no markings on it. However, the ruler in your instrument box is graduated into centimetres along one edge and into inches along the other edge.	To draw line segments and to measure their lengths.
2.	The Compasses Pencil Pointer	A pair-a pointer on one end and a pencil on the other.	To mark off equal lengths but not to measure them. To draw arcs and circles.
3.	The Divider	A pair of pointers	To compare lengths.

4.	Set-squares	Two triangular pieces, one of them has 45°, 45°, 90° angles at the vertices and the other has 30°, 60°, 90° angles at the vertices.	To draw perpendicular and parallel lines.
5.	The Protractor	A semi-circular device graduated into 180 degree-parts. The measure starts from 0° on the right hand side and ends with 180° on the left hand side and *vice-versa*.	To draw and measures angles.

■ **Circle** Circle is a boundary at an equal distance from its centre.

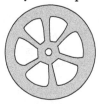

■ **Construction of a circle when its radius is known** Let us draw a circle of radius 3 cm. We need to use our compasses. Here are the steps to fallow.

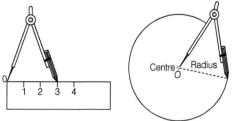

Step I Open the compasses for the required radius of 3 cm.

Step II Mark a point with a sharp pencil.

Step III Place the pointer of the compasses on *O*.

Step IV Turn the compasses slowly to draw the circle. Be careful to complete the movement around in one instant.

- **Line segment** A line segment is bounded by two end points. It is used to measure its length with a ruler.

  Construction of a line segment of a given length Let us draw a line segment of length 4.7 cm. We can use ruler and mark two points A and B and get $(\overline{AB})$. While marking the points A and B, we should look straight down at the ruler.

  Use of ruler and compasses A better method would be to use compasses to construct a line segment of a given length.

  Step I Draw a line l. Mark a point A on a line l.

  Step II Place the compasses pointer on the zero mark of the ruler. Open it to place the pencil point upto the 4.7 cm mark.

  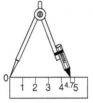

  Step III Taking caution that the opening of the compasses has not changed, place the pointer on A and swing an arc to cut l at B.

  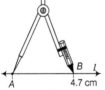

  Step IV $\overline{AB}$ is a line segment of required length.

- **Constructing a copy of a given line segment**

  Let us draw a line segment whose length is equal to that of a given line segment $\overline{AB}$.

  A quick and natural approach is to use you ruler (which is marked with centimetres and millimetres) to measure the length of $\overline{AB}$ and then use the same length to draw another line segment $\overline{CD}$.

A second approach would be to use a transparent sheet and trace $\overline{AB}$ onto another portion of the paper.

But these methods may not always give accurate results.

A better approach would be to use ruler and compasses for making this construction.

To make a copy of a line segment $\overline{AB}$, here are the steps to follow :

Step I   Given, a line segment $\overline{AB}$ whose length is not known.

Step II   Fix the compasses pointer on A and the pencil end on B. The opening of the instrument now gives the length of line segment $\overline{AB}$.

Step III   Draw any line l. Choose a point C on l. Without changing the compasses setting, place the pointer on C.

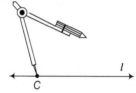

Step IV   Swing an arc that cuts l at a point, say D. Now, line segment $\overline{CD}$ is a copy of line segment $\overline{AB}$.

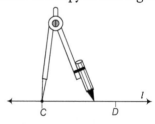

▪ **Perpendiculars**   As we know that, two lines (or segments) are said to be perpendicular, if they intersect such that the angles formed between them are right angles (90°).

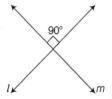

In the above figure, lines *l* and *m* are perpendicular.

Perpendicular to a line through a point on it Let a line *l* drawn on a paper sheet and a point *P* lying on the line. It is perpendicular to *l* through *P*.

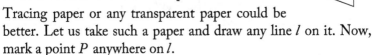

We can simply fold the paper such that the lines on both sides of the fold overlap each other.

Tracing paper or any transparent paper could be better. Let us take such a paper and draw any line *l* on it. Now, mark a point *P* anywhere on *l*.

Fold the sheet such that *l* is reflected on itself; adjust the fold, so that the crease passes through the marked point *P*. The crease is perpendicular to line *l*.

Checking points of perpendicular to line through a point Note that the line *l* passes through the point *P* as required.

Drawing perpendicular using ruler and a set-square Here, are the steps to follow :

Step I   A line *l* and a point *P* are given as shown alongside.

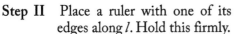

Step II   Place a ruler with one of its edges along *l*. Hold this firmly.

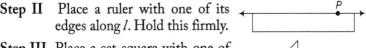

Step III Place a set-square with one of its edges along the already aligned edge of the ruler such that the right angled corner is in contact with the ruler.

Step IV Slide the set-square along the edge of ruler until its right angled corner coincides with *P*.

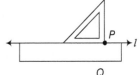

Step V   Hold the set-square firmly in this position. Draw $\overline{PQ}$ along the edge of the set-square, where *PQ* is perpendicular to *l*.

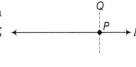

We can also use ruler in the place of set-square.

- **Method of using ruler and compasses** As is the preferred practice in geometry, the dropping of a perpendicular can be achieved through the 'ruler-compasses' construction as follows:

  Step I   Let a point *P* on a line *l*.

  Step II   With *P* as centre and a convenient radius, construct an arc intersecting the line *l* at two points *A* and *B*.

  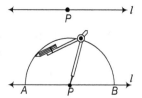

  Step III   With *A* and *B* as centres and a radius   greater   than   *AP* construct two arcs, which cut each other at *Q*.

  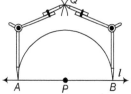

  Step IV   Join *PQ*. Then, $\overline{PQ}$ is perpendicular to *l*. We write $\overline{PQ} \perp l$.

  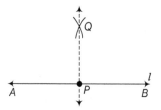

- **Perpendicular to a line through a point not on it** (paper folding) If we are given a line *l* and a point *P* not lying on it and we want to draw a perpendicular to *l* through *P*. We can do it by a simple paper (transparent) folding.

  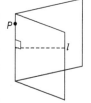

  For paper folding, take a sheet of paper and draw any line *l* on it. Mark a point *P* away from *l*. Fold the sheet such that the crease passes through *P*.

- **Method of using ruler and a set-square** For paper folding method, we can use ruler and a set-square. Here, are the steps to follow :

  Step I   Let *l* be the given line and *P* be a point outside *l*.

Step II Place a set-square on l such that one arm of its right angle aligns along l.

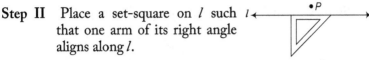

Step III Place a ruler along the edge opposite to the right angle of the set-square.

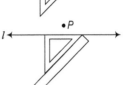

Step IV Hold the ruler fixed. Slide the set-square along the ruler till the point P touches the other arm of the set-square.

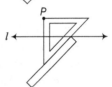

Step V Join PM along the edge through P meeting l at M. Now, $PM \perp l$.

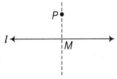

- **Method of using ruler and compasses** A more convenient and accurate method for drawing a perpendicular to a line through a point not on it is use of ruler and compasses method.

Step I Given a line l and a point P not on it.

Step II With P as centre, draw an arc, which intersects line l at two points A and B.

Step III Using the same radius and with A and B as centres, construct two arcs that intersect at a point, (say Q) on the other side.

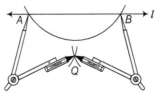

Step IV Join *PQ*. Thus, *PQ* is perpendicular to *l*.

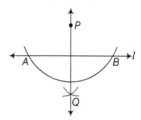

- **Perpendicular bisector of a line segment** For perpendicular bisector of a line segment fold a sheet of paper. Let $\overline{AB}$ be the fold, place on it (•) *X* anywhere.

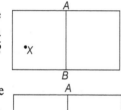

Find the image *X'* at *X*, with $\overline{AB}$ as the mirror line. Let $\overline{AB}$ and $\overline{XX'}$, intersect at *O*.

As we know, $\overline{AB}$ is the mirror line, this means that $\overline{AB}$ divides $\overline{XX'}$, into two parts of equal length. $\overline{AB}$ bisects $\overline{XX'}$ or $\overline{AB}$ is a bisector of $\overline{XX'}$.

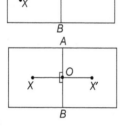

Here, $\angle AOX$ and $\angle BOX$ are right angles.

Hence, $\overline{AB}$ is perpendicular bisector of $\overline{XX'}$.

- **Method of constructing perpendicular bisector by using ruler and compasses** In the construction using ruler and compasses, some steps are as follow :

Step I   Draw a line segment $\overline{AB}$ of any length.

Step II   With *A* as centre, using compasses, draw a circle. The radius of your circle should be more than half the length of $\overline{AB}$.

Step III With the same radius and with *B* as centre, draw another circle using compasses. Let it cut the previous circle at *C* and *D*.

Step IV Join $\overline{CD}$. It cuts $\overline{AB}$ at O. Use your divider to verify that O is the mid-point of $\overline{AB}$. Also, verify that $\angle COA$ and $\angle COB$ are right angles. Therefore, $\overline{CD}$ is the perpendicular bisector of $\overline{AB}$.

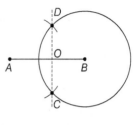

■ **Angles** Angles measuring is most important part of practical geometry. Angles are constructing by the use of ruler and compasses and protractor also.

Some methods of constructing an angle are as follow :

■ **Constructing an angle of a given measure** Suppose, we want to make an angle of measure 40°.

Some steps are as follow:

Step I Draw $\overline{AB}$ of any length.

Step II Place the centre of the protractor at A and the zero edge along $\overline{AB}$.

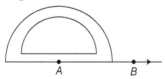

Step III Start with zero near B. Mark point C at 40°.

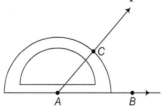

Step IV Join AC. $\angle BAC$ is the required angle.

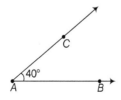

- **Constructing a copy of an angle of unknown measure** Suppose an angle (whose measure is not given) is given and we want to make a copy of this angle. We will have to use only a straight edge and the compasses.

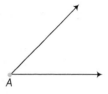

Let ∠A be an angle whose measure is not known. Here, we follow the steps as given below

Step I   Draw a line *l* and choose a point *P* on it.

Step II   Place the compasses at *A* and draw an arc to cut the rays of ∠*A* at *B* and *C*.

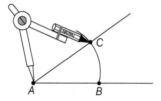

Step III   Use the same compasses setting to draw an arc with *P* as centre, cutting *l* at *Q*.

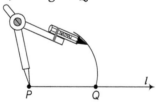

Step IV   Set your compasses to the length *BC* with the same radius.

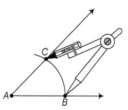

Step V   Place the compasses pointer at *Q* and draw the arc, to cut the arc drawn earlier in *R*.

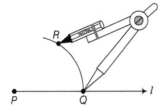

Step VI Join *PR*. This gives us ∠*P*. It has the same measure as ∠*A*.

This means ∠*QPR* has same measure as ∠*BAC*.

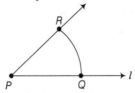

■ **Bisector of an angle** For making a bisector of an angle.

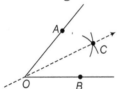

In the above figure mark a point *O* on it. With *O* as initial point, draw two rays $\overrightarrow{OA}$ and $\overrightarrow{OB}$. We get ∠*AOB*. Fold the sheet through *O* such that the rays $\overrightarrow{OA}$ and $\overrightarrow{OB}$ coincide.

Let *OC* be the crease of paper, which is obtained after unfolding the paper. *OC* is clearly a line of symmetry for ∠*AOB*. Measure ∠*AOC* and ∠*COB*. *OC* is line of symmetry, therefore it is known as the angle bisector of ∠*AOB*.

■ **Construction using ruler and compasses** For constructing bisector of an angle, we use ruler and compasses in this method.

Here are the steps to follow :

Let an angle, (say ∠*A*) be given.

Step I   With *A* as centre and using compasses, draw an arc that cuts both rays of ∠*A*. Label the points of intersection as *B* and *C*.

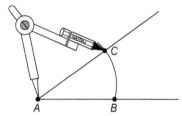

Step II With *B* as centre, draw (in the interior angle of ∠*A*) an arc, whose radius is more than half the length of *BC*.

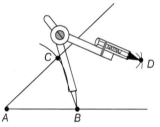

Step III With the same radius and with *C* as centre, draw another arc in the interior angle of ∠*A*.

Let the two arcs interesect at *D*. Then, $\overline{AD}$ is the required bisector of ∠ *A*.

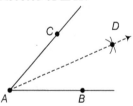

■ **Angles of special measures** There are some elegant and accurate methods to construct some angles of special measures, which do not require the use of the protractor.

Some of them are as follow:

Constructing a 60° angle

Step I   Draw a line *l* and mark a point *O* on it.

Step II Place the pointer of the compasses at O and draw an arc of convenient radius, which cuts the line $\overleftrightarrow{PQ}$ at a point, say (A).

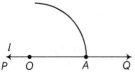

Step III With the pointer at A (as centre), now draw an arc that passes through O.

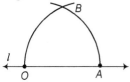

Step IV Let the two arcs intersect at B. Join OB. We get $\angle BOA$, whose measure is 60°.

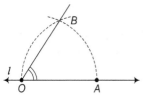

Constructing a 30° angle Construct an angle of 60° as shown in above construction. Now, bisect this angle. Each angle is 30° and verify it by using a protractor.

Constructing a 120° angle An angle of 120° is nothing but twice of an angle of 60°. Therefore, it can be constructed as follows:

Step I Draw any line $\overline{PQ}$ and take a point O on it.

Step II Place the pointer of the compasses at O and draw an arc of convenient radius which cuts the line at A.

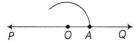

Step III Without disturbing the radius on the compasses, draw an arc with A as centre which cuts the first arc at B.

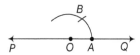

Step IV Again without disturbing the radius on the compasses and with B as centre, draw an arc which cuts the first arc at C.

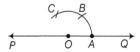

Step V Join OC, $\angle COA$ is the required angle, whose measure is 120°.

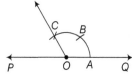

Constructing a 90° angle Construct a perpendicular to a line from a point lying on it, as discussed earlier. This is the required 90° angle.

Exercise 14.1

Que 1. Draw a circle of radius 3.2 cm.

Sol. To draw a circle of radius 3.2 cm, we use the following steps:

Step I Open the compasses to take a distance of 3.2 cm for the required radius of circle.

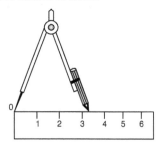

Step II   Mark a point with a sharp pencil for the centre of the circle and name it as O.

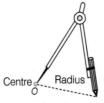

Step III   Place the pointer of the compasses on O.

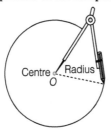

Step IV   Turn the compasses slowly to draw the circle.
Then, the figure obtained is of the required circle of radius 3.2 cm.

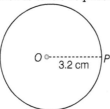

Que 2. With the same centre O, draw two circles of radii 4 cm and 2.5 cm.

Sol. Here, to draw two circles of radii 4 cm and 2.5 cm with the same centre O, we use the following steps:

     Step I   Open the compasses to take distance of 4 cm for the required radius of circle.

     Step II   Mark a point with a sharp pencil for the centre of the circle and name it as O.

     Step III   Place the pointer of the compasses on O.

     Step IV   Turn the compasses slowly, to draw the circle of radius 4 cm.

     Step V   Now, again open the compasses to take a distance of 2.5 cm for the required radius of circle.

     Step VI   Place the pointer of the compasses on O (since, both circles have same centre).

Step VII   Turn the compasses slowly, to draw the circle of radius 2.5 cm.

Thus, we get two circles with same centre O and radius 4 cm and 2.5 cm, respectively.

Que 3. Draw a circle with any two of its diameters. If you join the ends of these diameters, what is the figure obtained if the diameters are perpendicular to each other? How do you check your answer?

Sol. Firstly, draw a circle with O as centre and of any radius.

Then, draw any two diameters, say AOB and COD.

Now, join DA, AC, CB, and BD. It is clear from the given figure that $DACB$ is a rectangle.

When the diameter AOB and DOC are perpendicular to each other, then figure obtained by joining AC, CB, BD and DA is a square $ADBC$.

To check our answer, we can compare lengths of sides by using divider.

Que 4. Draw any circle and mark points A, B and C such that

    (i) A is on the circle.

    (ii) B is in the interior of the circle.

    (iii) C is in the exterior of the circle.

Sol.   On drawing, we get the following circle with O as centre and of any radius.

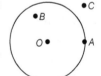

    (i) Take a point A such that A lies on the circle.

    (ii) Take a point B such that B lies in the interior of the circle.

    (iii) And take a point C such that C lies in the exterior of the circle.

Que 5. Let A and B be the centres of two circles of equal radii, draw them so that each one of them passes through the centre of the other. Let them intersect at C and D.

Examine whether $\overline{AB}$ and $\overline{CD}$ are at right angles.

Sol. To draw two circles such that each one of them passes through the centre of the other, we use the following steps:

Step I   Firstly, mark two points A and B on the paper.

Step II   Take the distance between A and B as radius and draw a circle with centre A.

Step III   Now, take B as centre and draw a circle with radius AB.

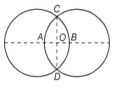

Thus, we get two circles which passes through the centres of each other. Let these circles intersect each other at C and D. Join C and D, which intersect AB at O. Then, we observe that, the $\angle AOC$ and $\angle COB$ are equal to 90°. Hence, $\overline{AB} \perp \overline{CD}$.

So, we can say that $\overline{AB}$ and $\overline{CD}$ are at right angles.

Exercise 14.2

Que 1. Draw a line segment of length 7.3 cm using a ruler.

Sol.   In order to construct a line segment of length 7.3 cm using a ruler, we use the following steps :

Step I   Mark a point A on the paper and place the ruler, so that zero mark of the ruler is at A.

Step II   Mark with a pencil a point B against the mark on the ruler which indicates 7.3 cm.

Step III   Join points A and B by moving the tip of the pencil against the straight edge of the ruler.

The line segment AB, so obtained is the required line segment of length 7.3 cm.

Que 2. Construct a line segment of length 5.6 cm using ruler and compasses.

Sol.   To construct a line segment of length 5.6 cm using ruler and compasses, we use the following steps :

Step I   Draw a line l and mark a point A on this line.

Step II   Place the pointer of the compasses at a zero mark of the ruler. Open it to place the pencil point upto the 5.6 cm mark.

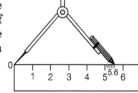

Step III Taking caution that the opening of the compasses has not changed, place the pointer on *A* and swing an arc to cut *l* at *B*.

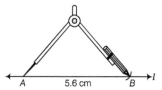

Step IV $\overline{AB}$ is a line segment of required length.

A   5.6 cm   *B*

Que 3. Construct $\overline{AB}$ of length 7.8 cm. From this, cut off $\overline{AC}$ of length 4.7 cm. Measure $\overline{BC}$.

Sol. Given, $\overline{AB}$ = 7.8 cm and $\overline{AC}$ = 4.7cm. Now, to construct a line segment of length 7.8 cm, we use the following steps:

Step I Draw a line *l.* Mark a point *A* on this line.

Step II Place the pointer of compasses at the zero mark of the ruler. Open it to place the pencil point up to the 7.8 cm mark.

Step III Without changing the opening to the compasses. Place the pointer on *A* and swing an arc to cut *l* at *B*.

Step IV $\overline{AB}$ is a line segment of length 7.8 cm.

A   *B*   7.8 cm

Now, to cut off $\overline{AC}$ of length 4.7 cm from $\overline{AB}$, we use the following steps:

Step V Now, place the pointer of compasses at the zero mark of the ruler. Open it to the place the pencil point upto 4.7 cm mark.

Step VI Without changing the opening of the compasses, place the pointer on *A* and swing an arc to cut *l* at *C*.

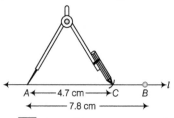

A 4.7 cm *C* *B*

7.8 cm

Step VII Now, $\overline{AC}$ is a line segment of length 4.7 cm. On measuring, we get $\overline{BC}$ = 3.1 cm

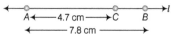

A 4.7 cm *C* *B*

7.8 cm

Que 4. Given $\overline{AB}$ of length 3.9 cm, construct $\overline{PQ}$ such that the length of $\overline{PQ}$ is twice that of $\overline{AB}$. Verify by measurement.

(**Hint** Construct such that length of $\overline{XQ}$ = length of $\overline{AB}$, then cut off $\overline{XQ}$ such that $\overline{XQ}$ also has the length as $\overline{AB}$).

Sol. Given, $\overline{AB}$ = 3.9 cm. Now, to construct required line segment by using compasses, we use the following steps:

Step I	Firstly, draw $\overline{AB}$ = 3.9 cm 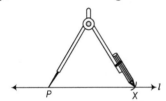
Step II	Now, to draw an another line l, mark a point P on it.
Step III	Place the pointer of compasses at the zero mark of the ruler. Open it to the place of the pencil point upto 3.9 cm mark.
Step IV	Without changing the opening of the compasses, place the pointer on P and swing an arc to cut l at X.

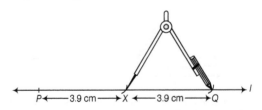

Step V	Measure $\overline{PX}$, we get $\overline{PX}$ = 3.9 cm = $\overline{AB}$.
Step VI	Again, without changing the opening of the compasses, place the pointer on X and swing an arc to cut l at Q.

Step VII	Now, measure $\overline{XQ}$, we get $\overline{XQ}$ = 3.9 cm = $\overline{AB}$
Step VIII	$\overline{PQ}$ = $\overline{PX}$ + $\overline{XQ}$ = (3.9 + 3.9)cm = $\overline{AB}$ + $\overline{AB}$ = 2 $\overline{AB}$
	Hence, $\overline{PQ}$ is twice that of $\overline{AB}$.

Verification : On measuring the length of $\overline{PQ}$ and $\overline{AB}$.
We get, $\overline{PQ}$ = 7.8 cm and $\overline{AB}$ = 3.9 cm and $\overline{PQ}$ = 2($\overline{AB}$) = 7.8 cm
Thus, twice of $\overline{AB}$ is equal to $\overline{PQ}$.

Que 5. Given, $\overline{AB}$ of length 7.3 cm and $\overline{CD}$ of length 3.4 cm, construct a line segment $\overline{XY}$ such that the length of $\overline{XY}$ is equal to the difference between the lengths of $\overline{AB}$ and $\overline{CD}$. Verify by measurement.

 TIPS

Firstly, draw $\overline{AB}$ and $\overline{CD}$, then cut length of $\overline{CD}$ from $\overline{AB}$ and remaining length of $\overline{AB}$ gives the difference between their lengths. Now, draw a line *l* and cut line segment $\overline{XY}$ from it, whose length is equal to the difference of length $\overline{AB}$ and $\overline{CD}$.

Sol. Given, $\overline{AB}$ = 7.3 cm and $\overline{CD}$ = 3.4 cm

Now, to construct required line segment $\overline{XY}$, we use the following steps:

Step I   Firstly, draw $\overline{AB}$ = 7.3 cm and $\overline{CD}$ = 3.4 cm

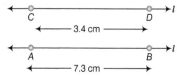

Step II   Now, place the pointer of compasses on C of pencil on D. The opening of the instrument gives the length of $\overline{CD}$ i.e. 3.4 cm.

Step III   Without changing the opening of the compasses place the pointer on A and swing an arc to cut $\overline{AB}$ at R.

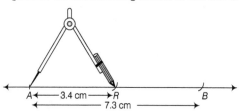

Step IV   Thus, $\overline{AR}$ = 3.4 cm and $\overline{RB}$ is the difference between the length of $\overline{AB}$ and $\overline{CD}$.

Step V   Now, draw a line *l* and mark a point X on it.

Step VI   Place the pointer of compasses on R and of pencil on B. The opening of the compasses gives the length of $\overline{RB}$.

Step VII   Without changing the opening of the compasses, place the pointer on X and swing an arc to cut *l* at Y.

Thus, $\overline{XY}$ is a line segment whose length is equal to the difference between the lengths of $\overline{AB}$ and $\overline{CD}$.

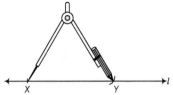

Verification By actual measurement, we have $\overline{XY} = 3.9$ cm

Now, $\overline{AB} - \overline{CD} = 7.3$ cm $- 3.4$ cm $= 3.9$ cm

$\Rightarrow$ $\qquad\qquad\qquad\qquad \overline{XY} = \overline{AB} - \overline{CD}$

i.e. length of $\overline{XY}$ = The difference of lengths $\overline{AB}$ and $\overline{CD}$.

Hence, verified.

Exercise 14.3

Que 1. Draw any line segment $\overline{PQ}$. Without measuring $\overline{PQ}$, construct a copy of $\overline{PQ}$.

Sol. To make a copy of $\overline{PQ}$, we use the following steps:

Step I   Firstly, draw $\overline{PQ}$ of any length because length is not known.

Step II   Fix the compasses pointer on P and the pencil end Q. The opening of the instrument now gives the length of $\overline{PQ}$.

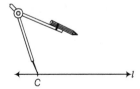

Step III   Draw any line l and choose a point C on it. Without changing the compasses setting, place the pointer on C.

Step IV Swing an arc that cuts *l* at a point, say *D*. Then, $\overline{CD}$ is copy of $\overline{PQ}$.

Que 2. Given, some line segment $\overline{AB}$ whose length you do not know, construct $\overline{PQ}$ such that the length of $\overline{PQ}$ is twice that of $\overline{AB}$.

Sol. To make $\overline{PQ}$, we use the following steps:

Step I   First of all, draw a line segment $\overline{AB}$, whose length is not known.

Step II   Fix the pointer of compasses on *A* and the pencils end on *B*. The opening of the instrument now gives the length of $\overline{AB}$.

Step III Draw any line *l*. Choose a point *P* on *l*, without changing the compasses setting, place the pointer on *P*, swing an arc that cuts *l* at point *R*.

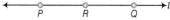

Step IV   Now, place the pointer on *R* and without changing the compasses setting, swing another arc that cuts *l* at a point *Q*.

Step V   Thus, $\overline{PQ}$ is the required line segment whose length is twice that of $\overline{AB}$. Hence, $\overline{PQ} = 2\overline{AB}$

Exercise 14.4

Que 1. Draw any line segment $\overline{AB}$. Mark any point *M* on it. Through *M*, draw a perpendicular to $\overline{AB}$. (use ruler and compasses).

Sol. To draw a perpendicular to $\overline{AB}$, we use the following steps:

Step I Firstly, draw a line segment $\overline{AB}$ and take any point *M* on it.

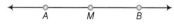

Step II With *M* as centre and a convenient radius, construct an arc intersecting the line $\overline{AB}$ at two points *X* and *Y*.

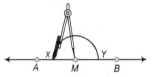

Step III With *X* and *Y* as centres and a radius greater than $\overline{XM}$ construct two arcs which cut each other at *D*.

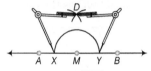

Step IV Now, join *MD*. Then, $\overline{MD}$ is perpendicular to $\overline{AB}$ and we can write it as $\overline{MD} \perp \overline{AB}$.

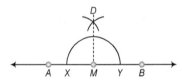

Que 2. Draw any line segment $\overline{PQ}$. Take any point R not on it. Through *R*, draw a perpendicular to $\overline{PQ}$. (use ruler and set-square).

Sol. To draw a perpendicular to $\overline{PQ}$ using ruler and set-square, we use the following steps:

Step I Draw a line segment $\overline{PQ}$ and take a point *R*, outside of $\overline{PQ}$.

Step II Place a set-square on $\overline{PQ}$ such that one arm of its right angle aligns along $\overline{PQ}$.

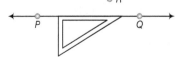

Step III　Place a ruler along the edge opposite to the right angle of the set-square.

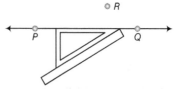

Step IV　Hold the ruler fixed. Slide the set-square along the ruler till the point R touches the other arm of the set square.

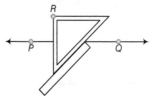

Step V　Join RS along the edge through R meeting $\overline{PQ}$ at S.

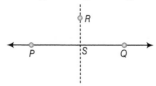

Hence, $\overline{RS} \perp \overline{PQ}$

Que 3. Draw a line l and a point X on it. Through X, draw a line segment $\overline{XY}$ perpendicular to l.

Now, draw a perpendicular to $\overline{XY}$ at Y. (use ruler and compasses)

Sol.　To draw $\overline{XY}$ perpendicular on l and then a perpendicular to $\overline{XY}$ at Y, we use the following steps:

Step I　Firstly, draw a line l and take point X on it.

Step II　With X as centre and a convenient radius, draw an arc intersecting the line l at two points A and B.

Step III　With A and B as centres and radius greater than $\overline{XA}$, draw two arcs, which cut each other at C.

Step IV　Join $\overline{XC}$ and produce it to Y. Then, $\overline{XY}$ is perpendicular to l.

Step V　With Y as centre and a convenient radius, draw an arc intersecting $\overline{XY}$ at two points E and D.

Step VI　With E and D as centres and a radius greater than $\overline{YD}$, draw two arcs, which cut each other at F.

Step VII   Join $\overline{YF}$, then YF is perpendicular to $\overline{XY}$ at Y. i.e. $YF \perp XY$ and $YX \perp l$.

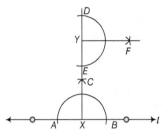

Exercise 14.5

Que 1. Draw $\overline{AB}$ of length 7.3 cm and find its axis of symmetry.

Sol. To find out the axis of symmetry of $\overline{AB}$ of length 7.3 cm, we use the following steps :

Step I   Draw a line segment $\overline{AB}$ of length 7.3 cm.

Step II   With A as centre, using compasses, draw a circle, whose radius is more than half the length of $\overline{AB}$.

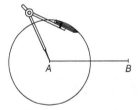

Step III   With the same radius and with B as centre, draw another circle using compasses. It cut the previous circle at C and D.

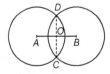

Step IV   Join $\overline{CD}$. It cuts $\overline{AB}$ at O.

Then, $\overline{CD}$ is the perpendicular bisector of $\overline{AB}$.

Also, it is the axis of symmetry.

Que 2. Draw a line segment of length 9.5 cm and construct its perpendicular bisector.

Sol. To construct the perpendicular bisector, we use the following steps:

  Step I   Draw a line segment $\overline{AB}$ of length 9.5 cm.

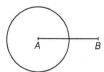

  Step II   With A as centre and radius more than half of $\overline{AB}$, draw a circle.

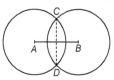

  Step III   With B as centre and same radius draw another circle which intersects the first circle at C and D, respectively.

  Step IV   Join CD, which intersects $\overline{AB}$ at O.

  Then, $\overline{CD}$ is the required perpendicular bisector of $\overline{AB}$.

Que 3. Draw the perpendicular bisector of $\overline{XY}$ whose length is 10.3 cm.

  (a) Take any point P on the bisector drawn. Examine whether $PX = PY$.

  (b) If M is the mid-point of $\overline{XY}$, what can you say about the lengths of MX and XY?

Sol. Firstly, we will draw the perpendicular bisector of $\overline{XY}$, so we use the following steps:

  Step I   Draw a line segment of $\overline{XY}$ whose length is 10.3 cm.

  Step II   With X as centre, using compasses, draw an arc of a circle whose radius is more than half of XY. (Here, we can draw a circle also but here more than half length of given line segment is long and circle will be very big, so we use arc in place of circle).

Step III With the same radius and with Y as centre, draw another arc of circle using compasses.

It cut the previous arcs at R and S.

Step IV Join $\overline{RS}$. It cuts $\overline{XY}$ at M.

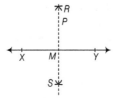

Then, $\overline{RS}$ is the perpendicular bisector of $\overline{XY}$.

(a) Let P be any point on the bisector, then join PX and PY.

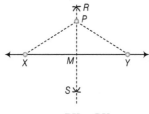

$$PX = PY \qquad \text{[using divider]}$$

(b) If M is the mid-point of $\overline{XY}$, then we can say that the length of XY is the twice of MX or MY (or MX or MY is half of XY)

i.e. $MX = \dfrac{1}{2} XY$ or $MY = \dfrac{1}{2} XY$ or $XY = 2MX$ or $XY = 2MY$

Que 4. Draw a line segment of length 12.8 cm. Using compasses, divide it into four equal parts. Verify by actual measurement.

TIPS

To divide the given line segment $\overline{AB}$ into four equal parts, firstly we draw the perpendicular bisector of $\overline{AB}$ which divide it into two equal parts. Then, draw perpendicular bisector of each part. Out of these two parts divide the given line segment into four equal parts.

Sol. To divide a line segment into four equal parts, we use the following steps:

Step I Draw a line segment $\overline{AB}$ of length 12.8 cm.

$\overset{\longleftarrow}{\underset{\longleftarrow 12.8 \text{ cm} \longrightarrow}{A \qquad\qquad B}}$

Step II With A as centre using compasses, draw an arc of a circle (we also draw circle here) of radius more than half length of $\overline{AB}$.

Step III With the same radius and with B as centre, draw another arc using compasses. It cut the previous arc at P and Q.

Step IV Join $\overline{PQ}$. It is the perpendicular bisector of $\overline{AB}$.

Step V Now, with A as centre, using compasses draw an arc of a circle of radius more than half of the length AO.

Step VI With the same radius and with O as centre, draw another arc of a circle which intersect the previous arcs at R and S.

Step VII Join RS. It cuts $\overline{AO}$ (or $\underline{AB}$) at C. Therefore, RS is the perpendicular bisector of $\overline{AO}$.

Step VIII Now, with B as centre, using compasses, draw an arc of a circle whose radius is more than half of the length of OB.

Step IX With the same radius and with O as centre, draw another arc of a circle which intersect the previous arc at M and N.

Step X Join $\overline{MN}$. It cuts $\overline{OB}$ (or $\underline{AB}$) at D. Therefore, MN is the perpendicular bisector of $\overline{OB}$.

Step XI Now, the line segment is divided into 4 equal parts

i.e. $\overline{AC} = \overline{CO} = \overline{OD} = \overline{DB}$

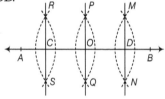

Verification By actual measurement, we get

$$\overline{AC} = \overline{CO} = \overline{OD} = \overline{DB} = 3.2 \text{ cm}$$

and $$\overline{AB} = 4 \times 3.2 \text{ cm} = 12.8 \text{ cm}$$

Que 5. With $\overline{PQ}$ of length 6.1 cm as diameter, draw a circle.

TIPS

Firstly, divide the given diameter into two equal parts i.e. draw its perpendicular bisector, then take any one part as radius and common point of both part as centre, draw a circle which gives the required circle of diameter 6.1 cm.

Sol. To draw a circle, of diameter 6.1 cm, we use the following steps:

Step I Draw a line segment $\overline{PQ}$ of length 6.1 cm.

Step II   With *P* as centre, using compasses, draw an arc of a circle (here, we can draw a circle also) with radius more than half of the length of $\overline{PQ}$.

Step III With the same radius and with *Q* as centre, draw another circle using compasses. Let it cut the previous circle at *M* and *N*.

Step IV   Now, join $\overline{MN}$. It cuts $\overline{PQ}$ at *O*.

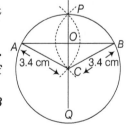

Therefore, $\overline{MN}$ is the perpendicular bisector of $\overline{PQ}$ and *O* is the mid-point of $\overline{PQ}$. Now, with *O* as centre and *OP* or *OQ* as radius, draw a circle. Thus, it is a circle whose diameter is the line segment $\overline{PQ}$.

Hence, the circle *PMQN* is the required circle.

Que 6. Draw a circle with centre *C* and radius 3.4 cm. Draw any chord $\overline{AB}$. Construct the perpendicular bisector of $\overline{AB}$ and examine if it passes through *C*.

Sol.   To construct the perpendicular bisector of chord $\overline{AB}$, we use the following steps:

Step I   Draw a circle with *C* as centre and radius 3.4 cm.

Step II Now, draw a chord *AB* of the circle (a chord of a circle is a line segment joining any two points on the circle)

Step III With *A* as centre, using compasses draw an arc (here, we can draw circle also) with radius more than half of the length of $\overline{AB}$.

Step IV With the same radius and with *B* as centre, draw an another arc using compasses. Let it cut the previous arc at *P* and *C*.

Step V   Join $\overline{PC}$ and produced upto *Q*. It cuts $\overline{AB}$ at *O*.Therefore, $\overline{PC}$ is the perpendicular bisector of $\overline{AB}$.

Also, the perpendicular bisector $\overline{PC}$ passes through the centre *C* of the circle.

Hence, the perpendicular bisector of chord *AB* passes through the centre *C*.

Que 7. Repeat Question 6, if $\overline{AB}$, happens to be a diameter.

Sol.   To construct the perpendicular bisector of diameter $\overline{AB}$, we use the following steps

Step I   Draw a circle with *C* as centre and radius 3.4 cm.

Step II   Draw diameter AB of the circle (a diameter is a   chord passing through the centre of the circle).

Step III   With A as centre, using compasses, draw an arc with radius more than half of the length of $\overline{AB}$.

Step IV   With the same radius and with B as centre, draw another arc using compasses. Let it cuts the previous arc at M and N.

Step V   Join $\overline{MN}$. It cuts $\overline{AB}$ at C.

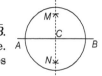

Therefore, $\overline{MN}$ is the perpendicular bisector of $\overline{AB}$.
Also, $\overline{MN}$ passes through the centre C of the circle.
Hence, perpendicular bisector of diameter passes through the centre of the circle.

Que 8. Draw a circle of radius 4 cm. Draw any two of its chords. Construct the perpendicular bisectors of these chords. Where do they meet?

Sol.   Here, we will use the following steps of construction:

Step I   Mark a point O on the paper and draw a circle of radius of 4 cm with O as centre.

Step II   Draw any two chords $\overline{AB}$ and $\overline{CD}$ of this circle.

Step III   Now, with A as centre, using compasses, draw an arc of radius more than half of the length of $\overline{AB}$.

Step IV   With the same radius and with B as centre, draw another arc using compasses. Let it cut the previous arc at P and Q.

Step V   Join $\overline{PQ}$. It cuts $\overline{AB}$ at M.

Therefore, PQ is the perpendicular bisector of $\overline{AB}$.

Step VI   Now, with C as centre and radius more than half of the length of CD draw an arc.

Step VII   With D as centre and same radius draw another arc which intersects previous arc at R and S.

Step VIII Join RS. It cuts CD at N. Therefore, RS is the perpendicular bisector of CD.

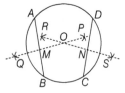

From the above figure, it is clear that these perpendicular bisectors also passes through O, the centre of the circle.

Hence, the perpendicular bisectors of these chords meet each other at centre of the circle.

Que 9. Draw any angle with vertex O. Take a point A on one of its arms and B on another such that $OA = OB$. Draw the perpendicular bisectors of $\overline{OA}$ and $\overline{OB}$. Let them meet at P. Is $PA = PB$?

Sol. Here, we will use the following steps of construction:

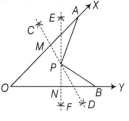

Step I	Draw any angle XOY with vertex O.
Step II	Take a point A on OX and a point B on OY, such that $OA = OB$.
Step III	Now, with O as centre, using compasses, draw an arc radius more than half of the length of $\overline{OA}$.
Step IV	With the same radius and with A as centre, draw another arcs using compasses. Which cut the previous arc at C and D respectively.
Step V	Join $\overline{CD}$. It cuts $\overline{OA}$ at M. Therefore, CD is the perpendicular bisector of $\overline{OA}$.
Step VI	Now, with O as centre and radius equal to more than half of the length of OB, draw arcs.
Step VII	With same radius and with B as centre, draw another arcs which cut the previous arcs at E and F.
Step VIII	Join $\overline{EF}$. It cuts $\overline{OB}$ at N. Therefore, EF is the perpendicular of $\overline{OA}$.

Also, both perpendicular bisectors meet at A.

On measuring, we get $PA = PB$.

Try These (Page 290)

Que 1. How will you construct a 15° angle?

Sol. To construct an angle of 15°, steps of construction are given below:

    (i) Firstly, construct an angle of 60°.

    (ii) Bisect this angle to obtain an angle of 30°.

    (iii) Finally, bisect the angle of 30° to obtain an angle of 15°.

Steps of construction

Step I   Draw a line l and mark a point O on it.

Step II   Place the pointer of the compasses at O and draw an arc of convenient radius which cuts the line at a point say A.

Step III   Without disturbing the radius on the compasses draw an arc with A as centre which cuts the first arc at B.

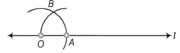

Step IV   Join OB. We get $\angle BOA$, whose measure is 60°.

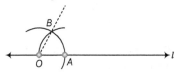

Step V   Now, bisect this angle. For this, take distance more than half of length AB as radius and A as centre draw an arc.

Step VI   Take B as centre and radius same as in Step V. Draw another arc which intersects the arc drawn in Step V at C.

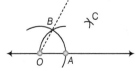

Step VII   Join OC by dotted line which intersects the arc AB at I. Then, $\angle COA = 30°$. Now, again we bisect this angle.

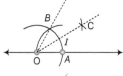

Step VIII   Take A and I as centres and radius more than $\dfrac{1}{2} AI$, draw two arcs, respectively such that both intersect each other at point D.

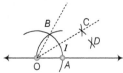

Step IX Join *OD*. Thus, ∠*DOA* = 15°.

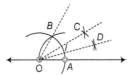

Try These (Page 291)

Que 2. How will you construct a 150° angle?

Sol. To construct an angle of 150°, steps of construction are given below

Step I Draw a line and mark point *O* and *A* on it such that *A* is in the right of *O*.

Step II With *O* as centre and with any convenient radius draw a semi-circle, cutting the line *l* at *P* and *S*.

Step III Now, take *P* as centre and radius same as in Step II and draw an arc which intersects the semi-circle at *Q*.

Step IV Now, take *Q* as centre and (same as step II) draw an arc which intersect the semi-circle at *R*.

Step V Now, bisect this angle, for this, take distance more than half of length *RS* as radius and with *R* and *S* as centre draw arcs such that both intersect each other at *T*.

Step VI Join *OT* and produce it upto point *B*.

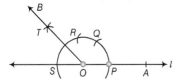

Thus, ∠*AOB* = 150°.

Try These (Page 291)

Que 3. How will you construct a 45° angle?

 Firstly, draw an angle of measure 90° and then draw its bisector to get an angle of measure 45°.

Sol. To construct an angle of 45°, steps of construction are given below:

Step I Draw a ray *OA* and take *O* as centre and with any convenient radius, draw an arc which cuts *OA* at *P*.

Step II   Without disturbing the radius on the compasses, draw an arc with P as centre which cuts the first arc at Q.

Step III   Again, draw an arc R with Q as centre and with same radius which intersects the arc drawn in Step I at P.

Step IV   Take Q and R as centre and with radius more than half of length RQ, draw two arcs respectively which intersects each other at B.

Step V   Join OB which intersects QR at I and produce upto C. Then, $\angle AOC = 90°$.

Step VI   Now, take P and I as centre and with radius more than half of length PI, draw two arcs respectively which intersect each other at D.

Step VII   Join OD.

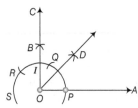

Then, $\angle AOD$ is the required angle of 45°.

Exercise 14.6

Que 1. Draw $\angle POQ$ of measure 75° and find its line of symmetry.

 TIPS

The line of symmetry of angle 75° is its perpendicular bisector.

Sol. So, to find the line of symmetry of angle 75°, we use the following steps:

Step I   Draw $\overline{AB}$ of any length.

Step II   Place the centre of the protractor at A and the zero edge along $\overline{AB}$.

Step III   Start with zero near *B*, mark point *C* at 75°.

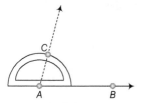

Step IV   Join *AC*. ∠*BAC* is the required angle of measure 75°.

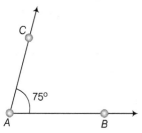

Step V   With *A* as centre and using compasses, draw an arc that cuts both rays of ∠*A* at *P* and *Q*.

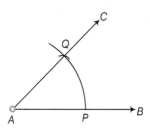

Step VI   With *P* as centre, draw (in the interior of ∠ *A* an arc whose radius is more than half of the length of *PQ*).

Step VII   With the same radius and with *Q* as centre, draw another arc in the interior of ∠*A*. Let the two arcs intersect at *D*.

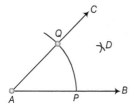

Step VIII Join AD, then $\overline{AD}$ is the required bisector of $\angle A$. i.e. AD is the line of symmetry of an angle of measure 75°.

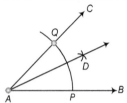

Que 2. Draw an angle of measure 147° and construct its bisector.

Sol. Here, we firstly draw an angle of 147° and then construct its bisector. So, we use the following steps:

Step I Draw $\overline{AB}$ of any length place the centre of the protractor at A and the zero edge along $\overline{AB}$.

Step II Start with zero near B. Mark a point C at 147°.

Step III Join AC. Then, $\angle BAC$ is an angle of measure 147°.

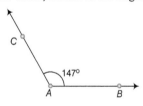

Step IV Now, with A as centre and using compasses, draw an arc that cuts both rays of $\angle A$ at P and Q.

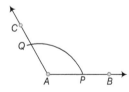

Step V With P as centre, draw (in the interior of $\angle A$) an arc whose radius is more than half of the length of PQ.

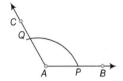

Step VI With the same radius and with Q as centre, draw another arc in the interior of $\angle A$. Let the two arcs intersect at D. Join $\overline{AD}$. Then, $\overline{AD}$ is the required bisector of $\angle A$.

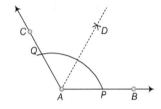

Que 3. Draw a right angle and construct its bisector.

Sol. Here, firstly draw an angle of measure 90° and then construct its bisector. For this, we use the following steps:

Step I Draw $\overline{AB}$ of any length. Place the centre of the protractor at A and the zero edge along $\overline{AB}$.

Step II Start with zero near B. Mark point C at 90°.

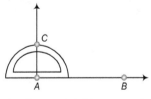

Step III Join AC. Then, $\angle BAC$ is an angle of measure 90°.

Step IV   With P as centre and using compasses, draw an arc whose radius is more than half of the length of PQ.

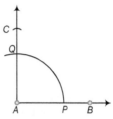

Step V   With the same radius and with Q as centre, draw another arc in the interior of $\angle A$, which intersects the previous arc at D. Join $\overline{AD}$. Then, $\overline{AD}$ is the required bisector of $\angle A$.

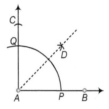

Que 4. Draw an angle of measure of 153° and divide it into four equal parts.

Sol. Here, to divide an angle of measure 153° into four equal parts, we use the following steps:

Step I   Draw $\overline{AB}$ of any length. Place the centre of the protractor at A and the zero edge along $\overline{AB}$.

Step II   Start with zero near B. Mark point C at 153°.

Step III Join AC, then $\angle BAC$ is an angle of measure 153°.

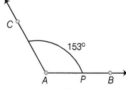

Step IV   With A as centre and using compasses, draw an arc that cuts both rays of $\angle A$ at P and Q.

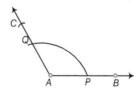

Step V   With P as centre, draw (in the interior of $\angle A$) an arc whose radius is more than half the length of PQ.

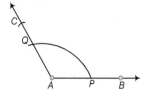

Step VI   With the same radius and with Q as centre, draw another arc in the interior of $\angle A$. Let the two arcs intersect at D. Join $\overline{AD}$. Let AD cut the arc PQ at I. Then, $\overline{AD}$ divides the $\angle BAC$ in two equal parts.

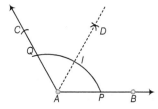

Step VII   Now, with P and I as centre and with radius more than half of length PI, draw two arcs respectively, which cut each other at R.

Step VIII   Join $\overline{AR}$. Then, $\overline{AR}$ divides $\angle BAD$ into two equal parts.

Step IX   Now, with Q and I as centre and with radius more than half of length QI, draw two arcs respectively, which cut each other at M.

Step X   Join $\overline{AM}$. Then, divide $\angle CAD$ into two equal parts.

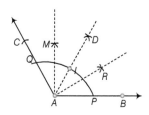

Thus, $\overline{AM}, \overline{AD}$ and $\overline{AR}$ divide $\angle BAC$ into four equal parts.

Que 5. Construct with ruler and compasses, angle of the following measures.

    (a) 60°   (b) 30°   (c) 90°

    (d) 120°   (e) 45°   (f) 135°

Sol. (a) For constructing an angle of 60°, we use the following steps of construction :

Step I　Draw a line *l* and mark a point *O* on it.

Step II　Place the pointer of the compasses at *O* and draw an arc of convenient radius which cuts the line *l* at a point say *A*.

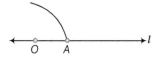

Step III　With the pointer at *A* (as centre), now draw an arc that passes through *O*.

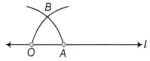

Step IV　Let the two arcs intersect at *B*. Join *OB*. Then, we get ∠*BOA*, whose measure is 60°.

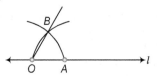

(b) For constructing an angle of 30°, we firstly construct an angle of 60° and then bisect it. Here, we use the following steps of construction:

Step I　Draw a line *l* and mark a point *O* on it.

Step II　Place the pointer of the compasses at *O* and draw an arc of convenient radius which cuts the line *l* at a point, say *A*.

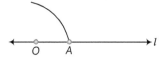

Step III　With the pointer at *A* (as centre), draw an arc that passes through *O*.

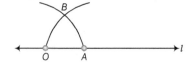

Step IV   Let the two arcs intersect at B. Join OB. Then, we get $\angle BOA$, whose measure is 60°.

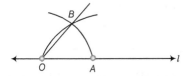

Step V   With A as centre, draw (in the interior of $\angle AOB$ an arc, whose radius is more than half the length of AB).

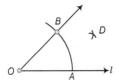

Step VI   With the same radius and with B as centre, draw another arc in the interior of $\angle O$. Let the two arcs intersect at D. Join OD. Then, $\overline{OD}$ is the bisector of $\angle BOA$.

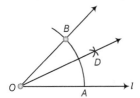

Thus, we get $\angle BOD$ and $\angle AOD$, which are equal in measure.

On measuring, $\angle BOD = \angle AOD = 30°$.

(c) To draw an angle of measure 90°, we use following steps of construction:

Step I   Draw a line l and mark point O and A on it.

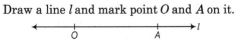

Step II   Place the pointer of the compasses at O and draw an arc of convenient radius which cuts the line l at a point P.

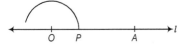

Step III Without disturbing the radius on the compasses, draw an arc with P as centre which cuts the first arc at Q.

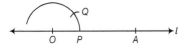

Step IV   Again, without disturbing the radius on the compasses and with Q as centre, draw an arc which cuts the arc (drawn in Step II) at R.

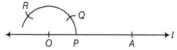

Step V   Now, with Q as centre and with radius more than half of length RQ draw an arc.

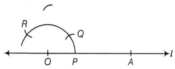

Step VI   Without disturbing the radius on the compasses, draw another arc with R as centre, which cuts the arc draw in Step V at B.

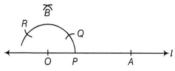

Step VII   Join OB. Then, we get $\angle BOA$ which is of measure $90°$.

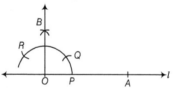

(d) To draw an angle of measure $120°$, use the following steps of construction:

An angle of $120°$ is nothing but twice of an angle of $60°$.

Therefore, it can be constructed by using the following steps of construction.

Step I   Draw any line PQ and take a point O on it.

Step II   Place the pointer of the compasses at O and draw an arc of convenient radius which cuts the line at A.

Step III Without disturbing the radius on the compasses, draw an arc with *A* as centre, which cuts the first arc at *B*.

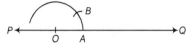

Step IV Again, without disturbing the radius on the compasses and with *B* as centre, draw an arc which cuts the first arc (drawn in Step II) at *C*.

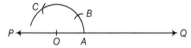

Step V Join *OC*, Thus, ∠*COA* is the required angle, whose measure is 120°.

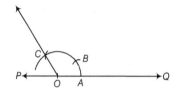

(e) To draw an angle of measure 45°, we use the following steps of construction:

Step I Draw a line *l* and mark points *O* and *A* on it.

Step II Place the pointer of the compasses of *O* and draw an arc of convenient radius, which cuts the line *l* at a point *P*.

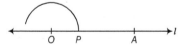

Step III Without disturbing the radius on the compasses, draw an arc with *P* as centre, which cuts the first arc at *Q*.

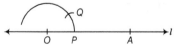

Step IV Again without disturbing the radius on the compasses and with *Q* as centre, draw an arc, which cuts the first arc (drawn in Step II) at *R*.

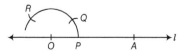

Step V   Now, with Q as centre and with radius more than half of length RQ draw an arc.

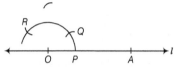

Step VI   Without disturbing the radius on the compasses, draw another arc with R as centre, which cut the arc drawn in Step V at B.

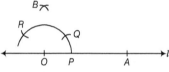

Step VII   Join OB, let it cut the arc QR at I. Then, we get $\angle BOA$ which is of measure 90°.

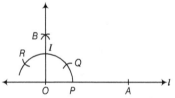

Step VIII Now, with P as centre and with radius more than half of length PI, draw an arc.

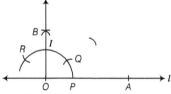

Step IX   Without disturbing the radius on the compasses, draw another arc with I as centre which cuts the arc drawn in Step VIII at C.

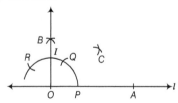

Step X   Join *OC*. Then, we get ∠*COA* which is the required angle of measure 45°.

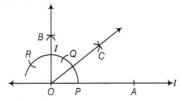

(f) To construct an angle of measure 135°, we use the following steps of construction :

We know that, $135° = 120° + 15° = 120 + \dfrac{30°}{2} = 120° + \dfrac{(150° - 120°)}{2}$.

So, firstly construct an angle of 120° and then angle of 150°. Then, bisect the angle between 120° and 150° to get required angle of measure 135°.

Step I   Draw any line *PQ* and take a point *O* on it.

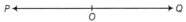

Step II   Place the pointer of the compasses at *O* and draw an arc of convenient radius which cuts the line at *A* and *D*.

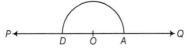

Step III   Without disturbing the radius of the compasses, draw an arc with *A* as centre, which cuts the first arc at *B*.

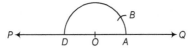

Step IV   Again, with the same radius draw an arc with *B* as centre which cuts the first arc (as drawn in Step II) at *C*. Join *OC* by dotted line. Then, we get ∠*COQ* = 120°.

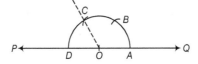

Step V   Now, with *C* and *D* as centre and radius more than half of length *CD*, draw arcs which cut each other at *E*.
Join *OE* by dotted line, we get ∠*EOQ* = 150°.

Also, *OE* cuts the arc *CD* at *I*.

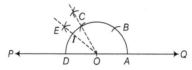

Step VI   With *C* and *I* as centre and radius more than half of length *CI*, draw arcs which cut each other at *F*.

Join *OF*. Then, we get ∠ *FOQ* = 135°

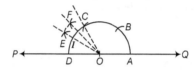

Que 6. Draw an angle of measure 45° and bisect it.

Sol.   Here we use the following steps of construction :

Step I   Draw $\overline{AB}$ of any length. Place the centre of the protractor at *A* and the zero edge along $\overline{AB}$.

Step II   Start with zero near *B*, mark point *C* at 45°.

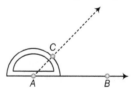

Step III   Join *AC*. Then, ∠*BAC* is an angle of measure 45°.

Step IV   Now, with *A* as centre and using compasses, draw an arc that cuts both rays of ∠*A* at *P* and *Q*.

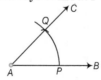

Step V With P as centre, draw (in the interior of $\angle A$) an arc whose radius is more than half the length of PQ.

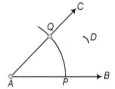

Step VI With the same radius and with Q as centre, draw another arc in the interior of $\angle A$. Let the two arcs intersect at D. Join $\overline{AD}$. Then, $\overline{AD}$ is the required bisector of $\angle A$. i.e. angle bisector of angle 45°.

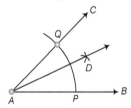

Que 7. Draw an angle of measure 135° and bisect it.

Sol. Here, to bisect an angle of 135°, we use the following steps of construction :

Step I Draw $\overline{AB}$ of any length. Place the centre of the protractor at A and the zero edge along $\overline{AB}$.

Step II Start with zero near A. Mark point C at 135°.

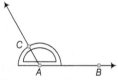

Step III Join AC. Then, $\angle BAC$ is an angle of measure 135°.

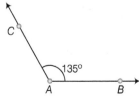

Step IV   With A as centre and using compasses, draw an arc that cuts both sides of $\angle A$ at points P and Q.

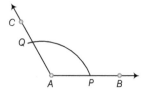

Step V   With P as centre, draw (in the interior of $\angle A$) an arc, whose radius is more than half of length PQ.

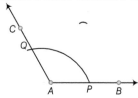

Step VI   With the same radius and with Q as centre, draw another arc in the interior of $\angle A$. Let the two arcs intersect at D. Join $\overline{AD}$. Then, $\overline{AD}$ is the required bisector of i.e. $\angle BAC = 135°$.

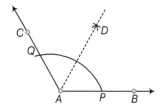

Que 8. Draw an angle of 70°. Make a copy of it using only a straight edge and compasses.

Sol. To draw an angle of measure 70°, we use the following steps of construction :

   Step I   Draw $\overline{AB}$ of any length. Place the centre of the protractor at A and the zero edge along $\overline{AB}$.

   Step II   Start with zero near B. Mark point C at 70°.

   Step III Join AC. Then, $\angle BAC$ is an angle of measure 70°.

   Now, to draw a copy of 70°, by using straight edge and compasses, we use the following steps of construction :

Step IV Draw a line *l* and choose a point *P* on it.

Step V Place the pointer at *A* and draw an arc to cut the rays of ∠*A* at *M* and *N*.

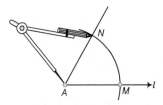

Step VI Use the same compasses setting to draw an arc with *P* as centre, cutting *l* at *Q*.

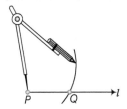

Step VII Set your compasses to the length of *MN*.

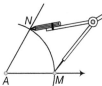

Step VIII Without disturbing the compasses. Place the compasses pointer at *Q* and draw an arc at *R* to cut the arc drawn in Step VI.

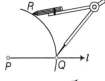

Step IX Join *PR*, then give us ∠*RPQ*. It has the same measure as ∠*BAC*. Hence,∠*RPQ* is required copy of an angle of measure 70°.

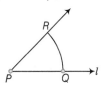

Que 9. Draw an angle of 40°. Copy its supplementary angle.

Sol. To draw an angle of measure 40°, we use the following steps:

Step I Draw a line *l* and mark three points *D*, *A* and *B* on it. Place the centre of the protractor at *A* and the zero edge along $\overline{AB}$.

Step II   Start with zero near B, mark point C at 40°.

Step III   Join AC. Then, $\angle BAC$ is an angle of measure 40°.

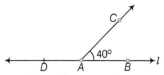

We know that, the sum of two supplementary angles is 180° and l is a straight line.

So, $\angle BAC + \angle DAC = 180°$ i.e. $\angle DAC$ is the supplementary angle of $\angle BAC$.

Now, to draw the supplementary of an angle 40°, we use the following steps of construction :

Step IV   To copy $\angle DAC$, draw a line l and choose a point P on it.

Step V   Place the compasses at A and draw an arc to cut the rays of DAC at P and Q, respectively.

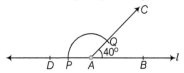

Step VI   Use the same compasses setting to draw an arc with P as centre, which cuts the line l at M.

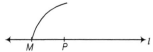

Step VII Set your compasses to the length PQ. Then, without disturbing the setting of compasses. Place the compasses pointer at M and draw the arc which cuts the previous arc (drawn in Step VI at N).

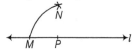

Step VII Join MN. Then, we get $\angle MPN$ which is the copy of $\angle DAC$ i.e. supplementary angle of 40°.

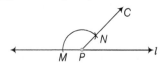

Selected **NCERT Exemplar Problems**

Que 1. Draw a line segment of length 10 cm. Divide it into four equal parts. Measure each of these parts.

Sol. To draw a line segment, we use following steps of construction :

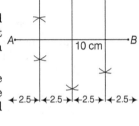

Step I	Firstly, we draw a line segment (*AB*) of length 10 cm.
Step II	By the help of compasses and ruler bisect the line segment and join both the points with line segment.
Step III	By the help of bisector of the line segment either side of line is also bisected by the ruler and compasses.
Step IV	Both bisector points of either side is joined.
Step V	By the help of ruler, we measure the each part of bisected line segment and each part is measured of length 2.5 cm.

Que 2. Draw an $\angle ABC$ of measure 45°, using ruler and compasses. Now, draw an $\angle DBA$ of measure 30°, using ruler and compasses as shown in figure. What is the measure of $\angle DBC$?

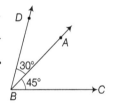

Sol. To draw an angle, we use following steps of construction :

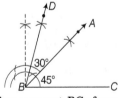

Step I	Draw a line segment *BC* of any length.
Step II	Place the compasses pointer at *B* and draw a right angle (90°).
Step III	Right angle (90°) is also bisected in 45° ($\angle ABC$) by the help of ruler and compasses.
Step IV	Place the compasses pointer at *B* and draw an angle of 30° ($\angle DBA$) between the right angle and bisected angle.
Step V	By the help of protractor, we get $\angle DBC = 75°$.

Que 3. Draw the images of points A and B in line l of figure and name them as A' and B', respectively. Measure AB and A' B'. Are they equal ?

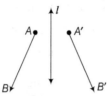

Sol.

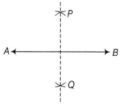

Yes, they are equal because by the rule of reflection of symmetry, the image of points. A and B in the line (l) is the points A' and B' and both are equal in length. Lines are measured by the help of ruler.

Que 4. Draw a line segment of length 6 cm. Construct its perpendicular bisector. Measure the two parts of the line segment.

Sol. To draw a perpendicular bisector, we use following steps of construction :

Step I	Firstly, we draw a line segment AB of length 6 cm.
Step II	With A and B as centre, draw arcs which intersect at points P and Q.
Step III	Join PQ, thus PQ is perpendicular to line segment AB.
Step IV	Measure the two parts of line segments with the help of ruler, it comes out to be 3 cm each.

Que 5. Bisect a straight angle, using ruler and compasses. Measure each part.

Sol. To bisect a straight angle, we use following steps of construction :

Step I	Firstly, draw a line of any length say AB.
Step II	With P as centre, draw an arc which bisects the line at X and Y.
Step III	With X and Y as centres, draw two arcs which cut each other at Q.
Step IV	Join PQ, thus PQ is a bisector of straight angle.

Step V By the help of protractor, the measure of the angle is 90°

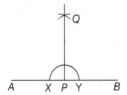

Que 6. Draw an angle of 60°, using ruler and compasses and divide it into four equal parts. Measure each part.

Sol. To draw an angle of 60°, using ruler and compasses, we use the following steps of construction:

Step I Firstly, draw a line segment *AB* of any length.

Step II Place the compasses pointer at point *A* and draw an angle of 60° by the help of ruler and compasses.

Step III Place the pointer at point *A* and bisect the angle.

Step IV Either side of bisected angle is also bisected by the help of ruler and compasses.

Step V Measure the bisected angles with the help of protractor, each comes out to be of 15°

Que 7. Draw a line segment of length 6.5 cm and divide it into four equal parts, using ruler and compasses.

Sol. Here, are the steps of construction:

Step I Firstly, draw a line segment *AB* of length 6.5 cm.

Step II Place the compasses pointer at points *A* and *B* and cut the arcs at points *P* and *Q*. Join *PQ* and it is the bisector of line segment *AB*.

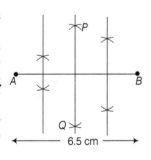

Step III The either sides of bisector length is also bisected by the help of ruler and compasses.

Step IV Join the arc points.

Step V Hence, the line segment *AB* is divided into four equal parts by using ruler and compasses.

Que 8. Draw a circle of radius 6 cm, using ruler and compass. Draw one of its diameters. Draw the perpendicular bisector of this diameter. Does this perpendicular bisector contain another diameter of the circle?

Sol. To draw a circle, we use the following steps of construction:

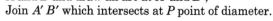

Step I   Firstly, draw a circle of radius 6 cm with the help of ruler and compasses.

Step II   Draw a diameter of 12 cm length in circle.

Step III   Place the compasses pointer at points A and B and draw an arc at A' and B', Join $A'B'$ which intersects at P point of diameter.

Thus, $A'B'$ is perpendicular at line segment AB.

Hence, the same circle is also draw by same length of diameter $A'B'$.

Que 9. Draw an angle of 65° and draw an angle equal to this angle, using ruler and compasses.

Sol. Here, are the steps of construction:

Step I   Firstly, draw an angle of 65°, by using protractor.

Step II   Draw a line segment AB of any length.

Step III   Place the pointer at point A and cut an arc with reference point.

Step IV   Join the cut arc at point A.

Hence, the given angle is of 65°.

Que 10. Draw an angle of 80°, using a protractor and divide it into four equal parts, using ruler and compasses. Check your construction by measurement.

Sol. Here, to divide an angle of measure 80° into four equal parts, we use the following steps of construction :

Step I   Draw $\overline{AB}$ of any length. Place the centre of the protractor at A and the zero edge along $\overline{AB}$.

Step II   Start with zero near B. Mark C at 80°.

Step III   Join AC, then $\angle BAC$ is an angle of measure 80°.

Step IV	With *A* as centre and using compasses, draw an arc that cuts both rays of ∠*A* at *P* and *Q*.	
Step V	With *P* as centre, draw (in the interior of ∠*A*) an arc whose radius is more than half the length of *PQ*.	
Step VI	With the same radius with *Q* as centre, draw another arc in the	

interior of ∠*A*. Let the two arcs intersect at *D*. Let the two arcs intersect at *D*. Join $\overline{AD}$, which cuts the arc *PQ* and *I*. Then, $\overline{AD}$ divides the ∠*BAC* in two equal parts.

Step VII Now taking *P* and *I* as centre, having radius more than half of length *PI*, draw two arcs respectively, which cut each other at *R*.

Step VIII Join $\overline{AR}$, which divides ∠*BAD* into two equal parts.

Step IX Now taking *Q* and *I* as centre, having radius more than half of length *QI*, draw two arcs respectively, which cut each other at *M*.

Step X Join $\overline{AM}$. Then, divide ∠*CAD* into two equal parts.

Thus $\overline{AM}$, $\overline{AD}$ and $\overline{AR}$ divide ∠*BAC* into four equal parts.

Que 11. Draw a line segment of length 7 cm. Draw its perpendicular bisector, using ruler and compasses.

Sol. To draw a perpendicular bisector of line segment of length 7 cm. We use the following steps of construction:

Step I Firstly, draw a line segment $\overline{AB}$ of length 7cm.

Step II With *A* as centre, using compasses, draw a circle. The radius of circle should be more than half the length of $\overline{AB}$.

Step III With the same radius and with *B* as centre draw another circle using compasses. Let it cut the previous circle at *C* and *D*.

Step IV Join *CD*. It cuts $\overline{AB}$ at *O*.

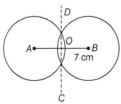

Use your divider to verify that O is the mid-point of $\overline{AB}$. Also, verify that $\angle COA$ and $\angle COB$ are right angles.

Therefore, $\overline{CD}$ is the perpendicular bisector of $\overline{AB}$.

Que 12. Bisect $\angle XYZ$ in figure given below.

Sol.

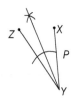

In the given figure, firstly cut the arc by compasses from point P and bisect as the shown in figure.

Direction *In questions 13 to 15 four options are given choose the correct answer.*

Que 13. The instrument in the geometry box having the shape of a triangle is called a

    (a) protractor   (b) compasses

    (c) divider   (d) set-square

Sol. Set-square has the shape of triangle.
    Hence, option (d) is correct.

Que 14. The instrument to draw a circle is

    (a) ruler   (b) protractor

    (c) divider   (d) compasses

Sol. Compasses is used to draw a circle by the help of ruler.
    Hence, option (d) is correct.

Que 15. The instrument to measure an angle is a

    (a) ruler   (b) protractor   (c) divider   (d) compasses

Sol. Protractor is used for measuring an angle.
    Hence, option (b) is correct.

Brain-Teasers

Que 1. From a basket of mangoes when counted in twos there was one extra, counted in threes there were two extra, counted in fours there were three extra, counted in fives there were four extra, counted in sixes there were five extra. But counted in sevens there were no extra. Atleast how many mangoes were there in the basket?

Sol. As per given information, when mangoes counted in **sevens** there were no extra. So, number of mangoes will be a multiple of 7. Then, number of mangoes may be 7, 14, 21, 28, 35, 42, 49, 56, 63, 70, 77, 84, 91, 98, 105, 119, 126,.... When mangoes counted in **twos**, then one mango is extra. So, number of mangoes will be an odd number. Then, number of mangoes may be 7, 21, 35, 49, 105, 119.

Now, when mangoes counted in **fives** there were four extra. So, unit place of number of mangoes will be either 4 or 9. But if unit place digit is 4, then it will divisible by 2. Which is not possible. So, the number of mangoes may be 49, 119.

When mangoes counted in **three** there were two extra, on dividing 49 by 3, we get remainder 1, So, it is not possible. On dividing 119 by 3, we get remainder 2.

Now, when mangoes counted in **fours** there were three extra on dividing 119 by 4, we get remainder 3.

So, 119 is the required value of number of mangoes.

Que 2. A boy was asked to find the LCM of 3, 5, 12 and another number. But while calculating, he wrote 21 instead of 12 and yet came with the correct answer. What could be the fourth number?

Sol. Let the fourth number be x.

Case I. When taking 21 instead of 12, then the LCM of 3, 5, 21.

3	3, 5, 21
5	1, 5, 7
7	1, 1, 7
	1, 1, 1

∴ LCM of 3, 5, 21 = $3 \times 5 \times 7$

Case II. Now, when taking the correct number 12.

2	3, 5, 12
2	3, 5, 6
3	3, 5, 3
5	1, 5, 1
	1, 1, 1

∴ LCM of 3, 5, 12 = $2 \times 2 \times 3 \times 5 = 4 \times 3 \times 5$

But the LCM in both cases are not same.

Since, LCM in both cases contains two dissimilar factor 7 and 4.

∴ Fourth number should be 7×4, i.e. 28.

Que 3. There were five pieces of cloth of lengths 15 m, 21 m, 36 m, 42 m and 48 m. But all of them could be measured in whole units of a measuring rod. What could be the largest length of the rod?

Sol. We know that, the largest length of rod is equal to HCF of 15 m, 21 m, 36 m, 42 m and 48 m.

We have,

3	15
5	5
	1

3	21
7	7
	1

2	36
2	18
3	9
3	3
	1

2	42
3	21
7	7
	1

2	48
2	24
2	12
2	6
3	3
	1

Thus,

$$15 = 3 \times 5$$
$$21 = 3 \times 7$$
$$36 = 2 \times 2 \times 3 \times 3$$
$$42 = 2 \times 3 \times 7$$
$$48 = 2 \times 2 \times 2 \times 2 \times 3$$

HCF of 15 m, 21 m, 36 m, 42 m and 48 m = 3

Hence, the largest length of the rod is 3 m.

Que 4. There are three cans. One of them holds exactly 10 litres of milk and is full. The other two cans can hold 7 litres and 3 litres respectively. There is no graduation mark on the cans. A customer asks for 5 litres of milk. How would you give him the amount he ask? He would not be satisfied by eye estimates.

Sol . The man takes an empty can other than these, with the help of 3 litres can, he takes out 9 litres of milk from the 10 litres can and pours it in the extra can. So, 1 litre milk remains in the 10 litres can. With the help of 7 litres can he takes out of 7 litres of milk from the extra can and pours it in the 10 litres can . The 10 litres can now has $1 + 7 = 8$ litres of milk.

With the help of 3 litres can he takes out of 3 litres milk from the 10 litres can. The 10 litres can now has $8 - 3 = 5$ litres of milk, which he gives to the customer.

Que 5. Which two digit numbers when added to 27 get reversed?

Sol. Let the digit of ten's place and unit (one) place be x and y respectively.

$\therefore$ Number $= 10x + y$

Now, interchange the digit, then digit at ten's place $= y$

and digit at unit's place $= x$

$\therefore$ New number $= 10y + x$

According to the question,

$$(10x + y) + 27 = 10y + x$$
$$10x - x + y - 10y = -27$$
$$9x - 9y = -27$$
$$x - y = -3 \qquad \text{[dividing by 9 on both sides]}$$
$$\Rightarrow \qquad y = x + 3$$

When	$x = 1$, then $y = 1 + 3 = 4$
$\therefore$ Number	$10x + y = 10 \times 1 + 4 = 14$
When	$x = 2$, then $y = 2 + 3 = 5$
$\therefore$ Number	$10x + y = 10 \times 2 + 5 = 25$
When	$x = 3$, then $y = 3 + 3 = 6$
$\therefore$ Number	$10x + y = 10 \times 3 + 6 = 36$
When	$x = 4$, then $y = 4 + 3 = 7$
$\therefore$ Number	$10x + y = 10 \times 4 + 7 = 47$
When	$x = 5$, then $y = 5 + 3 = 8$
$\therefore$ Number	$10x + y = 10 \times 5 + 8 = 58$
When	$x = 6$, then $y = 6 + 3 = 9$
$\therefore$ Number	$10x + y = 10 \times 6 + 9 = 69$

Hence, the required two digit numbers are 14, 25, 36, ...

Que 6. Cement mortar was being prepared by mixing cement to sand in the ratio of 1 : 6 by volume. In a cement mortar of 42 units of volume, how much more cement needs to be added to enrich the mortar to the ratio 2 : 9?

Sol. In mortar, ratio of cement to sand = 1 : 6

Sum of the ratio = 1 + 6 = 7

Given, volume of cement mortar = 42 units

Now, quantity of cement = $\frac{1}{7} \times$ volume of cement mortar

$$= \frac{1}{7} \times 42 = \frac{42}{7} = 6 \text{ units}$$

and quantity of sand = (42 − 6) units = 36 units

Let x units of cement be added to this mortar, so that new ratio becomes 2 : 9.

i.e. $\qquad \frac{6 + x}{36} = \frac{2}{9} \Rightarrow 9(6 + x) = 36 \times 2$

$\Rightarrow \qquad 54 + 9x = 72 \Rightarrow 9x = 72 - 54 \Rightarrow 9x = 18 \Rightarrow x = \frac{18}{9} = 2 \text{ units}$

Que 7. In a solution of common salt in water, the ratio of salt to water was 30 : 70 as per weight. If we evaporate 100 grams of water from one kilogram of this solution, what will be the ratio of the salt to water by weight?

Sol. Given, a solution of common salt in water

Ratio of salt to water = 30 : 70

Sum of ratio = 30 + 70 = 100

We know that, 1 kilogram = 1000 gram

∴ Quantity of salt in 1 kg solution = $\frac{1000 \times 30}{100}$ = 300 gram

and quantity of water in 1 kg solution = $\frac{1000 \times 70}{100}$ = 700 gram

Given, 100 grams of water evaporate, then remaining water in the solution

$$= (700 - 100) \text{ gram} = 600 \text{ gram}$$

∴ New ratio of salt to water become = 300 : 600 = $\frac{300}{600} = \frac{1}{2}$ = 1 : 2

Que 8. Half a swarm of bees went to collect honey from a mustard field. Three fourth of the rest went to a rose garden. The rest ten were still undecided. How many bees were there in all?

Sol. Let the total number of bees be x.

Number of bees went to collect honey from mustard field $= \dfrac{x}{2}$

$\therefore$ Remaining bees $= x - \dfrac{x}{2} = \dfrac{x}{2}$

Number of bees went to rose garden $= \dfrac{3}{4} \times \dfrac{x}{2}$

and number of bees still undecided $= 10$

According to the question, $= \dfrac{x}{2} + \dfrac{3}{4} \times \dfrac{x}{2} + 10 = x,$

$\Rightarrow \qquad \dfrac{x}{2} + \dfrac{3x}{8} + \dfrac{10}{1} = x$

$\Rightarrow \qquad \dfrac{4x + 3x + 80}{8} = x, \ \Rightarrow \dfrac{7x + 80}{8} = \dfrac{x}{1}$

$\Rightarrow \qquad 7x + 80 = 8x \ \Rightarrow 8x - 7x = 80 \ \Rightarrow \ x = 80$

Hence, the number of bees are 80.

Que 9. Fifteen children are sitting in a circle. They are asked to pass a handkerchief to the child next to the child immediately after them. The game stops once the handkerchief returns to the child it started  from. This can be written as follows :

$1 \rightarrow 3 \rightarrow 5 \rightarrow 7 \rightarrow 9 \rightarrow 11 \rightarrow 13 \rightarrow 15$
$\rightarrow 2 \rightarrow 4 \rightarrow 6 \rightarrow 8 \rightarrow 10 \rightarrow 12 \rightarrow 14 \rightarrow 1.$

Here, we see that every child gets the handkerchief.

(i) What would happen, if the handkerchief were passed to the left leaving two children in between? Would every child get the handkerchief?

(ii) What if we leave three children in between? What do you see?

In which cases every child gets the handkerchief and in which cases not?

Sol. (i) When the handkerchief was passed to the left leaving two children in between, then we can written as

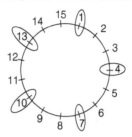

$$1 \rightarrow 4 \rightarrow 7 \rightarrow 10 \rightarrow 13$$

Hence, the all children would not get the handkerchief.

(ii) When the handkerchief was passed to the left leaving three children in between, then we can write as

$$1 \rightarrow 5 \rightarrow 9 \rightarrow 13 \rightarrow 2 \rightarrow 6 \rightarrow 10 \rightarrow 14 \rightarrow 3 \rightarrow 7 \rightarrow 11 \rightarrow 15 \rightarrow 4 \rightarrow 8$$
$$\rightarrow 12 \rightarrow 1$$

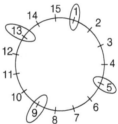

Hence, all children would get the handkerchief.

Que 10.   Take two numbers 9 and 16. Divide 9 by 16 to get the remainder. what is the remainder when 2×9 is divided by 16, 3×9 divided by 16, 4×9 divided by 16, 5×9 divided by 16 ... 15×9 divided by 16. List the remainders. Take the numbers 12 and 14. List the reminders of 12. 12×2, 12×3, 12×4, 12×5, 12×6, 12×7, 12×8, 12×9, 12×10, 12×11, 12×12, 12×13 when divided by 14. What do you observe?

Sol. **Case I.** Taking the numbers 9 and 16.

Here, $9 \times 1 = 9$

$$9 \times 2 = 18, 9 \times 3 = 27, 9 \times 4 = 36, 9 \times 5 = 45, 9 \times 6 = 54,$$
$$9 \times 7 = 63, 9 \times 8 = 72, 9 \times 9 = 81, 9 \times 10 = 90, 9 \times 11 = 99,$$
$$9 \times 12 = 108, 9 \times 13 = 117, 9 \times 14 = 126 \text{ and } 9 \times 15 = 135$$

∵ Dividing these numbers by 16.

∴ The respective remainders are 9, 2, 11, 4, 13, 6, 15, 8, 1, 10, 3, 12, 5, 14, 7.

Case II Now, take the numbers 12 and 14.

Here, $12 \times 1 = 12$

$12 \times 2 = 24, 12 \times 3 = 36, 12 \times 4 = 48, 12 \times 5 = 60, 12 \times 6 = 72,$

$12 \times 7 = 84, 12 \times 8 = 96, 12 \times 9 = 108, 12 \times 10 = 120, 12 \times 11 = 132$

∵ Dividing these numbers by 14. So, the respective remainders are 12, 10, 8, 6, 4, 2, 0, 12, 10, 8, 6, 4.

Here, these remainders goes on decreasing by 2 and on reaching zero they again occur in the same order.

Que 11. You have been given two cans with capacities 9 and 5 litres respectively. There is no graduation marks on the cans nor is eye estimation possible. How can you collect 3 litres of water from a tap ? (You are allowed to pour out water from the can). If the cans had capacities 8 and 6 litres respectively could you collect 5 litres?

Sol. Fill 9 litres can, remove 5 litres from if using 5 litres can. Now 9 litres can have only 4 litres water. Empty 5 litres can and transferred the water contained in 9 litres can. Now 5 litres can have 4 litres of water. Again fill 9 litres can, and transfer water into 5 litres can from it. Now, 5 litres wholy filled and 9 litres can have 8 liters of water remaining. Again empty the 5 litre can and fill it from the 9 litres can. Now, 3 litres left in the 9 litres can.

Que 12. The area of the east wall of an auditorium is 108 sq m, the area of the north wall is 135 sq m and the area of the floor is 180 sq m. Find the height of the auditorium.

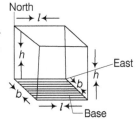

Sol. Let the length, breadth and height of the wall of an auditorium be l, b and h respectively.

According to the question,

Area of the East wall of auditorium, i.e.

$$b \times h = 108 \text{ sq m} \qquad \text{...(i)}$$

Area of the North wall of auditorium, i.e.

$$l \times h = 135 \text{ sq m} \qquad \text{...(ii)}$$

and area of the floor of a auditorium, i.e.

$$l \times b = 180 \text{ sq m} \qquad \text{...(iii)}$$

Dividing Eqs. (ii) by (iii), we get

$$\frac{l \times h}{l \times b} = \frac{135}{180} \Rightarrow \frac{h}{b} = \frac{135}{180} \Rightarrow \frac{h}{b} = \frac{135 \div 15}{180 \div 15} = \frac{9}{12} = \frac{3}{4} \Rightarrow \frac{h}{b} = \frac{3}{4} \Rightarrow b = \frac{4h}{3}$$

On putting $b = \dfrac{4h}{3}$ in Eq. (i), we get

$$\frac{4h}{3} \times h = 108$$

$$h^2 = \frac{108 \times 3}{4} = 27 \times 3 = 81$$

$$h^2 = 81 \qquad \text{(Taking square root both sides)}$$

$$h = 9 \text{ m}$$

Hence, the height of the auditorium is 9 m.

Que 13. If we subtract 4 from the digit at the units place of a two digit number and add 4 to the digit at the tens place, then the resulting number is doubled. Find the number.

Sol. Let the ten's digit and unit's digit be x and y respectively.

$\therefore$ Number $= 10x + y$

If subtract 4 from the digit at the unit place, then new unit's place number $= (y - 4)$ and if add 4 to the digit at the ten's place, then new ten's place number $= (x + 4)$

$\therefore$ New number $= 10 \times$ ten's place $+$ unit place

$$= 10(x + 4) + (y - 4) = 10x + 40 + y - 4 = 10x + y + 36$$

According to the question,

$$2 \times (10x + y) = 10x + y + 36 \quad \Rightarrow \quad 20x + 2y = 10x + y + 36$$

$$\Rightarrow \quad 20x - 10x + 2y - y = 36 \quad \Rightarrow \quad 10x + y = 36$$

Hence, the required number is 36.

Que 14. Two boatmen start with same speed simultaneously from the opposite shores of a river and they cross each other after 45 minutes of their starting from the respective shores. They  rowed till they reached the opposite shore and returned immediately after reaching the shores. When will they cross each other again?

Sol. Suppose, two boatmen A and B are standing on two shores M and N respectively.

Given, boatmen A and B move from respective shores and cross each other after 45 min at point H.

Therefore, after crossing, boatman A takes 45 min to cover the distance from point H to N and 45 min to come back from N to H. Similarly, boatman B takes 45 min to cover distance from point H to M and 45 min to come back from M to H.

A ——45 min—— H ——45 min—— B
M   N

∴ The total time taken (i.e. time taken to go and come back) by boatman A from point H to N = 90 min and total time taken (i.e. time taken to go and come back) by boatman B from point H to M = 90 min. Thus, boatman A and B will again cross each other after 90 min.

Que 15. Three girls are climbing down a staircase. One girl climbs down two steps at one go. The second girl three steps at one go and the third climbs down four steps. They started together from the beginning of the staircase leaving their foot marks. They all came down in complete steps and had their foot marks together at the bottom of the staircase. In how many steps would there be only one pair of foot mark?

Are there any steps onwhich there would be no foot marks.

Sol. For the first girl, where she puts her foot marks is as under

1 2 3 4 5 6 7 8 9 10 11 12 13 14 15

For the second girl,

1 2 3 4 5 6 7 8 9 10 11 12 13 14 15 16

For the third girl,

1 2 3 4 5 6 7 8 9 10 11 12 13 14 15 16 17

Here, number of pairs of foot marks shown as below

1 ② 3 4 5 ⑥ 7 ⑧ 9 10 11 ⑫ 13 ⑭ 15 16

∴ Steps with one pair (✓) of foot marks = 3, 4, 10, 11, 15
and steps with no pair of foot marks ② ⑥ ⑧ ⑫ ⑭.

Que 16. A group of soldiers was asked to fall in line making rows of three. It was found that there was one soldier extra. Then, they were asked to stand in rows of five. It was found there were left 2 soldiers. They were asked to stand in rows of seven. Then, there were three soldiers who could not be adjusted. At least how many soldiers were there in the group?

Sol. Let the number of soldiers in the groups be $3n + 1$, $5n + 2$ and $7n + 3$, where n is a natural number.

Now, putting $n = 1, 2, 3, 4, 5, \ldots$

Then, $3n + 1 = 4$, 7, 10, 13, 16, 19, 22, 25, 28, 31, 34, 37, 40, 43, 46, 49, ㊲, 55, 57

$5n + 2 = 7$, 12, 17, 22, 27, 32, 37, 42, 47, ㊲, 57

and $7n + 3 = 10$, 17, 24, 31, 38, 45, ㊲, 59

In above series, we observe that minimum number 52 is common.

So, least number of soldiers are 52.

Que 17. Get 100 using four 9's and some of the symbols like $+, -, \times$, etc.

Sol. We know that,

Largest two digit numbers $= 99$

Now, to make the 100, we have to add 1

and 1 can be written as $= 9 \div 9 = \dfrac{9}{9}$

So, the required result $= 99 + \dfrac{9}{9}$.

Que 18. How many digits would be in the product $2 \times 2 \times 2 \ldots \times 2$ (30 times)?

Sol. Given, $2 \times 2 \times 2 \times 2 \times \ldots \times 2$ (30 times)

$$= 2^1 \times 2^1 \times 2^1 \times \ldots 2^1$$
$$= 2^{1 + 1 + 1 + \ldots \text{(30 times)}} = 2^{30} = (2^5)^6$$
$$= 2^5 \times 2^5 \times 2^5 \times 2^5 \times 2^5 \times 2^5$$
$$= 32 \times 32 \times 32 \times 32 \times 32 \times 32$$
$$= 1024 \times 1024 \times 1024 = 1073741824$$

Hence, the number of digits are 10.

Que 19. A man would be 5 min late to reach his destination, if he rides his bike at 30 km per hour. But he would be 10 min early, if he rides at the speed of 40 km per hour. What is the distance of his destination from where he starts?

Sol. Let the required distance be x km.

Now, time taken at 30 km/h $= \dfrac{x}{30}$ h $\qquad \left[\because \text{Time} = \dfrac{\text{Distance}}{\text{Speed}}\right]$

$$= \left(\dfrac{x}{30} \times 60\right) \text{min} \qquad [\because 1\,\text{h} = 60\,\text{min}]$$

$$= 2x \text{ min} \qquad\qquad ...(\text{i})$$

Again, time taken at 40 km/h $= \dfrac{x}{40}$ h

$$= \left(\dfrac{x}{40} \times 60\right) \text{min} = \dfrac{3x}{2} \text{ min} \qquad ...(\text{ii})$$

Now, difference between two reach times

$$= 5 + 10 = 15 \text{ min}$$

$\therefore$ From Eqs. (i) and (ii), we get

$$2x - \dfrac{3x}{2} = 15$$

$\Rightarrow \qquad \dfrac{4x - 3x}{2} = 15 \Rightarrow \dfrac{x}{2} = 15 \Rightarrow x = 2 \times 15 = 30$ km.

Que 20. The ratio of speeds of two vehicles is 2 : 3. If the first vehicle covers 50 km in 3 hours, what distance would the second vehicle covers in 2 hours?

Sol. Let v_1 and v_2 be the speeds of two vehicles

Given, $\qquad v_1 : v_2 = 2 : 3$

$\Rightarrow \qquad \dfrac{v_1}{v_2} = \dfrac{2}{3} \qquad\qquad ...(\text{i})$

We know that, $\qquad \left[\text{Speed} = \dfrac{\text{Distance}}{\text{Time}}\right]$

$\therefore$ Speed of first vehicle, $v_1 = \dfrac{50}{3}$ km/h

From Eq. (i),

$$\dfrac{50}{3v_2} = \dfrac{2}{3} \Rightarrow v_2 = \dfrac{50}{2} = 25 \text{ km/h}$$

Now, distance covered by the second vehicle in 2 h

$$= \text{Speed}\,(v_2) \times \text{Time} = 25 \times 2 = 50 \text{ km}$$

Que 21. The ratio of income to expenditure of Mr. Natarajan is 7 : 5. If he saves ₹ 2000 a month, what could be his income?

Sol. Let the income and expenditure be $7x$ and $5x$ respectively.

We know that,

Savings = Income – Expenditure = $7x - 5x = 2x$

and given savings = 2000 per month

$\Rightarrow \qquad 2x = 2000 \qquad\qquad$ [dividing by 2 both side]

$x = 1000$

Now, income = $7x = 7 \times 1000 = 7000$

Que 22. The ratio of the length to breadth of a lawn is 3 : 5. It costs ₹ 3200 to fence it at the rate of ₹ 2 a metre. What would be the cost of developing the lawn at the rate of ₹ 10 per square metre.

Sol. Given, the ratio of the length to breadth of a lawn = 3 : 5.

Let the length of a lawn be $3x$.

and breadth of a lawn be $5x$.

Now, perimeter of a lawn = 2 [length + breadth]

$= 2\ [3x + 5x] = 2 \times 8x = 16x$

Also, cost of fencing at the rate of ₹ 2 per metre = ₹ 3200

and cost of fencing at the rate of ₹ 1 per metre

$= ₹\ \dfrac{3200}{2} = ₹\ 1600$

Here, perimeter of a lawn = 1600

$\Rightarrow \qquad\qquad 16x = 1600$

$\Rightarrow \qquad\qquad x = \dfrac{1600}{16} = 100$

Now, length of lawn = $3x = 3 \times 100 = 300$ m

and breadth of a lawn = $5x = 5 \times 100 = 500$ m

Area of a lawn = length × breadth

$= 300 \times 500$ sq m = 150000 sq m

∴ Cost of developing the lawn at rate of ₹ 10 per sq m

$= 10 \times 150000 = ₹\ 1500000$

Que 23. If one counts one for the thumb, two for the index finger, three for the middle finger, four for the ring finger, five for the little finger and continues counting backwards, six for the ring finger, seven for the middle finger, eight for the index finger, nine for the thumb, ten for the index finger, eleven for the middle finger, twelve for the ring finger, thirteen for the little finger, fourteen for the ring finger and so on. Which finger will be counted as one thousand ?

Sol. Let A, B, C, D and E denotes as indicated below.

Number appeared

Thumb	A	1		9		17		25		33		41		49		57		65		73	
Index finger	B	2	(8)	10	(16)	18	(24)	26	(32)	34	(40)	42	(48)	50	(56)	58	(64)	66	(72)	74
Middle finger	C	3	7	11	15	19	23	27	31	35	39	43	47	51	55	59	63	67	71	75
Ring finger	D	4	6	12	14	20	22	28	30	36	38	44	46	52	54	60	62	68	70	76
Little Finger	E	5		13		21		29		37		45		53		61		69		77

Thumb	A		81		89		97
Index finger	B	(80)	82	(88)	90	(96)	98
Middle finger	C	79	83	87	91	95	99
Ring finger	D	78	84	86	92	94	100
Little Finger	E		85		93		101

Here , We see that in index figure B series has a multipe of 8 (or we say it is a table of 8)

We know that, $8 \times 125 = 1000$.

Hence, Index figure counted as one thousand.

Que 24. Three friends plucked some mangoes from a mango grove and collected them together in a pile and took nap after that. After some time, one of the friends woke up and divided the mangoes into three equal numbers.There was one mango extra. He gave it to a monkey nearby and took one part for himself and slept again. Next the second friend got up unaware of what has happened, divided the rest of the mangoes into three equal shares. There was an extra mango. He gave it to the monkey, took one share for himself and slept again. Next the third friend got up not knowing what happened and divided the mangoes into three equal shares. There was an extra mango. He gave it to the monkey, took one share for himself and went to sleep again. After some time, all of them got up together to find 30 mangoes. How many mangoes did the friends pluck initially?

Sol. Let the total number of mangoes $= 3x + 1$

Case I On distributing the mangoes equally in three shares, by the first friend.

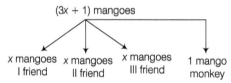

(3x + 1) mangoes

x mangoes   x mangoes   x mangoes   1 mango
I friend   II friend   III friend   monkey

1 mango is given to the monkey.

Number of mangoes in each equal part $= \dfrac{3x}{3} = x$

∵ First friend keeps 1 part from distributed mangoes with himself i.e. x mangoes

∴ The remaining mangoes $= x + x = 2x$

Case II on distributing the mangoes equally in three shares by the second friend

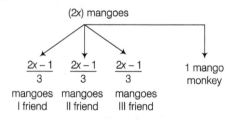

(2x) mangoes

$\dfrac{2x-1}{3}$ $\dfrac{2x-1}{3}$ $\dfrac{2x-1}{3}$ 1 mango
                                          monkey
mangoes   mangoes   mangoes
I friend   II friend   III friend

1 mango is given to the monkey.

∴ Number of mangoes in each equal part $= \dfrac{2x-1}{3}$

∵ Second friend keeps 1 part from distributed mangoes with himself.

∴ The remaining mangoes $= \dfrac{2x-1}{3} + \dfrac{2x-1}{3} = \dfrac{4x-2}{3}$

Case III On distributing the mangoes equally in three shares by the third friend

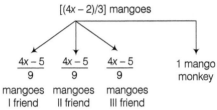

[(4x – 2)/3] mangoes

$\dfrac{4x-5}{9}$ mangoes I friend $\dfrac{4x-5}{9}$ mangoes II friend $\dfrac{4x-5}{9}$ mangoes III friend   1 mango monkey

1 mango is given to the monkey.

Number of mangoes in each equal part $\dfrac{1}{3}\left[\dfrac{4x-2}{3} - 1\right]$

$= \dfrac{4x-5}{9}$

∵ Third friend keeps 1 part from distributed mangoes with himself

∴ The remaining mangoes $= \dfrac{4x-5}{9} + \dfrac{4x-5}{9} = \dfrac{8x-10}{9}$

Now, according to the question, $\dfrac{8x-10}{9} = 30$

⇒ $\qquad 8x-10 = 9\times 30 \ \Rightarrow \ 8x-10 = 270$

⇒ $\qquad 8x = 270+10 \ \Rightarrow \ 8x = 280 \ \Rightarrow \ x = \dfrac{280}{8} = 35$

∴ Total number of mangoes $= 3x+1 = 3\times 35 + 1 = 105 + 1 = 106$

Que 25. There is a number which is very peculiar. This number is three times the sum of its digits. Can you find the number?

Sol. Let unit's digit and ten's digit be y and x respectively.

∴ The number $= 10x + y$

According to the question,

$\qquad 10x + y = 3(x + y)$

⇒ $\qquad 10x + y = 3x + 3y$

⇒ $\qquad 10x - 3x + y - 3y = 0 \ \Rightarrow \ 7x - 2y = 0$

⇒ $\qquad 2y = 7x \ \Rightarrow \ y = \dfrac{7}{2}x$

For $x = 2$, then $y = \dfrac{7}{2} \times 2 = 7$

$\therefore$ The required number $= 10x + y = 10 \times 2 + 7 = 20 + 7 = 27$

Hence, the required number is 27.

Que 26. Ten saplings are to be planted in straight lines in such way that each line has exactly four of them.

Sol. One arrangement could be as under

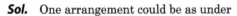

Que 27. What will be the next number in the sequence?

    (a) 1, 5, 9, 13, 17, 21, ...   (b) 2, 7, 12, 17, 22, ...

    (c) 2, 6, 12, 20, 30, ...   (d) 1, 2, 3, 5, 8, 13, ...

    (e) 1, 3, 6, 10, 15, ...

Sol. (a) Given, 1, 5, 9, 13, 17, 21, ...

      Here, $5 - 1 = 9 - 5 = 13 - 9 = 17 - 13 = 21 - 17 = 4$

      $\therefore$ Required number $= 21 + 4 = 25$

    (b) Given, 2, 7, 12, 17, 22, ...

      Here, $7 - 2 = 12 - 7 = 17 - 12 = 22 - 17 = 5$

      $\therefore$ Required number $= 22 + 5 = 27$

    (c) Given, 2, 6, 12, 20, 30, ...

      Here, this sequence can be written as

          $1 \times 2, 2 \times 3, 3 \times 4, 4 \times 5, 5 \times 6, ...$

      $\therefore$ Required number $= 6 \times 7 = 42$

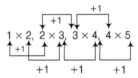

    (d) Given, 1, 2, 3, 5, 8, 13, ...

      Here, this sequence can be written as $1 + 2 = 3, 2 + 3 = 5, 5 + 8 = 13$

      $\therefore$ Required number $= 8 + 13 = 21$

    (e) Given, 1, 3, 6, 10, 15, ...

      Here, this sequence can be written as

          $1 + 2 = 3, 3 + 3 = 6, 6 + 4 = 10, 10 + 5 = 15$

      $\therefore$ Required number $= 15 + 6 = 21$

Que 28. Observe the pattern in the following statement: $31 \times 39 = 13 \times 93$. The two numbers on each side are co-prime and are obtained by **reversing the digits** of respective numbers. Then, write a pairs of such numbers.

Sol. One such pair is $13 \times 62 = 31 \times 26$.

Ingram Content Group UK Ltd.
Milton Keynes UK
UKHW021814060423
419751UK00014B/494